HOPE

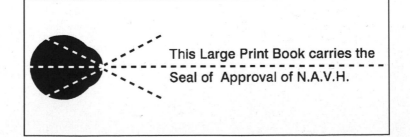

This Large Print Book carries the
Seal of Approval of N.A.V.H.

HOPE

ENTERTAINER OF THE CENTURY

RICHARD ZOGLIN

THORNDIKE PRESS
A part of Gale, Cengage Learning

GALE
CENGAGE Learning·

Farmington Hills, Mich • San Francisco • New York • Waterville, Maine
Meriden, Conn • Mason, Ohio • Chicago

GALE
CENGAGE Learning·

Copyright © 2014 by Richard Zoglin.
Thorndike Press, a part of Gale, Cengage Learning.

ALL RIGHTS RESERVED
Thorndike Press® Large Print Biography.
The text of this Large Print edition is unabridged.
Other aspects of the book may vary from the original edition.
Set in 16 pt. Plantin.

LIBRARY OF CONGRESS CATALOGING-IN-PUBLICATION DATA

Zoglin, Richard.
  Hope : entertainer of the century / by Richard Zoglin. — Large print
edition.
     pages ; cm. — (Thorndike Press large print biography)
  Includes bibliographical references.
  ISBN 978-1-4104-7521-3 (hardcover) — ISBN 1-4104-7521-2 (hardcover)
  1. Hope, Bob, 1903–2003. 2. Comedians—United States—Biography.
  3. Large type books. I. Title.
  PN2287.H63Z85 2015
  792.702'8092—dc23
  [B]   2014038588

Published in 2015 by arrangement with Simon & Schuster, Inc.

Printed in Mexico
3 4 5 6 7 19 18 17 16 15

For Charla

CONTENTS

V. LOSING HIS GRIP

VI. ENSURING THE LEGACY

INTRODUCTION

On a balmy October morning in 2010, one hundred people were gathered on a dock in Battery Park at the foot of Manhattan Island. They were a well-dressed group — the men in jackets and ties, the women in business suits. Many were quite old and needed help climbing into the boat that had been chartered to ferry them across New York Harbor to Ellis Island. Once there, they made their way to the second floor of the cavernous Immigration Museum building, where rows of chairs had been set up in a long, book-lined room, which was about to be dedicated as the Bob Hope Memorial Library.

Linda Hope, the late comedian's seventy-one-year-old daughter, stepped to the microphone to emcee the ceremony. She introduced the smattering of celebrities on hand — actress Arlene Dahl, baseball legend Yogi Berra, two US congressmen — and several clip reels highlighting Bob's life and career: his childhood years in England, where he was

9

born in 1903, and Cleveland, Ohio, where he and his family emigrated when he was four and a half; scenes from his movies and TV shows; excerpts from his tours to entertain US troops around the globe. His granddaughter, Miranda, accompanying herself on guitar, sang a folk ballad called "Immigrant Eyes." Dick Cavett popped up from the audience to tell a couple of impromptu stories about Hope, whom he had befriended in the comedian's later years. Michael Feinstein, the cabaret singer and musical archivist, closed the event with a wistful solo rendition of Bob's theme song, "Thanks for the Memory."

It was another chapter in what has surely been the most determined campaign of legacy building in Hollywood history. A few months before the Ellis Island ceremony, Hope's family and friends gathered in Washington, DC, to inaugurate a new Hope-centric exhibit on political humor at the Library of Congress, where the comedian's voluminous letters and papers are stored. A year earlier, the Hope legacy tour made a stop on the deck of the USS *Midway* in San Diego Harbor to mark the introduction of a postage stamp bearing Hope's likeness. Memorials to Hope have proliferated across the American landscape. You can walk down streets named for Bob Hope in El Paso, Texas, Miami, Florida, and Branson, Missouri; cross the

Cuyahoga River on the Hope Memorial Bridge in Cleveland, Ohio; and bypass the congestion at Los Angeles International by flying into the Bob Hope Airport in Burbank, California. Hope's name is memorialized on hospitals, theaters, chapels, schools, performing arts centers, and American Legion posts from Miami to Okinawa. The US Air Force named a transport plane for him, and the Navy christened a cargo ship in his honor. Bob Hope Village, in Shalimar, Florida, provides a home for retired members of the Air Force and their surviving spouses. The World Golf Hall of Fame, in St. Augustine, Florida, features an exhibit celebrating Hope's passion for the game, "Bob Hope: Shanks for the Memory." A dozen colleges offer scholarships in Hope's name. Another dozen organizations give out awards in his honor, among them the Air Force's annual Spirit of Hope Award and the Bob Hope Humanitarian Award, presented by the Academy of Television Arts & Science.

His punchy, two-syllable name, so emblematic of the optimistic American spirit; the unmistakable profile, with its jutting chin and famously ski-slope-shaped nose; the indelible images of Hope performing for throngs of cheering GIs in World War II and Vietnam — it was once impossible to imagine a time when the first question that needed to be answered about the most popular comedian

11

in American history would be: Who was Bob Hope, and why did he matter?

By the time he died — on July 27, 2003, two months after his hundredth birthday — Hope's reputation was already fading, tarnished, or being actively disparaged. He had, unfortunately, stuck around too long. The comedian of the century, who began his vaudeville career in the 1920s and was still headlining TV specials in the 1990s, continued performing well into his dotage, and a younger generation knew him mainly as a cue-card-reading antique, cracking dated jokes about buxom beauty queens and Gerald Ford's golf game. "World's Last Bob Hope Fan Dies of Old Age," the *Onion*'s fake headline announced a year before his death. Writer Christopher Hitchens expressed the disaffection of many of the baby-boom generation in an online dismissal of Hope just a few days after his passing: "To be paralyzingly, painfully, hopelessly unfunny is a serious drawback, even lapse, in a comedian. And the late Bob Hope devoted a fantastically successful and well-remunerated lifetime to showing that a truly unfunny man can make it as a comic. There is a laugh here, but it is on us."

Hope never recovered from the Vietnam years, when his hawkish defense of the war, close ties to President Nixon (who actively courted Hope's help in selling his Vietnam policies to the American people), and the country-club smugness of his gibes about antiwar protesters and long-haired hippies, all made him a political pariah for the peace-and-love generation. His tours to entertain US troops during World War II had made him a national hero. By the turbulent 1960s, he was a court-approved jester, the Establishment's comedian — hardly a badge of honor in an era when hipper, more subversive comics, from Mort Sahl and Lenny Bruce to George Carlin and Richard Pryor, were showing that stand-up comedy could be a vehicle for personal expression, social criticism, and political protest. Even before Hope became a doddering relic, he had become an anachronism.

Yet the scope of Hope's achievement, viewed from the distance of a few years, is almost unimaginable. By nearly any measure, he was the most popular entertainer of the twentieth century, the only one who achieved success — often No. 1–rated success — in every major genre of mass entertainment in the modern era: vaudeville, Broadway, movies, radio, television, popular song, and live concerts. He virtually invented stand-up comedy in the form we know it today. His face, voice, and stage mannerisms (the nose, the lopsided smile, the confident, sashaying walk, and the ever-present golf club) made him more recognizable to more people than any other entertainer since Charlie Chaplin. A tireless stage performer who traveled the country and the world for more than half a century doing live shows for audiences in the thousands, he may well have been seen in person by more people than any other human being in history.

His achievements as an entertainer, however, only hint at the breadth and depth of his impact. For the way he marketed himself, managed his celebrity, cultivated his brand, and converted his show-business fame into a larger, more consequential role for himself on the public stage, Bob Hope was the most important entertainer of the century. Viewed from the largest historical perspective — the way he intersects with the grand themes of the century, from the Greatest Generation's crusade to preserve democracy in World War II, to the social, political, and cultural upheavals of the 1960s and 1970s — one could argue, without too much exaggeration, that he was the *only* important entertainer.

His life almost perfectly spanned the century, and to recount his career is to recapitulate the history of modern American show business. He began in vaudeville, first as a song-and-dance man and then as an emcee and comedian, working his way up from the amateur shows of his Cleveland hometown to headlining at New York's legendary Palace Theatre. He segued to Broadway, where he costarred in some of the era's classic musicals, appeared with legends such as Fanny Brice and Ethel Merman, and introduced standards by great American composers such as Jerome Kern and Cole Porter. Hope became a national star on radio, hosting a weekly comedy show on NBC that was America's No. 1–rated radio program for much of the early 1940s and remained in the top five for more than a decade.

He came relatively late to Hollywood, making his feature-film debut, at age thirty-four, in *The Big Broadcast of 1938,* where he sang "Thanks for the Memory" — which became his universally identifiable, infinitely adaptable theme song and the first of many pop standards that, almost as a sideline, he introduced in movies. With an almost nonstop string of box-office hits such as *The Cat and the Canary, Caught in the Draft, Monsieur Beaucaire, The Paleface,* and the popular *Road* pictures with Bing Crosby, Hope ranked among Hollywood's top ten box-office stars for a decade, reaching the No. 1 spot in 1949.

Hope brought a new kind of character and attitude to the movies. He was the brash but self-mocking wise guy, a braggart who turned chicken in the face of danger, a skirt chaser who quivered like Jell-O when the skirt chased back. "I grew up loving him, emulating him, and borrowing from him," said

15

Woody Allen, one of the few comics to acknowledge how much he was influenced by Hope — though nearly everyone was. Hope played variations on his cowardly character in spy comedies, ghost stories, costume epics, Westerns — but always with a winking nod to the audience, an acknowledgment that he was an actor playing a role. Especially in his interplay with Crosby in the *Road* films, Hope often spoke directly to the camera or stepped out of character to make cracks about the studio, his career, and his Hollywood friends. This improvisational, fourth-wall-breaking spirit was a radical break from the stylized sophistication of the 1930s romantic comedies, or the artifice of other vaudeville comics who transitioned into movies, such as W. C. Fields or the Marx Brothers. And it perfectly met the psychological needs of a nation at a time of war and world crisis. As the newsreels broadcast scenes of thundering European dictators, jackbooted military troops, and docile, mindlessly cheering crowds, Hope's humor was both an escape and an affirmation of the American spirit: feisty, independent, indomitable.

When television came in, Hope was there too. Others, such as Milton Berle, preceded him. But after starring in his first NBC special on Easter Sunday in 1950, Hope began an unparalleled reign as NBC's most popular comedy star that lasted for nearly four decades. Other comedians who made the move into television — Berle, Jack Benny, Red Skelton, Jackie Gleason, Danny Thomas, even Lucille Ball — had their heyday on TV and then faded; Hope alone remained a major star headlining top-rated TV shows well into his eighties. His 1970 Christmas special from Vietnam was the most watched television program *of all time* up to that point, seen in a now-unthinkable 46.6 percent of all TV homes in the country. (The final episodes of *Dallas, M*A*S*H,* and *Roots* are the only entertainment shows ever to beat it.)

That would have been enough for most performers, but not Hope. Along with his radio, TV, and movie work, he traveled for personal appearances at a pace matched by no other major star. He was just one of many performers who went overseas on USO-sponsored tours to entertain the troops during World War II. Unlike most of the others, he didn't stop when the war ended. Starting with a trip to Berlin during a Cold War crisis in 1948, he launched an annual tradition of entertaining US troops around the world at Christmas — in wartime and peacetime, from forlorn outposts in Alaska to the battlefields of Korea and Vietnam. Stateside, he was just as indefatigable, making as many as 250 personal appearances a year, manning the microphone at charity benefits, trade shows, state fairs, testimonial dinners, hospital dedications, Boy Scout jamborees, Kiwanis Club luncheons, and seemingly any event that could pack a thousand people into a ballroom on the promise that Bob Hope would be there to deliver the one-liners.

On a podium, no one could touch him. He was host or cohost of the Academy Awards ceremony a record nineteen times — the first in 1940, when *Gone With the Wind* was the big winner, and the last in 1978, when *Star Wars* and *Annie Hall* were the hot films. His suave unflappability — no one ever looked better in a tuxedo — and tart insider wisecracks ("This is the night when war and politics are forgotten, and we find out who we really hate") helped turn a relatively low-key industry dinner into the most obsessively tracked and massively watched event of the Hollywood year.

The modern stand-up comedy monologue was essentially his creation. There were comedians in vaudeville before Hope, but they mostly worked in pairs or did prepackaged, jokebook gags that played on ethnic stereotypes and other familiar comedy tropes. Hope, working as an emcee and ad-libbing jokes about the acts he introduced, developed a more freewheeling and spontaneous monologue style, which he later honed and perfected in radio. To keep his material fresh, he hired a team of writers and told them to come up with jokes about the news of the day — presidential politics, Hollywood gossip, California weather, as well as his own life, work, travels, golf game, and show-business friends.

This was something of a revolution. When Hope made his debut on NBC in 1938, the popular comedians on radio all inhabited self-contained worlds, playing largely invented comic characters: Jack Benny's effete tightwad, Edgar Bergen and his uppity dummy, Charlie McCarthy, the daffy-wife/exasperated-husband interplay of George Burns and Gracie Allen. Hope's monologues brought something new to radio: a connection between the comedian and the outside world.

Hope was not the first comedian to do jokes about current events. Will Rogers, the Oklahoma-born humorist who offered folksy and often pointed commentary on politics and the American scene, achieved huge popularity in vaudeville, movies, and radio in the 1920s and 1930s, before his death in a plane crash in 1935. Fred Allen, the frog-voiced radio satirist, was aiming acerbic and literate barbs at the potentates of both Washington and his own network while Hope was still apprenticing. But Hope was the first to combine topical subject matter with the rapid-fire gag rhythms of the vaudeville quipster. His monologues became the template for Johnny Carson and nearly every late-night TV host who followed him, and the foundation stone for all stand-up comics, even those who rebelled against him.

Hope wasn't a political satirist. His jokes never hit hard, cut deep, or betrayed any political viewpoint. Mostly they took personalities and events from the news and lampooned them for superficial things, or with clever wordplay — an ironic juxtaposition or unexpected twist or jokey hyperbole. "Not much has been happening back home," Hope told a crowd of servicemen after the 1960 presidential election. "Hawaii and Alaska joined the union, and the Republicans left it." He poked fun at new California governor Ronald Reagan for his Hollywood pedigree, not his conservative politics: "California's back to a two-party system: the Democrats and the Screen Actors Guild." When Bobby Kennedy was thinking of running for president, Hope joked about the candidate's growing brood of kids: "He may win the next election without leaving the house." On hot-button issues such as gay rights, Hope's gags amiably skirted any potential land mines: "In California homosexuality is legal. I'm getting out before they make it mandatory."

He was the first comedian to openly acknowledge that he used writers — as many as a dozen at a time, turning out hundreds of potential jokes for each monologue. He saved them all, the keepers and the castoffs, in a

20

fireproof vault in the office wing of his home in Toluca Lake, California — more than a million of them by the end of his career, all filed alphabetically according to subject matter ("Fairs, Fans, Finance, Firemen, Fishing . . ."). The jokes were rarely memorable, trenchant, or even very funny, and his dependence on writers would later be scorned by younger comedians, who mostly wrote their own material. Yet the jokes were always the weakest part of his act; his impeccable delivery is what put them across. The lamest formula gags could get laughs through the sheer force of his style and stage presence: the confident manner, the rat-a-tat pace and clarion tone of his voice, the perfect weight and balance given to each word, the way he barreled through a punch line and began the next setup ("But I wanna tell ya . . .") until the laughter caught up with him — a technique that both bullied the audience into laughing and congratulated it for keeping up.

This was more than just the triumph of style over substance. Like the great pop and jazz singers of the pre-rock era, who performed songs written by others (before the Beatles came along, and singers had to become songwriters too), Hope was not a creator but a great interpreter. He didn't necessarily say funny things, but he said them funny. Larry Gelbart, who wrote for Hope on radio for four years, before creating the hit

TV series *M*A*S*H,* recalled watching Hope onstage at London's Prince of Wales Theatre in 1948 and being surprised at the belly laughs he got for a joke whose punch line mentioned a motel.

"Do you think anybody here knows what the word *motel* means?" Gelbart asked the pretty British girl he was with.

"No," she replied.

"Then why were you laughing?"

"Because he's so funny."

Hope sold an attitude: brash, irreverent, upbeat. He was a product of Middle America — "the unabashed show-off, the card, the snappy guy who gets off hot ones at shoe salesmen's conventions while they're waiting for the girls to show up," as humorist Leo Rosten once put it — who eased the country's anxieties through complex and difficult times. The message of his comedy was that no issue was so troubling, no public figure so imposing, no foreign threat so intimidating, that it couldn't be cut down to size by some good old American razzing. Hope's comedy punctured pomposity and fed a healthy skepticism of politics and public figures. It helped Americans process changing mores, from new roles for women during World War II to the counterculture revolution of the 1960s. If the jokes were sometimes corny, even reactionary, Hope could be excused. He transcended comedy; he was the nation's designated mood-lifter. No one else could perform that role; few even tried. Comedians for years did impressions of Jack Benny, Groucho Marx, George Burns, and other classic clowns. Almost no one did Bob Hope. His ordinariness was inimitable.

The machinelike impersonality of Hope's comedy mirrored the impenetrability of Hope the man. Even to intimates and people who worked with him for years, he remained largely a cipher. He was not given to introspection or burdened with inner angst. He was the last person in Hollywood one could imagine walking into a therapist's office. He never read books or went to art museums, unless he was dedicating the building. "Bob had no intellectual curiosity," said a younger writer who befriended him in his later years. "If it didn't concern him, he didn't care." He had just one hobby, golf — which provided him with access to presidents, corporate titans, and other power brokers, as well as the material for endless jokes. He authored several memoirs, but all were ghostwritten and filled with one-liners rather than revelations about his inner life.

In public he could be charming, charismatic, and surprisingly approachable. Always attentive to fans, he rarely turned down an autograph request or failed to acknowledge a compliment. He had a photographic memory for names and faces — people he had met at fund-raising events or on the golf course, even the officers of army units he had once entertained. In social gatherings, the room would galvanize around him. "Everybody came to attention when he walked into the room or when they were engaged in conversation with him," said Sam McCullagh, his former son-in-law. "He had a bright spirit — the way you say a saxophonist has a bright sound. The room lit up. His personality beckoned you."

He was funny even without his writers. Unlike some comedians, driven by insecurity and a need for constant attention, Hope was not always "on," rattling off one-liners in normal conversation. Yet he had a natural, unforced, possibly brilliant wit. His writers could see it in the material they *didn't* write for him. "He was funnier than the monologues," said Larry Gelbart. "He was original. He would rather die than call you by your real name — he called me Fringe because I used to have a very short haircut. He spoke the way Johnny Mercer wrote lyrics, always colorful, with a twist."

His TV and radio audiences could glimpse it in the ad-libs that popped so easily from him when slipups occurred on the air — the wisecrack after a fumbled line or missed cue, which made those now-clichéd "blooper reels" funnier than the sketches they supposedly ruined. Friends and colleagues saw it in his ability to respond in the moment, in ways no script could predict. A *Times of London* reader, in a letter to the editor a few days after Hope's death, recalled sitting behind Hope on a shuttle flight between New York and Boston in the 1960s, when hijackings to Cuba were in the news. Though it was an utterly routine one-hour flight, a starstruck stewardess fawned over her celebrity passenger. "Mr. Hope," she cooed, "I hope you will save your ticket and boarding pass, because I mean to make this one of your most memorable airline flights ever." Hope's dry response: "My God, not Havana again." A family member marveled at Hope's opening line at a luncheon for the Catholic diocese of St. Louis in the early 1970s. The bishop who was to introduce Hope launched unexpectedly into a long comedy routine of his own, cracking up the room. Finally the prelate wrapped up his monologue and introduced the comedian who was the guest of honor. Hope walked to the microphone and began soberly, "Let us pray."

Yet his personality had an essential coldness, a wall that prevented outsiders from getting behind the flip, impenetrable surface. For the writers who worked for him, he was an affable, good-humored boss, one of the boys. But the narcissism could be oppressive. He expected them to be on call at any hour of the day or night; he was known for his late-night phone calls, to suggest a new topic for jokes he needed by morning or simply to repeat a funny story he had just heard (often a dirty one). "Once you worked for Hope, you were his property, and just on loan to the rest of the world," said Hal Kanter, who wrote for him off and on for forty years. He was notoriously tight with a dollar, a boss who could complain about reimbursing employees for the cost of a cab ride. Yet he was generous with relatives and friends who were down on their luck, many of whom he quietly helped out financially for years.

He surrounded himself with a battalion of lawyers, agents, public relations men, and assistants of various kinds, who helped manage his public image and protected him from the rough edges of everyday life. Once he called up a neighborhood movie theater and asked what time the feature started. The theater manager replied, "What time can you get here?" He never wore a watch — others could tell Bob Hope the time. He never apologized and rarely said thank you. His longtime publicist Frank Liberman recalled Hope's unhappiness at the lack of press coverage for a special he was set to host at Madison Square Garden in the 1960s. Finally Liberman landed Hope a coveted interview with the *New York Times.* The star's only response: "Now you're talkin'."

For journalists, he was a frustrating interview, glib and stubbornly unrevealing. J. Anthony Lukas, who wrote a profile of Hope for the *New York Times Magazine* in 1970, at the height of the embattled Vietnam years, recounted a telling anecdote from one of Hope's publicists. A magazine reporter, interviewing Hope on an airplane, grew increasingly frustrated with his flip responses to her questions about what motivated him as a performer. When she got up to go to the bathroom, the publicist took Hope aside and told him, "Bob, this gal comes from New York, where they're very big on psychoanalysis. The only way to stop her is to tell her you work so hard because you're the fifth of seven sons and you had to compete for your mother's attention." When the reporter returned, Hope repeated the publicist's answer almost word for word. The reporter smiled happily, and her story wound up quoting his revelation — made "in a rare moment of introspective analysis."

It's not just that Hope was closed off. He seemed to regard the details of his biography and private life as fungible particulars, to be shaped and rewritten as needed for public consumption. He had one of the longest-running and most celebrated marriages in Hollywood — for sixty-nine years, to former nightclub singer Dolores Reade. But he was a lifelong womanizer, carrying on a string of extramarital affairs that were an open secret to friends and colleagues, but largely kept under wraps by his entourage and the press. He had a secret, short-lived first marriage, to his former vaudeville partner, which he never publicly acknowledged. And he almost certainly fudged the date and place of his marriage to Dolores — which, since there is no record of it, some family members suspected may never have taken place at all.

Yet it was, in its fashion, a good marriage. Bob depended on Dolores, a smart, strong-willed Catholic, for counsel, support, and the proper image of Hollywood domesticity. She ran the household, raised their four adopted children, and organized his social life. Hope was a playful, not uncaring, but distant and frequently absent father — a fleeting presence at family dinners, who would typically arrive late and dash off early, always running to appointments. His children had fond memories of their limited time with him, but also varying degrees of trouble coping with the burden of having Bob Hope as a father. It may have weighed most heavily on his youngest daughter, Nora, who broke with the family entirely after a dispute with her mother in the 1980s and remained estranged for the rest of her parents' lives.

If any of this caused Hope serious angst, he kept it well hidden. A *Los Angeles Times* profile in 1941 called him "the world's only happy comedian," and it may not have been far from the truth. He was energized by performing, never seemed stressed, and kept up an exhausting work schedule well into his eighties. He refreshed himself with frequent catnaps, daily massages, and long walks every night before he went to bed, no matter how late the hour or unfamiliar the terrain (usually with a companion — and in later years a golf club for protection). Though one of the wealthiest men in Hollywood, he had a relatively unpretentious lifestyle, raising his family not in the ritzy enclaves of Beverly Hills or Bel Air, but in the San Fernando Valley bedroom community of Toluca Lake. He had a second home in the desert resort of Palm Springs, but it was a relatively modest three-bedroom retreat until the 1970s, when Dolores oversaw the construction of a giant, modernist showplace, with a dome-shaped roof that reminded many of the TWA terminal at New York's JFK Airport.

He was on a first-name basis with presidents and generals, corporate leaders, and business titans. But his closest friends were the people he worked with — writers, old cronies from Cleveland, former vaudevillians, businessmen who joined him for golf and supplied him with clothes and other freebies. Until his later years he drove his own car — not a fancy Mercedes, but one of the middle-class Chryslers or Buicks given to him by his

TV sponsors. Despite a busier travel schedule than practically any other star in Hollywood, he didn't have a private plane until late in life, when his friend and San Diego Chargers owner Alex Spanos loaned him one. After seeing how much it cost to maintain, Hope gave it back.

To many he seemed hopelessly shallow: a gleaming perpetual-motion machine with a missing piece at the center. "Deep down inside, there is no Bob Hope," writer Martin Ragaway once said. "He's been playing Bob Hope for so long that everything else has been burned out of him. The man has become his image." But what seemed shallowness was merely a sign of how effectively Hope was able to guard his private life, and the almost superhuman intensity of focus on his public one. His manager, Elliott Kozak, liked to say that every morning Bob Hope would get up, look in the mirror, and say to himself, "What can I do today to further my career?" That relentless dedication to his own stardom allowed Hope to virtually redefine the notion of stardom in the twentieth century. Indeed, there is hardly an element of our modern celebrity culture that Bob Hope did not invent, pioneer, or help to popularize. He was largely responsible, in the age of celebrity, for setting the parameters of what it means to *be a celebrity.*

THE STAR AS BUSINESSMAN. Like nearly every movie star of the 1930s and 1940s, Hope was initially a salaried employee, signing regular contracts with his studio, Paramount Pictures, for a specified number of films per year at a fixed fee. But in the mid-1940s, when he was churning out box-office hits like clockwork, Hope set up his own production company, so that he could have an ownership stake in his movies and keep more of the profits. A few years later he made a similar deal with NBC, becoming the producer of his own TV specials and charging the network a license fee for them — enabling him to own his shows in perpetuity. Hope wasn't the first Hollywood star to become an entrepreneur of his own career; he patterned his Paramount deal after one that his friend Bing Crosby had made with the same studio a few years earlier. But his business arrangements were the most successful and highly publicized of his day, and a model for the production companies and packaging deals that have become routine for nearly every major star in Hollywood.

Hope's business acumen became part of his legend. By the late 1940s he was making more than $1 million a year, when that was real money. He invested it shrewdly, first in

31

oil and then in California real estate, buying up huge parcels of land in the San Fernando Valley and elsewhere; at one time he was reputed to be the largest private landowner in the state of California. *Fortune* magazine in 1968 estimated his net worth at over $150 million — making him the richest person in Hollywood, wealthier even than studio moguls. He was forever complaining that such estimates were too high, and he may have been right. After *Forbes* magazine put him on its list of America's four hundred richest people in 1982, he challenged the magazine to prove it and got his net worth downgraded from over $200 million to a measly $115 million. Still, Hope was rich, a canny businessman, and a key figure in the gradual shift of power in Hollywood away from the studio and network moguls and toward the stars who kept them in business, and who began taking control of their own financial destiny.

THE STAR AS BRAND. Hope was voracious in seeking out new audiences, marketing his fame across what would today be called multiple platforms. He had been a movie and a radio star for only three years when he published his first book — a jokey, illustrated memoir (penned largely by his gag writers) called *They Got Me Covered.* It was a surprise bestseller, and Hope went on to author or coauthor eleven more books, including another, more substantial autobiography, memoirs of his travels during World War II and Vietnam, and books about golf and his encounters with presidents. He promoted all of them tirelessly, in personal appearances around the country, on his own TV specials, and in guest spots on other TV shows — an early demonstration of the power of show-business synergy.

He was Hollywood's inventor of the brand extension. Along with the books, he had a daily syndicated newspaper column (ghosted, as always, by his writers), which began with dispatches from his World War II tours and continued for eight years afterward, into the early 1950s. He brought his name, prestige, and showbiz connections to a struggling Palm Springs golf tournament, renamed it the Bob Hope Desert Classic, and turned it into the most star-studded pro-am event on the PGA Tour. He was the star of a comic book: *The Adventures of Bob Hope,* launched in 1950 by DC Comics and published quarterly for the next eighteen years. He even had his own logo — the familiar line-drawn caricature of his concave-shape profile, instantly recognizable from Boston to Bangkok.

THE STAR AS PUBLIC CITIZEN. Hope was far from the only Hollywood star who used his talents to raise money for charitable causes. But no one else pursued his public-service mission so fervently or made it such an integral part of his image. He was awarded the first of five honorary Oscars in 1941, for being "the man who did the most for charity." He was the most celebrated of the stars who toured the Pacific and European theaters to entertain the troops during World War II. Back home after the war, he became a ubiquitous fund-raiser, host of charity events, and supporter of patriotic causes, securing his reputation as Hollywood's most tireless do-gooder.

All this had a careerist aspect, of course. Hope sincerely loved entertaining the troops, and it fed the patriotic pride of an immigrant who had lived a classic Horatio Alger success story. But his troop shows also provided him with huge, easy-to-please audiences, lofty TV ratings, and boundless good publicity. Still, no cynical view of his motives can diminish the impact that Hope had in setting a standard for public service in Hollywood. "Playing the European theater, or any theater of war, is a good thing for actors," he wrote in *I Never Left Home,* the memoir of his World War II travels. "It's a way of showing us that there's something more important than billing; or how high your radio [rating] is; or breaking the house record in Denver." Hope showed by example that Hollywood stars have an opportunity, even an obligation, to do more than just make movies, sign autographs, and buy oceanfront estates in Malibu. They can give back, do good, use their fame to make an impact in the public arena.

Hope's particular causes and conservative political views, of course, were not the same as those of many of the stars who followed his example. But he opened the way for celebrities to *have* causes and political views — to work for endangered whales or starving children in Africa or hurricane victims in Louisiana. They may not acknowledge or even realize it, but a direct generational line connects Bob Hope to the globe-trotting activism of Angelina Jolie and George Clooney, Madonna and Oprah Winfrey. Hope made it safe for celebrities to be taken seriously as public citizens.

THE STAR AS INSPIRATION. Even as he golfed with presidents, entertained royalty, and became one of the most famous people in the world, Hope maintained an unusually powerful and personal connection with his fans. This relationship was qualitatively different from that of most stars and their public, an intimate link that illustrated the symbolic role celebrities can play in the inner lives of their fans. "It is painfully obvious to us that our communications with our celebrated favorites is all one-way," wrote Richard Schickel in his book about fame, *Intimate Strangers.* "They send (and send and send)

35

while all we do is receive (and receive and receive). They do not know we exist as individuals; they see us only as the components of the mass, the audience." Bob Hope was different. When he went to do shows in a new town or college or military base, he would send advance men to scout the local scene — gathering information about the popular hangouts, names of local celebrities, and bits of local gossip. When he mentioned these in his monologue, the audience felt an instant bond. As an entertainer, he was the greatest grassroots politician of all time.

Hope got more fan mail than any other star of his day — thirty-eight thousand letters a week in 1944 by one estimate. That record may well have been broken in the age of rock idols and reality TV. But it's hard to imagine any other entertainment personality — Frank Sinatra or Elvis Presley or Justin Bieber — getting the volume of personal, heartfelt letters that Hope did. Servicemen thanking him for bringing a touch of home to a remote outpost during wartime. Parents of soldiers killed in action writing to thank Hope for providing a last glimpse of their son in the crowd at one of his Christmas shows. People who once met him or saw him onstage in vaudeville asking if he would stop by the house for dinner when he came through St. Louis. Old friends pouring out tales of woe and asking for loans or help in finding a job.

Birthday greetings and get-well cards by the truckload. When he had eye problems that threatened his vision, dozens of people wrote to offer one of their own eyes so that Bob Hope could see. "I believe this operation can take place without newspapers or anyone finding out," wrote one man, who said he had only months to live. "This will be my last gift to my fellow man."

To read through Hope's fan mail is to experience the sad drama of everyday human misfortune — illness, family problems, money troubles, disappointed dreams — and realize the beacon of inspiration, hope, and maybe even salvation that celebrities can represent. Hope must have understood this. He replied to an amazingly high proportion of his fan letters — with the help of a battery of assistants, to be sure, but with the kind of care and personal detail that only he could have supplied. Every letter from a serviceman who had seen him in World War II drew an attentive, individualized response — with a few jokes thrown in for good measure, something the letter writer could keep and cherish. A fan who sent a gift to Hope's hotel room in Oklahoma City before a concert in 1974 got this charming response:

This is just to thank you for the lemon pie you sent to the hotel and to let you know I really enjoyed it. It gave me energy to fight off the cold I had and to go ahead and do the Stars and Stripes show. There are several ways to make a lemon pie and you have the proper format because it was just tart enough to be good, almost like my Mother used to bake, which is high praise.

For any other star the first sentence would have been enough, a pro forma thank-you that an assistant could easily have handled. But Hope himself had to add the details — his cold, the tartness — that doubtless earned him a fan for life, one of millions.

In 1967 Hope got this letter from the friend of a seven-year-old Wisconsin girl, whom he had met a year earlier when she was a poster child for cystic fibrosis. Now, the letter writer told him, the girl was dying:

She is in the hospital fighting for her life. The doctors give her about four months to live. She learned a few years ago that she was going to die, but the word "die" had no meaning to her. She recently began to understand what was going to happen. She is taking it hard, Mr. Hope, very hard. She falls apart at the word "die." . . . It will help very much if you were to write a letter or note comforting her. I realize you are a very busy man and you don't have time to answer every letter you get. But please, Mr. Hope. It might help so much.

Hope wrote this to the girl in response:

Dear Kelly:
Remember me? I had my picture taken with you last year in West Allis. I just heard that you were in the hospital and so I wanted to send you a little letter to tell you I'm hoping that you're coming along all right and that you're putting on a good fight so you can get out of there very soon.

I was in Madison, Wisconsin, the other night for a big show at the new auditorium. I did enjoy it and certainly wish I'd had a chance to see you. Anyway, I just wanted to let you know I'm thinking about you, hoping you will get a lot better and get out and enjoy the beautiful Wisconsin country.

A lot of people are praying for you. I am, too.

My best regards,
Bob Hope

It would take a hard-hearted celebrity to ignore a request like that, and an oafish one not to write a sensitive reply. But the delicacy of Hope's response, its warmth and self-deprecating good humor ("Remember me?"), is a small work of art. Hope may have been a cold and driven man, a glutton for applause with an outsize ego. But he could also write a letter like that. In an era when stars routinely lament the tribulations of fame, complain about the loss of privacy, or lose their bearings to drugs and excess, Hope was one celebrity who loved being famous, appreciated its responsibilities, and handled it with extraordinary grace. His monumental role in our public life may have come at the expense of a private life that seemed, to many, stunted and incomplete. But for Hope, the sacrifice was worth it.

■ ■ ■ ■

I
THE MAKING OF AN
ENTERTAINER

GROWING UP, LEARNING THE TRADE, AND
TASTING STARDOM

■ ■ ■ ■

CHAPTER 1
OPENING

"HE WAS A BIG SHOW-OFF SINCE HE WAS ABOUT NINE."

When reporters first began to take notice of Bob Hope, a young comedian who was making a mark in radio and on Broadway in the mid-1930s, they learned some surprising things about the English-born entertainer. He was, early profiles of him reported, actually "Lord Hope, 17th baronet of Craighall, direct lineal descendant of that famous titled English family who at one time owned the ill-fated Hope diamond." His mother was a celebrated music-hall artist (in some accounts) or operetta singer (in others), and her charming voice had "lured the aristocratic scion of the Hope family away from the ancestral castle. From one of them anyway — there are several in the family, all covering miles of territory and impossible to occupy."

None of it was true. It's hard to know whether the aristocratic folderol was a serious attempt by Hope at autobiographical revisionism, or simply a practical joke played on reporters by a cheeky young comic trying to get attention. In fact, he remembered little about his first four and a half years in England, and his family background could hardly have been more drably middle-class. His father was a hard-drinking stonemason who kept the family on the move in search of work; his mother, a shy Welsh girl with a sweet voice who may have sung in local village festivals when she was growing up, but never, as far as anyone has recorded, appeared on a professional stage — operetta, music hall, or otherwise.

She was Avis Towns (Bob took his middle name from her, but for some reason he and everyone else spelled it incorrectly as *Townes* for his entire life), and she grew up in the village of Borth, on the western seacoast of Wales. She was orphaned at an early age, and little is known about her parents, John and Sarah (or possibly Margaret) Towns. By her own account, the family moved from Borth when she was young, to escape the seawater that would often flood their home at high tide, and settled a few miles inland, near Llancynfelyn. Avis had fond memories of walking there with her governess down a long pathway of stone steps to a lake below, where she would play with a pet black swan she nicknamed Chocolate. She remembered little about her parents, who were often traveling (she thought, or imagined, that they were in the diplomatic service in India) and would make occasional grand appearances in a magnificent horse-drawn carriage. Then one day Avis was told her parents would not be coming back. There was talk of a shipwreck, but she never knew for sure what happened to them. In any event, she was taken in by a foster family, a retired sea captain named Abraham Lloyd and his wife, Mary, and they soon moved to Barry, a larger town on the southern Welsh coast.

Even these few, sketchy memories are, however, suspect. No birth certificate has been found for Avis, and later census records indicate she was born in London, not Borth. Her age too is a moving target. According to family lore, she was only fifteen or sixteen when she married in 1891, but her age in the 1891 census (not always definitive) is listed as seventeen. The records of the parish school in Borth, which she attended after transferring from the public school in 1882, give her birth date as June 3, 1872, which is probably more reliable — and would make her nearly nineteen when she married. No records have been found of her parents, or of a supposed older brother named Jack. Alan Blackmore, a retired schoolmaster in England who has done the most extensive research on the Hope genealogy, suggests that Avis was most likely taken as an infant to a London orphanage and (as was common at the time) boarded out to a foster family when the orphanage became overcrowded. By the time she appears in the 1891 census for East Barry, Avis was living with David Lewis, a deputy dockmaster, his wife, Jane, and their five-year-old son, Baisil — and described as a "general domestic servant."

She was a shy, diminutive girl, no more than ninety pounds, with long brown hair and delicate, doll-like features. Her schooling was limited, but she learned to play the piano and the harp at an early age — suggesting an upbringing of some comfort and means. Still, the sheltered girl must have been excited, along with the rest of the girls in town, by the activity at the Barry waterfront in the winter of 1890–91, where the construction of new docks was under way. This major civic project drew workers from all over the surrounding area. Among them was a strapping twenty-one-year-old stonemason named William Henry Hope, known to everyone as Harry.

He had come from Weston-super-Mare, across the Bristol Channel, with his father, James, who was partner in a construction firm hired to work on the docks. A stonemason by trade, James Hope had worked on the Royal Courts of Justice in London as well as the Statue of Liberty when it was being carved in Paris. He had even spent some time working in America, but returned to England when his wife, Emily, refused to make the trip over and join him. They eventually settled in the southwest England resort town of Weston-super-Mare and raised ten children. Harry, the second oldest, was being groomed by his father to go into his trade, so when James moved to Barry for several months of work on the docks, he brought Harry along.

The father, a supervisor on the project, rented a room on Greenwood Street in town, while his son stayed in one of the sheds provided for the workers on the docks. There, young Harry was flattered by the attention paid him by pretty, little Avis Towns, and the two soon struck up a romance. His proud father didn't think much of the "spindly-legged little floozy," and he got Harry transferred to the other end of the docks, to keep the couple apart. Avis was heartbroken not to see him anymore. When Harry became ill and his father decided to send him home to convalesce, it looked as if she would never see him again.

Father and son were on the docks preparing for Harry's departure when a heavy rainstorm broke out. Amid the downpour, they suddenly caught sight of Avis, scurrying for cover and falling flat on her face in the mud. Harry dropped his tools and rushed over to pick her up and carry her to safety inside a shed. While she was recovering, he confessed to his father that she was the girl he wanted to marry.

"Why, she's just a baby," James said — at

least as Avis would tell the story years later. "What a man needs is a woman."

Avis, gathering herself from her swoon, replied, "I am a woman, sir!"

The elder Hope soon realized his objections were fruitless. "Get on with it then, Son," he said. "Marry her and be done with it. We've got work to do." A few days later, on April 25, 1891, the couple traveled to Cardiff, the Welsh capital, just a few miles away, and got married in a small civil ceremony.

For an orphaned, poorly educated Welsh girl with few prospects, it was a promising match. Harry was a skilled craftsman, with hopes of becoming an architect or going into business for himself, like his father. But their life together, almost from the start, was itinerant and financially precarious. When the construction work on the Barry docks was done, Harry and Avis moved to Newport, a few miles up the coast, where there was more work. There a son, Ivor, was born in 1892. A second son, Francis James (Jim), arrived a year later, followed by a daughter named Emily in 1895. When he ran out of work in Newport, Harry moved with the family back to Barry, where a fourth child, Frederick, was born in 1897.

Soon they were on the move again, this time across the country to Lewisham, a few miles south of London. Here the Hopes had as comfortable a life as they would ever enjoy.

They lived in a large stone house, complete with stables and a large, well-kept flower garden. When Harry came home from work, he would pick some bluebells and present them to Avis with a romantic flourish, singing, "I'll be your sweetheart if you will be mine!" Harry raised gamecocks and played the horses, and he would take the family on weekend excursions, to the beach or Covent Garden or the racetrack at Epsom Downs. They had a gardener and a maid, and Avis would entertain guests by playing the dulcimer, or a harp that had been given to her (according to family lore) by the actress Ellen Terry. Avis would often be singing around the house, and all the boys picked up her love for music.

A fourth son, William John (known as Jack), was born in Lewisham in 1900. But just before his birth, the family suffered a terrible loss, when Emily, the only girl, contracted diphtheria and died, barely four years old.

The death of their only daughter, Avis always believed, started Harry on a downward path. Before Emily's death, her older brother Jim remembered, Harry was a good-looking, well-read, charismatic man, with sandy hair and a handlebar mustache. "I still swear I have not seen a handsomer man than our dad in those days," Jim wrote in an unpublished memoir of the family's early life, "Mother Had Hopes." "Immaculately dressed in the

49

best of taste; five foot eleven [actually a bit shorter], 215 pounds of healthy flesh and muscle; full of confidence. And a gentleman in every way." After Emily's death, however, he began drinking more heavily (like many stonecutters, he justified it as needed to wash away the dust inhaled in his work), ignored his books, and started to pile up gambling debts.

In 1902, Harry moved the family yet again, this time to Eltham, a farming community southeast of London. The town was enjoying something of a boom, thanks to a railroad line that had been completed in 1895, connecting it to London and providing easy transportation for milk and produce from the area's rich Kent farmland. The Scottish developer Cameron Corbett had begun to build houses on a 334-acre tract of farmland, and he hired the construction firm of Picton and Hope — James and his partner, Percy Picton — to help with the job. So, once again, Harry followed his father for work, moving into one of the brick row houses that Hope and Picton had built on Craigton Road.

The Eltham house (which still stands today, a plaque marking it as Bob Hope's birthplace) was a comedown from Lewisham: a comfortable but far from luxurious row house in the middle of a gently upsloping block, a mile off the High Street. The tiled entryway led to a parlor to the right, and the three upstairs bedrooms each had a fireplace. The bathroom was outdoors — a plumbing setup that, amazingly, remained unchanged until the house changed owners in the 1990s. Harry had a greenhouse in the backyard, but had to dispense with the servants, due to the family's financial straits.

Still, the Hope boys had a good time in Eltham. The town's main attraction was (and still is) Eltham Palace, an eleventh-century manor house used as a royal residence through the time of Henry VIII. When the king would parade through town, the Hope boys would have front-row seats on a plot of land their grandfather owned at the foot of their street. For adventure, they rambled through a woodsy area to the northeast of their house dubbed the "wilds," where they would join the neighborhood kids looking for wild donkeys or scouring the trees in search of wild birds' eggs.

On May 29, 1903, while Harry was off at work, Avis told the boys she felt sick. Though pregnant, she thought she wasn't due yet and claimed it was just a touch of flu. But they called for the doctor, and by the end of the day he had delivered the Hopes' fifth boy. They named him Leslie — either for a famous soccer star of the day, or for a Hope relative who once served with "Chinese" Gordon, the British general killed by Sudanese rebels in Khartoum in 1885. Hope, typically, told it both ways.

Leslie Towns Hope missed the Victorian age by just two years. After the death of Queen Victoria in 1901, England was going through profound changes. The costly and debilitating Boer War in South Africa — one of the last gasps of the fading British empire — had ended in 1902. Liberal reform was on the ascent, with the passage of legislation that would provide the foundation for the modern welfare state, including guaranteed health care, free school meals, and unemployment benefits for workers. Yet the rapid industrial growth of the previous century had slowed, and Britain was losing its dominance in manufacturing to the United States and European countries such as Germany. Mass production, meanwhile, was rendering the old Victorian artisans increasingly obsolete. All of this was making it tough on people like Harry Hope.

With brick replacing stone on most buildings, jobs for specialists in stonework were growing scarce. Even the little stone used on the houses in Eltham was mostly precast and brought in from elsewhere. Harry had to spend more and more time away from home looking for work — or drowning his disappointments in liquor. Avis would often have to send the older boys into town to scour the pubs and bring their father home. Some nights she would sit up waiting for his return, listening to hear if he was bounding up the street on foot (often with a handful of flowers and a song for his sweetheart), meaning he was sober, or if his approach was heralded by the slow clop-clop-clop of a carriage, which usually meant he was coming home drunk.

One time, when Harry returned home after several days away, Avis emptied his pockets and found a woman's photograph inside, with the inscription "With all my love, Maude." Harry tried to deflect her rage with sweet talk: "You know you're the only girl in the world for me." Avis got so mad she broke a hairbrush over his head.

Though Bob adopted Eltham as his home-town (and years later raised money to restore the local theater, which was renamed for him), the town was one of the briefer stops on the Hope family's sojourn in England. Before Leslie was five months old they were gone, moving back across the country to Weston-super-Mare, where Harry had grown up. They moved into a three-story house on Orchard Street; then, to save money, into a less expensive place on the last street in town, Moorland Road. Harry was still having trouble finding work, and Avis went to work as a cashier in a tea shop to help out. When a sixth Hope boy, Sidney, was born in 1905, she took the baby in her arms and worked as a housekeeper from eight until four.

Their plight got worse. After returning from a job-hunting trip, Harry wandered over to a playground to watch two of his sons playing soccer. When a ball rolled near him and he ran over to kick it back, he stumbled in a hole and broke his ankle. He got right back up and tried to run, turning the simple fracture into a compound one that left him unable to work for more than a year.

The oldest boys, Ivor and Jim, now had to help out, going to work at a dairy. Jim would bring home extra milk for the family and pick up day-old bread and cakes from a bakery where he made deliveries. His mother scrimped to make ends meet. At one dinner, Jim noticed that all she had on her plate was a small portion of potatoes. He asked why she was eating so little. "Mom's not hungry," she replied. Later, when he went into the kitchen to help clean up, he found her eating the leftovers from all the plates. There had been only enough for the boys.

Harry, meanwhile, was a sorry figure, trying to keep busy as he convalesced: repairing the boys' shoes, cutting their hair, and tending to a small flock of caged canaries given to him by a neighbor. Much of the time he just wandered aimlessly around the house and garden. "When he would be in the house, he felt he was underfoot," recalled Jim. "It was pitiful to watch him." Even when he was well enough to look for work again, he had little luck. So once again the family picked up and moved, this time to Bristol, the large port city up the coast.

They lived for a time in a house on Church Road, then downsized to a smaller place on Whitehall Road, across the street from a woman who sold sweets through her window. But Harry again found little work, and Ivor and Jim picked up the slack with a variety of dreary and sometimes dangerous factory jobs. Meanwhile, Harry began thinking about a much more drastic move: to America.

Two of his brothers had already emigrated there and were living in Cleveland, Ohio. Frank, who had a successful plumbing business, had made the move in the 1880s; Fred, a steamfitter, had come more recently. When Harry wrote proposing that he join them, they both tried to dissuade him, warning him that jobs were scarce — you couldn't even find work digging ditches. Avis too pleaded with Harry not to attempt the move. But Harry — impressed by literature that promised gold mines, wide-open spaces, and unlimited opportunity in America — made up his mind to go. He told Avis and the boys that he would send for them once he found work.

The family scraped together enough money for his fare and saw him off at the Bristol station, where he took the train to Southampton and, on April 10, 1907, boarded the USS

Philadelphia for New York City. He arrived at Ellis Island a week later and made his way by train to Cleveland, to join his brothers and try to start a new life in America.

Not yet four years old, Leslie was surely unaware of the seriousness of his family's financial plight. Still, it must have imprinted itself on him profoundly. Psychologists know that stable attachments in the first two years of a child's life are crucial. Leslie lived those formative years in a household that was constantly on the move, with a father who was frequently absent or drunk, and a mother with five other sons and constant money worries that demanded her attention. Without an environment that provided him with the safety and security he needed, Leslie must early on have learned to protect himself by avoiding close attachments that could so easily be upended. He would retain that protective shell for the rest of his life.

He also learned to fight for what he wanted. Significantly, his one memory from his English childhood was of a neighborhood scuffle, when he got conked on the head by a rock thrown by some young toughs in St. George's Park, near their house in Bristol. "I was defending my dogs from a gang of Bristol kids," he recalled in his memoir *Have Tux, Will Travel.* "I've been leery of dog acts ever since." His brothers' early memories of Leslie also mostly involve mishaps and misadventures. His oldest brother, Ivor, once plucked Leslie from under a pier in Herne Bay, on the Kent seacoast, after the boy fell in the water and nearly drowned. Another time, Ivor and his uncle packed Leslie into the family's pony cart for a ride to a local food joint. When they came out, the cart and the pony were gone. They walked home — only to find that the police had been sent on a frantic search because the pony had trotted home alone, with the cart turned upside down and empty.

In the bustling, itinerant household, Leslie found that performing was a way to get attention. Jim recalled that Leslie would hang out with his older brothers on a busy street corner, drop his trousers, and burst into tears, telling a sob story to get passersby to cheer him up with a few coins. Once they did, he'd start the act all over again for the next group of pedestrians. He would do imitations of fat people for his great-aunt Polly, who gave him cookies as a reward. He liked to dress up in his mother's old clothes, shoes, and hats, delighting in the praise from neighbors: "Whose lovely little girl are you?" Ivor claimed that his precocious younger brother could recite an entire Irish poem, "The Burial of Sir John Moore after Corunna," at the age of four.

Without Harry, Avis was terribly lonely. For

weeks after he left for America, Jim recalled, she did the housework almost in a trance. To save money, she moved the family to an even smaller and more dismal house on Cloud's Hill Avenue, right next to St. George's Park. She got sick, was diagnosed with abscessed teeth, and had to have all of them extracted. Jack came down with rheumatic fever and almost died.

Avis waited anxiously for Harry's letters from America. When the postman had one, he would wave it at her from down the street, and Avis would run out to grab it before he even got to the house. Harry wrote newsy, romanticized accounts of the new country. The buildings in New York were so high, he said, they had to be lowered to let the moon pass by. All the women dressed like actresses and painted their faces like Indians on the warpath. Cleveland was on a lake as big as the Atlantic Ocean. "The very air in America is invigorating," Harry wrote. "Why, Avis, I've been here only a month, but I feel like a different man already!" He would write special messages to the boys, telling them to take care of their mother: "Remember sons, since I can't be there, I'm depending on you. You know, the Queen has an army of soldiers to protect her. It's up to you guardsmen to guard our queen!"

Harry was having little luck finding work in America, but Avis made up her mind to bring

over the family anyway. "We started planning
and figuring, even though Dad said things
were bad over there," Jim recalled. "Mom
decided it would be cheaper to maintain one
home anyway. And we'd never starved yet."
The family began saving up money for the
trip. Avis stopped buying the kids any new
clothes or shoes. During an especially frigid
winter, she scrimped on coal, and most of
the children caught colds. Finally she sold off
their furniture — including their cherished
grandfather clock, the only thing Harry had
asked his parents for when he and Avis got
married.

In March 1908, Avis and her six boys — all
dressed in double layers of shirts and underwear so they would have to pack less —
trekked to the Bristol station to catch the
train for Southampton. They left in a rainstorm, casting an extra pall on their departure. When they got to Southampton, Avis
discovered they had inadvertently packed
their boat tickets in one of the bags that had
been sent ahead; she had to corral a steward
to find their trunk in the pile of luggage waiting to be loaded, so they could rifle through
it and find the tickets.

Finally, on March 21, 1908, the Hope clan
boarded the USS *Philadelphia,* the same ship
that had taken Harry to America nearly a year
earlier. Back in Bristol, when the two eldest
Hope boys didn't answer the roll call at

59

school for a few days, the teacher asked where they were. A student's reply was entered in the logbook: "Gone to Canada."

The family had two cabins in steerage — though, because Avis hated to be apart from any of the children, they often squeezed together into one. The trip was rough, with the heat and the clanging from the engine room making it especially noisy and uncomfortable. Once they left their cabin unattended and returned to find it had been ransacked by an intruder. Luckily, a watch was the only thing missing.

"Everybody on the ship was in sympathy with this tiny lady traveling with her brood of six sons, three of them larger than she — and as a result the boys fared exceptionally well," recalled Jim Hope. "None of them were backward when encouraged to sing, usually to the accompaniment of someone's concertina, mouth organ, or Jew's harp, for the amusement of the passengers, who would in return often reward us generously."

Leslie, as usual, was the most troublesome of the brood. When all the kids on board were lined up for their smallpox vaccinations, the four-year-old bolted free and led the ship's crew on a mad chase around the deck before they found him hiding behind a ventilator and forced him to face the needle. Later his mom tried to calm him down with a bath, but he raised such a fuss that his bandage was dislodged and some of the vaccine inadvertently rubbed off on Avis's thumb, leaving a vaccination scar there for the rest of her life.

The ship docked at Ellis Island on March 30, after an eighteen-hour delay in New York Harbor because of fog. Leslie is the fifth of six Hopes listed on the ship's manifest (his age incorrectly recorded as two years old); their destination is given as Cleveland, to join "husband and father, William H. Hope," at 2227 East 105th Street — where Uncle Fred and his wife, Alice, were living. The manifest notes that their train fare to Cleveland was already paid for, and that they carried $50 in cash.

The immigrant train to Cleveland was slow, forced to give up the right of way to every freight train in its path. With no food on board, the family had to wolf down meals during the brief stops at stations along the way. With little clean water on the train, mothers would use the station stops to wash their children's clothes, then hang them out to dry on baggage racks or out the window once the train got going. A pair of Leslie's pants got snagged by a passing post and were ripped away, and Avis had to search through their luggage to find him another pair, to stop his crying.

After a two-day trip, they arrived at Cleveland's Erie Depot on the evening of April 1.

Harry and his older brother Frank were there to meet them, and Avis cried with joy as she embraced her husband. "I'll swear she looked as though she had shed twenty years," said Jim. The motley crew of three adults and six children then straggled with their luggage, much of it held together with string or wire and breaking at the seams, to the public square downtown, where they caught a Cedar Avenue streetcar and rode all the way out to Uncle Fred and Aunt Alice's house, on East 105th Street. Though it was the middle of the night, a feast was waiting for them at the dinner table, their first meal on solid ground in more than ten days.

Cleveland was not a bad place for an immigrant family to start life in the United States in 1908. In the waning months of Theodore Roosevelt's vigorous presidency, and despite the lingering effects of the panic of 1907, the American economy was thriving. And Cleveland — then the sixth-largest city in the United States, with a population of 560,663 in the 1910 census — was home to many of the industries that were making it hum. Until Detroit overtook it a few years later, Cleveland was the nation's No. 1 manufacturer of automobiles. It was among the leaders in iron and steel production, shipbuilding, and the manufacture of machine tools. Thirty-two banks were founded in Cleveland between 1900 and 1903 alone. The city was enjoying a construction boom, with new downtown office buildings, bridges, colleges, churches, and fine homes in the well-to-do residential neighborhoods along Euclid Avenue to the east of downtown. True, automobile exhaust was starting to befoul the streets, and development was encroaching on the greenery that had earned Cleveland its nickname the Forest City, but the metropolis was enjoying an economic heyday.

The booming city drew plenty of immigrants. At the turn of the century, fully one-third of Cleveland's population was foreign-born; another 40 percent had foreign-born parents. Most of them came from Western Europe — at least half from either Great Britain or Germany, followed in order by those from Sweden, Russia, Austria, and Italy. The Hopes, like many of these newcomers, settled in a neighborhood on the eastern fringe of the city known as Doan's Corners. The bustling area (named for Nathaniel Doan, from whose farm the area had been carved up, before being annexed by the city of Cleveland in 1872) was becoming known as Cleveland's "second downtown," and its vibrant center was the corner of Euclid Avenue and 105th Street, dominated by the four-story Cleveland Trust building. Just to the east were the adjoining campuses of Western Reserve University and the Case

School of Applied Science (decades later to merge into Case Western Reserve). To the west, along Euclid, was so-called Millionaire's Row, a stretch of mansions where Cleveland's richest industrialists and business leaders lived, among them Standard Oil tycoon John D. Rockefeller, mining magnate Samuel Mather, and Charles F. Brush, inventor of the arc light.

A working-class neighborhood bounded by opulence and higher education, Doan's Corners was home to small tradesmen, steelworkers, salesmen, clerks — along with the cooks, chauffeurs, and other household workers who helped tend the mansions on Millionaire's Row. Like so many other urban residential neighborhoods at the time, it was shedding its quaint nineteenth-century trappings and being transformed by the technology of a new century. A hand-drawn map of the area around 1900, annotated by a long-time resident, gives a good snapshot of the neighborhood that likely greeted the Hopes when they arrived in 1908:

Euclid and Cedar had Brush arc lights. Other streets were faintly illuminated by artificial gas lamps on posts: lighted in evening and turned off in early morning by the lamp lighters. Homes of the rich had electric lights, those of the well-to-do artificial gas, while the poor burned coal oil lamps. . . . Coal was king, but furnaces were few. Hard coal base burners warmed the living rooms, while the cook stoves in the kitchens helped out with their smoky soft coal fires. In the summer much cooking was done on gasoline stoves. Ice boxes were had by some. A telephone was a luxury, and if you owned a bathtub you were rich. . . . Electric cars — four wheelers — ran on Euclid and on Cedar; cable cars on Hough. Those had stone block pavement. Doan was a sandy road, while many of the others were yellow clay with coal-ash crosswalks for wet weather.

When they arrived in Cleveland, the Hope family had to temporarily split up. Ivor and Jim stayed with Uncle Frank and Aunt Louisa, who lived above Frank's plumbing and pipe-fitting business. Avis, Harry, and the rest of the boys moved in with Uncle Fred and Aunt Alice. It's unclear how long that arrangement lasted. According to Jim Hope's memoir, the family moved into their own home within a few weeks. But the August 1909 Cleveland City Directory still lists the family as living at 2227 East 105th Street — Fred and Alice's place. At some point, however, Avis rented a three-bedroom house from a Welsh doctor named Staniforth for $18.50 a month, and the family was together again, in their first home in America.

After buying furniture and stocking up on groceries, their money was nearly depleted, and they didn't have enough to pay for the second month's rent. Harry was no help: most days he came home with nothing in his pockets and liquor on his breath — much to the chagrin of Avis, who'd harbored some hope that his drinking problems had been left behind in England. Jim appealed to Uncle Frank for money, but he refused, saying the family shouldn't have come to America unless Harry could support them.

The Land of Opportunity, it turned out, had not provided much opportunity for Harry Hope. Jobs for a stonecutter were nearly as hard to find in America as they were in England. Architects who had previously designed buildings with limestone were switching to terracotta, and there were ten men for every stonecutting job. The frigid Ohio winters were another problem, limiting the number of days when stonecutting could be done. Even at the relatively good wage of $12 a day, Harry could not generate enough steady income to do much more than cover his bar bill. As in England, the job of keeping the family solvent was left largely to Avis and the boys.

Bob Hope, at least in his public recollections, had warm memories of his father. A jovial English gentleman, whose figure varied from "medium stout to happy stout," the man known in the neighborhood as 'Arry 'Ope was "not only an artist with the stone-cutting tools, he was a happy man," Hope wrote in his memoir *Have Tux, Will Travel.* "He loved to live it up. He was popular, and a great entertainer." He wasn't much for disciplining the kids, but would occasionally "take off his belt and salt us good." Yet he was having a hard time in America: "I remember Dad saying, 'The United States is a fine place for women and dogs. It's a poor place for horses and men.' He had trouble adjusting himself to this country. I don't think he ever did."

His drinking was not constant, and never in front of the family. When he was working and sober, the older boys liked to stop by his jobs and just talk to him. "For when he was sober he was so magnetic, he'd cause you to want to linger as long as possible," wrote Jim. "Maybe we'd ask his opinion on some current topic. He'd explain it in such a way that you'd feel proud to discuss it with the next person you'd meet, who would in turn credit you with being well-informed." He was a strong union man, popular among his fellow workers. "I have seen Harry in a great group of angry stonecutters debating and arguing in the most violent fashion," recalled one fellow worker, "and after listening for a while to their remarks he would rise to the floor and with all the true marks of a born orator would calm them down and show them the proper and logical approach to their problem."

His stonecutting skills were also admired. He worked on some major construction projects in Cleveland, including the Church of the Covenant, a Gothic Revival Presbyterian church at 112th and Euclid, and the Lorain-Carnegie Bridge, spanning the Cuyahoga River (and later renamed the Hope Memorial Bridge in his honor). Yet as a businessman he was fairly hapless. Once Harry and a fellow stonecutter formed a partnership and bid on a contract for the stonework on a high school. They won the job, but seriously underestimated the costs and wound up losing money.

Avis, as always, was the family rock, the diminutive, de facto head of the household, and her resourceful, can-do spirit, more than his father's old-country ways, imprinted itself most strongly on young Leslie Hope. Generous, self-effacing, unfailingly upbeat, she put up with Harry's misbehavior and took on the responsibility of managing the household finances. She was a painstaking shopper, carefully comparing prices at the city market and buying in bulk — butter, beans, several sacks of onions in the fall to last through the winter. She altered the boys' clothes so they could be passed down the line to each successive kid. (A seventh, George, was born in 1909, the only Hope son to be born in

America.) She kept the house bright with music, singing and accompanying herself on a secondhand piano she had saved enough to buy. She took the boys to services at a nearby Presbyterian church (after trying out an Episcopalian church that she found too uppity) and frowned on cardplaying, cigarettes, and public dancing. Unable to afford doctors except in dire emergencies, she treated every childhood malady, from measles to whooping cough, with a hot bath and a homemade brew. She kept their home immaculate, regularly scrubbing the floors, beating the rugs, and scouring the cooking stove. She always had fresh-baked pies and cakes ready for visitors, tradesmen, and the children's friends, who would frequently stop by.

"She had the kind of skin you love to touch very much and as often as possible," Jim Hope wrote lovingly in his memoir, "lustrous medium brown hair; beautifully smiling brown eyes with the light of the love of life shining through . . . a beautifully smiling mouth that had never uttered a harsh, unkind or inconsiderate word to or of anyone. With this, a perfectly proportioned body, with the carriage of a thoroughbred, down to a size three shoe." His words are somewhat at odds with photos of her in later years — a slight, plain-looking woman, often lurking in the background of family pictures, or bowing her head as if she wanted to shrink from view —

but understandable from an adoring son who watched his mother's valiant efforts to keep the family afloat.

The family's first two winters in Cleveland were "almost unbearable," Jim recalled, colder than any they had experienced in England. None of the boys even had overcoats. They learned to dress in layers — stuffing newspapers between their underwear and their shirts and trousers for extra insulation. They had a gas fireplace in the living room, but "unless we put our bare bottoms so close as to be dangerous, we'd not know the fire was lit," said Jim. Avis would get up early in the morning and light every burner on the kitchen stove, so at least the kitchen would be warm when the boys raced downstairs from their freezing bedrooms.

To make money, Avis moved the family to increasingly larger houses, so they could take in boarders — three different houses on one block of 105th Street in five years. She was a soft touch with tenants, always susceptible to anyone with a sob story for why he couldn't pay the rent. But the older boys worked at an assortment of jobs to help out: Jim and Ivor at the Van Dorn Iron Works, Fred and Jack at neighborhood stores such as Wheaton's Market and Heisey's Bakery. When one Hope boy would quit a job, another one would often step in and take his place. It got so that Avis couldn't keep track of who was working where. When she sent Sid down to the bakery one day to look for one of his older brothers, the German woman who ran the place exclaimed, "Ach! How many Hopes are there?"

"Looking back on my Cleveland boyhood, I know now that it was grim going," Hope wrote in *Have Tux, Will Travel.* "But nobody told us Hopes it was grim. We just thought that's the way things were. We had fun with what we had." It is a typically brisk assessment of what were certainly difficult times. Leslie, a grade-schooler during those tough early years in Cleveland, may well have been shielded from the worst anxieties of their hand-to-mouth existence. Still, he was clearly developing the tools for protecting himself from harsh realities: a thick skin, an ability to mask his feelings, and a relentlessly positive, can-do attitude in the face of precarious times.

He was a mischievous kid, a daredevil, small for his age — the size of a six-year-old at age ten, Jim recalled. (His father liked to joke that when he was being born and the doctor said, "Grab him," Leslie thought he said, "Stab him," and slipped back inside, thus retarding his growth.) His brothers called him "banana legs" because of his habit of moving so fast his legs couldn't catch up and falling on his face. He seemed to be constantly in motion. "You sat in front of me in one class," a schoolmate recalled in a letter years later, "and you never could sit still. I hit you on the head one time and asked if you had worms!" He and his younger brother Sid once found a giant umbrella and tried to use it as a parachute, leaping off the roof of the Alhambra Theater building into a pile of sand below, nearly breaking their necks. Leslie even walked in his sleep. One night a policeman found him two blocks away from home, knocking at the door of the neighborhood drugstore. After that, Avis would tie his feet to his older brother Jack at night to make sure he didn't wander.

At Fairmont grade school, where he arrived on the first day dressed in an Eton jacket and stiff white collar, his classmates flipped his name, Les Hope, and dubbed him Hopeless. He was never a very good student. The one subject he liked was music: he was the pet of his singing teacher, Miss Bailey, sang in a church choir, and joined his musical family in songs at the annual Welsh picnic at Euclid Beach.

Performing came easy to him, and early. "He was a big show-off since he was about nine," his brother Fred recalled. At age twelve, when Charlie Chaplin–imitating contests were the rage, Les would dress up as the silent-film tramp and walk like Chaplin past the local firehouse. Egged on by his brothers, he entered a Chaplin contest at Luna Park, the amusement mecca a mile away from their home. His brothers packed the audience with neighborhood kids to cheer him on, and he won either first prize (Bob's recollection) or second (Jim's version). According to Bob, he used the prize money to buy a new stove for his mom.

One of his first jobs, at age twelve, was selling newspapers on the corner of 105th and Euclid. He and three brothers — Fred, Jack, and Sid — would each take a corner of the busy intersection, valuable turf that they would often have to defend from rival newsboys in the neighborhood. One of Les's regular customers was an old gentleman in a chauffeur-driven limousine, who would stop by for a paper on his way home in the evenings. One day he rolled down the window and gave Les a dime for the penny paper. Les didn't have change and told the gentleman he could pay tomorrow. The man said no, he would wait for his change, so Les scurried into a nearby grocery store to get it.

When he returned, the old man gave the boy some advice: "If you want to be a success in business, trust nobody. Never give credit and always keep change on hand. That way you won't miss any customers while you're going for it." After he left, someone told Les the old gentleman was John D. Rockefeller.

It was one of Hope's favorite stories from childhood, repeated often. It may even have been true. Rockefeller, the philanthropist and founder of Standard Oil, was in his late seventies at the time, and dividing his retirement years between his Cleveland home and an estate in upstate New York. "As his leisure increased," noted Grace Goulder in *John D. Rockefeller: The Cleveland Years,* "he frequently had his chauffeur stop during afternoon automobile rides so that he might chat with farmers, tradesmen, and anyone who caught his attention." One of them could well have been a young newsboy named Les Hope.

He graduated from Fairmont and went on to East High School. He had a variety of after-school jobs — soda jerk, taffy puller, delivery boy, flower-stand attendant at Luna Park. He spent much of his free time at the Alhambra poolroom, above Dye's restaurant, with his pal George "Whitey" Jennings. Les became a sharpie at three-cushion billiards, good enough to make a few bucks hustling the newcomers, and entertaining the rest with his wisecracks. "We would hang around the corner of Euclid and East 105th Street," one neighborhood kid recalled, "until someone suggested that we go up and watch the 'funny kid' shoot pool." Aunt Louisa admonished Avis that her son was spending too much time in the poolroom, but Avis dismissed her concerns: "Don't worry about Leslie. He'll turn out fine."

Les and Whitey hung out together, coming

up with new schemes for making money. They competed for cash prizes in the foot-races held at the big company picnics every summer at Euclid Beach and Luna Park. When two races were scheduled at the same time, they would try to get one rescheduled so they could compete in both: one of them would call the organizers and pose as a news-paper reporter, saying the race would get covered in the paper if it could just be moved earlier or later. Then, once entered in the race, the two boys would work together, plot-ting for one of them to bump the fastest run-ner, so the other could speed ahead to vic-tory.

In the glow of nostalgia, Hope's early Cleveland years sound like a quintessential early-twentieth-century Norman Rockwell idyll. Childhood friends would write him in later years to reminisce about their youthful exploits and hangouts — places such as Hoffman's restaurant, with its famous ice cream (22 percent butterfat), where, as one neighborhood girl recalled, "you and 'Whitey' fattened me up on 'tin roofs,' walked me home, down past Wade Park, past Superior, to my home, where you played our piano till I almost had to throw you both out." Another neighborhood friend remembered, "My father had a Buick touring car, which I used most every night. Some warm evenings, we would put the top down and pile in and ride slow from 105th to the square and back again, singing barbershop, till the cops chased us off the street. I guess we weren't too hot."

The gritty side of those years has largely been airbrushed out. Les was a tough kid who was no stranger to trouble. He dropped out of high school when he was a sophomore, for reasons that Hope and his biographers have always been vague about. In fact, he was sent to reform school. Records of the Boys Industrial School, a state reformatory in Lancaster, Ohio, show that Lester Hope (in his teenage years he changed his first name from the more effeminate-sounding Leslie), height five feet, weight 105 pounds, residing with his parents at 1913 East 105th Street, was admitted there on May 18, 1918, a few days before his fifteenth birthday. His infraction is not specified — his full juvenile court records have, significantly, been removed — but he was apparently arrested, given a hearing, and "adjudged a delinquent" who was "in need of state institutional care and guardianship."

In interviews over the years, Hope sometimes alluded to incidents of shoplifting during his adolescent years. "I guess it's no secret, but I have a record in Cleveland," he said, only half-jokingly, at a Boys Club benefit in 1967. "They nabbed me for swiping a bike. . . . I pleaded for mercy, but the judge was an ugly, cruel, vindictive man. He turned me over to my parents." In fact, the punishment, for that or a presumably similar incident, was considerably more serious. Les spent seven months at the Boys Industrial School, was paroled on December 21, and then readmitted to the school on March 6, 1919, after violating his parole. The date of his final discharge is unclear, but he appears to have spent at least another year at the reformatory, before being discharged for good in April of either 1920 or 1921. There is no record that he ever returned to high school.

What's most interesting about Hope's stint in reform school is that he felt the need to keep it secret. Even his brother Jim, in his rosy but scrupulously detailed family memoir, doesn't mention it. An arrest for shoplifting and a stretch in reform school are hardly the most scandalous things that can happen to a teenager growing up in a tough urban neighborhood. It might even have added some raffish color to Hope's stories of his wayward youth. But his elimination of them from his personal history was another sign of Hope's capacity for denial, of the need to distance himself from the more unpleasant realities of his early life, and of his effort to construct a new persona that the world would someday know as Bob Hope.

World War I, which the United States entered when Les was fourteen, did not leave the

Hope family untouched. Two of the Hope brothers, Fred and Jack, enlisted in the Army and served overseas — Fred in a field artillery unit and Jack in the infantry. Some tense days in the Hope household followed the news that Jack was missing in action. He turned up in a military hospital, suffering from shell shock. According to accounts given the family, Jack was trying to rescue a fellow soldier when a shell exploded nearly on top of him. He recovered and returned home, but was again hospitalized and survived a near-fatal bout of what was described as trench fever.

In 1920 Harry Hope became a naturalized US citizen, which automatically made Les and his brothers US citizens as well. Harry's work prospects, however, remained bleak. Just to keep busy, he would take on small jobs such as cutting stepping-stones or garden fountainheads from material left over from previous jobs. For Avis he carved a birdbath with a sundial in the center, and a crescent-shaped stone bench that she placed in the garden and would sit on for hours, admiring the flowers. The eldest Hope boys picked up much of the slack, often helping one another in getting jobs. When Jim went to work for an electrical-power-line construction company, for example, he hired Les and two other brothers to string wire.

"Leslie was a good worker, always trying to

do a little more than his workmate," Jim recalled. When they got weekend breaks, however, Les might not show up at work until Tuesday — typically with an outlandish explanation of why. One time, when he was high up in a tree trimming back some branches, one of them snapped and he plunged to the ground, smashing his face. In later years it was occasionally suggested that the mishap — or the plastic surgery that followed — was the cause of his ski-slope nose, but Hope denied it. "It is not true my nose is the way it is as a result of having been broken in an accident," he wrote in *Have Tux, Will Travel.* "It came the way it is from the manufacturer."

Les bounced around to several other jobs in these years: selling shoes at Taylor's department store, filling orders in the service department at the Chandler Motor Car Company. (He got fired from that job when he and some of his pals used the company Dictaphone after hours to practice their singing — and inadvertently left it for their boss to discover the next morning.) He worked at the butcher's stall that his brother Fred had opened at the downtown Center Market. "Bob helped out weekends," recalled Fred. "Plucked chickens, did some waiting on. He was a born salesman, but he never bothered to learn the different meats. One time I heard him trying to sell a customer a ham — and he was showing her a leg of lamb. Honestly, he didn't know the difference. And he sold it to her too."

He even tried boxing. Always a scrappy kid, Les worked on his fighting skills at Charlie Marotta's Athletic Club on Seventy-Ninth Street. One day he found out that his friend Whitey Jennings had signed up to fight in the Ohio State amateur tournament, under the name Packy West. Hope decided to enter too — dubbing himself Packy East. In later years he would often joke about his brief boxing career ("I was the only fighter in Cleveland history who was carried both ways: in and out of the ring"), but he may have had more talent than he gave himself credit for. "He was a good young fighter," said Al Corbett, a local boxer who saw some of Hope's early fights. "He needed training, but he had natural ability. He was well built and his prospects were good." But for the state tournament he weighed in at 128 pounds, just missing the cutoff for the featherweight division, and was forced to battle fighters bigger than he.

Still, he won his first-round fight, got a bye in the second round, and found himself in the semifinals. There he was matched against a more experienced bruiser named Howard "Happy" Walsh. "I probably outweighed Hope by six or eight pounds and I'd been boxing two or three years," Walsh, who later

80

became the state's junior lightweight champion, told the *Cleveland Press*. "I sized him up when he entered the ring as a novice and decided to carry him along, make it look good for the fans. But in the second round he made me mad. I thought he was sneering at me, although I learned later he just unconsciously made faces. Anyhow, I had an exceptionally good right and I hooked him and he was counted out."

Hope remembered it pretty much the same way, with gags: "In the first round I played cozy," he wrote in his memoir. "Happy examined me as if to see what was holding me together. When I found out I was still alive, my footwork got fancier. I pranced around on my toes. In the second round I threw my right. I never got my arm back. Happy hit me on the chin. I fell in a sitting position, bounced and fell over. . . . Red [his manager] threw a bucket of water over me and carried me out." That was the end of his career in the ring.

But not the end of his fighting days. When he was nineteen, Les and Whitey were walking through Rockefeller Park when they got into a scuffle with some thugs who were harassing a girl from the neighborhood. When Jim and some friends found him, Les had cuts over his face and a knife wound in the shoulder, serious enough to require a blood transfusion and fourteen stitches. The inci-

81

dent made the *Cleveland Press* the next day.

For a teenager who couldn't seem to stay out of trouble or keep a job, show business provided a welcome escape. He soaked up all the entertainment available to a kid growing up in World War I–era America. He frequented the local nickelodeons, a fan of swashbuckling silent-film stars like Douglas Fairbanks. His mother would take him to the neighborhood vaudeville house, Keith's 105th Street, where they once saw the celebrated vaudeville star Frank Fay, a song-and-dance man who also did comedy monologues. After a few minutes of his act, Avis whispered to her son, loud enough so that everyone around them could hear, "He's not half as good as you."

Les and Whitey would earn money for the rides at Luna Park by singing for pennies on the bus ride over, and Les sang in a quartet with some neighborhood kids who would perform outside of Schmidt's Beer Garden. His most promising talent, however, was dancing. He practiced steps with his friend Johnny Gibbons, who worked with him at his brother Fred's meat market. (Fred later married Johnny's sister LaRue.) Les took dance lessons from King Rastus Brown, a former vaudeville hoofer, and later from Johnny Root, another ex-vaudevillian, who ran Sojack's Dance Academy, behind Zimmerman's dance hall. Then Root left town, and Les, not yet twenty, took over Root's dance classes and tried to run the school himself. He made up business cards advertising his services: "Lester Hope will teach you to dance — Buck and Wing, Soft Shoe, Eccentric, Waltz, Clog."

When dance marathons were sweeping the country in the early 1920s, Les even tried to hop on the bandwagon, starting his own contest at Sojack's. Unfortunately he was a little late. The grueling marathons (dramatized so memorably in the novel and movie *They Shoot Horses, Don't They?*) had spawned a backlash across the country, and Cleveland was one of several cities weighing a ban on them. In a front-page story on April 17, 1923, the *Cleveland Plain Dealer* reported that the city council had decided to take no action on a proposed ban, allowing those marathons that were already under way to continue, but barring any new ones. Hope made it into the story's last paragraph:

Lester Hope, of 2069 E. 106th Street, started a new contest at Sojack's Dancing Academy, 6124 Euclid Avenue, but the contest was called off after an hour, due to Dance Hall Inspector Johnson's ruling against permitting any new contests to start.

Les closed the school not long after. But he continued to work on his own dancing, competing in local amateur shows, first with Gibbons as a partner and then hooking up with Mildred Rosequist, a "cute little trick" he had met at Zimmerman's dance hall.

"Mildred was tall, blonde, willowy, graceful, and a slick dancer," Hope said. "I thought she was beautiful. She looked as if she'd done her hair with an egg beater. But I loved it that way." He would bring her sweetbreads from Fred's meat market and flirt with her at the cosmetics counter at Halle's department store downtown, where she worked. She became a frequent visitor at the Hope house, and the family liked her. "She worshipped Leslie," remembered Jim. "For some time we were all sure it was a hopeless, one-sided affair, but eventually Leslie also succumbed to her charm."

Mildred remembered the romance a bit differently, describing Les as the pursuer, not to say something of a pest. "He would follow me home from work some nights," she told Hope biographer William Robert Faith. "I mean, he would get on the same streetcar and I wouldn't even know it. When I got off at Cedar, he'd be walking right behind me. Then I'd walk in the front door and my mother'd ask if he was with me and I'd say, 'No,' and then he'd stick his head around the hallway door and say, 'Oh, yes I am.' " He said he wanted to marry her and even bought her an engagement ring. It was so small that she cracked, "Does a magnifying glass come with it?" Les didn't appreciate the joke, and Mildred apologized for hurting his feelings.

They were a smooth pair on the dance floor. They modeled themselves on Vernon and Irene Castle, the enormously popular husband-wife dance team who headlined in vaudeville in the midteens and sparked a national craze for social dancing. Les and Mildred won some amateur contests around the city and were good enough to get a few paying jobs, earning $7 or $8 for an evening. Hope said he split the money with her, but Mildred claimed that Les told her the performances were for charity and kept all the money himself.

Their act had a homey touch. Hope described it in his memoir: " 'This is a little dance we learned in the living room,' I'd tell the audience. Then we'd do that one, and I'd say, 'This is a little dance we learned in the kitchen.' Then we'd do that. We ended with, 'This is a little dance we learned in the parlor.' The parlor dance was a buck dance. We saved it for last because it was our hardest and it left us exhausted."

A little too exhausted for Mildred. She recalled one of their performances at a local social club: "When we came out to do the hard stuff, the buck and wings which were so fast, I just quit, and I said I was tired, and I walked off the stage. Les looked at me with

85

kill in his eyes — he was furious, but he ad-libbed. . . . He picked out a little old lady in the first row and said, 'See, Ma, you should never have made her do the dishes tonight.' "
It is the first recorded Bob Hope joke.

Les wanted to develop an act with Mildred and take it on the road. But her mother had no intention of allowing Mildred to travel with a man who clearly had more on his mind than dancing, and she nixed the idea. Les kept up a romance with Mildred, stringing her along for years to come as a hometown girlfriend. But for a professional partner, he had to look elsewhere.

He settled on Lloyd "Lefty" Durbin, a kid from the neighborhood he had gotten to know at Sojack's Dance Academy. Lloyd was a polished dancer, and together they came up with an act that mixed in a little comedy with their tap and soft-shoe routines. They made the rounds of amateur shows, played intermission spots at movie houses, and landed an occasional fill-in gig on local vaudeville bills. Then, in August 1923, an agent got them a spot at the Bandbox The-ater, as part of a vaudeville show headlined by Roscoe "Fatty" Arbuckle.

Arbuckle, the onetime silent-film comedian, was embarking on a comeback after one of the most sordid scandals in Hollywood his-tory. In 1921, at the height of his popularity, the portly film star was implicated in the mysterious death of a starlet who had been partying with him and some friends in a hotel in San Francisco. Amid tabloid accusations that he had raped or murdered her, Arbuckle was put on trial for manslaughter. Though he was ultimately acquitted (in a third trial, after two hung juries), his film career was finished. Now he was trying to start over, as the star attraction in a touring variety show called *Bohemia.*

Hope and Durbin worked up some fresh material for their spot in the show. They did soft-shoe and buck-and-wing dance routines, and closed with a comic Egyptian dance number. "We wore brown derbies," Hope recalled. "We pretended to go down to a well near the Nile, dip some water in a derby and bring it back. The gag was that afterward we poured actual water out of the derby. It was real crazy and it fetched a boff." By chance, it is one of the few Hope vaudeville routines that can actually be seen: Hope re-created it, with dancer Hal Le Roy as his partner, on his first TV special in April 1950. The two dancers strut around in stiff-armed, hunch-shouldered style, like ancient Egyptian hieroglyphics come to life, and do some neatly synchronized physical shtick, one behind the other. If not quite a boff, it is a slick and amusing piece of comedy business.

"The whole offering is built along familiar lines," the unimpressed reviewer for the

Cleveland Plain Dealer wrote of the Arbuckle show, "with some better-than-ordinary costumes and settings standing out as the distinguishing feature. The comedians are found wanting in many instances, but the musical chorus numbers are well up to snuff." Yet Arbuckle was impressed enough with Hope and Durbin to talk them up to Fred Hurley, a producer of vaudeville tabloid shows — musical-comedy revues that toured mostly small towns. These "tab shows" were considered the bottom rung of the vaudeville ladder, but they were a good place for newcomers to get a start. So, when Hurley a few months later offered Hope and Durbin parts in his new tab revue, *Jolly Follies,* which was set to begin a tour of the Midwest, they grabbed it.

It was Hope's first full-time show-business job. His mother was proud; his practical brothers skeptical that he could earn a living at it. But for Hope, at age twenty-one, it was a great opportunity. The job would give him a chance to travel and see if he could make it as an entertainer in front of more than just hometown crowds. It would pay him a decent salary of $40 a week, half of which he promised to send back home to his parents. What it wouldn't give him was a quick road to stardom. Hope's vaudeville apprenticeship would last for nearly a decade — longer than the ambitious young hoofer had probably anticipated. Yet it would give him plenty of time to learn the tools of his trade, discover how to survive in a changing show-business world, and invent Bob Hope.

CHAPTER 2
VAUDEVILLE

"NO, LADY, THIS IS NOT JOHN GILBERT."

When Les Hope and his partner Lloyd Durbin went on the road with their act in the fall of 1924, vaudeville was dying. But then it had been dying for years, and it would continue dying for many years to come, as movies and radio plundered its audience and lured away its star performers. Still, enough life was left in those old Olympic and Palace and Hippodrome theaters, which brought live stage entertainment to towns big and small across America, to give a young hoofer from Cleveland a chance to make his mark.

Vaudeville was Hope's irreplaceable school of show business. He loved his time there, and it instilled the qualities that would define him as an entertainer for the rest of his career: his love for stage performing, his ability to adapt to audiences of all kinds, his tireless work ethic. He came into vaudeville a novice, but he was smart and resourceful, doing whatever it took to survive — borrowing jokes, finding new partners, latching on to fads, even dancing with Siamese twins. But in that survival-of-the-fittest world, he evolved into something original, a fresh stage personality perfectly pitched to the changing times.

Vaudeville, even in its waning days, was still a great adventure for a young performer, a unique, if relatively short-lived, chapter in American entertainment. It was born in the 1880s, an outgrowth of the rambunctious, often racy variety shows that catered largely to men in the saloons and beer halls of post–Civil War America. A few prescient theater owners in New York City got the idea to clean up these shows, move them into larger and more respectable theaters (no liquor, no hookers), and market them to the family audience. These new family-friendly shows ("good clean fun" was the popular catchphrase) caught on almost immediately. In 1900 the United States had an estimated two thousand vaudeville houses; by 1912 the number had grown to five thousand. Giant theater chains sprang up with centralized booking so that acts could be mixed and matched and sent on nationwide tours efficiently. At one time, an estimated twenty thousand people were making a living — sometimes a handsome living — as vaudeville entertainers.

A typical vaudeville bill featured eight to ten acts, carefully assembled to appeal to as broad an audience as possible: young and old, male and female, highbrow and lowbrow. In a vaudeville show you could see singers, dancers, comedians, jugglers, magicians, acrobats, ukulele players, trained animals, female impersonators, and an assortment of wacky comics loosely categorized as "nut" acts. Celebrated stage actors such as Sarah Bernhardt and Ethel Barrymore appeared on the vaudeville stage. So did sports stars, among them Babe Ruth, and tabloid newsmakers such as Evelyn Nesbit, the former Floradora Girl whose lover, the architect Stanford White, was murdered by her jealous husband, Harry K. Thaw. Harry Houdini, the famed illusionist and escape artist, was a big vaudeville star. Even Helen Keller did a turn in vaudeville.

Vaudeville was America's first form of mass entertainment. It grew to maturity as waves of immigrants were transforming American cities, and it was both a reflection of the melting pot and an agent of assimilation. Comedians often got laughs from broad ethnic stereotypes: there were funny Germans, funny Irishmen, funny Italians, funny Jews — and funny Negroes, played in blackface by white comics, a throwback to the minstrel shows that were an important forerunner of vaudeville. Yet even as it spotlighted ethnic differences, vaudeville was helping draw the nation together — creating the first mass-audience entertainment stars, from Lillian

Russell, the 1890s chanteuse who was called the most beautiful woman in the world, to such pioneers of early-twentieth-century show business as George M. Cohan, Al Jolson, Will Rogers, Sophie Tucker, and the Marx Brothers.

For its performers, vaudeville wasn't just a job but a way of life, with its own traditions, protocol, and lingo. There was "big-time" vaudeville — the large theaters in the biggest cities where the top acts appeared, usually doing two shows a day, matinee and evening — and "small-time" vaudeville, the minor leagues, where less established acts worked, usually in continuous shows that were repeated four, five, or six times a day. Billing of the acts adhered to strict hierarchies and customs. The opening spot was the lowest in the pecking order — usually an acrobat or some other "dumb" act, to allow time for latecomers to get settled. The show's headliner typically had the second-to-last spot ("next to shut," in the argot of *Variety,* the show-business trade paper), leaving the finale for a lesser act whose primary job was to clear out the house for the next show (thus called the "chaser"). Performers traveled from town to town by train or bus and frequently stayed in run-down rooming houses or show-business hotels. It was a hard, exhausting life, which forever carried a kind of seedy romance for the performers who came of age in it.

Hope and Durbin's first vaudeville job was strictly small-time. Hurley's tab show *Jolly Follies* traveled the lowly Gus Sun circuit, a Chicago-based chain of some three hundred theaters that served small towns in the Midwest and South. The show's headliner, Frank Maley, doubled as a performer (teaming with a partner in a blackface comedy act) and the company manager — handling the books, overseeing the scenery, and sometimes even taking the tickets.

For Les Hope, it was a great learning experience. "Tab shows were a special part of show business," Hope wrote in his memoir. "There's no dollars and cents way I can measure the seasoning, the poise, the experience that being with Hurley gave me." Hope and Durbin started in the chorus and worked their way up to larger roles in sketches and musical numbers. Hazel Chamberlain, the company's top-billed singer, recalled the first time she heard Hope get a laugh — in Bloomington, Indiana, when he filled in as emcee for a sketch called "Country Store Night." "Frankly we had all thought Lefty Durbin was the more likely of the two to be a comic," she said, "but that night Les Hope was as much surprised as the rest of us."

The troupe of thirteen traveled together by bus, staying in cheap theatrical hotels and boardinghouses. When they arrived in a new town, Maley would often have to knock on doors to find lodgings that were willing to take "show folk." The living conditions were often dicey: cramped rooms, suspect food, linens that rarely got changed. "By the end of the week the towels would be so dirty you would usually bypass them and fan yourself dry," Hope said. As the junior members of the troupe, Hope and Durbin often got the worst of it. At a theater in Orangeburg, South Carolina, the two tiny dressing rooms (one for men and one for women) had no space for them, so they had to clean out the coal bin in the basement and do their makeup there amid the coal dust.

Life on the road had its pleasures too. Les began seeing a girl in the troupe named Kathleen O'Shay — the stage name of Ivy Shay, a pretty Irish girl from Morgantown, West Virginia. Their affair caused a bit of a stir in the straitlaced *Jolly Follies* troupe (Maley and several others were married and had their wives along). At a hotel in Bedford, Indiana, Les was visiting Kathleen's room when the hotel manager knocked at the door and ordered him out. He had a gun to put the point across. Kathleen left the troupe not long after and moved back to Morgantown, where she opened a dress shop. Les continued to stop in and see her when he passed through town, sometimes bringing dresses for her shop from New York. According to one Morgantown friend, she broke off the relationship because she was too embarrassed by his loud clothes.

Hurley's *Jolly Follies* toured for one season, closing in the spring of 1925. But the team of Hope and Durbin didn't last that long, broken up prematurely by an unexpected tragedy. Hope's partner died.

Hope always blamed it on a bad piece of coconut cream pie that Durbin had eaten in a restaurant in West Virginia. When he began complaining of stomach pains, a doctor told him he had food poisoning. But while Durbin was taking his bows after their last show in New Castle, Pennsylvania, he sank to the floor and began spitting up blood. "I'm sick," he muttered. "Get me home."

The company members quickly checked train timetables, while Les tried to reach Lloyd's parents. Jim Hope — who, by odd chance, was there, having dropped in to catch his brother's act while traveling — carried Lloyd four blocks to the station and put him on a midnight train, entrusting him to the care of the attendant in charge of the baggage car. (By some accounts, Les traveled back to Cleveland with him, but Jim's recollection seems more reliable.) Lloyd's parents were at the station to meet him when the train arrived, and they took him to the hospital. He died three days later.

The cause, it turned out, was tuberculosis, an illness Durbin had apparently either ignored or managed to hide. Hope remained convinced the culprit was food poisoning; forever afterward, he was wary of eating at greasy spoons on the road, and he usually opted instead for the relatively safe home cooking of local tearooms.

In later years, when reminiscing about his vaudeville days, Hope didn't like to dwell on, or even mention, Lloyd Durbin's death. He glosses over it in one paragraph in his memoir *Have Tux, Will Travel.* Some chroniclers of Hope's career have suggested that he willfully ignored his partner's deteriorating health, reluctant to jeopardize his big break in show business. That is probably unfair. Still, what might have been a traumatic blow to another entertainer, or at least a sobering interruption in a budding career, was little more than a hiccup for Les Hope. Within days of Durbin's death, he was back on the road with Hurley's show. Fred Hurley had found him a new partner.

George Byrne was a soft-spoken, slightly built, angel-faced hoofer from Columbus, Ohio — like Durbin, a mild-mannered counterpoint to the more driven and outgoing Les Hope. "George was pink-cheeked and naïve," Hope said. "He looked like a choir boy. He was real quiet. Real Ohio. He was a smooth dancer and had a likeable personality. We became good friends."

Hope and Byrne finished out the *Jolly Follies* season together, doing well enough to move up to third billing, dubbed "Dancers Supreme." Next, Frank Maley put them in a blackface revue called *The Blackface Follies.* As Hope tells it, on their first night in McKeesport, Pennsylvania, they blacked up with greasepaint instead of the usual burned cork and had to work all night trying to get it out. "After that we told Maley we thought we'd skip the blackface," said Hope. Instead, Fred Hurley cast them in a new tab show he was readying for the 1925–26 season, called *Smiling Eyes.*

The show was another mélange of sketches, songs, and dance numbers, with Hope playing leading roles and character parts, singing in a quartet with Maley and two others, and joining Byrne for a featured dance spot. The team added bits of comedy to their act — mostly corny, secondhand vaudeville gags, with Les typically playing the straight man. George, for example, might walk across the stage with a woman's dress on a hanger.

HOPE: "Where are you going?"
BYRNE: "Down to get this filled."

Or George would come in carrying a plank of wood.

HOPE: "Where are you going now?"

BYRNE: "To find a room. I've already got my
  board."

But their dancing, not their comedy, drew
the most attention. "The most versatile
couple of eccentric dancers who have ever
been seen at the Victoria," wrote a reviewer
in Wilmington, Delaware. In Newport, Kentucky, "they stopped the show with their
numbers and were called back for two en-
cores." They were a smash in Newport News,
Virginia. "For the premier honors of the
entire bill, Hope and Byrne came through
with flying colors in the eccentric dance,"
wrote the local critic. "Friends, it was a
regular knockout. There has never been
anything any better in this house of this kind."
  Hope and Byrne traveled with *Smiling Eyes*
for the entire 1925–26 season. At breaks
between engagements, they would stop in
Cleveland and practice dance routines in
front of the big mirror above the fireplace
in the Hopes' living room. "I taught myself
to play 'Yes, Sir, That's My Baby' on an
upright piano, while George stood on top of
the piano, plucking a banjo strung like a uke,"
Hope recalled. On the road, their adventures
were not always so homespun. Once, in Brad-
dock, Pennsylvania, they hitched a ride to
Pittsburgh with a stranger outside the theater
and found themselves in a highway car chase
with the cops. The driver ditched the car in a

gulley and ran off into the bushes, leaving Hope and Byrne to get hauled off to jail. The car had been reported stolen. They were released after a night in jail when the driver was identified as a doctor's chauffeur who had taken his boss's car for a spin without asking.

Their act caught the eye of Gus Sun, the theater-circuit owner, who thought Hope had possibilities as a single. But Fred Hurley was more skeptical and told a reporter covering the show in Springfield, Ohio, not to give Hope "any big puff." "Why not?" the reporter asked. "Because it'll go to his head," said Hurley. "Next thing he'll be wanting a raise, and I'm already paying him more than he's worth."

When *Smiling Eyes'* season was over in the spring of 1926, Hope and Byrne decided to strike out on their own. They billed themselves as "Dancemedians" and put together an act that featured as much comedy as dancing. One of their models was the vaudeville team of Duffy and Sweeney, a comedy duo known for wacky stunts: taking out a frying pan and making eggs onstage, for example, or lying underneath a piano sucking lollipops. Their shenanigans would often continue offstage. After one performance they staged a shouting match in their dressing room, climaxed by a gunshot and a thud — followed by Duffy stalking out of the room alone.

When company members nervously opened the dressing-room door to see what had happened, they found Sweeney calmly removing his makeup.

Hope and Byrne brought some of this madcap spirit to their act. "Our act opened with a soft-shoe dance," Hope recalled in his memoir. "We wore the high hats and spats and carried canes for this. Then we changed into a fireman outfit by taking off our high hats and putting on small papier-mâché fireman hats. George had a hatchet and I had a length of hose with a water bulb in it. We danced real fast to 'If You Knew Susie,' a rapid ta-da-da-da-da tempo, while the drummer rang a fire bell. At the end of this routine we squirted water from the concealed bulb at the brass section of the orchestra in the pit."

The act was good enough to get them two weeks at the State Theater in Detroit for $175 a week, with a late show at the Oriole Terrace for an additional $75 — a nice raise from the $100 a week they were getting from Hurley. They squandered most of their first week's pay at a gambling joint down the street from the theater. But the reviews were good and helped them get a few more gigs in Detroit. Then they moved on to Pittsburgh for a stint at the Stanley Theater for $300 a week, on a bill with Tal Henry and His North Carolinians, a popular swing band.

But Hope was itching to go to New York,

where the big-time bookers were. He bought the team Eton jackets with big white collars and spats and hired a top photographer in Chicago to take new publicity shots of them; even at this early stage, Hope was learning the value of marketing. In their boaters and bow ties, they looked like perfect 1920s dandies. Hope, with his slicked-back hair, lantern jaw, and hawklike gaze, was clearly the sharpie of the pair — lean, dapper, and good-looking, "the thinnest man in vaudeville," in Hope's words. "I was down to 130 pounds. I was so thin I always made sure the dog act was over before I came onstage."

The publicity shots apparently paid off. When Hope and Byrne got to New York and started pounding the pavement, they met with Abe Lastfogel of the William Morris Agency. "If you're only half as good as your pictures, you'll do," Lastfogel said. The job he had for them, however, was certainly the strangest of Hope's career. He and Byrne were hired to play second fiddle to a pair of Siamese twins.

Daisy and Violet Hilton, joined back-to-back at the hip, were born in Brighton, England, in 1908, to a barmaid who gave them up to her landlady shortly after birth. The twins' foster parents turned them into a sideshow attraction in England, and later, after moving to San Antonio, on the American vaudeville circuit. (Today they're best known for their featured roles in Tod Browning's 1932 film *Freaks*.) Sideshow freaks were hardly unheard of in vaudeville, but there was nothing quite like the sensation caused by the Hilton sisters. When they played Newark, the lines around the theater blocked traffic. They set a house record in Cleveland. *Variety* pronounced them "the greatest draw attraction and business getter that has hit vaudeville in the past decade."

In their relatively skimpy twelve-minute act, the sisters talked about their lives as Siamese twins, played a duet on saxophone and clarinet, and performed a closing dance number with two male partners. That's where Hope and Byrne came in — returning for the finale after their own featured dance number earlier in the show. Improbable as it seems, the act got good reviews. "The finish is a wow and a real novelty," said *Variety*. "The routining of the dance steps shows it perfectly possible for the twins to dance all of the present type of dances with partners who are familiar with close formation." Though the Hiltons were the obvious star attraction, Hope and Byrne got their share of attention. "They have some fast dances and several novelties, even singing a little," noted one reviewer. "Both Hope and Byrne stand out pleasantly on the program."

Hope was a little nonplussed at the whole experience. "At first it was a funny sensation to dance with a Siamese twin," he wrote. "They danced back to back, but they were wonderful girls and it got to be very enjoyable — in an unusual sort of way." But when the twins' manager wouldn't give Hope and Byrne a raise after six months, they quit the show in Providence and headed back to New York.

It was 1927, a pivotal year for show business. Hollywood's first talking picture, *The Jazz Singer* with Al Jolson, opened in October, giving vaudeville another push toward oblivion. Movies had been encroaching on vaudeville's turf since the early teens. At first, short silent films were added to vaudeville bills as a novelty — just another attraction, like a juggler or a comedy team. With the advent of feature-length films, however, more vaudeville houses began switching to movies as a primary attraction, with live entertainment as merely a supplement. By 1925, only a hundred all-live vaudeville theaters were left in the country. When talking pictures arrived, the trend accelerated, with more theaters adding movies and many dropping their stage shows altogether.

Vaudeville was also getting strong competition in 1927 from another quarter: Broadway. More than 260 shows, at least 50 of them musicals, opened on Broadway during the 1927–28 season, including such classic musicals as the Gershwins' *Funny Face* (starring

Fred and Adele Astaire), Rodgers and Hart's *A Connecticut Yankee,* and Jerome Kern's landmark *Show Boat.* It was also the heyday of the musical revue. These loosely structured shows (including such perennials as the Ziegfeld *Follies, George White's Scandals,* and *Earl Carroll's Vanities*) featured songs, sketches, and lavish production numbers — a kind of gussied-up vaudeville show — and provided a bounty of jobs for performers who might otherwise be touring in vaudeville, both well-known stars and up-and-comers.

Hope and Byrne were among those up-and-comers in the summer of 1927 when they landed parts in a Broadway show called *Sidewalks of New York.* With book and lyrics by Eddie Dowling and music by James Hanley — the team whose *Honeymoon Lane* had been a big hit the previous season — it was nominally a book musical, about a naïve girl from an orphanage who comes to the big city. But it had many revue-style elements, including topical jokes about current political figures such as New York governor Al Smith and New York City mayor Jimmy Walker, and a cast packed with veteran vaudevillians, among them the comedy team of Smith and Dale (the model for Neil Simon's bickering vaudeville duo in *The Sunshine Boys*). One of the show's female leads was a young dancer, soon to marry Al Jolson and move to

Hollywood, named Ruby Keeler.

Getting cast in the show was a big break for Hope and Byrne: just months after playing dance partners to a pair of Siamese twins, they were on Broadway. But their roles were minimal; except for a small dance bit in the opening production number, they were mostly lost in the gigantic cast of eighty. During the show's pre-Broadway tryout run in Philadelphia, a new number was written that featured them and Keeler, but it never made it into the show.

Sidewalks of New York opened at New York's Knickerbocker Theater on October 3, 1927, and got reasonably good reviews. But to keep the show running, the producers had to cut costs. Hope and Byrne were just one of two male dance teams in the show, and as the less experienced pair, they got the ax. *Sidewalks of New York* went on to have a respectable run of 117 performances, but the Broadway career of Hope and Byrne was over in eight weeks. By the end of 1927, they were back on the street, scrounging for vaudeville jobs.

They rented rooms in a series of theatrical hotels, sometimes sharing the same lumpy bed and filling their substantial downtime by trading stories with other out-of-work vaudevillians. They kept working on the act — Hope pushing, as always, to add more comedy. They landed the No. 2 spot at the B. S.

Moss Franklin Theater to showcase their act for bookers, but it didn't go well. After a while they had trouble getting bookers to even come see them. A top agent at William Morris, Johnny Hyde (later famed for his role in launching the career of a young Marilyn Monroe), gave them a blunt assessment: "You ought to go West, change your act, and get a new start."

Beaten down, Hope and Byrne decided to make a strategic retreat to Chicago and try to rethink their act there. Hope called an agent in Cleveland named Mike Shea, who found them a job along the way: a three-night weekend engagement in New Castle, Pennsylvania, third on a three-act bill, for a salary of $50. It would turn out to be an important stop for Hope.

Before their first show, the theater manager asked Hope if, at the end of his closing spot with Byrne, he would stay onstage to announce the next week's show. Hope, grabbing the chance for a little more stage time, ad-libbed a joke about the coming headliner, Marshall Walker. "Marshall is a Scotsman," said Hope. "I know him. He got married in the backyard so the chickens could get all the rice."

The wisecrack, playing on the stereotype of the frugal Scotsman, got a laugh, and the manager told Hope to keep it up for the next show. The following night Hope threw in a few more jokes. By the end of the weekend, an orchestra member told him he ought to drop the dancing act altogether and try to make it as an emcee.

Emcees were a relatively new phenomenon in vaudeville. In contrast to British music halls — where the performers were introduced by a host, or "chairman" — vaudeville acts traditionally just trooped onstage, announced only by a title card on an easel at the side of the stage. But that began to change in the 1920s, thanks largely to the success of a suave comedian named Frank Fay, vaudeville's best-known master of ceremonies. If anyone in vaudeville can be singled out as Hope's creative role model, it is Fay.

He first became popular as a vaudeville monologuist in the late teens. By the mid-1920s he was the most popular emcee at New York's Palace Theatre, once appearing there for an unprecedented ten straight weeks. His job was to introduce the performers, fill the spaces between acts with banter, and generally keep the show moving — or slow it down if there was a delay backstage. This required a new style of comedy. In contrast to most vaudeville comics, with their exaggerated stage personas, loud checked suits, and well-honed routines, Fay came onstage as himself and joked around in a casual, seemingly off-the-cuff manner.

Fay was a handsome Irishman, with a velvety manner and an aloof, almost aristocratic bearing — very different from the brash, fast-paced style that Hope developed. Fay's humor was often cutting, even mean. (Girl: "I just came back from the beauty parlor." Fay: "And they didn't wait on you?") He was, moreover, reputed to be something of a bastard offstage; anecdotes about his contemptuous behavior toward fellow performers abounded. (He later had a stormy marriage to the actress Barbara Stanwyck.) Though he appeared in several movie musicals in the early 1930s and starred in the original Broadway production of Mary Chase's hit 1944 play, *Harvey,* his later career never came close to the heights it reached in vaudeville.

Fay was a key inspiration for Hope, introducing him to a comedy style that was more natural and spontaneous, a style that would allow Hope to showcase his quick wit and stage presence, rather than his often mediocre material, and to establish a more intimate relationship with the audience. But it meant working alone.

By Hope's account, the end of the Hope-Byrne partnership was amicable, and not unexpected. Near the end of 1927, as Hope told the story, he simply went to Byrne and said, "I think I'll try it alone for a couple of weeks. If it works, we'll break up the trunk."

Byrne took the news in stride: "I don't blame you. I'll go back to Columbus and take it easy." According to Jim Hope, Byrne's father was ill, and George felt it was time to move home and get steadier work.

It may be a stretch to believe that the breakup of a relatively successful three-year stage partnership came with no more trauma than that, and some observers have seen it as an early example of Hope's self-centered careerism. Lawrence Quirk, author of the gossipy, unfriendly, and only marginally reliable biography *Bob Hope: The Road Well-Traveled,* claims that the breakup was a cruel blow to Byrne, who was too weak a personality to put up much of a fight with his domineering partner. Quirk quotes director George Cukor, a friend of Byrne's, describing a tearful phone call from Hope's partner, who was distraught over the prospect of splitting up the team. "Without him I'm nothing," Byrne supposedly said. Quirk also cites Cukor and others to suggest that Byrne was gay and had an unrequited crush on Hope.

(Quirk also hints, more dubiously, that Hope himself had repressed homosexual urges. A single young man traveling the vaudeville circuit in the fast-and-loose 1920s may well have done some experimenting. Hope once told his radio writers of an encounter he had on the road with a cross-dressing performer known as Umqualia the

Spanish Queen. The fellow knocked on Hope's hotel room door one night and offered to service him. "Why not?" Hope responded. Still, the suggestion that Hope was bisexual is hard to take seriously.)

If there was any bitterness between Hope and Byrne over the breakup of their act, it didn't last. After the split, Byrne spent a few years as part of a comedy-dance quartet, then retired from show business and went to work for the Defense Supply Company in Columbus. He and Hope remained friends. On a stop in Columbus a few years later, Hope invited Byrne to join him and his brothers for a family celebration at a local nightspot, and Byrne brought along his sister Mary. She hit it off with Hope's youngest brother, George, and the two ended up marrying — thus establishing a permanent family link between the onetime vaudeville partners.

Byrne never talked publicly about his partnership with Hope or their breakup. But family members discounted any suggestion that Byrne felt badly treated by Hope. "My mother told me that her brother George wanted to leave the act," said Avis Hope Eckelberry, the daughter of George and Mary Byrne Hope. "He wanted to go home. He was done with being on the road. There were no hard feelings." George Byrne died in 1966, at age sixty-two. Hope never had a bad word to say about him.

■ ■ ■ ■

Once he split from his partner, Les Hope was in uncharted territory. He accompanied Byrne on the bus back to Columbus, then continued on to Cleveland, where he moved back home for a while to get his bearings. Avis was glad to have him back; his letters from the road had made his hand-to-mouth existence all too apparent. "If I don't get any work by Saturday," he wrote in one, "I'll be starting home on Shank's pony." Avis fortified him with home-cooked meals and lemon pie.

Les called up Mike Shea, the Cleveland agent who had booked Hope in New Castle, and asked if Shea could find any work for him as a single. Shea got him a spot on a "rotary," a vaudeville show that moved around to different venues in town every night. For the first few days, Hope worked in blackface. "I went out, bought a big red bow tie, white cotton gloves like Jolson's, a cigar, and a small derby which jiggled up and down when I bounced onstage," he recalled.

It was an odd choice for Hope, but it may have helped loosen him up, easing the pressure of doing a single for the first time. "Audiences knew that white performers in blackface were not really blacks. But they associated blackface performers with a uniquely freer, more expressive style," wrote Robert Snyder in *Voice of the City,* his history of vaudeville in New York City. "In blackface, white performers found a liberating mask." But Hope's blackface experiment didn't last long. He would take the trolley from home each night to his various gigs. On the fourth night, he missed the streetcar and arrived too late to put on the burned cork. So he went on without makeup, and the act went over just fine. Afterward Shea told him, "Don't ever put that cork on again. Your face is funny the way it is."

After a few weeks in Cleveland, Les was ready to make the move to Chicago. The country's second-biggest entertainment center after New York, the city offered plenty of opportunities for a vaudeville performer — with lavish downtown theaters such as the Palace, Majestic, and State-Lake, along with many neighborhood movie houses that also offered live entertainment. But in early 1928, with no contacts and little money, Les Hope got a cold welcome.

"I couldn't get in anybody's door," he recalled. "I was living at a hotel on Dearborn Street and sharing a bathroom with a man who had a cleanliness complex. He only came out to eat. I couldn't get a date, and I owed four hundred bucks cuffo for coffee and doughnuts." Years later, while traveling through Chicago with his granddaughter

Miranda, he would point out the street corner where he used to gaze in the window of a fancy restaurant and watch the rich people dining. "I used to dance on that corner for tips," he said. It was probably the low point of Hope's career.

When spring came and there was still no work, he was about to give up. Then he ran into Charlie Cooley, a vaudeville hoofer he knew from Cleveland. Sorry to see his brash Cleveland pal down on his luck, Cooley took him into the Woods Theater Building to meet his friend Charlie Hogan, who booked vaudeville acts in movie theaters around town. Hogan told Hope an emcee spot was open on Memorial Day weekend at the West Englewood Theater, on the city's southwest side. The pay was only $25, but Les, hungry for anything, snapped it up.

He did well, and before the weekend gig was over, Hogan had lined up another emcee job for him: two weeks at the Stratford Theater, a popular neighborhood movie house at Sixty-Third and Halstead. The Stratford had just lost its longtime emcee, Ted Leary, and was trying out replacements. "Late of *Sidewalks of New York* Co.," read the ad in the *Chicago Tribune* on June 25, 1928, announcing Hope's debut there (on a bill with the Wallace Beery movie *Partners in Crime*). The ad was a notable milestone. For the first time, he was billed as Bob Hope.

The name change was fairly arbitrary, if euphonious. "I thought Bob had more 'Hiya, fellas' in it," Hope said. The name took awhile to catch on. Hope loved telling the story of a theater in Evansville, Indiana, that billed him on the marquee as "Ben Hope." When he complained, the theater manager shrugged and said, "Who knows?" Hope kept a photo of the marquee for the rest of his life.

At the Stratford, Hope made friends with a pint-size song-and-dance man named Barncy Dean, who talked up Hope's act with Charlie Hogan, and his two-week run was extended to four weeks. But the neighborhood regulars were a tough crowd. Harry Turrell, the Stratford's manager, reminded Hope in a letter years later of "the very unfair reception given you when you tried so hard to follow Ted Leary, who had been a fixture there for many years"; after six weeks "I had to tell you that you didn't make it." After his Stratford gig ended, Hope (who had kept his connections in the New York theater world) landed the small role of Screeves the butler in a short-lived Broadway musical called *Ups-a Daisy*. But on New Year's Eve he was back in Chicago, signing a contract with the Stratford for another stint as emcee, at $225 a week. This time Hope stayed for sixteen straight weeks, and the engagement was a turning point in his career.

At the Stratford, Hope had to develop a

comedy act on the fly. A vaudeville comic who traveled the road, appearing in a new city every week, could recycle material over and over. But the emcee of a neighborhood movie house faced many of the same patrons week after week, as the movie bills changed. That meant he had to keep coming up with new material. Hope scrounged for new gags anywhere he could. He mined vaudeville jokebooks and magazines such as *College Humor.* He stole bits from more established vaudeville comics like Frank Tinney. He begged new acts that came through town to throw a couple of extra jokes his way.

He improvised material, playing off the acts he had to introduce — such as the Great Guilfoil, who juggled cannonballs. He danced and sang, wading into the audience for numbers like "If You See Me Dancing in Some Cabaret, That's Just My Way of Forgetting You." He threw in some Duffy-and-Sweeney-style stunts: there would be a loud crash offstage, after which Hope would walk on, dust off his clothes, and straighten his tie as if he'd just finished a fight, snarling, "Lie there and bleed." He would poke fun at himself when his jokes bombed — "I found that joke in my stocking; if it happens again, I'll change laundries" — to disarm the crowd and get them on his side.

"I learned a lot about getting laughs and about ways of handling jokes of different types at the Stratford," he said. "I'd lead off with a subtle joke, and after telling it, I'd say to the audience, 'Go ahead; figure it out.' Then I'd wait till they got it. One of the things I learned at the Stratford was to have enough courage to wait. I'd stand there waiting for them to get it for a long time. Longer than any other comedian has enough guts to wait. My idea was to let them know who was running things."

He was brash, sophisticated, modern. Unlike so many of the vaudeville comics who preceded him, he didn't do accents or play an ethnic type. ("I simply can't tell a dialect joke," he often said.) He was an all-American wise guy, accessible to everyone. For the critic John Lahr — the son of actor Bert Lahr, a former vaudeville comic of the same era — Hope represented a clean break with the physical clowns and ethnic (often Jewish) comics who came before. "He was a bright package of assimilated poise and pragmatism — the all-American average guy," wrote Lahr. "In their manic bravado, the older generation of funnymen gave off a whiff of immigrant desperation and sadness at what had been left behind. Hope was all future. The wrinkles had been pressed out of his suits and out of his personality. He was an anxiety-free, up-to-the-minute, fast-talking go-getter on holiday."

With his urbane, fast-paced style, Hope also

exemplified the racier, more freewheeling comedy that was becoming popular at the Palace Theatre, the New York City showplace that opened in 1913 and quickly became the premier vaudeville house in the country. The entertainers who starred at the Palace blew away the last vestiges of Victorian prudishness — the era of "good clean fun," variety entertainment for the whole family. The Palace was "the focal point of a new twentieth-century aesthetic of shazz and pizzazz, of (as *Variety* abbreviated it) 'show biz,' " wrote D. Travis Stewart (under the pseudonym Trav S.D.) in his lively vaudeville history, *No Applause — Just Throw Money.* "This quality permeated every aspect of the era's entertainment. The breezy new spirit was perhaps embodied most successfully in the personality of Bob Hope — wisecracking, confident, comfortable. Here was the future."

Bob Hope's own future became clearer with his successful run at the Stratford Theater. Armed with a fresh load of material and a new comedy style, he set out in the spring of 1929 to try his act on the road. Charlie Hogan got him some bookings around the Midwest, mostly small-time theaters in such places as South Bend, Indiana, and St. Paul, Minnesota. He sported a brown derby and cigar and had the confidence of a headliner — and pretty soon he was one.

He also had a new partner in the act: a pretty, blond aspiring actress from Chicago named Louise Troxell. He began using her onstage at the Stratford in "Dumb Dora" routines, popular vaudeville bits in which a male comic is constantly flummoxed by his daffy female companion. Their material was a pretty standard example of the genre:

LOUISE: "The doctor said I'd have to go to the mountains for my kidneys."
BOB: "That's too bad."
LOUISE: "Yes, I didn't even know they were up there."

BOB: "What have you got in your bag?"
LOUISE: "Mustard."
BOB: "What's the idea?"
LOUISE: "You can never tell when you're going to meet a ham."

Louise quickly became a fixture in Hope's act, as well as in his life, in ways that would cause him some problems in the years to come.

Hope put together an act he called "Keep Smiling" and toured on the Interstate Vaudeville Circuit, moving through the Midwest and then into the South. There he hit a speed bump. The fast-paced Chicago personality who played so well up North seemed to befuddle his Southern audiences. In Fort

Worth, Texas, Hope felt totally lost. "When I walked out before my first Fort Worth audience with my fast talk," he recalled, "I might as well have kept walking to the Rio Grande. Nobody cared. I couldn't understand it. I came offstage, threw my derby on the floor and told the unit manager, 'Get me a ticket back to my country.' "

Bob O'Donnell, head of the Interstate circuit, was in the audience that night, and he came backstage after the show. "What seems to be the matter, fancy pants?" he said. When Hope complained about the audience, O'Donnell suggested, "Why don't you slow down and give them a chance? This is Texas. Let them understand you. Why make it a contest to keep up with your material?"

Hope, the cocky Midwesterner, bristled at the advice. But it registered. "I did slow down for the next show (as much as my stubbornness would let me) and the audience warmed up a little," he recalled. "I slowed down even more for the next show, and during the last show of the night, I was almost a hit. Before I moved on to Dallas, I was a solid click." If the Stratford Theater was where Hope developed his new, more spontaneous style of stand-up comedy, his Fort Worth experience showed him the importance of tailoring his act to each specific audience and locale. For a comedian who would go on to become the greatest grassroots entertainer of his era, it was a crucial lightbulb moment.

Still, he was playing mostly small-time theaters. His goal, ever since the Hope and Byrne days, was to crack the big-time houses that were part of the Keith circuit — the chain of vaudeville theaters founded by B. F. Keith and Edward F. Albee, encompassing most of the biggest and most prestigious venues east of the Mississippi (and after a merger with the West Coast–based Orpheum chain in 1927, across the country as well). For a vaudeville performer, playing "Keith time" meant you had made it.

Hope's breakthrough came in the fall of 1929, when he got a wire from a New York agent named Lee Stewart, who had heard about him from Bob O'Donnell. Stewart wanted to set up a showcase for Hope in New York — a tryout engagement where the Keith-circuit bookers could see his act. Bob grabbed Louise, hopped in his new yellow Packard, and sped to New York.

As Hope recalled the events, Stewart first offered to put him on a bill at the Jefferson Theatre on Fourteenth Street. But Hope balked at the downtown venue, which was known for its boisterous audiences, and held out for a classier uptown theater. A few days later Stewart called back with a theater more to Hope's liking: Proctor's 86th Street, on Eighty-Sixth and Broadway. Hope prepared for the engagement by testing out his mate-

121

rial in a smaller tryout theater in Brooklyn. Stewart came to see one of Hope's shows there and on the subway ride back to Manhattan seemed to have doubts. "Proctor's Eighty-Sixth Street is a pretty big theater, you know," said Stewart. "Look, Lee," Bob replied. "I open there tomorrow, and if I don't score, we won't talk to each other again, okay?"

That's Hope's version. A slightly different account comes from Dolph Leffler, who worked in the Keith office and recalled the events in a letter to Hope years later. No mention of Hope's rejecting the Jefferson Theatre. Indeed, the young performer appears all too eager to take whatever he can get. "I offered Lee Stewart $35 (all I had left of my budget) for your five-person act," recalled Leffler. (Along with Troxell, Hope had added several other comic foils, or "stooges," to his act.) "He almost fainted but decided to wire you the offer. We never expected you to accept, as $35 wouldn't buy your transportation from Cleveland — but you wired back accepting."

The Keith bookers arranged Hope's tryout in Brooklyn, and Leffler was there, along with Stewart, for the first, sparsely attended matinee. Despite the small crowd, Leffler liked what he saw, and he gives a lively firsthand account of Hope's zany vaudeville act at the time:

When you introduced your world famous International Orchestra which had just returned from playing before the Crown Heads of Europe — "and mind you, we are just getting rid of our sea legs before going to the Palace" — then the curtain went up and that joker sat on a beer keg in overalls playing a muted trumpet, no scenery, just the heating pipes, I fell off my seat. Then when the two boys started fishing from the balcony boxes I flipped. . . . One could never be sure, but I felt we had found something good. So we brought you into the Proctor's 86th Street the following week and raised you to $50 for three days.

His engagement at Proctor's 86th Street was Hope's big shot, and he was uncharacteristically nervous. When he arrived at the theater on the night of the show, he asked the doorman, "How's the audience here?" He replied, "Toughest in New York." Hope walked around the block twice to calm himself down.

He knew he needed something to win over the crowd right away. Just preceding him on the bill was Leatrice Joy, a silent-film actress who had recently been in the headlines for her divorce from screen idol John Gilbert. With typical resourcefulness, Hope used that as the springboard for his opening salvo. After Joy finished her act, Hope walked out on the stage, waited until his musical intro was done, turned to a woman in the front row, and cracked: "No, lady, this is not John Gilbert." The audience roared.

It was another defining moment in Hope's comedic evolution. The line wasn't just a good ad-lib. It also, importantly, showed Hope's willingness to break down the barrier between performer and audience, to cozy up to the crowd by gossiping with them about the backstage lives of the stars. The inside-Hollywood wisecracks that became such a staple of Hope's comedy, his constant ribbing of Bing Crosby and other showbiz pals, the Oscar-night jokes about nervous nominees and jealous losers — all of it can be traced back to that single line.

Variety's reviewer was higher on the performer than the material: "Hope, assisted by an unbilled girl [Troxell] appearing only in the middle of the act for a gag crossfire, has an act satisfactory for the time it is playing. If some of the material, especially where old gags are found, could be changed, chances are this would double strength of turn." Yet the Keith folks were impressed enough to book him for a tour almost on the spot. On November 7, 1929, Hope signed a contract with the B. F. Keith–Albee Vaudeville Exchange, guaranteeing him thirty-six weeks of work over the next year. The salary: a hefty $475 a week for the first fifteen weeks, bumped up to $500 after that, with an option for two more seasons at a salary that would slide upward to $700. He had to pay Troxell out of that amount — $100 a week, according to Hope.

It was a major boost in Hope's earning power, especially striking in view of the timing. In between Hope's arrival in New York for the audition with Keith and his signing of the contract, the stock market crashed.

The sudden end to the 1920s economic boom — splashed out on the front page of *Variety* with the memorable headline "Wall Street Lays an Egg" — was, strangely, something of a nonevent in Hope's career. Recounting his breakthrough with the Keith circuit in his memoir *Have Tux, Will Travel,* he never even mentions it.

But for the vaudeville business, it was a devastating, and ultimately fatal, blow. With the onset of the Great Depression, people still needed (more than ever) an escape through entertainment. But alternatives such as movies and radio were cheaper. What's more, vaudeville's economic model (driven partly by escalating salaries like the one that Hope landed in 1929) was making it an unprofitable business. Hope, with uncanny timing, had caught the last gravy train.

Over the next nine months, Hope crisscrossed the country on the Keith-Orpheum circuit. This classic vaudeville road trip was Hope's whistle-stop introduction to America. He started with a couple of New York City dates (at the Jefferson, the theater he had first shunned, and the Riverside, on Ninety-Sixth and Broadway); moved upstate to Rochester and Syracuse; made a swing through the Midwest to Chicago, St. Louis, Kansas City, and St. Paul; traveled northwest to Calgary, Spokane, Seattle, and Vancouver; headed down the coast to Portland, Oakland, Los Angeles, and San Diego; veered back east through Salt Lake City and Omaha; then south to Dallas, San Antonio, Houston, New Orleans, Atlanta, and Charlotte; before a final Midwest swing, to South Bend, Indiana, Cedar Rapids, Iowa, and Rockford, Illinois.

His act was another knockabout mix of songs and gags. Hope opened by singing "Pagan Love Song" while getting razzed by the orchestra, did a rapid-fire monologue, and mixed it up with Troxell, before going out with a song and dance. The reviewers were less impressed with Hope's "well-worn" material than with his showmanship and ingratiating personality. (It "sounded like a gagster's catalog, from auto jokes to synthetic Scotch witticisms," said *Billboard,* but "socked in heavy on the laugh register.") For much of the tour, he was on a bill headlined by Harry Webb and his orchestra, whom Hope would introduce and clown around with. "This act flows right into Harry Webb's turn," reported *Variety,* "so that it is impossible to tell where one ends and the other begins."

As he moved from city to city, Hope would throw in jokes tailored to the local crowd. In Chicago, he and Louise repurposed an old gangster joke for one of the city's more infamous residents:

BOB: "I come from a very brave family. My brother slapped Al Capone in the face."
LOUISE: "I'd like to shake his hand."
BOB: "We're not going to dig him up just for that."

After the show, Hope recounted getting a call in his hotel room from a gruff-voiced thug, who asked if he was the comic doing the Al Capone joke. When Hope said he was, the fellow warned, "Do us a favor, take it out." Hope obliged — and lived to tell the tale, endlessly.

Even when his material faltered, Hope's routines with Troxell usually got good reviews. She was a bigger asset to the act than he probably liked to admit. In November 1929, she got a mention in *Variety*'s "Clothes and Clothes" column, a survey of fashions onstage: "Girl with Bob Hope makes a very neat appearance in a simple black transparent velvet frock, unadorned but for a buckle at the natural waist and a crystal choker necklace. It hung longer in back and fitted well, showing good taste seldom met in the unbilled girl."

The unbilled girl, however, was getting restless. Louise pressed Hope to give her billing and even threatened to quit. Hope's response, astonishingly, was to contact his old girlfriend in Cleveland, Mildred Rosequist, and ask if she wanted to replace Louise in the act. According to Rosequist, he accompanied the offer with a marriage proposal. She wired back to say that she was sorry, but she was engaged to someone else. Hope then made up with Troxell — and promised to marry *her.*

The Hope-Troxell relationship remains one of the murkiest parts of Hope's life story. He had little to say about her, other than to give grudging credit to her skills as a comic foil. ("She was quick and intelligent," Hope wrote in his memoir, "but I'd trained her to hide all that.") They almost surely were romantically involved as they traveled together on the vaudeville circuit, with various interruptions, for more than three years. At least once he brought her home to Cleveland, to meet the family. The marriage proposal, however, would sit for a while.

After his successful 1929–30 tour, Hope signed a new three-year contract with the Keith circuit, at a salary that rose in steady increments toward $1,000 a week. But Hope realized that he needed to improve his material, and he had the foresight and the resources to hire a writer. No hack either, but Al Boasberg, one of the most respected gagmen in the business. A portly, Rabelaisian character who liked to think up jokes in the bathtub, Boasberg had written for Buster Keaton, Jack Benny, and Burns and Allen; a few years later he was credited with writing the famous cramped-stateroom scene for the Marx Brothers' movie *A Night at the Opera.* "He was a great joke mechanic," said Hope. "He could remember jokes, fix jokes, switch jokes around, improvise on jokes. He could even originate jokes."

Hope and Boasberg would brainstorm together at Lum Fong's, a Chinese restaurant in New York City, Hope jotting down lines on the back of the menu. Later, when Boasberg decamped to Los Angeles to work on movies, he would send suggestions to Hope by wire or letter. A typical Boasberg telegraphed pitch:

```
WHEN GIRL MAKES HER FIRST APPEAR-
ANCE YOU SAY WHERE WERE YOU ALL
LAST WEEK IN NEWARK AND SHE
ANSWERS MR. HOPE YOU TOLD ME NOT
TO COME OUT UNTIL YOU GOT YOUR
FIRST LAUGH STOP ASK ONE STOOGE
WHAT SCHOOL HE WENT TO AND HE
WON'T TELL AND YOU ASK HIM IF HE'S
```

129

ASHAMED AND HE ANSWERS THE PRIN-
CIPAL GAVE ME FIFTY DOLLARS NOT
TO TELL STOP PLEASE RECORD HOW
MATERIAL IS GOING.

With Boasberg's help, Hope came up with a new "afterpiece" for his act. These were miniature comedy revues, tacked on at the end of many vaudeville shows, in which the top-billed comedian and other performers in the show would return for a fast-paced string of comedy bits to close the show on a frantic high note. Hope called his afterpiece "Antics of 1930" (and later "Antics of 1931"), and it showed off his freewheeling, ad-libbing style to good effect. "Bob Hope closing 28 minutes opens with Hope playing around with the spotlight," *Variety* wrote of his show at Chicago's Palace Theatre in February 1931. "His easygoing smooth way of razzing himself soon ingratiated him to the audience for plenty of healthy laughs."

Hope brought his show to Cleveland in February 1931, playing the downtown Palace Theatre — a triumphal homecoming for the former scourge of Doan's Corners. Some of the old neighborhood gang came to see him, buying up the front seats and needling him by ostentatiously taking out their newspapers and reading during his act. He made a second visit to Cleveland a few months later, for an engagement at Keith's 105th Street, his old

130

neighborhood theater. This time his mom came to see him.

Avis, Bob had learned, was sick with what would eventually be diagnosed as cervical cancer. But she was beside herself with excitement to see her boy on the stage where she had once taken him to see Frank Fay. Bob's brother Jim accompanied her, and described the scene in his memoir, "Mother Had Hopes":

From the moment she took her seat, she just trembled from head to toe. The tears ran uncontrollably down her beautiful cheeks, and her little fingernails were cutting my hand. I was afraid she would pass out on us momentarily. And when her son made his appearance, her entire body stiffened until I'm sure had I not held her hand, she would have automatically stood up. Then when she heard the reception accorded him by the audience acknowledging him as a neighborhood product, she seemed to relax and, as a coach might at the debut of a very promising student, she listened to every syllable, nodding her head as though in approval to every word.

When Bob caught sight of her in the crowd, he gave her a big shout-out: "There she is, folks! There's my mom! With the lilies of the valley on her hat!"

Though Avis was a fan, Hope's brothers had long been skeptical of his show-business career. When he was still struggling to find work in New York, his brother Fred and Johnny Gibbons, Fred's brother-in-law and Bob's old dance partner, went there on a rescue mission, trying to talk him into coming home. He refused, saying he wanted to stick it out a little longer. His eldest brother, Ivor, still doubted that Bob would ever make a decent living in show business. When Bob showed him the paycheck for a week of shows in Cleveland, Ivor's eyes popped. Indeed, Bob was doing well enough to buy a new home for his parents, moving them from their aging place on Euclid Avenue to a smaller but more modern house on Yorkshire Road, a few blocks away in the more upscale neighborhood of Cleveland Heights.

Except for Jim — who was in Hollywood now, trying to get into the movie business — the brothers were all settled in Ohio, leading the kind of solidly middle-class, midwestern lives that Hope, while not looking down on them, was happy to have left behind. Fred, the most successful of the family, had turned his butcher shop into the United Provision Company, which supplied meat to most of the major hotels in the area. Ivor had a metal-products business, while Sid had moved to a farm near Ridgeville Corners, in the western part of the state, where he raised a family and dabbled in various small businesses. Only George, Bob's good-looking youngest brother, seemed interested in joining his brother in show business. Bob didn't see a lot of talent there, but at Mom's urging, he gave George a spot in his act.

He teamed George with an old friend from Toledo named Toots Murdock and used them as stooges in his "Antics" shows. They would sit in the audience boxes and heckle Hope and the other performers: "What's going on behind the curtain?" one would call out. "Nothing," Bob would reply. "Well, there's nothing going on in front of it either!" When Hope brought on a singer who did a parody of the popular crooner Rudy Vallee, the hecklers interrupted with insults. Hope snapped, "Don't you boys know you can be arrested for annoying an audience?" Their comeback, in unison: "You should know!"

This was more than just random silliness. Hope was slowly developing, if not a comic persona, at least a comic strategy: the self-assured wise guy who is continually cut down to size. "A part of my new idea was for my stooges to come out and start whipping at me," Hope said. "I figured it would be a great device for them to tear down this character on the stage who'd been so cocky, brash and bumptious." It was another step in Hope's transformation from generic vaudeville gag-man to a much more distinctive, fully formed stage comic — a modern comedian.

Bob and George were sometimes at odds. Bob tried teaching his brother to dance, but "I had to pound his eardrums to get him to do it." Once they had a fight and George walked out. He turned up at home in Cleveland, and Mom had to patch things up between them. George remained in the act (billed as "George Townes," evidently to disguise the family connection), as Bob toured through 1931, on a bill with a brother-sister roping act and twenty trained monkeys. (The monkeys got loose behind a theater in Minneapolis one night and caused a near panic in the audience before they were finally rounded up.)

Despite his success on the Keith-Orpheum circuit, Hope still had a big gap in his résumé: he had not yet played the Palace Theatre, still deemed the pinnacle of vaudeville success. When he appeared in New York, he found himself stuck mostly with movie-theater gigs — twice, no less, he was forced to follow the grim World War I drama *All Quiet on the Western Front.* Then, in February 1931, while he was appearing in Cleveland, he got a surprise call from Lee Stewart, telling him to scoot back to New York in a hurry: a spot at the Palace had opened up on a bill headlined by Beatrice Lillie.

"He almost kissed me," Stewart recalled. "I never saw such a happy and excited guy in my life." The engagement meant a lot to Hope, and it put him in self-promotional overdrive. On the day of his Palace opening, he arranged for a band of picketers to show up at the theater with protest signs: BOB HOPE IS UNFAIR TO STOOGES. The publicity stunt got him some ink, but Hope later disowned it, claiming it was "too much."

His Palace debut, on February 21, 1931, didn't go so well either. "I was numb," he recalled. "Not just scared, numb. I did my act mechanically." The reviews were only mixed. He was especially hurt by one slam in the *Daily Graphic:* "They say that Bob Hope is the sensation of the Midwest. If so, why doesn't he go back there?" The saving grace of his weeklong run was the chance to emcee the Palace's Sunday "celebrity night," where stars would often show up in the audience, and he got to banter with two of vaudeville's top comics, Ted Healy and Ken Murray.

On the road, however, his polish and crowd appeal were growing. When Boasberg got too busy with his film work, Hope hired another writer, a highly regarded young comic named Richie Craig. The sketches got tighter; the gags popped. In one routine, credited to Craig, Bob played a hotel desk clerk:

MAN: "Can you give me a room and bath?"
HOPE: "Well, I can give you a room, but you'll have to take the bath yourself."

135

MAN: "Is the elevator still broke?"
HOPE: "Aren't we all?"
MAN: "The last time I was here the elevator used to fall halfway down the shaft."
HOPE: "Oh, we had that fixed. It falls all the way down now."

As Hope's confidence grew, so did his daring. The Keith-Orpheum theaters were notorious for their prudish resistance to any racy material. (In the old days signs would be posted backstage listing the slang terms that performers were forbidden to use, such as *slob* and *son of a gun.*) Hope's material was considered borderline, and the censors kept a close eye on him. As early as 1929, in a review of Hope's tryout act for the Keith circuit, *Variety* had warned, "The sting of some of his gags stand a chance of being taken out if the Keith office feels badly the day they are heard or reported." By May 1933, Hope's risqué material was raising eyebrows at the Bureau of Sunday Censorship in Boston. A report on his act listed with disapproval such suggestive lines as "Had breakfast with an English girl and did she have a broad 'A.' " The report also noted, "Hell and God used quite a lot . . . men in boxes have cross talk and get very unruly." Its recommendation: "Act needs a lot of watching."

Hollywood was watching too. With the advent of sound, the movies were busy scouring vaudeville for new comedy talent. By 1930, the Marx Brothers had already adapted two of their Broadway hits, *The Cocoanuts* and *Animal Crackers,* for the screen; vaudeville comics such as Eddie Cantor and Joe E. Brown were starring in features; and W. C. Fields, Jack Benny, and Burns and Allen were all making comedy shorts. So it wasn't surprising that a West Coast agent named Bill Perlberg, who had heard about Hope from Boasberg, contacted Hope in the summer of 1930 and asked him to come in for a screen test.

Hope was on his West Coast swing for the Keith-Orpheum circuit, and he scheduled the test for the break between his bookings in Los Angeles and San Diego. He took a cab with Louise out to the Pathé lot in Culver City, where he did his vaudeville act for the cameras. He got laughs from the crew and was sure his Hollywood break was imminent. But after he and Louise continued on to San Diego and didn't hear anything for days, he called Perlberg to find out what the reaction had been.

Perlberg invited Hope to come see the test for himself. Hope stopped back in LA before his return East and found his way to the screening room on the Pathé lot by himself. He cringed as he watched the screen test, all alone in the darkened theater. "I'd never seen anything so awful," he said later. "I looked like a cross between a mongoose and a turtle. I couldn't wait to get out."

There's no telling how bad Hope's test really was. He had a habit of exaggerating his mistakes and missteps, both for comic effect and to cover up the pain of rejection. But his failure to get snapped up for the movies was certainly a blow to the ambitious vaudeville comic. It soured him on Hollywood for years and forced him to shift his focus back East. If he was to graduate from vaudeville, it now appeared, he had better concentrate on the entertainment center at the other end of the country: Broadway.

Since his debut in *Sidewalks of New York* in 1927, Hope had kept his ties to the Broadway theater. In addition to his brief stint in *Ups-a Daisy* in the fall of 1928, Hope got another small part in the chorus of *Smiles,* a Ziegfeld-produced revue, with a cast that included Fred and Adele Astaire, that opened in November 1930 and ran for two months. (Both roles were apparently so negligible, at least to Hope, that he omitted them from his résumé and never mentioned them in any of his reminiscences of his Broadway years.) But in the summer of 1932 he landed his most substantial Broadway part yet, in a musical revue called *Ballyhoo of 1932.* Hope was in the middle of his three-year contract with Keith, but the vaudeville circuit was perfectly willing to give him a leave of absence, on the promise that he would satisfy his touring obligations later. (The Broadway credit would only make him a bigger draw.) Hope, for his part, was happy to keep one foot in vaudeville, and he continued to tour sporadically, in between his Broadway gigs, for several more years.

Broadway came to Hope's rescue at just the right time. In November of 1932 the Palace Theatre, after reducing its admission price and boosting its number of daily shows to try to stay afloat, finally caved to the inevitable and switched over to showing movies — a milestone usually cited as the final curtain for vaudeville. Film palaces such as the Roxy and Radio City Music Hall (and the Palace itself, from time to time) would continue to offer vaudeville-style stage shows along with their movie presentations for years to come. But as a viable, autonomous business, vaudeville was all washed up.

Hope spent the next five years in New York, getting major roles in five Broadway shows and launching a radio career. Yet the vaudeville experience left an indelible imprint on him. It gave him all the tools — singing, dancing, sketch acting — that he would need as a performer. Some of the people he met, such as Charlie Cooley and Barney Dean from the Chicago days, became lifelong friends and members of his entourage. Vaudeville taught him the value of hard work, made him a nimble and inventive performer, and gave him a solid grounding in the *business* of show. His years on the vaudeville circuit also ingrained in him a basic insecurity as a performer. To survive the vaudeville grind you had to be resourceful, vigilant, watchful of money, always on the move. They were qualities Hope would never lose.

He was, moreover, the great ambassador of vaudeville to a new generation of entertainment consumers. Gags from his vaudeville days were recycled as wisecracks on his radio and TV shows for the next six decades. In the *Road* pictures, he and Crosby typically played small-time vaudevillians, reprising the cheesy routines and repartee of a bygone entertainment era. Like other ex-vaudevillians who became TV stars (but for longer than any of them), Hope kept the vaudeville format alive in his television specials: an emcee doing an opening monologue, introducing a series of variety acts, chatting with guest stars. "When vaudeville died," Hope once joked, "television was the box they put it in."

After nine years, Hope had wrung all that he could out of vaudeville. Broadway would give him the finishing-school polish that completed his show-business education. It would also, for the first time, give him a taste of stardom.

CHAPTER 3
BROADWAY
"DO WHATEVER YOU CAN TO GET LAUGHS."

New York City, like the rest of the nation, was suffering through the worst year of the Great Depression when Bob Hope moved there in the summer of 1932. More than a quarter of all employable New Yorkers were out of work. The city's public debt was nearly as large as that of all the forty-eight states combined. Hoovervilles — shantytowns of the homeless, named for the president who still promised that "prosperity is just around the corner" — had so overrun the Sheep Meadow in Central Park that police had to remove the sheep for fear they would be eaten.

Hoover himself would soon be gone, replaced by Franklin D. Roosevelt and the New Deal. Other icons of the Roaring Twenties were quickly passing from the scene as well. Jimmy Walker, New York's flamboyant flapper-era mayor (whom Hope would one day portray in a movie), was forced out of office in September 1932, the target of a corruption investigation. Florenz Ziegfeld, producer of the lavish musical revues that were the epitome of Broadway extravagance in the 1910s and 1920s, died in July, financially ruined by the stock market crash. Prohibition, which lent the decade so much of its disreputable glamour, was on its way out too, its repeal ensured by the Democratic victory in November and officially ended by constitutional amendment in 1933.

In the midst of the hard times, however, a parallel world of glittery excess was thriving. The 1930s were the heyday of New York's "café society," a fashionable world of socialites and show-business celebrities, on display in such Manhattan nightspots as the Colony, El Morocco, and the Stork Club — a scene chronicled by newspaper gossip columnists such as Walter Winchell and romanticized in the ritzy, art deco settings of so many Hollywood musicals and romantic comedies of the era. "For most Americans, 'café society' immediately triggered images of women in smart gowns and men in satin-collared tuxedos, of tiered nightclubs undulating in the music of swell bands, of cocktails and cigarettes, of cool talk and enervated elegance," Neil Gabler wrote in his biography of Winchell, "all of which made café society one of those repositories of dreams at a time when reality seemed treacherous."

Bob Hope was well outfitted for this glamorous scene: a dapper, good-looking, twenty-nine-year-old entertainer with an eye for the ladies and a budding career on Broadway. In those days Hope drank as much as he ever would (which was never much), chain-smoked cigarettes (until it began affecting his singing voice and he gave them up on doctor's orders), and had an apartment on posh Central Park West, just blocks away from the Broadway theaters where he introduced great American standards by Cole Porter and Ira Gershwin. In later years, Hope would come to epitomize the golf-playing, leisure-suited, suburban-Republican lifestyle of Southern California. But New York gave him a big-city edge and pace that would set him apart when he finally made his move to Hollywood.

Ballyhoo of 1932, his fourth Broadway show but the first in which he had a major role, was a musical revue inspired by a popular humor magazine called *Ballyhoo,* known for its cheeky parodies of popular advertising. The show was written by Norman Anthony, the magazine's editor; featured songs by Tin Pan Alley veteran Lewis Gensler and lyricist E. Y. ("Yip") Harburg (whose "Brother, Can You Spare a Dime?," written that same year, became a Depression-era anthem); and boasted a cast filled with well-known vaude-villians, most notably the comedy team of Willie and Eugene Howard.

When Hope arrived for rehearsals and two out-of-town tryouts, the show was something of a mess. Scenes were being added, dropped, and moved around so fast that the technical crew couldn't keep up. In Atlantic City, the electricity failed in the middle of a performance. "Actually it was rather frightening," recalled Hope's agent, Lee Stewart. "There was a blazing short circuit and the theater went dark. The management feared that the audience was ready to panic and rush the door." One of the producers, Lee Shubert (of the theater-owning Shubert family), grabbed Hope backstage and told him to go out front and keep the crowd calm until power could be restored.

He did it so well that Shubert called on him again two weeks later in Newark, when a new opening production number was being added to the show and the dancers weren't ready in time for the opening curtain. Hope again had to vamp for time, and he drew on all his experience as a vaudeville emcee. "Ladies and gentlemen, this is the first time I've ever been on before the acrobats," he cracked. He called out to someone in the box seats — "Hello, Sam!" — and then turned to the audience: "That's one of our backers up there. He says he's not nervous, but I notice he's buckled his safety belt."

Shubert suggested making the bit a permanent opening for the show. Hope balked, saying the device would seem too forced night after night. But he and writer Al Boasberg came up with another idea, which Shubert went for. To start each show, Hope would be discovered sitting in the box seats and would introduce himself as head of the show's Complaint Department. With the help of stooges planted in the crowd, he then poked fun at the show's well-publicized pre-Broadway troubles:

BOB: "Ladies and gentlemen . . ."
STOOGE: "My God, is this show really going to open?"
BOB: "Well, if we waited a couple of weeks longer, that tuxedo of yours would be in style again."
STOOGE: "I hope your gags are as new."
BOB: "Ladies and gentlemen, tonight we are inaugurating a new idea in the theater . . . the Complaint Department. Of course, we know there'll be no complaints because this show is as clean and wholesome as the magazine."
STOOGE: "Well, so long."
BOB: "You leaving?"
STOOGE: "Yeah, I'm going over to Minsky's."

After a few minutes, Hope turned to the orchestra and asked them to start the overture. He got no response. "Hey, fellas, wake up!" he shouted. All he got was snores. He fired a pistol in the air. More snores. Finally he rang a cash register. Suddenly the conductor and his team jumped to attention and began to play.

It was obvious vaudeville shtick, but it set the irreverent, self-mocking tone for the show, which otherwise was a so-so mix of songs and sketches: a Hollywood actress training like a boxer for a big role, the Howard brothers as a pair of Columbus Circle rabble-rousers, Hope and Vera Marshe as a couple of nudists (a sketch lost, alas, to history). Reviews were mixed, and Hope, billed sixth, got only passing attention. ("An agreeable but far from brilliant master of ceremonies," noted Howard Barnes in the *New York Herald Tribune.*) The show, which opened in early September, ran into money problems, missed a payday for the cast and crew, and closed at the end of November after ninety-five performances. But it was a win for Hope, proof that the cocky vaudeville comedian could hold his own on a Broadway stage.

After *Ballyhoo* closed, Hope went back on the road in early 1933 with his vaudeville act, fulfilling his contractual obligations to the Keith-Orpheum circuit. He also continued to make frequent appearances at the Capitol and other New York City theaters that still booked live entertainment. And he dipped his toe into the medium that would provide the third component, along with Broadway and vaudeville, of his showbiz résumé during the New York years: radio.

Commercial radio was barely a decade old, but it was quickly reaching critical mass. In 1932 one-third of American homes owned a radio, and two national networks had sprung up to supply them with programming — the National Broadcasting Company, created in 1926, and the Columbia Broadcasting System, formed two years later. *Amos 'n' Andy,* which began in Chicago in 1928 and was picked up by NBC the following year, was riding high as radio's first national hit show. Songwriters were discovering that radio airplay could turn their new tunes into instant chart-toppers. And comedians who saw work drying up on the vaudeville circuit were jumping into radio as a lifeboat. In 1932 alone, Ed Wynn, Fred Allen, Jack Benny, and the team of George Burns and Gracie Allen all made their network radio debuts.

Hope was a step behind these better-established stars. His first appearances on radio were little more than simulcasts of his vaudeville stage act, on such shows as the *RKO Theater of the Air* and the *Capitol Family Show,* a Sunday-morning broadcast hosted by Major Edward Bowes, a dour but good-hearted impresario who insisted on the military title because of his service in World War I. (He later became better known as host of radio's *Original Amateur Hour.*) Hope would give Bowes his script on the Friday

147

before each Sunday show, then watch in dismay as the Major appropriated most of the good jokes for himself on the air. But Hope noticed that every time he appeared on the *Capitol* show, the audiences for his stage appearances would spike. Like a lot of vaudeville performers, he was learning that the route to mass-audience popularity now ran through those boxy Philcos and Crosleys that were becoming fixtures in nearly every living room in the country.

Hope's first appearance in a studio show came on June 8, 1933, when he was a guest on *The Fleischmann Hour,* a weekly variety show hosted by singer Rudy Vallee. Hope came on as a slick boulevardier, doing jokes about his clothes, his cigars, and his girlfriends, with Vallee as the stuffy straight man:

BOB: "Here's a picture of a girl I can marry tomorrow. She has ten thousand dollars. Isn't she beautiful?"

RUDY: "Yes, she is. She's gorgeous."

BOB: "Here's a picture of another girl I can marry. She has fifty thousand dollars. Of course, she's not so pretty."

RUDY: "No, she's not so pretty, but fifty thousand dollars is a lot of money."

BOB: "But that's nothing. I know a girl I can marry with a hundred thousand dollars."

RUDY: "Where's her picture?"

BOB: "Nobody'll take her picture."

Hope didn't much take to radio at first. "It all seemed so strange, talking into a microphone in a studio instead of playing in front of a real audience," he said. "I got nervous on those first radio shows and the Vallee engineers couldn't figure out why they heard a thumping noise when I did my routines until they found out I was kicking the mike after each joke."

On the stage, however, his self-confidence and popularity were growing. "Goofy, self-assured, ingratiating and welcome as the flowers that'll be out in six weeks," *Variety* wrote of his show at Chicago's Palace Theatre in March 1933. "Hope diverted the customers with as tasty a dish of comedy hash put together from odds and ends." He was brash and irreverent, sometimes pushing the boundaries of vaudeville's still stodgy standards of good taste. At the Capitol, for example, he did a parody of sentimental mother songs called "My Mom." During the number, an old lady posing as his mother wandered onstage, pleading for food, only to be rudely pushed away by Hope:

OLD LADY: "Son, I haven't eaten in four days."

BOB: "Mom, I told you never to bother me while I'm working."

OLD LADY: "At least give me a few dollars to have my teeth fixed."

BOB: "You're not eating, Mom, what do you need teeth for?"

The bit didn't go over well with the Capitol's mostly older crowd, and Major Bowes himself asked Hope to take it out of his act. Hope, always worried about alienating any portion of his audience, obliged — and later chastised himself for the lapse of taste.

The Capitol Theatre was also where Hope teamed up for the first time with an entertainer to whom he would be linked for the rest of his career. In December 1932, shortly after the close of *Ballyhoo,* Hope was asked to emcee a two-week show at the Capitol headlined by a young singer who was fast becoming a national sensation.

Harry Lillis Crosby was born in Tacoma, Washington, in May 1903, just a few weeks before Hope. He grew up in Spokane and got the nickname "Bing" in third grade, owing to his fascination with a newspaper humor column called the Bingville Bugle. In high school and later at Gonzaga University, the local college, he sang in student vocal groups, acted in school theater productions, and formed a singing duo with his friend Al Rinker. After developing an act in local clubs, the two piled their belongings into a Model T in October 1925 and drove to Hollywood to see if they could break into big-time show business. A year later — with the help of

150

Rinker's sister, the jazz singer Mildred Bailey — they landed a job with the Paul Whiteman Orchestra, the most famous jazz band in America.

Unlike Hope, who plodded for years in the vaudeville trenches, Crosby's career caught fire instantly. Recording with the Whiteman band, he had a No. 1 hit with "My Blue Heaven" in 1927, followed by popular recordings of "Ol' Man River," "I Surrender Dear," and "Where the Blue of the Night Meets the Gold of the Day," which became his theme song. He brought something new, almost revolutionary, to popular singing. Unlike the belters of vaudeville and Broadway, who sang to the rafters, Crosby had a relaxed, intimate, jazz-inflected style that was perfectly suited to that new recording innovation, the microphone.

Crosby and Hope first met on October 14, 1932, outside the Friars Club on Forty-Eighth Street in New York City. Crosby was a much bigger star at the time — not just a well-known recording artist, but host of his own radio show and about to star in his first Hollywood feature, *The Big Broadcast.* Hope was impressed by Crosby's success, his easygoing self-confidence, and his willingness to play around onstage. For their appearance together at the Capitol, they came up with some vaudeville-style bits to liven up the show. They played two politicians who run into each other on the street; approaching each other from opposite sides of the stage, they would meet at the center and grope each other's pockets. Or they would be two orchestra leaders, who conduct each other's conversation with flourishes of their batons. In another bit, Hope would announce with a straight face that Crosby couldn't make the show because "some cad locked him in the washroom," at which point a fuming Crosby would emerge from the wings with a doorknob attached to a splintered piece of wood.

"The gags weren't very funny, I guess," Hope said, "but the audience laughed because Bing and I were having such a good time — and I guess it was clear that we liked each other. We would laugh insanely at what we dreamed up." In between shows, they would trade showbiz stories at O'Reilly's, a nearby bar, or over the billiards table at the Friars Club. They discovered a shared passion for golf — a sport that Hope had taken up during his downtime on the vaudeville road, and which Crosby played at close to a professional level. Living on different coasts, they wouldn't get back together again for a few years, but it was the start of a partnership that would change both their careers.

Hope was all over New York City in those days: on the radio, on the vaudeville stage, and on the dais for a growing number of charity benefits. Indeed, *Variety* made him exhibit A in a November 1933 article complaining about the overexposure of a few top performers on the withering vaudeville circuit. "One answer to what's wrong with Vaudeville that can be traced to the booking offices is the startling number of repeats played in the remaining first-grade variety theaters by certain acts during the past year," the trade paper wrote — noting that Hope had in just the past year played the State, the Paramount, the Roxy, and the Capitol twice. "In many instances they're playing the few fans to death."

One of the few entertainers who could rival Hope for ubiquity on the vaudeville-and-benefit circuit in those years was Milton Berle, the brash burlesque comic with whom Hope had a friendly, and sometimes not so friendly, rivalry. Berle even then had a reputation for stealing gags, and Hope was angry to find out that some of his best jokes were turning up in Berle's act at the Strand Theater. Hope and Richie Craig, his pal and sometime writer, devised a revenge scheme that became part of Hope's showbiz lore. On a Sunday night when Berle was scheduled to do four benefits back-to-back, Hope got himself booked at the same benefits earlier in the evening and delivered batches of Berle's material even before he got there. Berle, perplexed to find his jokes falling flat, caught on midway through the evening and turned the tables, leapfrogging Hope at the final benefit and stealing *his* material.

Hope always denied that he had any serious beef with Berle. Elliott Kozak, Hope's manager and producer in the later years, claimed Hope would always defend Berle against detractors, for one reason. In late 1933, when Berle was doing a show in Cleveland and Hope's mother was dying of cancer, Berle visited her nearly every day, a kindness Hope never forgot. (Something else Berle and Hope shared was an affection for Richie Craig, who died of tuberculosis in November 1933, at age thirty-one. They helped organize a benefit at the New Amsterdam Theater to raise money for his widow and parents. Hope made the largest single contribution, paying $300 for a photo of Craig.)

In the summer of 1933 producer Max Gordon was casting a new Broadway musical called *Gowns by Roberta.* It was a much-anticipated new show from composer Jerome Kern, with a book by Otto Harbach, about a college football star who inherits his aunt's dress shop in Paris. Gordon was looking for a comedian to play Huckleberry Haines, a bandleader and the football star's best friend. He had run through several candidates (Rudy Vallee reportedly turned down the role) before he saw Hope performing at the Palace Theatre. He brought Kern — who was set to direct the musical as well — to see him, and with the composer's assent signed Hope for the show that would be his Broadway breakthrough.

Roberta (as the musical was eventually retitled) had a cast studded with stars from Broadway's past, present, and future. Fay Templeton, the turn-of-the-century star of George M. Cohan musicals, was lured back to the stage, at age sixty-eight, to play the dress shop owner. (She dies after warbling one song, "Yesterdays.") The female lead was Lyda Roberti, a live-wire, Polish-born singer-comedienne of both stage and screen in the early 1930s, before her death of a heart attack in 1938, at age thirty-one. Also in the cast were Ray Middleton, who went on to costar in such Broadway hits as *Annie Get Your Gun* and *Man of La Mancha;* George Murphy, the future Hollywood song-and-dance man (and later US senator from California); and Fred MacMurray, who had a small role as a sax player and landed a Hollywood contract in the middle of the show's run.

The show had troubles out of town. After it got bad reviews in a pre-Broadway tryout in Philadelphia, Gordon decided the show needed a more opulent production — and more comedy. To fix the former, he had the sets and costumes redesigned and brought in Hassard Short, a highly regarded Broadway

155

hand, to replace Kern as director. To address the latter, he turned to Bob Hope. "Do whatever you can think of to get laughs," Gordon told him.

Hope hardly needed the encouragement. As the show's script was being tinkered with, he threw in gag lines wherever he could. "Long dresses don't bother me — I've got a good memory," he quipped in one scene. In another, an expatriate Russian princess (played by Tamara Drasin, a Ukrainian-born actress who went by the stage name Tamara), who has fallen for the football hero, sings the show's big ballad, "Smoke Gets in Your Eyes," as Hope listens, straddling a chair. To set up the song, she tells him, "There's an old Russian proverb: when your heart's on fire, smoke gets in your eyes." Hope suggested a new line as a comeback: "We have a proverb in America too: Love is like hash. You have to have confidence in it to enjoy it." Harbach hated the line, claiming it would spoil the mood. But Hope appealed to Kern, who told him to give it a try. When it got a big laugh, the line stayed in. (Harbach apparently never forgave Hope. "An impossible, impossible man," he told author Lawrence Quirk. "It was his way or no way.")

Roberta opened at the New Amsterdam Theater on November 21, 1933, to disappointing reviews. "Extremely unimportant and slightly dead," wrote John Mason Brown in the *Evening Post*. "The humors of *Roberta* are no great shakes," sniffed the *Times'* Brooks Atkinson, "and most of them are smugly declaimed by Bob Hope, who insists upon being the life of the party and who would be more amusing if he were Fred Allen." Even Kern's score (which also included such first-rate numbers as "I'll Be Hard to Handle" and "Let's Begin") got only a lukewarm reception.

Yet *Roberta* ran for 295 performances, longer than any other book musical in the 1933–34 season. Much of the reason was its big song hit, "Smoke Gets in Your Eyes," which was quickly picked up on radio and by dance bands across the country. Yet Hope's comedy also gave the mostly dreary script an important boost. "I've always said that Bob Hope had as much to do with *Roberta* being a hit as 'Smoke Gets in Your Eyes,' " said George Murphy. "He made the difference between a hit and a flop."

Hope left the cast in June 1934, before the show closed (and lost out to Fred Astaire to costar in the 1935 movie version, retooled as a vehicle for the dance team of Astaire and Ginger Rogers). But he always had a special place in his heart for *Roberta.* He reprised his role as Huck Haines for the musical's West Coast premiere at the Los Angeles Philharmonic Auditorium in 1938; again in 1958 at the Muny Opera in St. Louis; and one more time, age-defyingly, in an updated version staged at Southern Methodist University and telecast on NBC in 1969. *Roberta* was a milestone for Hope: a major role in a major musical by a major American composer. It made him a Broadway star.

His lifestyle began to reflect it. Hope bought a ritzy Pierce-Arrow automobile and hired a chauffeur to drive him around in it. He got a Scottish terrier, named it Huck, and brought it to the theater to help him get girls. "I had Marilyn Miller's old dressing room at the New Amsterdam, and Huck sat at the top of the stairs," he recalled. "He was a great come-on, great bait. When the girls went by they stopped and petted him. As a result, I did a nice business with those beauties."

One beauty, however, was about to monopolize his time. After one show in December, Hope's *Roberta* costar George Murphy and his wife, Julie, asked Bob to join them at the Vogue Club to see a singer named Dolores Reade. When they walked into the club, a tall, twenty-four-year-old brunette with a sultry contralto voice was singing "It's Only a Paper Moon." After finishing her set, she came over to sit at Murphy's table and met Bob Hope for the first time.

"I hadn't caught his name and wasn't the least interested," Dolores later recalled, "but to make conversation I asked him if he wanted to dance." Bob, equally blasé, turned her down, saying he did enough dancing in his Broadway show. But later, when the group moved to the Ha Ha Club and Murphy took Dolores out on the dance floor, Bob cut in. They ended the evening with a late-night sandwich together, and Hope invited her to come see him in *Roberta.*

He got her tickets for a matinee just after Christmas, and she saw the show with a girlfriend. She was startled to discover that Hope had one of the leading roles. Two days later Hope went back to the Vogue Club to ask why she hadn't come backstage to say hello. Dolores told him she was too embarrassed; she'd thought he was just a chorus boy. Hope then asked her to go out on New Year's Eve, and the romance blossomed.

Dolores De Fina was born in Harlem and grew up in a close-knit extended family in the Bronx. Her mother, Theresa, was one of seven daughters of Nora and Henry Kelly, who had emigrated from Ireland in the 1880s. Theresa married Italian-born John De Fina and had two daughters, Dolores and her sister, Mildred, fourteen months younger, and the family moved in with Theresa's parents, in a three-bedroom brownstone in the Bronx. Dolores's grandmother was the lively center of the family, a devout Catholic who would genuflect at any priest she passed on the sidewalk and regaled her grandkids with tales of Irish fairies and leprechauns.

"Nana was the heart and soul and strength of our family," Mildred wrote of her grandmother. "Her clothing spoke of her whole life. She wore black cotton dresses for the many funerals in and out of the family, and white cotton dresses for summer and visiting the sick. . . . After church, Nana would invite people over to eat, and we'd all end up in the parlor where we sang along with the player piano. Nana used to always say to us: 'Dolores, you're the singer and, Mildred, you're the dancer in the family.' "

Her father died when Dolores was just sixteen, and she quit school to help support the family. She worked for her seamstress aunt, then as a fashion model and a Broadway chorus girl, appearing in the road company of *Honeymoon Lane* and (along with Mildred) in the chorus of the 1929 Ziegfeld musical *Show Girl*. After a screen test with Richard Dix for Paramount failed to land her a movie contract, she concentrated on her singing, appearing with the George Olson and Jack Pettis bands, and on her own in nightclubs — without great success, though when she appeared at the Richmond Club in 1932, a columnist called her the female Crosby.

Hope pursued her avidly. He would meet her each night at the Vogue Club when she was finished working and drive around with her in his Pierce-Arrow. At the end of the night he would park in front of her Ninth

160

Avenue apartment, where she lived with her mother, and dismiss the chauffeur so they could talk and smooch.

Dolores's mother was doing what she could to discourage the romance. She was no fan of this Broadway sharpie who kept her daughter out until six in the morning and was non-Catholic, to boot. When Dolores went to Miami in mid-January for a nightclub engagement, Theresa came along too, hoping some distance would cool the relationship. Instead, Bob and Dolores talked by phone nearly every day. The romance hit a more serious snag when Dolores saw a newspaper gossip item suggesting Hope had another girlfriend. Bob smooth-talked his way out of that one. "I hadn't seen that particular girl for six months, but it almost broke up our romance," Hope wrote in his memoir. "It would have been finished if I hadn't convinced Dolores that the whole thing was a columnist's blooper."

Yet there was, in fact, a woman standing between Bob and Dolores. Hope was already married at the time — to his former vaudeville partner Louise Troxell.

Hope's first marriage was long kept secret, and much about it remains mysterious. But a few facts are clear. Bob and Louise were married in Erie, Pennsylvania, on January 25, 1933, in a civil ceremony that was obviously meant to be kept quiet. Their marriage

161

license, on file in the Erie courthouse, identifies the couple as Leslie T. Hope, a "salesman," and Grace L. Troxell (using her first name, which she dropped for the stage), described as a "secretary." When the marriage license was unearthed by Arthur Marx for his 1993 biography, *The Secret Life of Bob Hope,* Hope's publicists weakly suggested that the couple merely took out a license, but never actually married. Yet according to an Erie official, the document would not exist if the wedding had not taken place; an Erie alderman's signed affidavit confirms that he presided over the ceremony.

Just what prompted Hope to marry his vaudeville partner, after an on-again, off-again relationship that spanned more than four years, is hard to say. But it forced him to deliberately muddle the details of his subsequent marriage to Dolores. According to Bob and Dolores (and virtually all the profiles and official biographies of them, both during and after their lifetime), they were married on February 19, 1934 — in, of all places, Erie, Pennsylvania. The town was accurate, but not the bride: there is no record of Bob's marriage to Dolores in Erie — only his marriage to Troxell a year earlier. Nor is there any record of a marriage in New York City, where it would more likely have taken place, given that Bob was appearing on Broadway at the time. (Hope was always vague about why he and Dolores would travel to Erie to get married. "We picked Erie, Pennsylvania, for our wedding," he wrote in *Have Tux, Will Travel.* "I can't remember why. I was in a thick pink fog anyway." When comedian Alan King, interviewing Hope on TV in 1992, asked him to explain why they got married in Erie, Hope tossed it off with a quip: "Because I couldn't wait until I got to a bigger town.")

When were Bob and Dolores Hope married? Certainly not before August 4, 1934, when this item appeared in the *New York Herald Tribune:*

> Bob Hope, who played a comedy lead in *Roberta* last season, and Miss Dolores Reade, a nightclub singer, announced their engagement yesterday. They will be married about Thanksgiving.

Moreover, they could not have been legally wed until after November 19, 1934 — when a judge in Ohio's Cuyahoga County granted Hope a divorce. In the divorce petition, filed by Lester T. Hope against Grace Louise Hope on September 4, Hope charged that his wife was "guilty of extreme cruelty and gross neglect of duty," citing her "quarrelsome disposition" and claiming that she "habitually, during their married life, associated with other men in public and has caused plaintiff humiliation and embarrassment as a result thereof." The judge found in Hope's favor, granted the divorce, and denied Troxell any "claim for alimony, either temporary or permanent."

Hope was represented in the divorce by a Cleveland attorney named Henry B. Johnson. Years later Johnson wrote Hope a letter that suggests the lengths to which the Broadway star went to keep the whole affair quiet. "It was in the early 1930s that you walked into my office in the Standard Building Cleveland," Johnson recalled:

I was to represent you in the litigation which you later referred to as the "Troxell deal" and apparently in driving to Cleveland you had to change a tire or perform some other mechanical chore which left your hands, face and clothing very much in need of freshening. This service we were able to furnish, and on subsequent visits and in Court you were then as now the acme of sartorial elegance.

I recall that you requested that there be no publicity about the matter; I was perhaps a year or two older than you with no compunctions then about lying to reporters, and I did lie brazenly to the reporters that called. [One] inquired whether you were the Bob Hope who was appearing in *Roberta*. . . . I assured him that there was no connection whatever, that you were Lester Townsend

Hope and would certainly not be nicknamed "Bob," and that while you were an actor, you were a minor figure on the stage and probably out of work.

If Hope had any concerns about Johnson's unearthing this skeleton from the closet, he hid them well in his sanguine reply to the lawyer: "It was great hearing from you again, and you took me back a few years when you were talking about the 'Troxell case.' "

No marriage license for Bob and Dolores Hope has ever turned up. One person who claimed to have attended their wedding, Milton Berle, told Arthur Marx that it took place in a New York City church sometime in late 1934 or early 1935. In an interview with *American Weekly* magazine in 1958, Dolores said she and Bob got married "a year after we met," which would put the wedding around the same time. Yet there was never a wedding announcement, and when Dolores appeared with Bob onstage over the next couple of years, she was never identified as his wife. For an entertainer who rarely missed an opportunity for self-promotion, the notion that Hope would keep his marriage to a glamorous nightclub singer secret is hard to believe.

The lack of any record of the Hopes' marriage (not even a wedding photo) led some Hope family members to speculate over the years that a wedding may never have taken place. It seems farfetched that Dolores, a devout Catholic, would not at some point have dragged Bob into a church to exchange formal vows. By then, presumably, it would have been too late for announcements. Hope had already fudged so many details of his marital status that trying to untangle the web of untruths would have been all but impossible.

As for Louise Troxell, she stayed in vaudeville for at least another year, doing Dumb Dora routines with a new partner, Joe May. She later moved back to her hometown of Chicago and married Dave Halper, owner of the Chez Paree nightclub. In 1952 they had a daughter, Deborah, and, after the nightclub closed in 1960, moved to Las Vegas, where Halper worked for the Riviera Hotel until his death in 1973. Bob and Louise stayed in touch, and Hope quietly sent her money in her later years. In two letters written to Hope in 1976, Louise complained about her declining health and the difficulties she was having with her daughter: "When Deb went away . . . I had a sinking feeling that I would never see her alive again. A beautiful life, self-destroyed. It is so sad." Troxell died in Las Vegas in November 1976, at age sixty-five. Her daughter, Deborah, apparently still troubled, died in San Diego of a drug overdose in 1998.

Just how much Dolores knew about all this

is unclear, but probably more than she ever revealed. On the San Diego County death certificate for Deborah Halper, the "informant" — the person who supplies information about the deceased — is listed, intriguingly, as "Dolores Hope — Godparent."

On January 22, 1934, in the midst of Hope's whirlwind courtship of Dolores, his mother died of cervical cancer. Despite radium treatments, little could be done, and Avis had largely been bedridden for months. When Hope last saw her at Christmas, she was clearly failing, her already-frail body down to seventy-five pounds. He flew to Cleveland for the funeral, bringing along opera singer Kirsten Flagstad, who sang "Beautiful Isle of Somewhere," one of Avis's favorite hymns, at the service. His brother Jim, the family romantic, writes achingly of Avis's last days, silently mouthing the names of each of her boys as she lay near death. Bob couldn't muster quite the same sentiment, though the death of his mother, in the midst of his great success on Broadway, was clearly a blow. "It was murder," he wrote in his memoir, "that this should happen just when I was really able to take care of her."

Dolores, meanwhile, moved into Bob's apartment at 65 Central Park West, with its elegant, green-and-white living room overlooking the park, and they embarked on their life together in New York. They played golf together at Green Meadows, a golf club in Westchester County, or, when they couldn't get out of the city, at a driving range under the Fifty-Ninth Street Bridge. They took a cruise to Bermuda, Bob doing a show for the passengers en route. Dolores's dinner parties got mentioned in the gossip columns. Yet she was already learning how to fend for herself on the many nights that Bob was working, organizing weekly card games with a small group of friends and cousins. She desperately wanted children, but had no luck getting pregnant.

She continued to pursue her singing career, at least for a couple of years. When Bob, after leaving *Roberta,* took his vaudeville act back on the road in the summer of 1934, Dolores was on the bill as featured singer. After his monologue, Bob would introduce her and let her do one number straight. Then, during her second song, he would come back on-stage and clown around while she sang — mooning over her, lying on the ground and staring at her adoringly, stroking and nibbling her arm. "Don't let me bother you," he'd crack.

Like his other stage partners, going back to Mildred Rosequist, Dolores found that she had to be on her toes when teaming with Bob Hope. "What he expected was perfection," she said. "He never let down for a moment onstage, and heaven help me if I did. . . . Sometimes my mind would wander and that was fatal. Bob would get very angry, and right there in the middle of the act he'd crack, 'What's the matter with you, tired?' "

When Bob went to Boston for tryouts of his next Broadway show, Dolores came along and was booked for a solo engagement at the Loews State Theatre. But unaccustomed to a large vaudeville house, as opposed to the more intimate nightclubs where she usually worked, she had a difficult time. After her first show, she called Bob at their hotel in a panic.

"Come right over," she sobbed. "I'm going to quit. They didn't like me. The band played too loud and the lights were wrong. Everything was wrong." Hope went over and took charge. "They gave her a little more production and her act pulled together beautifully. Give her any kind of decent staging and my girl was good," he recalled gallantly.

Her regal good looks and alluring voice drew some admiring reviews when Hope featured her in his act. ("A likely picture bet, if she can speak on a par with her torching and looks," *Variety* wrote.) But as a solo, she had trouble registering. "On song values she's in the same category as many another femme warbler with any of the radio-dance bands extant, and actually suffers comparatively with Joy Lynne, who's merely a featured songstress with the Bestor combo," *Variety*'s critic wrote after her appearance at New York's State Theater in December 1934. Soon, except for sporadic appearances in Bob's tours or on his radio show, Dolores would stop singing professionally, devoting herself instead to the man whose career was proving to have considerably more upside.

That career was tooling along nicely on all three tracks: Broadway, radio, and vaudeville. To manage all of it, Hope had acquired a new agent: Louis "Doc" Shurr, who signed him up as a client while Hope was appearing in *Roberta* and would become one of his most effective and loyal advocates for the next three decades.

Shurr was a colorful New York showbiz character: a short, bald man who propped up his height with elevator shoes and wore a homburg over his fringe of dyed-black hair. He spent practically every night out on the town, impeccably dressed in a suit, tie, and crisp white handkerchief, reeking of Charbert cologne and with a buxom showgirl on his arm — usually towering over him and wearing a white fur coat, one of three (in sizes small, medium, and large) that Shurr supposedly kept for his dates. Called Doc because of his reputation for fixing troubled Broadway shows, Shurr was a hard-driving agent of the old school, with an office in the Paramount Building on Broadway, where he

170

was all but hidden behind rows of framed photos and a baby grand piano. His clients included such well-known stage stars as Bert Lahr, Victor Moore, and George Murphy, many of whom he was getting into motion pictures. He thought he could do the same with Bob Hope.

Hope was wary of Hollywood, still smarting from his failed 1930 screen test at Pathé. In 1933 he turned down an offer from Paramount to costar with Jack Oakie in a comedy called *Sitting Pretty,* reasoning that the money — $2,500 for four weeks' work — was less than the $1,750 a week he was making on Broadway and thus wasn't worth the move to Hollywood. But when Shurr got him an offer from Educational Pictures, to star in six comedy shorts — to be shot in Brooklyn during the day while he continued appearing in *Roberta* at night — Hope decided it was a relatively low-risk proposition and said yes.

Comedy shorts were still common on movie bills in the 1930s — cheaply made vehicles for fading silent-film stars such as Buster Keaton and Harry Langdon, but also important early showcases for W. C. Fields, Laurel and Hardy, and newcomers such as Jack Benny, Burns and Allen, and Bing Crosby. Hope's shorts were pretty low-grade examples of the genre. In his first, *Going Spanish,* Hope and Leah Ray play a pair of newlyweds on their honeymoon, motoring through Mexico with her mother tagging along. They stop in a town called Los Pochos Eggos on the day of an annual festival in which anyone is allowed to insult whomever they please, so long as the insult is followed by a song. Various comic high jinks and romantic mix-ups ensue, including a sight gag in which people hop around after eating Mexican jumping beans.

Hope, looking dandyish in a light-colored, double-breasted suit, with slicked-back hair parted high on his head, is crisp and self-assured in his film debut. But he can do little with the lamer-than-lame material. After a screening of the film at the Rialto Theater on Broadway, Hope ran into columnist Walter Winchell, who asked about Hope's film debut. "When they catch Dillinger they're going to make him watch it twice," Hope cracked. When Winchell printed the remark in his column, an angry Jack Skirball, head of Educational Pictures, called up Shurr and said the last thing he needed was a star bad-mouthing his own film. After Hope tried in vain to get Winchell to retract the item, Educational canceled Hope's contract.

But Shurr quickly got Hope another deal, to star in six more shorts for Warner Vitaphone, at a salary of $2,500 for each. Produced by Sam Sax, they were shot at Warner's studios in Astoria, Queens, on a rock-bottom budget. "Sam's ability to squeeze a buck

172

could make Jack Benny seem like Aristotle Onassis," Hope said. "He made those shorts in three days, rain or shine. In fact, if a director got three sprocket holes behind schedule, Sam would stick his head into the soundstage and say, 'What's wrong?' "

The Warner shorts were a step up from *Going Spanish,* but not by much. The first, *Paree, Paree,* released in October 1934, is probably the best, mainly because it provides a rare glimpse of Hope in his incarnation as a Broadway leading man. Adapted from Cole Porter's 1929 show *Fifty Million Frenchmen,* it casts Hope as a rich American playboy in Paris who bets some friends that he can get the girl he met on board ship to marry him without revealing that he's a millionaire. Though drastically truncated and ludicrously underpopulated, the film still squeezes in four Porter songs and two Busby Berkeley–style production numbers in just twenty minutes. Hope sings the lovely Porter ballad "You Do Something to Me" in a light, appealing tenor, before the girl he's wooing (Dorothy Stone) turns it into a high-kicking dance number — as Hope, disappointingly, just watches from a chair. But Hope gets another fine Porter song, "You've Got That Thing," all to himself, deftly managing Porter's tricky rhythms and demonstrating his skill at lyrically intricate "list" songs, which he would make a specialty

173

both on Broadway and later in feature films.

The other shorts for Warner, released over the next two years, were straight comedies, most of them crude farces that show Hope developing his skills as both comedian and straight man. In *The Old Grey Mayor,* he has to win over his fiancée's father, a gruff big-city political boss; in *Watch the Birdie,* he's a practical joker on a cruise ship; in *Double Exposure,* a pushy celebrity photographer; and in *Calling All Tars,* he and a pal (the Stan Laurel–like Johnny Berkes) dress up as sailors to get girls and wind up dragooned into the real Navy. *Shop Talk,* the last and probably the best of the nonmusical shorts, features Hope as a spoiled rich kid who inherits his father's department store. The comedy spins off his encounters with a string of wacky store employees, comic bits that both hark back to his vaudeville routines (dumb girl applying for a job asks, "Do you mind if I use your telephone?" — and then uses it to crack nuts) and anticipate the comic repartee between Hope and his sidekicks that would become a staple of his radio shows.

But the movie shorts were just a diversion for Hope, who still considered himself primarily a Broadway star. After his success in *Roberta,* he landed a costarring role in the 1934 musical *Say When.* The show was conceived as a vehicle for Harry Richman, the veteran song-and-dance star of the 1920s who was looking for a Broadway comeback; he not only starred in the show but invested $50,000 of his own money in it. (Gangster Lucky Luciano was reputedly one of the other backers.) Richman and Hope play vaudeville hoofers who romance two bankers' daughters aboard a transatlantic ocean liner. The songs were by Ray Henderson (composer of "Varsity Drag" and "Life Is Just a Bowl of Cherries") and lyricist Ted Koehler (Harold Arlen's collaborator on "Stormy Weather" and "I've Got a Right to Sing the Blues"), and the supporting cast included "Prince" Michael Romanoff, a flamboyant New York character who claimed to be a Russian royal (and later became a popular Beverly Hills restaurateur).

Richman was unhappy with the show almost from the start, distressed that he didn't have an obvious hit song, and that Hope was getting most of the laughs. Hope offered a sympathetic ear when Richman, on the train back to New York after the Boston tryouts, lamented, "I'm the star, and if I'm weak, it won't help any of us." Hope was grateful that Richman didn't go behind his back and steal his good lines, but the ambitious young costar didn't exactly shy away from the chance to hog the spotlight. "Harry was one of Broadway's greatest stars, but he was playing an unsympathetic lover and his part was thin," said Hope. "If he'd had a good score, he'd be all right, but he had no big songs. I was shortsighted and hamola enough to enjoy the situation."

Say When opened on November 8, 1934, and got surprisingly good reviews. Walter Winchell called it the "merriest laugh, song and girl show in town," and Hope's contribution was duly noted. "Mr. Hope, as usual, was amiably impudent, never offensive and a likable and intelligent clown, equal to all the emergencies of Broadway operetta," wrote Percy Hammond in the *Herald Tribune.* None of this assuaged Richman, who quit the show after eight weeks, forcing *Say When* to close prematurely in January.

That was enough time for Hope. In December, before the show closed, Hope landed an audition for his first weekly radio job: as emcee of *The Intimate Revue,* a Friday-night variety show on NBC sponsored by Bromo-Seltzer. Worried that he didn't have enough material for the audition, Hope got Richman to drive him out to his Long Island estate and let him go through Richman's extensive joke file and pilfer what he wanted. Hope got the job and for years afterward credited Richman as "the guy responsible for my success in radio."

The Intimate Revue lasted only thirteen weeks, and Hope's uneasiness with the new medium was apparent. It was primarily a music program, featuring the classically trained songstress Jane Froman and Al Goodman's mellow-toned orchestra. "Every week at this time, we present a show as sparkling and as easy to take as Bromo-Seltzer," went the show's weekly sign-off. The easy-to-take part usually trumped the sparkle. Hope carried most of the comedy, which consisted of weak sketches (Hope as a South Pole explorer, or the head of a travel agency, or Sergeant Hope of the Mounted Police) and strained banter with his on-air companions on topics such as the best way to dunk a doughnut. In one recurring bit, Hope delivered jokey "society notes" in a fast-paced, Winchell-like staccato: "Flash! Miami Beach! Young Puppy Wellington, missing for three days, lost his trunks while bathing and was forced to keep running in and out with the tide." Hope didn't yet have the confidence or the technique to recover when the jokes fell flat; often the only titters heard in the studio were those coming nervously from Hope himself. "Hope is intermittently very funny," said *Variety.* "At other times either his material falters or his delivery is a bit too lackadaisical. . . . Hope is easy to take but hard to remember."

The best thing to come out of *The Intimate Revue* for Hope was a new comedy sidekick — a Southern-fried Dumb Dora by the name of Honey Chile. She was played by a sixteen-year-old Macon, Georgia, beauty named Patricia Wilder. Bob had met her in Louis Shurr's office and was taken with her dark-haired good looks and "thick, spoonbread Southern accent." He tried her out in his act at the Capitol Theatre and liked the way she won over the crowd with her first line — wandering out to center stage and drawling, "Pahdon me, Mistah Hope. Does the Greyhound bus stop heah?"

He brought her on *The Intimate Revue,* playing straight man to her goofy non sequiturs. ("Where you from?" "The South." "What part?" "All of me.") Wilder's laid-back, countrified insouciance made her an audience favorite, even outshining Hope. "Bob Hope is a likeable fellow personally, and I'm sorry to say he hasn't clicked so well on the air," noted the *New York Radio Guide* on March 30, 1935, predicting that Hope would "be off the program soon. At this writing, the new talent hasn't been selected, but I'd like to suggest they keep Honey Child and give her some good material."

Both were off the air in April, when *The Intimate Revue* was canceled. But Hope wisely brought back Honey Chile when he landed his next radio job the following December, as emcee for a CBS variety show sponsored by the Atlantic Oil Company.

On the *Atlantic Family Show,* Hope played second fiddle to the program's ostensible star, tenor Frank Parker. Sketches were often

built around the straitlaced Parker's courtship of his on-air fiancée, Sue Fulton —
Frank and Sue are weekend guests at a
colonial mansion, for example, or Frank
shops for Sue's Christmas present, with Hope
as a wisecracking store clerk. (Parker: "Would
you help me around the store?" Hope: "Why,
are you drunk again?") When the show was
renewed in the spring, Parker left to take a
job on orchestra leader Paul Whiteman's
program, and Hope inherited the starring
spot. He brought in three writers to help
improve his material, added a couple of supporting players, and gave Honey Chile more
to do. And he began to develop a more
distinctive radio personality.

His pace was faster now, his voice brittle
and smart-alecky, drawing out the end of his
punch lines like a carnival huckster. As in
vaudeville, he tried to build up his pompous
character so that others could cut him down
to size. One of his sidekicks, for instance, a
rube character named Skunky, brings a horse
into the studio. Hope asks why. Skunky
replies, "He figures if you're a radio comedian, he's wastin' his time pullin' that plow
around." In his routines with Honey Chile,
Hope's ripostes to her nonsense ("You know,
Honey Chile, a mind reader would only
charge you half price") were usually topped
by her sucker-punch comebacks:

BOB: "I wish you'd be careful. Anything you say will be held against you."

HONEY: "Anything I say will be held against me?"

BOB: "That's right."

HONEY: "Mink coat."

Wilder became so popular as Honey Chile that she was soon gone, leaving for Hollywood in the summer of 1936 when RKO offered her a movie contract. Hope kept the character but replaced the actress, hiring a Dallas beauty named Margaret Johnson as the new Honey Chile, and then (when Johnson also left for the movies) replacing her with Claire Hazel. Hope and Wilder reunited later in Hollywood, when she made a couple of guest appearances as Honey Chile on his radio show and in two of his early movies. But her film career didn't go anywhere, and in the early 1940s Wilder returned to New York, where she became a flamboyant, Holly Golightly–style fixture on the Manhattan nightclub scene. Later she moved to Europe, married an Austrian prince, and became a well-known international hostess. Wilder denied that she and Bob were ever romantically involved, but they remained lifelong friends; Bob and Dolores would pay occasional visits to her home in Marbella, Spain, or attend parties she threw in the South of France, and she continued to write him long, effusive letters — always signed "Honey" — nearly until her death in 1995.

The *Atlantic Family Show* had a nine-month run on CBS, Hope's longest radio stint to date. He turned up frequently in the radio columns, which chronicled his show's changing cast and time slots, repeated his best jokes, and fed his reputation as the hardest-working comic on radio. "It's all right for the established comedians to take 'time out' for the summer to relax," he told an interviewer, explaining why he wasn't taking a summer vacation, as most radio stars did. "They've captured their listening public and merit a rest. But I'm a comparative newcomer to the airwaves and am glad I have the opportunity to keep plugging."

He worked hard to court the press and cultivate his image — which didn't always bear much resemblance to the real Bob Hope. First he made up bogus details about his supposedly titled English background. Then he gave himself an Ivy League make-over. For a *Radio Stars* profile in September 1936, Hope greeted the interviewer in his Central Park West apartment dressed in a yellow sweater, with two Scottie dogs on his lap and a fat book called *Education Before Verdun* on the coffee table. "He just doesn't look like a comedian," the reporter observed. "He's still in his twenties [actually thirty-three] and his cheeks are rosy and a couple of boyish cowlicks keep his brown hair from being the plastered cap he has tried to make it. He might be a tennis pro or a Yale undergrad or even a young doctor — but never a zany of the mikes."

He was getting some buzz as a radio up-and-comer. "Before 1940, don't be surprised if Bob Hope turns out to be the ace comic of radio," wrote one prescient radio columnist, Dick Templeton, in March 1936. "That may sound like a long shot and a long time prediction, but if it does happen, then Bob will have realized his ambition."

It would happen. But first he had a couple more stops on his Broadway tour.

In the fall of 1935, Hope signed on for his fourth Broadway show in as many seasons. This time he was cast in the *Ziegfeld Follies of 1936,* a new edition of the lavish, showgirl-studded revues staged by Florenz Ziegfeld every season from 1907 to 1925 and sporadically after that. The 1936 show was the second to appear since Ziegfeld's death in 1932 and was produced by his widow, Billie Burke, along with Lee and J. J. Shubert. The show's main attraction was Fanny Brice, the long-time *Follies* star, and it also featured Josephine Baker, the celebrated chanteuse just returned from Paris; singer Gertrude Niesen; the dancing Nicholas Brothers; and a statuesque young singer-comedienne named Eve

Arden. George Balanchine choreographed the ballet sequences, Vincente Minnelli designed the scenery, and Vernon Duke and Ira Gershwin wrote the songs. The show was so jam-packed with talent that some cast members had to be dropped during the Boston tryouts, among them ventriloquist Edgar Bergen and his dummy Charlie McCarthy.

Even in this heady company, Hope was a standout. He had two numbers with Brice, one in which he played a Hollywood director to her famous Baby Snooks character, the other a send-up of British snobs called Fancy, Fancy. Best of all, he was handed what would be the show's biggest hit song, "I Can't Get Started."

He sings it to Eve Arden, the two playing a posh New York couple saying good night after an evening on the town. In Gershwin's wistful-witty lyrics, Hope laments his inability to make any romantic headway with her: "I've flown around the world in a plane, I've settled revolutions in Spain/ The North Pole I have charted, still I can't get started with you." Arden ignores his entreaties, trying to hail a cab as he moons over her. When Hope starts panting, she quips, "What's the matter? Have you been running?" (Hope said he gave Arden the line after the doorman at the Winter Garden Theater suggested it.) When Hope finishes the song, she finally succumbs and they embrace — after which Hope straightens up, briskly adjusts his cuffs, and puts a comic button on the number: "That's all I wanted to know. Well, good night."

The number impressed two visitors from Hollywood, producer Harlan Thompson and director Mitchell Leisen, who came to see the show one night. A year later they cast Hope in his first Hollywood feature, *The Big Broadcast of 1938.* His performance of "I Can't Get Started" was surely on their minds when they handed him another wistful-witty romantic list song, the one that would launch his movie career, "Thanks for the Memory."

Ziegfeld Follies of 1936, after some delays and out-of-town tinkering, opened on January 29, 1936, at the Winter Garden Theater, to mostly excellent reviews. "A jovial and handsome song-and-dance festival, glorifying the Broadway tempo and style," wrote Brooks Atkinson in the *Times.* Though Brice got most of the praise, Atkinson noted that she "has a capital partner in Bob Hope, who is gentleman enough to be a comrade and comedian enough to be funny on his own responsibility."

Hope loved his time in *Follies.* The Winter Garden Theater was right in the middle of the Broadway action. Bob would get haircuts across the street at the Taft Hotel, from a barber who shaved Walter Winchell and would give Hope all the theater gossip. He walked to the theater each night from his Central Park West apartment. "It was a kick, whipping down to the theater and saying 'Hi' to the traffic cops and to people on the avenue and to the people in the show when you got there," he wrote. "That was really living. There was always something going on."

The show, however, ran into trouble because of Brice's fragile health. During a performance in Philadelphia, she took an overdose of sleeping pills — supposedly mistaking them for cold medication — and forgot the words to one of her numbers. The curtain had to be unceremoniously brought down on her, as the cast cringed in the wings. The Shuberts decided to close the show in June and give her the summer to recover, then reopened in September. But Hope, along with Arden and several other cast members, decided not to stick around. He already had another Broadway show waiting in the wings.

It was a new Cole Porter musical, the composer's much-anticipated follow-up to his 1934 hit *Anything Goes.* Originally titled *But Millions!* the show came from the same team of writers, Howard Lindsay and Russel Crouse, and was intended to reunite the same three stars, Ethel Merman, William Gaxton, and Victor Moore. But Gaxton, a popular Broadway leading man at the time, backed out when he felt that Merman's part was being elevated above his, and the role went to Hope instead. When Victor Moore also bowed out, his part was given to another, even bigger comedy star, Jimmy Durante.

The show, eventually retitled *Red, Hot and Blue,* had another rough voyage to Broadway. Merman and Durante had a famous battle over billing. Neither wanted the other to have the most prominent spot in the show's advertising, listed either on top or on the left. A compromise was worked out in which both their names were printed diagonally, like a railroad crossing sign. (Hope settled for a line of his own underneath.) In its first tryout performances in Boston, the show ran more than three hours. Porter walked out in a huff when the music director criticized one of his songs, "Ridin' High." Durante, the big-schnozzed, raspy-voiced ham, was a loose cannon onstage. One night he appeared to forget his lines, walked to the orchestra for help, then finally called into the wings, "Trow me da book!" Hope admired Durante's chutzpah, even after discovering that the bit was entirely planned.

Butting up against two Broadway egos even bigger than his own, Hope had to fight for stage time. Lindsay and Crouse were having trouble coming up with an ending to the first act and after several tries finally settled on one that featured only Durante and Merman. This rankled Hope, and he got Doc Shurr to argue his case with the writers. "I've been with Bob a long time," Shurr said. "He's going to feel bad about this. He'll go on depressed, and if he's not in that finale, maybe he won't be able to give a good performance." The writers relented and shoehorned Hope into the scene as well.

Like *Anything Goes, Red, Hot and Blue* had a madcap plot involving gangsters and society swells. Merman played "Nails" Duquesne, a former manicurist now a rich widow, who teams up with an ex-con (Durante) to stage a national lottery aimed at finding Hope's old hometown sweetheart — a girl whose identifying feature is a waffle-iron brand on her rear end. The show continued Hope's streak of good luck with musical numbers, teaming him with Merman on the song that became the show's most enduring standard, "It's De-Lovely." His light touch and crisp articulation got the most out of Porter's fizzy lyrics and provided a nice counterpoint to Merman's voice and bombastic stage presence. (The two made a recording of the number — the only one that remains of Hope's Broadway work.)

Merman had her problems with Hope. She hated improvising onstage and was thrown off when he would clown around during their numbers. Once, during "De-Lovely," she turned around to find him lying down on the stage. "He lay down by the footlights, with me standing behind him," Merman recalled in her autobiography. "I controlled myself with an effort that almost busted my stay strings, but afterward I had a heart-to-heart talk with [producer Vinton] Freedley. 'If that so-called comedian ever does that again,' I said, tight-lipped but ladylike, 'I'm going to plant my foot on his kisser and leave more of a curve in his nose than nature gave it.' " Asked about the incident later, Hope admitted, "I probably kidded around with her too much," but claimed the lying-down incident came not in "De-Lovely" but in another number, "You've Got Something," a weaker song that "needed some help."

Yet Hope admired Merman as a performer — and possibly as more than that. He used to walk her home from the Alvin Theater on Fifty-Second Street, dropping her off at her parents' apartment at 25 Central Park West, before continuing on to his place a couple of blocks up. Hope's longtime publicist Frank Liberman, in an unpublished memoir of his time with Hope, recalled: "In a rare moment of introspection, he told me that he and Ethel, both in their early thirties [Merman actually wasn't yet thirty] and with raging hormones, would walk home and make love standing up in darkened doorways on Eighth Avenue. They'd then proceed to their separate apartments." Of all Hope's reported liaisons, it surely ranks as one of the unlikeliest.

Red, Hot and Blue, which opened on October 29, 1936, had a bumpy ride with the critics, who found the book idiotic and the score a comedown from *Anything Goes.* Yet the stars won praise, and Hope got his share of it. *Time* found him "coyly engaging"; the *Times* "generally cheering"; and the *Evening Journal* "urbane, sleek, and nimble of accent. He knows a poor joke when he hides it and he can out-stare more of them." A few brief clips of his performance exist — silent footage shot by a young theater enthusiast from Jacksonville, Florida, named Ray Knight, whose home movies constitute the only filmed record of many Broadway shows from the 1930s. Hope is dapper and handsome, if a bit more filled out than in his vaudeville days ("the roly-poly Bob Hope," *Time* described him), prancing across the stage in a double-breasted suit with chin tucked in, a tight smile on his face, and the confident, wide-swinging gait that would later become a trademark.

The show lasted for most of the season, closing in April 1937, after 183 performances. The producers reopened it for a two-week run in Chicago, then it expired for good, bringing down a final curtain on Hope's Broadway career.

It was a great run, lifting Hope out of the vaudeville trenches and turning him into a front-rank Broadway star. But Broadway, in some ways, was an aberration for Hope: a high-style interlude on the way from vaudeville to the more informal, naturalistic, and personal comedy style he would develop on radio and in films. "I was an entirely different fellow on Broadway," he told an interviewer. "I was very chic and very subtle. I wouldn't do a double take for anything." More important, in terms of his comedy evolution during the New York years, were his many appearances at charity events (of the 125 major benefits in New York City during the 1936–37 season, Hope appeared, either as emcee or a performer, in fully half of them) and on the radio, where he was finally gaining some traction. In May 1937, just after *Red, Hot and Blue* closed, he landed another weekly radio gig, as host of a new NBC Sunday-night show called *The Rippling Rhythm Revue*, sponsored by Woodbury soap and featuring Shep Fields and His Rippling Rhythm Orchestra. By that time, however, Doc Shurr was already negotiating for Hope's next big career move: into the movies.

For most of his time in New York, Hope had maintained at least a pretense of disdain for Hollywood. The memory of his failed screen test in 1930 still burned, and he took the pragmatic approach that even a lucrative Hollywood contract would bring in less than the $5,000 a week he was making in his peak New York years. "Hollywood was for peasants, I decided. New York was my town," Hope said. "The New Yorkers were sophisticated enough to understand and enjoy my suave, sterling style. Hollywood was Hicksville."

But in July, Shurr got an offer from Paramount to cast Hope in *The Big Broadcast of 1938,* a musical-comedy revue starring W. C. Fields. Hope's part, as a radio broadcaster on an ocean liner embarked on a transatlantic race, had originally been offered to Jack Benny, who turned it down because he thought it was too similar to one he had played in another film, *Transatlantic Merry-Go-Round.* Shurr had to work hard to get Hope to accept, making his case in a telegram from Hollywood to his brother Lester, who worked with him back in New York: "Please advise Bob this is the great opportunity he has been waiting for, and we shouldn't let money stand in the way, as we can't afford to lose this proposition on account of a few thousand dollars."

In a follow-up telegram a day later, Shurr pressed the case: "Advise Bob Hope part Paramount has for him in *Big Broadcast* is light comedy lead and will give him every opportunity to show his ability as comedian and chance to sing several songs. . . . Zukor, LeBaron and Harlan Thompson [the studio chief, head of production, and the film's producer, respectively] most enthusiastic in Bob's future and will give him every opportunity to score."

Hope eventually agreed to the deal, signing a contract with Paramount for three pictures a year at $20,000 per film, with an option for seven years. But the option deal meant little since the studio could essentially drop him at any point. So when he and Dolores boarded the Super Chief for the cross-country train trip to California in early September 1937, he was not at all sure the move to Hollywood would be for good. "We've always hated the idea of leaving New York," Hope told a reporter before he left. "And this may not be permanent — probably won't be."

But it was.

■ ■ ■ ■

II
Inventing Comedy

FROM ENTERTAINER TO INNOVATOR: PIONEERING A NEW COMIC STYLE

■ ■ ■ ■

CHAPTER 4
HOLLYWOOD
"I ALWAYS JOKE WHEN I'M SCARED."

Mitchell Leisen didn't have much fun working on *The Big Broadcast of 1938*. The Paramount contract director, a former costume and set designer, was best known for stylish romantic comedies such as *Hands Across the Table* and *Easy Living* (the latter, with a script by Preston Sturges, one of the high points of 1930s screwball comedy). Now, however, he was stuck directing the fourth in a middling series of musical-comedy revues, which had begun in 1932 with *The Big Broadcast,* starring Bing Crosby. The top-billed star for the new film was W. C. Fields, returning to the screen after a year's health layoff, and the cantankerous comedy veteran gave Leisen nothing but trouble. "The most obstinate, ornery son of a bitch I ever tried to work with," said Leisen, who was so bored with some of Fields's recycled comedy routines that he fobbed them off on another director, Ted Reed. The film's initial screening for Paramount executives was "my most embarrassing moment," Leisen recalled. "The only part that was any good was 'Thanks for the Memory.' "

Leisen had ordered up the song from Leo Robin and Ralph Rainger, the Paramount songwriting team who had written "Please" for Bing Crosby and "Love in Bloom," Jack Benny's theme song. Leisen wanted a number for Bob Hope and Shirley Ross, cast as a divorced couple who find themselves together on the same ocean liner embarked on a transatlantic race. The song, Leisen told the composers, needed to reveal the feelings that the couple still had for each other, but subtly and with humor. "It's not easy to say, 'I love you,' without *saying* it," said Robin. "But we'll see what we can do."

The songwriters spent three weeks working on the number. After they were done, they worried that it wasn't funny enough. But when Leisen finished listening to the song for the first time, he was wiping away a tear. "No, it's not funny," the director said, "but I'll take it." He told them to slow down the tempo and asked for some additional lyrics. Then he made them promise not to come to rehearsals until he was ready to shoot the scene.

Rather than prerecord the song and have the actors lip-synch on camera, as was the usual practice, Leisen convinced the studio to let him record it live, to give it more feeling. That meant having a full orchestra onstage, and three cameras rolling simultaneously to capture the actors' reactions in real time. "I rehearsed Bob and Shirley over and over, until they could give it just the mood I was trying to get across," Leisen said. Ross was a rising young singing star at Paramount, with several films under her belt, including *Waikiki Wedding* with Bing Crosby. But Hope was a neophyte in films, and Leisen took him out to lunch to give him some pointers. "In pictures, everything comes through the eyes," he said. "Try to think through your eyes."

When Leisen was finally ready to shoot the number, he called in Robin and Rainger. By the end of the scene, Ross was nearly in tears, and so were the songwriters. "We didn't know we wrote that song," they said.

The number is set in the ship's bar, where Hope, playing a radio announcer named Buzz Fielding, meets his ex-wife, Cleo, for a friendly drink. After some talk about a bet Hope has made on the ocean-liner race, they drift into reminiscing about their failed marriage. Ross mentions that she just found "that green tie of yours" while cleaning out an old trunk. "You know something, Buzz?" she adds wistfully. "I kinda miss your singing in the bathtub." Hope joins in the reverie: "Good old bathtub." And she: "Good old singing." They toast, and then Hope begins the song:

Thanks for the memory
Of rainy afternoons, swingy Harlem tunes
Motor trips and burning lips and burning
    toast and prunes
[She] How lovely it was . . .

The melody glides up the scale with each line, reaching the top at the final "lovely." The lyrics, bandied back and forth by the two ex-spouses, tick off random memories from their marriage, in classic "list song" fashion. The wit lies in the juxtaposition of the romantic high points and the mundane low ones:

[She] Thanks for the memory
Of faults that you forgave, rainbows on a
    wave
[He] And stockings in the basin when a
    fellow needs a shave.

With gentle irony, the song pokes fun at the stiff-upper-lip sophistication of this "modern" couple, who can't quite acknowledge their own emotions:

[She] We said goodbye with a highball
[He] And I got as high as a steeple
But we were intelligent people
[She] No tears, no fuss, [together, toasting]
    hooray for us.

When he saw himself on screen later, Hope

cringed at how literally he had taken Leisen's advice about using his eyes: "When I saw the rushes, I was astonished at my galloping orbs. I did everything with them except make them change places." Hope does appear a little too stage-directed, raising his eyes dreamily toward the sky or forcing a laugh, and Ross actually delivers most of the emotion in the number, her face registering various shades of amusement, annoyance, hurt, and romantic longing. But Hope is charming. He is fully inside his character — toying distractedly with the lemon in his drink, slumping his chin onto his shoulder like a daydreaming kid, shooting an occasional alert glance at Ross in response to one of her lines. At a few points they slip out of the song into brief bits of spoken dialogue:

[She] Letters with sweet little secrets
That couldn't be put in a day wire
[He] Too bad it all had to go haywire
That's life, I guess. I love —

Here Hope turns to Ross and finishes the sentence in his normal conversational voice: "— your dress." "You do?" she responds, flattered. He: "It's pretty." She: "Thanks" — and then picking up the melody once again — "for the memory . . ."

This blend of song and conversation, one of the number's most engaging devices, artfully connects the stylized lyrics with the real, evolving emotions of the couple singing them. At another point, Ross reminisces about "China's funny walls, transatlantic calls," and Hope comes back with "That weekend at Niagara when we hardly saw the falls." Ross again steps out of the melody, reacting to the obvious sexual allusion with a dreamy, sincere "How lovely that was." Hope responds with a clipped, amusingly smug "Thank you." The memory of their best night together, evoked in a perfect confluence of song, dialogue, and acting.

In the final verse, the emotional arc is completed. The tone is more intimate, with a sweet diminuendo:

> [She] Strictly entre nous, darling how are
> you?
> [He] And how are all those little dreams
> that never did come true?
> [She] Awfully glad I met you, [He] Cheerio,
> tootle-oo.

On the final "thank you," Ross, in the midst of leaving the bar, suddenly stops and comes back, collapsing tearfully in Hope's arms. In just a few minutes, the song has told the story of their relationship, revealed emotions that thcy have long kept buried, and brought the couple back together. It is one of the most beautifully written and performed musical numbers in all of movies. It was the moment that made Bob Hope a star.

"I don't think it's so much," Dolores said when Bob first brought a recording of "Thanks for the Memory" home for her to hear. She thought he was getting a solo in the movie, not a duet. A born and bred New Yorker, Dolores was already leery of the move to Hollywood — where Bob was just another movie wannabe, not a Broadway star. She was annoyed that the first thing the studio wanted to mess with was his nose. After testing out various shading and highlighting techniques, the studio's chief makeup man, Wally Westmore, suggested plastic surgery. Dolores objected, "Bob, your whole personality is in your face. They want to turn you into another leading man. No."

Hope wasn't exactly sold on Hollywood either. He was thirty-four years old — practically middle-aged for an actor just starting out in films — and still had a "log-size chip on my shoulder" about Hollywood. He told his agent, Louis Shurr, that he had some money saved up, and if things didn't work out in California, he was more than ready to go back to New York. "It's amazing that you can be a star in New York and just another fellow elsewhere," Hope told a reporter from the *New York Daily Mirror.* "When my agent called to tell me that I had been signed for the *Big Broadcast,* I asked him what [Broadway] show he had me booked for after that assignment. 'Don't worry about shows,' he replied. 'You're going to be busy in Hollywood for the rest of the season.' "

Hope certainly hit the ground running. He and Dolores arrived from New York at the Pasadena train station on Thursday morning, September 9, 1937 — greeted by a Paramount publicist and a photographer for the *Los Angeles Daily News,* which ran a photo of the couple's arrival the next day. They checked into the Beverly Wilshire Hotel, and Bob went into the studio that same afternoon to meet people. Shooting on *The Big Broadcast* began the following Monday.

For an aspiring film comedian just arriving in Hollywood, Paramount Pictures was a good place to land. Run by an imperious but cultivated Hungarian immigrant named Adolph Zukor, Paramount was among the most prestigious of Hollywood studios, home to such pioneering directors of the silent and early sound eras as Josef von Sternberg, Ernst Lubitsch, Rouben Mamoulian, and Cecil B. DeMille. Its impressive roster of stars under contract included Gary Cooper, Bing Crosby, Maurice Chevalier, Marlene Dietrich, George Raft, and Cary Grant. The studio was especially strong in comedy, having signed up many of the ex-vaudeville comics who were getting into films, including the Marx Brothers (who did their first five films for Paramount before moving over to MGM), W. C. Fields, Mae West, Jack Benny, Martha Raye, and George Burns and Gracie Allen.

What Paramount wasn't especially good at was nurturing and grooming its stars. In contrast to a studio like MGM, Paramount's modus operandi, all too often, was simply to throw stars into projects willy-nilly and see what stuck. What's more, the studio had something of a split personality when it came to comedy. On the one hand, it produced some of the era's most sophisticated, high-style romantic comedies — the continental "Lubitsch touch." At the same time, it churned out a host of wild, ramshackle farces — *International House, Million Dollar Legs, Six of a Kind* — that mixed and matched its comedy stars in seemingly random fashion. Hope had one foot in both camps: he was a gagster from vaudeville, but a sophisticated Broadway-musical star as well. The studio took awhile to figure out just what to do with him.

After a few weeks at the Beverly Wilshire Hotel, the Hopes rented a house in Beverly Hills from Rhea Gable, Clark's wife. Dolores was homesick for New York. But even before *The Big Broadcast* finished shooting, Paramount was lining up more projects for Hope. In November he stepped into a role originally intended for Jack Oakie in an all-star musical comedy called *College Swing.* In December the studio tapped him to costar with Martha Raye in *The Wallflower* (later retitled *Give Me a Sailor*), scheduled to start shooting in the spring. He was being eyed for a Damon Runyon story called *Money from Home,* and there was talk of teaming him in a musical with Dorothy Lamour. "Bob Hope, fine Broadway comic, has clicked big out here," *New York Daily News* columnist Ed Sullivan reported in early January — still a month before *Big Broadcast* even opened.

Hope did his part to feed the buzz. He hired a publicist from New York named Mack Millar, a well-connected hustler who was close to the major newspaper columnists such as Sullivan and Walter Winchell. Millar planted Hope's name in the columns and came up with publicity stunts, including a charity golf match between Hope and Bing Crosby — who had reconnected when Hope moved West — with the loser agreeing to work as a stand-in for one day on the winner's next movie. (Hope lost, 76 to 72, and had to show up on the set of Crosby's *Dr. Rhythm.*) The studio played up the friendship between Hope and Crosby, touting Bob as a new challenger to Bing as the "easiest-going actor in Hollywood":

Hope, like Crosby, is just having a lot of fun out of life. He takes things as they come,

204

worrying more about the size of his golf score than the size of his movie roles. . . . The bizarre clothing of Crosby is completely eclipsed by Hope. As a matter of fact, where Bing's clothing is a rainbow, Hope's clothing is an Aurora Borealis. He just can't be bothered by such things as color ensembles. If he is dressing and needs a tie he picks up the nearest one and puts it on. The same is true in regard to everything from shirts to socks.

Hope's visibility in Hollywood also got a boost from his radio work. When he moved West in early September, Hope was still a regular on Woodbury soap's *Rippling Rhythm Revue.* The show was broadcast from New York on Sunday nights, but NBC agreed to let Hope do his opening monologue live from Hollywood, then feed it to New York via a transcontinental hookup.

But when Hope arrived at NBC's Hollywood studios for his first show, he was dismayed to find that no studio audience was waiting for him. Insisting that he couldn't do a monologue without one, he got the NBC ushers to rearrange the rope lines so that the audience leaving Edgar Bergen's show, taped an hour earlier in the studio next door, would be funneled directly into Hope's studio. Enough of the confused patrons stuck around to give Hope some live laughs, and the network had a full audience ready for him the following week. By the end of September, however, *The Rippling Rhythm Revue* was off the air, the latest in a growing trail of canceled Hope radio shows.

Eager to get his stop-and-start radio career on track, Hope hired a new agent back in New York, a young, cigar-smoking go-getter named Jimmy Saphier. "I found him a shrewd boy who knew the business, my kind of guy," said Hope. Saphier had more connections than Shurr with the ad agencies that controlled most of the programming on radio, and Hope decided to split duties between the two agents: Saphier negotiating his radio deals, while Shurr continued to handle his movie and stage work. Shurr was somewhat dismayed at the newcomer's taking away a chunk of his Hope business (though Shurr continued to get a share of Hope's radio deals), but the two agents made an effective and loyal tandem. Both would remain with Hope for the rest of their lives.

Saphier felt strongly that Hope needed to make some changes in his approach to radio, putting less emphasis on sketches and more on his monologues. "I had watched Hope at the Capitol and had seen him in a Broadway musical before I heard him on radio, and I felt it was a shame the home listeners weren't getting the best of him," Saphier said. "Radio simply wasn't using his talents properly. I knew this, and I sensed Bob knew it but didn't yet know how to overcome it. His work with [his radio foils] was funny, but his strength seemed to me and also to him — eventually — to be centered in what he did best, the monologue."

Hope took Saphier's advice and began talking up his new emphasis in the press. "The monologue is now showing signs of being a main comedy trend," he told Samuel Kaufman of the *New York Sun.* "I haven't discarded dialogue and sketches, and I don't expect to. But I intend giving short monologues prominent spots on all my programs."

They would, however, be monologues of a new kind — filled not with generic vaudeville-style gags, but with fresh jokes, drawn from the news and from his own real-life experiences. "A comedian won't be able to take the stage and rattle off story after story or spiel gags without especial point," he told another reporter. "That's gone forever. But the monologue in modern dress, clever and smart, is due for a comeback." Radio columnist Edgar A. Thompson caught the essence of Hope's new approach: "He had never been able to understand why he could get hearty laughs from the stage or at the banquet table and why his material seemed to fall short at the microphone. He remembered that big talks at parties went along smoothly without any gags or 'he and she' jokes. Many of them started out, 'On my way over here from home I' — and then Hope realized. Every time he got a laugh it was from a situation and not from a gag."

Hope explicitly invoked Will Rogers, the late monologuist beloved for his homespun commentary on politics and current events. "He took an old form and cloaked it with novelty, gave it vitality," said Hope. "There was a performer. You get only one like him in a generation." Yet Hope was Rogers's logical heir. He adopted the humorist's everyman approach and topical subject matter ("All I know is what I read in the papers," went Rogers's famous line), but added speed and moxie and a vaudeville gagster's instinct for the laugh line. In doing so, he invented a new kind of monologue — the seeds of modern stand-up comedy.

Hope's new approach evolved slowly, but it started to become apparent in his next radio job. In December 1937 Saphier convinced Albert Lasker, head of the powerful Chicago-based ad agency Lord & Thomas, to give Hope a couple of guest spots on *Your Hollywood Parade,* a one-hour variety show sponsored by Lucky Strike cigarettes, a Lord & Thomas client. Hosted by Hollywood musical star Dick Powell, the show was a leisurely mix of songs from new movies, "behind-the-scenes" features on moviemaking, and original playlets featuring Hollywood stars such as Edward G. Robinson. Hope's role in the show was limited to a single comedy spot, with Powell serving as straight man. Hope hired a writer named Wilkie Mahoney to help him come up with material, and the two would spend two or three late nights a week together, working long after Hope's day of shooting was done at Paramount.

Hope made his first appearance on *Your Hollywood Parade* on December 29, 1937, Powell introducing him as a "Broadway comedian exploring Hollywood with gagbook and funny bone." Hope made jokes about Christmas shopping, tours of movie-star homes, and his own recent arrival in Hollywood. It was hardly Will Rogers material, but at least it was pegged to the real-life Hollywood scene and his own place in it. He was rewarded with a regular spot on the show, and the reviewers began to take notice. "Hope appears too adaptable a comic to be kept out of the general proceedings and tucked away for a few minutes of dialogue," wrote *Variety.* The head of Lucky Strike, the show's sponsor, even wanted Hope to replace Powell as the program's host, but the movie star's contract had him locked in.

Your Hollywood Parade lasted only thirteen weeks. But Hope's stint there impressed Lasker, as well as another important person: Charles Luckman, the marketing wunderkind who had built Pepsodent toothpaste into the bestselling brand in America. Pepsodent, also a Lord & Thomas client, was about to end its nine-year sponsorship of *Amos 'n' Andy,* once the top-rated show on radio but now a fading franchise, and the company was looking to shift its dollars to a new program for the fall. Saphier began negotiating to get Bob Hope the starring job.

The Big Broadcast of 1938 finally opened in February of 1938. Hope's first feature film is a labored hodgepodge of comedy bits and musical numbers, linked by a silly plot about a transatlantic race between two mammoth ocean liners. Fields, playing a dual role as an ocean-liner magnate and his wastrel son, is at close to his worst, trudging through tired comedy bits (including variations on his pool-room and golf-course routines that he had done often before in films) and interacting little with the rest of the cast. Martha Raye turns up midway through the film, rescued from a lifeboat in the middle of the ocean, and gives it some spark with an acrobatic musical number, "Mama, That Moon Is Here Again," in which she's tossed about like a sack of potatoes by a bunch of sailors. There's a perfunctory romantic subplot involving Dorothy Lamour and Leif Erickson; a Busby Berkeley–style production number celebrating the waltz; a Wagnerian solo from Metropolitan Opera star Kirsten Flagstad; and even an animated cartoon, to go with a musical number by Shep Fields and His Rippling Rhythm Orchestra.

Hope has more screen time than anyone else but Fields, and he's considerably more lively. He opens the film in alimony jail: "I had a little trouble keeping a wife and the government on one salary," he quips, looking stylishly disheveled in a suit jacket and open-collar white shirt. Actually, there are three ex-wives, none of whom will bail him out. Ross plays wife No. 3, and the caustic push-pull of their relationship is established right at the start. "Remember the last time we were in jail?" Hope asks. "Our wedding night," she responds drily. "Did you ever manage to find the marriage license?" Hope: "Gee, that was about the maddest house detective I ever saw."

Hope eventually gets sprung from jail and boards one of the ocean liners, serving as radio broadcaster for the race and emcee for the shipboard entertainment. He has some uninspired comedy business with a sidekick played by Ben Blue, does a comedy bit with his old radio foil Honey Chile, and shows off some steps in the big waltz number. But his duet with Ross in "Thanks for the Memory" is the film's high point. Al Jolson had actually introduced the song on radio the previous December, predicting that it would be the "big hit tune of 1938." But it took Hope and

Ross's lovely handling of it on-screen to make the prediction come true.

The movie got mixed reviews. "All loose ends and tatters, not too good at its best, and downright bad at its worst," scoffed Frank Nugent in the *New York Times*. But nearly everyone singled out Hope and Ross's number as the film's bright spot. "You'll rave over Bob Hope and Shirley Ross warbling 'Thanks for the Memory,' " wrote Ed Sullivan. Hedda Hopper proclaimed, "Bob is our American Noël Coward." The song spent ten weeks on radio's *Your Hit Parade,* three weeks in the No. 1 spot. What may have put it over the top was a love letter from Damon Runyon, who raved about the song in his syndicated newspaper column, the Brighter Side, on March 13, 1938:

Our favorite gulp of the moment is something called "Thanks for the Memory." A gulp is a song of the type that makes you keep swallowing that old lump in your throat. We have always been a dead cold setup for a good gulp. . . . Mr. Hope is no great shakes as a singer, though he is as good a light comedian as there is around. He sort of recites his lyrics, but he does it well, and that Miss Ross really can turn on when it comes to singing a gulp. If we had a lot of money we would hire the pair of them to go around with us singing "Thanks

212

for the Memory" at intervals for the next month.

The Big Broadcast of 1938 was Paramount's biggest box-office hit of the winter season — and the highest grossing of all the *Big Broadcast* films (though it would be the last). The studio publicity machine churned out stories by and about the film's new star: Hope on the differences between Hollywood and Broadway, for example, or Hope's guide to comedy slang. He became a hot attraction at benefit dinners around town: emcee for a Film Welfare League dinner in February, host of a Temple of Israel benefit in March, guest of honor at the Professional Music Men of America banquet in April, where he was made an "honorary crooner" for singing "Thanks for the Memory." Hope was doing a monologue at the Turf Club Ball in Del Mar when Al Jolson turned to George Jessel and said, "Move over, boys." It was the old guard acknowledging a new star had arrived.

On-screen, however, Hope had trouble following up his *Big Broadcast* success. His second film, *College Swing,* which opened in April, was another star-packed musical comedy, with Gracie Allen as a student at a fusty New England college who must pass her final exams to earn an inheritance. Hope's part was originally so small that he went to producer Lewis Gensler — who had worked

213

with him on Broadway in *Ballyhoo of 1932* — to get it beefed up. Cast as Gracie's tutor and business manager (George Burns is also in the film, but on this rare occasion is not Gracie's partner), Hope has mostly straight-man duty — "a pleasant comedian completely bested by bad material," wrote Howard Barnes in the *New York Herald Tribune*. But Hope does get rewarded with the film's best musical number: a peppy Burton Lane–Frank Loesser duet, "How'd Ya Like to Love Me," which he sings with Martha Raye as they cavort around his office, tear through assorted props, and exit through a glass door, munching bananas.

Hope's next film, *Give Me a Sailor,* teamed him with Raye again. He and Jack Whiting play a pair of brothers in the Navy who battle over two sisters: one a good-looking prima donna (Betty Grable), the other a plain-Jane homebody (Raye). It is mainly Raye's picture, with Hope doing his best to make sense of a frantic and convoluted plot that culminates with Raye's winning a "beautiful legs" contest (in a movie with Betty Grable!). Hope shows some spirit, and even a little emotional depth, as a guy who discovers that the ugly duckling is really a swan. But it was another slapdash B-picture, which got a tepid reception and did little for Hope's prospects.

In the spring, Paramount was dithering on whether to pick up Hope's option for another year. There was talk that studio executives thought he was too similar to Jack Benny, or that his sashaying walk (which seemed modeled on Benny's) made him look too fey. Shurr tried to shop Hope to other studios, but all he got was an offer from Universal for $10,000 — just half of what he was getting at Paramount — to costar in a picture with Loretta Young. And Young vetoed him in favor of David Niven.

"Thanks for the Memory" saved Hope again. Paramount had the rights to a play by Frances Goodrich and Albert Hackett about a bickering married couple called *Up Pops the Devil.* To get some more mileage out of the song that had launched Hope in movies, someone had the bright idea to retool the story as a vehicle for Hope and his *Big Broadcast* costar Shirley Ross and retitle it, shamelessly, *Thanks for the Memory.* In June of 1938 the studio gave the film a green light and picked up Hope's option at the same time.

Secure in his future at the studio, at least for a while, Hope got set for a busy summer. In June he reprised his Broadway role as Huck Haines in the West Coast premiere of *Roberta* at the Los Angeles Philharmonic. As soon as the ten-day engagement was finished, he flew to New York to headline a stage show at the Loews State Theatre, with former child actor Jackie Coogan as his featured guest star.

Hope basked in his return to the New York vaudeville stage, sprinkling his monologue with cracks about his budding movie career ("Paramount signed me in one of my weaker moments — I was starving") and his new Hollywood surroundings ("Everyone goes to bed at nine o'clock out there — with each other").

Most notably, he closed the show with new lyrics for what had become his signature song:

Thanks for the memories
Good audience of the State, your welcome
  has been great
I hope I can return again on some near
  future date
I thank you so much

It was the first of thousands of renditions of "Thanks for the Memory" that Hope would use to close his TV, radio, and stage shows for the rest of his career. Only a few months after introducing the song in *The Big Broadcast of 1938,* Hope had discovered its amazing adaptability, as well as its value as a branding tool. Robin's delicately ironic lyrics would be replaced time and again by greeting-card sentiments, syrupy tributes, and outright plugs. But "Thanks for the Memory" proved to be the most enduring and versatile theme song in show-business history. And it was all Hope's.

Back in Los Angeles, Bob and Dolores were settling into their new life. Bob joined Lakeside, the golf club in Toluca Lake that Crosby had introduced him to, and whose members also included many other golf-playing (non-Jewish) Hollywood celebrities, among them Douglas Fairbanks, Wallace Beery, W. C. Fields, and Oliver Hardy. The Hopes rented a house on Navaho Street, just a few blocks from the club, while they looked to build a permanent home in Toluca Lake, just over the hill from Hollywood.

To help manage his expanding career, Hope gave a call to his brother Jack, who was back in Ohio working in their brother Fred's meat business. Three years older than Bob, Jack was the sibling he felt the closest to. They had shared a bedroom as kids and once stayed together in the same New York City hotel room when both were looking for work. (They had only enough money for one pair of dress pants, so they would trade off wearing it for job interviews.) Jack, an affable, blond-haired ladies' man, who was in between two of his eventual five marriages, quit his job, hopped in his 1937 Pontiac, and drove out to Los Angeles. Bob put him to work in various roles — producer, advance man, consigliere, and all-purpose assistant, another member of Hope's growing entourage who would remain with him for life.

In the meantime, Hope finally got the break he had been waiting for in radio. Early in the summer of 1938 Saphier closed a deal to give Hope the starring role in a new comedy-variety show sponsored by Pepsodent and scheduled to air Tuesday nights on NBC starting in September.

Pepsodent and its ad agency, Lord & Thomas, had considered Milton Berle and Fred Allen for the job, and they were taking something of a risk with Hope. They thought he would appeal to a young audience, but feared that his cocky, fast-talking radio persona might be too abrasive for Middle America. They told Saphier that Hope needed to be more self-deprecating — that he should make himself the butt of jokes, the way Jack Benny and Edgar Bergen did. Saphier relayed this in a letter to Hope, stressing that he should take care "to prevent your being a smart aleck . . . as only sympathetic comedians have a chance for long life on the air."

In launching his new show, Hope had a daunting task. Most comics in radio came equipped with an established character or familiar running gags: Jack Benny's cheapskate, or the comic sparring matches between Edgar Bergen and his monocled dummy, Charlie McCarthy. Hope had no such crutches; he had to build his show practically from the ground up, with jokes drawn, not from the comedian's self-contained radio community, but from the outside world.

To do that, he needed writers, and he hired more of them than anyone else in radio. They were mostly young guns, writers who were hungry and not too expensive. He paid them as little as $50 or $100 a week — low for the time, but a sacrifice for Hope, since it all came out of his starting salary of $1,500 a week. "No comic had ever tried to maintain a staff that size, especially not out of his own end," Hope said. "But I wanted to be number one, and I knew that jokes were the key. . . . All these comedy minds were necessary if I was to carry out my plan, which was almost unheard of at that time. It was to go on the air every week with topical jokes written right up to airtime. And some even after."

Hope's charter staff of writers included Wilkie Mahoney, his *Hollywood Parade* cohort; Al Schwartz, who had written gags for Walter Winchell in New York; and the team of Milt Josefsberg and Melville Shavelson, who had impressed Hope with some material they wrote for his stage show at the Loews State. A few weeks into the season he added Sherwood Schwartz, Al's younger brother, who was studying for a master's degree in biological sciences at the University of Southern California; Norman Sullivan, another New York radio writer; and Norman Panama and Melvin Frank, two aspiring playwrights from Chicago who had written for Milton Berle. The staff would grow and evolve over the years, as some left and others replaced them, but this was the founding core of the biggest and most storied writing crew in all of radio.

For his new show, Hope also knew he needed a strong supporting cast. He looked first for a bandleader with some personality who could also serve as a comedy foil. After coming close to hiring Ozzie Nelson, Hope settled on Edgar Clyde "Skinnay" Ennis, a drawling, rail-thin North Carolina native who had appeared in Hope's film *College Swing*. As announcer, Hope chose honey-voiced Bill Goodwin, who could also banter with him and take part in sketches. For more comic support, he hired Jerry Colonna, a former trombone player who looked like a refugee from Mack Sennett silent comedies, with bulging eyes, a walrus mustache, and a siren-like voice that could hold notes for longer than most opera singers. Colonna used to do Nelson Eddy parodies at parties, and Bing Crosby once brought him on his radio show, introducing him as a famous Italian tenor making his US debut and even inviting prominent music critics to the show. (Some of them apparently thought he was for real.) Colonna had done a funny bit in *College Swing,* playing a zany professor of music who does a florid rendition of the Crosby song

"Please," and he was one of Hope's most inspired additions. Rounding out the team of regulars was a close-harmony singing group, Six Hits and a Miss, who did backup vocals, an occasional featured song, and the commercials on the show (which, as was common in radio, were all performed live).

The Pepsodent Show debuted on Tuesday night, September 27, 1938, broadcast live from a rented NBC studio on Sunset Boulevard, at seven o'clock Pacific time — 10:00 p.m. eastern time, following NBC's popular comedy *Fibber McGee and Molly.* For his theme song, Hope had originally intended to use a rewritten version of "Wintergreen for President," a song from the Gershwin musical *Of Thee I Sing.* But when he found out the rights would cost him $250 a show, he opted instead for the cheaper, and more obvious, alternative, "Thanks for the Memory." The vocal group opens the show:

We bid you all hello, and welcome to our show
May we present for Pepsodent, a guy you ought to know.

Hope then chimes in:

Ah, thank you, so much . . .
Tonight is the night and I hope you will tune in on us every Tuesday

221

Let's make it your chase-away-blues day
By listening in, when we begin . . .

"Well, here we are," Hope begins his first
monologue, "with a brand-new sponsor, a
brand-new program, a brand-new cast, and
ready to tell some . . . jokes." The pause is
the first sign that Hope has taken his sponsor's advice to make himself the self-
deprecating butt of gags. (It's also accurate;
few of the jokes in the first show are new, or
very good.) The show follows the usual
format for comedy-variety shows of the era:
an opening monologue, followed by a musical number from the house band (Ennis and
his group do Irving Berlin's "Change Partners") and then Hope's introduction of the
week's guest star — Constance Bennett, of
the popular *Topper* films, on the opener.
There are two comedy sketches: Bob and
Connie go to a girls' baseball game, and Bob
plays the head of a detective agency assigned
to find a little girl's lost basket (a play on
Ella Fitzgerald's hit song "A-Tisket,
A-Tasket"). Colonna gets a featured spot,
trading quips with Hope and then launching
into a song with his trademark hyperextended
opening wail — "Ahhhhhhhhhhhhhhh, sweet
mystery of life . . ." The only topical joke is a
throwaway gag in the baseball sketch. "Who's
that girl going around and around without
stopping at home?" asks Bill Goodwin.

222

"That's Mrs. Roosevelt," says Hope — a reference to Eleanor Roosevelt's peripatetic travel schedule. Hope closes with a slower-tempo reprise of "Thanks for the Memory," and that's the show.

Variety was impressed: "That small speck going over the centerfield fence is the four-bagger Hope whammed out his first time at bat for Pepsodent. If he can keep up the pace he'll get as much word-of-mouth for 1938–39 as Edgar Bergen got for 1937–38. He sounded like success all the way." But Hope knew that the show needed to improve. In succeeding weeks, as he and the writers grew more comfortable, the material got better, as well as more current. When California had a lot of rain, there were rainstorm jokes: "Cop gave me a ticket for crossing a street against the tide." During Christmas shopping season, Hope talked about the crowds at the post office: "Somebody shoved me, I went right through the parcel post window. Cost me sixty dollars to get back to Hollywood." When he went to the racetrack at Santa Anita, he joked about his pokey horses: "I should have known better when I saw the jockey carrying an overnight bag."

The gag lines had more snap than wit, but Hope delivered them with crisp self-assurance, and faster than anybody else on the air. Soon they were calling him Rapid Robert. "My idea was to do [the monologue] as fast as I could and still have the listeners at home get it and let the live audience in the studio laugh too," said Hope. "Unless the live audience took the play away from me with their laughter, I raced." Hope was a good editor, with a sure sense of the quickest path from setup to laugh. "When you wrote for Hope, you learned not to put one word extra in," said Sherwood Schwartz. "Electronic sound, radio, was a new medium, and Hope was the smartest guy in it. He knew how to pack it in, pace it, and fill it. You had to write all bone and make a great joke in twenty-four words or less."

Everything about him was fresh and modern. Benny had the slow pace and fussy manners of your old spinster aunt, with gags about his underground money vault and antique Maxwell car. Radio's popular comedy teams — Bergen and McCarthy, Burns and Allen — sounded as if they might still be doing two-a-days at the Palace Theatre in New York. Fred Allen, probably the most brilliant radio wit of the era, was a more pointed satirist than Hope would ever be, but he was an acquired taste, too cerebral for the mob. Hope was brash but chummy, in the know but available to all.

As the season went on, the show began to develop recurring comic themes — Hope's cheapness, for example, and his obsession with Hollywood glamour girls such as Madeleine Carroll and Hedy Lamarr. Colonna became a big hit, opening his segments with a hearty "Greetings, Gate!" — an obscure bit of jazz-era slang that Colonna turned into a national catchphrase — and needling Hope with his insults, puns, and nonsensical stories. Hope joked easily with guest stars such as Olivia de Havilland, Chico Marx, and Betty Grable. He had a special rapport with Judy Garland, the sixteen-year-old MGM star best known (in her pre–*Wizard of Oz* days) for her schoolgirl love song, "Dear Mr. Gable." In her guest appearance in March 1939, Garland confesses a crush on Hope. He gently tries to dissuade her. She asks if he's "somebody else's crush." He replies, "I was, but she married me." Disappointed, Judy laments that she's "in between — not old enough to be a glamour girl, and too old to go around with dolls." Hope's retort: "I hope I'm never too old to go around with dolls."

Hope established a working routine with his writers that would change little through the years. For each week's monologue, Hope would suggest several topics — his trip to Palm Springs, say, or the Rose Bowl game, or a Hollywood star's wedding. Each writer or writing team (they worked mostly in pairs) would churn out a dozen or more jokes for each topic. Hope would then gather the writers in his living room and read all the jokes aloud, winnowing them down to his favorites and putting together a rough cut of the monologue. He would test out the jokes in a run-through of the entire show on Sunday night, done before a live audience and often running an hour or more — followed by a late-night session with the writers, in which he'd make the final selections for the monologue and do some more fine-tuning.

Hope's focus was intense and all-consuming. He was on the job 24/7, and he demanded the same from his writers. If he ran into one of them at a restaurant eating lunch, he'd ask why he wasn't working. When Shavelson and Josefsberg came to see Hope on the afternoon they arrived in Los Angeles, "he seemed a little concerned that we had spent the whole morning of our arrival without writing a line," Shavelson recalled. "Later in our career I learned that it was unwise to show up at a story conference with Hope sporting a tan, indicating a wasted day at the beach to his expert eye."

Hope could call at almost any hour of the day or night to suggest a new topic or ask for some new jokes, due first thing in the morning — or sooner. "He had no sense of time," said Sherwood Schwartz. "Whenever he wanted something, he wanted it." When they got together for meetings at his house, Hope wouldn't even offer snacks. If he got hungry, he'd send out Schwartz, the junior writer on the staff, with thirty-five cents to buy him a pineapple sundae, then eat the whole thing himself. (Years later, when Schwartz was no longer working for Hope, he walked in on a Hope writing session in New York and as a gag brought along a pineapple sundae for him. Hope didn't bat an eye. "What took you so long?" he said.)

He was a genial, easygoing boss, but often self-absorbed and insensitive. On payday, Hope used to stand at the top of the circular staircase in his house, make paper airplanes out of the writers' paychecks, and float them downstairs, forcing the writers to grovel on the floor for their wages. He joked that he wanted to give them some exercise. It was a gag, but some of the writers were offended, taking it as a sign of his disdain. (After the story got around, Hope stopped doing it.)

Hope had other ways of lording it over his writers. On Shavelson's first day on the job after arriving in California, he told Hope that he had just moved into an apartment and was waiting for his fiancée to come out from New York. Hope brightened and asked if he could borrow the key to his place that night. "I'll leave it in the mailbox when I leave around midnight," Hope said. The cowed young writer, in a real-life version of Billy Wilder's *The Apartment,* had to give up his apartment to his boss and wander the streets until midnight. When he returned, he found the key in the mailbox as promised, the bed unmade, and two sets of wet footprints leading from the shower to the bed.

Hope's sexual dalliances were well-known and discreetly ignored by his writers. "We'd go to a hotel, I swear to you, outside his room were three, four, five young, beautiful girls, waiting to be picked by him to come in," said Schwartz. "That's just how it was." Hope would often call writers' meetings for the evening, then arrive an hour or two late. "What we didn't realize for a long time was that it was Bob's excuse for getting out of the house," said Shavelson. "So when he finished with the girl, he'd show up at the meeting and we would have all the jokes ready for him." Such antics were taken for granted, regarded as a perk of fame. "It never occurred to us to be embarrassed or guilty," said Shavelson. "This was show business. He was a star enjoying his stardom. All men would do the same with his charm and opportunities."

Despite the indignities, the grueling hours, and the sometimes overbearing ego, most of the writers enjoyed working with Hope. Shavelson remained associated with him for years, writing and directing several of his movies and ghostwriting one of his books. (Yet he got bleeding ulcers while still in his twenties, and when asked what caused them, Shavelson would say, "Two things: Sam Goldwyn and Bob Hope.") Sherwood Schwartz left Hope to go into the Army during World War

II, and the star was not pleased when, on his return, Schwartz said he wasn't coming back to work for him. (Schwartz went into sitcoms and later created *Gilligan's Island* and *The Brady Bunch*.) Still, Schwartz loved his time with Hope. "There was no separation, no wall," he said. "He was detached, but you never had a feeling that he looked down on you just because you were a writer. He was really quite incredible."

No two writers had a more ambivalent attitude toward Hope than Norman Panama and Melvin Frank. They graduated together from the University of Chicago and intended to go to New York to write socially relevant plays. Instead, they moved to Los Angeles to see if they could make money writing for radio. After supplying gags for Milton Berle, they got hired by Hope at $50 a week, with a promised raise to $62.50 after three weeks. Frank, a left-wing political idealist who was attending Communist Party meetings at the time, scorned the radio show as "an amazing bit of capitalist excess" and had mixed feelings about his boss. "Hope is the ordinary actor type — and he's not bad as such," he wrote in his journal. "Spoiled, of course, and a complete egoist, he is inconsiderate of people close to him (he treats his older brother [Jack], a man shell-shocked in the war, with complete disdain) and has been working Norm and me 14 and 15 hours a day every day."

If Hope knew about their left-wing politics, it didn't seem to bother him; they could turn out the jokes. Panama and Frank left Hope within a year, unhappy over their low pay. Yet they were back two years later writing a movie for him, *My Favorite Blonde,* and continued to work on Hope films through the 1950s. "My father really loved Hope," said Frank's daughter, Elizabeth Frank, an author and literature professor at Bard College. "He thought of him as his creative father, as the embodiment of everything that moved my father about certain aspects of American identity, that transcended ethnicity, the heat that melted the melting pot."

Hope's own politics were largely undefined at this point: a conservative, but also a fan of President Roosevelt's and a union supporter. He was hardly a corporate lackey, often tangling with his sponsor and the network over his suggestive material. "He still had a tendency to go overboard on the sexy innuendos," recalled Wally Bunker, an NBC executive who was in the control room during *The Pepsodent Show*'s early years. "During rehearsals the NBC [censor] would say to Hope, 'You can't use that word.' And Hope would snap back, 'I'm going to use it anyway.' " Once the offending lines were bleeped out a couple of times, Hope would usually relent. But he always bristled at interference from the corporate suits. Sherwood Schwartz recalled a writers' meeting in which Tom McAvity, the ad-agency executive who oversaw *The Pepsodent Show*, suggested that Hope ought to downplay his girl-chasing gags and try to develop a more wholesome image. Hope exploded, according to Schwartz, pushing McAvity against the wall and telling him hotly, "This is what I do. I tell jokes. I'm not gonna sit down and invent a character because you think it's better."

Whatever Hope was doing was working. A 1939 poll of radio critics ranked Hope fourth on a list of the best comedians on the air (behind Jack Benny, Fred Allen, and Edgar Bergen), quite an achievement for a relative newcomer. His ratings, while still well behind the more established hit shows, were moving up steadily. After a string of false starts and ill-suited vehicles, Hope finally had a radio show that looked as if it was going to stick. And it did, for seventeen years.

The fourth Hope film to be released in his breakthrough year of 1938, *Thanks for the Memory*, opened in November. Hope and Shirley Ross play New York newlyweds who are having trouble paying the rent on their improbably ritzy penthouse apartment. He's a struggling writer trying to finish his novel, and she's a former model who goes back to work to support him. The film is a curdled bit of late-thirties romantic fluff, with a parade of stock Depression-era comic characters: the wisecracking best-friend couple (the wife played by gossip columnist Hedda Hopper, who gave the film plenty of coverage in her newspaper column); a kept man and his rich battle-ax of a wife; and a tipsy swell in top hat and tails who keeps wandering in and out. Patricia "Honey Chile" Wilder, Hope's old radio foil, even shows up as a flighty, flirty neighbor with bats in her apartment.

The marital misunderstandings are drawn out mainly to justify a reprise of the title song, inserted clumsily near the end and sung by the bickering couple from either side of a locked bedroom door. This time the lyrics are more bitter than ironic —

Thanks for the memory
Of quarts of gin and rye, how you'd alibi
And how you swore the night you wore my
   mother's Christmas tie

— before some last-minute contortions to get the couple back together.

The film's real musical highlight, however, comes earlier, when Hope and Ross are still in their lovey-dovey stage. After a night of partying, they collapse on their balcony, share a cigarette, and sing Hoagy Carmichael and Frank Loesser's wonderful "Two Sleepy People." Though it lacks the emotional complexity of "Thanks for the Memory," it is an even more affecting song, with its lovely, lulling melody and cozy, romantic lyrics:

Here we are, out of cigarettes
Holding hands and yawning, look how late
it gets

Hope and Ross recycle some of the same devices they used in their original version of "Thanks for the Memory" — bits of dialogue interspersed with the lyrics, a couple of jokes tossed in. But Hope is warmer and more relaxed than before — playful with some lyrics ("kaarazy in the head"), caressing others with real feeling, totally winning from start to finish.

Thanks for the Memory was the first Hope film in which he's the undisputed star, and the critics were pleased. "In previous pictures, in which he was smothered by poor scripts or Martha Raye, it has largely been a case of Hope deferred," wrote Frank Nugent in the *New York Times,* "but in *Thanks for the Memory,* with a feather-brained story, an arsenal of effective gags at his disposal and no 'Big Broadcast' trappings to stumble over, Bob assumes his rightful stature as the most debonair and delightful of the screen's romantic comedians." Though not a very good film or a big hit, *Thanks for the Memory* seemed to steady Hope and promise better things.

Hope's rising profile in Hollywood was confirmed in February 1939, when he made his first appearance at the Academy Awards. The Oscars were just ten years old, and the annual awards dinner, held that year at the Biltmore Hotel, was still largely a closed industry event. Hope's role was limited to handing out the awards for short subjects. But he was ushered in to the strains of "Thanks for the Memory" — which had won an Oscar for Best Original Song earlier in the evening — and he made a few jokes that went over well with the Hollywood insiders in the room: "Looks like Bette Davis's garage," he quipped when he saw the table full of Oscars, a reference to Davis's two Best Actress wins in the past four years. "Bob Hope didn't get an Oscar," wrote *Variety* the next day, "but deserved one for a slick bit of nonsense that injected persiflage into the ceremony when it showed signs of lagging."

Hope's own film career, however, was still struggling to get on track. *Thanks for the Memory* was followed in 1939 by two more negligible B-pictures: *Never Say Die,* with Hope as a rich hypochondriac at a Swiss spa who thinks he's dying, and *Some Like It Hot* (later retitled *Rhythm Romance,* to distinguish it from the infinitely better 1959 Billy Wilder film), in which he costars once again with

Shirley Ross and plays the fast-talking owner of a failing carnival. Both were duds at the box office, continuing Hope's string of disappointments since *The Big Broadcast*. All six of his films to that point, moreover, seemed like throwbacks to an increasingly outdated film era: stylized romantic comedies with glamorous settings (an ocean liner, a Manhattan penthouse, a European spa), stock comedy characters, and an air of effete, Depression-era escapism. Hope glided easily through these films, but they gave him little chance to develop a distinctive personality or establish any real connection with the audience. He said the funny lines, sang the songs, kissed the girl at the end, and moved on to the next project.

But in April 1939, he began shooting a new film that would change all that. It was an adaptation of John Willard's Broadway play *The Cat and the Canary,* a haunted-house melodrama that had been filmed once before, as a silent thriller in 1927. Paramount decided to retool it as a comedy for Hope and Martha Raye, but the female lead wound up going instead to Paulette Goddard, a Paramount star who was waiting to shoot *The Great Dictator* with her husband, Charlie Chaplin. When Hope met Chaplin, his boyhood idol, during the filming, the great comedian told Hope that he had seen some of the rushes. "I want you to know that you are one of the best timers of comedy I've ever seen," Chaplin said. Hope was thrilled, and Chaplin was right. The film would rejuvenate Hope's movie career.

But first he took a vacation. Hope had been working almost nonstop since arriving in Hollywood, shooting seven feature films and launching a new radio show in just twenty-one months. When *The Pepsodent Show* went on summer hiatus at the end of the 1938–39 season, he and Dolores decided to take a break with a trip to England — Hope's first visit to the country of his birth since sailing for America with the family in 1908.

Hope could never relax much on vacations, and he packed this one, typically, with plenty of work. On the way to New York, where they were scheduled to sail for England on August 2, Hope was booked for stage appearances in Minneapolis, Chicago, and Atlantic City. Joined onstage by Colonna and Dolores (and his brother Jack pitching in as a stooge), Hope drew big crowds, evidence of the growing popularity of his radio show. At the State Lake Theater in Chicago, Hope's show earned $44,500 for the July 4th week — beating Jack Benny, who took in $35,000 a week later. In Chicago, Pepsodent's top executives threw a dinner party for Hope aboard the company yacht on Lake Michigan. Along with an official renewal for a second season of *The Pepsodent Show,* they gave him a bon-voyage gift of two round-trip tickets to Europe and $25,000 in spending money once he got there. "A little pin money to keep you in cigars and cigarettes," wrote Pepsodent president Kenneth Smith. "Dolores," Hope told his wife, "start brushing four times a day."

After Chicago, Bob and Dolores made a stop in Cleveland to see the family. The Hope clan there had dwindled since Avis's death in 1934. His father, seemingly lost since his wife's death, outlasted her by only three years and died in 1937. Three Hope brothers (Jack, Jim, and George) were now living in California, leaving only Ivor and Fred holding the fort in Cleveland, with Sid raising a family on his farm 150 miles away in northwest Ohio. Bob and Dolores got the Ohio clan together for a family dinner at the Hotel Cleveland, before leaving for New York with one family member in tow: Bob's Uncle Frank, Harry's brother, who joined them on the trip to England.

In New York, Hope was honored with "Bob Hope Day" at the New York World's Fair, and then settled in for a two-week engagement at the Paramount Theater. "As always, Hope isn't inclined to work too hard, but he has an ingratiating personality and an effective comedy style," *Variety* wrote of his show. "He's even better than before he went to the Coast — and that's plenty good enough." In an interview backstage with a *New York Times* reporter, Hope was the picture of relaxed self-confidence, talking about his fast-moving career in between sprints on and off the stage. "I'm used to this sort of thing," said Hope, "I love it. Keeps a guy on his toes, you know. There's nothing as pleasant as the sound of applause when you're hitting on all six." And he was.

War clouds were gathering in Europe as the Hopes sailed for England aboard the French liner *Normandie* on August 2, 1939. The passenger list included such Hollywood stars as Norma Shearer, George Raft, Madeleine Carroll, Charles Boyer, and Edward G. Robinson, along with US Treasury Secretary Henry Morgenthau. After docking in Southampton, the Hopes took a train to London, where they checked into the Berkeley Hotel. They went to the theater, played golf (Hope hit five different courses during his two weeks there), visited Bob's hometown of Eltham, and took a trip up to Hitchin, in Hertfordshire, where his ninety-six-year-old grandfather, James, lived, still riding a bicycle every day. A crowd of relatives gathered in a local pub to see their famous American cousin, now the talk of Hollywood.

After their stay in Britain, Bob and Dolores sailed across the Channel to Paris. They had barely checked in at the George V Hotel when they got disturbing news. Adolf Hitler's army was threatening to invade Poland, and the Hollywood studios were suddenly nervous that so many of their traveling stars might be stranded in Europe if war broke out. "Studios Call Stars Back from War-Menaced Europe," read the headline in the *Los Angeles Times* on August 26: "Crisp instructions were sent to traveling motion-picture notables, most of them in England and France. 'Book passage on first available American-owned ship,' were the cabled messages."

The Hopes cut short their Paris stay, returned to England, and secured one of the last cabins left aboard the *Queen Mary,* set to sail from Southampton on August 30. Among the 2,331 passengers who jammed into the ship (including 250 who slept on cots in the public areas) were financier J. P. Morgan Jr., Hollywood studio chief Harry Warner, and Erich Maria Remarque, author of *All Quiet on the Western Front.*

On September 1, two days after they set sail, German forces invaded Poland. Two days later, at around eight o'clock on Sunday morning, Dolores was at mass when she heard the news that Britain had declared war on Germany. She rushed back to their cabin to tell Bob. He got dressed, went out on deck, and later recalled the tense scene: "Many of the British people were in tears; women and men too. Nobody was saying anything. They just sat around thinking. I guess they knew that a lot of their people and their relatives were going to be killed before things were better again." King George VI's speech to the nation was broadcast aboard the ship around lunchtime. When it was over, the passengers stood and sang "God Save the King." The captain announced that for the rest of the voyage the ship would sail without lights, for fear of German submarines.

The captain asked Hope if he would do a show for the passengers that night. He tried to beg off, saying he didn't think it was time for comedy, but Harry Warner convinced him that a little entertainment might boost morale. Hope did an impromptu show, ad-libbing a few jokes about their predicament. "My steward told me when I got on board, if anything happens, it's women and children first," he quipped, "but the captain said in your case you can have your choice." He closed with "Thanks for the Memory," with new lyrics he had penned himself that afternoon:

Thanks for the memory
Of this great ocean trip, on England's finest ship
Though they packed 'em to the rafters,
they never made a slip . . .

Thanks for the memory
Some folks slept on the floor, some in the

corridor;
But I was more exclusive, my room had
"Gentlemen" above the door
Ah, thank you so much

When the ship docked safely in New York on September 4, the captain gave every passenger a copy of Hope's lyrics as a memento of the trip.

Back in New York, Bob and Dolores found a message waiting for them. They had a new baby.

Dolores had grown increasingly frustrated at her inability to have a child. While they were still living in New York, according to a cousin, she even pleaded with her sister Mildred, who had one son and was pregnant again, not to go ahead with a planned abortion and to give her the baby instead. Mildred refused. Finally, Dolores began looking into adoption. At the suggestion of George Burns and Gracie Allen, she contacted the Cradle, a well-known adoption agency in Evanston, Illinois, founded in 1923 by Florence Walrath. During their stop in Chicago on the way to New York, she got Bob to go with her for a screening interview.

"We were getting along fine and I wasn't too keen on the idea," Hope wrote, with unaccustomed candor, in his memoir. "I was content with a wife and show business and golf. But after five years of being nudged by Dolores, I was talked into visiting the Cradle." While they were traveling in Europe, a baby girl was found for them, and they made a stop in Evanston on their way home to see her. They returned to Los Angeles while the legal arrangements were being completed, and Dolores came back later to pick up their new eight-week-old baby daughter, whom they named Linda Theresa.

The family addition didn't put much of a crimp in Hope's peripatetic work schedule. Just days after his return to Los Angeles, he went to San Francisco to do a week of stage shows at the Golden Gate Theater, also making several appearances at the San Francisco World's Fair and playing in a charity golf tournament. Then it was back to Los Angeles to start work on the new season of *The Pepsodent Show.*

Some important additions were made to the show in its second season. Judy Garland, who had worked so well with Hope when she guested the previous season, was brought back as the regular singer. "My schoolteacher's happy I'm on the program," the seventeen-year-old star of *The Wizard of Oz* said brightly on the season opener. "She says I ought to be glad to take anything to get started." Her rapport with Hope was obvious; she giggled girlishly at his jokes, and he playfully called her Jude or Judith. She often

242

poked fun at his image as a wannabe Romeo. In one sketch he takes her to the high school prom in a broken-down jalopy. Judy: "This car is uncomfortable. What's covering the springs?" Bob: "You." It was sweet, funny, and blessedly free of any sexual innuendo. (She was too young for any serious moves — though Hope years later confided to a friend that Garland showed up one night at his hotel room door, and he had to turn her away.)

Also joining the show in its second season were Elvia Allman and Blanche Stewart, who played two shrill-voiced, man-hungry society girls named Brenda and Cobina — a takeoff of two real-life debutantes, Brenda Frazier and Cobina Wright. They were the first incarnation of a favorite Hope comedy foil: the homely, sex-starved spinster, obsessed with landing a man. The sexist humor was redeemed by some slick gag writing:

BRENDA, *prepping Cobina for a big society party:* "Ya gotta act like a lady. When they pass the food, say ya ain't hungry. And when they pass the drinks, say ya ain't thirsty."
COBINA: "All right, but if they pass the men, I'm gonna ad-lib."

In the second season, Jerry Colonna also came into his own as the show's comedy spark plug. Hope began referring to him as

243

"the professor" and played a perfect straight man to Colonna's absurdist riffs. On one show, when cast members were trying to come up with names for expectant father Bill Goodwin's baby, Colonna blurted out, "Yehudi" — presumably a reference to violinist Yehudi Menuhin. The question "Who's Yehudi?" soon became a running gag on the show, and a national catchphrase. Sketches were built around it; Ennis and the singers even turned it into a novelty song.

Hope, meanwhile, was sharpening his radio persona. In the first season he would often use generic setups and gags — "My girlfriend wore a pillbox hat. A fellow with heartburn followed us all day with a glass of water." (No one was supposed to believe Hope actually *had* a girlfriend — he was just telling jokes.) He soon ditched those and began building jokes more organically from his real life, work, and daily activities — as well as the radio personality his writers were building for him, which was closer to reality than he probably liked to admit. "We took his own characteristics and exaggerated them," said Mel Shavelson. "The woman chaser. The coward. The cheap guy. We just put them in. He thought he was playing a character. He was playing, really, the real Bob Hope."

Yet even as his comedy moved closer to home, Hope kept a distance, making it clear that he was, above all, a *comedian* — an entertainer trying to make an audience laugh. He frequently made jokes about his sponsor, the network, or his movie studio. He was the first comedian to openly acknowledge his writers, often tweaking them in his "savers" when jokes didn't go over. *Variety* cited Hope as an example of "the extreme wisdom of comedians devoting a substantial amount of income for writers. The gag staff that Hope has surrounded himself with is one of the best." And the audience was catching on. In its first season Hope's show averaged a 16.2 Hooper rating, meaning that 16.2 percent of the nation's households were tuning in. By the end of the second season its rating had soared to 25.0 — the fourth most popular show on the air.

Hope's transformation from a generic radio wise guy to a fully developed radio personality was well under way. A similar transformation was taking place in his movie roles. But it would happen much more abruptly — with his seventh film, *The Cat and the Canary.*

The movie, released in November 1939, was a step up in class for Hope. Directed by the capable Elliott Nugent (a sometime stage actor and playwright who had also directed Hope in *Give Me a Sailor* and *Never Say Die*), it's a comedy-thriller with a mise-en-scène and a narrative coherence that sets it apart from any of Hope's previous films. In the atmospheric opening, a group of family

245

members are making their way in separate boats at night through a Louisiana bayou, heading to a lonely mansion where a wealthy relative's will is about to be read. The will, they soon learn, has left the entire fortune to one family member, played by Paulette Goddard. A storm forces the group to stay overnight in the spooky house, amid dark warnings that one of the passed-over relatives might be out to kill her. Lights flicker on and off, eyes in portraits move, hands emerge from hidden panels, while a sinister housekeeper, Gale Sondergaard, watches over it all with an icy glare.

The wild card in the family gathering is Hope. He plays Wally Campbell, a stage actor whose nervous wisecracks — "Even my goose pimples have goose pimples" — keep breaking the tension of the old-dark-house melodrama. "They do that when you don't pay your bill," he quips when the lights go out. "Don't big, empty houses scare you?" one of the family members asks. "Not me," says Hope. "I used to be in vaudeville." Someone asks Wally whether he believes in reincarnation: "You know, dead people coming back?" Hope's up-to-the-minute retort: "You mean like the Republicans?"

With his double-breasted suit and slicked-back hair, Hope still has the look of a high-style 1930s romantic-comedy lead. But he has discovered the character that he would

246

make his own: the brash coward, a nervous Nellie who uses jokes to ward off his fears, a braggart who talks big but melts when face-to-face with danger. "I always joke when I'm scared," he says at one point. "I kind of kid myself into being brave." But it's more than just jokes; Hope creates a rich comic character, recognizable and relatable — a coward you can root for.

A small scene with Goddard in the middle of the film shows how far he's come. Hope is in her bedroom, fighting off nerves while assuring her that he'll protect her. "You always did fight for me, didn't you, Wally?" she says gratefully. "Even back there in Whitford. Remember when you used to carry my books to school? And the time Big Jim Bailey pulled my hair? And you flew at him, and what a terrible beating —"

"— he gave me? I'll never forget it," says Hope, jumping in and timing the turnabout perfectly. "Seems I always got licked fighting for you," he adds, his tone shifting. "Well, maybe it was worth it."

There's a commotion outside the room, and Hope's bluster/fear response kicks in. He grabs her by the arms and says he'll go outside to investigate. "If there's a rumpus or anything, don't come out. You just sit tight and yell like the devil."

"Well, what will you do?"

"Why I'll" — clenching his fists and setting

his jaw for an instant, then relaxing them just as suddenly — "I'll run and get help. Don't worry."

She, affectionately: "I don't worry when you're around, Wally."

He, touched and taken a little aback: "Oh, really? Thanks." He turns tentatively to leave. "Good night." He goes out the door, then suddenly reopens it and repeats, more tenderly now, "Good night." She blows him a kiss.

With both delicacy and humor, Hope lets us feel every twinge of the inner battle between his manly duty and his cowardly instincts, all while conveying his emerging feelings for the woman in his care. (Since everyone in the house is related, it's not clear how the two can be kindling a romance — but never mind.) Little of this is in the actual dialogue; Hope accomplishes it with small gestures, subtle shifts in tone, posture, and facial expression. No need for Mitchell Leisen's advice anymore; Hope has learned how to act.

Chills and laughter were a potent combination with a long movie tradition. But Hope's constant comic chatter ("Don't you ever stop babbling?" someone exclaims) wasn't just a way of defusing the tension in a spooky old house. It also had resonance for an audience facing an increasingly scary world outside. It was no accident that *The Cat and the Canary* opened in theaters and became a hit just a few weeks after the outbreak of World War II in Europe, when the country was facing terrors of a more sinister, real-world kind. Hope's brash wisecracks were both a release and a coping mechanism for a stressed-out nation.

The Cat and the Canary was Hope's biggest box-office success yet and, despite his two duds earlier in the year, single-handedly boosted him into tenth place on the list of the top box-office stars of 1939. He would remain in the top ten — with a one-year interruption, when he was preoccupied by a world war — for more than a decade.

CHAPTER 5
ACTOR

"GO AHEAD, TALK TO EACH OTHER WHILE
WE REHEARSE."

The Cat and the Canary was an important film for Hope, but it was overshadowed in 1939 by an unprecedented bounty of Hollywood classics. It was the year of *The Wizard of Oz* and *Mr. Smith Goes to Washington;* the definitive John Ford Western, *Stagecoach;* and the classic Kipling adventure tale *Gunga Din.* Garbo laughed in *Ninotchka,* Olivier brooded in *Wuthering Heights,* and a slew of Hollywood's top leading ladies traded bons mots in Clare Boothe Luce's *The Women.* Towering above them all was *Gone With the Wind,* producer David O. Selznick's epic screen version of Margaret Mitchell's Civil War bestseller. Fittingly, the Oscar ceremony that commemorated what would become known as Hollywood's greatest year was the first one hosted by the entertainer who would do more than anyone else to make that annual event Hollywood's greatest night.

When Hope was asked to emcee the twelfth annual Academy Awards dinner, held at the Cocoanut Grove on February 29, 1940, it was still primarily a film-industry event, with no national radio coverage and, that year at least, little suspense. The names of the winners, which were typically given out to the press in advance under an embargo, had prematurely been revealed by the *Los Angeles Times,* which published the results in an early edition of the newspaper at 8:45 p.m., well before the 10:00 p.m. ceremony. The gaffe led the Academy to change its policy the following year: for every Oscar night thereafter, the names of winners would be kept inside sealed envelopes, guarded by the accounting firm of Price Waterhouse.

With or without the spoiler, *Gone With the Wind* was widely expected to be the big winner, and it was naturally the evening's hot topic. Walter Wanger, the Motion Picture Academy's new president, introduced Hope, the evening's master of ceremonies, as "the Rhett Butler of the airwaves." Hope began his monologue by echoing the handicappers — "What a wonderful thing, this benefit for David Selznick" — before turning his attention to other stars and trends of Hollywood's year: Bette Davis's Oscar collection (again), the ubiquitous teenage star Mickey Rooney ("the ten best actors of the year"), and the current vogue for big biographical dramas, such as *The Story of Alexander Graham Bell,* starring Don Ameche. "MGM plans to star

251

Mickey Rooney in a super-epic," said Hope, "portraying Don Ameche as a boy."

Gone With the Wind made its expected sweep, hauling in ten awards, including Best Picture. "David, you should have brought roller skates," quipped Hope on one of Selznick's trips to the podium. Clark Gable was a surprise loser for Best Actor (to Robert Donat in *Goodbye, Mr. Chips*), but Hattie McDaniel was in tears accepting her award for Best Supporting Actress, the first African-American performer to win an Oscar. "Over the Rainbow" won for best song, and Judy Garland got a miniature Oscar for "outstanding performance as a screen juvenile." Hedda Hopper, recapping the show in her column, criticized some of the boring acceptance speeches, but noted that "Bob Hope, as usual, was his lifesaving self."

He was the ideal Oscar host: a movie star who could also tell jokes; a Hollywood insider with the irreverence of an outsider; a suave, elegantly dressed ambassador for Hollywood to the rest of the world. When the Oscar shows began to be covered live on radio a few years later, his monologues played an important, often overlooked role in shaping the image of Hollywood for the American moviegoing public. It was a glamorous world, filled with people who were richer and more beautiful than you and I, but Hope brought it down to earth — reporting its gossip, popularizing its jargon, satirizing its mores and morals. Hollywood stars had storybook love affairs, but their marriages didn't last. They were charming in public, but jealous and backbiting in private. They lived in lavish homes with big swimming pools, but this glittering gated community had a small-town camaraderie, where everybody seemed to know one another. Over the next thirty-five years, Bob Hope, who went on to host or co-host the Oscar show a record nineteen times, provided our annual peek inside it.

Hope's role at the Oscars in demystifying Hollywood — ribbing its stars and puncturing its pretensions — was paralleled by an evolution that was taking place in his movie roles. He was developing a new kind of comedy, one that helped redefine the relationship between ordinary moviegoers and those remote figures on the silver screen. That evolution, which began with *The Cat and the Canary,* took a giant leap forward in Hope's next movie, which opened just a few weeks after his inaugural stint as Oscar host. It was the first of the famous *Road* pictures, co-starring his friend and most enduring show-business partner, Bing Crosby.

After their first appearance on stage together in 1932, at the Capitol Theatre in New York, Hope and Crosby returned to separate coasts and didn't see much of each other for five years. But they reconnected when Hope

253

arrived at Paramount in the fall of 1937. They would meet for lunch on the studio lot and play golf together at Lakeside, the club where Crosby belonged and Hope soon would join too. Crosby had Hope as a guest on his popular radio show, *The Kraft Music Hall,* and invited Bob and Dolores down to Del Mar, the racetrack near San Diego that Crosby owned a large share of.

On Saturday night, August 6, 1938, Bing was master of ceremonies for a special Hollywood night at Del Mar when he called Bob to join him onstage. The two horsed around together, rehashing some of the bits they had done at the Capitol Theatre six years before. Their chemistry so impressed William Le-Baron, Paramount's production chief, who was in the audience, that he suggested putting the two of them together in a movie.

The idea took more than a year to come to fruition. The studio may have had second thoughts about teaming Crosby, one of its biggest stars, with Hope, who in mid-1938 was still an unproven quantity. But the project was assigned to screenwriters Frank Butler and Don Hartman, who had written for both Hope (*Never Say Die*) and Crosby (*Waikiki Wedding*). They dusted off a script they had done years earlier for Crosby called *Follow the Sun* and had refashioned for Jack Oakie and Fred MacMurray, with the new title *The Road to Mandalay.* When Oakie and

MacMurray bowed out, the screenwriters retooled it once again for Hope and Crosby and changed the title to *Road to Singapore,* supposedly because the new locale sounded more sinister.

To round out the team and provide a romantic interest for both Hope and Crosby, Paramount cast one of its top female stars, Dorothy Lamour. A native of New Orleans, Lamour (originally Lambour, before the *b* got dropped on a marquee) had moved to Chicago with her divorced mother and began her show-business career as a singer with Herbie Kaye's big band. Following a short-lived marriage to Kaye, she moved to New York and worked solo in nightclubs — where Hope often used to see her when he was starring on Broadway. But she got the call from Hollywood first, and in 1936 moved west to costar in *The Jungle Princess,* playing a native girl who falls for Ray Milland. She was cast as exotic, scantily clad beauties in several more tropical adventures, among them John Ford's *Hurricane,* as well as in the musical *High, Wide, and Handsome* and Hope's debut film, *The Big Broadcast of 1938.* Her dark beauty, sultry voice, and trademark sarong had made her one of Paramount's most recognizable stars, and she got second billing in *Road to Singapore* — after Crosby but before Hope.

Shooting began in October 1939 on the

Paramount lot, with some location work at the Los Angeles County Arboretum and Botanic Garden in Arcadia. The director was an old studio hand, Victor Schertzinger. A former concert violinist, Schertzinger had more experience with musicals than comedy (he even composed two of the movie's four songs, with lyricist Johnny Burke). But no director could have been prepared for a comedy quite like this.

Hope and Crosby wanted to re-create the wisecracking spontaneity of their stage appearances together. So they treated the Butler-Hartman script as merely a jumping-off point. They brought in gag writers from their radio shows to add new jokes, tossing them in willy-nilly during rehearsals. "For a couple of days," Crosby recalled, "when Hope and I tore freewheeling into a scene, ad-libbing and violating all of the accepted rules of movie-making, Schertzinger stole bewildered looks at his script, then leafed rapidly through it searching for the lines we were saying." Lamour, who prided herself on knowing her lines, was nonplussed when Crosby and Hope kept departing from the script she had learned. "I kept waiting for a cue that never seemed to come," she recalled, "so finally, in exasperation, I asked, 'Please, guys, when can I get my line in?' They stopped dead, broke up, and laughed for ten minutes." She finally gave up trying to learn the script in advance. "I would read over the next day's work only to get the idea of what was happening. What I really needed was a good night's sleep to be in shape for the next morning's ad-libs."

Butler and Hartman were not happy when they saw the shambles Hope and Crosby were making of their lines. "If you recognize any of yours, yell bingo!" shouted Hope when the writers showed up on the set. They complained to the studio, but got nowhere; Hope and Crosby's antics, unorthodox as they were, seemed to be working. Hope described the creative process that began on *Road to Singapore* and was honed in succeeding *Road* pictures: "I had a great staff [of writers] on radio . . . all these marvelous people. I would give them the script, and they would bring the jokes in, and I would edit them and call Bing into my room and say, 'What do you think of this? What do you think of that?' We'd go to the set, and the stagehands were waiting for us to do nutty stuff. We wouldn't disappoint them."

They were playing to the crew, the writers, and anyone else who was on the set. "The *Road* pictures had the excitement of live entertainment," Hope said. "Some stars banned visitors, but Bing and I liked to have people around. New visitors sparked new gags." One visitor was an ex-vaudeville song-and-dance man named Barney Dean, whom

Bob had first met at the Stratford Theater in Chicago. A short, bald-headed Jewish immigrant from Russia, born Barnett Fradkin, Dean showed up on the set of *Road to Singapore* one day selling Christmas cards. He made Crosby and Hope laugh, and Crosby persuaded Paramount to hire him as a writer on the film. Dean did little actual writing, but he would kibitz on scenes, occasionally suggesting a line or bit of business and in general keeping Bob and Bing amused. Dean was legendary among Hollywood gagmen for his ad-lib wit. (Once a policeman stopped him for jaywalking across Hollywood Boulevard. "How fast was I going, Officer?" said Dean.) He became a regular member of the *Road* picture crew, and a frequent companion for Hope when he toured — writer, court jester, and all-purpose good-luck charm.

Hope and Crosby were fortunate to have a director who indulged their loosey-goosey style. For one scene, Hope recalled, Schertzinger shot just one take, yelled, "Cut and print," and started to move on. An assistant director pointed out that Hope had stepped out of the light for a few seconds and asked if Schertzinger didn't at least want to reshoot part of it from other angles, to cover himself. "No," said Schertzinger. "That scene was like a piece of music; it was well orchestrated and it flowed beautifully. Maybe the flutes were off-key or the cellos didn't come in at the right time. But the total performance was great."

No one knew that *Road to Singapore* would be the first of a series, and the film in some ways is atypical of the *Road* pictures that followed. Crosby is clearly the central character, with a conventional backstory. He plays Josh Mallon, the son of a shipping magnate (Charles Coburn), who chafes at going into the family business, spurns an engagement to his high-society fiancée, and escapes to a South Seas island with his free-spirited pal Ace Lannigan (Hope). His father's efforts to bring Josh back home provide a framing device for the comic adventures — a plot obligation jettisoned by future *Road* pictures, in which Hope and Crosby were simply plopped down in an exotic setting and let loose.

But *Road to Singapore* introduces most of the key elements of the series' successful formula. Hope and Crosby are usually hucksters or con men of some sort, trying to earn money by duping the locals. At some point they meet up with Lamour, who becomes both a partner and an object of romantic rivalry, with Crosby nearly always the victor. When danger threatens, Bob and Bing play a childlike game of patty-cake, distracting the villains just long enough to sucker punch them and make their escape. There are four or five songs, including at least one romantic ballad for Crosby and Lamour, and a buddy number for Hope and Crosby.

Most crucially, *Road to Singapore* establishes the contours of the Hope-Crosby screen relationship. They're close friends, but always at odds. Hope is the patsy, Crosby the schemer. Hope is a worrier, brash but insecure, all nervous motion. Crosby is the cool customer: easy-going, self-possessed, unflappable. Hope is an overeager puppy with women, chasing but rarely catching them. Crosby merely has to take out his pipe and give them a *bu-bu-boo,* and the girls can't resist.

Road to Singapore doesn't have the comic highs of the later *Road* pictures; there's too much plot and not enough nuttiness. Lamour plays a native girl rescued by Hope and Crosby from her bullwhip-wielding boyfriend (Anthony Quinn). She moves in with them as their (chaste) housekeeper, and the three try to make money by hawking a bogus cleaning solution to the locals, predictably ruining the suit of an unsuspecting customer (Jerry Colonna). In the farcical climax, they find themselves in the middle of a native wedding ceremony, where Bing is picked by one of the local girls for marriage and they must make a fast escape — not just from the natives but from Josh's father and fiancée, who turn up in the jungle looking for him.

The delights of *Road to Singapore* are in

the margins: the fizzy, freestyle repartee between Hope and Crosby. There are relatively few actual jokes. (Trying to wrestle a sailfish into their fishing boat, Crosby shouts, "He won't give up!" Hope responds, "Must be a Republican!") The laughs come from the way they bounce off each other so effortlessly, in their idiosyncratic, jazzy slang — so natural that it sounds adlibbed, but so fast and perfectly timed that it can't be. After they arrive at their tropical isle destination, for example, the two travelers check their money supply in a few throwaway lines:

BING: "How much you holdin' there, Bubbles?"
BOB: "We're loaded, chum. A dollar twenty-eight."
BING: "One-two-eight."
BOB: "Net."
BING: "Well, that should be enough to light a fire under a couple of short beers."

Or, more elaborately, a scene in which the boys decide that Lamour's overeager housekeeping is ruining their laid-back bachelor lifestyle, and they have to tell her to leave. Crosby forces Hope to break the bad news — and then, after Lamour has left and both of them are feeling remorseful, tries to take the credit:

BING, *seated and puffing on his pipe:* "You

261

know, I thought I handled that pretty well, didn't you?"

BOB, *stopping short, in the midst of moving their furniture back in place:* "You did what?"

"I handled the situation here pretty well."

"What was *I* doin' in there?"

"Well, you were weakening, I'll tell you that. I had to back you up."

"I only gave her the whole idea! I packed her bag and put her on the bus!"

"Yeah, but I was the menace, I was the heavy in the whole piece."

"I had my whip, right there, I just gave it to her like that!"

"I was the man who really accomplished the final brush-off."

BOB's *exasperation turning to sarcasm:* "Oh, you want the bow? Take a bow."

BING, *obliging with a flourish:* "A little light bow — a-da."

BOB, *now spent, giving up and settling back into a chair:* "That's fine, that's fine — you did it all!"

"I think so."

"I'm snookered again."

"Possibly."

"Thank you very much."

"Thank you. Good night."

"Leave a call."

The exchange is propelled by nothing but

262

the momentum of two performers feeding off each other, like riffing jazz musicians. None of the dialogue is in the film's shooting script — it was apparently improvised on the set. Crosby is hilariously smug, but Hope's exasperation is the real engine for the comedy. Dressed in a long-sleeved black T-shirt — which flatters his fit, five-foot-eleven-inch frame — he paces frantically, bends insistently over Crosby, uses his hands to italicize points (poking Bing in the chest, miming the cracking of a whip). The lines aren't funny in isolation. Often they don't even make much sense ("Leave a call"?). But it is character comedy of a high order.

There had been comedy teams in movies before, of course, and fast-paced dialogue, but this was something new. The interplay between Groucho and Chico Marx, say, or George Burns and Gracie Allen, had an abstract, almost surreal quality. The witty repartee of 1930s screwball comedies such as *My Man Godfrey* or *Bringing Up Baby* was too polished and stylized to be mistaken for anything but movie dialogue. Hope and Crosby seemed like ordinary guys — like Hope and Crosby, in fact — perfectly attuned to each other's thoughts, moods, obsessions, and vulnerabilities. In later *Road* pictures they would loosen up even more, breaking down the fourth wall and talking to the camera. But even here, still hemmed in by the conventions of 1930s romantic comedy, they are a breath of fresh air, with a spontaneity and intimacy that the movies had never before seen.

Road to Singapore opened nationally in March of 1940 and broke two-year box-office records in New York, Chicago, Los Angeles, and Miami. Hope helped out by plugging the film constantly on his radio show. By April, Paramount was already planning a sequel, reuniting the trio in a film originally called *Blue Lagoon,* before someone realized the obvious and retitled it *Road to Zanzibar. Road to Singapore* wound up earning $1.6 million at the box office — Hollywood's highest-grossing movie of 1940. The teaming of Hope and Crosby was a smash.

Their real-life relationship was a little more complicated. Hope and Crosby got along well, enjoyed working together, and shared a passion for golf. (Crosby was the better golfer — a three-time winner of the Lakeside club championship — though Hope could occasionally beat him.) But they were not close friends. Though they lived near each other in Toluca Lake, the families rarely socialized. (Bing and his wife, the former actress Dixie Lee, had four sons before Bob and Dolores adopted their first child.) The two men were, moreover, sharp contrasts in temperament. Hope loved being a Hollywood star, enjoyed socializing, and was a workaholic who got antsy on vacations. Crosby seemed more ambivalent about his fame, was often lackadaisical about work, and enjoyed getting away from the Hollywood scene — with his racehorses at Del Mar or, in later years, in Northern California, where he moved with his second wife and family. "Bing loved to hunt and fish, and Bob wouldn't be caught hunting or fishing anything but a golf ball. Bob had no interest in horses," Dolores told Crosby biographer Gary Giddins. "They lived entirely different lives, but they respected each other and loved working together."

Many in Hope's entourage did not like Crosby, finding him cold and standoffish. Hope, though hard to get close to, at least had a superficial bonhomie. Crosby kept his distance from all but the closest friends. "Bing was a cold tomato," said Sherwood Schwartz. "He was aloof. Bob was friendly. He'd say hello to everybody. I saw many people come up and put an arm around Bob, say, 'How you doing?' I never saw anybody touch Bing." Once, when they were leaving their hotel in New York City after an appearance together to promote *Road to Singapore,* Crosby saw Hope stuffing some fan mail into a pillowcase. "What the hell are you doing that for?" he asked. Hope said he was taking the letters back home so that his secretary could answer them. "I'll show you what I do with my fan mail," said Crosby. He felt through some envelopes, found a quarter in one that had been enclosed by a fan for postage and photos, pocketed the change, and tossed the letter into the wastebasket.

In many ways Hope looked up to Crosby. Bing was college educated, well read — on radio and in movies he often affected a comically erudite British accent. Bob was a high school dropout who read little but the sports pages and the show-business trades. Bing was a bigger star, and Hope envied his clout and his business savvy. "Bob wanted everything that Bing had, and more," said Hal Kanter, who was a writer for Crosby before Hope hired him away. They ribbed each other like brothers — Crosby joked about Hope's nose and his stinginess, Hope made cracks about Crosby's broad hips and slow racehorses — but the jokes could touch a nerve. Once, when Hope was a guest on Crosby's radio show in San Francisco, Crosby's writer Bill Morrow, who got perverse enjoyment out of mocking Hope, wrote some jokes about Hope breaking out of his cage on the plane and being fixed up on a blind date with an ape from the zoo. Hope thought it was too insulting, and he exploded. "It was the only time I saw Bob really get mad," said Kanter. "He threw down the script: 'What are you doing to me?'" Crosby had to calm him down and tell Morrow to cool it.

Yet they brought out the best in each other, both onstage and off. Hope loosened up Crosby, unleashed his sense of humor. Crosby gave Hope a role model, both as a businessman and as a manager of his own career. Crosby was arguably the greater artist. But Hope was more driven, more responsive to the changing entertainment landscape, and, in the end, had a broader and more lasting impact on the world of show business. He simply tried harder.

With two career-defining movies released in the space of four months and a radio show steadily climbing in the ratings, Hope's career shifted into a new gear. His surging popularity was evident when he made an eight-week personal-appearance tour in the spring of 1940, taking his radio show on the road for the last five weeks of the season. His stage show — which also featured radio sidekicks Jerry Colonna, Brenda and Cobina, and the singer who was still billed as Dolores Reade — drew unprecedented crowds. On his first stop in Joliet, Illinois, two shows were scheduled, but a third had to be added to accommodate the overflow. At a Chicago theater, there were lines around the block, and Hope convinced the theater manager to cut a reel out of the featured movie, so they could squeeze in more performances. In Atlantic City, Hope broke a forty-four-year attendance record at the Steel Pier. He played to packed houses in Detroit, Boston, and New York City. With a guarantee of $12,500 a week (up from $4,500 just a year earlier) plus 50 percent of the gate over $50,000, Hope's gross take was close to $20,000 a week.

Variety, reviewing his show in Chicago, gave a vivid account of the rock-star frenzy Hope was stirring up:

> Bob Hope is blazing hot, and the king can do no wrong. He can come in with last year's gags; can stall, forget his gags — and yet the audience laps it up. Comedian has a splendid manner; makes a great appearance and handles an audience with the assurance born of years of experience. The box office is whirling itself dizzy. Anything that Hope says or does seemingly is a howl for this mob. He only just started to introduce "two glamour girls" and the audience broke out into a roar before he could finish the introduction. The very mention of "Yehudi" rocked the house. It is a sample of spontaneous public exuberance that fires every gag, every bit of mugging, every gesture, walk-on or walk-off into something that might be construed as brilliant.

Even Hope was taken aback by the reception. "It was my first experience with the power of radio," he wrote later. "I had no idea that the millions of numbers that made up the ratings every week were actually *people.*" He drank in the adulation. "This kind of success was brand-new to me, but I felt I could get used to it. I must have been pretty difficult to live with, because when somebody in the mob of autograph hounds outside the stage door asked Dolores if she was connected with Bob Hope, she replied, 'No, I'm his wife.' "

Just what it meant to be Bob Hope's wife was becoming increasingly clear to Dolores. She still had the remnants of a singing career, thanks to Bob, who used her in his stage shows and occasionally on the radio. After a couple of radio appearances in the spring of 1940, Hope even tried to hire Dolores as the show's regular singer, to replace the departed Judy Garland, but his sponsor nixed her. Yet Dolores was phasing out her show-business career and starting to put most of her energy into the job that would consume the rest of her life: being Mrs. Bob Hope.

She performed the job with flawless grace. Dolores gave Bob more than just a socially adept partner and a picture-perfect Hollywood home life. She was a stabilizing influence, providing a commonsense sounding board, anchored by her bedrock Catholic values. She was intelligent, opinionated, better read than Bob, more capable of conversing knowledgeably on a range of subjects, from the arts to politics. (She started out as a Democrat and only in later years tacked toward his conservative views.) She had a sense of humor, and she was one of the few who could tell him off — something that became more important as the years went on and the circle of sycophants grew larger and more insulating. Most of all, she was fully on board for his great life endeavor: building the brand known as Bob Hope. "He had his job, and she had her job," said Dolores's nephew Tom Malatesta. "They were both on the same page as to where they were going. And they were a hell of a team."

If she was bothered by his many absences, his sometimes dismissive treatment of her, the rumors of other women, she kept it to herself. On rare occasions there were glimpses of the frustration. "She longed for romance from this man, and he was cold as ice to her," Elliott Kozak, Hope's agent and producer in later years, told John Lahr in the *New Yorker.* "We were in London one time. Bob, Dolores, and I were walking at night. All of a sudden, out of the clear blue sky, she pushed him up against the wall and said, 'Kiss me, Bob. Tell me you love me.' I was so embarrassed I didn't know what to say. I turned my back on it. . . . I never saw him go to her and give her a peck on the cheek. I was with him for twenty-five years."

Yet shows of affection of any kind were rare

for Bob Hope. Whatever bond he and Dolores shared went beyond pecks on the cheek — and was never on display for outsiders, or even family members. She adored him, and he needed her. They had a partnership, an understanding, a marriage that neither ever seriously considered ending, maybe even a love affair. They endured.

The family grew. After adopting Linda in the fall of 1939, the Hopes told the Cradle they wanted a son as well. In the spring of 1940 the agency said it had found a boy for them, and Bob stopped in to see the baby during a stop in Chicago. When he saw that the boy had a ski nose just like his, he was sold. They named him Anthony Jude, known as Tony.

Along with a second child came another move: from their rented place on Navaho Street to a fifteen-room English Tudor–style house in Toluca Lake that they built on a former walnut grove on Moorpark Street — just a short drive from the Lakeside Golf Club and a few blocks away from St. Charles Borromeo Church, where Dolores would become a daily regular at mass. The unpretentious, tree-lined neighborhood was home to a small cadre of movie-industry people who preferred the relatively low-profile San Fernando Valley community to the showier, starrier neighborhoods in Beverly Hills and elsewhere. The Hopes would renovate and expand the house several times, buying up the lots around it, creating a five-acre compound with a one-hole golf course in the backyard (with two different tee boxes, so Bob could play it as two holes), indoor and outdoor swimming pools, and a separate four-thousand-square-foot office wing, added to the main house a few years later. Grand yet homey, decorated in Dolores's tasteful all-American style (with a Grandma Moses painting among the artwork on the walls), the Toluca Lake house would remain the Hopes' main residence and the nerve center of Bob's working life for more than sixty years.

With a new home, a growing family, and an expanding retinue of writers, assistants, and other support people, Hope turned his attention to money. His phenomenally successful 1940 tour had opened his eyes to his drawing power. When the crowds were circling the block for him in Chicago, Hope called his agent, Louis Shurr, and told him to get on a plane and come see for himself. Hope told Shurr he wanted Paramount to boost his salary to $50,000 a picture. Shurr not only got him the raise, but went one better. When Samuel Goldwyn wanted to borrow Hope to star in a picture for his own independent studio, Shurr told him Hope's price was $100,000.

Goldwyn turned him down flat. But Hope took the negotiations public when the two found themselves on a stage together in Fort Worth, Texas. Hope was there to host the opening of *The Westerner,* a film that Gary Cooper had made for Paramount, on loan from Goldwyn. When Hope saw Goldwyn in the audience, he called him up on-stage. The sixty-year-old Hollywood mogul announced proudly that he was about to make a film with Hope. "I haven't made a comedy since Eddie Cantor left me," he said. "I haven't found a comedian I want to work with, but I think I've found one in Bob Hope."

"That's all fine, but let's talk money," said Hope, grabbing the microphone. The studio boss demurred. "Why don't we just lie down and talk things over," Hope said, pulling Goldwyn down on the floor with him. As Goldwyn protested, the crowd roared. After a whispered colloquy, the two got up, and Hope announced, "It's going to be a pleasure making a picture with Mr. Goldwyn." Whether or not the deal was actually consummated there, Hope ultimately got his $100,000.

It would be nearly two years, however, before the Goldwyn film finally went into production. Paramount was keeping Hope too busy. After the success of *The Cat and the Canary* and *Road to Singapore,* the studio was dismayed to find that it had only one more

273

Hope movie in the pipeline for the rest of 1940 — *The Ghost Breakers,* due to open in June — thus wasting an opportunity to cash in on the buzz over Hope's smash personal-appearance tour in the spring. Determined not to be caught short again, the studio put him on a nearly nonstop shooting schedule starting in the fall, teeing up four pictures in quick succession, all of which would be released in 1941.

The Ghost Breakers did nothing to dampen the studio's confidence in Hope. Another haunted-house comedy-thriller, the film is an obvious attempt to repeat the winning formula of *The Cat and the Canary.* But whereas *Canary* put Hope in the middle of an ensemble, in *The Ghost Breakers* he is the clear center of the action. He plays Larry Lawrence, a Winchell-like gossip columnist who comes to the aid of another frightened heiress — Paulette Goddard again — who is saddled with another spooky old house, this time a supposedly cursed castle in Cuba. Adapted, evidently quite freely, from a play by Paul Dickey and Charles Goddard and directed by George Marshall (a silent-film veteran who had recently directed *Destry Rides Again,* with James Stewart and Marlene Dietrich), the film probably has more laughs than *The Cat and the Canary,* but is a more scattershot effort, with a confused story line and tacky special effects, and thus less satisfying overall.

Hope is fast, flip, and engaging as the reluctant hero, joking away his jitters in the face of malefactors ranging from mob thugs to an assortment of spooks, both real and imagined. He has a sidekick this time, a valet played by Willie Best, the quavering black comic actor whose exaggerated, bug-eyed fright takes actually make Hope look restrained by comparison. (Hope, getting ready to climb a spooky staircase, flashlight in hand: "If a couple of fellows come runnin' down the stairs in a few minutes, let the first one go. That'll be me.")

The jokes sometimes step outside the film, puncturing the supernatural doings with abrupt references to the mundane real world. A stranger, for example, is warning Hope and Goddard about zombies: "A zombie has no will of his own. You see them sometimes walking around blindly, with dead eyes, following orders, not knowing what they do, not caring." Hope's retort: "You mean like Democrats?" (One out-of-context political joke per film, it seems.) On their boat trip to Cuba, Hope and Goddard run into a sinister passenger, played by the Hungarian-born actor Paul Lukas, who says he wants to buy Goddard's castle, warning her about the curses and dead spirits that lurk there. Hope chimes in, greeting each gloomy warning with a cheeky wisecrack:

LUKAS: "Are you the one who's advising Miss Carter not to sell the castle?"

HOPE: "No, my advice is to keep the castle and sell the ghosts."

LUKAS: "I myself have heard of only one ghost — the spirit of Don Santiago."

HOPE: "Does he appear nightly, or just Sundays and holidays?"

The lines are trivial, but the psychological resonance isn't. In mid-1940, with Nazi troops on the march in Europe, Hollywood was debating just how much of the real world ought to be reflected in its movies. While a few films, such as *The Mortal Storm* and Chaplin's *The Great Dictator,* took note of the sobering headlines, far more common were escapist comedies such as *The Ghost Breakers.* And yet the laughs provided more than just escape. Hope's breezy, self-confident mockery of the glowering villain — with a Middle European accent, no less — was a tonic for a nation on the verge of war against real foreign enemies: the triumph of the brash, irreverent, can-do American spirit in a world getting darker and more threatening by the day.

"Its lightness and levity throughout, in these times of war, provide added impetus to bright biz prospects," wrote *Variety* in its review. *The Ghost Breakers* was another box-office hit for Hope, and the trade paper noted that it was doing especially well with "the under-21 mob." Hope wasn't just hot; he was hip.

On radio too Hope was blazing. Now one of the most popular stars on the air, he put the squeeze on Pepsodent over the summer to double his salary, to $8,000 a week — even threatening to quit radio for a year if he didn't get it. He wound up settling for $6,000 and was back on the air in September.

The show was reaching a comfortable cruising speed. Hope would always open with a corny rhyming product plug for his sponsor ("If you've got preserves in the cellar, use Pepsodent and you'll preserve what's under your smeller"). There were weekly jokes about Skinnay Ennis's beanpole frame, and back-and-forth insults with "Professor" Colonna. (Bob: "Colonna, this is the last straw." Jerry: "All right, you use it — I'll drink from the bottle.") The monologue jokes were increasingly tied to the news, or the season, or anecdotes from what at least sounded like Hope's own life — paying his income tax, for example, or fighting the crowds at the Motor Vehicle Department to get new license plates. "I wouldn't say the line was long," said Hope. "All I know is when I got to the end of the line, I had to buy Colorado plates." Hope was having more fun now. He was so fast and sure-footed that on the rare occasions when he stumbled on a line, or a laugh didn't come as fast as he expected, he got even bigger laughs with his self-mocking comebacks: "Go ahead, talk to each other while we rehearse, will ya?"

Part of Hope's brilliance was to make these often scripted lines sound like ad-libs. The ruse was common in radio. "Everyone would write down their ad-libs and we wouldn't tell each other," said George Burns. "The way to become a star was to ad-lib without rattling your paper." But Hope could improvise when he had to; his reactions were quick and his ability to roll with the punches impressive. When Chico Marx, a guest on one show, dropped his script in the middle of a bit, there was an awkward stretch of silence as he fished around for it. After a few seconds Hope broke in, "Who do you think you are — Harpo?" Close to a perfect ad-lib — and no one could have written it.

During the 1940 presidential campaign, with Roosevelt running for a third term against Republican candidate Wendell Willkie, Hope made a few tentative forays into political humor. It was the first presidential campaign to feature heavy political advertising on the radio, and that provided an obvious target. "I want to thank both political candidates for giving up their time so this program can be heard," Hope began one show. "The Democrats really put on a demonstration last

Tuesday night," he said after Roosevelt's election victory. "But you can't blame them. It's not every day that Roosevelt gets elected president. It just seems like it." Even his few mild political jokes, however, were enough to raise concerns at the network. A telegram from an NBC executive on November 19, 1940, complained about Hope's jokes on political topics, among them President Roosevelt's plan to move up the Thanksgiving holiday by a week:

We are getting many protests about Bob Hope from both Democrats and Republicans — concerning his reference to the "Republicans waiting until a week from next Thursday to celebrate Thanksgiving, hoping by that time to have something to be thankful for" and his "Willkie button" crack. Each time he refers to things political, and that's been pretty consistent for some weeks, we've had protests. Can't we do something about it?

Still, political jokes were relatively rare for Hope in those days. Indeed, many of the headlines were too ominous for humor. At the end of 1940, fears that the United States would be drawn into the war overseas were mounting. President Roosevelt, in the face of isolationist opposition, launched a massive war mobilization effort and began sending arms to Britain under the Lend-Lease Act.

In September 1940, Congress passed the nation's first peacetime draft, requiring every American male between the ages of eighteen and thirty-five to register for military service. When Hope returned to host the Academy Awards dinner on February 27, 1941, the war took center stage. President Roosevelt had been invited to attend the event, but he begged off, saying the tense world situation demanded he remain in Washington. Instead, he delivered a six-minute address to the audience at the Biltmore Hotel, praising Hollywood for its role in supporting his mobilization efforts and for promoting "the American way of life." Bette Davis followed him onstage to deliver the movie community's response — "We thank you for the unique honor you have bestowed upon us" — and Judy Garland sang "America."

Hope, emceeing his second Oscar show, lightened the mood with another batch of Hollywood jokes. He harked back to the previous year's sweep by *Gone With the Wind,* pointing to the table filled with Oscar statuettes: "What's the matter, did Selznick bring them back?" (Producer David Selznick would, in fact, get one of them back, when his film *Rebecca,* directed by Alfred Hitchcock, won for Best Picture.) Hope joked about the secrecy surrounding the winners, whose names were now guarded in sealed envelopes by Price Waterhouse: "When the last envelope was sealed, Price Waterhouse had to open it again to let [columnist] Sidney Skolsky out."

Hope got his own award that year: a plaque in recognition of his "unselfish services for the motion picture industry" and for being the "man who did the most for charity in 1940." He was taken by surprise and fumbled for words ("I don't feel a bit funny," he said) as the audience of fourteen hundred applauded wildly for nearly a minute. In a year that saw two popular stars, Jimmy Stewart and Ginger Rogers, win the top acting awards (for *The Philadelphia Story* and *Kitty Foyle* respectively), Hope got the biggest ovation of the night.

It was testimony to the stature he had achieved in Hollywood after just three years. Other stars, such as Eddie Cantor, were well-known for their charity work and frequent benefit appearances. But no one was as tireless as Hope. In two years he entertained at a reported 562 benefits, raising money for domestic charities such as the March of Dimes and the American Red Cross, but also, as the war in Europe spread (and his home country of England was fighting for survival), for such war-related causes as the Greek War Relief Committee and Bundles for Britain.

Altruism, to be sure, was only one of Hope's motivations. Entertaining at charity events provided him with the enthusiastic live audiences that he craved, and it was also — as the Academy honor validated — great for his image. But Hope also recognized, more acutely than any other star of his day, the power of his celebrity and felt a calling to use it. The rest of Hollywood would learn from him.

A long ten months passed between *The Ghost Breakers* and the release of Hope's next film, *Road to Zanzibar,* in April 1941. The second *Road* picture reunited most of the same creative team from *Road to Singapore.* Screenwriters Frank Butler and Don Hartman again took an old script, originally titled *Find Colonel Fawcett,* and repurposed it for Hope, Crosby, and Lamour. Director Victor Schertzinger was back too, along with lyricist Johnny Burke — though teamed this time with a new composer, Jimmy Van Heusen.

The film was shot in November and December of 1940, and the set was the usual mix of chaos and camaraderie. The impish Barney Dean would shuttle back and forth between the stars, feeding them new lines. Lamour (whom Bob and Bing nicknamed Mother because of her habit of adopting young actresses on the set) tried to keep up with the mayhem, getting a makeup man to black out two of her teeth and startling Hope and Crosby with a gap-toothed smile in the middle of one scene. A studio press release claimed that when the film was screened for its first test audience, it got *too many* laughs — and seventy-two of them had to be removed, "so that the spectators would be able to follow the story."

Road to Zanzibar was, indeed, a more rollicking trip than the first *Road* film — one of the best of all the *Road* pictures and the one that firmly established the winning format of the series. There is no cumbersome backstory for Crosby this time; he and Hope are a team of equals (Hope has moved up to second billing, ahead of Lamour) and are plunged into their adventures from the very first frame. Even before the first frame: over the opening credits we hear Crosby singing a Burke–Van Heusen ditty called "You Lucky People, You." When the credits finish, he is revealed to be singing on a carnival stage somewhere in Africa, trying to entice the locals to plunk down their money for a daredevil act called the Living Bullet.

That would be Hope. Dubbed Fearless Frazier, he has been stuffed inside a giant cannon, wearing a dorky crash helmet with a skull and crossbones on it. "I don't mind being drafted, but not as ammunition," Hope gripes when Crosby comes over to check on him. Scoffing at Hope's fears, Bing fires off the cannon, sending Bob flying through a ring of fire. Actually, he's hiding in a secret compartment inside the cannon, but the flaming dummy fired in his place sets the carnival tents ablaze, forcing Crosby and Hope to make a fast getaway, pursued by the police.

The next few minutes deftly establish the modus operandi of these carnival hucksters. There's a quick travel montage, punctuated by town signposts and newspaper headlines: Hope as the Human Dynamo, dressed in superhero tights and holding a lightbulb in his mouth, as a jolt of electricity is pumped through him; Hope as the Human Bat, wearing the same dumb outfit but now with giant bat wings attached, getting ready to leap off a hundred-foot cliff. Finally, back in their tent — Hope now nursing a broken arm — Crosby has a giant fish tank carted in, with an octopus inside. His latest idea: Hope will put on a diver's suit and wrestle the beast, "like you did with Bonzo the Bear." Hope goes ballistic, and what follows is another of their bristling comedy duets:

BOB: "That thing's got eight arms! I only got one little hand!"
BING: "What's the matter with that?"
"I don't like the odds."
"Well, if it bothers you, we'll snap a couple off him."
"Those things are murderous! That ain't spaghetti he's wavin'. Besides, they're poisonous. They spit ink!"

"All the better. You can wrestle him and write home at the same time." *(Then switching tacks, taunting.)* "You're really slippin'. I'm trying to make a big fellow outta you! A famous man! They'll write books about you."

"Yeah, and I know three words that won't be in 'em: *ripe old age.*"

"Why, it's a cinch, we'll train him."

"Train him? I'd look fine runnin' around with a chair and a whip. You can't train an octopus. They only know one thing: grab you quick and suck the blood outta you. How would I look goin' around with no blood?"

After peering into the octopus tank, the pair turn toward each other and deliver the kicker in perfect unison: "Just the same."

It's a brilliant scene, capturing the essence of their comic relationship: always at odds, yet perfectly in sync; Hope the panicked prey, Crosby the cool predator. In *Singapore,* there was still a distance between them: Crosby the rich kid chafing under family obligations, Hope the gadabout friend who lures him to the South Seas. Now Crosby is the schemer, and Hope the one who wants to go home to Birch Falls. There's a sadistic streak in Crosby's cavalier treatment of his friend. When Hope convinces him to take the money they've earned and buy ship's passage back home, Crosby instead squanders it on a phony diamond mine. Hope is so angry that he wants to end the friendship for good. "I've stood plenty from you," he says, sincerely hurt, "but now we're through, know what I mean?"

"Now look here, Junior," says Crosby, a bit chastened and using the diminutive nickname that symbolizes their relationship. "We've been through a lot together since we were kids. We've been through thick and thin. I never figured it was your dough or my dough. I always thought it belonged to both of us. It was share and share alike."

Hope, who has started to soften, suddenly perks up: "What about that blonde in Brooklyn?"

"Oh, you didn't want a share in her. You wanted to be the whole corporation."

"Yeah, and you wound up as the holding company."

All the actors up their game in *Road to Zanzibar.* Lamour, cast as a meek native girl in the previous film, is funnier here, more integrated into the comedy action, playing an American who is running her own con game — posing as a girl about to be sold in a slave auction and then, after Hope and Crosby shell out to save her, splitting the proceeds with her friend (Una Merkel) and the bogus slave trader. Crosby too seems energized by the more sharply defined relationship with

Hope and a more equal romantic partner in Lamour.

Hope is better than ever: faster, more animated, with a broader repertoire of double takes and panic reactions — true to his character even as the farcical shenanigans grow more outlandish. As they plunge deeper into the jungle, the boys are captured by cannibals and put inside giant birdcages to be eaten. (The stereotypical Hollywood treatment of African natives, alas, has to be overlooked.) Then Hope, to win his freedom, is forced to wrestle a gorilla, in a ludicrous but very funny slapstick climax: Bob and the beast trade wrestling holds while Bing distracts the ape by lighting matches and the gorilla keeps running over to blow them out.

The film introduces another signature element of the *Road* pictures: the first of Hope's out-of-character, self-mocking asides to the camera. When two thugs barge into Hope and Crosby's quarters, looking to reclaim the money Hope has bilked from them (by reselling the phony diamond mine), Bob and Bing do a reprise of their patty-cake routine from *Road to Singapore.* But just as they are about to throw their punches, the chief muscleman conks them both on the head. Hope, on the floor, looks up dazed: "He musta seen the picture!"

Time, using the film as the occasion for a cover story on Crosby, called it "some of the most uninhibited, daffy nonsense to hit the US screen since the heyday of Harold Lloyd." *Road to Zanzibar* was another hit at the box office, and within weeks Paramount had announced plans for a third in the series: *Road to Moscow.* The politically charged destination would later be changed to the more benign Morocco, but Hope and Crosby clearly had a buddy act that could travel anywhere.

Hope's next film, *Caught in the Draft,* was ginned up quickly, to capitalize on the vogue for military comedies in the wake of the reinstatement of the draft in September 1940. (Abbott and Costello's *Buck Privates,* released in January, beat Hope's film to the theaters and was a big hit.) Based on an idea by producer Buddy DeSylva and a script by Harry Tugend, it casts Hope as Don Bolton, a vain Hollywood actor who stars in war pictures but is scared to death of gunshots. To evade the draft, he decides to get married and sets his sights on a gruff army colonel's daughter, played by Dorothy Lamour. When she questions his patriotism, Hope concocts a scheme to "enlist" with a fake recruiting officer, played by an actor he's hired. But the plan backfires when Hope enlists with an actual recruiting sergeant by mistake and winds up in the army for real.

As a pampered, self-centered movie star, Hope was playing more to type than he was probably ready to admit. *Caught in the Draft* was shot during January and February of 1941 and suffered many delays because of bad weather. When the skies finally cleared, director David Butler — a portly, easygoing veteran of Shirley Temple films, working with Hope for the first time — scheduled a key scene to be shot in the afternoon in Malibu. Driving to the location with his makeup man, Hope decided to stop off and see some property he was thinking of buying. They misjudged the time, and when Hope finally got to the set, the light was nearly gone and Butler was furious. "I thought David was going to knife me," said Hope. They finished the scene with the help of lights, and Butler apparently forgave him — he did three more films with Hope and became one of his favorite directors — but he wasn't the last director to learn that working around Hope's schedule could be a challenge.

As a service comedy, *Caught in the Draft* is merely serviceable, putting Hope through a predictable gauntlet of army indignities: peeling potatoes, pulling guard duty, trying to overcome his nerves at the rifle range. But Hope gives the character some real dimension and empathy, as he sucks it up and tries to prove — to his fellow soldiers, to Lamour and her father, and most of all to himself — that he's not a coward and a bumbler. After he loses control of a tank and crashes it into the colonel's car, there's something touching about the way Hope surveys the wreckage, smartly salutes, and issues a crisp apology: "I'm terribly sorry about the car, sir. I hope you haven't kept up the payments."

Caught in the Draft opened in June 1941 to terrific business. On July 4, it set an all-time box-office record for a matinee at New York's Paramount Theater. With patriotic sentiment growing and broader slapstick comedies making a comeback, supplanting the more refined drawing-room comedies of the 1930s, Hope's film was perfectly pitched to the mood of the country. It earned $2.2 million at the box office, more than any other Hope film yet.

Hope's Hollywood winning streak continued with his next film, *Nothing But the Truth,* released in October. Directed by Elliott Nugent (who, after *The Cat and the Canary,* had taken a year off from Hollywood to star on Broadway in James Thurber's *The Male Animal*), it gives Hope another chance to show off his maturing skills as a comic actor. Once again he gives a farcical character some human dimension, playing a shallow egotist who discovers unknown reserves of courage and moral fiber.

Hope plays a stockbroker who goes to work for a tony Miami brokerage firm. On his first day on the job he arrives in a dapper white suit, accompanied by a valet and looking forward to a cushy job. But he balks when his first assignment is to sell unsuspecting customers a worthless mining stock. After a debate with his colleagues over whether it's okay to tell "necessary lies" to do business, Hope makes a bet that he can tell nothing but the truth for twenty-four hours. This puts him in a predictable series of tight spots. At a dinner party aboard the company yacht, he has to bite his tongue to avoid offending the high-society guests at the table, including his boss's pretty niece (Paulette Goddard, for once unaccompanied by spooks). His jutting chin never looked so defiant, or so vulnerable, as he tries to navigate the polite conversation without losing the bet.

"Cat got your tongue?" the hostess says after he's been quiet for too long. "You haven't said very much. And I've put you between two of Miami's most attractive women. Don't you agree?"

Hope, sitting between two dowagers, turns to look at one — then swivels his head an extra half-turn, pricelessly, looking for the person the hostess might be referring to. He recovers quickly: "Why, you're right. I *haven't* said very much."

You can see the wheels turning, as he tries to maneuver through each treacherous conversational pass with evasions and euphemisms. Finally, he gives up and lets loose a torrent of truth-telling — blurting out that one guest at the table "couldn't pass for thirty unless she had a bag over her head." Scandalized, the haughty hostess lectures him, "We should weigh our words very carefully before we speak." Hope cries, "I do!" Indeed, no one in movies weighed them better.

Al Capstaff, a producer on *The Pepsodent Show,* was the first to suggest to Hope that he broadcast one of his radio shows from a military camp. Capstaff's brother was stationed at March Field, the Air Force base in Riverside, California, and the men there needed entertainment, Capstaff said. Hope was initially cool to the idea: "Why should we drag the whole show down there?" But the appeal of a captive audience of a thousand bored servicemen — plus a chance to promote his upcoming movie, *Caught in the Draft* — helped change his mind.

On Tuesday, May 6, 1941, Hope and his radio troupe were bused to Riverside to do a remote broadcast from the base. Autograph seekers mobbed them as soon as they were inside the gates. Once they were onstage, nearly every joke was greeted with howls of laughter. "I want to tell you I'm thrilled to be here," Hope said. "I came up to look at some of the sweaters I knitted." And: "One of the aviators here took me for a plane ride this afternoon. I wasn't frightened, but at two thousand feet one of my goose pimples bailed out."

Hope recalled, "I got goose pimples myself from the roar that followed that one. Then I started to understand. What I said coincided with what these guys were feeling, and laughter was the only way they could communicate how they felt to the rest of the country. I was their messenger boy." Hope returned to the studio the following week, but he missed the fired-up military crowds and went back on the road for several more troop shows — at the San Diego Naval Station, the Marines' Camp Roberts in San Luis Obispo, and the Army's Camp Callan in Torrey Pines — before the season ended in June.

To get a reaction from the men, Hope would send out an advance team of writers to find out the popular hangouts, names of commanding officers, and other local gossip so that he could plug them into the monologue. "It was our job to talk to the men, and anyone else, to find out which captain they didn't like, or what terminology we could use," said Sherwood Schwartz. "We were all civilians. We didn't know about army stuff at the time." A line on one show made a reference to the "head of the Navy," and it got an unexpected laugh — Hope and company didn't know that *head* meant "bathroom." Even the term *GI,* standing for "government issue," was not in common usage until Hope began using it to refer to the soldiers. For a nation being dragged reluctantly toward war,

Hope's shows played an important, if rarely acknowledged, role in getting Americans accustomed to the military mind-set, and providing a link to the servicemen who would soon be defending them on the battlefield — his own contribution to the war mobilization effort.

One member of Hope's troupe who was a particular hit with the servicemen was his new singer — a pretty, petite brunette named Frances Langford. She had grown up in Florida and originally wanted to be an opera singer before a tonsillectomy changed her voice from soprano to contralto and she switched to pop. Langford began singing on radio and had appeared in a few movies, but she reached her career apotheosis when Hope began using her on his radio show in the spring of 1941 and made her a regular the following season. Langford had a mile-wide smile and a brassy, emotionally charged voice that could carry over an expanse of thousands of men. She was sexy, but had the open-hearted wholesomeness of an older sister. Along with his other contributions to the war effort, Hope had discovered the iconic singing voice of World War II.

With a string of hit movies, a radio show that was moving up steadily in the ratings (*The Pepsodent Show* finished in third place for the 1940–41 season, trailing only Jack Benny and Edgar Bergen), and the start of his military-camp shows, Hope was riding higher than ever. But he didn't rest. Even as his career was still in its formative stages, Hope set himself apart from nearly every other Hollywood star by the aggressive and creative ways in which he sought to promote himself and market his fame.

Hope noticed how many fan letters he was getting, many with requests for bios and photos, and over the summer he came up with the idea of writing a humorous memoir, timed to come out at the start of his fall radio season. Pepsodent, seeing the promotional possibilities, agreed to back the project, and Hope's writers spent the rest of the summer churning out a ninety-six-page, joke-filled paperback called *They Got Me Covered.* Pepsodent printed 4 million copies and sold them for ten cents apiece (plus a box top from a tube of Pepsodent toothpaste). Free copies were handed out to Hope's studio audiences; Paramount distributed ten thousand more to the press to promote his fall movie *Nothing But the Truth;* and Hope flogged the book constantly on his radio show. It was a marketing masterstroke.

The book gave Hope not just his first brand extension, but an early opportunity to take control of his own life story. The accounts of his boyhood in Cleveland and early show-business career are lighthearted, gag-filled, and all but useless for anyone looking for real insights into Bob Hope:

> I was such a beautiful baby. My parents had me kidnapped twice a week just so they could see my picture in the papers.
> I remember my first appearance as a comedian. I had them rolling in the aisles. Then the usher came and took away the dice.
> Fan mail is like bread and butter to an actor. That reminds me — we're having postcards for dinner tonight.

Hope would write other, marginally more revealing memoirs in later years. But he was already constructing a wall around his private life and taking charge of his public image. In July 1941 he was the subject of a laudatory profile in *Time* magazine, but he was unhappy because of a few comments about his wealth and his reputation for cheapness. Asked by *Time* how much he earned in a year, Hope replied, "You can say it's about a quarter of a million, and I don't like it." The magazine estimated his net worth at around $800,000 and noted, "Around the Paramount lot he is known as a 'hard man with a dollar.' "

Nothing got under Hope's skin more. He had his publicists feed stories to the press about his charitable donations (a reported $100,000 in 1940) and his busy schedule of benefit appearances. Crosby even wrote a letter to *Time,* identifying himself as the source of the "hard man with a dollar" crack, but insisting that the reporter had not recognized it as a joke. "It's not very often that I get mad," he wrote, "but to speak of the 'appealing avarice' of Hope, the one man in the business who does not deserve such snide reporting, is fantastic." But the portrait stuck: Hope's wealth and reputed tightness with money became touchstones for nearly every profile of him.

Hope's fourth film of 1941, the year that vaulted him to the front rank of American entertainment stars, was *Louisiana Purchase.* It was a screen adaptation of Irving Berlin's Broadway musical, with Hope playing a Louisiana businessman caught up in a graft investigation. Though a relatively big-budget production with a Broadway pedigree, it was Hope's weakest film of the year — with one of Berlin's most negligible scores, and the tedious Victor Moore taking up way too much screen time as a graft-investigating senator. But Hope gives the film his all, particularly in a climactic filibuster on the floor of the Senate (with its obvious echoes of Jimmy Stewart in *Mr. Smith Goes to Washington*), and the movie, which opened on Christmas Day, earned $2.75 million at the box office, another record high for a Hope film.

It was an amazing year for Hope. He was Paramount's No. 1 star and ranked fourth on

Variety's annual list of Hollywood's top box-office draws — behind Gary Cooper, Abbott and Costello, and Clark Gable. According to SEC figures, he earned $294,000 for his movie work in 1941 — second only to Bing Crosby, with $300,000. A poll of 450,000 radio listeners named him the top comedian on the air, beating out Jack Benny for the first time. *Radio Daily* gave him its "No. 1 Entertainer" award, and the Women's Press Club even named him the "most cooperative star in Hollywood." In December the *Los Angeles Times* ran an adulatory story on him, portraying an upbeat Hollywood star at the top of his game: "Other top-line funnymen either complain of overwork or feel that stage and screen have passed over their 'real' dramatic talents. Bob thinks his work is swell, life is grand, everything is hunky-dory. And he doesn't want to play *Hamlet.*"

It was the last time for a while that he could appear so carefree. The *Times* story appeared, by chance, on Sunday morning, December 7, 1941. Hope was at home, having just finished working with his writers on his radio monologue, when Dolores came into his bedroom to tell him the news that the Japanese had bombed Pearl Harbor. Hope thought it was a joke at first, and it still hadn't quite sunk in when he went to a Hollywood Stars football game in the afternoon. At halftime an announcement was made for all men in uniform to report to their units. Hope went ahead with the usual Sunday night run-through of his radio show ("We were all too shocked to react normally by canceling it," he said) and told jokes about Christmas shopping as if nothing had happened. "The audience laughed in little spurts," he recalled, "on the edge of their seats in case they had to make a hasty exit."

The show never aired. Hope's Tuesday-night broadcast was pre-empted for an address to the nation by President Roosevelt, telling the country to get ready for war.

■ ■ ■ ■

III
Finding a Mission

HOLLYWOOD'S GOODWILL AMBASSADOR,
FROM THE BATTLEFIELD TO
THE BANQUET HALL

■ ■ ■ ■

CHAPTER 6
WAR

"HE WAS SPEAKING OUR LANGUAGE."

Hollywood was a changed place after Pearl Harbor. For days following the attack, Los Angeles was on edge — fearful that the Japanese, having so brazenly attacked our naval base in Hawaii, might next target Southern California, where two-thirds of the nation's aircraft production was located. There were rumors of Japanese planes buzzing California. Blackouts were ordered, and radio stations were shut down. Japanese Americans were rounded up, suspected of being potential saboteurs. The Army moved uninvited into the Walt Disney lot in Burbank so that it could stand watch over the huge Lockheed plant nearby. The studios, meanwhile, made contingency plans to pool their facilities in case of an enemy attack — "to ensure completion of films in event of loss of life during production of any important screen personalities," *Variety* reported.

The start of the war didn't mean a halt to making movies. On the contrary, Hollywood quickly reassured itself that continuing to make them was more important than ever. "Sacrifices will have to be made," *Daily Variety* editorialized on the day after Pearl Harbor, "but the show industry must keep functioning, to preserve morale, to keep up the spirits of this country and its allies with top-rung entertainment and beneficial propaganda." Yet, like the rest of the country, Hollywood had to adapt to the new wartime restrictions. All guns used on movie sets were confiscated. With rubber and gasoline strictly rationed, car chases were banned. For security reasons, shots of airports, harbors, or bridges were forbidden, as was the filming of battle scenes after 5:00 p.m., so as not to alarm civilians.

With the Japanese attack on Pearl Harbor, the national debate over whether the United States should get involved in a "foreign war" came to an abrupt end. Now was the time to band together in an all-out war effort, and Hollywood was eager to play its part. Many stars — Jimmy Stewart, Henry Fonda, William Holden, Tyrone Power — enlisted in the service. Directors such as William Wyler, Frank Capra, and John Ford got officer commissions and went overseas to make war documentaries and propaganda films. Those who stayed home found other ways to contribute. John Garfield and Bette Davis helped set up the Hollywood Canteen, a former livery stable on Sunset and Cahuenga Boulevard converted into a recreation center for servicemen, where movie stars pitched in as waiters, dishwashers, and even dance partners for the boys getting ready to be shipped overseas. Clark Gable was recruited to head the actors' division of the Hollywood Victory Committee, which lined up stars to travel the country selling war bonds. (Coming back from one of these tours in January 1942, Gable's own wife, Carole Lombard, was killed in a plane crash.) Hollywood beauties such as Hedy Lamarr and Lana Turner sold bonds by offering kisses in return for pledges of $25,000 or $50,000. Dorothy Lamour reportedly sold $30 million worth of bonds in just four days.

At thirty-eight, married, and the father of two, Bob Hope was safe from military service. (With the start of the war, the age of eligibility was raised from thirty-five to forty-five, but in practice no men over thirty-five were ever drafted.) And given his radio show's many visits to military camps, no star had staked out a clearer role for himself on the home front. But Hope, surprisingly, took a little while to realize it. For the first few weeks after Pearl Harbor, his show remained in the studio, trying to conduct comedy business as usual. "We feel that in times like these, more than ever before, we need a moment of relaxation," Hope said, opening his first show to air after Pearl Harbor. "All of us in this studio feel that if we can bring into your homes a little laughter each Tuesday night, we are helping to do our part."

Yet he could hardly ignore the war. Hope's radio monologues were now peppered with jokes about blackouts, gas rationing, and other wartime privations, such as the ban on women's girdles to save rubber. Then, on January 27, Hope took his radio show to the San Diego Naval Base and followed it with six straight weeks of military-camp shows. After returning to the studio for one week, he went back on the road and continued to do shows for military audiences virtually nonstop until the end of the war. Jack Benny, Hope's chief radio rival, did some shows at military bases too, but he found the raucous crowds too disruptive of his timing and carefully scripted material. For Hope, louder, looser, and faster on his feet, they were energizing. "I find these audiences of soldiers and sailors like a tonic," he told a reporter. "They get so excited at times that they can't resist trying to join in the performance themselves, which is okay with me because then you know you are getting audience response."

The servicemen loved him. Hope spoke their language, sympathized with their gripes, and brought sexy movie stars for them to ogle. He would introduce himself by explicitly identifying with whatever group or base he was visiting — "This is Bob Soldier-in-the-

Desert Hope," or "This is Bob San-Diego-Naval-Base-Hospital Hope." When he was entertaining marines, he'd make jokes about the Navy; in front of Navy men he'd take potshots at the marines. In front of everyone, he would dwell on topic A: sex. "I really don't think there are enough girls around this base," he joked in San Diego. "Today I saw twenty-six sailors in line to buy tickets to see a hula dancer tattooed on a guy's chest."

Offstage too Hope was at the front lines of Hollywood's war effort. When the studios made plans in January for a Red Cross War Emergency Drive, Hope helped rally studio employees at Paramount. "We are all soldiers now," he said at an organizing meeting. "It is the part of some of us to fight with dollars instead of guns." He traveled with Crosby for a series of exhibition golf matches to raise money for war relief. For a match in Sacramento he formed a twosome with Babe Ruth, playing against Crosby and California governor Culbert Olson. In Houston, the crowds packed the fairways so tightly that Hope and Crosby barely had room to drive. One Hope shot hit a spectator standing in a sand trap and bounced onto the green. When he found his ball, Hope shouted, "Who do I pay? Who do I pay?"

At the end of April, Hope joined the Hollywood Victory Caravan, a star-packed variety show booked on a whistle-stop tour of thirteen cities in three weeks, to raise money for the Army and Navy Relief Funds. The all-star troupe — which included Cary Grant, Groucho Marx, Claudette Colbert, Merle Oberon, James Cagney, Betty Grable, and Laurel and Hardy, among others — set out by train from Los Angeles on April 26 and arrived in Washington three days later to start the tour. Hope, who was too busy with his radio show for the cross-country train ride, hopped a plane instead and met them in Washington, in time for a welcoming tea at the White House, hosted by Eleanor Roosevelt.

Their first show, at Washington's Capitol Theatre, was a little ragged and under-rehearsed, running nearly three hours long. But Hope, sharing emcee duties with Cary Grant, was a hit. "If anything it was Bob Hope's Victory Caravan," *Variety* said in its review. "As long as Hope was on the stage, the show had zest and lift. With his departure it dropped to varying levels of mediocrity." The caravan continued on to Boston and Philadelphia, made a swing through the South and Midwest, and finished up in San Francisco on May 19. The trip was grueling enough for most of the Hollywood stars-turned-vaudeville vagabonds. But for Hope, typically, it was little more than a part-time job. He broadcast his radio show from various stops on the tour, played in more exhibition golf matches, and entertained at dozens of military bases along the way. And when the caravan was over, Hope kept on going — doubling back through the South and East, doing his radio show along the way and winding up the season at Mitchel Field on Long Island and the submarine base in New London, Connecticut. His camp-show broadcasts helped propel his radio show into first place in the Hooper ratings in June, the culmination of a remarkable four-year climb. The BBC picked up transcriptions of his show, and Hope became a radio hit in Britain as well.

After ten weeks of traveling and appearances at nearly a hundred military camps, Hope came home physically exhausted. His doctors warned him to slow down. But there was little chance of that. The rush of adrenaline that Hope got from being onstage was multiplied by the wild reception he got from the servicemen — and the feeling that he had found his role in the war effort.

The war didn't deter a record crowd of sixteen hundred from packing into the Biltmore Bowl for the annual Academy Awards banquet on February 26, 1942. But it cast a sobering light on the affair. In keeping with the national mood of austerity, the Academy urged attendees to avoid fancy formal wear (though several actresses came in evening gowns anyway). The guest of honor was former presidential candidate Wendell Willkie, author of a new bestselling book urging international cooperation called *One World,* whose speech was broadcast nationally on CBS radio.

Hope, emceeing the event for the third year in a row, revealed a Willkie button under his lapel. "I haven't given up yet," he joked. "And there's one for Hoover under it." The wartime anxieties didn't deter him from his usual Hollywood wisecracks. About a recent air raid in Los Angeles: "That was no air raid; that was John Barrymore coming home from W. C. Fields's house." When Hope presented a fake Oscar to Jack Benny, for impersonating a woman in *Charley's Aunt,* Hope quipped, "Benny will no longer play any of these female roles because the government's taking his rubber girdle away from him."

Hope's own movie career, meanwhile, was rolling along. He was developing a consistent screen character — the wisecracking, girl-chasing, blustering coward — but the movies themselves had a pleasing variety: service comedies, buddy movies, comic horror films, retro-thirties romantic comedies. With *My Favorite Blonde* — which began shooting just before Pearl Harbor, finished up in January and was released in April — he discovered a new genre that showed him off especially well: the comedy spy caper.

The movie had its origins in Hope's radio show. His obsession with the glamorous, blond British actress Madeleine Carroll became a running gag on the show, and one day Carroll, a fellow Paramount star, telephoned to thank Hope for all the publicity. She suggested they ought to do a picture together, and Paramount liked the idea. As a vehicle, the studio chose a script by two of Hope's former radio writers, Norman Panama and Melvin Frank, rewritten by Don Hartman and Frank Butler, the *Road* picture team. Sidney Lanfield, a comedy veteran working with Hope for the first time, got the director's assignment. The result was one of Hope's best films of the early forties.

He plays a small-time vaudeville song-and-dance man who does a cheesy act with a roller-skating penguin. Carroll is a British secret agent who shows up at his dressing-room door ("Too late, sister, I've already got an agent," he tells her) and drags him into a Hitchcockian spy plot. The MacGuffin is a brooch with a secret code, needed to launch a fleet of British bombers from an air base in California. Carroll surreptitiously plants the brooch on Hope, then accompanies him on a cross-country train trip to deliver it, with enemy spies in hot pursuit. (The silly premise was close enough to reality to disturb some British military officers, who complained about the film's suggestion that the launching of an RAF fleet would be dependent on such a harebrained scheme.)

My Favorite Blonde puts a comic twist on a familiar Hitchcock formula: the average Joe drawn unwittingly into life-or-death intrigue. Some of the scenes consciously echo *The 39 Steps,* the 1935 Hitchcock film in which Carroll raced around the Scottish countryside with Robert Donat, trying to foil an enemy spy ring. Hope does an amusing parody of their stiff-upper-lipped derring-do: he's a quavering, reluctant hero who wants no part of the adventure but is too moonstruck by Madeleine to avoid it. Their first encounter in his dressing room is Hope at his babbling, glassy-eyed best:

> MADELEINE: "Do you know what it feels like to be followed and hounded and watched every second?"
> BOB: "Well, I used to. Now I pay cash for everything."
> MADELEINE *(urgently):* "Look at me."
> BOB *(hypnotized):* "I'm looking."
> MADELEINE: "You've got to trust me."
> BOB: "I'm not through looking."

Hope gets the most out of every gag line, even the most obvious ones. Being dragged away by the authorities: "They can't do this to me! I'm an American citizen! I pay taxes!" Beat. "Well, I'm an American citizen." But the film also shows off his skills as a physical comedian as never before. Riding the train in one scene, he hides behind a newspaper as a trio of threatening characters silently join him in the compartment. Hope fidgets, peeks timidly from behind the paper, fans himself nervously with his hat, opens his cigarette case, and spills all of them on the floor. It's Hope's version of a classic comic archetype — the childlike naïf, flustered by an intimidating adult world — harking back to Chaplin and ahead to Jerry Lewis.

Though Hope stays admirably committed to character, he steps outside of the film at several points, with self-mocking references to his offscreen life and career — a device that would become common in his films. At one point he turns on the radio and hears an announcer introducing *The Pepsodent Show.* He quickly switches it off. "I can't stand that guy," he snaps. And Crosby turns up for the first of many unbilled cameos in Hope films, as a truck driver who gives Hope directions to a Teamsters picnic. After getting the directions and giving Bing a light for his pipe, Hope walks away, then stops and does a double take. "Couldn't be," he mutters, before moving on.

"Not only the funniest Bob Hope picture, but the funniest comedy within memory — that is the verdict of New York critics (and of New Yorkers) on *My Favorite Blonde,*" reported the *Los Angeles Times* when the film opened in April. "Unless everybody hereabouts is wrong, this is an almost perfect feature." It broke records for its four-week run at the Paramount Theater in New York and outdrew Hope's previous hits *Caught in the Draft* and *Nothing But the Truth* at theaters around the country. Once again, it was an escapist comedy with potent echoes of the real world. Though conceived before the United States was drawn into the war, Hope's comic face-off with the vaguely identified (but obviously German) spies was a welcome release for a nation now fighting real-life foreign enemies.

The early months of 1942 were the darkest of the war. After the attack on Pearl Harbor, Japan's war machine moved with frightening speed — overrunning Hong Kong, Burma, Thailand, Singapore, and the Philippines in a matter of weeks. American merchant ships, speeding across the Atlantic to supply the European Allies with war matériel, were being sunk by German submarines faster than new ships could be built. With America's war-production efforts still gearing up, a much-anticipated counteroffensive by the Allies was many months away.

Hollywood's first efforts to bring entertainment to the troops were, by necessity, confined to the home front. The United Service Organizations (USO), created in 1941 by six nonprofit groups to provide recreation and entertainment for America's men in uniform, set up clubs near military camps around the country where soldiers could eat, drink, and dance with local volunteer girls. Later, through its Camp Shows subsidiary, run by Abe Lastfogel, head of the William Morris talent agency, the USO began sending stars such as Al Jolson, Mickey Rooney, and Martha Raye on entertainment tours of domestic military bases.

Armed Forces Radio also began producing radio variety shows expressly for the troops and broadcast overseas via shortwave. Hope was a frequent host of one of them, *Command Performance,* a weekly show that featured top Hollywood guests supposedly picked by its GI listeners — "the greatest entertainers in America as requested by you, the fighting men of the United States armed forces throughout the world." Hope hosted his first broadcast for the troops on July 7, 1942, and did two more that year, sending along jokes from back home and motivational pep talks for the job they were doing over there: "This is Bob rubber-drive Hope, telling you guys out there that we're all gonna keep turning in our rubber suspenders till we've caught the Axis with their panzers down." And: "Hitler's always talking about his spring offensive, but, brother, that guy's offensive all year round." He could be a little racier than he could on

NBC, where his jokes were closely monitored by the censors. One example was his notorious crack about the rubber shortage and Kate Smith, the amply proportioned singer whose theme song was "When the Moon Comes over the Mountain." "Kate Smith finally turned in her girdle," said Hope. "You should see the moon come over the mountain now." NBC censors nixed the line, but the troops got to hear it.

In the summer of 1942, one of Hope's former movie stand-ins, now an army sergeant, dropped by the Paramount lot and suggested that Hope pay a visit to the US troops stationed in Alaska, guarding the Aleutian Islands against a possible Japanese attack. A few entertainers, among them Joe E. Brown and Edgar Bergen, had already traveled to that frozen territory, and Hope was eager to join them. He told his brother Jack to arrange a trip there during the one small window of time he had on his busy schedule — after his current film, *They Got Me Covered,* finished shooting on September 5, and before his first radio show of the season, on September 22.

Bob got two of his radio costars, Frances Langford and Jerry Colonna, to join him. With no room for a band, Langford suggested that Hope bring along a guitarist named Tony Romano, who had worked with Morey Amsterdam on the radio and as Dick Powell's vocal arranger at Warner Bros. A small, wiry Italian-American from Fresno, California, known as one of the top arrangers in Hollywood, Romano signed on as the fourth member of Hope's first troupe of wartime entertainers.

The trip was almost scrubbed before it got started. Just as the quartet was getting ready to leave from San Francisco, Hope got a telegram from the military brass in Alaska calling off the tour. The weather looked dicey, they said, and they couldn't guarantee that Hope would be back in time for his radio show. Hope wired back quickly, all but begging to come: "Four thespians, bags packed with songs and witty sayings, ready to tour your territory. Have been informed, due to lack of time, trip is off. Please let us make trip and will take our chances." Twelve hours later he got a reply from Major General Simon Buckner, overall commander of US troops in Alaska: "You leave Tuesday."

Hope and his entertainers flew first to Fairbanks, where they were assigned a Lockheed Lodestar aircraft and two pilots to ferry them around the territory. Their first stop was Nome, the remote town nicknamed Devil's Island by the GIs stranded there. Hope entertained in Quonset huts for men jammed inside and standing on tiptoes to see. He did a show for three thousand troops in the rain on Unimak Island in the Aleutians and for thirteen hundred mud-caked construction engineers working on the Canadian-Alaskan Highway in the Yukon Territory. At a refueling stop in Northway, he did an impromptu show for forty men, using a tree stump as a stage. With communications spotty in these forlorn outposts, the arrival of a troupe of Hollywood entertainers often came as a surprise and prompted some emotional reactions. At one show in the Aleutians, when Langford was singing "Isn't It Romantic," a general nudged Hope and pointed to two airmen listening to her in the crowd. One had his arm around his buddy, who was silently crying.

Hope and his little band grew close on the trip, as they endured the below-zero weather, bare-bones accommodations, and often treacherous plane flights. Their two pilots, Marvin Setzer (the younger, whom Hope nicknamed Junior) and Bob Gates (the tall one, dubbed Growing Pains), became part of the family too, especially after a perilously close call on a flight from Cordova to Anchorage. The troupe was supposed to be in Anchorage by evening, but with darkness falling — and flying at night in Alaska considered too dangerous — the pilots wanted to wait until morning. But Hope and Langford, intent on getting to Anchorage in time for a welcoming party that had been planned for them, prevailed on the pilots to leave that night.

A few minutes after taking off, the plane was enveloped in fog and sleet. As they headed toward Anchorage, the right engine conked out, and so did the radio. The plane was losing altitude at a rate of two hundred feet a minute and couldn't find the airport. Back in the main cabin, Hope and company knew something was wrong when they heard shouting from the cockpit. The crew chief came back and told them to put on their parachutes and "Mae West" life vests.

As he watched Langford being outfitted, Hope felt a wave of guilt: he had prevailed on her husband, actor Jon Hall, to let Frances take the trip. Colonna nervously stroked his mustache and quipped drily that the station wagon probably wouldn't be there. It was a reference to a joke Hope told, about a nervous recruit making his first parachute jump. The sergeant instructs him to pull the rip cord and ride the parachute to the ground, where a station wagon will be waiting to pick him up. But when the recruit pulls the cord, the parachute doesn't open. Hurtling toward the earth, he grumbles, "I'll bet the station wagon won't be there either."

"It was a pretty scary night," Gates, the copilot, recalled years later. "Bob came up to the cockpit, tapped me on the shoulder, and said, 'They're all on their knees praying back there.' I said, 'Tell 'em to keep going, 'cause we're gonna need all the help we can get.' " The ground crew at Elmendorf Air Force Base near Anchorage, learning of the plane's troubles, turned on all their searchlights, in violation of security rules. The plane had dropped to about two thousand feet when Gates and Setzer finally caught sight of the beams and headed the plane toward the airport.

"We saw this big glow, circled, and landed," said Gates. "We couldn't taxi, because we only had one engine. There was ice all over the airplane. All the generals and base commanders came running out. Bob was one of the first ones out. I was the last one. He came over, put his arms around me, and said, 'Okay, let's go to the barracks and change our drawers.' "

Hope later gave each pilot a watch, with the inscription "Thanks for my life." He wasn't exaggerating the danger. Gates, who became a colonel in the Air Force and logged eighteen thousand hours of flying time (including several more overseas trips with Hope), said that of all the flights he made in his career, that was the worst.

Bad weather of a more benign sort nearly kept Hope from getting back in time for his first radio show of the season. Pepsodent had lined up Edgar Bergen and bandleader Kay Kyser to fill in for him, in case Hope didn't make it. But the weather cleared just in time for Hope and company to fly to Seattle on Monday, and they did a show on Tuesday night from nearby Fort Lewis. Then they turned around and flew back to finish the Alaska tour, making a few final stops in the Aleutians before heading home to Los Angeles.

The Alaska trip made a powerful impression on Hope, and he talked soberly about it afterward. "I wouldn't trade this trip for my last five years in show business — my lucky years," he told a reporter. "I tell you, a guy gets to seeing himself in the proper focus in a setup like that. It's touching to think that the visit of a mere human being can mean so much." He promised to make another trip to Alaska, launched a drive to raise money for athletic gear and other recreational equipment for the men up there, and said he planned to go next to the British Isles. "Yes, Hollywood won't see so much of Hope from here on out. I've got other plans."

Questions were occasionally raised as to why Hope, Hollywood's greatest cheerleader for the troops, wasn't in uniform himself. He batted away the criticism fairly easily, with the help of friendly newspaper columnists. Dorothy Kilgallen reminded her readers how much Hope had done for the war effort, entertaining the troops and selling war bonds, and reported that he had tried to enlist six times (unlikely). "He was rejected every time," she wrote, "because the Army would rather have him doing what he is doing than carrying a gun." Ed Sullivan, after a golf game with Hope and heavyweight champion Joe Louis, now a sergeant in the Army, quoted Louis as telling Hope that it was more important for him to stay out of the line of fire. "The greatest good you can do is by making soldiers and sailors laugh," said Louis. "Us younger boys will take care of the fighting. You take care of the laughing."

He was taking care of it quite well. His *Pepsodent Show,* riding high on Hope's wartime gags, was now the No. 1 program in radio's Hooper ratings, just ahead of *Fibber McGee and Molly,* the show that followed Hope on Tuesday nights. And in November 1942, Paramount released a third *Road* picture, *Road to Morocco,* probably the most famous and fondly remembered (if not necessarily the best) of the entire series.

One reason is the film's title number, sung by the boys while riding on the back of a two-humped camel — the iconic image of the raffish camaraderie that sparked the films. The two, who have washed up on a desert shore after their ship has exploded and sunk (thanks to a match tossed inadvertently by Hope into the engine room), look as good as they ever have: sailor caps perched jauntily on their heads, Crosby trimmer and more animated than usual, Hope looking fit and manly in a white T-shirt and stubble of beard. Johnny Burke's lyrics, batted back and forth by the two stars, are a high point of the *Road* films' self-parodying, in-joke humor:

> Where we're goin', why we're goin', how
>   can we be sure?
> I'll lay you eight to five that we meet
>   Dor-o-thy Lamour . . .
> [Bing] For any villains we may meet, we
>   haven't any fear
> [Bob] Paramount will protect us 'cause
>   we're signed for five more years.

The entire Burke–Van Heusen score, which includes the standard "Moonlight Becomes You," is probably the best of all the *Road* pictures. The comic plot — from another screenplay by Frank Butler and Don Hartman, directed by David Butler (replacing Victor Schertzinger, who had died unexpectedly in October 1941) — is a satisfying pile-on of schemes and counterschemes. First, to make some money, Bing sells Bob into slavery. When Bob winds up being pampered in a harem and engaged to marry a desert princess (Lamour, naturally), Bing tries to horn in on the action. Then, when

Hope finds out that any man who marries the princess is cursed to die, he tries to con Bing into taking his place. The thrust and parry of their back-and-forth has been polished to a fine edge:

BING: "We'll have to storm the place."
BOB: "You storm, I'll stay here and drizzle."

BING: "You got red blood, ain't you?"
BOB: "Yeah, but I don't want to get it all over strangers."

BING: "I wanna have a talk with you, man-to-man."
BOB: "Who's gonna hold up your end?"

Road to Morocco is the wackiest and most anarchic *Road* picture yet. There are talking camels ("This is the screwiest picture I was ever in," one says) and fourth-wall-breaking gags. In a scene near the end, for example, an exasperated Hope quickly recaps all the troubles that Bing has gotten them into. "I know all that!" says Bing after he finishes. "Yeah," Bob replies, "but the people who came in the middle of the picture don't." (Bing's retort: "You mean they missed my song?") And the movie has one of the only truly adlibbed moments in the entire *Road* series. In the middle of a scene with a camel they've found in the desert (the one they'll

324

hop onto for the "Road to Morocco" number), the beast suddenly spits in Hope's face. As Hope reels back out of camera range, Crosby laughs and pets the animal: "Good girl, good girl." The camel improvised the spit — but when director Butler saw the spontaneous reaction, he kept it in the film.

The Morocco setting turned out to be unfortunately timed — Allied troops invaded North Africa just days before the film's release — but that mattered little. *Road to Morocco* earned $4 million at the box office, the best ever for a *Road* picture and the fourth highest for any film of 1942.

By early 1943, the tide in the war had turned in the Allies' favor. Starting with the Battle of Midway in June 1942, Japan's advances in the Pacific were being steadily reversed. The German invasion of the Soviet Union had bogged down in the bitter Russian winter. The long-awaited Allied offensive in the European theater, the invasion of North Africa in November 1942, had succeeded beyond expectations, with Rommel's forces driven out and Allied troops now securely in control of the region. So secure, in fact, that the USO was able to start sending entertainers there. Hope, tied up with his radio show until the summer, must have looked on enviously as stars such as Martha Raye and Carole Landis were in the first wave of entertainers to travel to North Africa in the early months of 1943.

Hope did his bit back home, making a ten-week tour in the spring of military camps in the Midwest and South. His pace was unflagging, his energy almost uncanny. "There were never less than three telephones in our rooms, and all of them rang at the same time every second of the day and night," said Barney Dean, who accompanied Hope on the trip. "And people, people, people. It was maddening. But Bob didn't seem to mind." When his exhausted troupe reached Atlanta, looking to rest up before the next day's radio broadcast, Hope got a call from a Paramount wardrobe boy who had been drafted and was now stationed in Albany, Georgia. Hope grabbed Barney Dean and made a hundred-mile drive there, just to do a show for the fellow's unit.

Back in Hollywood, Hope made a cameo appearance in *Star Spangled Rhythm,* a flag-waving Paramount musical revue, and played a newspaper reporter in Washington who stumbles on a German spy plot in *They Got Me Covered,* his long-delayed picture for Goldwyn. On March 4 Hope emceed his fourth Academy Awards banquet, held at the Cocoanut Grove. The war once again took center stage. The evening began with privates Alan Ladd and Tyrone Power unfurling an American flag containing the names of

26,677 members of the Hollywood community who were in uniform, and ended with the Best Picture award going to *Mrs. Miniver,* the inspirational wartime drama about an English family during the German Blitz. In between, Hope made jokes about the many Hollywood leading men who were off fighting in the war. "Pretty soon," he said, "we'll see Hedy Lamarr waiting to be kissed while they put a heating pad on Lewis Stone" — Mickey Rooney's screen father in the Andy Hardy films.

Hope was about to become one of those missing Hollywood stars. For his summer radio hiatus in July and August of 1943, Hope made plans for his first overseas tour of military bases: a two-month trip to the British Isles and North Africa, under the auspices of the USO Camp Shows. He wanted to reassemble the same group he had taken with him to Alaska and managed to recruit both Langford and guitarist Romano. But Colonna had movie commitments and a family to support, and he had to beg off. In his place Hope brought along Jack Pepper, a pudgy former vaudeville entertainer (once married to Ginger Rogers), who was in the Army and stationed in Texas, where Hope reconnected with him while traveling on his spring tour.

The four entertainers flew to New York in mid-June, to get their inoculations and await word on when they could depart. Dolores came along too, joining Bob for a few nights at the Waldorf Astoria. During the days, he went over material, which included some special songs written for the tour by Johnny Mercer. In the evenings he and Dolores would take in a nightclub or a Broadway show, including the hit new Rodgers and Hammerstein musical *Oklahoma!* Hope even squeezed in some last-minute reshoots for *Let's Face It,* the movie version of Cole Porter's Broadway musical that he had shot in the spring. Paramount had decided the film needed a better ending and sent second-unit director Hal Walker all the way to New York to get two new scenes on film before Hope left for Europe.

After six days of waiting, Hope and company finally got the word to be at LaGuardia's Marine Air Terminal at 1:00 a.m. There, Bob and Dolores had an anxious but subdued parting. A few months earlier, in February 1943, a similar USO flight headed for North Africa had crashed near Lisbon, killing Tamara, Hope's former costar in *Roberta* on Broadway, and severely injuring singer Jane Froman, who had appeared with him on his early radio show *The Intimate Revue.*

"Take care of yourself," Dolores said, as Bob got ready to board the plane.

"You know I will," he replied. They kissed, and he was off.

For Dolores the partings were becoming sadly familiar. In one of her few interviews around that time, with *Screenland* magazine, she put a typically upbeat face on it, praising Bob's dedication and energy, and touting her own volunteer work during the war — as head of the Southern California chapter of the American Women's Volunteer Services, in charge of agriculture. "I couldn't let this exciting world fly by without doing my share, and I'm busy," Dolores said. "You have no idea how many angles this involves. We spend days and nights rounding up workers, both men and women — thousands and thousands of them, to harvest the fruit and vegetable crops. Also, the vast vineyards. We have to work fast, you know, and it is a tremendous task. But we are so elated over our success that we forget to be tired."

She was circumspect, as always, about their marriage — though, in the coded language of 1940s Hollywood wives, one can detect hints of the accommodations she had to make: "It is the woman who makes the marriage, and like any career, one must work at it." She laughed off any suggestion that she might be jealous over "all those beautiful movie girls" her husband worked with. But she added, "Marriage can become complicated. Nothing is stationary, least of all emotions. But when a couple has built up understanding and companionship, along with the love, they find little difficulty in bridging the various evolutions." She was good.

Hope and his troupe were among the thirty passengers and crew aboard the Pan Am Clipper that took off from LaGuardia, lights blacked out for security reasons, early in the morning of June 25, 1943. They made a stop in Newfoundland and were on their way to Britain when they were forced to turn back because of high winds. Grounded for an extra day, the troupe did its first show of the tour at a Royal Canadian Air Force command station.

The next day they flew to Foynes, Ireland, and from there to Bristol — the Hope family's last home in England, before sailing for America in 1908. They caught a train to London, where they were greeted by a throng of fans, reporters, and newsreel photographers. Also in the welcoming party: William Dover, chief of the USO in England, and Hal Block, a radio gag writer supplied by the Office of War Information to help visiting entertainers with their comedy material. Seeing London for the first time since his trip there in 1939, Hope was startled at the damage wrought by the German bombing, and by the impact the war was having on everyday life. When he checked into Claridge's Hotel, Hope called up room service and said there wasn't any soap in the bathroom. "Sorry, sir," came the reply, "there is no soap in the King's bathroom either."

On his first day in London, Hope had a driver take him to Hitchin, forty miles away, to see his ninety-nine-year-old grandfather, James. The old man had slowed down considerably since the family get-together back in 1939, but he and his grandson still spent some time together talking about the family. "I was sorry I wasn't able to tell him more about the children," Bob noted. "I'd been traveling around the country so much that when I came home, it was just like doing another personal appearance, only with meals." A week later, while Hope was still in England, his grandfather died, just a few weeks short of his hundredth birthday. "He finished out of the money," said Hope.

After a night of theater in London, the "Hope gypsies," as Hope dubbed them, embarked on an eleven-day, thirteen-hundred-mile swing through the English countryside. They traveled in two cars, a 1938 Hudson and a 1938 Ford, with drivers supplied by the English Women's Corps, navigating roads from which the road signs had been removed, a precautionary measure to thwart a potential German invasion. They entertained at air hangars, supply depots, and bomber bases, doing three or four shows a day, sometimes for pilots who were going out on bombing runs the next day. An advance truck would typically arrive at each location twenty minutes ahead of the performers to set up the sound system. When the shows were finished, the entertainers would spend the night at local inns, with and without plumbing, or private farmhouses.

"I've just arrived from the States," Hope would begin. "You know, that's where Churchill lives." Then after the laugh: "He doesn't exactly live there. He just goes back to deliver Mrs. Roosevelt's laundry." He joked about the Brits and their customs ("They drive on the wrong side of the street here — just like in California") and about barracks life: "Were the soldiers at the last camp happy to see me! They actually got down on their knees. What a spectacle! What a tribute! What a crap game!" He talked about the Hollywood stars who were now in uniform (one of them, Clark Gable, was stationed at an air base in England that Hope visited) and the pinup girls who were waiting back home. "We soon discovered you had to be pretty lousy to flop in front of those guys," Hope said in his memoir of the trip, *I Never Left Home.* "They were so glad to see somebody from home that they yelled and screamed and whistled at everything. And for a little while, they were able to forget completely their own problems and what they'd been through, or what they might be expecting to go through."

Hope and his entertainers visited military

hospitals nearly everywhere they went. "Don't get up!" Bob would shout when he entered the wards. He would walk among the beds, making small talk with the men, dishing out wisecracks to cheer them up — "Did you see our show or were you sick before?" In one ward, Hope did a few quick dance steps, slipped on a wet floor, and sprained his wrist — an injury that bothered him the rest of the trip. He instructed his fellow entertainers to keep the mood light and their emotions in check, but sometimes it was hard. In one ward Langford began to sing "As Time Goes By," but had only got through eight bars when a soldier with a head wound began to cry. She finished the song in a whisper and went outside, where she burst into tears.

After their first eleven-day swing, Hope and his troupe returned to London to rest, before making several more hops around the country. They flew to Belfast for a tour of army camps, submarine bases, and aircraft plants in Northern Ireland. Hope returned to Bristol to take part in an international radio broadcast and, to cap off the tour, appeared in a gala variety show at London's Odeon Theater, with other USO performers who were in the country, including Adolphe Menjou, Hal Le Roy, and Stubby Kaye. Afterward, with help from Senator Happy Chandler, who was in London with a group of visiting US dignitaries, Hope wrangled an invitation to a reception at 10 Downing Street, where he met Winston Churchill. The prime minister did a double take on seeing the Hollywood star, then autographed Hope's "short snorter," a five-pound note commonly used by travelers during the war to collect signatures as souvenirs.

Hope spent a total of five weeks in Britain, covered five thousand miles, and gave nearly a hundred performances, not counting the hospital visits. No other USO performer moved as fast or left as big an impression. "The most wonderful thing about England right now is Bob Hope," wrote Captain Burgess Meredith in a letter to Paulette Goddard. "The boys in camp stand in rain, they crowd into halls so close you can't breathe, just to see him. He is tireless and funny, and full of responsibility too, although he carries it lightly and gaily. There isn't a hospital ward that he hasn't dropped into and given a show; there isn't a small unit anywhere that isn't either talking about his jokes or anticipating them."

Novelist John Steinbeck, covering the war for the *New York Herald Tribune,* saw Hope too and paid him a memorable tribute:

When the time for recognition of service to the nation in wartime comes to be considered, Bob Hope should be high on the list. In some way he has caught the soldiers' imagination. He gets laughter wherever he goes, from men who need laughter. . . . It is hard to over-estimate the importance of this thing and the responsibility involved. The battalion of men who are moving half tracks from one place to another, doing a job that gets no headlines, no public notice, and yet which must be done if there is to be a victory, are forgotten, and they feel forgotten. But Bob Hope is in the country. Will he come to them, or won't he? And then one day they get a notice that he is coming. Then they feel remembered.

Other reporters, from *Time* and *Esquire* and *Vogue,* tagged along with Hope, documenting his trip and the extraordinary reaction to it. By the time he left Britain, he was America's most celebrated wartime entertainer. And he was just getting started.

Hope had just appeared on the screen in *Road to Morocco,* and his next stop, improbably, *was* Morocco. He and his troupe took off from Prestwick, Scotland (where Hope got in his only golf game of the trip — most of the courses in England having been covered with barbed wire to prevent enemy planes from landing on them), and landed in Marrakech. Hope's wardrobe, geared for the blustery British weather, was too heavy for the North African heat, so an officer lent him a light-weight, green linen suit. Hope wore it for the rest of the trip.

They flew first to Tunis, operational head-quarters for the bomber groups that were preparing for an invasion of Sicily, and embarked on a fast-moving tour of the region, doing shows at every air base, tank corps, and military hospital they could reach. "Hiya, fellow tourists," Hope would greet the crowds. "Isn't this a great country, Africa? It's Texas with Arabs." No matter how corny or stale the jokes, the men roared.

Though North Africa was firmly under Allied control, German bombing raids were continuing, and Hope's troupe got caught in several of them. In Bizerte — just a short hop from Sicily and thus a major target of German bombers — they were rousted out of bed at the Transatlantique Hotel by an air raid in the middle of the night. They watched another raid on the city from a road a few miles away, as they were driving back from a tour of hospitals. "Frances and I were standing next to our parked car," Hope recalled. "We had on helmets. I've never heard such noise. Every once in a while we'd see one of the big German planes burst into flame and come plunging down." When the planes came so close they could hear the whistles, an MP hustled them to cover. Romano dove under a car, Pepper got inside an ambulance, and Hope and Langford piled on top of each other in a ditch — Hope spraining a ligament as he dove in.

As he had in Britain, Hope showed remarkable reserves of energy. He kept himself fresh with frequent catnaps — he could drop off to sleep seemingly anywhere. Riding with him in a bumpy jeep in Tunisia, Jack Pepper was amazed: "I was bouncing like a rubber ball and losing everything I'd ever eaten in my life. But when I turned to look at Hope, the guy is fast asleep." Reporting on the trip for *Esquire,* Sidney Carroll compared Hope to another famously tireless world traveler, Eleanor Roosevelt. "He is what the psychologists call an 'energist,' or one who seems to possess unfailing reserves of the magic motive power. . . . It is as much of a miracle as the burning bush. Hope never burns out."

Just three days after the successful Allied invasion of Sicily, Hope's troupe got aboard a B-17 and flew to Palermo, the first American entertainers to arrive on the European continent since the start of the war. Hope did a show for sixteen thousand men jammed into a soccer field, and another in a gulley for nineteen thousand soldiers from the Forty-Fifth Army Division, with P-38s circling overhead for protection. ("It not only gives you a feeling of security," said Hope, "it gives you a feeling your jokes aren't being heard.") General George Patton, hero of the Sicily campaign, invited Hope and his troupe to dinner at King Victor Emmanuel's palace, where Patton had taken up residence. The general asked Hope about his travels, showed off his pearl-handled six-guns, and impressed Hope with his quick wit. "A very wonderful guy," Hope recalled. "Never opened my kisser but that he topped it." Patton may have had his own agenda in inviting Hope to the palace. The hard-driving general was under fire for slapping two soldiers, and he asked Hope for a favor when he got back home: "I want you to tell the people that I love my men." Hope, who didn't know about the controversy, was puzzled: "I looked at this guy and I thought he was suffering from some kind of battle fatigue."

Footage of Hope's shows in North Africa and Sicily is all but non-existent. But seeing him must have been a powerful experience for American soldiers just days out of battle. An Army lieutenant named John D. Saint Jr., who saw Hope in Sicily, wrote a vivid description of his show in a letter home to his parents:

Bob came on the grandstand as a man on the street, baggy trousers, an ordinary coat, and an open-neck collar. Nothing fancy at all. His nose was really sunburned and caught the brunt of a lot of his own jokes. He started his patter and all of us laughed until tears were just streaming down and we couldn't see a darned thing. He has been playing Army camps a lot and has picked up the lingo. He can tell you all about lister bags, atabrine tablets and armor artificers. That made his comments much funnier to us. He was speaking our language. . . .

And all of a sudden Bob said, "Here's Frances Langford!" There was a din you would not believe. She was stunningly dressed, though simply. It was good to see a clean, neat American girl who spoke our language and thought like we do. She sang and she sang from the very bottom of her heart. It could not have been otherwise. First it was "You Made Me Love You." Then "Tangerine" and then "Night and Day." The songs were mixed with patter between Hope and her, clever and funny as you can imagine. We thought it was all over, and Bob asked her back to sing "Embraceable You." Every one of those thousands of men then went home to their wives and sweethearts. It was almost more than a man could stand.

Much of the impact came from the knowledge that these Hollywood stars were taking real risks in being there. No entertainers had ever been closer to the action. At the Excelsior Hotel in Palermo, Hope and his troupe were again jolted awake in the middle of the night by an air raid. Too late to make it to the bomb shelter, Hope gritted it out in his hotel room, watching tracer bullets whiz across the sky and a big piece of red-hot flak fly by his window. "After you've listened to a raid for a little while you begin to be afraid that just the noise will kill you," he wrote. "Then after you've listened to it a little while longer you begin to be afraid it won't. You want to curl up in a ball." When the raid was over, Hope crawled out of bed and checked on his traveling companions. Langford had also been trapped in her room; Pepper was the only one who made it to the bomb shelter. Hope called it "the most frightening experience of my life."

War stories can be exaggerated, but Hope's wasn't. "I was in two different cities with them during the raids, and I will testify they were horrifying raids," wrote war correspondent Ernie Pyle, in one of his dispatches for the *New York World-Telegram.* "It isn't often that a bomb falls so close that you can hear it whistle. But when you can hear a whole stack of them whistle at once, then it's time to get weak all over and start sweating. The Hope troupe can now describe that ghastly sound."

After Sicily, Hope and his gypsies flew back to Bône, Tunisia, and continued their North African tour. Hope had one bad moment, when a heckler in a crowd of British and American troops yelled, "Draft dodger! Why aren't you in uniform?" Hope shouted back,

"Don't you know there's a war on? A guy could get hurt." Their last stop was Algiers, where Hope did another international radio broadcast and met General Dwight D. Eisenhower, overall commander of the North African forces. Ike was another general who impressed Hope enormously (his voice reminded Hope of Clark Gable's). "He flattered us not only by being so gracious, but by knowing where we'd been and what we'd been doing," Hope said. Eisenhower knew that Hope's troupe had been through several air raids and assured them they would have a safe night in Algiers. "We haven't had a raid in three months," Ike said. "We're too strong for 'em."

But that night at the Aletti Hotel, Hope and company were again jolted awake in the middle of the night by German bombers. This time Hope made it down to a wine cellar with the rest of his band to take shelter. They spent an hour and forty minutes there, listening to the bombs, and for the first time he saw Frances Langford lose her composure. "When we were lost over Alaska, during the raids on Bizerte and Palermo, she'd stayed perfectly calm," he said. "But cooped up in a bomb shelter under Algiers she began to tremble and cry. For once I had the chance to be the big strong man. I put her head on my shoulder and held her close to me, so we sort of trembled in unison."

The raid wasn't over until 6:00 a.m. They were supposed to leave Algiers that morning at eight, but had to put it off until the evening. They finally made it to London and then to Iceland — where they were again delayed by weather and filled the extra time by doing three more shows. Descending at last over the familiar skyline of New York City, Hope felt an understandable letdown. All told, he had spent eleven weeks overseas, doing some 250 shows for an estimated 1.5 million men. He came back with scores of names and addresses scrawled on pieces of paper — of the mothers and wives and sweethearts of the men he had entertained, who asked Hope if he would contact their loved ones and send greetings. Which he did.

Back home, Hope was hailed as a hero. He recounted his experiences to columnists such as Ed Sullivan and wrote about his tour in a syndicated newspaper article, "I Saw Your Boys." *Time* magazine celebrated him in a cover story, with the headline "Hope for Humanity." "From the ranks of show business have sprung heroes and even martyrs," the magazine wrote, "but so far only one legend. That legend is Bob Hope."

It sprang up swiftly, telepathically, among US servicemen in Britain this summer, traveling faster than even whirlwind Hope himself, then flew ahead of him to North

Africa and Sicily, growing larger as it went. Like most legends, it represents measurable qualities in a kind of mystical blend. Hope was funny, treating hordes of soldiers to roars of laughter. He was friendly — ate with servicemen, drank with them, read their doggerel, listened to their songs. He was indefatigable, running himself ragged with five, six, seven shows a day. He was figurative — the straight link with home, the radio voice that for years had filled the living room and that in foreign parts called up its image. Hence boys whom Hope might entertain for an hour awaited him for weeks. And when he came, anonymous guys who had had no other recognition felt personally remembered.

He went to work on a book for Simon & Schuster about his tour, collaborating with a ghostwriter named Carroll Carroll, an adman who had written for Crosby's *Kraft Music Hall.* The two worked together through the fall, meeting every Wednesday in Hope's living room — Carroll writing up chapters from Hope's recollections, Hope editing them and handing them over to his gag writers for punching up. The book, *I Never Left Home,* has plenty of jokes, but also much vivid detail, as well as passages of elegiac and often moving prose. It begins:

I saw your sons and your husbands, your brothers and your sweethearts. I saw how they worked, played, fought and lived. I saw some of them die. I saw more courage, more good humor in the face of discomfort, more love in an era of hate, and more devotion to duty than could exist under tyranny. I saw American minds, American skill, and American strength breaking the backbone of evil.

I Never Left Home was published in June 1944 — the first hundred thousand copies in paperback, aimed at servicemen and priced at $1, followed by a hardback edition for $2. Hope donated all the proceeds to the National War Fund, which was coordinating relief for the countries being reoccupied in the war. The book got admiring reviews, not just from Hope's many friends in the Hollywood press but from serious book critics too. "A zany, staccato but often touching account," wrote Tom O'Reilly in the *New York Times Book Review.* It sold more than 1.6 million copies, the bestselling nonfiction book for all of 1944. The wartime legend of Bob Hope was born.

Returning to Los Angeles on September 7 after his life-changing trip, Hope tried to adapt to the new normal. He took Dolores and the kids to Del Mar for a rest, then began preparing for the September 21 debut of his sixth radio season. "I think I was suffering from adrenaline withdrawal," he said. "I had gotten hooked on fear, the real thing, not the sort you felt when a joke didn't play, or a movie got panned."

Hope's radio show — with Langford and Colonna back as regulars, and Stan Kenton replacing bandleader Skinnay Ennis, who was in the service — was now virtually all military, all the time. He tailored his comedy for each base or military unit he was visiting: the Navy aviators at Terminal Island, the marines at Camp Pendleton, the gunnery specialists in Las Vegas. The jokes were broad and chummy, aimed squarely at the soldiers — endless variations, for example, on Hope's favorite "you know — that's" formula: "You know what a bunk is — that's a bookshelf with a mattress." "You know what a Wave is — that's a Wac with salt water in her blood." "You know what a tank is — that's a coffee percolator that made good." With the help of a new writer, Glenn Whedon, Hope added serious patriotic messages at the end of the shows, urging listeners to buy war bonds or write a serviceman overseas, or paying tribute to the particular service branch or specialty he was entertaining that week — Navy nurses, say, or the Coast Guard. His No. 1 ratings soared to new heights. On February 19, 1944, Hope scored an astonishing 40.9 in the Hooper ratings — meaning 40.9 percent of all the radio homes in the country were tuned in, the highest audience ever for a half-hour radio program.

On March 11, 1944, he went to Washington to emcee the annual White House Correspondents' Association dinner, with President Roosevelt as guest of honor. It was the first time Hope entertained a president — a coveted assignment that he almost missed. Hope and his radio cast had just done a show at an officers' training school in Miami, and before flying to Washington, Hope decided to stop at Brookley Field in Mobile, Alabama, for a golf game with the base commander. But the weather turned bad, the golf was canceled, and it looked likely that Hope would be stranded in Alabama. He got to Washington only after a telegram from General Henry "Hap" Arnold was delivered to the base commander: "Have plane coming north tonight. Make sure Hope is on it."

He got to the dinner an hour late, and the show had already started, with *Duffy's Tavern* star Ed Gardner filling in as emcee. But after Fritz Kreisler, Gracie Fields, and Fred Waring and the Pennsylvanians entertained, Hope was there in time for his closing monologue. He joked about the president's battles with Congress, Eleanor's peripatetic traveling, and the First Couple's least favorite newspaper, the conservative *Chicago Tribune.*

Hope joked that Fala, the Roosevelts' Scottish terrier, was "the only dog housebroken on that paper." When Hope glanced over nervously to see the president's reaction, FDR's head was tilted back in laughter.

In these heady and dramatic times, Hope's movies seemed almost like an afterthought. When shooting began in November 1943 on *Road to Utopia,* the fourth in the *Road* series, signs of the star's inattention and self-involvement were becoming apparent. The script, set in the 1890s Alaska gold rush, was by Panama and Frank (their first screenplay for Hope, after getting only story credit for *My Favorite Blonde*), and the writers had to revise it several times to please both stars. "In those days they were *enormous* stars," said Frank. "You really had to have their okay on the script, even though they were under contract and could be forced to do what you wanted. So we would sit down with Crosby and explain our ideas and we would make it sound like it was going to be *his* picture. Then we'd tell Hope the story and make it attractive from his point of view." On the set too Hope and Crosby moved at their own leisurely pace, forcing director Hal Walker to work around their golf games and trips to the racetrack. "Some days I became almost as nonchalant as Bing," Hope admitted. "Together we were a deadly combination."

Lamour often bore the brunt. One Saturday

morning she spent two hours getting into her period gown, hair, and makeup for a musical number with Hope and Crosby, scheduled to start shooting at 9:00 a.m. But neither showed up. She was still waiting in the afternoon when Gary Cooper dropped by the set and told her she should just go home. She did — a few minutes before Hope and Crosby finally sauntered in. They had spent the day at a charity golf match and claimed to have forgotten about the scene. "The next day it was all patched up," Lamour wrote, charitably, in her autobiography. "Of course, Bing and Bob took turns teasing the life out of me, calling me 'that temperamental Lamour woman who stormed off the set.' But they didn't pull another stunt like that ever again." Still, it was a sign of how thoroughly Hope and Crosby had turned the *Road* films into their own private playground. For Lamour, the slights would accumulate.

In the spring of 1944 Hope shot another film for Goldwyn, initially called *Sylvester the Great* and later changed to *The Princess and the Pirate* — Hope's first costume picture and his first movie in color. But his war-related activities were taking up more and more time and attention. He hosted a bond drive and charity golf tournament with Crosby at Lakeside and did several more *Command Performance* broadcasts for Armed Forces Radio.

In March he made a four-day tour of US military bases in the Caribbean. And he prepared to make his next major overseas tour, during his radio show's summer vacation, this time to the Pacific theater.

His last show of the season was scheduled for June 6, 1944. Early that morning, Allied forces landed on the beaches of Normandy, launching the long-awaited invasion of Western Europe. Hope scrapped the show he had planned, from the Van Nuys Air Field, and instead delivered a tribute to the invasion forces of D-day. His wartime prose was never more eloquent, his brisk, plain-spoken delivery rendering it even more powerful:

What's happened during these last few hours not one of us will ever forget. How could you forget? You sat up all night by the radio and heard the bulletins, the flashes, the voices coming across from England, the commentators, the pilots returning from their greatest of all missions, newsboys yelling in the street. And it seemed that one world was ending and a new world beginning, that history was closing one book and opening a new one. And somehow we knew it had to be a better one. We sat there, and dawn began to sneak in, and you thought of the hundreds of thousands of kids you'd seen in camps the past two or three years. The kids who scream and whistle when they hear a gag and a song. And now you could see all of them again, in four thousand ships in the English Channel, tumbling out of thousands of planes over Normandy and the occupied coast. And countless landing barges crashing the Nazi gate and going on through to do the job that's the job of all of us. The sun came up, and you sat there looking at that huge black headline, that one great black word with the exclamation point — *Invasion!* The one word that the whole world has waited for, that all of us have worked for.

It was only fitting that Hope, the man who had brought the war home to America, would be the one to capture the nation's relief and pride in the military triumph that would help bring it to an end.

Much was still left to do in the Pacific, however, where the United States was embarked on a painfully slow, island-by-island march toward what seemed an inevitable invasion of Japan. Again Hope assembled an entertainment troupe and headed for the action. Langford and Romano were back, and Colonna, who had to pass on the European trip the year before, was on board this time. For some added sex appeal, Hope hired Patty Thomas, a pretty, leggy dancer who had been working in USO shows in the States and got the job after an interview with Hope. He added one more member to the troupe: his crony, sometime writer, and *Road* picture jester, Barney Dean. "We had Barney along in case we had to trade with the natives," Hope cracked.

The group left San Francisco on June 22 aboard a C-54 medical transport plane. They stopped first in the Hawaiian Islands, where they spent nine days and did some thirty-five shows, the largest for twenty-five thousand civilian employees at the Pearl Harbor Naval Yards. Then they flew off to Christmas Island and began hopscotching islands on the "pineapple circuit."

Ferried around by a Catalina seaplane, they went to Kwajalein, Bougainville, and Eniwetok (where Navy lieutenant Henry Fonda was stationed), doing five, six, or even seven shows a day. They visited the site of bloody battles such as Tarawa and Guadalcanal, doing shows near unmarked graves and pillboxes full of weapons abandoned by the Japanese. Hope joked often about the tiny islands and the swampy, bug-infested conditions. "You're not defending this place, are you?" he cracked on one. "Let them take it!" Hope picked up jungle rot on the trip, a skin disease that would plague him for years.

For Hope the most memorable stop was the island of Pavuvu, where the Marine First Division was preparing for an attack on Peleliu, a nearby Japanese stronghold. For six months the fifteen thousand men there had seen no entertainment. The island was so small there was no airstrip, so Hope and his crew had to fly in on tiny Piper Cubs, the men cheering as each plane buzzed the baseball field. Eugene B. Sledge, one of the marines who was there, described Hope's visit in his classic combat memoir, *With the Old Breed:*

> Probably the biggest boost to our morale about this time on Pavuvu was the announcement that Bob Hope would come over from Banika and put on a show for us. . . . Bob Hope, Colonna, Frances Langford, and Patty Thomas put on a show at a little stage by the pier. Bob asked Jerry how he liked the trip over from Banika, and Jerry answered that it was "tough sledding." When asked why, he replied, "No snow." We thought it was the funniest thing we had ever heard. Patty gave several boys from the audience dancing lessons amid much grinning, cheering and applause. Bob told many jokes and really boosted our spirits. It was the finest entertainment I ever saw overseas.

Weeks after their show on Pavuvu, the assault on Peleliu began. An operation that was supposed to take four days stretched out for two months — one of the bloodiest battles of the war, with more than sixty-five hundred men killed or wounded. Months later, Hope was visiting a hospital in Oakland when one of the patients called out, "Pavuvu!" Hope went over to shake the man's hand and found out the ward was full of marines who had seen Hope at Pavuvu and survived the campaign. One injured soldier awakened after an operation to see Hope standing over the bed. "Bob!" he exclaimed. "When did you get here?"

In the tight-knit family of traveling entertainers, Hope was nicknamed Dad, and Langford was known as Mother. Thomas, the youngster in the group (she celebrated her twenty-second birthday on Pavuvu), developed a close, sisterly bond with Langford. They shared bedrooms and often went to the bathroom together in the rough-hewn latrines, where the men would put up a sheet to give them privacy. Frances gave Patty advice on clothes (slacks, not skirts, and sweaters for the cool nights), food (eat as little as possible before flying), and avoiding sticky situations with the sex-starved servicemen — a little-mentioned peril for female entertainers traveling through the war zone. "You had to be careful," said Thomas. "Not talk to them alone, only in groups. These kids wanted to meet someone. But I wouldn't dare lead them on. One guy came up to me and said, 'I'd like to ---- you.' He was beaten up by the other soldiers."

(The GIs weren't the only problem for Thomas. She also had to fend off advances from Colonna, until Hope stepped in to help. "Bob would tell people, 'This is my girl.' I was not Bob's girl, but he did that for my protection." When she got back to the States, Thomas made a point of assuring Dolores that any rumors about them weren't true. Dolores was satisfied. "Honey, I know what you're like," she said. "I've seen you in church.")

The few film clips from his Pacific tour show how confident and charismatic Hope was onstage — tanned, often chewing gum, hair slightly mussed, as deft a straight man as he was a gagster. He and Romano had an easy, bantering relationship, doing patter songs together or parodies of the Ink Spots along with Colonna. Hope matched dance steps with Thomas, whose skimpy outfits and knockout figure always got a big reaction. Said Hope, introducing her to the crowd, "I just want you boys to see what you're fighting for."

The sex was never far from the surface, but Hope somehow made it seem innocent and wholesome. When Langford, who would close the show with some rewritten lyrics to "Thanks for the Memory," got to the lines "I wish that I could kiss / Each and every one of you," Hope stepped up to the microphone and cried, in mock-horror, "You want to get us trampled to death?" For men trying to survive grueling conditions in lonely outposts, sometimes days away from battle, it must have been marvelous.

After six weeks of island hopping, the troupe flew to Australia for a few days of shows. There, they had their closest call of the trip. Flying from Brisbane to Sydney, Hope asked the pilot of the Catalina seaplane if he could take the controls. While the plane was on automatic pilot, one engine conked out and the plane began dipping. Patty Thomas was looking out the window and saw black smoke. "Hey, Dad, I think we're in trouble," she said to Hope. "We're only working on one propeller!" The pilot hurried back to the cockpit and ordered the passengers to jettison whatever they could — luggage, souvenirs, cases of liquor. Barney Dean, who was petrified of plane flights even in the best of circumstances, told Hope to dump his wallet, since it was the heaviest thing on the plane.

The pilot located a small body of water near the village of Laurieton and maneuvered the seaplane to an emergency landing, skidding to a stop on a sandbar. A fisherman saw them and rowed over to rescue them. The first thing he asked for was some American cigarettes. Hope and his troupe did a show that night at the local dance hall in gratitude. The crash landing made headlines all over Australia, as well as back in the United States. When Hope flew the next day to Sydney, a mob of thousands was there to greet him at the hotel, pressing in so hard that Hope had to be rescued by the military police.

After Australia, Hope and his troupe continued on to Hollandia, New Guinea, recently recaptured from the Japanese. During the day they did a show for twenty thousand troops, the biggest crowd Hope had ever entertained in a war zone, and at night did a second show for five thousand Seabees. Then they hopped onto PT boats to entertain in the tiny Woendi islands. Among those in the audience, Hope learned years later, was a PT boat captain named John F. Kennedy.

The Pacific tour generated nearly as much attention back home as Hope's tour of Europe and North Africa had the year before. King Features, the Hearst newspaper syndicate, asked Hope if he would send back some dispatches from his trip, and midway through the tour (with help from a war correspondent, Frank Robertson, he met in Australia) Hope turned out several newspaper columns recounting his experiences. The War Department nixed Pepsodent's request to let Hope broadcast his radio show from the trip. But on August 12, he hosted a special NBC broadcast from a naval hospital "somewhere in the South Pacific." After joking about the bug-infested islands and harrowing plane flights ("It was so rough the automatic pilot bailed out"), Hope concluded with a sober tribute to the men he had visited, and an appeal to the nation to pull together for final victory:

Sure, a lot of citizens in the States have it pretty tough, with the rationing of meat, shoes, gasoline, and other items. But we've been deprived of these things while at home. How'd you like to be deprived of these things while crouched in a foxhole, ducking that lead with your initials on it? Where a bottle of Coke or a beer is a luxury, and hot water and linen are a dim memory, and your bathroom just ain't. . . . We've seen kids smile for the last time, and other boys spending long, monotonous, pain-filled hours fighting for their lives, after fighting for yours. Ladies and gentlemen, it might surprise you to know that these boys, who have made the sacrifice, are also buying bonds. Think it over.

Throughout the war, President Roosevelt had sought to convince the nation that the battles overseas and the war effort back home, from recycling rubber to buying war bonds, were inextricable, all part of the same great national crusade. Hope, with his blunt, no-nonsense wartime prose, brought that message home like no one else.

The long trip back to the United States went through Wake Island and took fifty hours. In all, Hope's Pacific tour had encompassed thirty thousand miles and 150 shows in eight weeks. Arriving in Burbank on Saturday, September 2, at the Lockheed Air Terminal, Hope was welcomed home by Dolores and the kids, along with a gaggle of reporters and photographers. His bags were filled with souvenirs of the trip — Japanese swords and guns, a native chieftain's cane. Four-year-old Tony greeted his father, "Goodbye, Daddy." Dolores had to explain: "He's so used to seeing Bob going away, he can't get used to his coming home."

Though his wartime tours were a high point of his performing life and a mission he passionately believed in, they were a financial sacrifice for Hope. The USO paid its performers only a nominal amount, and by spending two months out of the summer entertaining the troops overseas, Hope was giving up a lot of potentially lucrative paydays. Still, he was one of Hollywood's top earners in these years. He was making $100,000 per picture, and that, combined with his radio show, stage appearances, and other ventures, brought his income close to $1 million a year. But Hope was chafing under the three-picture-a-year pace that Paramount was keeping him on —

and was dismayed that so much of the money he made was going to the government in taxes.

His lawyer, Martin Gang, suggested a creative solution. Hope could improve his bottom line, Gang said, by setting up his own production company and, instead of getting a salary, taking a share of the profits from his films, thus allowing him to pay taxes at the lower corporate rate. Hope liked the idea and took Paramount chief Y. Frank Freeman to lunch to propose it. Freeman, a gentlemanly Southerner, listened politely, but refused flatly: "I don't see how we can let you do that, Bob."

Hope responded by going on strike. He refused to do the next two films that Paramount had lined up for him: a cameo appearance in *Duffy's Tavern* (an all-star screen version of the popular radio series) and a starring role, with Paulette Goddard, in a film called *My Favorite Brunette.* When Hope didn't show up for the scheduled first day of shooting on *Brunette,* on Monday, November 6, 1944, the studio suspended him.

Hope quickly took charge of the spin, claiming that *he* was suspending the studio. He was too busy with his war-related work, he said, to do three films a year for Paramount. "Just now I've been to Toronto, New York, Akron, Chicago, and Topeka — all war-benefit appearances," he told a reporter. "In the next month I do six more shows — three in Chicago and one each in Atlanta, Cleveland, and Independence, Kansas. . . . And I've got five or ten wires on my desk, asking me to give shows at other service camps along the way. These things are important. There are thousands of kids waiting there." In an interview with the *Los Angeles Times,* he added, "I'm not underrating the importance of motion pictures to a career. But there is a big horizon to the present situation that has to be recognized. Now is the time above all others to give to the war effort, and if what entertainers do is helpful and morale building, then this is the time for them to concentrate on that sort of helpfulness."

It was a shrewd appeal to patriotism in what was essentially a contract dispute. For six months there was a stalemate, as Hope refused to work. *My Favorite Brunette* was shelved. (Hope made a picture with the same title three years later, but with a different script and another costar, Dorothy Lamour.) *Road to Utopia,* which had finished shooting in February 1944, was held back from release, ostensibly because Paramount had a logjam of wartime films. Moviegoers were about to experience something they hadn't since Hope made his feature-film debut in *The Big Broadcast of 1938:* after the release of *The Princess and the Pirate* in the fall of 1944, more than a year passed without a Bob Hope picture.

While Hope was fighting with his movie studio, he was embroiled in a different sort of dispute over his radio program. In November 1944 an editorial in the *Pilot,* the weekly newspaper of Boston's Roman Catholic archdiocese, raised objections to the sexually suggestive jokes that Hope was doing for his military audiences. The editorial called Hope's material "artful filth," claiming it encouraged promiscuity among married servicemen and put lewd thoughts into the heads of young, impressionable ones. "Some of the servicemen are boys barely past adolescence," the Catholic paper said. "Their mothers knew that they were delivering their cherished sons to danger of death. They accepted that. But they never supposed that their boys would be exposed to 'entertainment' which might ruin their souls."

Battles over Hope's allegedly lewd material had been going on for years, though mostly behind closed doors. Notes from a 1942 meeting of NBC executives revealed that serious consideration was given to pulling Hope's show from the air after complaints from several New England stations about his off-color jokes. One NBC executive even proposed leaking news of the stations' complaints to the press, to pressure Hope and other radio comics to tone down their material:

I think if we came out with some publicity, stating that 11 New England stations threaten to cancel a certain program of a certain well-known comedian and give the reasons for it, you are not hurting the comedian and you are making four or five of them [radio comedians] sit up and take notice, why then you are drawing first blood in this and they are on the defensive. And I don't know that [CBS] would be willing to take a show that we threw off the air or which we cancelled because we wouldn't go for stuff which we regarded as being lewd.

There's no evidence NBC came close to acting on this rather outlandish suggestion. But the Catholic complaints, aired in public, presented a more delicate problem for Hope. "I think it is only fair to me to point out that if my shows were offensive," he responded carefully, "I could hardly have reached the position of where a great nationwide audience hears my radio program regularly, considering what public taste means." The controversy percolated for several weeks. Another Catholic paper, Chicago's *Novena Notes,* published the results of a poll of ten thousand readers, who voted Hope the entertainer who "most consistently violates" Christian principles. (Milton Berle was second.) Both supporters and foes inundated Hope with letters. ("Risqué stories — phooey!" said one defender. "I'll bet that editor loves them.") *Boxoffice* magazine came to his defense, declaring the attacks "as unfair a charge against a great entertainer and a good American as has been treated to printer's ink in many years." In the end, the campaign made little dent in Hope's enormous popularity. For the 1944–45 season, *The Pepsodent Show* finished first in the Hooper ratings by its biggest margin ever — drawing 34.1 percent of the radio audience, more than 3 points higher than the show in second place, *Fibber McGee and Molly.*

The only thing that could possibly slow down the Bob Hope juggernaut was his health. In May 1944 he had to take off five days for an eye operation — its exact nature unclear, but possibly the first sign of the eye problems that would plague him in later years. In January 1945 Hope's doctor, Hugh Strathearn, raised concerns about an electrocardiogram that, while in the normal range, "showed that you have been under a terrific strain, as far as your heart muscles are concerned." In a letter to Hope, who was traveling, the doctor added, "I do not feel that this condition is serious at this time, but I do think that it would be wise for you to plan to cut down on some of the activities which keep you under a nervous tension, and take a good rest when you come back to

California. . . . After all, no human being can stand the strain that you must have been under the past few years."

Yet he seemed incapable of cutting back. In January 1945, Hope traveled East for several war-related benefits and to accept the Gold Medal of Achievement from Philadelphia's Poor Richard Club. He did more shows for Armed Forces Radio, including a celebrated musical parody of Dick Tracy for *Command Performance*, with an all-star cast that included Bing Crosby, Jimmy Durante, Judy Garland, and Dinah Shore (Hope played Flattop). He even became a newspaper columnist.

After seeing the columns that he had sent back from his 1944 Pacific tour for the Hearst syndicate, William Randolph Hearst personally urged Hope to continue them when he returned. Now Hope (meaning his writers, of course) was turning out a five-day-a-week column called It Says Here, with breezy observations on everything from buying tires and picking out a Christmas tree to visiting a veterans' hospital in Atlanta. More than seventy newspapers picked up the column, and Hope got 50 percent of the gross proceeds. At a time when several other Hollywood stars, such as Orson Welles and Gracie Allen, were experimenting with newspaper columns, Hope's was, as usual, the most successful, and it continued for several years after the war, until he walked away from it in the early 1950s.

On March 15, 1945, Hope returned to host the Academy Awards ceremony, after a year off. (Jack Benny had replaced him for the 1944 awards, explaining, "I'm here through the courtesy of Bob Hope's having a bad cold.") The event was no longer a banquet, but now took place at Grauman's Chinese Theatre, and for the first time it was broadcast nationally, by ABC radio. Hope, who took over the show after director John Cromwell handled some of the early awards, was in fine form throughout. When eight-year-old Margaret O'Brien was given a special Oscar, Hope lifted her up so she could reach the radio microphone. After holding her for a few seconds, he quipped, "Would you hurry and grow up, please?" When Paramount's production chief Buddy DeSylva came up to accept the Best Picture award for *Going My Way,* Hope got down on his hands and knees, pulled out a handkerchief, and started shining DeSylva's shoes — a reference to the star's well-publicized dispute with the studio. When his friend Bing Crosby won the Best Actor award for *Going My Way,* Hope cracked that Crosby winning an Oscar was "like Sam Goldwyn lecturing at Oxford." But Hope got an award too — his second honorary one, a life membership in the Academy of Motion Picture Arts and Sciences, presented to him by Walter Wanger. "I guess I get the consolation prize," Hope said.

The impasse with Paramount came to an end on May 6, 1945, when Hope signed a new seven-year contract that allowed him to set up his own production company. Hope Enterprises, the new company, was allowed to produce one film a year on its own and to partner with Paramount on the rest. A few stars — notably James Cagney and Bing Crosby — had already set up similar production companies. But Hope's very public victory in his battle with Paramount was considered a watershed. "When a star of Hope's stature announces he doesn't want to work for nothing, who can blame him?" wrote Florabel Muir in the *New York Daily Mirror*. "Which is why we are going to see more and more top stars going as independent as they can." And they did. Over the next decade more top actors such as Burt Lancaster and Kirk Douglas started their own production companies, and by the 1980s nearly every major star in Hollywood had a production deal modeled on the one that Hope set up in 1945.

Before returning to the Paramount lot, however, Hope had more war work to do. World events were moving swiftly. On April 12, President Roosevelt died suddenly from a brain hemorrhage in Warm Springs, Georgia. Hope gave up five minutes of airtime on his show the following Tuesday for an address to the nation by the new president, Harry Truman. On April 30, Adolf Hitler committed suicide in his Berlin bunker, and a week later Germany surrendered unconditionally, ending the war in Europe. Yet Hope pressed on. On May 12 he was in Washington to host a three-hour NBC radio show kicking off another war bond drive. Afterward, Hope got a tour of the White House from President Truman and did a show for the new first family. Hope finished his radio season on the road, then prepared for one last wartime tour — to entertain the American troops still in Europe, now an occupying force itching to come home.

One familiar companion was missing. Frances Langford had parlayed her wartime popularity into a summer radio show of her own (after a legal battle with Pepsodent, which claimed she was exclusively bound to Hope's show) and couldn't join him on the tour. In her place, Hope brought along a pinup-pretty, redheaded singer named Gale Robbins, along with Colonna, Romano, Patty Thomas, and Jack Pepper. With fewer restrictions on the size of his troupe, Hope also added two more singer-musicians, June Bruner and Ruth Denas, and even a writer, Roger Price.

They took the slow route to Europe this time, sailing aboard the *Queen Mary* — the ship Hope had last taken in 1939, when the first guns of World War II were sounding. They visited air bases in England and did a show for ten thousand GIs at London's Albert Hall, then went to Paris, which was crawling with American entertainers, from Mickey Rooney to Alfred Lunt and Lynn Fontanne. Hope entertained the 438th Troop Carrier Group in Amiens, near the site of the Normandy landing, then headed south to Arles and Marseille. He was emceeing an all-star benefit at a soccer park in Nice when he spotted Maurice Chevalier in the audience. The French star had drawn harsh criticism for cooperating with the German-backed Vichy government during the war. But when Hope called him to the stage, the former Paramount star got a warm reception and sang a medley of his songs. Chevalier never forgot Hope's kindness.

Hope and his troupe then flew to Bremen for a tour of occupied Germany — Hope sending back dispatches for his newspaper column at every stop. They performed for throngs of US troops in Potsdam, Heidelberg, and Berlin. Unlike on his previous tours, however, Hope found many of his GI audiences restless, distracted, eager to get home. At one stop, Hope referred to the American soldiers as "occupation troops" and was greeted with a howl of protest. "Well, that's what they told me," he responded weakly. "Everything was different from the last time we'd played the European theater," Hope wrote. "Last time the men who saw our shows were hopped up with the anticipation of impending combat. They wanted to like everything. This time they listened to us while packing."

The war ended in the middle of his tour. Hope was playing Ping-Pong in his billet in Nuremberg when the word came that Japan had surrendered. An announcement was made to the crowd gathered at Soldiers Field, formerly Nuremberg Stadium, for the GI Olympics. "Those boys in the stadium rose twenty-five feet in the air and yelled for twenty minutes," Hope wrote in his column. "What a thrill it was to hear those American cheers for victory in a place where Adolf used to hold yearly heiling practice." Hope's official itinerary had him continuing on the tour for two more weeks, but he wrapped up early, flying back to New York on August 21 and returning to California a week later. It's not clear why Hope cut his tour short. The end of the war may have taken the wind out of his sails, or he may simply have been worn-out. But his great World War II adventure was over.

It had been a transforming experience for Hope. He carried the memories, and the patriotic glow, of his World War II tours with him forever. He brought back souvenirs — a piece of Hitler's stationery from the Führer's Berlin bunker, a photo of General Patton peeing in the Rhine that Patton himself had given him. Hope had a photographic recall of places and dates, the officers he had met, and the units he had entertained. He got letters, thousands of them, from servicemen and their families, thanking him for being there. He answered nearly all of them, often with personal comments and jokes, establishing a permanent bond with the soldiers who had seen and been moved by him. "It was a pleasure to hear from you and as much of a surprise," one GI stationed in Iran wrote him in December 1944, after getting one of Hope's personal replies. "Can't we become pals and write? I've always enjoyed your screen and radio acting, but never once did I think that you would step down to write to a common US soldier."

Hope's wartime tours, critics would later point out, were also a brilliant career move. Hope cloaked himself in patriotism at a time when patriotism was in fashion, and it made him the most popular entertainer in America. He would try to re-create the experience again and again, in times that had changed without his realizing it. Yet no cynical view of his motives, nothing that happened later during the Vietnam years, could diminish his extraordinary achievement during World War II. He grabbed the moment, and the mission, as no other entertainer ever had.

Now all he had to do was learn how to live with peace.

CHAPTER 7
PEACE

"YOU KNOW, THIS PICTURE COULD END RIGHT HERE."

"Well, here I am starting my eighth year for the same sponsor," said Bob Hope, opening his new season for Pepsodent on September 11, 1945. "I reenlisted." The war was over, but as far as his radio show was concerned, Hope was still on a war footing. He broadcast his first show of the season from the Corpus Christi Naval Training Station and continued traveling to military bases throughout the fall — the Victorville Army Air Field, the Santa Ana Army Separation Center, the battleship *South Dakota* in San Francisco Bay. In the euphoria that followed the war's end, the military crowds were so raucous and responsive that even Hope was taken aback. "Is it that good, really?" he mewled after the outburst for one mild joke on his season opener.

He wasn't about to tamper with a formula that had made him the No. 1 show in radio. Colonna and Langford were back as regulars, and so was bandleader Skinnay Ennis, returning from the service. Far from downplaying the military humor, Hope seemed to revel in it — adding new segments with Mel Blanc as a stuttering Private Sad Sack, based on the popular wartime comic-book character. In place of the patriotic appeals urging listeners to write a serviceman or buy war bonds, now he closed the show with calls to unite in the postwar rebuilding effort. "Nobody would ever deny that we owe those men a great debt," he said, referring to the soldiers who had won the war. "But our first and biggest payment toward this debt, and the prescription for veterans' readjustment, ought to be American unity — unity of purpose among labor and management and government. Peace with a purpose."

Postwar "reconversion" was the watchword now. Factories were gearing up production of the consumer goods that Americans had been without for so long during the war. The men who fought were back home — starting families, becoming homeowners, buying cars and washing machines. Some thought Hope wasn't changing fast enough. Even before the war's end, NBC was getting complaints from some listeners about his continuing military orientation: "Why isn't Hope doing shows for us now?" Not until December 4, 1945, did Hope finally bring his show back into the studio, for the first time since early 1942. "This is Bob Broadcasting-from-NBC-Again-It's-Been-a-Long-Long-Time Hope," he opened. Then it was back to jokes about Bette Davis's wedding and W. C. Fields's drinking.

Yet Hope still missed the large, enthusiastic crowds that he got on the road. He started taking his show to college campuses — the University of Southern California, Pomona College, the University of Arizona — getting screams of laughter for his local references. ("This is a beautiful campus. That noise you hear is the wind in the acacia trees, and that silence you hear is the nightlife in Claremont.") In Arizona he joked about rodeos; in Reno about divorces; in San Francisco about the steep hills. Like so much of network radio — which was still dominated by the same prewar stars (Benny, Bergen, Fibber McGee and Molly) and well-worn gags, as if the war had never happened — Hope's return to peacetime sounded more like a throwback than a step forward.

In the fall, after his dispute with Paramount was resolved, Hope was back on the studio lot, shooting his first movie in two years, *Monsieur Beaucaire.* In the meantime, Paramount was able to tide over Hope fans with a film that had been sitting on the shelf for more than a year: *Road to Utopia,* the fourth in the *Road* series, and one of the best.

Directed by Hal Walker, who had been assistant director on the two previous *Road* pictures, and written by Norman Panama and Melvin Frank, it has a slicker production than any of the earlier films, some of the wildest gags, and the most brazen riffs of self-parody. Set in the frozen Yukon, instead of Africa or the South Seas, the film avoids the sometimes uncomfortable racial stereotyping of the other films. It also boasts the best of the Hope-Crosby buddy songs: Burke and Van Heusen's "Put It There, Pal," with the pair razzing each other's radio shows and movies as they glide through the snow on a dogsled.

The story, uniquely for the *Road* series, is told in flashback. The film opens with Hope and Lamour, in old-folks makeup, as an aged married couple being reunited after many years with a white-haired Crosby. As the three of them reminisce, we flash back to turn-of-the-century San Francisco, where Hope and Crosby are working in a carnival, scamming customers with a bogus psychic act called Ghost-O. When their con game is exposed, they're forced to flee, and Crosby suggests they hop a boat for Alaska, to join the gold rush. Hope, as usual, balks. Crosby, as usual, cons him into going — by pick-pocketing his boat ticket home. En route north, they stumble onto a map leading to a valuable gold mine, a gang of crooks determined to get it back, and Lamour.

The self-referential, fourth-wall-breaking gags come thick and fast. Humorist Robert Benchley appears on-screen at the outset to

375

introduce the film, then pops up throughout to make wry comments on the action. Hope and Crosby step out of character repeatedly, poking fun at the film and their roles in it. In one scene they're shoveling coal in a ship's engine room. A man dressed in top hat and tails casually passes through and asks for a light. "You in this picture?" asks Crosby. "No," the fellow says, "taking a shortcut to Stage Ten." Lamour, trying to wheedle the map out of Hope, gives him a big smooch; after catching his breath, Hope turns to the camera and says, "As far as I'm concerned, this picture's over right now." While riding through the snow on a dogsled, Hope sees a mountain in the distance. "Get a load of that bread and butter," he says. "Bread and butter? That's a mountain," Crosby replies. "May be a mountain to you, but it's bread and butter to me," says Hope, as the peak is encircled by lights, re-creating the Paramount logo. There is a talking fish, and a grizzly bear that invades the boys' tent looking for its mate, then trudges off silently, before turning to the camera: "A fine thing. A fish they let talk. Me they won't give one stinking line."

It is subversive nonsense, satirizing the artifice of filmmaking itself. Yet it doesn't destroy the integrity of the comic relationship at the core of the film. Hope is more put-upon and overheated than ever, with bug-eyed double takes, hat-grabbing panic reactions, and wolflike growls in the presence of sexy gals. He gives every wisecrack just the right pitch and weight. "You wouldn't do this to me if I was in shape!" he cries as he's being carted off by the ship's officers — the perfect expression of his hapless bluster. In one scene, the boys swagger into a Klondike saloon, and Crosby tells Hope to act tough, so they can blend in with the crowd. At the bar the chief villain asks what they want to drink. "A couple fingers of rotgut," says Crosby gruffly. "I'll have a lemonade," Hope responds brightly. A quick poke from Crosby and Hope snarls, "In a dirty glass!" Panama and Frank get credit for the line, but Hope's perfect delivery, the split-second turn from milquetoast to roughneck, is what makes it perhaps the most famous joke in all the *Road* pictures.

Road to Utopia ends with a clever twist on the perennial Crosby-Hope romantic rivalry. In the climactic scene, as the villains are closing in on the boys in the arctic wilderness, the ice pack beneath them suddenly breaks and splits apart, and Crosby and Hope are separated — Hope on one side with Lamour, Crosby on the other, with the bad guys. Here the flashback ends, and Crosby, back in present time, recounts how he escaped, while Hope and Lamour bring him up-to-date on their life together since — which now includes a son. They call the boy downstairs to say hello. It is Crosby. As Old Bing fidgets uncomfortably, Old Bob turns to the camera and confides, in the film's capper, "We adopted him."

When Paramount production chief Buddy DeSylva proposed the ending, to replace one that Panama and Frank had written, Hope said it would never get past the censors. But it did. And *Road to Utopia* went on to gross $5 million at the box office, the most ever for a *Road* picture, or for any Hope movie to date.

With the war over, and his largely volunteer work for the USO completed, Hope focused once again on his finances. In January 1945 he signed a new contract with Pepsodent that raised his salary to $18,000 a week, guaranteeing him $7.5 million over ten years — the largest contract for radio talent ever negotiated to that point. His 1946 income was projected to reach $1.25 million. But he was pouring much of it into real estate and other investments, and in the spring of 1946 he found himself cash poor, unable to pay the $62,000 he owed in income tax.

For a quick payday, Hope got his agent Louis Shurr to book him on a personal-appearance tour in June. It was a fast-paced trip — twenty-nine cities in thirty days — in which Hope played auditoriums, stadiums, and state fairgrounds from Seattle to Topeka.

His traveling company included sexy Latin singer Olga San Juan, his wartime tour buddy Jack Pepper, another former vaudevillian and old Cleveland pal named Eddie Rio, Skinnay Ennis and his band, and a bevy of Paramount starlets — more than forty entertainers in all.

They were ferried from city to city on two DC-3s, the first domestic vaudeville tour to travel by plane rather than train. The pace was frenetic. Hope would typically arrive in town around noon, play a charity golf match in the afternoon, have a massage before dinner, put on a three-hour show in the evening, and often end the night at an after-show party thrown by a friend or local businessman. A phalanx of five Hope staffers, among them his brother Jack, handled arrangements and publicity for the tour at every stop. "I can't even remember what city I'm in," Jack said in an interview with the *St. Louis Globe-Democrat.* "I don't even know where I'm going next. Tonight, for example, I'll call Bob and tell him I'm through in St. Louis and ask where he wants me to go next. Your idea is as good as mine."

The tour was a huge success, grossing $500,000 in ticket sales (earning Hope $200,000 after expenses). Nearly as much as his World War II tours, his 1946 domestic tour was a defining event in Hope's career. It rekindled his love of vaudeville-style road trips, even when the audiences weren't raucous servicemen, and showed that they could be big moneymakers. It enabled him to get up close and personal with his fans — the show-business equivalent of retail politics, which Hope mastered better than anyone else in Hollywood. He would continue doing it for as long as he could still walk out on a stage. And even longer.

Hope, meanwhile, was busy getting his financial house in order. He split his show-business endeavors into three corporate entities: one, Hope Enterprises (with twenty-five stockholders, among them Bing Crosby), for his movies and personal appearances; another for his books (a sequel to his wartime best-seller, *I Never Left Home,* was in the works, entitled *So This Is Peace*); and a third for records (Capitol was planning an album of highlights from his World War II broadcasts). His business arrangement drew widespread attention — "Hope Inc.," read the headline in *Time.* Some cynicism began to creep into his press coverage. "Wherever he goes, the whole board of directors ambles right along with him," wrote Robert Welch, interviewing Hope for the *Seattle Post-Intelligencer* in July 1946. "Even when he goes to the gentlemen's retiring room he looks like a platoon. He is constantly surrounded with busy, worried and preoccupied people, with briefcases, papers and knitted brows."

Yet Hope was a hands-on manager of his

business affairs. Board meetings for Hope Enterprises would be held in his dressing room during the shooting of *Monsieur Beaucaire.* "We made him remove the wig because it didn't look dignified," said his attorney, Martin Gang. Whenever Hope was considering whether to buy a piece of land, he would always take a drive and walk the property himself. He was a micromanager of everything from his movie publicity campaigns to the placement of his newspaper column, It Says Here. The columns "have been doing pretty well here in Los Angeles lately, keeping it on page five," Hope wrote Ward Greene, his contact at King Features, in 1946. "If they would give me one spot and keep it there, I do think we could make it a habit." After Hearst renewed Hope's contract in October 1946, Greene wrote back, "Mr. Hearst is very pleased. He has instructed me to see that the papers carry your column in the news section and that the papers give it uniform position."

Hope could indulge in some personal whims as well. In June 1946 he joined a syndicate headed by Bill Veeck and acquired a one-sixth share of the Cleveland Indians, Hope's hometown baseball team, for around $1.75 million. "I used to climb over the fence at League Park to see a ball game. I'd like to come through the front gate for a change," Hope said. "Cleveland has been my home, I have other property interests there, and aside from my share as an investment, this is a matter of sentiment with me." Investing in the Indians not only satisfied his hometown pride and his interest in sports, it provided years of good comedy material — especially when Crosby, around the same time, became part owner of the Pittsburgh Pirates.

Hope took little active role in running the Indians. But he brought some Hollywood glamour to a franchise run by the most celebrated baseball promoter of his era. Veeck put Indians games on the radio for the first time; signed Larry Doby as the first black player in the American League; and famously (a few years later, when he owned the St. Louis Browns) hired a midget to pinch-hit as a publicity stunt. Under his guidance, the Indians rose from a lowly sixth place in 1946, when Hope acquired his share in the team, to the American League pennant in 1948. Hope came to Cleveland for the World Series, filling a box with family and friends as he watched the Indians beat the Boston Braves 4 games to 2.

Back home in Toluca Lake, the Hope family, like millions of others in America, were settling into a new postwar routine. First came expansion. Dolores had been eager for years to adopt another child, but the war had intervened. Finally, in the fall of 1946, she and Bob went back to the Cradle in Evanston to pick up a new two-month-old baby girl. Once there, they were told that a baby boy had also become available. They decided to take both — naming the girl Honorah (Nora, for short) and the boy William Kelly (known as Kelly). Dolores had requested a baby of either Italian or Irish heritage; she got one of each.

Linda and Tony were grade-schoolers by now, a picture-perfect, blond-and-brunet matched set of Hollywood children, trotted out for photo ops when their father came back from overseas, dressed up in their best clothes for an occasional dinner at the Brown Derby, often accompanied by Louis Shurr, Bob's man-about-town agent. Yet they had a more grounded, less pampered upbringing than many Hollywood children. They lived not in Hollywood or ritzy Beverly Hills but "over the hill," in the less pretentious San Fernando Valley. Their Toluca Lake circle included a few show-business families (Jerry and Flo Colonna and their son Robert; John Wayne's ex-wife Josie and their kids), but they largely avoided the catered birthday parties and junior social whirl that marked the childhood of so many Hollywood youngsters. "We didn't really do the Hollywood-celebrity-kid thing," said Linda Hope. "I don't know if it was something my parents decided between them, that they weren't going to have us be part of the Hollywood scene. But I think they wanted us to grow up normal."

The family dynamic was, in many respects, not unlike that of many other postwar families. Bob was the busy working father, traveling for his job, gone much of the time, emotionally detached when he was there. ("Hello, Bob Hope," Tony once called out when his father walked in to meet them in a restaurant.) Dolores took on most of the child-rearing and household-management duties. The children had governesses, who got them dressed for school and ready for dinner. But Dolores was the disciplinarian, enforcing strict manners and codes of conduct, strongly influenced by her Catholic faith.

"She wasn't easy," said Linda. "She knew what was right, and she had a very strict moral code and sense of honor and all of that." "Dolores had a voice," recalled Rory Burke, songwriter Johnny Burke's daughter, who regarded Dolores as a surrogate mother after her parents' divorce. "She was very assertive. She didn't like certain things — things that were shades of gray she saw in black and white. At the table you had to have your manners. You didn't reach. You wait for the food to be served to you. But she was very warm, funny. She had a batty side to her."

"She was a mother of the period," said Robert Colonna, another close friend of the family. "Very strict. We had to know how to behave, when to keep our mouths shut. A lot had to do with show business and the strictures of public life. And a lot had to do with her Catholicism." (Her strict Catholic values didn't prevent an embarrassing run-in with the law in the spring of 1946, when Dolores held an outdoor carnival on their lawn in Toluca Lake as a fund-raiser for some Carmelite nuns. The police were alerted that games of chance were being played, and the carnival was raided for gambling.)

With Dolores as the tough cop, Bob could play the childish cutup. "My mother would say, you know, sit up straight, and my dad would be at the end of the table hunched over or in some wacky pose, so it was kind of counterproductive," said Linda. He would entertain the kids by playing an imaginary friend, using the drapes as a curtain and adopting a falsetto voice: "Hello, Mr. Hope, this is Bessie. Can Tony and Linda come out to play?" Yet he was not a father to depend on for advice or heart-to-heart talks. "He was not somebody you'd sit and tell your troubles to," Linda said. "Dad didn't deal well with illness and other bad things. Not that he wasn't caring. He'd just say, 'You'll work it out.' "

The Toluca Lake house was the center of a large and close extended family. Dolores's younger sister, Mildred, lived just a few blocks away with her husband and two sons, and she was around often. The two sisters were a study in contrasts: Dolores was tall, attractive, with an almost regal bearing; Mildred was more plain-looking, feisty, outspoken. "Dolores was gracious, more formal," said Tom Malatesta, the younger of Mildred's two sons. "Mother was a pistol. She liked attention. She'd speak her mind." Mildred and Dolores's mother, Theresa, who came out from New York in the late forties and moved in with Bob and Dolores, was another formidable presence in the household. She was tough and opinionated, a streetwise Irish Catholic with a sense of humor — the kids called her "Mrs. Malaprop," for her frequent verbal miscues. Bob got along well enough with her, though having a mother-in-law in the house may have been a source of some sensitivity. Hope was one comedian who *never* did mother-in-law jokes.

Bob was relatively close with his own brothers as well, giving most of them jobs or helping out financially at one time or another. Jack was on Bob's payroll full-time. George, his youngest brother and former vaudeville stooge, worked for him from time to time as a writer and producer. Ivor, back in Cleveland, had a metal-products business that Bob backed financially. Younger brother Sid, who lived on a farm in northwest Ohio, would occasionally ask Bob for loans for various small-business ventures. When Sid died in 1946, of cancer at the age of just forty-one, Bob helped support his wife and children, who moved to Mount Gilead, Ohio, where they managed a motel and restaurant owned by Bob and his brother Fred. Fred, who ran United Provision Company, a successful meat-supply business with offices in both Cleveland and Columbus, was the one Hope brother who never needed Bob's financial help.

Bob's most complicated sibling relationship was with Jim, his cantankerous older brother, who had moved to Los Angeles in the 1930s, hoping to break into show business. Though he got some vaudeville and movie work (including a small role in a 1943 Monogram cheapie called *Spotlight Revue*), Jim sounded a bit desperate in 1946 when he wrote a letter asking for Bob's help in finding a job. "I've worn out four agents, patiently trying to get me picture work," Jim wrote. "I've tried vaudeville, so far very little success. . . . Naturally I would like something in the studios or in Hollywood, [but] I don't care what it is, so long as it's an honest living for honest effort."

The two brothers were drawn into an embarrassing legal dispute in 1942, when Jim's first wife, Marie, who had done secretarial work for Bob, claimed she had been underpaid and sued for $2,900 in back wages. (Bob countersued for $1,425, which he claimed Marie owed him as repayment for a loan. The suit was settled out of court.) And the brothers had an awkward near-encounter in the spring of 1946, when Jim and his second wife, Wyn, were doing a small-time vaudeville act in Spokane, Washington. During his 1946 tour, Bob was booked in Spokane at the same time, and he was surprised to learn from a reporter that Jim was doing a show in town too, billing himself as Bob Hope's brother. Apparently miffed that Jim might be trying to cash in on the family connection, Bob turned down the paper's request for a photo of the two together and left town without speaking to his brother.

Bob later regretted the snub. "It was a silly thing, silly and thoughtless," he told his biographer William Robert Faith. "As I look back, I remember thinking something secret was going on. But I was wrong." Bob eventually came to Jim's aid, giving him a job managing the White Oak Ranch, one of the large tracts of land that Hope acquired years later in the Santa Monica Mountains.

Paramount released *Monsieur Beaucaire,* the first film Hope had made since the end of the war, in September 1946. It was an auspicious return for him — a first-rate production, with a good supporting cast, a relatively sustained and coherent story, and plenty of opportunity for Hope to demonstrate his growing assurance as a comic actor. It remains one of his most celebrated films and inaugurated a rich, new postwar phase in his movie career.

Loosely adapted from a Booth Tarkington novel and play set in eighteenth-century France (filmed once before, in 1924, as a swashbuckler with Rudolph Valentino), the film had a bumpy road to the screen. Producer Paul Jones didn't like the original script by Panama and Frank and assigned a new writer to it. After Panama and Frank complained to the Writers Guild, the studio (backed by Hope) forced Jones to revert to their original script. Then, when the finished film, directed by comedy vet George Marshall, got a tepid reception at a test screening, the studio brought in Frank Tashlin, a director of Bugs Bunny cartoons at Warner Bros., to punch it up with more physical gags. The result was a Hope romp that had more formal integrity than most of his films — no talking animals, no asides to the camera — and plenty of good laughs too.

Hope plays a barber in the French court of King Louis XV who is sentenced to the guillotine for insulting the king. A duke helps him escape to Spain, where the two trade identities, pursue their separate romantic liaisons (Hope is after a court chambermaid played by Joan Caulfield, who has, conveniently, also been banished to Spain), and get entangled in a plot by a devious Spanish general (Joseph Schildkraut) to start a war between the two countries. The powdered wigs and poofy shirts suit Hope's comedy well, emphasizing the classic roots of his farcical character: the poseur, always playing a role (swordsman, lover, hero, even the king) to hide the timid "real" self underneath. Even the most predictable gags seem somehow ennobled — the inevitable comic turnabout, for example, when his girlfriend suggests that they elude the bad guys by splitting up:

> "We'll never make it together. You go on alone."
> "What, and leave you behind? Never!"
> "But you must!"
> "I said never!"
> "They'll cut you to pieces!"
> *(Beat. Gulp. Dropping the pose.)* "I'll send for you."

The sheer brilliance of Hope's voice as a comic instrument is often overlooked: that sharp, crystal-clear tenor, slicing through the confusion even when he's swallowing his words, gasping in panic, or fleeing up a staircase. Hope's physical comedy has the same kind of precision and clarity: powdering the king's wig, for example, and blubbering his apologies as he powders the king instead. Or in the climactic sword fight (one of Tashlin's additions), as he wields nearly every instrument in the court orchestra to pummel the villain: wedging the fellow's head between the strings of a harp, slamming a piano lid on his hand, and conking him on the head with a bull fiddle that has attached itself to Hope's back.

For latter-day fans such as Woody Allen, *Monsieur Beaucaire* was a high point of Hope's comic acting (and an obvious model for the nervous, cowardly character Allen played in such early films as *Bananas* and *Sleeper*). "He was a wonderful comic actor," said Allen. "He's totally committed to his character: he's scared when he's supposed to be scared, leching when he's supposed to be leching, playing someone more grand than he is. He was not a sufferer, like Chaplin, or even as dimensional as someone like Groucho Marx, who suggested a kind of intellect. Hope was just a superficial, smiling guy tossing off one-liners. But he was amazingly good at it." Even his best films were never more than competent vehicles for him, and Hope was rare among top Hollywood stars in that he never worked for a major director. But none of his comedy contemporaries — Groucho Marx or Jack Benny or Red Skelton — could match his command of both verbal and physical comedy, or his ability to create recognizable, sympathetic, and very human characters in essentially farcical movies.

"*Monsieur Beaucaire,* as now enacted by no less a clown than Bob Hope, is an item that bears a fair comparison with the best of screen travesties," wrote Bosley Crowther in the *New York Times.* "Charlie Chaplin as Don Jose in *Carmen* or Will Rogers as *A Connecticut Yankee in King Arthur's Court* have only the advantage of fond memory over Mr. Hope's barber in Madrid." "That rumbling yesterday," wrote John L. Scott in the *Los Angeles Times,* "wasn't thunder or an explosion; it was laughter shaking the walls of Paramount Downtown and Hollywood theaters, where Bob Hope's newest comedy *Monsieur Beaucaire* began runs which will prove extensive and profitable." The film earned a solid $3 million at the box office, proving that Hope's wartime break from Paramount had done little to dampen his popularity.

His next film, *My Favorite Brunette,* was another milestone: the first picture produced by Hope's own company, under the deal he had worked out with Paramount in 1945. With a financial interest in the film, Hope stuck to business on the set. "He used to say that he carried two watches with him, one set to Paramount time and the other to his own," said Dorothy Lamour, his costar. "He kept comparing them in order to discover how much time he'd be wasting if he were working for Paramount. It was a joke, but we didn't mess around as much as usual." His attentiveness paid off: Hope brought the film in for $1.69 million — $72,000 *under* budget.

Hope also made sure the first movie from his own production company got a full-court press of publicity. Paramount orchestrated a promotion in which fourteen brunette beauty queens were selected from around the country, brought out to Los Angeles by train, and feted with parties and radio appearances. Pepsodent ran a contest on Hope's radio show asking listeners to complete a jingle beginning "My favorite brunette is . . ." and giving away four Chevrolets every week to the winners. For the film's Hollywood opening, Hope hosted an all-star show to benefit the Damon Runyon Memorial Cancer Fund, broadcast nationwide on ABC and around the world over Armed Forces Radio.

The title had been floating around for a couple of years — first attached to the film with Paulette Goddard that had been scrubbed when Hope went on strike, then for a movie with Hope and Signe Hasso, which eventually became *Where There's Life,* released later that year. Directed by Elliott Nugent from a script by Edmund Beloin and Jack Rose, *My Favorite Brunette* was obviously meant as a companion piece to Hope's 1942 hit *My Favorite Blonde.* But the two films are quite different: the first a breezy spy caper, the second a more heavy-handed parody of private-eye films.

The movie starts, a little jarringly, with Hope on death row, narrating the story in flashback. He plays Ronnie Jackson (one of the least inspired of Hope's character names), a baby photographer who longs to be a private eye. He gets his chance when the gumshoe next door (Alan Ladd in an unbilled cameo) goes on vacation. "It only took brains, courage, and a gun," Hope says in the tough-guy voice-over. "And I had the gun." Lamour is the inevitable mystery woman who shows up in the office and lures him into a danger-ous spy plot. Peter Lorre plays a knife-throwing villain, and Lon Chaney Jr. takes a break from horror films to play the bad guys' slow-witted muscleman. The movie has some funny sequences, such as a scene in which Hope, the bumbling investigator, searches for clues in an empty house and keeps overlook-ing the one that Lorre keeps surreptitiously shoving in front of his face. And Crosby gets another cameo at the end — playing the prison executioner who is thwarted when Hope gets a last-minute pardon. "Boy, he'll take any kind of part," quips Hope.

But the noirish parody isn't Hope's strong suit, and the film isn't as fleet and fun as some of his others of the period. Still, it pleased his fans ("The best picture Monsieur Robin le Hope has ever made in his happy and prosperous life," said Louella Parsons) and was another hit at the box office. And for the first time, Hope was getting a piece of the action.

Hope stuck close to home in early 1947, shooting *Road to Rio,* the fifth in the series, in January and February and then spending six weeks with the family in Palm Springs, where he now owned a small house on Buena Vista Drive — the first of three homes Hope would acquire in the desert community, which was growing in popularity as a winter retreat for Hollywood's rich and famous. There was talk of Hope's returning to Broadway in a new Irving Berlin musical, or making a trip to Europe and North Africa in the summer, retracing his first World War II tour. But neither materialized. Instead, in June, Bob took Dolores and the two older kids on a vacation to South America. They visited Rio de Janeiro, Buenos Aires, and a half dozen other capitals; in Montevideo they stayed at the palatial estate of Alberto Cernadas, the most recent husband of Hope's former radio foil Patricia "Honey Chile" Wilder. On the boat ride back to New York, Hope got so sunburned (aggravating it with a golf game when he got back) that he had to delay the start of his next film — *The Pale-*

face, ironically enough.

On radio, meanwhile, Hope was hitting a rough patch. First came more criticism from religious groups over his risqué material. Jimmie Fidler, one of the many entertainment columnists with whom Hope was friendly, gave Hope an early warning of trouble in November 1946, passing along a letter from a Catholic high school student, who said her teacher had requested the class "not to listen to his program because it is so unclean." Fidler told Hope, "It is one of many letters I have received, voicing the same charge. If such a thing as this should gather momentum, Bob, it could be disastrous." In a poll of twenty thousand Catholic and Protestant college students in late 1947, Hope was branded the most tasteless comedian on the air.

The bad publicity was upsetting to Hope — and, he felt, unfair. Hope's material was often suggestive, but rarely over the line. On the few occasions when he let himself go, the censors were usually there to protect him. In April 1947 he hosted an hour-long radio special for Walgreens drugstores, with Groucho Marx among the guests. The show was running long, and by the time Groucho was introduced, a half hour late, he was annoyed. "Why, Groucho Marx! What are you doing way out here in the Sahara Desert?" Hope asked, following the script. "Desert, hell! I've been standing in a drafty corridor for forty-five minutes," Groucho ad-libbed. Hope cracked up, and what followed was an innuendo-laden free-for-all between the two comics, little of which could be used on the air. (John Guedel, producer of the radio show *People Are Funny,* who was in the studio, was so impressed with Groucho's ad-libbing that he created a game show for him, *You Bet Your Life,* which revived Groucho's career.)

Hope's biggest run-in with NBC censors, however, had nothing to do with racy material, only corporate sensitivities. On Fred Allen's show of April 20, 1947, NBC censored about thirty seconds in which Allen made some wisecracks about an (unnamed) NBC programming vice president. The incident was widely reported, and Hope made a joke about it on his own show two nights later. Las Vegas was a town "where you can get tanned and faded [at the craps tables] at the same time," Hope cracked. Then he added, "Of course, Fred Allen can get faded [censored] anytime." The network bleeped out Hope's line.

The network's hypersensitivity (Red Skelton was also censored on the same night for making a wisecrack about the Allen incident) prompted derisive criticism in the press. NBC president Niles Trammell eventually issued a conciliatory statement, calling the censoring of Allen's original lines a mistake. But Hope got into more hot water a few weeks later, in a segment with guest star Frank Sinatra. In saying his good-nights, Hope told Sinatra, "I'll be seeing you tomorrow night on your show." The line got bleeped because Sinatra's show was on CBS, and NBC had a ban on plugs for the rival network. (NBC didn't apologize for that one, reiterating its policy against cross-network plugs.)

Hope's battles with the network got plenty of publicity, but didn't do much to perk up a radio show that was beginning to sound a little tired. In the fall of 1946 Hope tried freshening up the old format with a new bandleader (Latin nightclub star Desi Arnaz, Lucille Ball's husband, who replaced Skinnay Ennis); a new sidekick, Vera Vague (another shrill, man-chasing spinster character, played by Barbara Jo Allen); and a few new comedy twists, such as a recurring bit in which Hope has conversations with his "conscience." (It didn't last long.) In a more important symbolic break with the wartime years, Hope said good-bye to the singer who had been identified with him for five years, Frances Langford, replacing her with a series of guest vocalists.

But the following season even that mildly innovative spirit seemed to be gone. Arnaz was replaced by Les Brown and his more traditional big band, and the show's formula was sounding increasingly stale and predictable: the weekly back-and-forth jousts with "Professor" Colonna; the man-chasing gags from Vera Vague; even the "Poor Miriam" musical jingles for Irium, the new whitening ingredient in Pepsodent — sung by a group called the Starlighters, which included a young Andy Williams.

The critics were starting to grouse. "You could enjoy it if you had not heard it the first, second, third, fourth, fifth, sixth, seventh, and eighth times," wrote the *New York Times'* Jack Gould, reviewing the premiere of Hope's ninth season, in September 1946. A year later, *Variety* was even more cutting. "Here's the epitome of radio's 'sad saga of sameness,' " began its review of Hope's season opener in 1947:

Apparently it's just too much to expect that Hope would veer an inch from his time-tested routine. His answer, it goes without saying, is: Why get out of the rut when there's pay dirt in it? And top pay dirt at that! By Hooper's count, too, Hope seems to be justified. His routine is apparently one of the things we fought the war for, like Ma's apple pie. Question simply is: Who's going to outlive the other: Hope or the listening public?

Hope's ratings were still strong (though no longer consistently No. 1), but he was encountering something he hadn't since *The Pepsodent Show* first went on the air back in 1938: a growing sense that Hope was old hat.

Hope's relations with his sponsor were also deteriorating. Pepsodent chief Charles Luckman — now the president of Lever Brothers, the British conglomerate that had acquired the toothpaste company — was Hope's original radio patron and considered himself a fan and a friend. But he and Hope were increasingly at odds — over Hope's demands for more money ("I can tell the seasons of the year and the Crossley ratings just by the tone of Hope's voice when he phones me for a raise," Luckman said), his resistance to making changes in the show after the war, and more recently his constant traveling. Hope liked taking the show on the road, where he always got a great reception from the live audiences. But each location show cost about $25,000 more than a studio show, and Luckman thought it was getting too expensive.

The travel issue came to a head in November 1947, when Hope was invited to attend the royal wedding of Princess Elizabeth in London and to headline a gala for the royal family at the Odeon Theater. Luckman objected to the trip since it would take Hope away from the studio for three weeks. But Hope refused to cancel, promising to do his radio shows from London while he was away.

Luckman's fears were realized when the transatlantic crossing aboard the *Queen Mary* was delayed, and Hope had to miss the first week's broadcast — the first time in ten years that Hope was a no-show on his own radio program. (Eddie Cantor replaced him, joined by an array of NBC guest stars, including Red Skelton, Fibber McGee and Molly, and Amos and Andy.)

The London trip may have been a flash point for Pepsodent, but it was a triumph for Hope. He brought along Dolores, as well as three writers (among them Fred Williams, an alcoholic rapscallion who keeled over drunk in front of the royal family in the lobby of the Odeon Theater), and the Odeon show was a hit with the royal audience. Queen Elizabeth reportedly "laughed so hard at some of Bob's cracking that she nearly split her seams." After the show, Hope presented the royal family with a book of autographed photos of Hollywood stars.

As Hope was leafing through the book, King George piped up, "Look at him. He's hurrying to get to his own picture."

"Why not?" Hope replied. "It's the prettiest."

"Is Bing's autograph there too?"

"Yes, but he doesn't write. He just made three *X*s."

The ad-lib session between Hope and King George made headlines around the world.

While he was in London, Hope met with US Secretary of State George C. Marshall, who asked if Hope would make an impromptu trip to West Germany, to do some shows for US occupation forces there. Dolores objected that he was too exhausted, but Hope jumped at the chance to entertain his favorite audiences once again. He did several shows in Frankfurt and Bremerhaven for the troops, before his voice gave out and he had to cancel the last couple of appearances. He flew back to London, where he broadcast one more radio show before taking a flight back to New York. Dolores returned separately by ship.

Hope was thrilled to be called into service by his country once again. Back in Los Angeles, he held a press conference to talk up his trip and urge more US aid to Europe. "The most important thing for us in America today is to maintain our friendship with the people of Europe," he told reporters. "We have to support the Marshall Plan. This is a wonderful Shangri-la we're living in over here, and we should share it with the Europeans before other forces move in and make them our enemies."

Hope's political views were well in the mainstream internationalist spirit of the times. Though always a political conservative, Hope liked and admired President Truman — joking often about his fights with Congress, his Missouri roots, and his daughter Margaret's musical ambitions. (The jokes about Margaret drew angry mail from some listeners, who thought Hope was disrespectful.) He was a strong anticommunist, but again hardly outside the mainstream in those early Cold War years, when fears of the Soviet threat were at a peak. "The Russians say they can't do anything until they get international cooperation," went a typical Hope joke. "International cooperation — that's 'Show us how to make the atom bomb and we'll show you where New York City used to be.' "

In the fall of 1947, when Congress was probing alleged Communist infiltration in Hollywood (an investigation that resulted in the blacklisting of the so-called Hollywood Ten), Hope took his show to Claremore, Oklahoma, the birthplace of Will Rogers. In paying tribute to the beloved political humorist, Hope did little to disguise his anti-Red sentiments: "The only sad thing about coming to Claremore," he said, "is that Will Rogers isn't here to say a few things about our troubled times with the tolerance and humor that made him an all-time great. 'I see by the papers,' he might have said, 'they've uncovered a few Reds out in Hollywood. Personally I've never preferred my politics in Technicolor, and when boy meets girl in the movies, I like to have them riding on the Freedom Train.' "

Hope was growing bolder in speaking out — cloaking himself in the unabashed patriotism of the war years, even as the world was growing more complicated. He was still groping for a role for himself in the postwar years, and fighting a perception that he and his radio show had not changed with the times.

In one area, however, Hope's audience was happy to see how little things had changed. Paramount had initially vowed that *Road to Utopia,* filmed in 1944 and released in early 1946, would be the last of the *Road* pictures. The movies were getting too expensive, and working around Hope's and Crosby's schedules too difficult. But the two stars wanted to continue, and they worked out a three-way coproduction deal with Paramount to film a fifth in the series, *Road to Rio.* Released at the end of 1947, it was another first-rate comedy, and one of the most successful of the whole series.

With a financial stake in the film, Hope and Crosby were unusually businesslike on the set: no more extended lunch breaks or afternoons playing hooky on the golf course. "Bing and I hardly left the set, except to go to the men's room," said Hope. "At precisely sixty minutes after lunch was called, Bing would say, 'All right, let's get moving. What are we waiting for?' " Yet the film, directed by Norman Z. McLeod (whose comedy credits included two early Marx Brothers films and

W. C. Fields's masterpiece *It's a Gift*), was a relatively elaborate production, with a large supporting cast that included the Andrews Sisters (who sing "You Don't Have to Know the Language") and the Wiere Brothers, doing a funny turn as a Brazilian street band impersonating American jazz musicians. Hope even threw in a part for his radio pal Colonna, who leads a cavalry charge that comes up empty in the film's last reel.

The boys, once again, are carnival entertainers, with Hope again conned by Crosby into performing a daredevil stunt, this time riding a bicycle across a high wire. ("You know, this picture could end right here," he quips while hanging on for his life.) Bing and Bob stow away on a ship to Rio and meet Lamour, who shows a mysterious split personality: flirting with them seductively one minute and rejecting them coldly the next. Turns out she's been hypnotized by her evil aunt (Gale Sondergaard) so that she will go through with an arranged marriage. "I found myself saying things I didn't know why I was saying them," she says, emerging from one of her hypnotic trances. Hope: "Why don't you just run for Congress and leave us alone."

Hope is fast, funny, and fully engaged, nailing every exasperated reaction and outshining Crosby almost every step of the way. (In their song-and-dance routines, Hope shows off some still agile hoofing, while Crosby merely goes through the motions.) The film is the most polished and least manic of the *Road* pictures, with more care taken in setting up the story and the running gags. If *Road to Utopia* was Hope and Crosby's *Duck Soup* — their surreal high point — *Road to Rio* is their *Night at the Opera,* the *Road* film for everyone. It took in $4.5 million at the box office — the top-grossing movie for all of 1947.

The only sour note involved Lamour, who was upset when she found out the three-way production deal did not include her. "They could have considered a four-way split, but no one ever asked me," she wrote in her memoir. "My feelings were hurt. (And, as it would prove later, so would my pocket-book.)" It confirmed her growing feeling that she was an unappreciated third wheel on the *Road* picture express, and she nursed the resentment for the rest of her life.

Her relations with Hope remained friendly, if hardly close. (She and her husband, Bill Howard, lived nearby in Toluca Lake — "two blocks from his garbage entrance," she liked to say.) But Crosby was openly disdainful of her, barely acknowledging her when they met at public events. "Crosby's attitude toward Dorothy Lamour was deplorable," said Frank Liberman, Hope's longtime publicist. "He didn't even try to hide his feelings about her in public. Bing felt that he and Hope were the mainstays of the *Road* pictures and that Dorothy was just 'a dumb, lucky broad.' "

Yet Crosby was aloof with a lot of people, and even Hope could feel dissed by him. On November 2, 1947, the Friars Club threw an all-star roast for Hope, with Jack Benny, George Burns, Eddie Cantor, Al Jolson, and George Jessel among the stars on the dais. Crosby was supposed to be there too, but he didn't show up. When reporters pressed him about it later, Crosby defended himself coolly: "My friendship with Bob doesn't depend on appearing at testimonials for him." Some said that Hope was hurt by the no-show, and he may well have been. Though he always had words of affection for Crosby in public, in private he was less charitable. Many years later, shortly after Crosby died, Hope was sitting in an NBC editing room, looking over film clips for a TV special he was preparing on their screen work together. Associate producer Marcia Lewis was startled when Hope turned to her and made a blunt admission:

"You know, I never liked Bing. He was a son of a bitch." In all their years of working together, Hope said, "He never had Dolores and me to dinner."

The year 1948 marked a turning point for Hope on several career fronts. In the fall, he finally made a major overhaul of his radio show, the first since it went on the air in 1938. He starred in just one feature film during the calendar year, but it was an important one: *The Paleface,* his biggest box-office hit to date and a film that signaled a new direction for him on-screen, both for good and ill. And at the end of the year he was called on to entertain US troops overseas during an international crisis, launching a Christmas tradition that would define the rest of his career.

On his way back from London in November 1947, Hope met with Pepsodent's Luckman, and the two at least temporarily patched up their differences. Hope agreed to cut back on the show's traveling and to make major changes for the following season. He also promised to steer clear of any more controversy over his material. "Bob is very much worried about the bad press he has been getting of late, and means to do everything he can to keep himself above criticism from here on in," Hugh Davis, an executive at Pepsodent's ad agency, Foote, Cone & Belding (the former Lord & Thomas), wrote in a memo. The critics' gripes about the show were finally starting to be reflected in the ratings, which had fallen from first place to fifth for the 1947–48 season. Lever Brothers was reportedly close to dropping Hope altogether (though other sponsors, among them Campbell's soup, were ready to snap him up). In the end, Lever decided to stick with Hope for another season, but switched products on him. Instead of Pepsodent, the brand he had been associated with for a decade, Hope would in the fall be pitching Swan soap, which Lever was promoting hard in an effort to catch the market leader, Ivory.

Hope was hardly the only radio personality feeling pressure in 1948, the breakthrough year for television. The new medium, whose development had been put on hold during World War II, was making rapid progress in the first years after the war. Hope was an early pioneer, serving as host on January 22, 1947, of Los Angeles's first commercial television broadcast, over Paramount-owned station KTLA. "This is Bob First-Commercial-Television-Broadcast Hope," he said, opening the show in front of a makeshift curtain, with an industrial-size bank of cameras and klieg lights pointed at him, "telling you gals who've tuned in, and I want to make this emphatic, if my face isn't handsome and debonair, please blame it on the static." Only about five hundred TV sets were able to pick up the crude broadcast, which was sponsored by a local Lincoln-Mercury dealer and also featured such Paramount stars as Dorothy Lamour, William Bendix, and director Cecil B. DeMille.

Hope, like most of radio's other top stars,

was holding back from taking a full plunge into TV. Although the new medium was gaining viewers fast, radio still had the bulk of the audience and the advertising dollars. It took an entertainer who had enjoyed little success on radio and thus had little to lose to be the groundbreaker. On Tuesday night, September 14, 1948, Milton Berle made his debut as host of a new weekly variety series on NBC-TV, the *Texaco Star Theater*. The show was an instant hit, igniting the sales of TV sets and launching a scramble by the four major TV networks — NBC, CBS, ABC, and DuMont — to roll out full schedules of national programming.

On the very same Tuesday night that Berle made his TV debut, Hope introduced his revamped radio show for Swan soap. He had done a thorough housecleaning over the summer, hiring an almost entirely new writing staff, and dumping his two main sidekicks, Jerry Colonna and Barbara Jo Allen, as Vera Vague. (Colonna, who had been with Hope for ten years, was ready to leave and strike out on his own, according to his son Robert, but the parting must have been difficult, both for him and for Hope, who genuinely liked Colonna and valued his contribution to the show's success.) Only Les Brown and his orchestra were kept on. Brown's Band of Renown was known for its high-quality players and clean-cut image — no drugs, no drinking — and they were one of the few traditional big bands to survive much beyond World War II. Hope would keep the group, and their easygoing, unobtrusive bandleader, close by his side for virtually the rest of his career.

At Brown's urging, Hope also added a new singer to the show: Doris Day, who had sung with Brown's band during the war (they had a hit recording of "Sentimental Journey") and who replaced the guest vocalists who had filled in ever since Langford's departure in 1946. Several other newcomers were added to the show, including Irene Ryan, the latest incarnation of the shrill, wisecracking spinster character that Hope was so fond of; a young baritone from Cleveland named Bill Ferrell; and a new announcer, Hy Averback. Even Hope's signature opening monologue had a fresh coat of paint. Now it was repackaged as "Bob Hope's Swan's Eye View of the News," with announcer Averback introducing each news headline ticker-tape style — Truman campaigns for reelection, Detroit unveils its new cars, the Soviets blockade Berlin — followed by a string of Hope jokes on the subject.

The newly revamped Bob Hope show debuted on September 14 and was marginally improved. The writing was a little sharper, and Day's addition was a big plus: she had a fresh, girlish soprano — in contrast to the smoky contraltos (Frances Langford, Dolores Reade) that Hope seemed to favor — and was a lively companion for Hope in sketches. Some reviewers noted his efforts to avoid stirring any controversy: "He is definitely out to remove any basis for criticism of the 'color' of his material," wrote one, "even if it means bending over backwards to do so."

He was still cautious about political material. Hope did surprisingly little, for example, on the 1948 presidential race between Harry Truman and New York governor Thomas E. Dewey. But after Truman's upset victory, Hope had plenty of fun with the pollsters (George Gallup's reaction to the results, said Hope: "That's the last time I take a house-to-house survey; from now on I'm gonna ask *people*") and the surprised first family. "Now Margaret Truman has to go back to the White House," Hope said. "And she had it all set to be the fourth Andrews sister." His most memorable postelection quip, however, was the one-word telegram he sent to the White House on the morning after Truman's victory. It read, simply, "Unpack."

In overhauling his show, Hope also streamlined his working process. His staff of writers was downsized from a dozen to just six, working in three teams. There was more division of labor: rather than having each team write a draft of every sketch (Hope would then mix and match the best material), each sketch was now assigned to just one writing team. All the writers still contributed to the monologue, which drew the lion's share of Hope's attention. Every week he would suggest five or six topics, and each writing team would turn out a dozen jokes or more for each. Hope would then assemble the writers in his wood-paneled office — now located in a new office wing, which was added to the Toluca Lake house in 1948 — and go through the resulting pile of a couple of hundred jokes. He would put a check next to his favorites; read over them a second time and put a cross through the check for the ones he liked best; and, on a third read-through, draw a circle around the best of those. The final selections would then literally be cut into strips and spread out on the floor or a pool table, so they could be put in final order.

"He was trying something quite novel for him," said Larry Gelbart, one of the new writers who joined the staff in 1948. "He was used to having a platoon of writers and didn't enjoy a particularly good reputation among writers. But he was terrific with us. He was a great editor. He knew what he should do and knew what he shouldn't do. He cared about the rest of the show, but nothing received the personal attention and that kind of involvement that the monologue did."

Despite his reputation for cheapness, Hope paid his top writers well. Gelbart and his partner Larry Marks, who had worked together previously on the radio show *Duffy's Tavern,* started out at $750 a week and worked their way up to $1,250. If Hope could get away with less, he did. Mort Lachman, an aspiring journalist from Seattle who joined the staff as an apprentice in 1947, started at just $75 a week. The writers were on call for anything Hope needed — monologues for his personal appearances, newspaper and magazine articles that carried Hope's byline, punching-up duty on his movie scripts. At almost any hour of the day or night Hope might call with a request for a new joke — "I need a bigger kid for the finish" — or to summon them for a meeting in the morning: "Ten o'clock. Tomorrow. My house. Bring your own orange juice."

Hope kept a close eye on every aspect of the show, and that included the freebies that the writers often got from companies in return for plugs on the air. "In those days there were product payoffs," said Si Rose, another young writer who joined the staff in 1948. "We'd get a General Electric gag on, and one of us would get a refrigerator. Bob found out and got in on the deal. Or a script would have a line about a hotel, and he would make it a line about a specific hotel in Palm Springs. He didn't need any of this stuff. But he was greedy. He wanted in on everything."

For all his demands, he was not a difficult

boss, and most of the writers enjoyed working for him. But his ego needed tending. "He was demanding, but not temperamental," said Gelbart. "He only got angry with me twice. Once I made a joke about his nose. That was personal, and he took it as such. Then one day we were writing a monologue for the opening at Santa Anita racetrack, and I wrote three lousy jokes: 'My horse is so old, they're betting him to win, place, and live.' Hope picked 'em, and I said, 'You're kidding! It's gonna sound like a goddamn Hope monologue!' He really got pissed."

Day, his new singer, found Hope a "joyous man to be around. He radiated good cheer." But she was bothered by the sycophantic treatment by his underlings. After each broadcast, she wrote in her memoir:

> Bob's staff would circle around him and tell him what a dynamite show it was. Week after week they'd squeal with delight after every show and Bob preened in the glow of their hyperbole. . . . I knew very well that some of those shows were quite awful. Allegedly funny lines that weren't funny at all. And I couldn't believe that Bob, wise about show business as he is, didn't know it — but I guess it was easier for him to defer his judgment to the uncritical accolades of his aides.

As the ego got puffed up, so did the sense of entitlement, especially when it came to women. The writers had to tolerate Hope's many sexual escapades, which he felt little need to hide. "When we traveled on the road, we'd always see a gal with him," said Rose. "We'd laugh because she often didn't even have a bedroom; she'd be in a cot. Or we'd see her riding on the train when we were going on a radio tour. The miracle of the century is how he never got caught."

Some in Hope's entourage joined in the fun, but others were put off by it. On a trip to New York City with Hope, Rose once walked into the star's hotel room and found an "orgy" under way. "Broads all over the place," Rose recalled. "Some of the guys are participating. Bob's eating ice cream. One of his assistants is on the floor boffing this girl. It was revolting. Ugly stuff." Rose left and returned to his hotel room, joining his wife in bed. A few minutes later, the phone rang. Assuming it was Hope, Rose told his wife to answer and say he was out. She picked up the phone, heard the familiar voice, and said, "I thought he was with you, Bob." Hope didn't skip a beat: "Oh, he must be in one of the other rooms. I'll find him."

It became a famous anecdote in Hollywood comedy circles, repeated often — though with varying details, attributed to different writers, and with the orgy left out. But the point was always the same: Hope, hearing a wife say she didn't know where her husband was, automatically assumed he was tomcatting around — and instinctively covered for him, as his writers so often did for him.

The Paleface was shot in the late summer of 1947, but Paramount waited more than a year to release it, until just before Christmas in 1948. The studio had come up with the idea of doing a Western comedy teaming Hope with Jane Russell, the buxom brunette who had made an R-rated screen debut in Howard Hughes's *The Outlaw.* Russell — who had done only one other film, a bomb called *Young Widow,* also for Hughes — was forever grateful to Hope for giving her a chance to show off her comedy talents, and to escape the mercurial, director-devouring Hughes. His films took months to shoot; on Hope's set, "they did one take, and if it worked, fine. If not they did two," Russell recalled. "I thought I had died and gone to heaven." Even Hope's lackadaisical working style was refreshing. One afternoon, as director Norman Z. McLeod was getting ready to shoot a scene, Hope suddenly announced he was through for the day and left for a golf game. The soft-spoken McLeod waited until the star was across the soundstage and out of hearing, then commanded, in a voice barely above a whisper, "Bob, you get back here!"

Russell and the crew cracked up.

The movie had a hit song before it even opened. Jay Livingston and Ray Evans, Paramount songwriters who had done the music for *Monsieur Beaucaire* and *My Favorite Brunette,* were asked to write a song for Hope, playing a frontier dentist named "Painless" Peter Potter, to sing to Russell, as Calamity Jane. They came up with the bouncy "Buttons and Bows," a comic lament for the delights of the "civilized" East, set to the clip-clop of a horse-drawn wagon. Impatient over the long delay before the film's release, Livingston and Evans got Dinah Shore to record it for Capitol, and the song was No. 1 weeks before the film opened. (It later won an Oscar for Best Song.) Hope's rendition, tossed off in a mock-Western twang as he sits on a buckboard playing a concertina — "Don't bury me on this prairie / Take me where the cee-ment grows . . ." — is understated and almost anticlimactic, but nonetheless charming.

The Paleface was a departure from Hope's previous films. Shot in candy-colored Technicolor, it is bigger and broader, full of burlesqued gunfights and slapstick chases. Hope's familiar nervous Nellie character seems quite at home in the land of cowboys and Indians, quaking in his boots one minute ("You're not afraid are you?" "No, I can always get another scalp"), swaggering around town the next when he thinks he's single-handedly fought off an Indian attack (Russell has done all the shooting). But *The Paleface* hits a few discordant notes that foreshadow a turn in Hope's film comedy.

With a script by Edmund Hartmann (a Hope first-timer who had written for Abbott and Costello), Frank Tashlin (the former cartoon director who had worked on *Monsieur Beaucaire*), and Hope's former radio writer Jack Rose, the laughs often depend on physical gags that are little particularized to Hope. In one running gag, for instance, Hope grabs the reins of his wagon and is yanked out when the horses bolt, dragged along the ground like a rag doll. It's both jarring and a little unseemly; it could just as well come from a Three Stooges short. In another scene, Hope and Russell get married in a quickie ceremony. As they repeat their vows, the camera remains fixed on the couple's hands — Bob fumbling with the ring, putting it on the wrong finger. After the minister pronounces them man and wife, he says, "And now the kiss." There is a loud offscreen smooch. "Not me, you fool!" says the minister. It gets a laugh — but it's pure, untethered nonsense. No matter how foolish or flustered a Hope character might be at the altar, he would never kiss the minister by mistake.

Still, the Western burlesque was a good showcase for Hope, and most of the critics loved the film. "A triumphant travesty," raved Howard Barnes in the *New York Herald Tribune.* "There could scarcely be a more joyful show for the Yule season." *The Paleface* grossed $7 million at the box office, a new record high for Hope.

While he was gearing up for the Christmas release of *The Paleface,* Hope got a phone call that would alter the course of his career and revive his commitment to a mission that had seemingly ended with the war. Stuart Symington, secretary of the Air Force and a sometime golfing buddy, asked if Hope would make a Christmas trip to entertain US troops taking part in the Berlin airlift.

The former German capital — partitioned by the Allies after the war, but surrounded by Soviet-controlled East Germany — had been under a Soviet-imposed blockade since the spring, with all road and rail access cut off. In response, Britain and the United States launched a daily airlift to keep the city supplied with food and other essential supplies. Symington told Hope that President Truman thought a delegation of entertainers at Christmas would be an important morale boost and a show of support from back home.

Though he had been planning to take Dolores and the kids to Lake Tahoe for the holidays, Hope had little trouble saying yes.

He quickly put together a troupe of entertainers, including most of his radio cast (minus Day, who had a film commitment), singer Jane Harvey, songwriter Irving Berlin, radio personality Jinx Falkenberg, and the Radio City Rockettes. Vice President–elect Alben Barkley and General Jimmy Doolittle also came along, courtesy of the US government, and so did Dolores — leaving the kids at home for Christmas.

They left a few days before Christmas, made a refueling stop at the US air base at Burtonwood, England, and then flew to Wiesbaden, West Germany, the embarkation point for planes carrying supplies into Berlin's Tempelhof Airport. The group was scheduled to fly to Berlin on Christmas morning, but the weather looked bad, so Hope and a few members of his troupe were rushed onto an earlier flight there on Christmas Eve. The rest of the group (including Dolores, who went to Christmas mass at 5:30 a.m., driven there in an Air Force jeep) flew in the next morning on a series of cargo flights. "It was an adventure," said Si Rose, one of three writers Hope brought along. "We were flying on a broken-down C-47. There was a board listing all the things that were wrong with the plane. We were standing up, not strapped in or anything, holding on to rods. We were all cargo."

In frigid Berlin, Hope went to meet incoming airlift pilots, before doing a big show at

421

the Titania Palast theater, an old vaudeville house. He talked about his flight through the tightly guarded air corridor: "Soviet planes started to buzz us, but the first Russian pilot took one look at me and said, 'They're okay — look at the hammerhead and sickle.' " Barkley, a former senator from Kentucky, told the airmen trying to outlast the Russian blockade that they were taking part in "the greatest filibuster of all times." Irving Berlin closed the show by singing "White Christmas."

General Lucius Clay had an after-party at his West Berlin quarters for Hope and visiting dignitaries, among them Walter Bedell Smith, the US Ambassador to the Soviet Union. Riding back to the hotel with Dolores, Hope insisted on making one more stop. An Army sergeant who hosted a radio show in Berlin had asked if Hope would drop by the studio for an interview. Though it was after midnight, Hope asked his driver to find the radio station. With gasoline in short supply in Berlin, the car ran out of fuel a few blocks from their destination — forcing Bob, Dolores, and the driver, flashlight in hand, to trudge the last few blocks in the snow to the station, where Hope took over the mike from the startled DJ.

Hope and company returned to Wiesbaden and made stops in London and Paris before flying back to New York on New Year's Eve.

The following May the Soviets lifted the blockade, ending one of the first major confrontations of the Cold War. Hope had played his part.

Just a few days after returning from Berlin, Hope began a busy stretch of domestic travel. In January and February of 1949, he and his radio cast went on a thirty-three-day, thirty-four-city tour across the South, East, and Midwest, playing big venues such as the Boston Garden and the Orange Bowl in Miami. He was back on the road in April for another, even more jam-packed tour — twenty-one cities in just over two weeks. He and his troupe flew from city to city aboard a United Airlines DC-6. At the time such short-hop air travel was rare for entertainers, and United used Hope's tour as a promotional tool. "Here is a perfect example of how air travel opens new opportunities for the entire show business," read an ad in *Variety,* accompanied by a photo of Hope posing with United pilots.

In her memoir, Doris Day, who suffered from stage fright even in the best of circumstances, recalled the nerve-rattling flights and the hectic scenes on the ground when they landed:

We often flew through storms and turbulence that had me praying more than once.

We made landings where I couldn't see the airfield until I was on the ground; sometimes the pilot had to circle a few times to find the landing strip. Then when we thankfully got off the plane, there would invariably be a mob of people waiting at the bottom of the steps. Bob was first off and I was in back of him with my hands full of traveling gear; as his fans moved in and mobbed Bob, I'd always get clobbered by the backwash of his faithful, virtually shoved off the steps, and an hour or so later, still spooked by the harrowing airplane ride and the clobbering fans, I'd have to go out on the stage of whatever mammoth auditorium we were playing with my pipes in good condition and my personality bubbling. I really learned what the expression "tough it like a trouper" means.

Something else may have contributed to Day's stress on the tour. Around the studio Hope liked to tease her with sexual banter — he called her "jut-butt" — but it may not have been entirely innocent. Hope claimed to a friend years later that he and Day had a brief romantic fling while they were touring together in 1949. If so, it was uncharacteristic of Hope, who usually avoided entanglements with his movie and radio costars, and it didn't last long. When they returned home to Burbank, Dolores was at the airport to greet them, giving Bob an ostentatious welcome-home hug. According to Hope, Day saw the gesture as a wife's symbolic marking of her territory, and she ended the relationship then and there. Day never commented on the alleged affair.

Not all of Hope's extramarital activities were discreet. During a stop in Dallas in the spring of 1949, Hope met a blond twenty-one-year-old Universal starlet named Barbara Payton, and the two began a relationship that lasted for several months. According to Payton, one of Hollywood's most notorious party girls, and her biographer, John O'Dowd, she followed Hope around the country, moved into a furnished apartment that he rented for her in Hollywood, and, when the affair ended in August, was paid off by Hope to keep quiet about it. If so, it didn't stop Payton — whose film career was tainted by scandal and over by the mid-fifties — from selling her story to *Confidential* magazine in 1956, a rare breach in the wall of secrecy that surrounded Hope's sex life.

Hope's 1949 personal-appearance tours were huge moneymakers for him, grossing a total of $870,000, of which Hope kept 75 percent. "You can't make money like that on Broadway. You can't make money like that anywhere," Hope told John Crosby of the *New York Herald Tribune*. At a time when Hollywood was having anxiety attacks over the threat from television, Hope's success was viewed as a heartening sign that movie stars could still be big draws with the public. "The Hope success should inspire some of our other better entertainers," said the *Hollywood Reporter,* "to get a show together and go out, first, of course, to grab some good moola, but more important to hypo show business generally that now needs all the dynamite that can be blasted at the public to get them going back to the theaters."

Between his radio show, his movie work, and his lucrative concert tours, Hope was probably earning more money than any other star in Hollywood. He was investing much of it in real estate. He also owned a stake in several broadcasting ventures, including Du-Mont Television and KOA radio in Denver. And in 1949, with his friend Crosby, he got into the oil business.

Years earlier, he and Crosby had met a Fort Worth oilman named Will Moncrief at a golf benefit in Texas. They stayed in touch, and in mid-1949 Moncrief cut them in on a deal to lease seventeen hundred acres of West Texas oil land. Hope put up $50,000, and another $50,000 when the first well came up dry, before they hit a gusher that was soon producing a thousand barrels a day. Hope, always a hands-on businessman, flew to Texas for a weekend in August to inspect the well. (Crosby, just as characteristically, stayed home fishing.) It was one of Hope's shrewdest investments. When he and Crosby sold out in the early 1950s, each earned a windfall of $3.5 million.

Big money was still being tossed around in radio as well. In late 1948 and early 1949, CBS chairman William Paley launched a series of talent raids on rival NBC, offering lucrative contracts to lure away many of the network's top comedy stars, including Jack Benny, Edgar Bergen, Red Skelton, and Burns and Allen. After he added Bing Crosby to his stable (hiring him away from ABC, where Bing had moved his radio show in 1946), Paley set his sights on Hope, envisioning a Hope-Crosby tandem airing back-to-back on CBS.

It's not clear how far the negotiations went, but Hope was one major NBC star who stayed put. His instinctive loyalty to the network that had helped make him a star doubtless played a role. But NBC also stepped up as it hadn't for some of its other defecting talent, promising to bankroll various Hope Enterprises projects and dangling a seven-figure salary when Hope made the all-but-inevitable move into television. Hope never seriously considered switching networks again.

Relations with his sponsor, Lever Brothers, weren't quite so tranquil. In the spring of 1949 Hope got into another fight with Luckman, this time over the taping of his radio show. Though most radio programs were still broadcast live, some stars (notably Crosby, who owned a piece of the Ampex audiotape company) were beginning to record shows in advance, and Hope wanted the option of doing the same when he was traveling. Luckman objected, complaining about the cost and worrying that radio listeners wouldn't sit still for "canned" shows. The dispute went to an arbitration panel, which ruled against Hope. Lever renewed its sponsorship of Hope's show for the 1949–50 season — encouraged, possibly, by a Gallup poll in September that named him America's favorite comedian (beating Milton Berle, the new TV sensation, by a two-to-one margin). But the disputes were taking their toll, and it would be Hope's last season for his longtime sponsor.

Back at Paramount, Hope spent most of the summer of 1949 filming *Where Men Are Men* (later retitled *Fancy Pants*), a remake of *Ruggles of Red Gap,* the 1935 Charles Laughton comedy about an English butler in the old West. While shooting a scene in which he rides a bucking mechanical barrel, Hope was thrown off the machine, fell six feet to the floor, and was knocked unconscious. A stay in the hospital revealed no serious injuries, but he needed a week off to recuperate from the bruises. Hope got plenty of publicity mileage out of the accident, writing an open letter to studio chief Henry Ginsberg: "If your economy-minded production heads had used a real horse instead of putting me over a broken-down barrel I would not have landed on my back on Stage 17 with an injury which you will see from the bill was not cheap."

Paramount could afford to have a sense of humor. The accident came a month after the release of *Sorrowful Jones*, an unexpectedly big hit for Hope and a real advance for him as a screen actor — the first film in which he plays something close to a dramatic role.

Based on a Damon Runyon story first filmed in 1934 as *Little Miss Marker*, with Shirley Temple, *Sorrowful Jones* is hardly devoid of comedy. Indeed, screenwriters Ed Hartmann, Mel Shavelson, and Jack Rose added gag lines to suit Hope's wisecracking screen personality, much to the dismay of some Runyon purists. Hope plays a bookie who finds himself saddled with a little girl (Mary Jane Saunders) when her father leaves her as a marker for a racing bet and gets bumped off by gangsters before he can retrieve her. The role was unlike any Hope had played before. Instead of his usual bumbling, girl-chasing coward, he is a hard-boiled, cynical, thoroughly citified Runyon wise guy. He even has a relatively adult, smoldering-at-arm's-length romantic rela-

429

tionship — with his ex-girlfriend, now a local mobster's girl, wonderfully played by Lucille Ball, in the first of four films she would do with Hope. They meet by chance, apparently for the first time in years, in front of a department store window, and the entire history of their relationship is told in one brief, brittle exchange:

"You know, it's been almost four years since I saw you, Sorrowful. But I recognize the suit."
"It's been lucky for me — up to now. Some people seem to forget what some people spend on some people."
"*Spend?* Where did you ever learn that word? I always figured you invented the dutch treat."

The film's chief love story, however, is between Sorrowful and little Martha Jane, the tyke in his care who disrupts his comfortably disordered bachelor's life. Their first night together in Sorrowful's apartment is a Hope gem. Martha Jane bursts in on him while he's undressing, and he scrambles for his pants like a ten-year-old surprised by his big sister. She asks where the bathroom is; he grits his teeth and stabs his finger toward the facilities: "Get you a floor plan later." When she takes too long to get to bed, he barks at her in tough-guy Runyonese: "Hey, Shorts, drag your royal chassis outta there and hit the sack."

Predictably, the little girl soon breaks down his resistance and awakens his fatherly instincts. Hope's underplaying — with the help of a sensitive director, Sidney Lanfield — keeps the transformation honest and touching, especially in the memorable bedtime scene, when Sorrowful teaches the little girl to pray. It begins when he mentions God, and Martha Jane tells him casually, "My daddy says there's nobody named God."

SORROWFUL: "When did he say that?"

MARTHA JANE: "When my mommy went away."

SORROWFUL *takes a moment to register this — the girl is an orphan:* "I guess your daddy got a bad break. But what he said wasn't right. Not *just* right. He kind of forgot a little. I mean, there is somebody named God."

"Do you know him?"

"I heard about him. And from what I hear he's a pretty good sport. Always tryin' to give a citizen a break. If there's something you want and can't promote for yourself, you ask God for it. And as often as not, he comes through."

"Do you write him letters, like Santa Claus?"

"No. That's where prayin' comes in."

The scene is beautifully played — not a hint of condescension or cuteness. Hope seems to be working it out for himself, even as he explains it in language that his little charge will understand. It's Hope the communicator, sizing up his audience and talking its language. He would have made a good father.

Sorrowful Jones skips along brightly toward a rather overwrought farcical-sentimental climax: Martha Jane has an accident and falls into a coma, and Sorrowful has to sneak her favorite racehorse into the hospital to save her. But the film is less treacly than the earlier screen version, *Little Miss Marker,* with Shirley Temple overdoing the adorableness and Adolphe Menjou as a more sorrowful Sorrowful. *Time* said the film "lifts comedian Bob Hope out of an accumulated litter of silly scripts, props and costumes, and gives him a new grip on the US public's funny bone." *Sorrowful Jones* was the top-grossing film in the country for the month of July, and one of Hope's biggest hits of the forties — the culmination of his long road from farceur to fully mature comic actor.

Hope had one more movie left to come in 1949, *The Great Lover.* It's relatively minor Hope, but a delightful film nonetheless, and a fitting coda to Hope's extraordinary decade. Directed by Alexander Hall (who had, coincidentally, directed the original *Little Miss*

Marker), the film in some ways is a look back for Hope, to the comedy-thrillers that were his bread and butter earlier in the decade, but with some fresh twists. Hope plays a newspaper reporter chaperoning a Scout troop on a tour of Europe. On the boat going home he gets entangled with a murderous cardsharp (Roland Young) and a gold-digging European duchess (Rhonda Fleming, the latest Paramount beauty to get matched with Hope). Hope is boyishly engaging as he tries to elude the watchful eyes of the straight-arrow Scouts while making time with the down-on-her-luck duchess. Released near the end of 1949, *The Great Lover* wasn't as big a hit as Hope's two previous films, *The Paleface* and *Sorrowful Jones.* But the three combined to boost Hope, for the first time, into the No. 1 spot in two annual film-industry polls of the top box-office stars of the year.

Hope's decade was capped off with another phone call from Stuart Symington. Hope had attended a Hollywood screening of *Twelve O'Clock High,* the story of the World War II hero Air Force general Frank Armstrong Jr., and Symington wanted to know if Hope would spend Christmas entertaining the troops now under Armstrong's command up in Alaska. Hope was hesitant, saying that he couldn't be away from his kids for a second Christmas in a row. Symington said to bring them along. Dolores was game, and Tony and

433

Linda were excited at the prospect of a snow vacation, so the family (minus the toddlers, Kelly and Nora) made the trip together.

With just a few hours to put together a troupe, Hope recruited Patty Thomas, his dancing companion from World War II; cowboy singing star Jimmy Wakely; and Les Brown's pianist Geoff Clarkson. Then he called up his head radio writer, Norm Sullivan, and told him the writers would have to put together the following week's show on their own because Hope was going to Alaska. After a pause, Sullivan deadpanned, "We'll move your pin on the map."

Hope and the family flew aboard Armstrong's B-17 to Seattle, where they caught Symington's plane to Anchorage. From there, Hope did twelve shows in three days and had five Christmas dinners. "You know who you are, don't you?" Bob told the troops freezing in twenty-below temperatures. "God's frozen people." He caught a cold on the trip and by the end could barely talk. When he climbed aboard the plane headed home, he said, "Get me some soup and some sleeping pills."

The brief trip was an important one for Hope, solidifying his status as the Pentagon's go-to entertainer and Hollywood's ambassador of holiday cheer for US troops around the globe. "The Bob Hope Christmas stint for the troops in Alaska had the entire Pentagon going sentimental with delight," reported

Variety, "and reminiscing over last year's junket at the height of the Berlin Air Lift — a trip still remembered here as an all-time high in public relations." Berlin, however, had been a special assignment — Hope heeding his country's call in a world crisis. The Alaska trip was more in the realm of routine duty, establishing the Christmas tradition that would become Hope's calling card.

As the 1940s ended, Hope was riding higher than ever. "His professional jaunts have astonished several branches of science, having the same kind of monumental energy normally associated with nuclear fission," the *New York Times* wrote in January 1950. "Today Hope's backlog of good will and public favor is of a size and quality most public figures can only dream about." He was the No. 1 movie star in America, a stage entertainer without peer, and still one of the most popular stars on radio, who was about to enter the medium that would replace it. What's more, he had laid the groundwork for his annual Christmas tours to entertain the troops, the patriotic missions that would ensure his legacy — and, two decades later, unexpectedly tarnish it.

Left: The house in Eltham, England, where Leslie Towns Hope was born. *(Photograph by author)* *Right:* His parents, Avis and Harry, in Cleveland. *(© Hope Enterprises, Inc.)*

A family portrait, taken in England: Leslie is front and center; younger brother Sidney, in a dress, is on Avis's knee. *(© Hope Enterprises, Inc.)*

With his first dance partner—and sometime
girlfriend—Mildred Rosequist.
(© Hope Enterprises, Inc.)

Hope started out in vaudeville with partner
Lloyd Durbin (left); the pair was broken up
early by tragedy. *(© Hope Enterprises, Inc.)*

Hope and George Byrne formed a successful comedy-dance team before Hope decided to strike out on his own. (© *Hope Enterprises, Inc.*)

Hope in *Roberta*, the show that made him a Broadway star, with Tamara, Fay Templeton (seated), and George Murphy (far right). (© *Underwood & Underwood/Corbis*)

When Hope finally moved out to Hollywood in 1937, at age thirty-four, he was ready for his close-up. *(© Bettmann/Corbis)*

Paramount teamed him with Martha Raye in several routine B pictures, including 1938's *College Swing.* *(© Bettmann/Corbis)*

In *My Favorite Blonde*, with British star Madeleine Carroll, Hope began to develop his distinctive screen persona: the brash coward, always chasing women but helpless in their grasp. (© *Bettmann/Corbis*)

On the *Road to Morocco* with Bing Crosby and Dorothy Lamour, third in the greatest buddy series in movie history. (© *Bettmann/Corbis/AP Images*)

With the help of sidekick
Jerry Colonna, Hope finally
broke through on radio in
1938 with *The Pepsodent
Show.* (© *Associated Press*)

Bob and Dolores sail for England in August 1939, just weeks before the outbreak
of World War II. (© *Bettmann/Corbis/AP Images*)

Hope in his World War II glory, entertaining servicemen in New Caledonia on his tour of the Pacific theater in 1944. (© *Bettmann/Corbis*)

"Don't get up": Hope and his "gypsies" (from top: Jerry Colonna, Frances Langford, Tony Romano, and Patty Thomas) visit with wounded soldiers. (© *Bettmann/Corbis*)

Heading west, with Jane Russell, in *The Paleface* (1948). (© *Boulevard/Corbis*)

Getting serious, with Mary Jane Saunders,
in *Sorrowful Jones* (1949). (© *Getty Images*)

They weren't close friends, but in movies, onstage, and in front of any camera that happened by, Hope and Crosby were a matchless team. (© *Popperfoto/Getty Images*)

Marilyn Maxwell appeared with Hope in three movies and nearly two hundred times on radio, TV, and the stage. They also had a long-running romance. (© *Hulton-Deutsch Collection/Corbis*)

Hope, with Bea Lillie, dons Western garb for a sketch on his first TV show, sponsored by Frigidaire, in April 1950. *(© Corbis)*

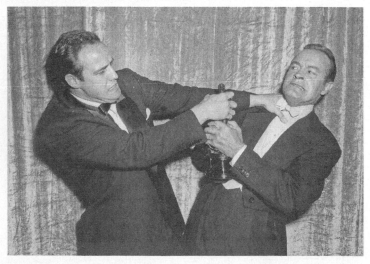

By 1955, when he wrestled playfully over a statuette with Best Actor winner Marlon Brando, Hope had made his Oscar snubs a running gag. *(© Associated Press)*

Dolores and Bob with the family in the mid-1950s. From left to right: Tony, Nora, Kelly, and Linda. *(© Bettmann/Corbis/AP Images)*

Mother had Hopes: Bob and his brothers, from left to right (and oldest to youngest), Ivor, Jim, Fred, Jack, Bob, and George. *(© Hope Enterprises, Inc.)*

The Facts of Life, with Lucille Ball, showed a new, more mature side of Hope on screen, but it was his last good film. (© *John Springer Collection/Corbis*)

Among his multitude of awards, none pleased Hope more than his Congressional Gold Medal, presented to him by President Kennedy in September 1963. (© *Corbis*)

Carroll Baker was just one of a string of beauties Hope brought to Vietnam for the troops to ogle. (© *Corbis/AP Images*)

With Phyllis Diller on his 1966 trip to Vietnam: the crowds grew with America's commitment to a troubling war. (© *Bettmann/Corbis*)

Hope's corny spoofs of the counterculture (here with Steve Lawrence and Eydie Gormé) planted him firmly on the geriatric side of the generation gap. (© *Bettmann/Corbis*)

Nixon hugs Sammy Davis Jr. (with Les Brown looking on), as Hope's Republican politics become more open. (© *Bettmann/Corbis*)

Hope in Hawaii with two of his later writers, Bob Mills (left) and Gene Perret, and the cue cards that by then had become indispensable.
(© Robert L. Mills)

The old guard: Hope and two presidential pals, Ronald Reagan and Gerald Ford.
(© Bettmann/Corbis)

On the golf course, as nearly
everywhere else, the picture
of determination and class.
(© Time & Life Pictures/Getty Images)

■ ■ ■ ■

IV
INVENTING STARDOM

CONQUERING TELEVISION, EXTENDING
THE BRAND, AND SHOWING HOW TO BE
A CELEBRITY

■ ■ ■ ■

CHAPTER 8
TELEVISION
"I'M BEING UNDERPAID, I'LL TELL YOU THAT."

Bob Hope drove fast. Passengers in the car with him would sometimes be hanging on for dear life when he was speeding along the highway between Toluca Lake and Palm Springs, a trip he made often. But Fred Williams, his hard-drinking writer pal, was dozing in the front seat next to him in January 1950, on the way back from Palm Springs after a weekend of golf and working on script revisions for Hope's film *Fancy Pants*. Doing 75 mph on rain-slicked Highway 60, Hope suddenly swerved and lost control of his Cadillac, which hit a ditch and rolled over, throwing both men from the car.

"I remember how my head jerked, and how I thought, 'This is it. I'm going to die,' " Hope recalled. "I remember everything that happened until I got hit on the head and blanked out." He was standing in the mud by the side of the road testing his golf swing when a passing motorist stopped to help and drove them to a hospital in Riverside. Williams had only bruises, but X-rays showed that Hope had suffered a broken collarbone.

It was a shaky start to a promising new decade, one in which Hope would master a new medium, say good-bye to an old one, and pioneer a new kind of stardom — enterprising, relentless, spanning all media, embracing a public role as well as that of mere entertainer. Show business had seen nothing like it.

The accident forced him to scuttle plans to play in Bing Crosby's celebrity golf tournament in Pebble Beach and to cancel a few weeks of public appearances. But in early February he was back on the road: flying with Dolores to Washington, where he picked up an award from the Air Force for his work during the Berlin airlift, appeared at a Women's National Press Club luncheon, and emceed another White House Correspondents' Association dinner. "Never trust a politician who knows how to measure your inseam," Hope cracked about the former haberdasher now in the White House, as President Truman laughed along on the dais.

Then Hope prepared for a return to vaudeville. In March, he was booked for a two-week stage show at the Paramount Theatre in New York City, accompanying the premiere of the Paramount film *Captain China*. Unlike his personal-appearance tours of the late forties — hopping from city to city, doing mostly one-nighters — this would be an old-style, continuous vaudeville run: six forty-minute shows a day, the sort of grinding schedule few Hollywood stars would take on. Hope was guaranteed $50,000 per week, plus a percentage of the gross receipts — more money than a performer on Broadway had ever before been paid. Joined onstage by his favorite glamour girl of the moment, Jane Russell, along with Les Brown's orchestra, Hope reveled in the chance to revisit his vaudeville roots, polish his stage skills, and get some face time with his fans. "I started in this sort of racket, and I feel that you've always gotta go back to where you came from every so often, to sharpen up," he told the *New York Herald Tribune.* "At the end of this run, I should have improved my comedy timing and everything else about the act, under all kinds of conditions."

His show was a smash hit. Despite bitter-cold weather in New York City and brownouts due to a coal strike, Hope set house records for the opening day, opening week, and second week of his Paramount run. "Where was Hope when the lights went out?" trumpeted an NBC ad in the trade papers. "Packing them in at the Paramount." When the two-week engagement was finished, Hope took the show on the road for another week, traveling to Cincinnati, St. Louis, and several more cities.

For the tour Hope added a new performer

— a young Italian American singer he had seen at Pearl Bailey's nightclub in Greenwich Village, who was going by the stage name Joe Barry. Hope told him he ought to change it to something closer to his real name, Anthony Benedetto — and suggested Tony Bennett. "It was very intuitive and correct," said Bennett, who would always credit Hope with giving him his first big break in show business, along with his stage name. "He took me on the road for six or seven days and ended in Los Angeles, where he introduced me to Bing Crosby. It was the first time I ever sang in front of a huge crowd."

Hope made one other important change in his stage show on the road. Because of a movie commitment, Jane Russell couldn't stay on, so Hope replaced her with a twenty-nine-year-old blond singer and actress named Marilyn Maxwell. Born in Clarinda, Iowa, as Marvel Marilyn Maxwell, she had traveled the road with her mother, a piano accompanist for the dancer Ruth St. Denis, and started in show business as a big-band singer. She puttered around Hollywood, getting supporting parts in mediocre films through much of the 1940s, before landing her best role as the sultry girlfriend of Kirk Douglas's ruthless boxer in the 1949 film *Champion.* Maxwell filled all the résumé requirements for a Hope stage partner: sexy good looks, a pleasant singing voice, and a "fun girl" who could trade quips with him. Maxwell became one of his favorite partners onstage, on radio, and later on TV. She also, most likely at some point in 1950, became his girlfriend.

By early 1950, any doubts that television was going to transform the entertainment world were all but gone. In May 1948, four months before the debut of Milton Berle's *Texaco Star Theater,* there were only 325,000 TV sets in American homes, nearly half of them in the New York City area. By the end of 1949, that number had grown to more than 4 million. Within another year it had nearly tripled again, to 11.6 million. The radio audience was dropping just as swiftly, from an 81 percent share of the broadcast audience at the start of 1949 to just 59 percent at its end.

Radio wasn't the only medium feeling the heat from television. College and professional sports leagues feared (amazingly, in retrospect) that TV coverage would mean doom because it would cut into stadium attendance. Hollywood was seeing movie attendance plummet — from a peak of 90 million in 1946 to less than 60 million in 1950 — and TV was the main culprit. The studios warned their top stars to stay away from the new medium, lest TV exposure damage their value on the big screen, and scrambled for ways to make their films stand out from the TV competition: wide-screen epics, splashy Technicolor musicals, and a few years later such gimmicks as 3-D and Cinerama.

Television, meanwhile, was busily minting new stars. Not just Berle, whose breakout success in the new medium earned him the nickname Mr. Television, but personalities such as Arthur Godfrey, the folksy, mellow-voiced host of not one but two popular TV shows, and Ed Sullivan, the stiff, almost comically untelegenic New York newspaper columnist who hosted the popular Sunday-night variety show *Toast of the Town.* TV spawned new Western heroes such as Hopalong Cassidy, kids-show stars (Howdy Doody, Kukla, Fran, and Ollie) and showmen of the wrestling ring such as the flamboyant, blond-tressed Gorgeous George.

Television was a frequent target of Hope's radio jokes in those early years — the old movies that filled up so much of the early TV schedule, the ubiquitous Godfrey and his many sponsors. But Hope could hardly afford to laugh off television. The decline in his audience was among the most precipitous in radio. For the 1948–49 season, Hope's Hooper rating stood at 23.8, good for third place; one season later it was down to 13.9 and tenth place, one spot behind Gene Autry's program of cowboy music. "The only radio comic who chooses to ignore television as a part of his future is the comic who wants to quit — to lie down — to retire with the loot

444

the government has allowed him to hold onto," wrote Walt Taliaferro in a May 1949 story on Hope in the *Los Angeles Daily News.* "And this is a description of everything Bob Hope isn't."

But Hope was approaching the new medium warily. In June 1949 an NBC vice president named John Royal offered a friendly prediction in a letter to Hope: "I want to take a little bet — in fact, a goddam big bet — that the first time Hope gets into television, he will do to this industry what Jolson did in talking pictures. He will make it." Hope was dismissive at first. "Berle can have that medium all to himself for the next year," he wrote back. "Then I shall have my head blocked and we'll all go back into vaudeville!" But he foresaw the inevitable: "Without a doubt television will really be going in a couple of years and we will have to put on our very best manners and do a nice half-hour show every week. I don't think any less than that will do, as television will have to become a habit . . . maybe one of the nastier habits, but nevertheless an interesting one."

The day of reckoning came sooner than he expected. In January 1950, Hugh Davis, of the ad agency Foote, Cone & Belding, came to visit Hope while he was convalescing from his car accident in Palm Springs. He asked Hope if he would consider hosting a TV variety show for Frigidaire, one of the agency's clients. Hope threw out what he thought was an outrageous amount of money, $50,000. A few days later Davis called back to ask if Hope would do it for $40,000 — more than had ever been paid to any entertainer for a one-time performance. Hope, who always liked breaking records, agreed.

Frigidaire signed him up for five ninety-minute specials, to air throughout the year around holidays. After the initial $40,000, he would get a total of $150,000 for the next four specials — out of which he had to pay his writers and travel expenses to New York, where the shows would be done live. The total cost to Frigidaire for each special: $135,000, more than had ever before been spent on a single hour of television. Max Liebman, who had just begun working on *Your Show of Shows,* with Sid Caesar and Imogene Coca, was brought in to direct (on the one week out of the month Caesar and Coca had off), and Douglas Fairbanks Jr., Beatrice Lillie, and Dinah Shore signed up as guests for the first show, scheduled for Easter Sunday, April 9.

Hope flew to New York five days early to prepare. Rehearsals were hampered by a technicians' union slowdown. Hope was unsure of himself in the new medium, and the writers too were feeling their way along. "I'm being underpaid, I'll tell you that," Hope told a reporter during the hectic rehearsals. "This is positive murder." Mort Lachman, one of four writers Hope brought to New York to work on the show, recalled the chaos: "It was very difficult. There was so much technical trouble — it took hours and hours to prepare. I went to Bob's dressing room before the show and couldn't get inside, there were so many people yelling and carrying on." Carl Reiner, who appeared in sketches on the show, met Hope for the first time backstage just before the broadcast. "His hand was soaking wet," Reiner recalled. "He was a nervous wreck. He was literally shaking."

The Star-Spangled Revue, as the special was called, went on the air at 5:30 p.m. eastern time, broadcast live to twenty-eight NBC stations across the country, with another thirty-two getting it on kinescope a week later. Viewed today, the show looks downright prehistoric. It opens with appliances: the camera panning across a display of Frigidaire products, including the new 1950 model refrigerator ("Just look at the beauty of that full-length door . . . that new target latch with its golden trim"). After a jerky hand-roll of the opening credits, Hope enters through a theater curtain, formally attired in a white, cutaway tuxedo, with a cane and top hat (the same one he wore in *Roberta* on Broadway). "Television," Hope begins. "Well, they finally got me."

447

Hope is obviously tense. When jokes fall flat, he is too unsure of himself to react and reach for a saver; he just barrels ahead. His monologue includes jokes about Eleanor Roosevelt, New York's well-traveled mayor, William O'Dwyer, and, most of all, the unfamiliar new medium he's just dived into. "I must tell you how I got into television," he says. "It's rather sneaky. I lied to them. I told them I was an old-time movie." The excess verbiage is probably a reflection of his nervousness.

The show has an old-style vaudeville feel. Hope's first guest is a stand-up boogie-woogie pianist. Another is former vaudeville hoofer Hal Le Roy, who joins him in a comedy Egyptian-dance number — the same one that Hope did with Lloyd Durbin when he was starting out in vaudeville. The sketches are broad and crudely staged. In one, Hope, playing himself, is wined and dined by NBC executives, who fumigate the room every time "CBS" or "Godfrey" is mentioned. In another, Fairbanks and Lillie join in a British burlesque of American Westerns called "Dragalong Cavendish." Hope and Dinah Shore have a little fun as Eskimo lovers, shivering in an igloo as they trip over their lines and sing "Baby, It's Cold Outside." Hope quips, "Like to see Milton Berle steal this."

Saying his good-byes at the end of the show,

Hope appears visibly relieved. "I do hope that we got away with it this afternoon. This really sells me on TV. In fact, from now on I'm gonna quit peeking through my neighbor's window and go out and get a small set of my own." Hope ends the show, as he often did on radio, with a patriotic sign-off, reflecting the anxieties of the early Cold War years.

> Tomorrow, when I get home, people are gonna say, "What did you do on Easter Sunday?" And I can say, well, we spent Easter with the family. A big family that believes in the American way of life, those folks that have never pulled down an Iron Curtain between their hearts and the Christian ideal called brotherhood of man.

Hope was the first major radio star to take the plunge into television, and his debut, not surprisingly, was a huge hit in the ratings. The show got a 49.4 Hooper score, meaning that nearly half of all homes in the country with television sets were watching — roughly 10 million viewers, the most for any TV special in the medium's short history. The reviews were mixed — *Life* said Hope "seemed subdued and uncertain in his new medium," and the *New York Journal-American* thought he looked "petrified with fear" — and Hope himself was not happy with his performance. "I couldn't believe how nervous and jumpy I was," he said. "I worried about my material, and especially the pacing of it. I knew that this was a quite different medium from either radio or film, but I hadn't figured it out yet." He was distracted by the constantly moving cameras — "like trying to do a nightclub act with three waiters with trays walking in front of you every time you reached the punch line" — and he thought the writing needed to be better. "It was really caveman TV," said Larry Gelbart, one of the show's writers. "We were not television writers by any stretch of the imagination. Our idea of television was to find the biggest twenty-gallon hat we could find for him and strap on a dozen six-shooters for a Western sketch. The writing was terrible. I see those shows and cringe."

The Frigidaire shows improved as they rolled out through the rest of the year. For his second special, which aired in May, Hope's top-billed guest was Frank Sinatra — the former bobby-socks idol who was in a career slump and was grateful to Hope for giving him the TV exposure. Hope, who often joked on the radio about Sinatra's scrawny frame, notices that he has filled out: "After I saw you on camera I had to throw away a lot of skinny jokes." Sinatra sings "Come Rain or Come Shine" and joins Hope in two sketches: as a pair of baseball players primping themselves for the TV cameras, and in a

Road picture parody, with Sinatra paddling a canoe and wearing big ears to impersonate Crosby.

Hope was learning the new medium, slowing down his pace and relaxing in front of the camera. "I used to work very fast on radio because I found out when I was working for service audiences that they wanted it fast," he wrote in his memoir *Have Tux, Will Travel.* "They didn't want situation comedy; they wanted jokes and they wanted them right now; they wanted them to go bang-bang-bang. I was successful with them that way. I carried this technique over into my first days on television, but it wasn't too successful. With that particular type of material and a civilian audience, I was ahead of them, and working too fast for them. I've slowed down for television, especially with my monologue."

Having broken the ice in TV, Hope began a complicated series of negotiations over his future on both radio and television. Relations with his radio sponsor, Lever Brothers, were continuing to deteriorate — despite the departure of Charles Luckman, the company president with whom Hope had often clashed, who resigned in January after a dispute with his corporate bosses in London. Now Hope wanted out of his ten-year contract, which still had four years to run. In June, after months of wrangling, Lever finally agreed to let him go, and Hope signed with a

451

new radio sponsor, Chesterfield cigarettes.

Separately, NBC worked to lock up Hope with an exclusive contract for both radio and TV. Those negotiations too dragged on, but concluded in the fall with a deal that guaranteed Hope $3 million over the next five years. All of his TV specials would be produced by Hope Enterprises, and NBC and Hope became partners in each other's company: NBC agreed to invest $1.5 million for a 25 percent share of Hope Enterprises, while Hope acquired a large block of NBC stock. At the same time, Hope struck a new deal with Paramount, promising eight pictures over the next four years — half produced by Hope Enterprises, the other half by Paramount, but giving Hope a one-quarter share of the profits. By the end of the summer, Hope had set himself up with a profit-sharing stake in everything he did in movies, radio, and television.

Then it was back to work — lots of it. Hope seemed to be everywhere. He spent most of the summer on the Paramount lot shooting *The Lemon Drop Kid,* adapted from another Damon Runyon story, with Marilyn Maxwell as his costar. On his weekends off he entertained at state fairs. In August he hosted an all-star benefit at the Hollywood Bowl, raising $48,000 for the United Cerebral Palsy Association. In September he flew to New York for his third Frigidaire TV special, then returned to LA for the fall premiere of his radio show. He recorded a single for Capitol with Margaret Whiting called "Blind Date," in which a couple on a first date exchange polite conversation interspersed with their "real" thoughts about each other (with "Home Cookin'," a song from his new movie *Fancy Pants,* on the flip side). He continued to turn out his daily newspaper column, It Says Here, for the Hearst syndicate (though he was growing tired of it and would finally call it quits in 1951). Hope even became the star of a comic book.

At the end of the 1940s, with the sales of superhero comics sagging, DC Comics began experimenting with a new genre: comic adventures based on the screen characters of movie and TV stars such as Ozzie and Harriet and Dean Martin and Jerry Lewis. In 1949 DC made a licensing deal with Hope and in January 1950 brought out the first bimonthly issue of *The Adventures of Bob Hope.* Each issue featured a cartoon version of Hope wisecracking through different exploits — Bob invents a new golf club, say, or joins the French Foreign Legion. Hope and his writers had nothing to do with the comic, but it was another extension of his brand and made his ski-nosed caricature instantly recognizable to a new generation of kids. *The Adventures of Bob Hope* had a surprisingly long run, appearing every other month for eighteen years — well into the Vietnam era, when young people were reading other kinds of comics, and Hope's adventures weren't quite so funny anymore.

The five years of peace since the end of World War II had been good to Bob Hope. His career was blazing, he was making lots of money, and he occasionally got home to see the wife and kids. But when North Korean troops, backed by the Soviet Union, invaded South Korea on June 25, 1950, Hope's war-fueled adrenaline began flowing again. Almost as soon as UN troops under the command of General Douglas MacArthur turned back the North Korean offensive, Hope began lobbying to make a trip there. MacArthur had requested that no entertainment units of larger than six people — and no women — be allowed into the war zone. But Hope prevailed on his friends among the military top brass to let him take a troupe of fifty there in October. It was hard to say no to Bob Hope.

His big troupe included cowboy singer Jimmy Wakely (who had accompanied Hope to Alaska the year before), dancer Judy Kelly, the Tailor Maids singing trio, a dance act called the Hi-Hatters, and Les Brown's band. Also joining the entourage were Hope's brother Jack, old vaudeville pal Charlie Cooley, four writers, and Hope's masseur from Lakeside Country Club, Fred Miron. For a leading lady, Hope's first choice was Jane Russell, but she again had to bow out because of a film commitment, so he asked singer Gloria DeHaven to come along for the first part of the trip, before Marilyn Maxwell could take over midway through the tour.

They stopped first in Hawaii, then island-hopped to Kwajalein, Guam, and Okinawa, before landing in Tokyo. Hope was a big celebrity in Japan, thanks largely to *The Paleface,* the most popular American film to open in the country since the war. (While he was being driven through the Tokyo streets, a car full of Japanese fans pulled alongside and serenaded Hope with "Buttons and Bows.") Hope and his entertainers were guests at a luncheon given by General MacArthur — another charismatic general who impressed Hope greatly. "He held us spellbound," Hope wrote in his newspaper column, "as he talked with authority and humor on subjects ranging from Bataan to baseball batting averages." Hope visited injured American soldiers at Tokyo General Hospital ("Most of them are so young you'd think they were drafted on the way to school," he wrote); flew to Yokota Air Force Base to entertain fliers under the command of General Emmett "Rosie" O'Donnell; and did his weekly radio show for an audience of three thousand GIs in Tokyo's Ernie Pyle Theater.

From Tokyo, Hope and his band crossed the Sea of Japan and landed at an airfield near Seoul, the South Korean capital that had just been retaken from the Communists. Military trucks carried them over ten miles of rough road to Seoul Stadium, where they entertained twenty thousand GIs in the frigid cold. Hope joked about a war in which the battlelines were shifting almost daily: "Some of these towns are changing hands so fast, one soldier bought a lamp with three thousand won and got his change in rubles. Seoul has changed hands so many times the towels in the hotel are marked 'His,' 'Hers,' and 'Who's Sorry Now?' "

After Seoul, Hope crisscrossed the country, going as far south as Pusan and north across the thirty-eighth parallel to Pyongyang, the North Korean capital now in friendly hands. Hope heard that the First Marine Division, which he had entertained in Pavuvu during World War II, was at the port of Wonsan, and he asked if he could do a show for them. He and his troupe were flown to Wonsan in two C-54s, only to find the airport nearly deserted when they arrived. They were waiting in an empty hangar, wondering what to do, when some officers finally arrived, among them General Edward Almond.

"How long have you been here?" asked Almond.

"Twenty minutes," said Hope.

"Are you kidding? We just made the landing." Weather had delayed their arrival, and Hope's troupe had actually beaten the Marines there. "Bob Hope and Marilyn Maxwell in Wonsan before Leathernecks," blared the headlines back home. Actually, the South Koreans had retaken the port two weeks earlier, so the marine landing was something of an anticlimax. "The only thing we're going in for is to give Bob Hope an audience," grumbled one marine.

Hope did shows on the deck of the battleship *Missouri* and the aircraft carrier *Valley Forge,* then returned to Pyongyang to entertain fifteen thousand troops in front of the former Communist headquarters. The tour ended with a swing through Alaska and the Aleutians, where Hope did the last of four radio broadcasts from the trip. He returned home to a big reception at the Lockheed Air Terminal in Burbank, with Dolores and all four kids there to greet him. Hope had traveled twenty-five thousand miles and done fifty-four shows in his four weeks abroad. He wasn't the first Hollywood entertainer to go to Korea; Al Jolson had preceded him in September (and had suffered a fatal heart attack a couple of weeks later, caused at least partly by the strain of the trip). But Hope was once again in his glory, the nation's most celebrated soldier in greasepaint.

Inspired by the trip, Hope resumed his

wartime routine of bringing his radio show to a different military camp each week. For his Frigidaire TV special in November, he featured the entertainers from his Korean trip, showed film clips from the tour, and closed the show with another of his inspirational messages, full of patriotic swagger:

The Iron Curtain boys thought they'd thrown a Sunday punch when they backed us up to Pusan. But they forgot one little detail. Ever since Plymouth Rock, Americans have had something to fight for — and, yes, die for if necessary. It's ten thousand miles from Westchester to Wonsan, but the flame of freedom in the human breast defies all distance and brings men together in a fight for the common ideal of a free and democratic world under God.

The Korean War dragged on for nearly three more years, settling into a stalemate and provoking a political firestorm when President Truman fired General MacArthur for "insubordination." Hope stayed away from the political controversy, but he was privately frustrated at the lack of military resolve. "I always had the feeling that if the US had used the air power it had standing by in Japan and the Philippines to bomb across the Yalu River line, a lot of American lives would have been saved," he wrote later. "But

458

it would have meant attacking Red China, and that was a political no-no." For Hope the battle lines were as clear-cut as they were in World War II. One of his writers, Larry Gelbart, came back with more ambivalent feelings about the war. His experiences traveling with Hope in Korea — especially their visits to mobile army hospital units near the front lines — supplied the raw material for his hugely successful antiwar sitcom of the 1970s, *M*A*S*H.*

By the early 1950s, Hope's image and attitude were undergoing a subtle but unmistakable shift. For much of the 1940s he was something of a renegade: an irreverent radio comedian and movie star, full of American moxie and impudence. Now he was show-business royalty: feted by generals, honored by presidents, entertaining queens. He grew more protective of his image and reputation, sensitive to criticism, notoriously litigious. In June 1950, he was sued for making jokes — by the Forrest Hotel in New York City, which claimed Hope had defamed it with some wisecracks about his stay there when he was playing the Paramount Theater. In November, Hope sued *Life* magazine for making jokes — in an article called "Radio's Seven Deadly Sins," by TV critic John Crosby. "Writers got $2,000 a week in Hollywood for copying down Fred Allen's jokes and putting them on Bob Hope's program," Crosby wrote. Hope sought $2 million in damages, claiming the line gave readers the serious impression that he was a plagiarist. (*Life*'s editors smoothed things over, and Hope eventually dropped the suit. His attorney Martin Gang said in a statement, "Hope had become convinced that the offending paragraph had been left in the story inadvertently and that there was no intention to harm him.")

With a greater role in producing his own films, Hope grew bolder in throwing his weight around. Just before he left for Korea in October, Paramount screened his just-completed film, *The Lemon Drop Kid,* which the studio wanted to have ready for a Christmas release. But Hope was unhappy with several scenes, and he insisted that Frank Tashlin, who had helped punch up *Monsieur Beaucaire,* be brought in again for rewrites. This time Tashlin was also allowed to direct the new scenes — infuriating director Sidney Lanfield, who never forgave Hope for taking the film out of his hands. "He was the worst egomaniac I ever worked with," Lanfield told author Lawrence Quirk, "a back-knifing son of a bitch, mean as sin. His way was the only way. I tried to buck him, and he took it out on me."

Another sign of Hope's growing power was the openness of his philandering. A tacit acceptance of Hollywood stars' extramarital activities was standard operating procedure in that prefeminism era. But the ability of Hope, along with his army of publicists and protectors, to keep his very open affairs out of the press was a real achievement. When rumors of his relationship with Marilyn Maxwell were rampant during the filming of *The Lemon Drop Kid,* Hollywood gossip doyenne Louella Parsons devoted a column to dismissing them. "In an exclusive interview with Dolores Hope," she wrote, "I have learned that there is absolutely no truth to the current rumors that Bob Hope and his leading lady, Marilyn Maxwell, are serious about each other just because they have been seen together so much."

Keeping Hope's womanizing under wraps was part of the job description for members of his entourage. Frank Liberman, a former studio publicist who began working for Hope in 1950, recalled an early conversation with Hope's longtime agent Louis Shurr. "Our mission in life," Shurr told him, "is to keep all news about fucking and sucking away from Dolores." Mark Anthony, an old friend from Cleveland who later took charge of arranging Hope's tours, as well as many of his assignations, said, "The boss knew a number of people, including newsmen, who were wise to his playing around on the side, but he counted on their loyalty to keep it quiet.

461

When I told him he was pushing his luck, he would say, 'Don't worry about it,' and I figured if he didn't, I wouldn't." Still, many in his inner circle were shocked at how brazenly Hope chased women. "You didn't know him in his frisky days," Charlie Lee, an acerbic British writer who joined Hope's staff in 1950, confided years later to a younger writer. "If the guy had any class, he'd commit suicide."

Dolores almost certainly knew about his sexual escapades, but she played the role of good wife to perfection. On the rare occasions when a reporter got near the subject, she would dance around it gracefully — though with more candor as the years went on. "I think he's a great man," she told *Life* magazine in 1971. "No person living has the kind of unspotted life that is the perfect example of clean living." "If he's had romances, I don't know about it," she told a *Washington Star* reporter in 1978. "I have read it in the paper. The paper loves to print things like that." Yet asked if she thought Bob was "one hundred percent true-blue," Dolores replied, "I doubt it. I think he's perfectly human and average and all that." When John Lahr raised the subject of Hope's womanizing in a 1998 profile of Hope for the *New Yorker,* Dolores gave this sweetly accepting response: "It never bothered me because I thought I was better looking than anybody else."

Clearly, she did what was needed to keep together a marriage that offered many compensations and was, in most other ways, sincerely close. She knew Bob was a rover from the start, she would tell people in later years, and simply made the best of it. "You can do anything you want," she told him, "as long as you don't bring any of it home." Said Linda Hope, "I'm sure that my mother knew what was going on. And she just decided that he was worth going through whatever she had to go through, to have the life and be Mrs. Bob Hope. But I don't think any of [the other women] had the significance to him that she did and that the family did. The stability, coming from a large family himself, was sort of an anchor that allowed him to go and do the kinds of things that he did."

If there were tensions in the marriage, they were kept well hidden from outsiders. Rory Burke, who as a child spent a good deal of time at the Hope house, caught a rare glimpse of discord — a sarcastic crack from Dolores, a snappish response from Bob, and quick orders for the children to leave the room. Most of the time, however, Dolores maintained a brave front. "She had grace under fire," said Burke. "She turned away from it. The main message was, you make your bed, you stay in it. If you're Catholic, you never get divorced."

Catholicism was Dolores's refuge and solace. She attended mass once a day, sometimes more, at St. Charles Borromeo Church, down the street from their house in Toluca Lake. She raised money for Catholic charities and surrounded herself with men of the church (like another family, the Kennedys, whose friendship with Catholic prelates seemed a way of atoning for family indiscretions). She had a passion for decorating and channeled her energies into the Toluca Lake house, undertaking a series of renovations, which she would typically have carried out while Bob was traveling. He joked that he hated to go away because he never knew what the house would look like when he came back.

But he did go away, often. In the spring of 1951 he spent a full two months abroad, on a personal-appearance tour that took him to London, Ireland, France, and Germany. Dolores had gone with him on his three previous non-wartime trips to Europe — in 1939, 1947, and his 1948 Christmas trip to Berlin. But this time she stayed home. His traveling companion, instead, was his costar on the tour Marilyn Maxwell.

Hope's intimate relationship with Maxwell was well-known to most of the people who worked with him. Writers traveling with Hope would find Maxwell in his hotel room when they met him there for meetings. On the road for a military-camp show, publicist Frank Liberman once saw Hope and Maxwell check in for the night at a cheap motel decorated with tepees and a neon sign reading SLEEP IN A WIGWAM TONIGHT. The two were together so often that people on the Paramount lot began referring to Maxwell as Mrs. Hope. For a time, according to some, she thought she might be.

Just how serious Hope was about Maxwell is hard to say. Twice married (she and her second husband, Andy McIntire, split in early 1951) and a former girlfriend of Frank Sinatra's (who was said to be jealous when Hope took up with her), Maxwell was unusual among Hope's girlfriends in being a high-profile leading lady, rather than one of the lesser known chorus girls, beauty queens, and showbiz wannabes he more typically hooked up with. Liberman, the publicist who helped cover up his affairs for many years, called Maxwell the second most serious of Hope's many girlfriends. (First place went to Rosemarie Frankland, a British-born beauty queen Hope was involved with in the 1960s.) Maxwell was one girlfriend who could hold her own with him onstage: until their relationship ended in 1954 (when Maxwell married her third husband, TV writer Jerry Davis), she and Hope appeared together, on radio, TV, and the stage, nearly two hundred times.

Hope's 1951 trip was the first of four visits he would make to England in four successive years. He felt a bond with the country of his birth, where he was nearly as popular as he was in the United States. (A *Motion Picture Herald* poll ranked him as Britain's No. 1 box-office star of 1951, followed by Jimmy Stewart and John Wayne.) London also had a great music-hall tradition, and Hope longed to play the Palladium, the last outpost for full-time vaudeville entertainment on either side of the Atlantic. But when the dates he wanted in April were already promised to Judy Garland, he agreed instead to a two-week engagement at the smaller Prince of Wales Theatre.

He gave himself a televised going-away party: a TV special for Frigidaire on April 8, 1951, that featured an all-British cast of guest stars, including Rex Harrison and Lilli Palmer, the husband-wife acting couple then appearing on Broadway in *Bell, Book and Candle.* In a sketch with Arthur Treacher, Hope shops for clothes for his trip, and in a big finale an all-star parade of "surprise" visitors — among them Ed Wynn, Eddie Cantor, Milton Berle, Sid Caesar, Jimmy Durante, and Frank Sinatra — drop by Hope's state-room to wish him bon voyage.

He sailed for London aboard the *Queen Mary* and did three one-nighters — in

Manchester, Blackpool, and Dudley — before making his way to London for the Prince of Wales engagement. On the bill with him were British comic actor Jerry Desmonde and an array of vaudeville acts, including a trick cyclist, a juggler, and a one-legged dancer named Peg-Leg Bates. Some of the London critics griped that Hope went on too long and that his material "had lapses into feebleness, surprising in a man who travels with a small army of gag men." But the two-week run was a sellout, and the Brits were impressed with his vaudeville pluck. "If little that Hope gave us was either inimitable or dazzling," said the *Guardian,* "much in the act was delightfully funny and as truly the stuff of the music hall as any film star has yet offered us."

Hope got an extra round of applause for donating the proceeds from the engagement to charity. A year earlier, on the Paramount lot, he was introduced to a diminutive Anglican priest named James Butterfield, who ran a center for underprivileged boys in South London called Clubland. The building had been badly damaged during the war, and Butterfield was trying to raise enough money to rebuild it. Hope impulsively promised that the next time he came to London he would do a benefit for the club. True to his word, he donated the bulk of the $50,000 he was paid for the Prince of Wales engagement, handing over a check personally on a visit to the club in its seedy South London neighborhood. One of the reformed delinquents who accepted Hope's gift talked years later about how much the gesture meant. "Bob was really great to us kids," said actor Michael Caine. "You can always send money. But to leave the West End and come right down to the Walworth Road, which isn't the Beverly Hills of London, takes a really charming man."

Hope finally made it to the Palladium a year later, headlining a two-week engagement in August 1952 with singer Betsy Duncan, and again in September 1953, with Gloria DeHaven. He built up a loyal support staff in London — a publicity team, two writers to help him tailor his material for his British audiences, and an agent, Lew Grade, who arranged British and European bookings. Hope's visits were widely covered in the British press and his London shows were nearly all sellouts.

There were some bumps, however. During his 1951 trip, Hope played in the British Amateur Golf Championship in Porthcawl, Wales, a year after Crosby had entered the same event. But Hope didn't play well, and the following year a columnist for the *London Star* publicly urged him not to come back: "Last year Hope never looked like a serious contender. His first match was a nightmare of gagging and tomfoolery. He departed leaving behind many sighs of relief."

Hope responded with jokes ("How hard can you hit a wet tea bag?"), while friends such as David Niven and golfer Jimmy Demaret wrote letters in his defense. But Hope skipped the tournament in 1952 and instead played a benefit match with Crosby against two British entertainers, Donald Peers and Ted Ray, at the Temple Golf Club in Maidenhead. That evening Crosby made an unbilled guest appearance with Hope at a benefit he was emceeing at London's Stoll Theatre — the first time Crosby had ever appeared on a London stage.

Hope's movies in the early 1950s were a mixed bag. Some harked back to his modest black-and-white comedies of the 1940s; others were more lavishly produced Technicolor farces, replete with sight gags typical of his broad, increasingly degraded later comedies. *Fancy Pants,* his 1950 Western comedy, was an unfortunate example of the latter, with Hope out of his comfort zone playing a British butler in the old West, Lucille Ball miscast as a frontier gal, and a lot of people getting hit over the head with crockery. *The Lemon Drop Kid,* released in April 1951, was a middling example of the former: another Damon Runyon story, featuring Hope as a racetrack tout who claims to get his tips directly from the horses, but with more farce and less warmth than *Sorrowful Jones.*

The Lemon Drop Kid does, however, boast one classic sequence: Hope and Maxwell's performance of "Silver Bells," the pretty, waltz-time Christmas song that Livingston and Evans had written to order for the movie. (It was originally called "Tinkle Bells," before someone thought better of it.) Hope was unhappy with the original staging of the number — he and Marilyn Maxwell sang it in a gambling parlor, with the gamblers providing choral accompaniment — and got his rescue man, Frank Tashlin, to totally reconceive it. Hope's instincts were right. The new scene, with the camera following the couple as they stroll along a snowy, movie-set re-creation of the New York City streets at Christmastime, has a lovely, nostalgic glow, and "Silver Bells" soon became a holiday standard, a perennial feature of Hope's Christmas TV specials, and a close second to "Thanks for the Memory" as Hope's great contribution to the American popular songbook.

My Favorite Spy, released in December 1951, was another throwback to Hope's classic style: the third in the *My Favorite* series, but actually an improvement over the last one, *My Favorite Brunette.* Hope has a role that is right in his wheelhouse — a cheesy burlesque comic named "Peanuts" White, who is a look-alike for an enemy spy from

Tangier — and costar Hedy Lamarr, the Vienna-born beauty whose movie career was on the wane, shows a surprising flair for comedy. But Hope's next film, *Son of Paleface,* was a more significant harbinger of things to come. A sequel to his hit 1948 Western spoof, the movie did a robust $3.4 million at the box office (one of the top-ten grossing films of the year), tickled most of the critics ("95 minutes of uninhibited mirth," said *Variety*), and remains one of the most popular Hope films of the fifties. Yet it doesn't hold up well and marks another step in the dumbing down of Hope's movie comedy.

He plays the son of his *Paleface* character, "Painless" Peter Potter — a snooty Harvard grad who has come West to claim his inheritance. Again Hope meets up with Jane Russell, this time playing the ringleader of a gang of gold thieves (a bigger star now, she has much more to do in this film, including a couple of musical numbers), as well as Roy Rogers, as a federal marshal on her trail. Playing a puffed-up "Harvard man," sneering at the townspeople while they're laughing behind his back, Hope is more effete and buffoonish than ever before. Russell, dressed in busty dance-hall outfits, looks ready to devour him. (Her steamy come-ons and revealing outfits prompted the Catholic Legion of Decency to slap the movie with an "objectionable" label, for "suggestive costuming, dialogue and situations.") In one creepy scene, Hope even finds himself in bed with Trigger, Roy Rogers's horse.

Son of Paleface was the first Hope film directed in full by Frank Tashlin, and the former cartoon director loads it with slapstick gags and camera gimmickry. When he first arrives in town, Hope loses control of his jalopy and sprays all the townspeople with mud. When he downs a strong drink, his body spins around like a top, steam blows out of his ears, and his head disappears into his torso. In a big chase scene, he trips the Indians by throwing banana peels in their path; in another he escapes by flying his car across a giant chasm, with the help of an umbrella. Some of this gets laughs, but it demeans Hope. Never before has he seemed so incidental to his gags.

"Let's see 'em beat this on television!" says Hope in the movie's last scene, as his car rears up on its hind wheels, like Trigger. And television, to be sure, was consuming most of Hope's attention in these years.

His flirtation with the new medium did not sit well with Paramount, which feared that its No. 1 comedy star was damaging his value on the big screen by doing television. But Hope too was hesitant about fully embracing the new medium. Like other radio stars, he feared getting overexposed on TV, which had shown how quickly it could burn up material and burn out performers — even Milton Berle's ratings were already slipping badly. In the 1951–52 season Hope hosted a couple of half hours for Chesterfield, his radio sponsor, including a December show from the deck of the USS *Boxer,* an aircraft carrier just back from Korea. But when Chesterfield wanted to put him on a more regular schedule, appearing once a month on Thursday nights (alternating with the popular police show *Dragnet*), Hope turned it down and said he was going to lay off television, except for occasional guest shots, for the rest of the season.

In the spring he starred in two installments of TV variety shows with rotating hosts, the *All-Star Revue* and the *Colgate Comedy Hour,* one filmed at the Presidio in San Francisco and the other at a Douglas Aircraft plant. And in June he and Crosby, making his television debut, were cohosts of a fourteen-hour televised fund-raiser — one of the first nationwide telethons — for US athletes headed to the 1952 Olympic Games in Helsinki. The show was carried on two networks, CBS and NBC; attracted dozens of top stars; and toted up more than $1 million in pledges (though only $300,000 was actually raised, an embarrassing shortfall that forced the fund-raisers to scramble for more donors to get the athletes to the Olympics).

The show was most memorable, however,

for the rare sight of Hope getting upstaged. The manic comedy team of Dean Martin and Jerry Lewis were at their peak of popularity — starring in hit movies, drawing top ratings on TV's *Colgate Comedy Hour,* and attracting huge crowds for their nightclub appearances and stage shows. (Their week at New York's Paramount Theater in July 1951 grossed $150,000 — $30,000 more than the record Hope had set a year earlier.) Hope saw their potential early on, inviting them as guests on his radio show in 1948, before their first movie was even released. But when he introduced them on the telethon, Lewis's frenetic, demented-child antics so unnerved Crosby that he fled backstage, leaving Hope to vainly try to get a word in, before he too gave up and left them alone onstage. The contrast between show-business generations — "It's time for the old-timers to sit down!" cried Lewis — was hard to miss. Martin and Lewis brought a jolt of anarchic energy to TV. Hope and Crosby, with their easygoing japery, were starting to look a little tired.

That impression was reinforced, alas, on their sixth *Road* picture, *Road to Bali.* Released in November 1952, five years after their last *Road* trip, to Rio, it was the first *Road* film in color, and the first of the television age. (Hope and Crosby even shot seven TV commercials to promote the movie.) But for the first time, the series was showing signs of wear.

It was another three-way joint production, between Hope, Crosby, and Paramount, and Lamour again felt left out. When she was asked to join Hope and Crosby in recording an album of songs from the film, she refused. "I didn't think it fair that I get less for the album than they did, and told them so," she said. "It was never mentioned again." Later she found out they went ahead and did the album with Peggy Lee. "It would have been nice if I had been informed," she commented sourly.

Most of the familiar ingredients of the series are here. Hope and Crosby once again play a small-time vaudeville team on the run — this time from Australia to the South Seas, in search of sunken treasure. The best laughs come from the stars' self-mocking asides. When Crosby and Lamour (back in a sarong as a South Seas princess) head offscreen together for a number, Hope turns to the camera: "He's gonna sing, folks. Now's the time to go out and get popcorn." While they're trekking through the jungle, a hunter walks on, fires his rifle, then leaves. "That's my brother Bob," explains Crosby. "I promised him a shot in the picture." A few minutes later there's a clip of Humphrey Bogart lugging his boat through the swamps in *The African Queen*. "Boy, is he lost," says Hope.

The trouble with *Road to Bali* is that it's

almost all diversions. The plot is virtually nonexistent, and the interplay between Hope and Crosby, both looking a little paunchier, lacks the improvisational zip that enlivened their earlier films. More than ever, the film seems to exist largely to indulge and showcase its two stars — a Scottish number called "Hoot, Mon," for example, so they can dress up in kilts. Still, *Road to Bali* did relatively well at the box office, and it would have been a respectable wrap-up for the great series. Unfortunately, there would be one last unnecessary chapter.

It took another decade to unfold. Plans for another *Road* film were in the works almost as soon as *Road to Bali* opened. A screenplay called *Road to the Moon,* written by Ken Englund (who had worked on Hope's first film, *Big Broadcast of 1938*), was set to be filmed in the fall of 1953, but it was shelved. The series lay dormant until eight years later, when Norman Panama and Melvin Frank wrote an entirely new script, still featuring a space trip, but now titled *The Road to Hong Kong.* With their film work getting more scarce, both Hope and Crosby were eager to recapture a little of their past glory, and the movie was scheduled to be shot for United Artists in the summer of 1961, at Shepperton Studios in London.

The production was a rare bonding experience for the Hope and Crosby families. Dolores came along, and she brought all four of the children, during their summer school vacations (Linda, the oldest, had just finished college). Crosby's second wife, Kathryn — pregnant with their third child — also joined them, along with their three-year-old son, Harry Jr. The two families rented a house together in Surrey — an English estate called Cranbourne Court, with twelve bedrooms, a croquet court, and a staff of proper English servants. Each morning Bob and Bing would eat breakfast with the wives, take a chauffeured car to the studio just a few minutes away, and wrap up the workday at 3:00 p.m. so they could get in a round of golf. On Friday nights the two couples went into London for dinner, took in the races at Ascot on Saturday afternoons, and spent one weekend together in the south of France. "I haven't seen this much of Bob since we were married," Dolores told Kathryn.

The odd woman out on this final *Road* trip was Dorothy Lamour. She had not done a movie of any kind since *Road to Bali* and was living in Baltimore with her husband, Bill Howard. But she was understandably hurt to discover that a new *Road* film was being planned without her. In the brutal casting calculus of Hollywood, Lamour — at forty-seven, more than a decade younger than Hope and Crosby — was deemed too old to play the love interest for them anymore. She was replaced with Joan Collins, a striking, twenty-eight-year-old British film actress who had appeared with Hope in one of his TV specials.

At the last minute Norman Panama gave Lamour a call and said there was a part for her in the film. After he dropped off a script in Baltimore on his way to London, she was disappointed to find that it was only a cameo — a single scene with Hope, with a song — and refused to do it. A series of pleading phone calls from London followed, asking her to relent: Panama and Frank had promised United Artists that Lamour would be part of the film and desperately needed her. "Realizing how important it was that I accept," she wrote in her memoir, "and remembering all the good times we went through together, I came to their rescue — but at a price, with a few zeroes attached to it."

The Road to Hong Kong was a sad last wheeze for the memorable series. Hope and Crosby, nearly sixty, look too old to be playing footloose con men (Hope has put on more weight, but Crosby has aged more). Their banter occasionally has some of the old spark. (Bing: "Ask your patriotic conscience what to do." Bob: "I already did." "What did it say?" "Yankee go home.") Frank Sinatra and Dean Martin, among others, make cameo appearances, and Peter Sellers has a funny bit as an Indian doctor treating Hope for amnesia. The film also boasts one of the best buddy songs of the entire series — "Teamwork," by Sammy Cahn and Jimmy Van Heusen.

But Hope and Crosby perform the number, significantly, not while riding a camel or on a carnival stage in darkest Africa, but over the opening credits, dressed in gaudy striped jackets in a spotlight on a generic stage — a sort of abstract idealization of their *Road*-picture camaraderie. References to earlier *Road* pictures are sprinkled throughout the film. "Not dangerous?" exclaims Hope, after hearing one Crosby scheme. "That's what you said when you shot me out of a cannon, when you dropped me in a tank with an octopus, when you had me wrestle a gorilla." Yet the out-of-character asides and fourth-wall-breaking stunts that made the earlier films so much fun are, strangely, almost entirely missing. Instead, Bob and Bing are put through a silly, way-too-consequential Cold War plot, with a shadowy superpower called the Third Echelon trying to launch a rocket to the moon to enslave the world. Bob and Bing wind up substituting for two chimpanzees being shot into orbit, providing the pretext for some crude fast-motion slapstick, as the strapped-in astronauts are force-fed food and drink by robotic machines that go haywire.

The Road to Hong Kong opened in May

1962 and got a deserved drubbing from the critics. Still, hopes for yet another reunion lived on. In the early seventies screenwriter Ben Starr wrote a treatment for a new film called *Road to Tomorrow,* but Hope scrapped it, and Starr had to threaten to sue to get his money. Then Mel Shavelson came up with a new script, titled *Road to the Fountain of Youth,* which was gearing up to start production in 1977 when Crosby died of a heart attack in Spain. Even after that, Hope toyed with recruiting George Burns to play the Crosby role in one last entry in the series. Thankfully, it never materialized. The greatest buddy series in movie history was finally put to rest.

Lamour never got over the feeling of being left out, her contribution to the series unappreciated to the end. Hope treated her better than Crosby did, giving her occasional guest spots on his TV specials in later years, as his career soared and she played dinner theaters. But when he included her in a 1966 special called *Bob's Leading Ladies,* she was offended to find herself just one of a dozen former movie costars given equal billing. "That was demeaning to her," said a friend. "She wasn't part of the crowd." Her resentment boiled over at a dinner at New York's Lincoln Center in the 1980s, when she let forth a tirade at the mention of Hope's name. "He still holds Hollywood like King Kong in the grip of his hand," she vented, according to film critic Carrie Rickey, who was at her table. "He treated all women with contempt. He never paid me any respect for my role in the *Road* movies and never helped me find work later. I was a totally replaceable part." It was always about the boys.

In July 1952, NBC asked Hope to do a series of daily five-minute monologues for its coverage of the Democratic and Republican National Conventions — the first political conventions to be televised nationally. Political material was becoming a bigger part of Hope's comedy repertoire: jokes about President Truman's testy relations with Congress, for example, or General Eisenhower's move into politics. "I happen to know why he's running for president," Hope said of Ike. "It's the only way to get out of the Army." As usual, Hope took aim, not at his targets' political views, but rather at superficial aspects of their popular image, such as Eisenhower's military background. "The Democrats are really determined to win this election," he said. "They're afraid if they don't win, Eisenhower will put 'em on KP."

When Hope took on more controversial figures, he was careful to avoid offending — usually poking fun at the mere fact that they were controversial. "General Eisenhower said that if he was elected, he was going to give

General MacArthur a very important job," Hope said. "Do you think we need an ambassador at the north pole?" Senator Joseph McCarthy's anticommunist witch hunts were lampooned with gibes that even McCarthy could laugh at: "Senator McCarthy is going to disclose the names of two million Communists. He just got his hands on a Moscow telephone book." There were endless jokes playing off the color red: McCarthy investigating red caps at the train station, or Congress appropriating money "for Red Skelton to dye his hair black." The Army-McCarthy hearings, said Hope, were "a new kind of television show. It's sort of a soap opera where everyone comes out tattletale gray."

Hope kept his own views on McCarthy private, but they surfaced unexpectedly in an audience question-answer session at the London Palladium in 1953. When one audience member asked what he thought about McCarthyism, Hope replied with unusual candor: "I think it's Americanism. Some people think McCarthy is wrong. Personally I think he's right ninety-nine times out of a hundred." Many in the audience booed, and Hope shut up after that.

For the 1952–53 season, Hope finally committed to a regular monthly TV show: as one of the rotating hosts (along with Martin and Lewis, Abbott and Costello, and Eddie Cantor) of NBC's popular *Colgate Comedy Hour* on Sunday nights. Hope's Colgate hours regularly trounced the tough competition on CBS, Ed Sullivan's *Toast of the Town.* Then, for the 1953–54 season, General Foods sponsored him in a once-a-month variety hour on Tuesday nights, alternating with Milton Berle's *Buick Show.* Hope consistently outperformed Berle, and for the season ranked fifth in the Nielsen ratings. In those two years Hope ended any doubts that he was in television to stay and established the variety-show format that he would stick with for the rest of his TV career.

He was hardly an innovator. While Sid Caesar and Imogene Coca were pioneering satirical sketch comedy on *Your Show of Shows,* and Martin and Lewis were bringing their improvisational anarchy to the *Colgate Comedy Hour,* Hope merely transferred his old radio format to television: an opening monologue, scripted patter with his guest stars, a song from the musical guest, and two or three comedy sketches. The shows were more elaborately produced than his early Frigidaire specials, often with a choreographed musical opening (a baseball-themed number for opening day, for example, or an Irish dance for St. Patrick's Day). Hope was now fully at ease with the camera: striding confidently to the microphone with his long-gaited, slightly effeminate, palms-facing-backward walk; reeling off the jokes at a brisk, metronome-steady pace; setting his jaw and locking in his gaze as he waited for the laughs, then breaking into a crooked, upcurled-to-the-left smile when they came, as they nearly always did.

The jokes were timely and topical, a chronicle of the issues, news makers, fads, and fears of early-1950s America: the A-bomb and 3-D movies, Christine Jorgensen's sex-change operation and Senator Kefauver's organized-crime hearings, the Cold War and color television. "NBC wants to get the color perfect before they release it to the public," Hope said. "We don't want the Russian who's inventing it next week to make any mistakes." (Hope was slated to host TV's first commercial color broadcast, on November 17, 1953. But the FCC at the last minute withheld its approval, allowing only a closed-circuit colorcast of the dress rehearsal. Hope was disappointed to miss out on the historic first — which came a week later on a Donald O'Connor–hosted segment of the *Colgate Comedy Hour.*)

On television, unlike radio, Hope couldn't hold a script, so he read his lines from cue cards — scrawled out for him by Barney McNulty, an Army Air Corps veteran who used to transcribe Morse code messages in block letters. McNulty came up with the idea of using cue cards for Ed Wynn's TV show in

1949, and he began doing them for Hope in 1953, putting them on stacks of thirty-by-forty-inch poster board. (Hope wanted the cards as big as possible, so they would have to be flipped less often.) An affable Irishman, McNulty became another loyal member of the entourage, often a whipping boy for Hope when things went wrong on the set, and all but inseparable from him for the next forty years.

In later years, Hope was notorious for being tied to the cue cards for virtually every moment of his shows. But in the early fifties he wasn't using them in sketches, and it showed. The skits were broad and crudely staged, with an overreliance on funny costumes and incongruous settings — Hope as a caveman, say, or a college frat boy, or a movie director named Orson Von Hope. But Hope was focused and well rehearsed, and at their best the sketches had the same wisecracking zing of his better movies of the period. In a 1954 bit with Rosemary Clooney, for example, he plays a turn-of-the-century bachelor who's being roped into marriage by his high-society girlfriend:

ROSEMARY: "Oh, Robert, don't you realize we're the only ones in our set that haven't been married?"

BOB: "Yeah, I was thinking about that."

"What do you think we should do about it?"

485

"Join a new set?"

"Can't you see what I'm hinting at? We have so much in common, haven't we?"

"Well, it's true that we have one important thing in common. We both like me."

"We could be so happy together. The two of us could be one."

"Won't there be some parts left over?"

The unscripted moments were even better. Animals were always good for some unrehearsed laughs, such as a sketch in which Hope plays poker with Trigger, or a funny *This Is Your Life* parody in which Hope cracks up as a parade of trained dogs troop onstage to pay tribute to Lassie. Blown lines and mishaps were common, and the spontaneous reactions to them were often funnier than the scripted lines: Jack Benny, as a violinist who wanders into Hope's New Orleans jazz club, breaking character to complain about his bad lines; or Fred MacMurray, as a college jock, grabbing a ukulele and serenading Hope's girlfriend (Janis Paige), then flubbing a line and nearly crushing his two costars as they stifle laughter on a couch underneath him. The sight of big Hollywood stars grappling with an unpredictable live medium was part of the fun of these early fifties TV variety shows. And no one had more fun with them than Hope.

Even as he was growing more comfortable with television, Hope was hedging his bets in radio, continuing to host his Tuesday-night show even as the audience steadily dwindled. In the spring of 1952 Chesterfield pulled out as Hope's radio sponsor, and for the first time in fifteen years he was left off NBC's fall schedule. But General Foods picked up the show, and he was back on the air in January, now pitching Jell-O, the dessert product so long associated with Jack Benny. With a new sponsor came other changes. His show was moved from its familiar Tuesday-night slot, where it had been a fixture since 1938, to Wednesdays at 10:00 p.m. What's more, Hope suddenly had a new radio program: a fifteen-minute daytime talk show, to air every weekday morning on NBC. Far from giving up on radio, Hope would now be on the air six times a week.

Hope's move into morning radio was a sign of the medium's desperation. As the audience for radio's long-running nighttime hits was fleeing for television, there was a brief flurry of hopeful speculation that the old radio favorites could have new life in daytime. The model was Arthur Godfrey, who, in addition to his two prime-time TV shows, was the host of a popular morning show on CBS radio. "It's not only a challenge, but it gives Bob a better chance to get closer to the people," said Hope's agent Jimmy Saphier, explaining the rationale behind the morning show, "and it's my strong conviction that daytime radio will outlast nighttime." Hope, with his inexhaustible appetite for work, was game to try anything.

His morning show, which debuted in November 1952 and was taped in the evenings at NBC's Hollywood studios, was a mix of celebrity chatter (Zsa Zsa Gabor was his first week's guest), musical numbers, and banter with the audience. "The new arrangement should make me very popular," Hope joked on his opening show. "When I did my show just once a week, people used to say, 'Wasn't Hope lousy last Tuesday?' Now they can say, 'If you think he was lousy on Tuesday, you should have heard him on Wednesday.' " *Variety,* reviewing the show's first week, was encouraging: "Hope at his old-time radio best — and that's good. It may well set the pattern for a complete reshuffle in network radio programming, in that a number of name personalities may follow Hope into the after-breakfast hours if he can draw a rating."

He didn't. After a few weeks NBC moved the show from 9:30 to 11:30 a.m., where it hoped more stations would pick it up. But Hope's daytime show never rose above a modest 3 or 4 Nielsen rating and couldn't challenge the formidable Godfrey. In July 1954, after two seasons on the air, NBC pulled the plug, ending this odd, forgettable cul-de-sac in Hope's career.

Hope continued his nighttime show for another season, but his radio career was stumbling to an end. In March 1953 the ratings for his prime-time show sank to a lowly forty-fourth place in the Nielsens. That fall General Foods dropped out as Hope's sponsor, replaced by the American Dairy Association, and NBC moved the show yet again, to Thursday nights. Still, Hope plodded on, with Margaret Whiting joining as regular singer and Bill Goodwin, a charter member of the original *Pepsodent Show* crew, back as announcer.

On his last show of the 1954–55 season, Hope's guest was his old sidekick Jerry Colonna. In the featured comedy sketch, Hope has a meeting with a snooty NBC executive, played by Jim Backus, who breaks the news that Hope's show has been canceled. (The punch line is that Colonna is replacing him.) It was meant to be a joke, but Hope's sign-off on April 21, 1955 — "Thanks from all of us for the memory of a grand season, and good night" — were the last words he would ever speak as the host of a network radio show. When the season was over, American Dairy dropped his program, and this time no new sponsor was waiting to pick him up.

After seventeen years, without a whimper or a formal good-bye, Bob Hope's radio career was over. Jack Benny's show ended its twenty-three-year run that same spring. Edgar Bergen and Charlie McCarthy lasted just one more season. The golden age of radio had faded years earlier, and now even its last relics were gone.

Nothing gave Hope's TV profile a bigger boost in the early 1950s than the night of March 19, 1953, when he was host for the first televised Academy Awards ceremony. He had emceed the Oscar show six times before, but not since 1946 — a reflection, most likely, of the movie studios' unhappiness over Hope's plunge into television. (Danny Kaye and Jack Benny were among the hosts in the interim.) But when NBC offered to pay $100,000 for the rights to televise the 1953 awards, the Academy decided it was time to make peace with television — and with Bob Hope too.

It was an ambitious broadcast for the young medium. Nine tuxedo-clad cameramen were stationed at the Pantages Theater in Hollywood, while another crew was dispatched to the International Hotel in New York City, where Conrad Nagel hosted the East Coast segments of the show. (Several nominees were appearing on Broadway, including Shirley Booth, who won the Best Actress award for

Come Back, Little Sheba.) The broadcast, marking the Oscars' twenty-fifth anniversary, opened with a clip from the first Best Picture winner, *Wings,* followed by shots of modern jets in flight. "Like the streaking jet plane," announcer Ronald Reagan intoned, "the Academy Award ceremony itself has been streamlined, has become a major news event, originating tonight on two coasts of a great continent and beamed around the globe."

Rain was falling in Los Angeles as the live broadcast began with a few quick shots of the red carpet arrivals. "We're having some unusual California weather," noted Reagan, before handing off to the orchestra, which opened the show with "The Continental," winner of the first Oscar for Best Song. Academy president Charles Brackett made some introductory remarks, and then came Hope.

Dressed in dinner jacket, white vest, and white tie, he was the picture of Hollywood elegance. Glancing down at a script in front of him (no cue cards yet), he opened with jokes about television: "I want to thank all the wrestlers for relinquishing their time. Just shows you, there's nothing that one group of actors won't do for another." He was a little patronizing to the new medium — "Television, that's where movies go when they die" — but also eager to call a truce in the industry feud. "This is indeed a wedding of two great entertainment mediums, motion pictures and television. And with Oscar twenty-five years old, it's high time he got married. While it's true he has a child bride, it's a comfort to note the kid is loaded."

Hope then reverted to his usual barrage of Hollywood jokes, tailored for the new TV audience: "Keep your eyes on the losers tonight as they applaud the winners. You'll see great understanding. Great sportsmanship. Great acting." He harped, as usual, on his favorite running gag, getting passed over for his own Academy Award: "There was a rumor going around last year that I might win an Oscar. But nobody paid any attention, so I stopped spreading it."

In fact, Hope did get an Oscar that year — his third honorary award, for "his contribution to the laughter of the world, his service to the motion picture industry, and his devotion to the American premise." Hope could even claim a tiny share of credit for the year's winner for Best Picture. In a mild upset, the Oscar went to *The Greatest Show on Earth,* the Cecil B. DeMille circus extravaganza, in which Hope had a brief cameo, sitting in a circus audience next to Crosby, watching Dorothy Lamour on the trapeze.

The first Oscar telecast was a triumph for both television and the movies. "Seldom has the immediacy and actuality of television been used so advantageously," said Jack

Gould in the *New York Times.* "As a TV show," cheered *Variety,* "it was socko almost all the way. . . . Certainly it dramatized the future course of show biz on how TV and pix must 'go steady' whether they like it or not." The show was watched by nearly 50 million people, the largest audience for any TV show in the medium's short history. For this vast audience, Hope would be the face of Hollywood, a guide to its glamour and a deflator of its pretensions, for the next two and a half decades.

He was Hollywood's First Citizen, its most acclaimed goodwill ambassador, an entertainer who transcended mere entertainment. In February 1953, to mark his fifteenth anniversary at both Paramount and NBC, the Friars Club threw him a testimonial dinner at New York's Waldorf Astoria Hotel. Along with the usual Friars regulars — Milton Berle, George Jessel, Fred Allen (but again, no Crosby) — the dais was filled with the sort of dignitaries only Bob Hope could attract, among them Senator Stuart Symington, former vice president Alben Barkley, New York City mayor Vincent Impellitteri, and eighty-three-year-old former presidential adviser Bernard Baruch — who got out of his sickbed for the event.

What's more, Hope now had a friend in the White House: his old World War II comrade Dwight D. Eisenhower. He played golf with the new president for the first time in April 1953, when Hope was in Washington for the White House Correspondents' Association dinner. Hope and Eisenhower formed a twosome, playing against senators Stuart Symington and Prescott Bush. Hope shot an 85, and he and Ike lost $4 on the match. The next day they played again, this time on opposite sides — Hope paired with Bush, and Ike with General Omar Bradley. Hope shot a 75, and Eisenhower lost again. "Why didn't you play this well yesterday?" Ike said. Recalled Hope, "He wasn't laughing either."

Even as Hope hobnobbed with the rich and powerful, he never stopped thinking of himself as a working stiff. In 1952 friends talked him into running as a write-in candidate for president of the American Guild of Variety Artists (AGVA), the union representing stage performers. He was elected by a landslide — though, at a time when the union was involved in several contentious labor disputes, Hope didn't attend a single meeting and quit when his one-year term ended. Meanwhile, as he reached his fiftieth birthday in 1953, Hope made his most serious attempt at an autobiography, collaborating on a memoir with ghostwriter Pete Martin, who had just helped Bing Crosby write his autobiography, *Call Me Lucky.* When Hope's book was serialized in the *Saturday Evening Post* beginning in February 1954, the first monthly installment (with a Norman Rockwell painting of Hope on the cover, the first time a Hollywood celebrity had ever been a *Post* cover subject) sold 5.2 million copies, a magazine record.

The book, published by Simon & Schuster the following December under the title *Have Tux, Will Travel,* was breezy, joke-filled, and only minimally revealing. But it was as candid as Hope would ever get in print. "That breezy Bob Hope — that Hope with a bounce you see on the screen or on your TV set — is me," he wrote in the introduction. "I get peeved as easy as the next guy — unless the next guy is Donald Duck. Occasionally I'm disillusioned with people I've liked and trusted. But I don't make a hobby of mental turmoil. . . . I know it's hard for people to believe a man in my business is normal emotionally and mentally. If they don't, there's nothing I can do about it."

The neglected stepchild in Hope's extended family of show-business activities in these years was his movie career. His two releases for 1953 were both oddities, neither very successful nor very good. In *Off Limits* Hope plays a boxing trainer who enlists in the Army when his new champion is drafted — then gets stuck there on his own when the champ is rejected as psychologically unfit. He finds another young recruit (Mickey Rooney) to train, while falling for his aunt, a nightclub singer played by Marilyn Maxwell. Hope is engaged and energetic, but too old to be playing an Army recruit, and the film, with its familiar service gags, feels like a weary retread of *Caught in the Draft.*

Next came *Here Come the Girls,* Hope's only full-scale movie musical. Set in turn-of-the-century New York, it cast him as Stanley Snodgrass, the "world's oldest chorus boy," who is given the starring role in a Broadway musical (opposite diva Arlene Dahl) as a decoy to catch a serial killer. Despite a couple of bright Livingston-Evans tunes — including "Ya Got Class," which Hope sings with Rosemary Clooney — the script is ludicrous, and Hope again seems too old for the part (he's living with his parents!). His bulging schedule of TV, radio, and personal appearances may have been taking its toll. He didn't rehearse much, and Arlene Dahl was most impressed with his ability to take catnaps between scenes. "He told me he starts with his feet and tells them to relax," she said. "Then his calves and thighs, up his body, gets to his head, and he's asleep. Very yoga-like." Rosemary Clooney recalled, "Bob was doing about twelve other things at the same time. It seemed to me that he would show up for about an hour a day and we would shoot around him the rest of the time." Clooney called *Here Come the Girls* "one of the world's worst pictures"; coming in the midst of the early-fifties heyday of the movie musical, it was certainly one of the most forgettable.

Casanova's Big Night, his next film, was at least an improvement, a return to one of his most successful genres, the costume swash-buckler. As in *Monsieur Beaucaire,* Hope dons period garb, playing a tailor's apprentice who poses as the famed eighteenth-century lover. Directed by Norman Z. McLeod, the film is another glossy production with an impressive supporting cast that includes Joan Fontaine, Basil Rathbone, and an unbilled Vincent Price as the real Casanova. Though less winning than *Beaucaire,* the film has its plea-sures. Hope is in top form as a commoner with pretensions, sharp-tongued and physi-cally graceful (when he bows low, his hat falls off his head and drops effortlessly into his waiting hand), and there's a clever, tongue-in-cheek double ending. Just before the guil-lotine is about to fall on Hope, he stops the action and replays it with his own alternate happy ending — then asks the audience to vote on which one it wants, his or the studio's. Hope loses.

Yet *Casanova's Big Night,* released in March 1954, got a surprisingly sour reception from the critics. *Variety* said the film "misses as often as it clicks," and the *Hollywood Reporter* complained, "Aside from a few scattered laughs, which come from Hope's wonderful gift for clowning rather than any wit in the script, there is little entertainment." Though it earned a respectable $3 million at the box office, better than most other Hope films of the period, it was a sign that Hope's formula was starting to wear thin.

Unhappy at the slump in his film career, Hope decided to break out on his own. In October 1954 he announced that he was leaving Paramount, the studio that had brought him to Hollywood and where he had spent seventeen successful if sometimes stormy years. After one final film, all his future movies would be produced by Hope Enterprises, giving him the right to peddle them to any studio for distribution. He wanted more leeway to pick his projects, set his schedule — and, he hoped, keep more of the profits. He played down the breakup the next day in an interview with columnist Hedda Hopper, saying he'd be happy to continue working with Paramount for another seventeen years, but was "only asking for good stories through my own company, Hope Enterprises. That's the kid I want to fatten up."

Hope was showing his independent streak with his TV network as well. In the fall of 1954, Hope accepted an invitation for another command performance for the royal family at the London Palladium. Because of the trip, he told NBC he would have to skip his regularly scheduled special for November. The network bosses objected, since it meant losing General Foods' sponsorship of the hour. But Hope refused to cancel the trip, telling Jimmy Saphier, "Let them sue me if they want."

In place of his November special, Hope told NBC, he would put together a big event for December: an international variety special featuring entertainers never before seen on American television. He arrived in London on October 15, two weeks before his Palladium appearance, and began lining up stars for the show. He hired the 182-member Cologne Choir after hearing them at Festival Hall. He flew to Paris (almost getting thrown in jail because he left his passport in London) and recruited Maurice Chevalier to make his American TV debut. While there he also signed up twenty-one-year-old ballerina Liane Dayde, whom he saw at the Paris Opera Ballet, and later added his old cohort Bea Lillie, traveling all the way to Glasgow to do rehearsals with her.

The special was filmed over two nights, November 7 and 8, by a BBC crew at the Empire Theatre in Shepherd's Bush. "In television in America we've got to such a difficult state with these big commercial shows that you see the same stars on four or five shows in the same week," he told the audience. "It's become impossible to do anything new. That's why we are over here." The show was edited in the United States and telecast on December 7, accompanied by a network publicity campaign heralding it as "the first truly global television show."

The ratings were only fair, and the critical response polite at best. "As an evening's entertainment, it should have been received in good grace if not with screams of joy," said *Variety*. But Hope was proud of the show, which gave him a chance to reaffirm his status as an international star and champion of global understanding. "Entertainment will continue to be the common denominator expressing mutual comprehension among the world's peoples," he told a reporter. "There's only one world for television."

Yet Hope was restless, making noises about slowing down. He turned down lucrative offers from Texaco and General Motors to sponsor his TV shows for the 1955–56 season, saying he wanted to take a break from television. He may simply have been playing hard to get in advance of negotiations for a new contract with NBC. But it's possible he was also feeling a whiff of mortality. In January 1955 his pal Charlie Yates, an agent who had helped Hope in his early vaudeville days, dropped dead of a heart attack while playing golf with Hope in Palm Springs. "It didn't really affect me for three days," Hope told the AP's Bob Thomas. "Then the shock set in. I was terribly upset. I began to feel all sorts of pains and things wrong in my body."

Even after the doctor gave him a clean bill of health, Hope decided he should take it easier. "The gang at Lakeside will tell you that Bob Hope is dead serious about slowing down," reported *Variety*. "Too many of his friends have crossed the border and, while still in his early 50s, he feels that the grueling pace of past years may catch up with him too."

In mid-1955 Hope agreed to a new five-year contract with NBC, which called for a scaled-back schedule of only six specials a year. Hope may well have wanted to slow down, but he also realized that the key to survival on TV was limiting his exposure, and making his fewer appearances as special as possible. It was a shrewd calculation that would pay off in the years ahead.

In early 1954, Mel Shavelson and Jack Rose, two of Hope's favorite writers, came to see him in Toluca Lake, bringing along a quart of ice cream as a peace offering. They told him about a movie they wanted to do: a biography of Eddie Foy, the turn-of-the-century vaudeville star who created an act with his seven children after their mother, an Italian dancer he had met and married in vaudeville, died of cancer. They wanted Hope to star as Eddie Foy.

Hope liked the idea. He had seen the Foys in vaudeville and welcomed a chance to do a challenging, semidramatic role. Then the

501

writers told him their conditions. Shavelson wanted to direct the film himself (he had never directed a movie before), and Rose wanted to produce it (he had never produced a movie before). "That's okay," said Hope. "My last picture was so lousy, you guys can't possibly do one lousier." There was one more condition: Paramount agreed to back the film, but only if Hope took no money up front, just a share of the profits. After some consideration, Hope agreed to that as well — the first time he had ever done a movie for no salary — and the film was produced jointly by Paramount, Hope Enterprises, and the partnership of Shavelson and Rose.

The Seven Little Foys was the first film in which Hope played a real-life character, and he did some homework for it, reading up on Foy and watching old silent movies of him. He also brushed up on his dancing, especially when James Cagney agreed to a cameo in the film as George M. Cohan — reprising his Oscar-winning role in *Yankee Doodle Dandy* — for a scene in which he challenges Foy to a dancing contest at the Friars Club. (Cagney took no salary for the part. When he was a starving Broadway chorus boy, he explained, the Foys would invite him to their house in Westchester County for Sunday dinner. Often it was the only good meal he got for a week. This was his payback.) The filming took place in August and September of

1954. During it, Hope paid a visit to his friend Barney Dean, who was in the hospital dying of cancer — sad motivation for the dramatic scenes he was in the midst of shooting.

No movie he had done meant more to Hope than *The Seven Little Foys,* and when it was released in May 1955, he went into overdrive to promote it. He made a tour of Australia in conjunction with the film's world premiere — the first time an American star had ever come to Australia to open a major Hollywood film. Back in the United States, Hope went on a four-week, twenty-five-city promotional tour for the movie, doing live stage shows and TV interviews in every city he visited. Paramount estimated that Hope's personal stumping added $1 million to the film's box office. "I think the way things are going, an actor is very foolish not to help sell his pictures," Hope told Louella Parsons. Hollywood was discovering the potential of using stars to promote their own films with personal appearances and media interviews — sellebrities, they were dubbed — and Hope, once again, was a pioneer.

The Seven Little Foys earned $6 million at the box office, Hope's biggest hit in years. Its mix of comedy and sentiment left a few critics uneasy, but most of them generally admired the movie and praised Hope's performance. "A commanding abandonment of the buffoon," said *Variety.* The *New York Daily News* raved, "Hope can now hold up his head with Hollywood dramatic thespians; for the first time in his career, Hope isn't playing Hope on the screen." In truth, Hope isn't exactly playing Eddie Foy either. He does a sort of half impersonation — imitating Foy's hoarse, laid-back, cigar-chomping swagger, but never quite disappearing into the role. He's still best being Bob Hope — trading wisecracks with his acerbic kids, and in the justly celebrated dance sequence with Cagney, in which they match steps atop a banquet table. (Cagney is clearly the better dancer, but he graciously allows Hope to outshine him.)

Hope's innate charm cheats a bit on the dark side of Foy's character — his self-regard, his emotional detachment, and his inattention as a father. But his stoic underplaying is effective in the big courtroom scene in which Foy laments his failings as a father, the culmination of his battle for custody of the kids against his former sister-in-law. He's even better in the quieter, earlier scenes when Foy comes home from traveling to find that his wife (whose illness he has willfully ignored) has died in his absence. Hope silently goes from bedroom to bedroom to check on his sleeping children. One daughter rouses from her sleep and asks groggily, "Who is it?" Hope's blank, poignant response: "Nobody."

The film may have had more real-life resonance than Hope was willing to admit. "How can you stay all these years with this man?" Foy's sister-in-law complains to his wife at one point about his frequent absences. "A stranger in his own home. A visitor to his children. Nothing to show how he feels." It's almost too obvious to note the parallels to Hope's own family life in the middle of the 1950s.

The older kids, Tony and Linda, were now attending Catholic high school in Hollywood. The younger two, Nora and Kelly, were in grade school and struggling to get attention (Nora, the more outgoing, with better luck than Kelly). Quality time with their father, always at a premium, grew even scarcer as their home life became grander and more public. "The family changed in the 1950s," said nephew Tom Malatesta. "Bob became enormous. There were more people around the house with bigger names. At a party Marilyn Monroe and Joe DiMaggio might walk in the door, or Ray Milland or Lana Turner. It was a larger environment, and the family relationship was more formal. More people came into the intimate setting."

There was occasional family time — fishing trips to British Columbia or Colorado, and the annual get-together of the extended family during the Christmas holidays, when relatives from Cleveland would come to town for a New Year's party and pile into a chartered bus for a trip to the Rose Bowl, with a police escort and seats on the fifty-yard line. Dolores, as always, picked up the slack when Bob was away, keeping the house organized and the kids in line. "She looked at the report cards and got us to school on time," said Kelly Hope, "and made sure the lunches were ready to go, and whoever was going to pick us up at three o'clock, and what doctor did we have to go to and why. For lack of a better word, she ran the show." Dolores could be tough, and her discipline unforgiving. Once when Kelly misbehaved, all the furniture was removed from his bedroom as punishment, except for his bed and a lamp. And their father's mere presence could be intimidating: when playing hide-and-seek in the library, the kids would often be shushed because Bob might still be sleeping in the bedroom above.

Dolores tried to shield them from the perils of being a celebrity's child — the constant press attention, the schoolmates who wanted access to their famous father, and sometimes worse. When *Confidential* magazine in 1956 published Barbara Payton's steamy account of her five-month affair with Hope in 1949, Dolores had to warn the children in advance. "This trashy magazine is coming out with an article about your dad," Linda recalled her mother telling them. "I just want you to know, in case they bring it up at school or some of your friends say something. But it's not true. You know your dad, and that's what's important."

Just how well they knew him was harder to say.

CHAPTER 9
AMBASSADOR

"I'M NOT HAVING ANY TROUBLE WITH THE LANGUAGE. NOBODY SPEAKS TO ME."

On November 14, 1955, Bob Hope applied for a visa to visit the Soviet Union. The request, made at the Soviet embassy in Washington for himself and a TV crew of ten, might have seemed strange coming from a staunchly anticommunist Republican at the height of the Cold War. Hope often cast the rigid and ruthless Soviet dictatorship as a comic villain in his monologues. "I saw a Russian ad for cold cream," he joked when the Soviets aired their first TV commercials. "It had a picture of a beautiful girl, and underneath it said, 'She's lovely, she's engaged, she's gonna be shot in the morning.'" But for Hope, entertainment always trumped ideology, and he wanted to score another show-business coup by becoming the first entertainer to do an American TV show from behind the Iron Curtain.

He got the idea while he was in London in the fall of 1955, shooting his movie *The Iron Petticoat,* in which Katharine Hepburn played a Soviet pilot who defects to the West. Hope, quixotically, wanted to shoot the movie's ending at a Moscow airfield. The US State Department turned down the request, even before the Russians had a chance to say no. Then, intrigued at the idea of bringing Soviet entertainment to American audiences, Hope sent his brother Jack to Brussels to get footage of the Moscow Circus, intending to use clips of the troupe ("the greatest I've ever seen," Hope said) in one of his TV specials. But both NBC and his sponsor, Chevrolet, vetoed the idea, apparently fearful of the political fallout.

Hope's next idea was to bring a TV crew to the Soviet Union to shoot an entire special there, featuring Soviet artists and entertainers who had never performed in the West. "I've seen many a curtain go up in my time," he said. "My greatest thrill would be to see this one, the Iron Curtain, go up." At a time when the Cold War was at its frostiest, the idea would take two and a half years to come to fruition. But it was the centerpiece of Hope's efforts in the 1950s to secure his role as America's leading show-business emissary to the world.

Hope had not taken an entertainment troupe abroad since his Far East swing during the Korean War in 1950. Then, in late 1954, Secretary of the Air Force Harold Talbott asked Hope if he would make a New

Year's Eve trip to Greenland, where five thousand US troops were manning a Strategic Air Command post at Thule Air Base, part of the nation's early-warning system against a potential Soviet nuclear strike. The lonely and forbidding outpost was 750 miles north of the Arctic Circle, but Hope jumped at the chance.

To join him, he recruited a big Hollywood star, William Holden (winner of the Academy Award for Best Actor that year for *Stalag 17*); two of his World War II traveling companions, Jerry Colonna and Patty Thomas; his radio singer, Margaret Whiting; and newspaper gossip columnist Hedda Hopper, who did double duty by writing about the trip in her syndicated column and joining Hope onstage for some banter about Hollywood. He tried to get Marilyn Monroe, Hollywood's top glamour girl of the moment, but she was embroiled in a contract dispute with her studio, Twentieth Century–Fox, and didn't even return his phone calls. (Monroe was the one major Hollywood sex symbol Hope never appeared with.) Instead, as the requisite piece of cheesecake, he tapped a well-endowed former Miss Sweden whom he had met at a Big Ten Football Conference banquet in Los Angeles, named Anita Ekberg.

In a brief trip of just forty-eight hours, Hope and his troupe landed at Thule (pronounced *TOO-lee*) in thirty-six-below weather and for two days never saw the sun. They did two shows, one at a gymnasium at Thule on New Year's Eve and a second the next day in Goose Bay, Labrador. Both were filmed and later edited together into an hour show for NBC's *Colgate Comedy Hour,* which aired on January 9. The telecast drew a protest from the cameramen's union, which was unhappy that government crews had been used instead of union cameramen. (Hope said he had nothing to do with the decision; he prided himself on supporting unions and regularly refused to cross picket lines.) But it was a landmark for Hope: the first time one of his military tours was televised.

"I can't tell you how happy I am to be up here on the moon with you," Hope says in his opening monologue, standing in front of a curtain on the makeshift stage in the converted gym at Thule. "It's the only place in the world where you get a good-conduct medal just for being alive." A half dozen dancing girls, dressed in parkas and skating skirts fringed in white fur, sing, "Why do they call it Greenland when everything looks so white?" Holden, adopting his swaggering, cigar-chomping *Stalag 17* persona, joins Hope for some repartee and later runs around supplying the props as Hope and Whiting do a patter-and-song number, "Make Yourself Comfortable." In a sketch, Hope and Holden (joined by the scruffy Robert Strauss, one of Holden's costars from *Stalag 17*) play stir-crazy servicemen who vie for the chance to give a tour of the base to Ekberg (as a *New York Times* reporter!). The familiar jokes about lonely, sex-starved servicemen, along with the sight of big Hollywood stars working with makeshift sets and community-theater production facilities, were a warming touch of home for the men stuck in this forlorn outpost. The special that was edited from the trip drew more viewers than any other Hope TV show yet, with a whopping 60 percent share of the viewing audience.

Hope recognized a winning formula when he saw one. The following year, in the midst of filming *The Iron Petticoat* in London, he took a break at Christmas to do some shows for the US troops stationed in Iceland, bringing along blond British sexpot Diana Dors as a guest star. Excerpts from the shows were edited into a special that Hope had already recorded back in Hollywood.

The Iceland trip was notable mainly for a mishap that didn't make it into the show. Among the entertainers Hope brought along was a blond, five-foot-ten-inch strongwoman named Jean Rhodes, who bent steel bars and did a bit with Hope in which she lifted him on her shoulders while they sang "Embrace-able You." Her tacky vaudeville act (testimony to Hope's low standards for entertainment when it involved curvaceous gals) went well enough until the last show, when Rhodes lost her balance after lifting up Hope, plunging him headfirst to the floor. He cut his nose and wrenched his neck and was flown immediately back to London for X-rays. There were no broken bones (and he was well enough to host a British TV show the next day), though Hope later speculated that the accident may have triggered the eye problems that began to plague him a few years later.

The trip that decisively established Hope's Christmas tours as an annual tradition came a year later, in December 1956, when he made a more extensive tour of US bases in Alaska. His top-billed guests were Hollywood star Ginger Rogers and New York Yankees slugger Mickey Mantle (who played a mama's boy Army recruit in one sketch, with Hope as his hard-bitten sergeant). The entertainment seemed a little retro for an audience of young servicemen in the early years of rock 'n' roll: Hope donned top hat and tails for a dance number with the forty-five-year-old Rogers; housemother Hedda Hopper was back, gossiping about old Hollywood; and Hope's idea of a young act for "you cats who dig talent" was pert vocalist Peggy King, from the *George Gobel Show,* who sang "I've Grown Accustomed to His Face." Still, it was a glittery package of stars, songs, and comedy, for an audience that was starved for it.

His popular Christmas shows helped send Hope's ratings soaring. For the 1955–56 season, his specials aired on Tuesday nights, sponsored by Chevrolet and alternating with Milton Berle and Martha Raye. Hope was the only one of the three who regularly beat the hot new sitcom airing opposite them on CBS — Phil Silvers as Sergeant Bilko in *You'll Never Get Rich.* For the 1956–57 season, still sponsored by Chevrolet, Hope moved to Sunday nights, alternating with Dinah Shore and Ray Bolger, and drew even mightier ratings. By early 1957 his shows were averaging 41 million viewers a week, and *Variety* was marveling at his staying power after seven years on television. "In an era when even the best of 'em consider they've 'had it' after a three-four-season TV span, the multiplying payoff on Hope's seven-year itch for the Top 10 continues as the TV Ripley of the Decade."

Hope's shows in these years were probably the best of his TV career. The sketches, though hardly comedy classics, were more elaborately staged and better written, at their funniest when spoofing current movies and TV shows: a 1956 parody of *The Desperate Hours,* for example, with Hope in the Bogart role as an escaped convict holding a suburban family hostage, but having trouble getting their attention away from the TV set. Or

Hope as a Colonel Parker–like rock 'n' roll impresario, trying to turn meek Wally Cox into a teen idol. (When Cox asks where all his money has gone, Hope responds indignantly, "Have you ever heard my honesty questioned?" Cox: "I've never even heard it mentioned.")

In his monologues, Hope seemed more conscious of his role as a comedic barometer of current events and national concerns. "There's been a lot of exciting news these past couple of weeks," Hope began one monologue in the fall of 1955. "The stock market is holding its own, Archie Moore is holding his head, Perón is holding the bag, and Eddie and Debbie are holding each other, for release at a more convenient time" — surely the only comedian who could combine a defeated heavyweight boxer, an ousted Argentine dictator, and a newlywed Hollywood couple into one gag line. He took note of world crises ("How about that Suez Canal?") and presidential politics ("Adlai made so many campaign promises, Ike voted for him"). He poked fun at big-money quiz shows and Hollywood epics such as *The Ten Commandments* and, endlessly, Elvis Presley, the pelvis-shaking rock 'n' roll sensation who was about to go into the Army. "He'll be the only private the Army ever had that can roll the dice without taking them out of his pocket," said Hope. And: "Can't wait to see

515

Elvis on guard duty, yelling, 'Halt, who goes there, friend or square?' " And: "Elvis is asking for a deferment, on the grounds that it would create a hardship for Ed Sullivan."

Sometimes the jokes could ruffle feathers. In 1956, when Britain's Princess Margaret broke off her engagement to the divorced Captain Peter Townsend under pressure from the Church of England, Hope joked about the thwarted affair as he prepared for a trip to London. Among the sights he was looking forward to seeing, he said, was "Buckingham Palace, the guards out front, and Margaret's handkerchief drying out the window." His quips drew protests from both Canadian and British fans, who thought Hope was disrespectful. He got complaints of a different kind from NBC station executives, who objected to his frequent use of product names in his jokes — plugs that often resulted in free merchandise for Hope and his writers.

Hope may have felt entitled to a few perks, for he claimed that he was losing money on his television work. Hope Enterprises received a fixed amount from NBC for each special, meant to cover the talent, writers, and other production costs. When Hope looked at the books in the fall of 1956, he realized that he was losing money on the deal — a total of $93,000 in the red for his first three NBC specials for the 1956–57 season, according to his accounting. "I'm a hit but going broke, as far as TV is concerned," he told reporters. "I wish I could afford TV, but judging from the losses so far this season, I don't think so."

It was somewhat disingenuous; even if the shows were running a deficit, Hope personally was still raking in plenty from the network — upward of $1 million a year. But it was a fine negotiating tactic. In early 1957 Hope got NBC to renegotiate his contract, retroactive to 1955. Under the new deal, NBC would pay $15 million for forty TV specials over five years — an average of $375,000 for each show. With the specials budgeted at around $130,000 apiece, that meant Hope cleared at least $200,000 per show, putting his yearly income from NBC at around $1.5 million. As part of the new deal, NBC also pledged to invest $10 million in five Hope films, thus becoming a partner in his movie-making for the first time.

Hope would renew his contract with NBC every five years, and he always drove a hard bargain. Hope was such a ratings powerhouse that NBC had little choice but to make him happy, and he squeezed the network wherever he could. NBC had a rate card for the use of its production facilities, for instance, and the costs went up steadily over the years — for everyone but Hope, whose charges were grandfathered at the mid-1950s rate. NBC designed an entire studio to Hope's specifications, with the seats steeply raked so that the audience would be as close to him as possible. (It later became the home of Johnny Carson's *Tonight Show,* but was always Hope's for the asking.) What's more, as a sweetener for each contract renewal, Hope would demand a side deal in which NBC purchased one piece of property from him — a way for him to realize some profits from his steadily appreciating real estate holdings. "The land purchase was done directly between me and Bob," said Tom Sarnoff, NBC's West Coast vice president of business affairs during most of those years. "He was a tough negotiator. He knew what he wanted."

Hope began accumulating real estate on a large scale in the 1950s, using the money he and Crosby earned from their lucrative Texas oil wells. In 1955, Hope bought a 1,695-acre ranch in Ventura County from Jim and Marian Jordan, radio's Fibber McGee and Molly, for $400,000. Hope picked up several more large parcels over the next few years in the San Fernando Valley, Malibu, and the desert communities around Palm Springs, as well as smaller pieces in Arizona and Ohio. He also owned several undeveloped lots in Burbank, including one adjoining NBC's headquarters and another next door to Universal Pictures — the site of a golf driving range run for years by Hope's brother-in-law and eventually sold to Universal, which turned it into the entrance to its new theme park. He bought most of this land cheap and held on to it for years. "Bob was known to hang on to his real estate," said Art Linkletter, who partnered with Hope in several deals. "In fact, I stopped doing deals with him because he never wanted to sell anything." At his peak Hope owned more than ten thousand acres of Southern California real estate, reputedly more than any other private landowner in the state.

He had an array of other investments as well. He was still part owner of the Cleveland Indians, and in 1949 he bought an 11 percent share of the Los Angeles Rams football team. He headed a group that owned Denver TV station KOA and in 1957 acquired WREX-TV in Rockford, Illinois. Yet he always downplayed his business successes, complaining about how much he had to pay back to the government in taxes. (Hope, with his old-fashioned, Main Street approach to business, never went in for sophisticated tax-shelter arrangements, which might have reduced his tax burden.) He loved to gripe about the business opportunities he'd passed up — an offer to get in on the ground floor of Polaroid, for example, or the time Walt Disney asked if Hope wanted to invest in the big theme park Disney was building in Anaheim. Hope turned him down, convinced that Disneyland would be a flop. If he had only said yes, Hope would tell friends, "I could have been a rich man."

The business that took up most of his time and attention, however, was the enterprise known as Bob Hope. He gathered around him a large and devoted support staff: his two agents, Louis Shurr and Jimmy Saphier; attorneys Martin Gang and Norman Tyre of the law firm Gang, Kopp & Tyre (surely the most aptly named in Hollywood); and a corps of well-connected publicity agents. Hope's brother Jack became the nominal producer of his TV shows, while old cronies from Cleveland and vaudeville, such as Eddie Rio and Mark Anthony, were brought on in various capacities. At the center of the operation was Marjorie Hughes, a prim and poised graduate of UCLA who joined his staff in 1942 and served as Hope's chief assistant for thirty-one years. "Miss Hughes," as she was always addressed by everyone in the office (including Hope), ran the office, oversaw his schedule, and helped answer his voluminous mail — answers that Hope would usually dictate personally, but which always bore her delicate and dignified touch. Watching over it all was Hope, a hands-on CEO of the most sophisticated star-managing enterprise of the twentieth century.

It is hard to overstate Bob Hope's achievement as a multimedia star in the 1950s. Success in movies and television in those years was almost mutually exclusive. Top movie stars (Cary Grant, Katharine Hepburn, Kirk Douglas, Ava Gardner — practically anyone you could name) almost never did television, while TV's biggest stars, for the most part, had either left their movie careers behind (such as Lucille Ball or Red Skelton) or never had one to begin with (Sid Caesar, Jackie Gleason). The only other stars besides Hope who achieved major success in both movies and TV in the 1950s were Dean Martin and Jerry Lewis — but Lewis's TV career went nowhere after the duo split in 1956, and Martin didn't get his own variety show until the late 1960s, when his movie career was winding down. No one came close to matching Hope's two-decade run as a star of both major Hollywood movies and top-rated TV shows.

To be sure, by the mid-1950s Hope was no longer the box-office kingpin that he was back in the 1940s. But his 1955 hit *The Seven Little Foys* proved that he could still, with the right vehicle, attract big crowds to the theaters. What's more, his critical and popular success with *Foys,* in a meaty, semidramatic role, encouraged Hope to stretch himself and look for more ambitious film parts. The second half of the 1950s was a time of experimentation for him — not always successful, but also not the mark of a comedian who was resting on his laurels.

That Certain Feeling, his first film after *The Seven Little Foys,* was a return to more conventional romantic comedy. But it was unusual for Hope in being based on a Broadway play — *The King of Hearts,* by Jean Kerr and Eleanor Brooke, which ran for eight months in 1954 — and casting him in a relatively realistic, contemporary role. He plays Francis X. Dignan, a neurotically insecure cartoonist who is hired to "ghost" the popular comic strip of a pompous colleague named Larry Larkin, played by George Sanders. The instigator of this arrangement is Larkin's assistant and fiancée, who also happens to be Dignan's ex-wife — played by Eva Marie Saint, in her first movie after her Oscar-winning film debut in *On the Waterfront.*

Written and codirected by former Hope writers Norman Panama and Melvin Frank, *That Certain Feeling* is a more sophisticated romantic comedy than anything Hope had done before. His familiar skittish, nervous-Nellie character now has real psychological underpinnings: he's seeing a psychiatrist (a first for Hope) to deal with his pathological fear of confrontation. Sanders does a funny caricature of a smug, bleeding-heart New York intellectual, giving Hope's deflating wisecracks more satiric bite. "When you pick up that pencil, my friend," Sanders lectures

Hope, "you draw Larkin, you think Larkin, you *are* Larkin." Says Hope: "All right, but I insist on separate toothbrushes."

In a superfluous subplot, Larkin adopts an orphan, played by Jerry Mathers, later of TV's *Leave It to Beaver.* (Hope's nine-year-old son, Kelly, also appears in one scene as Mathers's playmate.) And a youthful, honey-voiced Pearl Bailey, in the thankless role of Larkin's maid, gets a couple of nice songs, including the film's title number, resurrected from a 1925 Gershwin musical. But the heart of the movie is the reawakening romance between Dignan and his ex-wife, and Hope plays it with restraint and feeling. This is one of his few screen romances that actually gives off some sexual heat, and he's an indulgent straight man for Saint's big comedy scene, when the neatly tailored ice princess gets drunk and flounces around her apartment in silk Chinese pajamas.

"He was very patient as an actor, very generous and giving," said Saint, who also found Hope's easygoing working style refreshing. In contrast to the intensity of Elia Kazan and Marlon Brando on the closed *Waterfront* set, Hope's set was open and relaxed; one day an entire football team came to watch. "Thank God I had grown up in live television, where tours would come through and watch from behind the glass," said Saint.

"As an actress I had learned how to concentrate."

As he did for *The Seven Little Foys,* Hope went all out to promote the movie, which opened in June 1956. He did four stage shows a day at the Paramount Theater for the film's New York opening; made nearly a dozen TV guest appearances; and hosted premiere screenings around the country to benefit United Cerebral Palsy. One of his NBC specials, *The Road to Hollywood,* was little more than a long plug for the movie. Thinly disguised as a tribute to Hope's Hollywood career (with former leading ladies such as Jane Russell and Dorothy Lamour among the guests), the show featured Hope's first use of one of his publicity innovations: a clip reel of flubs and outtakes from his new movie. "Leave it to Bob Hope to show 'em how to plug a picture," said *Variety,* in its review of the show. "If NBC is willing to give away 90 minutes of prime time for a plug, and audiences are willing to take it with the palatable grain of sugar it was mixed with, more power to Hope."

Yet *That Certain Feeling* was a disappointment at the box office. *Variety* theorized that Hope's movie wisecracks were "too much the type of entertainment he offers on television." More likely, the relatively sophisticated New York relationship comedy was a little too rarefied for Hope's audience. Still, it was one of his most enjoyable and underrated films of the 1950s. After it, things began to go seriously awry.

The Iron Petticoat began with a script by veteran screenwriter Ben Hecht (*Scarface, The Front Page*): a Cold War–era update of *Ninotchka* about a female Soviet pilot who defects to the West and has a romantic and ideological awakening while being shown around London by an American Air Force captain. Katharine Hepburn was cast as the pilot, and Cary Grant was originally envisioned as her costar. But when Grant turned it down, producer Harry Saltzman came up with the notion of pairing Hepburn, Hollywood's classiest leading lady, with Hope, its most popular movie clown. Intrigued with the idea of working with Hepburn (as well as plans to shoot the movie in England), Hope signed on. Against the advice of friends, Hepburn agreed too.

It was an ill-starred project. Hecht and Hope were at odds from the start. According to Hope, the script was unfinished when he arrived in London for the start of shooting (Hecht no doubt rewriting it to suit the casting of Hope), and Hope merely suggested a few "hokey thoughts" to help it out. In Hecht's view, Hope was wreaking havoc on his script, bringing in gag writers to add jokes where they didn't belong. Hepburn was just as dismayed. "I had been sold a false bill of goods," she said later. "I was told that this was not going to be a typical Hope movie, that he wanted to appear in a contemporary comedy. That proved not to be the case." Ralph Thomas, the film's British director, was caught in the middle. "After only two days I realized there was no point of contact between the two of them," he said. "There was Bob inserting his one-liners — and she telling him, very forcibly, very chillingly, what she thought of his lack of professionalism."

Hope, who never liked to bad-mouth a colleague, was polite in retrospect, saying Hepburn was "a gem" during the filming. "She played the Jewish mother on the set, fussing over everyone who happened to sneeze." Hepburn did not return the compliment, calling Hope "the biggest egomaniac with whom I have worked in my entire life." Hecht, for his part, demanded that his name be removed from the credits and ran a full-page "open letter" to Hope in the *Hollywood Reporter* disavowing the film. "This is to notify you that I have removed my name as author from our mutilated venture, *The Iron Petticoat.* Unfortunately your other partner, Katharine Hepburn can't shy out of the fractured picture with me." Hope replied with his own sarcastic ad: "I am most understanding. The way things are going you simply can't afford to be associated with a hit."

The Iron Petticoat, which opened in December 1956, wasn't a hit, or anything resembling a good film. Hepburn complained that Hope wanted to turn the picture "into his cheap vaudeville act with me as his stooge," but her strident, humorless performance as the dogmaspouting Soviet pilot (with one of the worst Russian accents ever recorded) is what ruins the film. Hope at least tries to keep it grounded in recognizable human behavior, and he has some nice moments when Hepburn is offscreen — doing some deft flimflammery at the Soviet embassy, for example, to help her escape from the authorities who have arrested her. But the movie is heavy-handed and charmless, with not a smidgen of romantic chemistry between the two stars. "The notion of these two characters falling rapturously, romantically in love is virtually revolting," wrote the *New York Times'* Bosley Crowther. "If this was meant to be a travesty, it is."

Hope's next project, *Beau James,* at least brought him closer to home turf. Mel Shavelson and Jack Rose, who had given him one of his best roles in *The Seven Little Foys,* came up with the idea of casting Hope as Jimmy Walker, the colorful and corrupt 1920s mayor of New York City, in a biopic based on a recently published biography of Walker by Gene Fowler. For an essentially dramatic role, it was especially well suited to Hope. Walker had been a songwriter before getting into politics (he wrote the lyrics to "Will You Love Me in December as You Do in May?"), and as New York mayor was a bon-vivant symbol of the Roaring Twenties, who let speakeasies flourish in the city, allowed Tammany Hall corruption to run rampant, and left his wife for a showgirl.

Hope does well in the role, his flip, wise-cracking persona perfectly suited to the raffish mix of showbiz and politics that Walker embodied. The film's depiction of New York City politics is simplistic but often witty — a montage of Walker campaigning across the city, for instance, tailoring his campaign song to each ethnic group he encounters. "What kind of mayor is this guy going to make?" asks one bystander. "A lousy mayor," his campaign chief responds, "but what a candidate!" *Beau James* doesn't ignore the corruption that marred Walker's administration, or the personal indiscretions that enlivened it. (Alexis Smith plays Walker's wife-in-name-only, and Vera Miles is the showgirl he has an affair with.) The problem, as in *The Seven Little Foys,* is that Hope's opaqueness as an actor doesn't give us much insight into Walker's character or motives. Hope got respectful reviews, but the movie grossed just $1.75 million, his third box-office disappointment in a row.

Hope took his next movie into his own hands. He wanted to shoot another film overseas and came up with a bare-bones story idea in which he would essentially play himself, an American comedy star who sails to Paris in pursuit of a script for his next picture. Hope got United Artists to back the film, cast the French comedian Fernandel (who had guested on one of Hope's TV shows from London) as his costar, and hired screenwriters Edmund Beloin and Dean Riesner to flesh out a script. He also decided, for the first time, to serve as his own producer — a decision he came to regret.

Filming was scheduled to begin in Paris in April 1957. But Fernandel, who spoke no English, didn't see the script until Hope was about to arrive for the start of shooting, and he wasn't happy to find that his role was clearly secondary to Hope's. Hope made an emergency call to two of his writers, Mort Lachman and Bill Larkin, and ordered them to Paris, where they quickly reworked the script to pacify the French star — delaying the start of filming for ten days as the crew sat idle. The production fell further behind thanks to various technical snafus, bad weather (snow in May and a heat wave in June), and the French crew's habit of starting work late and taking long lunches. "At present we're three weeks behind on film and three weeks ahead on wine," Hope joked at a benefit for French war orphans that he hosted while in Paris. When their twelve-week lease on the Boulogne studios outside of Paris was up and the film still wasn't done, the crew had to relocate to another studio in Joinville to finish up. In the end, Hope claimed the production went $1 million over budget.

The results on-screen were just as discombobulated. *Paris Holiday* is a slovenly mix of Hope one-liners, silent-comedy set pieces for Fernandel (he pretends to be seasick, for example, to get some ship passengers to vacate a couple of deck chairs), and a slapdash story involving spies (among them Anita Ekberg) who are after the same film script that Hope is trying to buy. The film's director, Gerd Oswald, appears to be missing in action, and Hope was apparently too distracted by the production problems to pay much attention to the comedy. *Paris Holiday* was not just Hope's worst film to date; it was his laziest performance.

In December 1957, Hope made his most ambitious Christmas trip yet, a two-week tour of the Far East, with blond bombshell Jayne Mansfield as his top guest star and a far-flung itinerary that climaxed with a show before seven thousand infantrymen perched on a snowy hillside near the thirty-eighth parallel, the border between North and South Korea. The NBC special that resulted became the model for all of Hope's Christmas shows that followed. Unlike his previous three Christmas shows from the Arctic — essentially Hope variety shows done on location for military audiences — this one was a more elaborately produced travelogue: shots of the cast getting on and off planes, excerpts from their performances at each stop on the tour, all linked by Hope's voice-over narration and ending with his patriotic tribute to "our boys in a foreign land, there to preserve our way of life."

The trip was widely covered by several entertainment columnists whom Hope had cleverly invited along, and the special, which NBC aired on Friday, January 17, drew Hope's highest ratings of the season. Hedda Hopper (who again doubled as a guest star and chronicler of the trip) hailed the selfless work Hope was doing, anointing him, more explicitly than ever before, as Hollywood's finest role model for public service:

> Each time I pack my bags and turn my back on the wreathed door and the piles of gaily wrapped gifts, I have a warmer, more satisfying feeling in my heart. I can remember a day when Hollywood didn't think much about serious things. I remember the time of the mammoth Christmas party, the $5 Christmas card and the exchange of valuables which meant Yuletide in the movie colony. I remember too the first Christmas when a sober note was struck, when someone reminded us what we owed the rest of

the world. The time was 1943 and, you guessed it, the someone was Bob Hope.

Hope's status as Hollywood's most celebrated public servant and goodwill ambassador, however, would reach its high-water mark a couple of months later. After more than two years of trying, Hope finally got approval to make his trip to the Soviet Union.

He had renewed his application for visas in November 1957, while he was in London for some personal appearances and a screening of *Paris Holiday.* He told Ursula Halloran, a pretty young publicist who had gone to work for him in New York, to pursue the request with the powers in Washington and asked NBC's Moscow correspondent, Irving R. Levine, to press the matter from his end. Hope also appealed for help from the American ambassador in London, Jock Whitney, who personally brought up the trip with Russian ambassador Jacob Malik. "What does your Mr. Hope want to do," Malik said, "entertain our troops in Red Square?" Hope was disappointed that the approval didn't come before he had to fly home from London. But a few weeks later, he was summoned to the Soviet embassy in Washington. The Soviets had approved his trip, and six visas were waiting for him.

The State Department gave its blessing for the trip — the first to be scheduled in the wake of a cultural-exchange agreement between the United States and Soviet Union, signed in January. Yet Cold War suspicions were still high, and the Russians placed severe restrictions on the trip. Hope was not allowed to travel outside Moscow. All negotiations for Russian talent had to be conducted through the Soviet government, and only Russian film crews could be used. Moreover, with visas for just six, Hope had to severely limit his entourage. He brought along two writers, Mort Lachman and Bill Larkin; two PR people, Ursula Halloran (with whom he was having a fairly open affair) and Arthur Jacobs (a United Artists publicity man whose job was to arrange a Moscow premiere of *Paris Holiday*); and a top cameraman from London named Ken Talbot.

Hope, accompanied by the two publicists, flew to Copenhagen on March 14, 1958, and from there boarded a Soviet airliner for Moscow. (The writers and Talbot came separately.) Before the flight their passports were checked three times: at the gate, at the bottom of the ramp, and at the top of the ramp. ("This was to prevent us from changing identities halfway up the stairs," Hope noted.) Arriving in Moscow, they were greeted by NBC's Irving R. Levine and a handful of journalists, including two reporters for *Look* magazine, and taken to Moscow's newest luxury hotel, the Ukraine, where most of the lobby furniture was still covered with sheets.

Hope met first with top officials from the Ministry of Culture and gave them his wish list for the visit: a tour of a Russian TV or movie studio, a visit with students at a Russian university, and a theater where he could do a monologue for an English-speaking audience. The Russians politely took his requests and granted none of them. His efforts to arrange a Moscow opening for *Paris Holiday* also came to naught. For the entire trip Hope suspected that his hotel room was bugged. One night when he returned to the room, he found his suitcase open and his monologue jokes spread out over the bed. "I still don't know who went through those jokes," Hope wrote later, "and I guess I never will unless Molotov starts doing my act in Pinsk."

Hope began his sightseeing in Red Square, accompanied by Lachman and with Talbot filming as he visited such landmarks as St. Basil's Cathedral and Lenin's tomb, unnoticed by passersby. "Can you believe it? Not one person knows who I am," Hope marveled. "Congratulations," replied Lachman. "Now you know what it's like to be me." Talbot was allowed to film freely in most of the approved locations, but when the group wandered off the itinerary to a nightclub to see a popular all-girl orchestra, he had to sneak in his camera and film surreptitiously while a reporter distracted the maître d'.

Hope attended a performance of the Bolshoi Ballet, saw a Russian jazz combo, and went to a Russian puppet show (though most of the footage of these acts used in the show was supplied by his Soviet hosts, shot a year earlier for the fortieth anniversary celebration of the Soviet revolution). When Hope was having no luck making arrangements for a theater for his monologue, US ambassador Llewellyn Thompson offered his residence, Spaso House, for the show. Three hundred people — mostly embassy personnel, their families, and other English-speaking residents of the city — were in the audience as a Russian camera crew filmed Hope making jokes about the Cold War, the cold weather, and his cold reception in Moscow. "I got a wonderful tribute at the airport," he quipped. "They fired twenty-one shots in the air in my honor. Of course it would have been nicer if they'd waited for the plane to land." He added, "Surprisingly enough, I'm not having any trouble with the language. Nobody speaks to me."

Officials at the Ministry of Culture went over his jokes afterward and raised objections to several of them. One was a wisecrack about *Sputnik,* the Soviets' new space satellite, orbiting the earth every ninety minutes or so.

"The Russians are overjoyed at their *Sputnik,*" Hope said. "It's kind of weird, being in a country where every ninety-two minutes there's a holiday. Anybody without a stiff neck is a traitor." The Russians were sincerely proud of their space achievement, he was told, and "traitor is a very serious charge in Russia." Hope tried to explain: "What we are trying to do is to state in a humorous way how proud the people are of their *Sputnik.*" To placate the officials, Hope told them to submit a list of the jokes they were unhappy with and he would consider removing them. Like so much else in his bureaucracy-encrusted visit, the list never came through.

In all, Hope spent six days in Moscow. But he left without his film footage. Talbot had brought forty thousand feet of film from London, intending to process it back home, but the Russians insisted on using their own film and processing it there — adding another layer of uncertainty to the trip. Hope made Lachman and Larkin stay behind, to wait for the processed film and personally bring it back in their luggage. The writers arrived safely with it a day later. So did a bill from the Russians for $1,200, to cover the processing, camera crews, and film clips used in the show. Hope never paid the bill, claiming he didn't get all the clips he ordered. (He did, however, get the title for a memoir he eventually produced on the trip, *I Owe Russia $1200,* ghostwritten by Lachman.)

The TV special edited from his Soviet trip, *Bob Hope in Moscow,* aired on Saturday night, April 5, 1958, and was one of his finest achievements. Clips of Hope sightseeing in Moscow are interspersed with footage of Soviet entertainers — ballerina Galina Ulanova, violinist David Oistrakh, Russian circus clown Oleg Popov, a selection of folk dancers from various Soviet republics. Hope's voice-over plays on American stereotypes of the stolid Russians and stern Soviet dictatorship. Over shots of a beefy all-female orchestra, Hope comments, "They're playing this year's hit tune, 'When My Tractor Smiles at Me.' " As he gets ready to visit Moscow State University, he notes that it is "located on Stalin or Lenin or Bulganin Boulevard — I'm not sure which, I haven't seen today's newspaper." He has self-deprecating fun with his anonymity on the Moscow streets. As he is wandering through Red Square, a crowd of pedestrians approaches. "We'll cut across the square, if we can just get past this pack of autograph hounds," Hope narrates. The group walks right through him, oblivious. "Hmmpf. Guess they never heard of me."

He closes the show with a call for understanding between the two Cold War superpowers: "For five days and nights I stared and I walked and I wandered. It's a strange city. I missed the street signs, the advertisements, the neons gleaming in the night, everybody owning their own car." The words were almost surely written by Lachman — Hope's most trusted writer, whose thoughtful manner and big, round glasses got him nicknamed the Owl. As the street scenes of Moscow dissolve into shots of smiling Russian children, Hope concludes hopefully:

I found out that the little kids with the fur hats and the sticky faces have no politics, and that their party line is confined to "please pass the ice cream." You know, it would be wonderful if these children would someday grow up in a world that spoke the same language and respected the same things. . . . Take these characters right here. In a few years they'll be in school. Will they teach him that Communism is his friend, his salvation? And that democracy is his deadly enemy? Twenty years from now, will he be a violinist? A shopkeeper? A teacher? Or will he be the one at the countdown who pushes the button which shakes the crust of the earth? I certainly don't envy Mr. Dulles the job at hand. But it would be nice if somebody could work out a plan for peaceful coexistence, so that human beings like these don't become obsolete.

The critics had their reservations about Hope's stab at international diplomacy. "I wish there'd been a lot more Russia and a lot less Hope," said Cecil Smith in the *Los Angeles Times.* The *New York Times'* Jack Gould complained that Hope's chauvinistic wisecracks at the expense of the Soviets were in poor taste. But Hope's achievement was hard to dismiss. "Who would have thought even a few years ago," said Gould, "there could be such a change in the world climate that a viewer would be hearing Mr. Hope broach such subjects? In the universality of cultural artistry there indeed may be a ray of hope for a divided world."

Bob Hope in Moscow drew solid, if not sensational, ratings, won a Peabody Award for its "contribution to international understanding," and had a highly publicized rerun telecast on NBC the following January. The show was the first of several groundbreaking cultural exchanges between the United States and Soviet Union. In June, Ed Sullivan presented the American TV debut of the famed Moiseyev Dance Company; a year later impresario Sol Hurok brought the Bolshoi Ballet to New York City. And in September 1959 Soviet premier Khrushchev made his much-heralded first visit to the United States.

Hope was among the Hollywood celebrities invited to a lunch for the Soviet leader when he visited the Twentieth Century–Fox studios in Los Angeles. Sitting next to Mrs. Khrushchev (with Frank Sinatra on her other side), Hope suggested that she and Mr. K. ought to visit Disneyland. Khrushchev requested a visit, but the LA police turned him down (claiming it could not guarantee security), and the Soviet premier had a highly publicized temper tantrum. "What do you have there — rocket launching pads?" he bellowed to reporters. Hope would later joke that his casual comment to Mrs. Khrushchev started the Cold War. Not quite — Khrushchev had in fact requested the Disneyland trip well before the luncheon — but Hope's landmark show from Moscow surely melted some of the ice.

"Guys ask me all the time about what happened to Sid Caesar or George Gobel or Jackie Gleason or Wally Cox," Hope said in a 1957 interview, trying to explain the secret of his long-running TV success. "You've got no idea what a tremendous strain it is trying to be funny week after week. The American audience is the sharpest, most sophisticated, and fickle audience in the world. You can't get away with old jokes, old routines, second-class material. Trying to satisfy the public — honestly, it can tear you apart."

In truth, Hope got away with plenty of old jokes — tired, knee-jerk gags about Gleason's weight and Benny's cheapness and Crosby's many kids — and his material was often

540

second-class. But throughout the 1950s his TV popularity never flagged. He outlasted every TV trend and fad: the rage for Westerns and big-money quiz shows, the emergence of sitcoms and the glut of me-too variety shows. He stayed in the top ten despite changing nights, challenging time periods, and revolving sponsors. In the fall of 1957, Timex replaced Chevrolet as Hope's sponsor — paying $360,000 for an hour of airtime, highest ever for a variety show — but dropped him after just one month, upset over his guest appearance on a Frank Sinatra show, which was partly sponsored by Bulova, a Timex competitor. (Hope's agent Jimmy Saphier claimed Hope did the show only after being assured that the Bulova ad would not air until after the show's closing credits.) NBC had to postpone Hope's November special while another sponsor was found. Plymouth eventually picked him up for the rest of the season, before Hope switched to yet another car company, Buick, for the 1958–59 season.

One reason for his durability was his wise decision to carefully ration his TV exposure. Where other comedians, such as Caesar and Berle, did weekly shows and either burned themselves out or overstayed their welcome, Hope limited himself to just six or eight specials a year and tried to make them as special as possible — with big-name guest stars, foreign locales (he did two shows from

London in 1955, another from Morocco after shooting *Paris Holiday* in 1957), and special events, including a reprise of his stage role in *Roberta* at the St. Louis Muny Opera, taped in the summer of 1958 and broadcast as his season opener in September.

Just as important was Hope's dogged and creative efforts to promote his shows. "It's getting out there in person and selling each show like there's not going to be any tomorrow," Hope told Pete Martin in the *Saturday Evening Post.* "I get behind every show I'm in and push it as if it's a new musical comedy or a new feature-length movie." Before each special Hope would get his publicists to line up phone interviews with TV columnists around the country, and the one-on-one conversations would generate reams of coverage. "I sit in my office out there in Burbank and shove those calls through," he said. "It's a wonderful idea. They ask me about my next show, and I tell them a few intimate things about it. Then they give the fact that I called them a lot of space."

The quality of his shows in these years was spotty. The best sketches poked fun at popular TV shows and trends (Hope playing a tough private eye, for example, working "the most crime-ridden street in Hollywood — eighteen crime shows on one block"). The attempts at more ambitious social or cultural satire were pretty crude. When women were still a novelty in politics, Maureen O'Hara played a newly elected congresswoman, who interrupts a meeting with a top Army general to paste Green Stamps in her coupon book and suggests decorating Army tanks with wallpaper. When beatniks became a media obsession, Hope donned goatee and beret and played a bass-playing hipster, waiting in the maternity ward for his jive-talking wife to deliver their new baby. (The baby has a goatee too.) But the seat-of-the-pants spirit of the comedy, the self-mocking ad-libs making fun of the bad jokes or missed cues, even the tacky production values, all enlisted the audience in the artifice. This wasn't satire; it was show business.

The monologues were still the high point, a running chronicle of the headlines and hot topics of the era. When Soviet No. 2 man Anastas Mikoyan made a diplomatic visit to the United States, he "brought back everything he could that might give them a clue to our defenses," said Hope. "They've been up in Siberia for three weeks now trying to launch a Hula-Hoop." When President Eisenhower took a vacation in the California desert, Hope joked, "He wanted some peace and quiet, and La Quinta is the perfect hideaway. The Russians can't find it; the Democrats can't afford it." In the wake of his trip to Moscow, Hope savored his role as a comedy statesman, and the quips sometimes turned serious. During Khrushchev's 1959 visit to the United States, Hope closed one show with praise for a trip that allowed the Soviet leader "to show his sharp mind and tongue to the American people. Freedom of speech is a basic American principle, and so Khrushchev was allowed to come to this country to speak his mind and attempt to sell us Communism. I just hope that when our president visits Russia, they give him equal time to sell freedom."

Hope's stature in the show-business world was never higher, ratified by a growing stack of awards: a Meritorious Public Service Citation from the Navy, the Murray-Green Award for community service from the AFL-CIO, a humanitarian award from the American College of Physicians for "healing without resorting to pills or medicine." He was named honorary mayor of Chicago and hosted a TV special for the Boy Scouts' new Explorer program. He set attendance records almost everywhere he went, from the Canadian National Exposition in 1957 to a concert at the Lubbock Coliseum in 1958, the biggest one-nighter in the city's history. He told his publicist Mack Millar to make inquiries about getting him a Congressional Gold Medal, the nation's highest civilian honor, for his work entertaining the troops. When the White House initially turned down the request, explaining that it would be unfair to single out Hope when so many other entertainers had done their share, Hope told Millar (without irony) to try for the Nobel Peace Prize.

Hope's Christmas tours to entertain the troops were by now national events, coordinated by the Defense Department and the USO and watched by some of the biggest audiences in television. In December 1958, a year after his successful tour of Korea and the Far East, Hope was booked on an equally ambitious tour of North Africa and Europe. This time, however, he ran into a problem that had been looming for years, but that he had managed to keep at bay: his health.

The trip had an especially grueling itinerary of eight countries in just twelve days. To join him, Hope wanted to book a major European sexpot such as Brigitte Bardot or Sophia Loren, but the best he could get was an appearance by Gina Lollobrigida, who was shooting *Solomon and Sheba* in Spain and agreed to meet the troupe for one day, for $10,000 in cash up front. To fill out his troupe, Hope brought along Molly Bee, a singer on Tennessee Ernie Ford's TV show, and folk singer Randy Sparks, along with the reliable Jerry Colonna, the inevitable Hedda Hopper, and the indefatigable Les Brown and his band.

The trip ran into problems from the start. Hope and company took off from Burbank on December 17 in two Air Force planes, headed for McGuire Air Force Base in New Jersey, but one of the aircraft had engine trouble and had to return to California. After a day's delay, the reunited troupe flew to the Azores and then headed for Morocco, on a flight so stormy that even Hope, usually able to sleep through anything, couldn't catch a nap. He arrived in Morocco exhausted, then went straight to a charity golf match, followed by a visit to King Muhammed's palace, a tour of Rabat, and a show in the evening. The next morning he was back on a plane to Spain. During the first seventy-six hours of the trip, Hope figured he got only seven hours of sleep.

He was being greeted by the commanding officer at the Morón Air Base in Spain, when he suffered his first dizzy spell. "The walls of the room we were standing in started closing in on me," he recalled. "I shook my head to clear it, but the haze was still there." He was taken to the base hospital for an examination, but after some sleep felt well enough to join that night's show, which the rest of the cast had started without him.

He soldiered on as the tour resumed its relentless pace: to Madrid, where Lollobrigida made her guest appearance; to Naples, where they did two Christmas Eve shows in the rain aboard the aircraft carrier *Forrestal;* and to Frankfurt, Germany, where they were feted at a reception thrown by

General F. W. Farrell. There Hope had another attack, passing out in the middle of the party. His earlier health scare had been kept quiet, but this one was in public and in front of the journalists along on the trip, and it soon became worldwide news.

Hope vetoed the idea of another hospital visit and, after a night's sleep, again felt well enough to continue, doing a show at Rhein-Main Air Base and then flying with the troupe to West Berlin. There he got a call from Dolores, who had read the news of his illness and was worried. He told her that he was fine. "Stop lying to me and put your doctors on the phone," she said. Hope struggled through three more days in Germany and a trip back home through Scotland and Iceland. Dolores was waiting to greet him at the Lockheed Air Terminal in Burbank with all four kids, a Christmas tree, and an appointment to see his doctor, Tom Hearn.

Hearn found Hope's blood pressure elevated and ordered him to rest. But the comedian was soon back at work, overseeing the editing of footage from his Christmas tour. The dizzy spells continued, felling him during a golf game with his friend and PGA tour pro Jimmy Demaret. Now convinced that the ailment related to his eyesight, Hope went to an eye specialist, who diagnosed a blood clot in his left eye and prescribed blood thinners and more rest. Hope canceled a promotional trip to Florida, but continued to work on his next NBC special. During a rehearsal he suffered yet another attack, and his doctors, concerned about the eye's worsening condition, sent him to New York for a consultation with Dr. Algernon Reese at New York's Columbia Presbyterian Medical Center.

News of his worsening eye problems prompted alarmist headlines. "Bob Hope to Fly East in Fight to Save Eye," read one. Doctors in New York confirmed the diagnosis of a blood clot — a blockage in a retinal vein, which caused hemorrhaging and thus his blurred vision. They thought it could be cleared up without surgery, but warned that he could lose his eyesight unless he seriously cut back on his activities.

Hope's eye troubles prompted an outpouring of concern from his fans. He got thousands of get-well cards, many with medical advice or suggestions of doctors for him to see. Several people offered to donate (or sell, at prices ranging from $3,000 to $50,000) one of their own eyes, to replace the orb that ailed Hope. Shaken by the seriousness of his condition, he talked frankly about his need for rest. "If I had taken a day off in Spain or Africa, I think I would have been okay, but I worked when I was sick," he told Louella Parsons. Hope "seemed depressed" as he discussed his condition with UPI's Vernon

Scott, who found a changed attitude in the comedian. "He's quieter now. Less brash," wrote Scott. Hope seemed determined, finally, to cut back on his frenetic pace. "Nobody moved as fast as I did," he said. "My physical problems began a few years back when I was doing morning and evening radio programs, a weekly television show, movies, and personal appearances. . . . It was ridiculous. I used bad judgment. The folly was I couldn't keep the money and I was fighting myself on all mediums."

Yet Hope's idea of a slower pace was still enough to wear out most performers. He continued to do his monthly NBC specials for Buick (which continued to bury the competition in the ratings) and made personal appearances throughout the year, including a two-week run at the Cain Park Theater Summer Festival in Cleveland. But he put all his movie work on hold, canceled a promotional tour for his recently completed film *Alias Jesse James,* and spent more time resting in Palm Springs — even cutting back his golf games from eighteen to nine holes. During the summer he and Dolores vacationed in Scotland, and he took the family on a fishing trip in British Columbia.

It might have been a nice time to bond with the children, but he was past that. The two oldest kids were in college now — Tony at Georgetown University in Washington, DC, and Linda at Mount St. Mary's College in Los Angeles. The two youngest, Nora and Kelly, were just entering their teens, grabbing what little quality time they could with the Hollywood superstar who sometimes showed up for dinner. "Nora was better able to get his attention," said a cousin. "She laughed at his jokes. She was cute, very vivacious, funny. Kelly was at sea. He was not doing well in school. Being the son of Bob Hope was a difficult role for both of them."

Although Tony accompanied his father on Hope's 1957 Far East tour, and Linda appeared with him in 1956 as a mystery guest on the TV game show *What's My Line?*, Hope didn't push the kids to join him in show business. But it was hard for them to escape the shadow of his overwhelming fame. "I felt, growing up, that people were always looking past me, at him," Linda said years later. "I remember inviting people over to the house, as kids always do, and them making a big fuss, and the parents wanting to get inside and see as much as they could. They were more interested in the whole Bob Hope situation, and they weren't being my friends." While at Mount St. Mary's, Linda — an attractive blonde whose cool good looks reminded some of Grace Kelly — was nominated for homecoming queen of nearby Loyola University. "I was just thrilled that finally *my* moment had arrived," she said.

"And then I found out that I could be guaranteed to be picked as the queen if my father would show up." He didn't, and she wasn't.

After a year of sporadically enforced rest because of his eye problems, neither Dolores nor his doctors were happy when Bob insisted on doing another Christmas tour at the end of 1959. The trip was at least more manageable — a relatively short jaunt to Alaska (just admitted to the union as the forty-ninth state), with Jayne Mansfield and young film star Steve McQueen along for the ride. Hope turned the trip into a reunion of his old World War II troupe, bringing along Frances Langford, Patty Thomas, and Tony Romano as well as Colonna, by now a regular on Hope's tours. When Les Brown's band was not available, Hope even got Skinnay Ennis, his first radio bandleader, as a replacement, just for old times' sake.

The publicity-savvy Mansfield hogged most of the spotlight, posing for photographers with a lion cub and taking the stage in a gown so low-cut the men nearly rioted. (When Hope asked if they wanted her to sing, one yelled out, "Just let her breathe!") At a show in Fairbanks, Hope had another flare-up of his eye problems. When AP reported the story, Hope chewed out Bill Faith, the NBC publicist who had let the news slip out. But

551

otherwise the trip went off without incident, and the show that resulted, which aired on January 13, drew Hope's highest ratings of the season.

His TV popularity continued to soar — not just on his own show, but also on the many variety shows where he made guest appearances. In February 1960, *Variety* did an analysis of the ratings for TV's most frequent guest stars. Hope was ranked No. 1 — beating not only such TV personalities as Jack Benny and Red Skelton but also top movie stars such as Rock Hudson, Ingrid Bergman, and Jimmy Stewart. "Bob Hope is the champ of them all in audience pulling power," said *Variety,* "emerging as television's No. 1 personality."

In April 1960 he got another crack at the biggest TV guest spot of all: host of the Academy Awards show. He had not hosted the ceremony on his own since 1955 (when he grappled playfully over an Oscar with Best Actor winner Marlon Brando). For the next two years his sponsor, Chevrolet, barred him from the Oscar show because rival Oldsmobile was one of its sponsors. He returned as one of multiple hosts in both 1958 and 1959. But the 1959 show was a notorious disaster. In a once-in-a-lifetime miscalculation, the show came in twenty minutes *short,* and Jerry Lewis, the last of six hosts, was forced to ad-lib desperately to fill the time — stretching out a closing sing-along to "There's No Business Like Show Business," clowning around and picking up a baton to conduct the orchestra himself — until NBC mercifully cut away. Reviews of the show were scathing. The following year, Hope was back as host all by himself.

"Many changes have been made since our last show," Hope said at the start of the April 4 telecast from the Pantages Theatre. "We have a new director, a new producer, and a new watch." He was sharp and fully in control. The show was taking place during an actors' strike. "What a country," said Hope. "Only here would you wait in your swimming pool for the boss to improve working conditions." One of the year's Oscar-nominated films was *On the Beach,* based on Nevil Shute's bestseller about nuclear Armageddon. "The Russians loved it," said Hope. "They thought it was a newsreel." He was ubiquitous throughout the evening: introducing each presenter, sprinkling in quips everywhere, both planned and unplanned. When the Best Short Subject award was announced, Ann Blyth accepted for the absent winner, while a bald-headed man was left wandering uncertainly onstage, apparently thinking the duty was his. Hope gently ushered the confused man offstage: "There's nothing left over."

As if to thank him for his job in righting

the ship, the Academy gave Hope another honorary Oscar — the prestigious Jean Hersholt Humanitarian Award. *Ben-Hur* was the evening's big winner, taking home a record eleven awards, but the applause for Hope was the longest and loudest of the night.

Hope would return as solo host of the Oscars for seven of the next nine years, the greatest run of any host in Academy history. His monologues became don't-miss events: an eight-minute encapsulation of the major films, hot trends, and celebrity gossip of the year in Hollywood — written and rewritten by Hope and his regular crew of writers (with help from others, such as Oscar-show specialist Hal Kanter) right up until airtime and guarded like a state secret.

He joked about big-budget movie spectacles ("Right now Sam Spiegel has more men under arms than NATO"), Liz and Dick's affair on the set of *Cleopatra* ("I don't know how the picture is, but I'd like to make a deal for the outtakes"), the growing sexual frankness on-screen ("One picture got the seal of approval, and the director said, 'Where have we failed?' "). He came armed with good lines, but he had the quickness and agility to handle the unscripted moments too. When a gate-crasher disrupted the 1962 ceremony, bounding onstage to give Hope a bogus Oscar, the host was unflappable: "Who needs Price Waterhouse? All we need's a doorman."

When the winner of a short-subject award went on too long in his acceptance speech (in the days when acceptance speeches were rarely longer than a few seconds), thanking his wife, his son, and a friend back in Bronxville, Hope commented impeccably, "Well, that saves a telegram." Even as the shows grew longer and drearier, Hope made them sparkle.

By early 1960 Hope was back to a nearly full schedule of work. He signed a new five-year contract with NBC, after the usual protracted negotiations. He was the network's eight-hundred-pound gorilla, and he could be demanding and peevish when he didn't get his way. When NBC couldn't deliver a Saturday-night time slot that Hope wanted for one of his specials, his agent Jimmy Saphier raised a ruckus and threw Hope's weight around. "Don't you think this is a rather strange way for NBC to treat its number one piece of talent," he wrote the network, "particularly in view of the fact that your contract with Bob Hope is in its final year?"

After a self-imposed layoff of more than a year, Hope's movie career was also getting back on track. His last film before the layoff, *Alias Jesse James,* was released in March 1959, and the Western spoof — with Hope playing a New York insurance man who mistakenly sells a policy to Jesse James, then

has to go out West to try to keep him alive —
was a mild uptick from the disastrous *Paris
Holiday.* Following it, a year and a half later,
came a movie that showed a new side of
Hope on-screen.

The Facts of Life began with a script by
Norman Panama and Melvin Frank about
two married suburban neighbors, bored with
their respective spouses, who try to have an
affair. Panama and Frank originally wanted
to cast William Holden and Olivia de Havilland as the couple, but had trouble selling it
to a studio. Then they had the idea to refash-
ion it for two comedians: Bob Hope and
Lucille Ball.

Hope was wary of the idea at first. "It's a
little straight, isn't it?" he said of the script.
But he told Panama and Frank that he would
do it if Lucy agreed. Ball, Hope's favorite
costar, had largely dropped out of movies
since her huge success on TV with *I Love Lucy*
and was now partners with her (soon-to-be
ex-) husband, Desi Arnaz, in Desilu Studios.
She had her own reservations about the film,
worried that it would turn into a typical Hope
farce. "I don't want it to be the *Road to
Infidelity,*" she told the screenwriters. But she
agreed to do it, and the movie began shooting in June 1960, with co-screenwriter Frank
as the director.

The production had its share of problems.

Climbing into a rowboat for one scene, Ball slipped and fell, gashing her leg and bruising her face so badly that the production had to shut down for two weeks. While she was recuperating, Frank sprained his ankle on the golf course, and Hope jammed his thumb in a door. The film also posed creative challenges for the two stars. Ball, a more meticulous actor than Hope, worked hard to create a realistic character distinct from her farcical TV persona: "Was I Lucy? Was I Lucy?" she would ask after scenes. At times she pushed director Frank too far. "If you want to direct the picture, I'll go play golf," he snapped one day when she became too overbearing.

Hope, on the other hand, had to be steered away from his natural inclination to go for the easy laugh. In one scene, the couple check into a motel to consummate their affair, and the script has Hope making small talk when he enters the room — nice closet, good lamp — to show his nervousness. Hope wanted instead to come into the room and surreptitiously test out the springs of the bed. Frank indulged his star by shooting both versions; Hope's got more laughs, but Frank ended up using his own.

The Facts of Life is an enjoyable romantic comedy, proof that the two comic stars can handle relatively sophisticated adult material. It is handicapped by Hollywood's 1950s prudishness about sex (there is none) and by its farcical predictability (on the night of their assignation, Hope's convertible top won't go up and they're drenched in the rain). Hope is restrained and credible in a role that, for once, suits his middle-aged spread, and he has some funny moments: stuck at a Boy Scout meeting, for example, when he's late for a rendezvous with Ball, squirming as he has to sit through a Scout's interminable report on smoke signals. But Ball outshines him nearly all the way; indeed, she exposes some of his limitations as a serious actor. Every nuance of her character's conflicting emotions is registered in her animated face, body language, and line readings. Hope's inner life, hidden beneath his cool-wiseacre façade, is pretty much a cipher.

Yet *The Facts of Life,* released in November 1960, earned a healthy $3.2 million at the box office, more than any other Hope film since *The Seven Little Foys.* Rare for a Hope film, it even picked up five Academy Award nominations, including one for Panama and Frank's screenplay. (The film won one Oscar, for Edith Head's costumes.) It was a promising step forward for Hope as a film actor, a move into more intelligent, age-appropriate romantic comedy. Unfortunately, it was the last good film he would ever make.

The start of the 1960s augured big changes for both Hope and the nation. He joked often about the charismatic young senator from

Massachusetts who was running for president in 1960: "Do we really want a president who rides for half fare on the bus?" When John F. Kennedy entered the White House, the generational shift registered acutely for Hope — from Dwight D. Eisenhower, Hope's personal link to World War II, to a new and unfamiliar band of Ivy League–educated New Frontiersmen.

Hope, now fifty-seven, was becoming keenly aware of the passage of time. When he was entertaining the troops in Germany in 1958, a young solider came up to him and brought greetings from his father, who had seen Hope at Guadalcanal. "I entertained his father! That one line really aged me," said Hope. His old movies were now on TV — Paramount had sold all of its pre-1948 films, including most of Hope's classics, to television for $50 million (a deal that Hope publicly complained about, since it gave the actors no residuals) — and the contrast between the brash young movie star of the 1940s and the paunchier, middle-aged Hope was there on the small screen for all to see.

In the world of comedy, too, times were changing. By the end of the 1950s, a new wave of stand-up comics was emerging from the folk clubs and hip nightspots of New York, San Francisco, and Chicago. These comedians — Mort Sahl, Lenny Bruce, Jonathan Winters, Shelley Berman, Bob Newhart,

Mike Nichols and Elaine May — rejected the impersonal, joke-driven style of Hope and the comics of his generation who came out of vaudeville and the borscht belt. The new comedians wrote their own material and developed more individualized styles: doing characters and improvising scenes, using stand-up comedy to explore their own lives, experiences, and neuroses, and to express their often dissenting social and political views.

Hope was a fan of many of these comedians (though he had few of them on his shows). He saw Bruce, the infamous "dirty" comic, perform several times and thought he was brilliant. Once in the early sixties he went to see Bruce at a Florida nightclub. Bruce introduced Hope in the audience and after the show ran into the parking lot to flag him down, asking Hope if he would give Bruce a guest spot on one of his TV shows. Hope laughed him off: "Lenny, you're for educational TV."

Yet Bruce and the other new-wave comics were beginning to make Hope look old-fashioned. He was the older generation now, a friend of presidents and court jester for the Establishment — a symbol of everything the younger comics were rebelling against. It was not a role that Hope welcomed, or that would treat him very well.

560

CHAPTER 10
KING

"I FEEL VERY HUMBLE, ALTHOUGH I THINK I'VE GOT THE STRENGTH OF CHARACTER TO FIGHT IT."

For his 1960 Christmas tour, the Defense Department gave Hope a break from the arctic cold and the grueling long-distance treks through the Far East and Europe. His destination this time was the sunny Caribbean, for a visit to US bases in Panama, Puerto Rico, Antigua, and El Salvador. The climax of the trip, and its chief raison d'être, was a Christmas Eve visit to the US naval base at Guantánamo, on the southeastern coast of Cuba. Communist leader Fidel Castro had taken control of the island country and was ratcheting up anti-American rhetoric, nationalizing US businesses, and prompting fears that the Soviets were gaining a base of influence just ninety miles from US shores.

Hope brought a troupe of nearly sixty with him aboard the Military Air Transport Service (MATS) plane that left on December 19, among them Hungarian-born beauty Zsa Zsa Gabor, musical-comedy star Janis Paige, singer and former Miss Oklahoma Anita

Bryant, and a young crooner named Andy Williams. The flight into Guantánamo had some tense moments, as the pilot had to stick to the approved flying corridor or risk being fired upon by the Cubans. At one point, the entertainers looked out their windows and saw two Cuban planes flying alongside them. "It was scary," Janis Paige recalled. "There was an awful silence. Nobody knew what to say or what to do — when suddenly they peel off and in their place come four of our fighter planes, with the guys giving us the thumbs-up signal. You could see their faces, they were that close."

But for many in the group, the most stressful part of the trip was dealing with the prima donna known as Zsa Zsa. Hope appreciated performers who could tough out the often harsh conditions, and he was usually lucky in finding them — troupers such as Frances Langford and Patty Thomas, who didn't complain about the rough accommodations or having to do their hair and makeup on the fly. Even Jayne Mansfield, the blond bombshell who'd joined him on two previous trips, had her husband, Mickey Hargitay, along to buffer any diva behavior. But Gabor, a minor movie actress better known for her jewels, her accent, and her many husbands, was a high-maintenance problem, complaining about the accommodations, throwing tantrums in her dressing room, and monopolizing the hair dryer.

"Everybody hated Zsa Zsa," said Andy Williams. "On the trip I got crabs from sitting on a toilet seat, and everybody signed a proclamation wanting me to sleep with Zsa Zsa, so I could give them to her." Paige, the Broadway musical star who had top billing on the tour, was given the best quarters at Guantánamo, a small house on the base, while the rest of the troupe were assigned Quonset huts. Gabor flew into a rage when she found out, and assistant producer Silvio Caranchini had to plead with Paige to trade rooms with her. "He said, 'Jan, she's throwing hysterics. She demands that she has to have your quarters. I'm asking you to do this for Bob's sake,' " Paige recalled. "So I stayed in a Quonset hut with bugs that looked liked B-17s on the ceiling. It was hot and miserable. And she slept in an air-conditioned house that night."

Hope did two shows at Gitmo, on the day before Christmas and on Christmas night. "Guantánamo," he began his monologue, "that's a Navy term meaning 'Hear you knocking but you can't come in.' " In one sketch Hope and Williams played the husbands of two Waves (Paige and Bryant) who sneak them onto the base in violation of Navy orders. A few days after Hope's return from his tour, outgoing president Eisenhower formally broke off diplomatic relations with

Cuba, and Hope reedited the special to give even more time to the Guantánamo segments. The show, which aired on January 11, 1961, drew some of Hope's highest ratings yet. Just a few days later John F. Kennedy took office.

The early 1960s, with a glamorous and youthful new president in the White House, were Camelot years for Hope as well. Kennedy and his circle gave Hope a rich new load of comedy material. He joked about the president's wealth, his family, his hair, and his Ivy League brain trust. "There are so many professors in the cabinet," Hope said, "you can't leave the White House without raising your hand." He took note of the president's political battles, such as his face-off with the nation's steelmakers over rising steel prices: "Kennedy is still mad," Hope said. "He just ordered a plywood Chrysler." When the president's youngest brother, Ted Kennedy, won a Senate seat from Massachusetts, Hope told an audience overseas, "It's been a slow year back home. Only one Kennedy got elected." As Cold War flash points proliferated around the globe, Hope defused the tension with homegrown wisecracks: "There's trouble in Cuba, Laos, Vietnam. Things are so bad, last week Huntley tried to jump off Brinkley." When the Soviets launched their first cosmonauts into orbit and fears mounted that America was losing the space race, Hope tried to buck up morale with gallows humor: "It just proves one thing: their German scientists are better than our German scientists."

He was more than a comedian; he was a national institution. NBC paid tribute to his life and work in an hour biographical special, featuring behind-the-scenes footage from his 1960 Caribbean tour, interviews with associates such as Mort Lachman and Jimmy Saphier, and reverent narration by the mellow-toned Alexander Scourby. It was Hope's apotheosis as the nation's comedian laureate. He narrated a TV documentary on Will Rogers, reinforcing his generational link to the beloved humorist. He continued his tours of military bases during the holidays — back up north to Labrador and Greenland in 1961, another swing through Korea and the Far East in 1962. One of the men who kidnapped Frank Sinatra Jr. in 1963 told an FBI agent that the gang had first considered snatching Hope's oldest son, Tony, but opted for young Sinatra instead because "Bob Hope is such a good American and had done so much in entertaining troops."

The awards and honors poured in, growing ever more weighty and prestigious. The senior class at Notre Dame named him the 1962 Patriot of the Year. He was the first actor to get the Screen Producers Guild's Milestone Award, in a ceremony beamed to US armed forces around the world and highlighted by a congratulatory phone call from President Kennedy. "If there is anybody who has, and still is, doing more to project a shining image of Hollywood," said *Variety,* "and he doesn't answer to the name Bob Hope, who could that party be?" After some initial resistance, the Senate voted to award him the Congressional Gold Medal, in recognition of his work entertaining the troops. But the measure got bottled up in the House Banking Committee, over concerns that singling out Hope (only the third show-business personality to receive the award, after George M. Cohan and Irving Berlin) would open the floodgates to too many other entertainers. Hope was the only comedian in America who could prompt a congressional fight.

As an entertainer, he was in a class by himself. Other comedians played nightclubs or the big Las Vegas showrooms. Not Hope. He preferred stadiums, civic auditoriums, state fairgrounds — venues more fitting for a comedian of the people. He did a week of shows at the 1962 World's Fair in Seattle, drawing crowds so big that an extra matinee had to be added and overflow spectators were seated in boats moored on a lagoon below the stage. In October 1962 he gave another command performance at the London Palladium, entertaining Queen Elizabeth and Prince Philip with jokes about America's own royal family: "We don't have titles in the United States. No, sir, in America we have just two classes — the people and the Kennedys." And Bob Hope.

Yet he was still the hardworking vaudeville trouper, traveling the country for one-nighters — both paid concerts and unpaid charity gigs, raising money for local hospitals and Boys Clubs, supporting the projects and worthy causes of friends. One of his favorite cities was Dallas, where his pals included Bob Bixler, a former vaudevillian who did PR for him, and Tony Zoppi, a columnist for the *Dallas Morning News,* who would take Hope on late-night jaunts to Jack Ruby's nightclub. When Hope canceled a January 1962 concert at the Dallas Coliseum, Bixler prevailed on him to help bail out the local promoter who got burned, Iva D. Nichols of the Dallas Theater Guild, by doing a makeup concert in June. Hope did the show, unaware that Nichols was being pursued by the IRS and numerous angry creditors. On the night of his concert, federal marshals and sheriffs deputies were at the box office confiscating the ticket proceeds. Hope ended up getting only $4,500 of the $10,000 fee he was promised and found himself dragged into an embarrassing local scandal. "Let's face it, Bob," an executive for Neiman Marcus, another participant in the show, wrote him later, "both of us got had."

As his sixtieth birthday approached, the life milestones were starting to accumulate. In June 1962, his son Tony graduated from Georgetown University, with plans to go to Harvard Law School in the fall. Hope gave the commencement address, accepting an honorary doctorate in front of three thousand graduates, family members, and friends gathered outdoors on the tree-lined campus. "I can't wait till I get home and have my son read this to me," Hope said of the Latin diploma. "I did recognize one word — something about 'negligence.' "

Later that summer his brother Jack, a drinker who suffered from liver problems, went into a hospital in Boston for an operation to remove his spleen. After the surgery his organs began to fail and he fell into a coma. He died on August 6, 1962. His unexpected passing was a blow to Hope, who depended on his easygoing and well-liked brother, less for his titular role as producer of Bob's TV specials than as an adviser, fixer, and all-around security blanket. "He was just a doll," said Jack Shea, a director of Hope TV shows in those years. "He was the only person who could go in and tell Bob he was full of it."

Three months later another key member of Hope's inner circle, longtime publicist Mack Millar, died suddenly of a heart attack. Millar was an old-school hustler, pals with the veteran newspaper columnists who were rapidly being replaced by younger and less compliant TV journalists. Still, he was one of Hope's most loyal and hardworking advocates, and a mainstay of his powerful publicity team since the early days in Hollywood. Unfortunately, he wasn't around to see the culmination of one of his biggest projects: his campaign to get Hope the Congressional Gold Medal.

The bill to award Hope the medal was finally extricated from committee and passed by Congress in June 1962. President Kennedy promptly signed it into law. But it hit yet another snag when Congress failed to pass an appropriations bill that included $2,500 for the medal. That left the award hanging for months. Hope was on a fishing trip with his family in British Columbia in September 1963 when a call came that the medal would finally be presented to him at the White House in two days. He hurried to Washington with the family and was at the White House for the ceremony on September 11.

President Kennedy made the presentation before a crowd of two hundred congressmen and other dignitaries on the White House lawn, reading an inscription that praised Hope for his "outstanding service to the cause of democracy throughout the world." "This is one of the only bills we've gotten by lately," the president joked, getting a big laugh before handing off to the comedian being honored. Hope noted that Kennedy had seen him entertain in the South Pacific when the future president was a PT boat captain during World War II. "The president was a very gay and carefree young man at that time," Hope said. "Of course, all he had to worry about then was the enemy." After the ceremony, Milton Berle, who was there for a White House lunch, playfully grabbed the award from Hope and exchanged a few quips with him, giving reporters some fodder for their morning stories. It was a great day for Hope, who cherished the award as the highest recognition of his achievement as a humanitarian and entertainer. "I feel very humble," Hope said, "although I think I've got the strength of character to fight it."

Hope was well past humility. In the 1950s, despite his success in movies and radio, he was still something of a comedian on the make, trying to prove himself in the new medium of television. By the early sixties, his dominance in TV was no longer in doubt. He was NBC's biggest ratings powerhouse and most indispensable star. In 1961 *Variety* did an analysis of the ratings for the sixty-eight Hope specials since his first one aired in April 1950. Hope won his time period fifty-seven times — a level of consistency that no other

TV star could match over such a long stretch. "Hope is the closest anybody has come to batting 1000, over a more-than-decade span in walloping the competition," the trade paper marveled.

On camera he was thicker around the middle, a little graying at the temples. The posture was more regal (always a half turn to the right, so the camera would highlight the curling-up-to-the-left smile), the pauses longer and more defiant, almost daring the audience not to laugh. His shows took on a more formalized, almost institutional quality: Hope's annual presentation of the Hollywood Deb Stars, for instance (a selection of up-and-coming movie starlets that Hope began featuring back in the mid-1950s), or, beginning in the 1960s, the college football all-American team, with a Hope one-liner for each player as he trotted onstage to be introduced. The old variety-show format was starting to look a little stodgy. Well after most other NBC shows had switched to color, Hope's remained in black and white, probably because it was cheaper. (He finally made the changeover in December 1965.) His humor too was sounding more middle-aged, with smug, older-generation quips about rock 'n' roll fads such as the twist ("the only dance I know where you wear out your clothes from the inside") or sketches about those crazy, nonconformist beatniks, always with Hope in his fake goatee, doing hepcat jive talk.

His production team was stocked with people who had been with him for years: prop man Al Borden, who first worked with Hope on his Broadway show *Roberta;* assistant producer Silvio Caranchini and sound technician John Pawlek, who did the advance production work for his overseas tours; cue-card man Barney McNulty and longtime talent coordinator Onnie Morrow. The writing staff too congealed into a tight-knit group that remained remarkably unchanged: Mort Lachman, Hope's confidant and house intellectual, and his writing partner, Bill Larkin; Les White, who started out writing jokes for Hope in vaudeville, and his partner, Johnny Rapp; Charlie Lee, a corpulent, acid-tongued Englishman whom Hope nicknamed Lipton (because he drank tea), and Gig Henry, a former US intelligence officer in World War II; and Norm Sullivan, a crew-cut member of Hope's original *Pepsodent Show* radio team and the only writer who worked solo.

The writers complained a lot, but they mostly enjoyed their indentured servitude with Hope. He was a demanding boss, insatiable for material and possessive of their time. But he always appreciated their skills, credited their work, and knew he couldn't do without them. "This is all the talent we have, fellas," he once said, pointing to a script. Said Lachman, "When things go wrong, Hope takes the whip. He'll work you like a dog. But when the show's over, he doesn't get down on his guys. And he won't let anyone else do it either."

Lachman was the closest to him. They would play golf together in the afternoons; when Hope would call and bark into the phone, "Now," Lachman would rush over to meet him at Lakeside. Lachman was typically the last one left in Hope's dressing room before a show, after everyone else had cleared out and Hope was making final edits to the script and maybe a last-minute change in his wardrobe. Waiting backstage to go in front of the cameras, Bob would sometimes squeeze Mort's arm until it was black-and-blue — before striding out in front of the audience, the picture of cool. Their relationship was not always smooth. After Jack Hope's death, Lachman inherited many of the producing duties on Hope's TV shows. But when Hope didn't give him the title of producer (it went instead for a time to Hope's youngest brother, George), Lachman was miffed and quit to work for Red Skelton. Hope quickly made amends, and Lachman tore up his Skelton contract and went back to Hope.

Hope's sponsors weren't quite so loyal. As production costs for TV shows increased during the 1950s and early 1960s, it was becoming harder to find sponsors willing to take on one show for an entire season. Hope's show was one of the costliest on TV — around $350,000 per hour, plus another $50,000 that Hope demanded the sponsor kick in for publicity. That was too steep for Buick, which ended its sponsorship of Hope's shows in 1961 (switching instead to *Sing Along with Mitch,* which was cheaper). Hope shopped around for another company willing to sponsor him for the entire season. When he couldn't find one, he relented and began making deals on a show-by-show basis. His first special of the 1961–62 season (which didn't air until Christmas) was sponsored by Revlon, and later ones by Beech-Nut, Timex, and even, during the 1962–63 season, his old radio sponsor Pepsodent.

Then, in early 1963, Hope negotiated a major sponsorship deal with Chrysler. The automaker not only agreed to sponsor Hope's entire 1963–64 season; it wanted to put him on the air every week, as host of a dramatic anthology series, *Bob Hope Presents the Chrysler Theatre.* Hope would film introductions for each of the weekly dramas and star himself in two scripted comedies during the season, along with six of his usual variety specials. The $14 million deal also made Hope Chrysler's spokesperson and "image man," the start of a fruitful, decade-long association with the automaker.

Hope's *Chrysler Theatre,* which aired on

Friday nights during the 1963–64 season, was one of several new network shows (along with *The Richard Boone Show* and *Kraft Suspense Theater*) that augured a brief comeback for the dramatic anthology series, in eclipse since the passing of the 1950s golden age of live TV drama. Hope had little to do with the dramatic hours, which were produced at Revue Studios (later Universal Television) and overseen by writer-producer Dick Berg. But they included such notable programs as *One Day in the Life of Ivan Denisovich,* a TV adaptation of Alexander Solzhenitsyn's novel, starring Jason Robards; an original teleplay by Pulitzer Prize–winning playwright William Inge; and new work by such top writers as Rod Serling and Budd Schulberg. The scripted comedies that Hope starred in were negligible — laugh-track farces such as *Have Girls, Will Travel,* with Hope playing a frontier marriage broker, and *Her School for Bachelors,* in which he's the editor of a *Playboy*-style girlie magazine. But with his name on one of TV's most prestigious dramatic series — the winner of three Emmy Awards in its first season — Hope's TV profile was never higher.

Coping with enormous fame can be a challenge for any Hollywood celebrity. The adulation, the loss of privacy, the reluctance of underlings to tell you bad news, the shell that forms to protect against the onslaught of people who want favors or money — all can make it difficult, if not impossible, to stay grounded, human, in touch with the world outside of your own narcissistic bubble. In some ways, Bob Hope handled his fame better than most. He wasn't insecure or uncomfortable in the limelight; he wasn't a temperamental monster to work for; he didn't turn to drink or drugs. He played around with women, but never broke up his family. He had a relatively unpretentious lifestyle: a house in Toluca Lake that was spacious but not flashy, pet German shepherds, utilitarian American cars (usually supplied by his sponsors) that he liked to drive himself. He was always happy to greet fans who approached him on the street or in airports, chatting with them and signing autographs.

Yet decades of being one of the most recognizable people in the world, combined with his natural English reserve and an aversion to introspection, led Hope to wall off a great part of himself from outsiders, even those quite close to him. In social settings he could be convivial and charismatic, but also detached and programmed — a rote "How about that" or "Innat great" substituting for real conversation. He would deflect probing questions with jokes or by changing the subject. "He's shallow in the sense that he's never taken the time to look into himself," said Martin Ragaway, who wrote for him in the early 1960s, "and he won't let others do it either." Being interviewed by reporters, he could be remote and ungiving. "When he's not quipping, his conversation is flat, faceless, withdrawn," wrote a *Time* magazine reporter who spent time with him in 1963. "He appeared vague and preoccupied, lost in thoughts he couldn't articulate. He was courteous, gracious and removed. He wasn't uncooperative. One felt there just wasn't much there."

He had a temper, which could erupt when technical foul-ups or other problems occurred on the set. He could get nervous before shows and had show-business superstitions — no whistling in the dressing room or hats on the bed. But pressure never seemed to upset him or ruffle his cool. His calm self-possession had a way of assuaging the insecurities of others. Peter Leeds, a sketch actor who worked with him on TV and tours for years, recalled pitching Hope an idea for a TV show and getting no response for weeks. His anger steadily rising, Leeds finally blew his top and cursed out his boss. "Take it easy," said Hope, unperturbed. "We'll get to it." Leeds was later horrified that he had exploded at Hope. "If it were Danny Thomas or Milton Berle," he said, "they would've thrown me out on my ear." Hope didn't.

Yet he expected deference. Art Schneider, who edited many of Hope's early TV specials, was working late at night on a Christmas show when he got a phone call. "This is Bob," came the voice on the phone. "Bob who?" said Schneider, who also had a son named Bob. "Don't ever do that to me again," Hope snapped. Hal Kanter, who directed some of Hope's filmed introductions for his Chrysler hours, had a tiff with the star over his wardrobe. Since the intros for several shows were taped in one sitting, Kanter told Hope he needed to change neckties for each. Hope dismissed the idea, saying no one would notice. After Kanter pressed the matter, Hope took him into his dressing room and lectured him, "From now on, don't argue with me in front of the help. Just do it. Do you get my message?" Kanter said he did — and quit.

Hope hated confrontations. When he was unhappy with a performer or a staff member, he got others to deliver bad news. He wanted to be loved by everyone. He couldn't understand criticism and would complain to his publicists when he got a bad review or a negative story: "Are you telling these interviewers how much I raise for charity each year, or how much I pay in property taxes?" (The standard answer for each was $1 million.) He never bad-mouthed fellow performers in public and chastised those who repeated nasty gossip. "There's always some guy who wants to chop a comedian," Hope told a reporter. "I've met these guys everywhere. I've heard all the chops. I don't go in for that. I can understand these guys because I was one of them." He wasn't any more. He was Bob Hope.

His cheapness was legendary, if sometimes exaggerated. As producer of his own shows, he watched over expenses like a hawk, signed all the checks, and could balk at the cost of a cab ride or late-night pizzas for the crew editing his specials. Director Sid Smith, who worked on Hope specials in the 1980s, once submitted a $39 receipt for a taxi ride to the airport. Hope objected that the same trip only cost him $27. "I never put in another expense account in all my years with Bob Hope," said Smith. Bob Alberti, Hope's musical director in the later years, once finished a recording session in New York City after midnight and had to deliver the audiotape to Hope at a production studio across town. When Alberti arrived and turned in his cab receipt, Hope asked why he couldn't have taken a crosstown bus. Even a family member, after a stay at the Toluca Lake house, was startled to get a bill from Hope's office — for a $3.75 long-distance phone call he had made while there.

Lachman and others would leave tips for Hope at restaurants, just to make sure he didn't shortchange the waiters. Often it wasn't stinginess so much as sheer inattention. Hope once walked into the officers' club at Keesler Air Base in Mississippi and ordered "drinks on the house." Then he left, forgetting to settle the tab. "We were paying it off for the next year," recalled an officer's wife who was there.

Bob Mills, a Hope writer in the 1970s and 1980s, saw Hope's frugality as a function of his competitiveness. Hope hated to miss out on a deal or to feel that he was being taken advantage of. When his writing staff convinced him in the 1980s to get a fax machine (ending the tradition of personally dropping off jokes at the Hope compound), they bought the boss an expensive, fully loaded machine, while the writers got cheaper models at the fleet rate. When Hope found out about it, he asked why he hadn't gotten the same good deal. "Why did he care? He cared because we are sitting here with a deal that he didn't get," said Mills. After he explained to Hope why he needed the more expensive machine, the boss appeared satisfied. Then he thought for a minute and asked, "Why do I need a separate phone line?"

At the same time, Hope raised millions for charity (most of it through the Bob and Dolores Hope Foundation, which he set up in 1962) and was generous in helping out relatives and friends — supporting family members who were broke, staking former colleagues in business ventures, and giving work to old vaudeville pals such as Charlie Cooley and Jack Pepper. Hope appreciated professionalism and would reward it. When Arlene Dahl failed to show up for a guest appearance on one of Hope's TV shows in the mid-1950s, Hope got Janis Paige to fill in at the last minute. She quickly learned Dahl's part in a sketch and rehearsed a new musical number. Later she got two paychecks — hers, and the one that Dahl was supposed to get. "Thanks a lot, kid," Hope wrote in a note. He stayed loyal to his longtime agents, Louis Shurr and Jimmy Saphier, even when MCA made a pitch to take over all of his representation. After Hope read the proposed contract, he asked if MCA would be willing to buy out Shurr and Saphier. "Name a figure," came the reply. Said Hope, "Well, if they settle for anything less than ten million dollars, I'll never talk to them again." That ended the discussion.

He had a Depression-era mind-set. He never forgot his family's hand-to-mouth existence, and his years of struggle in vaudeville. Though his real estate holdings and other investments made him one of the wealthiest people in Hollywood, he never thought of himself as rich. "Emotionally he's still the vaudevillian who fought his way up during the Depression," said Lachman. "To vaudevillians, and to Hope, the only thing that matters is how much money you've got in your pocket, how much food in the kitchen, how much you can charge and get away with. The rest is crap."

Hope ran his sprawling enterprises like a mom-and-pop operation. Though he paid decent salaries and gave generous Christmas gifts to his employees, he provided no medical insurance or retirement benefits for his office staff until the 1990s. He was a hands-on manager of his many ventures, and only he knew the full extent of them. "Dad was always of the mind to divide and conquer," said his daughter Linda. "He would have all these different compartments and different people handling different things. And he was sort of the hub of the wheel. He knew the whole picture, but not too many other people did. And he kind of liked it that way."

He was always busy. His appearances at home carried a sense of occasion. When he arrived at family dinners, nearly always late, the clan would often stand to greet him, or his daughter Nora would sing a joking welcome song for him. When the larger extended family got together at the holidays, he could be funny and voluble or drift into stretches of impenetrable silence. "Even within the family it felt like he was special," said Justine Carr, a cousin. "It didn't feel like he was a dad; he was always Bob Hope. Everyone was on notice when he was around — waiting to see, was he going to be attentive, or aloof?"

"He was an impersonal guy in a lot of ways," said nephew Tom Malatesta. "I think everything else in his life was not as important as what he was doing for a living. Could he sit at the table and tell jokes and entertain? Absolutely. But that's what he did. He was Bob Hope, twenty-four/seven."

One houseguest who got an inside look at the Hope home life in those years was John Guare, the future playwright (*The House of Blue Leaves, Six Degrees of Separation*), who was best friends with Hope's son Tony at Georgetown. After graduating in 1963, Guare drove cross-country with Tony and was about to start an intern job at Universal Studios when he got his draft notice. While he was trying to sort out his draft status and enlist in the reserves, Dolores gave Guare an open-ended invitation to stay with the family in Toluca Lake. He wound up living there for nearly ten months.

His first Hope family dinner was memorable. "We sat down for dinner, and everybody turned quiet," Guare recalled. "Suddenly doors open on either side of the fireplace, and maybe eight men come in with enormous white cards, with jokes written on them. They stood around us at the table, and one by one Mr. Hope would say, 'Yes, no, yes . . .' No reaction to the jokes — just

'That's funny' or 'No, put that over there.' He was building his act. And that's what you did for dinner."

Yet Guare found it a warm and bustling household, thanks largely to Dolores and her spirited family — her mother, Theresa, who lived with them, and her sister, Mildred, who was often around. Both were streetwise, no-nonsense New Yorkers who helped keep the home lively and grounded. "You could imagine Theresa out on the sidewalk on Tenth Avenue playing cards with the girls," said Guare. "They were rich people; they were stars. But in a sense they weren't used to it. They had this glamorous house, but they were determined to keep the Tenth Avenue-ness of it." Dolores ran a tight ship, with a large household staff and a sign-up sheet for family members who would be joining for dinner, and even when Bob was around, one had a sense that his bags were never unpacked. But any tension over his frequent absences was kept well hidden. "It was not a house full of undercurrents," said Guare. "There was not a threat in the air, or wariness. It was a genuinely pleasant house."

Another outsider who got a close-up glimpse of the Hope household in those years was Tony Coelho, an aspiring seminary student and later a six-term California congressman. After graduating from Loyola University in 1964, he was diagnosed with

584

epilepsy, a disease that disqualified him from seminary school and estranged him from his parents, Portuguese-born Catholics who regarded it as evidence of possession by the devil. Unable to get a driver's license or a job, Coelho was close to suicide when a psychologist at Loyola connected him with Dolores Hope. She offered to give him a place to live while he tried to piece his life together.

Coelho spent nine months with the Hopes, living in their guest suite above the garage and becoming close friends with Kelly, the one Hope child still living at home. It was a heady experience: dinner with Martha Raye, phone calls from Barry Goldwater and Lyndon Johnson during the 1964 presidential campaign. (Hope was a Goldwater supporter; Johnson was trying to make sure that support stayed private.) The Hopes had other houseguests, among them a Standard Oil heiress who hired a pianist to play for her while she painted in the Hope backyard. "They obviously had a lot of money," said Coelho. "But they didn't flash it or try to impress you with it. They were regular people, fun to be around."

The stay helped turn his life around. "The Hopes were very supportive, just by accepting me. After going through suicide and family rejection and questioning the Church and my religion, all of a sudden getting this opportunity — I was just overwhelmed." After Hope suggested that Coelho go into politics instead of the ministry, he landed a staff job with a Democratic congressman from California, Fred Sisk. When Hope found out, he was dismayed that it was a congressman he'd never heard of. "If I knew you were serious about it," he told Coelho, "I could have got you with somebody who had a name."

"He was very kind to me," said Coelho. "He seemed to be a guy who knew himself and was in control of himself. I never felt that he was hiding anything. The only thing I picked up was that he was protecting himself. I think he always expected people to take advantage." When Coelho moved out, Hope sent him to a Bank of America branch and told him to borrow as much money from Hope's account as he needed. Hope asked only one thing in return: that Coelho promise never to write anything about his time living there. "There was no contract; he knew that he couldn't stop me," said Coelho. "But I felt it was interesting that he had to ask. It told me that he had been hurt. I don't think he let many people get to know the real Bob Hope."

As he entered his sixties, Hope continued his almost superhuman work pace: star of TV comedy specials and host of a weekly drama series, a couple of feature films a year, and a full schedule of personal appearances that kept him constantly on the move. Requests for his presence to help one worthy cause or another poured in at a rate of fifty a day, and he accepted as many as he could pack in. "Your hospital needs a new wing? Your church a vestry? You've got a flock of juvenile delinquents and no gymnasium? Or a Man of the Year Award that's not working? Your man is Bob Hope," wrote Dwight Whitney in a *TV Guide* profile. "At times the world seems made up exclusively of 'people I can't disappoint.' "

The nonstop travel satisfied an ex-vaudevillian's love of the road (and gave him more freedom for his extramarital dalliances), but it became a drain on his time and energy. "It was something that obviously called out to him," said his daughter Linda. "But many times he would leave his television shows and films sort of orphan children out there. They kind of got done, but they weren't necessarily his main interest." Movies had always been Hope's top priority; he considered himself a Hollywood star first, while TV was simply what he did for a living. By the 1960s, the movies too seemed to be getting short shrift. The scripts were getting worse, and Hope's performances more perfunctory and distracted — a far cry from the energetic, committed comic actor of twenty or even ten years earlier.

After his well-received 1960 romantic

comedy *The Facts of Life,* Hope continued to flirt with more mature romantic-comedy roles, but with much less success. In *Bachelor in Paradise,* released in November 1961, he plays an author of bestselling books about his globe-trotting bachelor lifestyle. When he is forced to return to the United States because of income tax problems, his publisher convinces him to move into a California bedroom community and write about American suburban mores. There he encounters a lot of nosy neighbors and randy housewives (and one conveniently available single, played by Lana Turner). But the comedy is mostly hackneyed sitcom stuff: washing machines overflow when they're filled with too much detergent, dinners go up in smoke when the oven is left on too long, and neighbors are always walking in on each other without knocking at just the wrong moment. Hope delivers his wisecracks mechanically and can't muster a real reaction to anything on-screen. Never before has he seemed so disengaged.

Following his reunion with Crosby in *The Road to Hong Kong,* Hope starred in another romantic comedy, *Critic's Choice,* released in April 1963. Adapted from a Broadway play by Ira Levin, it casts Hope as a New York theater critic who must decide whether to review a play written by his wife (Lucille Ball in her fourth and last film with Hope). The part seems all wrong for Hope — the last person one could imagine sitting down to write a theater review — and the contortions to turn it into a Hope vehicle destroy any sliver of credibility. In a ludicrous slapstick climax, he shows up sloshed for his wife's Broadway opening (one of Hope's rare drunk scenes), gets shunted to the balcony because the show has already started, winds up dangling from his heels over the orchestra seats — and still manages to get back to the office in time to write a devastating pan of the play for the morning paper.

In *Call Me Bwana,* released two months later, Hope was at least more in his comfort zone. He plays a travel writer who is sent to Africa by the US government to find a moon rocket that has crashed in the jungle. The character harks back to Hope's lecherous cowards of old: a timid New Yorker whose bogus adventure-travel books were actually written from the safety of his apartment. "The only wild animal I wanna see is the cigarette girl at the Stork Club," he says. "And I carry a gun when I'm with her." But with a lumpy script, lazy direction by Gordon Douglas, and a costar, Anita Ekberg, who provides little but decoration, the safari hits a dead end pretty quickly. The self-indulgence of the whole enterprise is epitomized by a cameo appearance by Arnold Palmer, who shows up in the middle of the jungle for a game of golf with Hope. He's there because Hope needed a golf partner during the filming.

Produced by Harry Saltzman and Albert "Cubby" Broccoli — who were just finishing up their first James Bond film, *Dr. No* — *Call Me Bwana* was originally supposed to be shot in Kenya, but political instability there forced a switch to London's Pinewood Studios. Hope didn't mind too much since he had begun a relationship with Rosemarie Frankland, a Welsh beauty who had won the title of Miss World, at age eighteen, at a ceremony hosted by Hope in the fall of 1961.

Hope took Frankland on his 1961 Christmas trip to the Arctic, supported her when she moved to Los Angeles to pursue a film career, and gave her a small part in his 1965 movie *I'll Take Sweden.* "Bob admitted to me that the great love of his life was Rosemarie Frankland," said Hope's publicist Frank Liberman, who was often on the receiving end of phone calls from Frankland when she needed money and couldn't reach Hope. The relationship, according to Liberman, lasted for nearly thirty years, but her movie career never took off, and Frankland died of a drug overdose in 2000. (She wasn't the only former Hope girlfriend to meet a similar sad end. Ursula Halloran, the publicist he was involved with in the late fifties, was found dead of a drug overdose in November 1963.

Barbara Payton, the former starlet who told the tale of their 1949 fling in *Confidential* magazine, turned to drugs and prostitution as her career fell apart and drank herself to death in 1967, at age thirty-nine.)

Hope's next film, *A Global Affair,* was a more high-minded project. He plays a low-level employee at the United Nations who inherits a baby abandoned there late on a Friday when he's the only one left working. When no one can decide what to do with the infant, Hope announces he will give the baby to the most deserving nation, then gets plied by an array of international beauties, each trying to get him to pick her country. Shot partially on location at the UN, the movie is a mix of curdled sex farce (Hope's bachelor neighbor, played by Robert Sterling, uses the infant to rouse the mothering instincts of every sexy gal in the vicinity) and promotional brochure for the United Nations — it was nominated for a Golden Globe for Best Film Promoting International Understanding. Swiss actress Lilo Pulver brightens up the movie with a charming turn as a Russian agent trying to persuade Hope of the glories of the Soviet state. (Katharine Hepburn could have taken a few lessons from her in *The Iron Petticoat.*) But Hope once again looks bored with the whole sorry affair.

Director Jack Arnold hated the film so much that he demanded his name be taken off the credits (though it's still there), complaining that producer Hal Bartlett ruined the film in the editing. But Hope was a problem too — so wedded to his cue cards that Arnold instructed his cameraman to make up technical problems so they would have to shoot each scene at least six times, by which point Hope would presumably have learned his lines. "Bob Hope lives in his own world," said Arnold. "He comes in, and does his work, and doesn't socialize with any of the cast — which doesn't mean that he's mean, or doesn't joke around with people. It's just that he is a very self-centered gentleman. He doesn't bother to even learn the script, and sometimes, I think, he hasn't read it."

Even as the quality of his work was declining, Hope continued to be a master at promoting it. Every NBC special would be preceded by a slew of newspaper stories, drawn from Hope's round of phone interviews with TV columnists across the country. He played an active, hands-on role in planning the publicity campaigns for all of his movies. Before the release of his 1959 Western comedy *Alias Jesse James,* for example, Hope proposed a gala premiere in St. Louis, complete with a Western-style fashion show, and wanted to fly to three cities for simultaneous premieres on the same day. He suggested a magazine feature story on "Friendship in Show Business," in which some of the Western actors who had cameos in the film, such as Gary Cooper and Roy Rogers, would talk about their longtime friendship with Hope, and told his publicists to get a magazine to do a cover story on him and costar Rhonda Fleming. "I explained to Bob that the magazines are going for stars like Natalie Wood and the younger set," Hope PR man Arthur Jacobs wrote in a memo relaying Hope's wishes to the Paramount publicists, "but Bob has something to offer and that is, if we can get a cover he will plug the magazine on his Buick specs."

Hope also pushed the novel idea of promoting his movies on television. He and Crosby had done TV ads for *Road to Bali,* and in 1962 Hope got satirist Stan Freberg to film some commercials for *The Road to Hong Kong.* "The film industry needs a positive approach to sell its pictures on TV," Hope told *Variety.* "They're still sort of laying back and not reaching people like they should. Why aren't they selling pictures on station breaks, for example? They should have TV campaigns to make the people want to go out and see films." Thirty years later, such saturation TV campaigns would become de rigueur for every major Hollywood release. Hope, once again, was a pioneer.

Meanwhile, he was expanding his brand

more aggressively and with more ingenuity than anyone else in Hollywood. Hope wasn't just a movie and TV star. He was a bestselling author (his fifth book, *I Owe Russia $1200,* came out in May 1963) and a recording artist too (the monologue from his 1958 Moscow trip was released as a Decca LP in 1963, with a Hope appearance at Notre Dame University on the flip side). He got his name plastered on countless awards, honorary diplomas, and an occasional building — donating $800,000 to Southern Methodist University for the Bob Hope Theater, which broke ground in 1965. He bought a sixteen-hundred-acre ranch in Simi Valley, once used as a set for movie Westerns, and renamed it Hopetown, with ambitious plans to turn it into a Western-themed amusement park. "It'll be Southern California's answer to Mount Rushmore," Hope said. And in perhaps his greatest marketing coup of all, Hope got his own golf tournament.

The Bob Hope Desert Classic had its origins in the old Thunderbird Invitational, which began in 1952 at the Thunderbird Country Club in Rancho Mirage, California. When the tournament ran into money troubles and had to shut down in 1959, a group of Palm Springs area golf boosters, not wanting to give up a valuable weekend on the PGA Tour, got together and fashioned a new tournament to replace it, the Palm Springs

Golf Classic. The plan was to make it a pro-am event, played over five days on four different courses in the Palm Springs area; each foursome of pros and amateurs would play one round on each of the four courses, with the fifth and final day reserved for the pros alone.

The tournament debuted in 1960 and struggled financially for a couple of years, until two of its founders, Milt Hicks and Ernie Dunlevie, came up with the notion of recruiting Hope as its celebrity front man, to compete with the other major pro-am tournament on the PGA Tour, the Bing Crosby Invitational in Pebble Beach. In 1963 they approached Hope with the idea in the locker room at the O'Donnell Golf Club in Palm Springs. Always competitive with his friend Crosby, Hope didn't take long to agree. After a year's delay while the tournament worked out some tax problems (the backers didn't want Hope to be linked to any negative publicity), Hope came on board, bringing along Chrysler as tournament sponsor.

The Bob Hope Desert Classic made its debut the first week of February in 1965. NBC paid $100,000 for the rights to televise it (matching the amount it paid for Crosby's tournament), and Hope wrangled dozens of celebrities to play in the event, among them Kirk Douglas, Lawrence Welk, Bob Newhart, and New York Mets manager Casey Stengel.

The mammoth field included 128 PGA pros and 384 amateurs; a battalion of 160 NBC executives and production people were on hand for the TV coverage; and the week's festivities included a lavish Saturday-night dinner-dance hosted by Hope. Billy Casper won the tournament by a stroke over Arnold Palmer, and former president Dwight D. Eisenhower was there to congratulate the winner at the eighteenth green.

In the years that followed, the Hope Desert Classic surpassed the Crosby as the most star-studded event on the PGA Tour. Hope lured in not just top Hollywood celebrities, but sports stars such as Johnny Bench, astronauts such as Alan Shepard, and even presidents. Gerald Ford, who retired to the Palm Springs area after leaving the White House, was a regular participant, as well as a frequent golfing partner for Hope (and target of many jokes about Ford's errant golf shots). Eisenhower never played in the tournament, but he was a regular guest of honor. When he died, proceeds from the tournament went to build a hospital in his name, the Eisenhower Medical Center in Rancho Mirage, which broke ground in 1969 on eighty acres of land donated by Hope.

The Hope Classic was not a favorite of many of the PGA touring pros, mainly because it forced them to play for four days with celebrity amateurs, who were not always the best golfers. (Crosby, a more serious golfer, had higher standards for the amateurs he invited to play. Hope was more willing to let duffers play if they had big names and could entertain the crowd.) But as one of the first events of the PGA year, with a stellar lineup of golfers playing in the golden desert sunshine while the rest of the country shivered, Hope's tournament became one of the highest-rated TV events on the PGA Tour — and an invaluable marketing tool for the booming Palm Springs area.

In the early years, Hope would play all four of the amateur rounds. Later he scaled back to just an opening-day round, and eventually, as swinging the club got to be harder, to just ceremonial duties, hitting an opening drive to launch the tournament and then retiring until a final appearance to crown the winner. Each year he would host a Monday-night black-tie gala at the Riviera Hotel, always with surprise Hollywood guest stars. Though he used his clout and connections to keep the tournament packed with celebrities, Hope left the actual running of it to others. "He never came to a board meeting," said Dunlevie. "He never told us what he'd like to do or how he'd like to do it." One year the tournament was played on the new, extremely difficult PGA West Stadium Course in La Quinta, and fifty-two pros later signed a letter complaining about the course and refusing to play it again. "Milt and I went over to see Hope and said, 'Bob, did you see all the complaints? We gotta find another golf course.' And he said, 'Why? Look at all the publicity we got.' I think that was the only meeting of substance we ever had with him."

Hope was a good amateur golfer and worked hard at his game, getting tips from every pro he knew, and he knew practically all of them. At his peak, in the early 1950s, he carried a 6 handicap, though it was edging into the low double digits by the mid-1960s. He could drive the ball around 230 yards, had a graceful swing (once compared to Fred Couples's) and was "without doubt one of the best chippers and putters I've ever seen," according to Lakeside caddy Eddie Gannon. Golf relaxed Hope and provided his main form of exercise, along with the late-night walks that he would routinely take before bed in later years. He shared a love of the game with Dolores, who was almost as good a golfer as he. "He could hit the ball farther, but around the green, her short game was impeccable," said Mort Lachman, who played with both.

Hope used golf to cement relationships with powerful people — politicians, generals, corporate bigwigs. "He would do a benefit for, say, John Deere tractors," said Linda Hope, "and then he'd go out on the golf course with the people in the company who played golf. And the head of John Deere might bring along other people who were also company heads, and so Dad would make a nice connection there. In years later it gave him access to a lot of these corporate guys, who had planes and could fly him where he needed to go. He was very smart with that kind of thing."

He was a walking advertisement for golf, from his widely publicized fund-raising matches with Crosby during World War II, to his constant jokes and references to the game in his radio and TV monologues. Along with Eisenhower, the golf-playing president, and Arnold Palmer, golf's first TV superstar, Hope was one of the three people who did the most to popularize golf in America during its boom years of the 1950s and 1960s.

"He was a fair golfer," said Palmer. "He shot mostly in the eighties. But he worked hard at it, and he was a great fan of the game. He and his tournament brought untold benefits to the game of golf." Palmer, a greenskeeper's son who learned to play golf on a public course in Latrobe, Pennsylvania, was golf's great working-class hero. Hope, by contrast, was a country-club guy. But his zeal for the game played a major role in raising the sport's profile and attracting new players to it. "Palmer got the blue-collar guys," said Dunlevie. "Hope got the white-collar guys. People could say, 'He's an ordinary golfer —

he's not any better than I am.' That encouraged a lot of people who weren't interested before."

He played on more than two thousand courses over his golfing lifetime — from Palm Springs to Scotland, in Korea and Vietnam, once on a course that filled the inside of a racetrack in Vienna. He made five holes in one and reputedly once beat Ben Hogan in a round. He published a bestselling memoir about the game, *Confessions of a Hooker: My Lifelong Love Affair with Golf,* cowritten by *Golf Digest* editor Dwayne Netland. Hope started bringing a golf club onstage with him when he entertained, an ever-present prop that became, along with his ski-slope nose, his most recognizable trademark. He even began carrying a golf club with him on his late-night walks — ostensibly for protection. As the tumult of the 1960s began to engulf him, he would need it.

V
LOSING HIS GRIP

FROM PATRIOT TO PARTISAN IN THE QUAGMIRE OF VIETNAM

CHAPTER 11
PATRIOT
"I'D RATHER BE A HAWK THAN A PIGEON."

By the early 1960s, Hope's annual Christmas tours to entertain the troops overseas were starting to draw some criticism. A few wondered why they were still necessary in peacetime. Cynics suggested that Hope was simply using the military to create top-rated TV shows. Objections were raised in Congress about the tours' cost to the military — which had to plan them, provide the facilities, and pay most of the travel and accommodations expenses. For his 1961 tour of Labrador and Greenland, the Air Force limited Hope's troupe to just one plane to save money, barring any journalists or even Hope press agents from coming along.

Inside the military too some grumbled that Hope's tours were taking too much money away from other, more mundane but equally important projects. "Hope did a valid service. But it was an expensive project, and it took a good deal of the budget," said Dorothy Reilly, whose husband, Colonel Alvin E. Reilly, as head of entertainment and recreation for the

Air Force, argued internally that the trips ought to be cut back. "That budget had to cover everything — libraries, R-and-R centers. There were so many ways that money could be used." She couldn't forget the sight of thousands of GIs in Korea in 1957, waiting on a hillside for hours in the subzero cold while Hope and his troupe were preparing and rehearsing. "I thought it was kind of a selfish use of the military," said Reilly.

What Hope needed to stifle the criticism was a real shooting war. And in 1962 he found one — in South Vietnam, where government forces were fighting a stubborn Communist insurgency backed by North Vietnam. The United States had only about nine thousand military "advisers" in the country, and the war was still beneath the radar for most Americans. But Hope made a request to go there as part of a Far East tour in December 1962.

Pentagon officials initially approved the trip, but at the last minute reversed themselves and nixed it as too dangerous. Hope went ahead with his Far East tour, visiting US bases in the Philippines, Guam, Okinawa, Japan, and South Korea. But the war in Vietnam shadowed the trip. At Iwakuni Air Base in Japan, a marine who claimed he had "hitchhiked" from Vietnam gave Hope a scroll with hundreds of signatures from soldiers there, asking him to come entertain.

Hope put in another call to the Pentagon, asking for last-minute permission to go, but again he was turned down.

Echoes of Vietnam also were unmistakable when Hope and his troupe visited that other divided Asian country, Korea. On the heavily guarded border between North and South, Hope saw a Christmas tree that had been planted by the United Nations and that the North Koreans were demanding be removed. "The commies just stared at us," Hope said, narrating his NBC special on the tour. "They claimed it was a capitalist weapon. In a way they were right. . . . But that tree is still there. And while it stands, there's hope for all."

A year later, with the US military presence in Vietnam growing, Hope again asked to make a trip there at Christmas. Again he got an initial okay. But after the assassination of South Vietnamese president Ngo Dinh Diem in November 1963, in a military coup backed by the CIA, the Pentagon again called off the trip as too risky. Instead, Hope switched the itinerary to the eastern Mediterranean, where Greece and Turkey were locked in a dispute over the island of Cyprus.

Just before the trip, Hope had another flare-up of his eye problems. On the advice of his doctors, he went to San Francisco to see another specialist, Dr. Dohrmann Pischel, who had developed a new laser treatment for his condition. Hope received two treatments in early December at San Francisco's Children's Hospital and was forced to lie nearly immobile in a darkened room for days. During his hospital stay, he got so many get-well calls that two extra switchboard operators had to be added to handle them. President Johnson, barely two weeks in office following the assassination of President Kennedy, sent him a handwritten get-well note: "Christmas without Bob Hope is simply not Christmas. God be with you."

Hope returned to Palm Springs to recuperate, and his Christmas troupe began the tour without him — flying to Turkey, with Jerry Colonna handling the emcee duties and teen-movie star Tuesday Weld as the top-billed guest. But Hope wouldn't stay grounded. He joined the company in Ankara and continued with them to Greece, Libya, and Italy. In between shows he had to wear a pair of dark glasses with pinholes to protect his eye. Hope tired easily, and the trip was "one of the roughest we've ever had," said a veteran of his tours. But Hope got stronger as the trip went on, and for the last show, against doctor's orders, he did a strenuous dance routine with old-time vaudevillian John Bubbles. The special that resulted drew some of Hope's best reviews yet. "Bob Hope is so established an institution that he necessarily runs the risk of being taken for granted; he shouldn't be," wrote Jack Gould in the *New*

York Times. "His annual Christmas tour of overseas bases . . . remains one of the enduring demonstrations of the star's special niche in contemporary Americana."

Hope had no reason to believe the cheers wouldn't continue the following year, when he finally got approval to go to South Vietnam. The intensifying war there still enjoyed strong support back home. After an attack on US ships in the Gulf of Tonkin, Congress in August 1964 overwhelmingly passed a resolution authorizing President Johnson to take any action necessary to counter threats to US forces or allies in the region. The war was not a major issue in the 1964 presidential election, which Johnson won in a landslide over Republican Barry Goldwater. By the end of the year the official US presence in the country was still only around twenty-three thousand men. For Hope, South Vietnam was simply another global hot spot where American troops needed a lift.

He assembled a large outfit of seventy-five cast and crew members, including five sexy females: red-haired movie starlet Jill St. John, Italian actress Anna Maria Alberghetti, Hope-tour veterans Janis Paige and Anita Bryant, and the current Miss World, Ann Sydney. Colonna was back as well, along with Les Brown's band. The cargo also included nearly a ton of thirty-by-forty-inch poster board, which Barney McNulty would lug around from show to show and turn into Hope's cue cards.

The troupe stopped first in Guam and the Philippines, then paid another visit (Hope's fourth) to Korea. A helicopter carrying some of the entertainers developed engine trouble and had to make a forced landing in a blizzard, causing a show in Bupyeong to be delayed while another chopper was sent to rescue them. From frigid Korea they flew to sweltering Thailand, where they were invited to a formal dinner by the king and did shows at US air bases in Udorn, Takhli, and Ubon. Then, on Christmas Eve, they flew into the combat zone of Vietnam.

Hope had never faced more danger. His arrival in South Vietnam was shrouded in secrecy "greater than that normally used to veil the movements of generals and cabinet officers," UPI reported. His exact itinerary was kept under wraps until the last minute, and for each show a stage was set up in two different locations, to confuse the enemy and thwart any potential terrorist attacks. Director Jack Shea was told that for every five thousand men Hope entertained, another five thousand were on alert outside the perimeter to protect them. But when Hope walked onstage at Bien Hoa Air Base — dressed in shirtsleeves, his tie loosened, wearing a baseball cap to shield his eyes from the sun, and casually twirling a golf club (the first ap-

608

pearance of Hope's favorite stage prop, two months before the first Bob Hope Desert Classic) — the response was tremendous.

"Hello, advisers," Hope began, a sardonic reference to the euphemism for US troops, who were officially there only to advise South Vietnamese forces. He recycled a favorite line he used when venturing into hostile territory: "As we flew in, they gave us a twenty-one-gun salute. Three of them were ours." He made jokes about the new kind of guerrilla war that was already confounding US military planners: "I asked Secretary McNamara if we could come here. He said, 'Why not, we've tried everything else.'" Henry Cabot Lodge had just been replaced as US ambassador to South Vietnam. "We're on our way to Saigon, and I hope we do as well as Henry Cabot Lodge," said Hope. "He got out."

From Bien Hoa they were supposed to travel to Saigon, twenty miles away, in a convoy of armed personnel carriers, but at the last minute the road was deemed too dangerous, and they were flown instead to Tan Son Nhut Air Base, just north of the city, and driven in from there. But as they inched their way through the clogged streets and neared the Caravelle Hotel, where Hope and the entertainers were to stay, they found a chaotic scene: billows of smoke, piles of rubble, people running, and sirens wailing. Minutes before, a massive explosion had gone off in the Brinks Hotel, a billet for US officers just a block away from the Caravelle. The blast killed two Americans and wounded another sixty-three people, both Americans and Vietnamese.

The shaken entertainers made their way to the hotel, where glass littered the lobby and the electricity was out. There was talk of canceling the tour. But after MPs searched the entire hotel for explosives and assured Hope they could provide security, he forged on. "We had no electricity all the time we were there and no water," recalled Butch Stone, Les Brown's saxophonist. "We just had candles. And all the glass from the windows had been blown into our beds. So before we could get in bed, we had to turn the beds over to get the glass out."

Ambassador Maxwell Taylor had invited Hope and the cast to his house for cocktails that night, and the ones who weren't too shaken by the bombing showed up with Hope. Afterward Hope, Colonna, and Brown were driven to a Navy hospital to visit servicemen who had been injured in the Brinks blast. To end the trying day (and keep a promise he had made to Dolores), Hope went to midnight mass. For safety reasons, it had been moved from the downtown cathedral to a small hotel nearby, where the service was conducted in a cramped single room and a priest heard confessions in the hallway.

The troupe spent two more days in South Vietnam, doing shows in Vinh Longh, a small base in the Mekong Delta; Pleiku, in the central highlands; Nha Trang, the seaside headquarters of the Green Berets; and the air base at Da Nang. The memory of their near-miss in Saigon dominated the trip. "Just as we got to town, a hotel went the other way," Hope cracked. "If there are any Cong in the audience, remember: I already got my shots." They returned to Tan Son Nhut Air Base for a show in front of ten thousand soldiers, their largest audience of the tour, and got an official welcome from General William C. Westmoreland, the new chief of operations in Vietnam.

The living conditions were even rougher than usual for Hope's traveling crew. In Pleiku, mirrors had to be specially brought in so the women could do their makeup. Janis Paige recalled arriving at her "tiny room, with one Coke bottle of water — for your teeth, drinking, everything — and a twin bed covered with mosquito netting. When I got in, it was still warm and covered with sand. Somebody had just gotten out of it. Believe it or not, I didn't care. I got in and went to sleep." The entertainers were impressed by the beauty of the country — and startled by the extent of the US presence there. "We supposedly had thirty thousand men there," said Jill St. John. "But I saw thirty thousand men everywhere we went. It was clear we had been misinformed. It was a much bigger commitment than we had been told." After they returned home, St. John tried to speak out during a press conference: "I started complaining. Suddenly there was no microphone in front of me. It was just removed." Still, St. John saw Hope's mission, at least at that early stage of a war she later opposed, as beyond politics: "He was definitely not a hawk. He was thinking of the servicemen."

Footage from Hope's twenty-three-thousand-mile tour was edited into a ninety-minute NBC special that aired on January 15, 1965. An evocative mix of documentary and variety show, it featured most of the elements that would become fixtures on his Vietnam specials. Hope narrates as the cameras show his entertainers boarding and exiting military planes, being greeted by generals, visiting with wounded men in military hospitals. There are clips of his stage shows, recorded by four cameras — three focused on the stage and a fourth handheld camera roaming the audience. The bug-eyed Colonna turns up in the crowd at each stop, dressed in a different costume or service uniform, for some back-and-forth with Hope. Each female guest star gets a musical number and some comedy shtick with Hope, and they appear onstage together for some banter at the star's expense:

"How'd he get you to go on this trip?"

"He asked me to go on a walk in the moon-light."

"He threatened me too."

Anita Bryant closes the show by singing "Silent Night," asking the men to join in — a sentimental moment that would be repeated on all of Hope's Vietnam specials. For his studio shows Hope never wanted reaction shots of the audience; he felt they disrupted the timing of his gags. But in Vietnam the re-action shots are constant — men applauding and laughing wildly, often shirtless, cigarettes dangling from their lips, iconic faces of the GIs Hope felt so close to. He pays tribute to them at the end, offering support for a military mission that was still considered no-ble and necessary:

> Even though they're putting up a great fight against tremendous odds in this hide-and-seek war, they're not about to give up, because they know if they walked out of this bamboo obstacle course, it would be like saying to the commies, "Come and get it." That's why they're layin' their lives on the line every day.

The NBC special chronicling Hope's first Vietnam tour was seen in 24.5 million TV homes, according to Nielsen — the largest audience for any Hope show to date, and the fourth-most-watched special of the season. Hope had enough outtakes from the tour to put together a second hour-long special, which aired in late March. He even released a record album, *On the Road to Vietnam*, featuring highlights from the trip — though its sales were disappointing.

A startling footnote to the trip came two years later. In March 1967, US troops captured a cache of secret Viet Cong documents, which revealed that the Brinks Hotel blast had, in fact, been directed at Hope and his group, but had detonated ten minutes too early. "Shortly after the explosion the cars of the Bob Hope entertainment group arrived," the document recounted. "If the bomb exploded at the scheduled time, it might have killed an additional number of guests who came to see the entertainment. . . . Basically the results were not satisfactory."

Looking back at their close call, members of Hope's troupe recalled that, on the day of the bombing, they were held up for ten minutes at Bien Hua Air Base because of Barney McNulty. The cue-card stand had collapsed during their first show, and McNulty was hastily trying to put the cards back in the proper order before boarding the plane. McNulty's ten-minute delay may have saved their lives.

■ ■ ■ ■

Hope had no way of knowing, when he made his first trip to Vietnam in December 1964, that the battle against a stubborn Communist insurgency in the remote jungles of Southeast Asia would become the longest war in American history, or that he would return there every Christmas for nine straight years and become embroiled in the most divisive political fight of a generation. The country's, and Bob Hope's, Vietnam nightmare didn't begin in earnest until 1965, when President Johnson, in response to mounting Communist attacks on US bases in the region, sent combat troops there for the first time and began a rapid buildup of forces. The US military presence in Vietnam grew from less than thirty thousand troops at the beginning of 1965 to nearly two hundred thousand by year's end. The escalation sparked antiwar protests back home, and opposition from such public figures as Dr. Martin Luther King Jr., a foretaste of the convulsive political battles ahead.

A political, social, and cultural revolution was brewing in the country, but for Hope it was simply more comedy material. He joked about long hair on men ("It's very confusing; everybody looks like Samson and talks like Delilah"), and protests on college campuses

("The Defense Department gave me a choice of either combat zone — Vietnam or Berkeley"), and those crazy mop-tops from England, the Beatles ("Aren't they something? They sound like Hermione Gingold getting mugged"). In his one movie released in 1965, *I'll Take Sweden,* Hope played the father of a very now teenager (Tuesday Weld), whom he transplants to Sweden to get her away from her motorcycle-riding boyfriend (Frankie Avalon), only to run headlong into the swinging Swedish sex scene. The ham-handed sex farce (an "altogether asinine little romp," said the *New York Times*) placed Hope firmly on the Geritol side of what would soon be called the generation gap.

For the Defense Department, however, Hope was still the go-to guy as a morale booster for the troops, wherever they might be. Near the end of April 1965, President Johnson sent fourteen thousand marines to the Dominican Republic to help quell a left-wing uprising that some feared might result in "another Cuba" close to US shores. Three months later, after order had been restored, Hope arrived with a troupe of entertainers, headed by his *I'll Take Sweden* costar Tuesday Weld. He did six scheduled shows and three impromptu ones in three days. When he saw signs on the streets of Santo Domingo saying YANKEE DOGS GO HOME!, he opened his show with "Hello, Yankee dogs!" and got a big laugh. In those days, it was still a joke.

With the buildup of US forces in Vietnam, there was little doubt that Hope would return there for his 1965 Christmas tour. He again assembled a big cast packed with pulchritude, including Carroll Baker, the sexy, blond star of *Harlow* and *The Carpetbaggers;* Joey Heatherton, a miniskirted go-go dancer from the *Dean Martin Show;* Anita Bryant, the former Miss Oklahoma returning for her sixth Hope Christmas tour; Kaye Stevens, a redheaded comedienne who did a faux striptease to "Take Me Out to the Ballgame"; and the new Miss USA, Diana Lynn Batts. Also along on the tour: singer Jack Jones, the dancing Nicholas Brothers, perennial sidekick Jerry Colonna, Les Brown and his band, twenty-six production people, three writers, two hairdressers, a makeup artist, a publicist, and Hope's trusty masseur, Fred Miron.

They took off aboard a Lockheed C-141 transport plane and made a refueling stop on Wake Island, before landing in Bangkok, Thailand. It was a rough trip from the start. Les Brown's band members, onstage for hours in the broiling sun without protection, got terrible sunburns. Trumpeter Don Smith's lips swelled so badly he couldn't touch his mouthpiece, and Joey Heatherton had to cut her performances short because of sun blisters. Hope had a nasty accident just before a show in Korat, Thailand, when he was jostled off a narrow, overcrowded stage and tumbled backward five feet to the ground. Though his fall was broken by a security man standing nearby, he tore two ligaments in his left ankle and was hobbling for the next several days.

The already worn troupe flew into South Vietnam's Tan Son Nhut Air Base on Christmas Eve, the plane doing a steep dive into the landing strip — a routine security precaution that always rattled Hope and his gang. After a press conference and lunch with General Westmoreland, they did a show for ten thousand troops on a nearby soccer field, with a temporary stage set up on the bed of a military truck-trailer. In his monologue, Hope captured some of the cynicism already building over a war that was proving to be more complicated than advertised: "The situation's improved; things couldn't be better." Beat. "Well, who am I gonna believe — you or Huntley and Brinkley?" He told the troops, "Last year you were all advisers. And now that you see where it's gotten us, maybe you'll keep your trap shut." Nor did he ignore the antiwar demonstrations that were getting more attention back home: "You men have a very important job: making the world safe for our peace pickets."

In Saigon, Hope and the entertainers once again stayed at the Caravelle Hotel, while the rest of the crew were put up at the Meyer-

618

cord, a new, fortresslike hotel with concrete abutments and armed guards on the balconies. Hope again attended midnight mass, which was conducted at the downtown cathedral by Frances Cardinal Spellman, the New York prelate who was also a frequent visitor to the troops in those years. With memories still fresh of the previous year's hotel bombing, nerves were on edge. At five in the morning on their first night at the Meyercord, members of Hope's troupe were jolted awake by the sound of an explosion. Fearing the worst, they burst from their rooms, half undressed — only to find out that the rope lowering a load of dishes from the rooftop garden had snapped, sending the dishes crashing to the concrete below.

Security precautions were high everywhere. On Christmas Day, Hope and company rode in helicopters to the First Infantry's base at Di-An. With a Vietcong staging area just a mile away, a thousand soldiers were stationed around the base to protect it during the show. When Hope went to the latrine, an armed guard went with him; when Hope asked why, the guard told him the Vietcong were close and some "might even be in the audience." Before the show got under way, an officer gave instructions to the crowd on evacuation procedures in case of a mortar attack. Jack Jones turned to bandleader Les Brown and said drily, "In case of an attack, you can cut my second number."

As Hope's troupe moved around the country, the massive buildup of US forces was unmistakable. The day after Christmas they did a show for seven thousand troops at Bien Hoa Air Base; a year before, at the same base, the crowd numbered fifteen hundred. The troupe flew to Cam Ranh Bay, where docks, roads, and airstrips were under construction, to create what would soon be the biggest port in all of Southeast Asia. They visited An Khe, which had been nothing but virgin jungle six months before, but now was home to sixteen thousand troops and 480 helicopters. In Da Nang, Hope's troupe did a late-afternoon show in the rain for eight thousand men, many of whom had been waiting in torrential downpours since eight in the morning.

On the aircraft carrier *Ticonderoga,* the entertainers had to compete with the roar of fighter planes taking off and returning from combat missions. At night they watched as one F-8 Crusader trying to land missed its arresting wires, overshot the deck, and plunged in flames into the sea. They waited in horror as rescuers raced to find the pilot. "Tension became almost unbearable," Hope wrote later. "I heard a sound behind me, looked around and saw Joey Heatherton sobbing uncontrollably. Kaye Stevens was hanging on desperately to an officer's arm, her face registering shock and disbelief. And to tell the truth I felt pretty weak myself." There were cheers when the pilot, who had ejected just before the crash, was pulled from the sea unhurt. Hope later visited him in sick bay. "I can't tell you how glad we all are that you decided to stick around for the show," Hope cracked. He was so keyed up that he couldn't sleep that night and found himself wandering the deck at two in the morning.

Hope was hardly the only entertainer going to Vietnam in those early years of the war; on his 1965 trip he ran into another USO troupe headed by Martha Raye, Eddie Fisher, and Hollywood "mayor" Johnny Grant. But no one connected with the troops like Hope. On the ninety-minute special drawn from his 1965 tour, the frequent cutaways to Hope's audiences — soldiers laughing, applauding, cheering — may well have been edited to Hope's best advantage. But the live, raw sound of the tremendous response could not have been doctored. The men roared as Joey Heatherton did a frenetic Watusi onstage and brought up several GIs from the crowd to join her. They laughed at the corny sketch in which Hope played a wounded soldier being treated by Kaye Stevens's officious nurse and Colonna's nutty doctor. They hooted in all the right places at the leering banter between Hope and Carroll Baker:

BOB: "I loved you in *Harlow.*"

CARROLL: "I was a little hoarse when I made that movie, didn't you notice?"

BOB: "I didn't even know it was a talkie."

The trip made a powerful impression on those who came along. "It was one of the most emotional experiences I ever had in my life," said Jack Jones. "I was a dove when I left. I became a hawk when I was there. It took me about two weeks to calm down." Jones later campaigned for antiwar presidential candidate Eugene McCarthy — and had a testy encounter with Hope over it when they ran into each other at a benefit in Washington, DC. But, like St. John and most of the other entertainers who traveled to Vietnam with Hope in the early years, he found the mission inspiring and Hope's spirit uplifting. "What he was doing was nonpolitical," said Jones. "He was a happy, positive force."

Hope too saw himself as a spirit lifter, not just for the troops in the field but also for Americans back home. At the close of his special, he made an emotional plea for support of the war, trying to recapture the patriotic spirit of his World War II appeals, even as he hinted at the divisions that were starting to grip the country. "You hear a few people say, 'Get out of Vietnam.' Here's some of our kids who are getting out the hard way," he intoned, over shots of the wounded men he had visited in military hospitals. He went on:

In their everyday job of fighting this treacherous war, they know there's no alternative. They know that in this shrinking world, the perimeter of war is boundless. They know that if they backed off from this fight, it would leave all of Asia like a big cafeteria for the Communists to pick up a country at a time. There are no reservations in their dedication. Our fighting men have confidence in the decisions of their leaders. It's hard for them to hear the rumblings of peace over the gunfire, but when peace comes, they'll welcome it.

Patriotic rhetoric and foxhole humor, however, couldn't hide the grim realities of this new kind of war. While Hope was in Vietnam, Bing Crosby sent him a letter, through an old friend named Gordon J. Lippman, a colonel who was serving with the First Infantry at Lai Khe. Enclosed was a photo of Bing swinging a golf club and a joking message: "Dear Bob, don't you wish you had a finish like this? And a waistline?" Bing asked Lippman to pass along the letter when Hope came through. The letter arrived safely, but before Lippman could deliver it, he was cut down by a sniper's bullet and died thirty minutes later in the camp's hospital tent.

The letter was delivered to Hope later in Toluca Lake, after he had returned home.

Hope's Christmas tours, and the TV shows that resulted from them, were enormous undertakings. After the itinerary was set in the fall — by the Defense Department, in consultation with the USO and Hope's people — two Hope advance men, associate producer Silvio Caranchini and soundman John Pawlek, would travel to scout the locations, set up production facilities, and gather local gossip and other tidbits for the writers to use in creating Hope's monologues. For the entertainers and the crew, the trips meant two weeks of rough accommodations, sporadic sleep, and holidays away from the family. Jack Shea, who directed most of Hope's Christmas shows in the late 1950s and early 1960s, reluctantly told Hope after the 1964 trip to Vietnam that he could do no more of them; he needed to stay home with his family at Christmas. Hope was taken aback, then wistfully sympathetic. "I'm past that," he said. Mort Lachman, Hope's most trusted writer, took on the added duties of directing the Vietnam specials after that.

Each trip produced more than 150,000 feet of film, which had to be boiled down to around 8,000 feet for the ninety-minute special that would typically air on NBC in mid-January. That meant a two- or three-week siege of round-the-clock work, to wrestle the massive amount of material into shape. "On January first I would take a thirty-day leave of absence from NBC to edit the show," said film editor Art Schneider, who worked on many of them. "There was an enormous amount of film. It would be shipped to us, and we'd spend two twelve-hour days looking at every single foot of film. Bob would be there, Mort [Lachman], Sil [Caranchini], eight editors, and eight assistants. We used to edit at Universal. They would have cots, beds for us to lie down and sleep. I don't think we even left for several days at a time. They'd bring in all the food we wanted, anything we wanted to keep us happy. Money was not spared. There was a big placard in the editing room, white letters on a black background: 'We traveled thirty thousand miles to get these laughs. Don't cut 'em.' "

The Hope Christmas specials are irreplaceable documents of the Vietnam era. The sight of Hope entertaining vast oceans of men brought home more vividly than anything on the evening news the enormity of America's commitment in Vietnam. The TV specials were patriotic, corny, inspiring, self-serving — and unmissable. The show edited from Hope's 1965 Vietnam tour, which aired on January 19, 1966, drew an Arbitron rating of 35.2, with a whopping 56 share of the viewing audience — the biggest audience for any TV show of the season, and the most watched Bob Hope show ever. A week after it aired, Senator Stuart Symington paid tribute in the *Congressional Record* to Hope, whom he had recruited for his first Christmas trip, to Berlin back in 1948: "Because of his continued and patriotic unselfishness over the Christmas holidays for a number of years, and the happiness he has brought to millions of people in this country and all over the world, Bob Hope could well be the most popular man on earth."

It was hard to argue. He was certainly popular at the White House. On March 31, 1966, Hope was honored at a black-tie dinner at the Washington Hilton to commemorate the USO's twenty-fifth anniversary. President Johnson made a surprise appearance, presenting Hope with a plaque and telling him that it was nice to honor a "frequent visitor to Vietnam who has never been asked to testify before the Senate Foreign Relations Committee" — a reference to the televised hearings being conducted by Senator William Fulbright, one of the war's chief critics. When Hope launched into his prepared jokes about LBJ and his battles with Congress ("It's nice to be here in Washington — or as the Republicans call it, Camp Runamuck"), the president, sitting on the dais, played a perfect straight man, glowering at Hope after each wisecrack. "I have to do it, sir," Hope said in mock dismay. "It's on the paper."

The antiwar protests disturbed Hope. He found it unthinkable that US troops fighting a tough war would not get unqualified support back home, and he became bolder in speaking out. He taped a half-hour TV program for Affirmation: Vietnam, a series of patriotic events in support of the war spearheaded by students at Atlanta's Emory University. He penned (with the help of his writers) an article for *Family Weekly,* the Sunday supplement for the conservative Hearst newspapers, lambasting the peace protesters: "Can you imagine returning from a combat patrol in a steaming, disease-infected jungle, tired, hungry, scared and sick, and reading that people in America are demonstrating against your being there? That people in America are burning their draft cards to show their opposition and that some of them are actually rooting for your defeat?"

In June he did the usual round of publicity for his new movie, *Boy, Did I Get a Wrong Number!* It was perhaps his most wretched vehicle yet, a slapstick sex farce with Hope as a married real estate broker who gets mixed up with a Hollywood sex kitten (Elke Sommer) hiding out from the press. But interviewers seemed less interested in the movie than in grilling him on Vietnam. Asked his opinion of the growing protest movement,

Hope sounded a more strident note. "One group is fighting for their country and one group is fighting against it," he told the *New York Post.* "They're giving aid and comfort to the enemy. You'd call these same people traitors if we declared war." He told Peter Bart of the *New York Times* that he was too "charged up" about the antiwar protests to stay silent: "People seem to forget we're at war."

Hope never had serious political aspirations, but some were beginning to have them for him. In 1963 Jack Warner had written Hope a letter urging him to run for the US Senate from California in 1964. "They call you a comedian, but that is not my definition," Warner wrote. "My definition of you is that you are a great American with a big heart. You have the feeling of the human race, which is needed in Washington for the good of our country and the world." (Hope declined, but his old friend and costar from the Broadway show *Roberta,* George Murphy, ran for the seat and won.) In May 1966 a Seattle radio station conducted a poll asking listeners if they would vote for Bob Hope for president. More than 62 percent said yes. Around this time, Hope related, "a couple of the Washington boys" came out to see him in Palm Springs and urged him to consider running for the Republican presidential nomination in 1968. Hope had to remind them that he was born in England and thus, according to the Constitution, not even eligible.

But what made him attractive to some as a political candidate was starting to cause problems for Hope the entertainer. As a comedian, he had always kept himself above politics, never taking sides, aiming his barbs at all. Now his open support for the war was making him a polarizing figure. Though he continued to draw big crowds on more conservative college campuses such as North Carolina State and the University of Florida, only 60 percent of the seats were filled for his appearance at the Yale Bowl in July 1966. When he began booking his 1966 Christmas tour, some stars turned him down because of their reservations about the war. The new Miss World, Reita Faria of India, accepted an invitation, but nearly backed out after protests in her country and a request from the Indian government that she pass up the trip because of its official opposition to the war.

Hope managed to recruit Joey Heatherton and Anita Bryant, two returnees from 1965, for the 1966 tour, along with singer Vic Damone. Without a Hollywood sex symbol on hand, Hope went in another direction — inviting Phyllis Diller, the fright-haired comedienne whom he had first seen at a Washington nightclub in the late fifties and had cast in *Boy, Did I Get a Wrong Number!* Diller, who became a Hope favorite, had trouble onstage at first, but with the help of Hope's writers, she developed a self-mocking routine with Hope that went over well. (Phyllis: "All the other girls got bouquets." Bob: "What'd they give you?" Phyllis: "A machete and a map of the jungle.") "He played the straight man, I got all the lines," said Diller. "Very, very generous. That got me through the tour." Hope just missed getting another big name for the trip: Lynda Bird Johnson, the president's daughter, who called from the White House in November and asked if she could join the tour. LBJ had apparently given his assent, but General Westmoreland vetoed the idea, saying that ensuring her security would be too difficult.

One familiar face was missing from the 1966 tour. Jerry Colonna, Hope's favorite second banana and his compatriot on every Christmas tour since 1948, suffered a major stroke in August, which left him paralyzed on his left side and unable to go. Colonna was too incapacitated to work much after that — though Hope, loyal to the man who had served him so well comedically for nearly three decades, continued to give him small parts on his TV specials (always positioned to hide his paralyzed side) and sent regular "royalty" checks to help him and his wife, Flo, until Jerry's death in 1986.

The 1966 tour also turned into a rare family Christmas for the Hopes. Dolores, who hadn't accompanied Bob on a Christmas tour since 1959, invited herself along this time, bringing their two college-age kids, Kelly and Nora. Kelly worked on the production, helping out assistant stage manager Clay Daniel, and Nora, the bubbly member of the brood, got up onstage at one show and did the Watusi. Hope introduced Dolores at Takhli Air Base in Thailand and asked her to sing "White Christmas." When she pleaded that she didn't know all the lyrics, Bob fed them to her. "She was charming and lovely," wrote Mort Lachman in his journal of the tour, "and when she changed the tempo in the second chorus and wound up with the words 'And may all your Christmases be at home,' the boys cheered and cheered and waved and whistled."

Hope didn't give his wife quite as good a review. "The last thing those guys needed was sentiment," he said years later. "Dolores became their mother. What they needed was the Golddiggers and Raquel." Hope's treatment of Dolores was often the most callous when she tried to share the spotlight with him onstage — a mixture of hardheaded showbiz calculation and, perhaps, some resentment that she was putting a damper on his freewheeling life on the road. Dolores's number was omitted from the NBC special on the tour, and she didn't join Bob again in Vietnam until his last trip there, in 1972.

In Bangkok, Hope and his troupe were

invited to the king's palace for dinner with the royal family, for the third year in a row. The king, who played the saxophone, had learned "Thanks for the Memory" in Hope's honor. For security reasons, the troupe spent only one night in Saigon, on Christmas Eve; the rest of the time they were based at the Erawan Hotel in Bangkok, shuttling back and forth for their shows in Vietnam. The heat, always oppressive, was especially brutal that year. Barney McNulty fainted at one show, and Lachman had to handle the cue cards. At another, Nora Hope acted as a runner, carrying ice-cold towels to the band members, so they wouldn't pass out from heat prostration. (Dolores, Kelly, and Nora left when the conditions got too difficult, finishing out the tour in the Philippines.) The crowds were bigger than ever: ten thousand at Tan Son Nhut, twelve thousand at Di-An, fifteen thousand at Qui Nhon. Flying into soggy Da Nang, Lachman was awestruck: "We saw the show site from the air, and then we saw the hills covered and covered with men — all the way up to Marble Mountain. We've never seen such a sight. In the rain — in their hooded ponchos, or bareheaded but coated — in the mud — there were thousands and thousands and thousands of them. Would you believe 20,000? They looked like more."

Hope said he was happy to be back in Vietnam, wearing "my Sunday-get-shot-at clothes." Again, he took note of the political storm that was brewing over the war: "If you don't get better ratings, this whole war may be canceled." He told the troops he brought them good news from back home: "The country is behind you, fifty percent." Dressed in tropical shirts and pants hiked up high on his waist, swinging his now ubiquitous golf club, Hope looked more and more like a middle-aged emissary from the Palm Springs Chamber of Commerce. In World War II he had been one of the boys. Now he was one of their father's friends.

In his TV special chronicling the tour, Hope seemed more intent than ever on rousing the nation's patriotic spirit and making a case for the war. Hope does an on-camera interview with Marines general Lew Walt, who says Vietnam is "a war we must win," to free the people of South Vietnam, who "have been enslaved by the Communist forces that have come into the country." Billy Graham, who crossed paths with Hope on the trip, appears in Da Nang to assure the troops, "Millions of Americans are very proud of what you fellas are doing." Anita Bryant sings a lugubrious version of "The Battle Hymn of the Republic" (Les Brown was tearing his hair out at her slow, ponderous tempos). "Nobody wanted this war, but we can't wish it away," Hope says in closing. "The boys fighting in Vietnam want peace as much as we do, and they're fighting to get it."

Some who were close to him said it was his 1966 Vietnam trip that hardened Hope's views on the war. He was taken to a Vietnamese village to witness the military's "pacification" program — the effort to win the allegiance of the people by helping local villages become self-sustaining — and came back enthusiastic. "This is what has to win it," he raved. "Wonderful what they're doing!" He had dinner with General Westmoreland in Saigon and met with other top generals, absorbing their view that the war needed to be pursued more aggressively. "Bob and Westy would sit up talking a lot that trip," said General Emmett "Rosie" O'Donnell, Hope's friend and golfing buddy, who was now head of the USO. "They'd talk about the war, what was happening at home, what it all meant. And this reinforced what Bob was seeing in hospitals. He was terribly torn up by those wards, trying to be gay with a guy whose guts are coming out. Hope put on a bold front, but when he got in the back room with his drink — vodka and orange juice — he'd ask why we subject our boys to this, to get killed, to get maimed, for what — to fight and not to win?"

When he came home, Hope seemed charged up by the experience, more outspoken than before. "Everybody I talked to there wants to know why they can't go in and finish it," he told Hal Humphrey of the *Los Angeles Times,* "and don't let anybody kid you about why we're there. If we weren't, those commies would have the whole thing, and it wouldn't be long until we were looking at them off the coast of Santa Monica." Asked at a press conference if he was a hawk on the war, Hope — who had resisted the term until then — replied, "I'm afraid I am. But I'd rather be a hawk than a pigeon."

Hope's position on the war was simplistic, emotional, and unsurprising. He had become a national hero during World War II and, like many members of his generation, could not conceive that his country would get into a war it couldn't, or shouldn't, pursue to victory. He fully subscribed to the Cold War dogma that stopping Communism in Vietnam was essential to preventing the rest of the dominoes from falling in Southeast Asia. Most of all, he backed his nation's leaders. One of the strongest arguments in favor of the war, in Hope's view, was that it had been supported by every president since Eisenhower. "When you get guys like Eisenhower and his staff," he said, "Kennedy and his staff, Johnson and his staff, all of whom thought it was important enough to save this little nation from Communism or enslavement, then you have to think maybe they know something."

"He was very supportive of the American

government, the president, no matter who it was," said Tony Coelho, the future Democratic congressman from California, who lived with the Hopes for nine months in 1964 and 1965. "That was true of a lot of people of his generation. I don't think it was so much naïve as patriotic. He supported the troops. He'd come back from those Christmas trips and he was emotionally worn, torn, elated — he was part of their effort. So I think it was hard for him to stand back and critique or question. He became part of it."

Obviously reflecting the views of the generals he talked to, Hope argued that the war could have been won quickly if only the military had not been hamstrung by politicians. "If Kennedy had lived, I guarantee that the war would have been over in four weeks," he said in 1977. Yet he never talked about the politics of the war with the entertainers he brought with him to Vietnam — and rarely, in any sustained way, with friends and family back home. "It was difficult for him to really give voice to the emotions that were going on," said his daughter Linda. "He didn't really talk much about the trips when he got back. He'd just say, 'It was something else' or 'It was very moving.' He said, 'People don't have any idea what goes on. And I see it.' "

What he couldn't see, however, was the political and cultural shift that was taking place in the country: a new skepticism of the nation's leaders and the military, a questioning of middle-class values and Cold War assumptions. Even more than most Hollywood stars, he lived in a rarefied world — enjoying the adulation of millions, with a direct pipeline to the people in power and a loyal entourage that shielded him from dissenting views. He was too far above the political turmoil roiling the country to realize that the ground was shifting beneath his feet.

In early December of 1967, Bob and Dolores celebrated their first family wedding. Their oldest son, Tony, a graduate of Georgetown University and Harvard Law School, had been engaged once before, to a nursing student he'd met at Georgetown, but the family didn't like her and he soon broke it off. Now, after serving a stint in the Air Force, he was engaged to Judith Richards, a minister's daughter from Ohio whom he had met in law school and who was now an attorney in Washington, DC.

The wedding was the biggest thing ever to happen in the bride's hometown of Defiance, Ohio. Her father gave the blessing at the ceremony, held in a Methodist church (though Dolores packed it with fourteen priests). The wedding party of nearly six hundred was too large for the town's hotels, so most of the guests stayed in Toledo, an hour's drive away. Bob and Dolores flew in

637

from Los Angeles on a chartered plane (along with Kathryn Crosby and other Hollywood friends) and arrived an hour late for the ceremony. On the ride back to Toledo for the reception, their car was stopped and Bob was "arrested" by a local sheriff — a joke orchestrated by Judith's father. Hope kept his sense of humor for the toast: "Isn't it wonderful. Have you ever seen two lawyers kiss?" The couple skipped a honeymoon and after the wedding flew back to Los Angeles, where Judith relocated and Tony was working in the business affairs department at Twentieth Century–Fox.

A few weeks later Hope was on his way back to Vietnam, for the fourth time in as many years. In a cast that included singer Barbara McNair, Phil Crosby (Bing's son), and columnist Earl Wilson, the big attraction was Raquel Welch, the buxom star of such movies as *One Million Years B.C.* Welch was the quintessential piece of Hope cheesecake. He coached her on how to get a rise out of the men ("When you come onstage, take the long walk, because the guys want to see you"), and she was the perfect foil for his leering wisecracks:

RAQUEL: "I'm most happy to be here and see all these boys."

BOB: "They were boys before you came out. Now they're old men."

He taught her how to behave at the hospitals they visited — no tears, no pity, only good cheer — and impressed her with his dedication and work ethic. "He never got ruffled," she said. "He was absolutely tireless. He was good with the boys — he knew their hometowns and would give them ball scores and talk guy talk. He didn't phone it in. I had nothing but admiration for the man." Like other performers who joined Hope in Vietnam, she ignored the political controversy and embraced the mission: "I was over there to entertain the guys, not to talk politics. This was something you could do for them."

They visited twenty-two bases in fifteen days, from Pleiku in the mountains to the aircraft carrier *Coral Sea*. Once again, the company set up base camp at the Erawan Hotel in Bangkok, making short hops to and from Vietnam — though Hope split off from the group to spend Christmas Eve in Saigon, where he had a private dinner with General Westmoreland. The next day Hope entertained his biggest crowd yet in Vietnam: twenty-five thousand troops at Long Binh, headquarters of the US Army in South Vietnam. All the top brass were in the audience: Westmoreland, US ambassador Ellsworth Bunker, and even South Vietnamese vice president Nguyen Cao Ky.

The US military presence in Vietnam was nearing its peak of a half million troops.

"Welcome to the land of rising commitment," said the Army specialist who introduced the show. Hope joked again about the antiwar protests back home, though with a more derisive edge: "Can you imagine those peaceniks back home burning their draft cards? Why don't they come over here and Charlie will burn 'em for them." But in his closing remarks for the TV special, he sounded a more conciliatory, even hopeful note:

Despite the millions of words that have been spoken and written, we know that there are no easy answers to this conflict. But an answer there must be. Somehow we must get through to Hanoi, in one way or another, that it's all such a waste, that it's better to build than to destroy. There are now some faint glimmers of hope, a few telltale signs that reason may yet prevail. We hope and pray that before too long the peace for which we're all yearning will become a reality. With God's help, this will be the year.

But it wasn't. On January 31, just two weeks after Hope's Christmas show aired, the Communists launched the so-called Tet Offensive — a massive, coordinated series of attacks on cities, bases, and airfields throughout South Vietnam. Though taken by surprise, US and South Vietnamese forces retaliated strongly, and the offensive wound up being a military defeat for the Communists. But it was a turning point for the war effort back home, casting fresh doubts on the optimistic reports of the war's progress and intensifying calls for the United States to get out of Vietnam. The next few months were the most traumatic of a turbulent decade: President Johnson, facing a strong primary challenge from antiwar candidate Eugene McCarthy, announced he would not run for reelection; Dr. Martin Luther King and Robert F. Kennedy were assassinated; violent protests rocked college campuses from Columbia to Berkeley; and the Democratic National Convention in Chicago descended into chaos when police beat demonstrators on the streets outside the convention hall.

Hope tried to stay out of the cross fire, but he couldn't entirely. For the fourth year in a row he was back to emcee the Academy Awards ceremony, scheduled for Monday, April 8. King was assassinated just four days before, and since Monday was the day of his funeral, the show was postponed out of respect. Two days later, Academy president Gregory Peck opened the delayed ceremony on a reverential note, acknowledging, "This has been a fateful week in the history of our nation." He noted that two of the five films nominated for Best Picture, *In the Heat of the Night* and *Guess Who's Coming to Dinner,* dealt with race relations and credited King's work for helping bring about the "increasing awareness of all men that we must unite in compassion in order to survive." Then he turned the evening over to Hope, "that amiable national monument who pricks the balloons of pomposity, evokes laughter even from the targets of his wit, and adroitly displays America's sense of humor to the world."

But for once, the national monument misjudged the national mood. He opened with some quips about the two-day postponement: "It didn't affect me, but it's been tough on the nominees. How would you like to spend two days in a crouch?" Kodak, the show's sponsor, was also upset at the delay, Hope said, "afraid it would hurt their image — a show that took three days to develop." The wisecracks were innocent enough, but they offended many in the audience, who thought they made light of a national tragedy. Jack Gould, in the *New York Times,* called the show "embarrassing" and Hope's quips "ungracious." *Time* scolded, "It was difficult to be funny under the circumstances. . . . Judging by Hope's monologue, it would have been better not to try."

The reaction was a sign of how frayed the nation's nerves had become. And it obscured what was, paradoxically, one of the best performances of Hope's Oscar-hosting career.

He found plenty of material in the new wave of American films that were up for awards, such as *Bonnie and Clyde* and *The Graduate*. ("They nominated a kid like Dustin Hoffman — he made a picture he can't get in to see.") He made a clever bank shot from his own Oscar deprivation to the upcoming Vietnam peace talks: "For thirty years I've been trying to get the Academy to sit down and talk. And they've always given me the same answer: they'll negotiate if I stop bombing." He was everywhere on the show: gabbing with the presenters, introducing the film clips, quipping when the evening dragged on, "I've never seen six hours whiz by so fast" — a joke repeated, in some version or other, by practically every host who followed. His most memorable line, however, came at the beginning of the show. "Welcome to the Academy Awards," Hope said. "Or as it's known at my house, Passover." He still got mileage out of the running gag, even though Hope by this time had received a record five honorary awards — the last one, in 1966, a gold medal for "distinguished service to our industry and the Academy."

By his 1968 Christmas tour, some Vietnam fatigue appeared to have set in, for the war seemed to be downplayed a bit. Vietnam was just one stop in an itinerary that also took him to Japan and South Korea — where tensions had risen following North Korea's seizure of a Navy spy ship, the USS *Pueblo*. Hope again landed a top Hollywood glamour girl for the tour, song-and-dance star Ann-Margret, along with singer Linda Bennett and retired football star Roosevelt Grier. A former Robert Kennedy aide, Grier was a rare Hope traveling companion who openly opposed the war. "I went with Bob because I felt he was doing something I could relate to," Grier explained to reporters. "I wanted to show the servicemen we cared about them."

Hope's Christmas shows were by now well-oiled productions, a mix of news documentary, patriotic rally, and vaudeville show. There were Hope's formula jokes playing off the exotic places he visited ("Os-San — that's Korean for 'take it and stuff it' "); his playfully suggestive patter with the new Miss World or Miss USA (inevitable question: "What are your measurements?"); his acknowledgment of the vast crowds, always pointing out the men perched on telephone poles or watching from distant hilltops ("Are you on our side?"). Hope would call up servicemen from the audience and read letters from home — and maybe plant a kiss on their forehead from Mom, or a girlfriend. He commiserated with their plight ("Twenty-one thousand men, all dedicated to one purpose — to get to Bangkok"), brought them news from home, and tugged at their heartstrings with the closing chorus of "Silent Night," by now a Hope tradition. "What a boon he is," wrote *Variety,* "to the sinking spirits of the men who defend our way of life." His Christmas special of January 16, 1969, drew a mammoth 38.5 Nielsen rating, yet another Hope record.

Back home, Dolores spent most of the Christmas holidays in 1968 preparing for the biggest party the Hopes had ever thrown: the wedding of their oldest daughter, Linda. After graduating from St. Louis University, Linda had worked as an English teacher, toyed with going back to school in psychology, and was now pursuing a career in filmmaking. The groom, Nathaniel Greenblatt Lande, the son of a prominent Georgia doctor, was a former Time Inc. executive who had helped launch Time-Life Films and now worked as a producer for Universal. He was Jewish, which meant that Dolores's retinue of priests had to share the stage with a rabbi for the ceremony at St. Charles Borromeo Church on January 11, 1969. But it was the Cecil B. DeMille reception afterward that got everyone's attention: a thousand guests under a billowing tent in the Hopes' backyard, with a who's who of celebrities on hand, including Governor Ronald Reagan and Vice President–elect Spiro Agnew.

"I wanted to get married under a tree in Carmel. Dolores wanted a big show," recalled

Lande. "I can't say I enjoyed it. But it was a grand affair, and beautifully done." Hope presided with his usual aplomb, and a fusillade of gags. "We had the wedding reception at home because Texas wouldn't rent us the Astrodome," he joked. He serenaded the couple with a rewritten version of "Daisy, Daisy," titled "Linda, Linda": "You've just had a stylish marriage / But don't expect a carriage / You must look sweet / Upon the seat / Of a Chrysler that's built for two." Hope left before the party was over, hopping a plane to Miami with Agnew, to see the Super Bowl game the next day.

Richard Nixon couldn't make the wedding, but he phoned before the ceremony with his congratulations. When Hope handed the telephone over to his new son-in-law, Lande joshed with the president-elect: "You'll make a Republican of me yet." Hope just glared at him. In the Hope family, some things were no longer funny.

CHAPTER 12
PARTISAN

"SHUT UP, BOB HOPE."

Richard M. Nixon's election as president in November 1968 marked the start of a new, more strident phase in Hope's tour of duty in the domestic war over Vietnam. He had gotten to know Nixon during the Eisenhower administration ("Ike's caddy," Hope jokingly called the vice president) and his unsuccessful 1962 run for governor of California, so they were already friends when Nixon entered the White House. Hope had struck up a more recent, even closer friendship with Spiro Agnew, Nixon's surprise choice as vice president. Hope and Agnew first met in June 1968, at a Variety Clubs International dinner in Baltimore where Hope was honored and Agnew, then governor of Maryland, gave a speech. Two months later, after he was picked to be Nixon's running mate, Hope sent Agnew a congratulatory telegram: "See what one dinner with me will do?"

They talked frequently on the phone during the 1968 campaign, with Hope feeding jokes to the vice presidential candidate. "The humorous 'one-liners' which you sent me for spicing up my tedious speeches were most successful," Agnew wrote to Hope after the election. "For a fellow who was having problems with the press, these efforts at light relief were most helpful." Hope ordered his writers to continue supplying jokes for Agnew speeches after the inauguration — a task some of them resented. "We hated writing for a repressive reactionary like Agnew," said one writer at the time. "But when you work for Hope these days, that's part of the job."

Nixon, meanwhile, began using Hope, more aggressively than Johnson ever had, to help sell his Vietnam policies to the American public. "He took natural advantage of the friendship," said Dwight Chapin, Nixon's special assistant, who often acted as a liaison between the two. Shortly after taking office, the president stepped up the bombing of North Vietnam and announced a policy of "Vietnamization" — gradually withdrawing US troops while handing over most of the fighting to the South Vietnamese army. Protests against the war only intensified, climaxing on October 15, 1969, with the Moratorium to End the War, a coordinated series of nationwide protests and teach-ins. Two weeks later, on November 3, Nixon addressed the nation on TV, laying out his plan to end the war and appealing to the "silent majority" of Americans for support. The next day, at a White House dinner for Britain's Prince Philip, Nixon asked Hope if he would serve as honorary chairman of National Unity Week, a series of rallies and patriotic displays across the country, intended to counter the next big antiwar demonstration, a march on Washington scheduled for November 15. Hope, who could never resist a presidential call to service, agreed.

National Unity Week — cast as a nonpartisan event, but clearly orchestrated by the White House — was overshadowed by the November 15 peace march, which drew 250,000 people, the largest crowd ever to march in the nation's capital. But Hope's involvement in the White House–backed effort to blunt the protest seemed to be a tipping point. The comedian who wanted to be loved by everyone was now a symbol of a war many people hated.

Suddenly, Hope found himself a target of protests. "Where There's Death, There's Hope," read a leaflet handed out to students arriving for a Hope appearance at the University of Michigan. At the University of Washington in Seattle, seven hundred protesters staged a peace vigil outside the auditorium where Hope was appearing. "Hell, I'm for peace, but not at all costs," Hope told a reporter afterward. "Why don't they march against the North Vietnamese?" Some colleges canceled Hope appearances, for fear of the protests he might spark.

Like his friend Agnew, Hope blamed the press for overplaying the antiwar protests. "It's those small minorities on campus that make the headlines," he said in response to a student reporter's question at Clemson University. "The news media are guilty of blowing this kind of disturbance way out of proportion." At a press conference for National Unity Week, he even lashed out at his own network, claiming that an NBC News report on unequal treatment of black soldiers in Vietnam used "rigged clips" and was "not honest." (NBC News president Reuven Frank sprang to the show's defense: "I have no doubt that Hope spoke his criticism of our Vietnam coverage sincerely. But his comments are wrong.")

Family and health concerns distracted Hope for much of 1969. The hemorrhaging in his left eye returned, and he was hospitalized twice for treatment, in January and May. Then in June, while he was accepting an honorary degree at Bowling Green University in Ohio, he got word that his oldest brother, Ivor, seventy-seven, had died suddenly of a heart attack in Cleveland. Only a few days after the funeral, his youngest brother, George (still employed by Bob as a "production coordinator" on his specials), died of lung cancer, at age sixty. Shaken by the loss of two siblings in just a week, Hope cut short

650

a four-day engagement at the Pikes Peak Festival in Colorado Springs, returned to Palm Springs, and took most of the next month off.

In August the Hopes celebrated a happier family occasion, the wedding of their youngest daughter, Nora, to Sam McCullagh, an assistant dean of admissions at the University of San Francisco. Nora, who was a favorite of her father's but whose relations with her mother were strained, had graduated from San Francisco College for Women and worked for a time in New York City, before returning to San Francisco to marry McCullagh, whom she had dated in college. Their wedding reception in the Hopes' backyard was a more modest affair than the extravagant party for Linda seven months earlier. Still, Bob did his usual stand-up routine, Dolores sang "On a Clear Day You Can See Forever," and the 250 guests included such notables as Stuart Symington and Phyllis Diller.

Hope's 1969 Christmas tour was a departure in two ways. For the first time, it was a round-the-world trip, with stops in Berlin, Italy, and Turkey before the usual series of shows in Thailand and Vietnam. And for the first time, Hope and his troupe (which included perky pop singer Connie Stevens, Teresa Graves of *Rowan & Martin's Laugh-In,* and the Golddiggers, the singing-dancing troupe from the *Dean Martin Show*) got an

651

official presidential send-off, with a formal dinner and performance at the White House — a sign that President Nixon was actively embracing the Hope tours as part of his campaign to rally Americans behind his war policies.

At the dinner in the Blue Room, Stevens sat next to Nixon at one end of the table, while Hope sat at the other end beside the first lady (who asked Hope for his autograph). One of the Golddiggers caused a minor disturbance when she unfurled a napkin with a STOP THE WAR slogan on it. Undeterred, Hope and his entertainers did a run-through of the show for the Nixons and a VIP crowd in the East Room. Hope got laughs with jokes about administration figures such as Martha Mitchell, the outspoken wife of Attorney General John Mitchell. "She's the one who makes Agnew look like Calvin Coolidge," Hope quipped. The next afternoon the troupe took off from Andrews Air Force Base, with Secretary of State William Rogers, Defense Secretary Melvin Laird, and General Westmoreland on hand to wish them bon voyage. Hope, who woke up late and was complaining about his eye again, was so late getting there that Rogers had left.

At their first stop in Germany, Hope was joined onstage by sexy Austrian actress Romy Schneider — and in the audience by Dolores and their son Kelly, now in the Navy, who came over to meet him. Hope did a show aboard the aircraft carrier *Saratoga* in the Mediterranean, and another at Incirlik Air Force Base in Turkey, where the WELCOME BOB HOPE banner was the same one they had used when Hope was there in 1963 — the 3 changed to a 9. Then it was on to Thailand and Vietnam, where Hope returned to familiar spots such as Long Binh, Lai Khe, and Da Nang, but ventured farther north than ever before, to Camp Eagle near Hue, just seventy-five miles from the DMZ.

The real star of the 1969 tour was Neil Armstrong, the astronaut who had just walked on the moon. (NASA opposed sending any of the Apollo astronauts to Vietnam with Hope, but President Nixon insisted on it — and threatened to fire any NASA employee who objected.) Armstrong was a big hit with the troops, bantering onstage with Hope and answering questions from the crowd, a few of them pointed. "I want to know why the US is so interested in the moon and not the conflict here in Vietnam," asked one serviceman. Armstrong replied evenly that the American system "works on many levels" to promote peace, and that "one of the advantages of the space activity is that it has promoted international understanding and enabled cooperative efforts between countries."

In his closing remarks on the NBC special

showcasing the tour, Hope once again made a plea for support of the war, trying to shift the focus from politics to the men doing the fighting: "One of the things that never changes is the unbelievably good spirit of our fighting men. Yes, in all this sorry business, it's the guys who are making these sacrifices who complain the least." Over shots of US soldiers with Vietnamese orphans, he continued, "The number of them who devote their free time, energy, and money to aiding Vietnamese families would surprise you. And don't let that image get tarnished by the occasional combat-disturbed casualty who may freak out and create the horrible headline" — a reference to the My Lai massacre of South Vietnamese civilians, which had recently come to light. "These are the men who lay their lives on the line every day. And in return they ask for one thing: time to do a job. For us to be patient, to believe in them, so they can bring us an honorable peace."

The 1969 tour, however, was most notorious for an incident that called into question just how in touch Hope really was with the troops he claimed to speak for. At his first show in Vietnam, before ten thousand men of the First Infantry at Lai Khe — so near the fighting, said Hope, "we had to give the Vietcong half the tickets" — Hope told the troops he had just been at the White House and assured them President Nixon had "a plan to end the war." He was greeted with boos.

The extent of the booing was disputed. The first reports called it a "barrage of boos." Hope, along with his publicist and later biographer Bill Faith, who accompanied him on the tour, described it as only a "smattering." Richard Boyle, a war correspondent for *Overseas Weekly,* recounted a more threatening scene in an interview with *Rolling Stone* a few years later (though he recalled it as taking place at Long Binh, not Lai Khe): "After about fifteen minutes of Hope's show, he was being drowned out by the boos. When the TV cameras panned the crowd, the GIs were standing up and giving the finger and making power salutes. Then the troops started throwing things and tried to rush the stage. They brought out about fifty-four MPs to guard the stage, and it was getting very menacing . . . pretty close to a riot. Hope, who was visibly shaken, had to stop the show and leave."

Connie Stevens, who was there, confirmed that the booing was loud enough to drive Hope from the stage — and that he turned to her in distress. "I happened to be walking by the stage," she said. "And he said, 'Connie, come here,' and he threw me out there." She wrestled with the unruly crowd for a few minutes and only managed to settle them down when she began singing "Silent Night." Yet the boos, she claimed, were a reaction not to Hope, but to his invocation of Nixon and his supposed plan for ending the war: "They weren't booing Bob. They were booing the idea that there was any help coming. The war had gone on too long. They were frustrated at what he was saying. They didn't want to hear it." Yet the outburst clearly took Hope by surprise. "It threw Bob, because I don't think he had ever experienced anything like that," said Stevens. "And I think that was a rude awakening for him."

Stevens, whose younger brother was serving in Vietnam, never spoke with Hope about the incident afterward. But she was already having her own doubts about the war. She was disturbed at a scene of jubilation she witnessed at one camp when some captured Vietcong soldiers were brought in. When she went to see the commotion, she found a couple of frightened kids of fourteen or fifteen being held up as trophies. "They were severely wounded and they were shaking and they were babies," she recalled. "I said, 'You guys, stop this, turn the cameras off.' I just didn't like it. And I thought, 'Oh my God, is this what this war is about?' I couldn't go along with that." Like Jill St. John after Hope's 1964 tour, she tried voicing her opinions at a press conference. "I was asked not to attend any more press conferences, right then and there."

When the booing incident was reported,

Hope was infuriated. "A few kids, about five, went 'Boo!,' which they will do, you know?" he said. "If you say, 'Second Lieutenant,' they go 'Boo!' " Yet in an account of the episode in his 1974 memoir *The Last Christmas Show,* Hope conceded that he had problems with the crowd that day at Lai Khe, calling it "the coldest, most unresponsive audience my show had ever played to." He found out later that many of the soldiers "were in a state of shock" because they had come to the show directly after a fierce morning of fighting that had resulted in many casualties. "It had been a wipeout day for a lot of them," he said. "They had lost a lot of friends, and they had been rushed in from a firefight to catch my show. After a morning like that, who could expect them to be in a mood for laughing it up at my jokes?"

Whether overblown or not, the booing incident exposed an undercurrent of frustration among at least a portion of the servicemen Hope entertained. Some of their gripes were trivial: complaints about being shunted to the back rows, for example, so that injured soldiers could be placed up front for the cameras. Some charged that entire units were ordered to attend Hope's shows, whether they wanted to or not, to ensure huge crowds for TV. Most of the soldiers looked forward to Hope's appearances; they appreciated the gags, the girls, and the break from their grinding routine. Others were more cynical. "Our response to him came out of fear and loneliness — convicts in a prison would have done the same thing," said Ron Kovic, the author of *Born on the Fourth of July,* who served two tours of duty in Vietnam before suffering injuries that left him a paraplegic. "I remember not wanting to go to the show, and the men who did go came back very cynical. People didn't laugh at his jokes; the war wasn't funny anymore, and a hundred Bob Hopes wouldn't have made any difference."

Some even questioned Hope's patriotic motives. As far back as the 1950s there were suggestions that Hope's military tours were big moneymakers for him. To be sure, the TV shows were produced and owned by Hope's company, a profit-making enterprise. But Hope always insisted that his Vietnam shows actually lost money. Although the military picked up the costs of travel and accommodations, Hope Enterprises still paid the sizable talent and production costs, which were much higher than for a typical studio show. According to figures supplied by Hope Enterprises to NBC in 1971, Hope's company made a profit of $165,000 on its five one-hour variety specials for the 1970–71 season. His one ninety-minute Christmas special from Vietnam, however, showed a loss of $274,000. Hope, of course, earned his own fee for these shows (around $200,000 per show during the Vietnam years), and the trips had incalculable public-relations value for him. Yet Bob Hope had easier ways to make money than by spending two grueling weeks a year traveling through military camps in a war zone.

What's more, while the shows clearly served Hope's purposes, they also were serving the needs of a huge audience back home. For supporters of the war, Hope's specials were a patriotic booster shot; for opponents, a reminder of the vast waste of men and resources wrought by the war; for everyone, a communal wallow in the quagmire that was tearing the nation apart. The ninety-minute NBC special edited from his 1969 Christmas tour, which aired on January 15, 1970, drew an almost inconceivable 46.6 rating — meaning that 46.6 percent of all TV homes in the country were tuned in to Hope on that Thursday night. It was the largest audience for any entertainment show in television history.

A peculiar irony of the Vietnam years was that, even as Hope became an increasingly partisan and controversial figure, his TV popularity was never greater. Chrysler ended his weekly dramatic anthology series in 1967 after four seasons, but the company remained the sponsor of his comedy specials, which continued to draw spectacular ratings. Maybe it was the "silent majority" speaking, or simply the escape that Hope's shows provided from the stressful, politically explosive times. During the 1966–67 season Hope's specials averaged an impressive 29.3 Nielsen rating — higher than TV's top-rated weekly series, *Bonanza.* For the 1969–70 season, his average rating soared to a phenomenal 32.3 — the highest of Hope's career.

It didn't seem to matter that the shows were growing more rote and predictable, with their old-fashioned variety format, hokey sketches, and cue-carded patter between Hope and his guests. The monologues were still topical, and occasionally funny, but there were an awful lot of potted jokes about Jackie Gleason's weight and Dean Martin's drinking and Zsa Zsa's husbands. Hope's musical guests would sometimes include a Smokey Robinson or Ray Charles, but mostly he stuck with middle-of-the-roaders such as Tom Jones, Eydie Gormé, and Andy Williams. He did one show paying tribute to old-time vaudeville, with guests George Burns and Lucille Ball; in another he reprised his original stage role in *Roberta,* in a live performance taped at the Bob Hope Theater at SMU. (With Hope playing the same role that he had originated thirty-five years earlier, it was a stodgy relic — and Hope's lowest-rated show of the season.) Sometimes the comedy material was literally recycled: in one February 1971 sketch, Hope played a man being roped into marriage by his fiancée, with Petula Clark taking the role that Rosemary Clooney had played in the virtually identical sketch back in 1954.

His jokes about the counterculture were sounding increasingly smug and out of touch. "Hey, did you read about that rock festival in upstate New York that was attended by four hundred thousand hippies?" he said in his 1969 season opener, a month after Woodstock. "It was held in a cow pasture. I can't think of a better place for it. Four hundred thousand hippies. Since the dawn of man that's the most dandruff that was ever in one place." He poked fun at the feminist movement in an October 1970 special, imagining what would happen if women took over the country. It was not a pretty sight. Hope meets a new female network chief, played by Nanette Fabray, who dusts the furniture during their meeting, and the Indianapolis 500 is canceled because "all thirty-nine women drivers crashed into the pace car." The show prompted an onslaught of angry mail. "I am not part of 'women's lib,' " said one letter writer, "but I have never felt so insulted nor so infuriated."

The critics were getting snippier too. A review in the *Hollywood Reporter* called his March 1970 special "one of those curiously lackadaisical Hope efforts of late, in which he seems to be living a cruel fantasy that he's Dean Martin." Another *Reporter* critic, reviewing Hope's special the following month, said it looked as if "everyone has hurriedly gotten together to do the show between holes at Lakeside." Jimmy Saphier, Hope's agent, sent both reviews over to the boss, with a note: "They are so prejudiced and vicious and unfair that there may be something more here than meets the eye. I don't know Tichi Wilkerson Miles [the *Reporter*'s editor], but if you know somebody who knows her well, she should be spoken to." No telling if she was, but she did get some letters in Hope's defense. "This kind of bitchy, ill-tempered effluvium hardly qualifies as a review," one reader wrote of another *Reporter* attack on Hope's poor material. "Anyone who knows anything at all about Mr. Hope's career knows that his writers have helped make him one of the wealthiest men in all of show business." The author, using a pseudonym, was Charlie Lee, one of Hope's writers.

His movies were no better: increasingly tired farces, with Hope looking more disengaged than ever, and doing little business at the box office. In the vapid, sitcom-like *Eight on the Lam,* released in 1967, he plays a single father running from the law with his seven kids and housekeeper Phyllis Diller. In 1968's *The Private Navy of Sgt. O'Farrell,* he's an army sergeant trying to get beer and girls for his men on a South Pacific island during World War II — a dated service comedy that was Frank Tashlin's last film. Hope's 1969 film *How to Commit Marriage* at least tried to look a little more with it. Hope and Jane Wyman play a middle-aged couple who decide to divorce, but hold off so as not to set a bad example for their newly engaged daughter. The twist is that the daughter's fiancé is a straitlaced classical pianist who is rebelling against his father, a pot-smoking, free-love-spouting rock-music producer, played by Jackie Gleason. The film's satire of the peace-and-love generation was hackneyed even then (a new-age guru touting "peace through protein"; rock groups with funny names like the Five Commandments and the Post-Nasal Drips), but the movie did marginally better at the box office, and Gleason's energy at least forced Hope to pay more attention.

During the summer of 1970, Hope again found himself in the center of the Vietnam fray. Following another wave of campus protests in response to the US invasion of Cambodia in May — and the killing of four students at Kent State University by members of the Ohio National Guard — backers of President Nixon organized a daylong series of patriotic events across the country on July 4, dubbed Honor America Day. Though billed as a nonpartisan celebration of America, the event was another effort to blunt the antiwar protests, orchestrated behind the scenes by the White House.

Hope agreed to cochair the event along with the Reverend Billy Graham, and to host an entertainment gala on the Capitol Mall in the evening. "This is one day we're not trying to sell any political message," Hope insisted at a press conference. But opponents such as radical activist Rennie Davis charged that the event was "designed to show a phony national consensus for Richard Nixon's foreign and domestic policies." In response the organizers recruited some prominent Democrats to endorse the event, among them Senators George McGovern and Edmund Muskie. But Honor America Day became another lightning rod for antiadministration protests.

The festivities began on the morning of July 4 with an interfaith religious service and an address by Graham on the Capitol Mall. Demonstrators trying to disrupt the event started early as well, with a band of a thousand Yippies staging a "pot smoke-in" and bathing nude in the Reflecting Pool. When Kate Smith began to sing "God Bless America," antiwar chants nearly drowned her out. Protesters and police clashed throughout the day, with at least thirty-four people arrested and twenty policemen injured. When

Hope was driven to the site in the afternoon, for a run-through of the evening's show with bandleader Les Brown, a group of hippies stood by hollering at him. Hope invited them to the show.

Some 350,000 people, mostly families with no interest in demonstrating on one side or the other, crowded onto the Mall in the evening for Hope's show. "What a gathering," Hope said when he came onstage. "Nixon took one look at the crowd and said, 'My God, what has Agnew done now?'" The entertainers on the bill were mostly old-timers, known conservatives, or people who owed Hope favors — among them Jack Benny, Red Skelton, Dinah Shore, Glen Campbell, Pat Boone, and Connie Stevens. Hope was distracted by sporadic disturbances throughout the show. When it was over, demonstrators broke through a police cordon and pounded on the trunk of the Chrysler limousine that was driving him back to safety. Hope was the emcee for what was looking more and more like a national nervous breakdown.

Even once-friendly venues were becoming trouble spots for Hope. The Oscar ceremony in April 1970 was a microcosm of the nation's cultural divide: new-generation films such as *Easy Rider* and the X-rated *Midnight Cowboy* were competing for awards, while John Wayne, nominated for *True Grit,* was greeted at the theater by a picket sign reading JOHN WAYNE IS A RACIST. "This is not an Academy Awards, ladies and gentlemen; it's a freakout," said Hope, one of sixteen "friends of Oscar" who shared hosting duties that year. A *Time* magazine reporter watched the ceremony at an Oscar party at the home of producer Don Mitchell and writer Gwen Davis, attended by a gaggle of Hollywood insiders. The mostly liberal crowd booed when Wayne won for Best Actor. And when Hope closed the show with a plea for the nation to come together ("Perhaps a time will come when all the fighting will be for a place in line outside the theater"), Shirley MacLaine yelled at the TV screen, "Oh, shut up, Bob Hope."

In the ultimate insult, even Hope's cherished bond with the troops was called into question. Kenneth D. Smith, chief of the Special Services agency for the entertainment of troops in Europe, complained to reporters in Ohio that not enough young entertainers were willing to go to Vietnam, and that old-timers such as Bob Hope were "unacceptable" to the younger generation of soldiers. The comments caused an uproar in the Hope camp and prompted some fast damage control. The Pentagon issued a disclaimer, Smith said he had been misquoted, and a USO spokesman wrote a letter to *Variety* asserting that Hope was still "socko" with the troops.

"I have seen Bob Hope operate in three wars," wrote Colonel Edward M. Kirby, "and if there is anyone in show business who is persona grata it is Bob Hope, the nearest thing to a court jester of class and distinction."

The press, meanwhile, was taking a more skeptical look at the nation's court jester. In a *New York Times Sunday Magazine* profile, journalist J. Anthony Lukas suggested that some of Hope's own writers were uneasy with his political activities and felt he was growing out of touch with the servicemen in Vietnam. "He just doesn't understand how the GI of today feels," said one unnamed Hope writer. "When he sees a V sign in his audience he thinks two guys want to go to the bathroom." Hope was furious at the Lukas article. He talked to his attorney Martin Gang about a libel suit and demanded that his New York publicist, Allan Kalmus, supply a list of all the people Lukas had talked to. Nothing came of it.

The bad press made Hope more defensive and intemperate. In an interview with the *Washington Post,* Hope called campus violence "a ridiculous thing" and said he was speaking out because he felt the United States was being undermined by left-wing dissenters and the press. "I just hated to get involved in politics," he said. "I stayed away from it until this past year, when I figured that it had to be pretty important. I got a very negative feeling that the country was getting very little support from the news media." In an interview with London's *Guardian* newspaper, he insisted, "It's not American students who are blowing up buildings or shooting people. It's the Communists who are doing it."

He spent a week in London in November 1970, but got only a brief respite from the political fire. He hosted two benefits for the royal family, including a cabaret show for the World Wildlife Fund that attracted a galaxy of European royalty. ("I'm the only one here who doesn't have his own army," quipped Hope.) He was the guest of honor for a segment of the British *This Is Your Life,* with all four Hope children and other relatives and old friends flown in to pay tribute. (Hope, inevitably, learned of the show in advance and faked his "surprise" reaction.) He capped off his busy week by emceeing the Miss World pageant, an event that usually produced a glamorous guest for his Christmas tour. This year, however, it produced only chaos.

Shortly after Hope took the stage at the Royal Albert Hall, he was interrupted by a handful of women's liberation activists, who set off noisemakers and smoke bombs, threw tomatoes across the auditorium, and unfurled signs attacking the beauty contest for "selling women's bodies." Hope, who had braved

Vietcong rocket fire in Vietnam, was forced to flee the stage under the feminist barrage. When order was finally restored, he returned and wisecracked, "I'll say this, it's good conditioning for Vietnam."

Talking to reporters afterward, he called the fracas "the worst theatrical experience of my life." As for the feminists' complaints about beauty contests, he was dismissive: "You'll notice about the women in the liberation movements, none of them are pretty, because pretty women don't have those problems. I don't get it." He clearly didn't.

A month later he was headed back to Vietnam, for the seventh straight year. Once again, it was a round-the-world jaunt, including stops in Germany and the Mediterranean. With most big stars staying away, his relatively low-wattage cast included dancer Lola Falana, singer Gloria Loring, and Cincinnati Reds catcher Johnny Bench. In response to news reports of widespread marijuana use among soldiers in Vietnam, Hope was big on pot jokes that year. "I hear you go in for gardening," he said at one show. "The commanding officer says you all grow your own grass." Bantering with Johnny Bench, Hope cracked, "Where but in baseball can you spend eight months on grass and not get busted?"

' "I didn't talk to the military brass about doing it," Hope told AP reporter Bob

Thomas, who asked about the pot jokes. "I just went ahead. I think it's better to get this thing out in the open. Then it can be treated as the problem it is." NBC didn't agree: the network ordered the marijuana references edited out of the special, a rare instance of censorship of Hope's Vietnam shows. This time the press jumped to Hope's defense. "Hope is not only an entertainer and his trip not just a show in the usual sense," said Jack Gould in the *New York Times.* "He also doubles as a reporter, a journalist in greasepaint, and the public would seem entitled to share in what he found out."

Hope, the journalist in greasepaint, was typically upbeat in his report to the nation on his January 14, 1971, special. Again he used scenes of orphaned Vietnamese children — youngsters who "will have to rebuild and live in the Vietnam of tomorrow" — to make his case for uniting behind the war and pursuing it to an honorable conclusion, an echo of President Nixon's refrain of "peace with honor." "Everyone agrees that this most unpopular of wars has lasted too long," Hope said. "But now for the first time we can see the light at the end of the tunnel."

At least one home viewer gave the show a rave. "I thought your closing remarks on the recent NBC broadcast of the highlights of your Christmas tour were sensational," President Nixon wrote Hope. "Your eloquent call for unity was deeply moving, and I wanted to add the Nixons' congratulations to the many others you must be receiving." Other viewers, however, were starting to feel some battle fatigue. "The growing unpopularity of the war in Vietnam seems to have stolen some of the bloom off the rose insofar as Bob Hope's annual Christmas season trek to entertain the troops is concerned," wrote *Variety.* "The electric excitement of past treks did not come over the tube this time." Still, the show drew another huge rating — 44.3 percent of the nation's TV homes, just a shade behind the previous year's all-time high.

Back home, Hope continued to be a target for opponents of the war. In early 1971, Jane Fonda announced that she and a group of antiwar actors, including Elliott Gould and Donald Sutherland, would make a tour of US military installations, expressly to counter Hope's shows, which she called "superhawkish" and "out of touch with today's soldier." Students at Valley State College in Northridge, California, marched in protest of plans to award Hope an honorary degree. For the first time in five years, Hope was *not* invited to appear at the Ohio State Fair. And in March the Council of Churches of the City of New York, representing seventeen hundred Protestant congregations, rescinded its own decision to give Hope its Family of Man award, after antiwar clergymen objected to his "uncritical endorsement of the military establishment and the Indochina war." The council voted instead to give the award posthumously to civil rights leader Whitney Young.

The group's executive director, Dan M. Potter, tried to smooth over the embarrassing turnabout, claiming it was not a snub of Hope but a tribute to Young, who had died a week earlier. Hope was gracious in public, praising the choice of Young: "I couldn't say anything against that man, and I was glad he got the award instead of me." Still, getting an award taken back was galling. "I appreciate the Americans who have laid down their lives for our country," Hope said. "If that stops me from getting awards, then I'll have to live with it."

Nothing, however, got under Hope's skin more than a caustic profile of him that ran in *Life* magazine in January 1971. Writer Joan Barthel had accompanied Hope on a personal-appearance tour of the Midwest in November, and her story was a revealing portrait of an entertainer under siege. When he was introduced at halftime of the Notre Dame homecoming football game, boos rained down from the upper grandstand. (Hope contended, with a straight face, that the crowd was actually crying, "Moo, moo"

— for Edward "Moose" Krause, the school's athletic director, who introduced him.) At an appearance in Flint, Michigan, Barthel reported, Hope called the Vietnam War "a beautiful thing — we paid in a lot of gorgeous American lives, but we're not sorry for it."

Hope went ballistic over the article, particularly the suggestion that he would call the Vietnam War — any war — "a beautiful thing." He claimed he had been misquoted, and that he had actually said "our guys fighting the war were beautiful Americans who have set aside their own lives to fight for their country." Again, he mobilized his lawyers, who questioned witnesses at the event and demanded Barthel's audiotapes. (Her tape recorder had actually run out before Hope's "beautiful thing" remark.) But Barthel stood by the quote, and no legal action was ever taken.

It's impossible to know for sure whether Hope was accurately quoted, but the fragmentary quote — with the subject for "a beautiful thing" left out — does seem ambiguous and framed to cast Hope in the worst light. Yet the *Life* piece was damaging in other, more subtle ways. Accompanying Hope on his visits to three cities, Barthel gave an up-close portrait of a chilly and inscrutable celebrity, accustomed to deference and unwilling to engage. While being driven to a benefit dinner in downtown Chicago, Hope and his escort, a man named John Gray, director of the Protestant Foundation of Chicago, have a one-sided conversation about Hope's schedule for rest of his visit:

"Do you have a lunch date tomorrow?" Gray asked. "No," Hope said. "Will you go to lunch with some people?" Gray asked. "No," Hope said. Gray paused. "There'll be a small reception after the dinner," he said. "But you don't have to stay long. About an hour." Hope said nothing. "Forty-five minutes," Gray said. Hope said nothing. "As long as you want," Gray said. Hope laughed, and Gray began talking about salmon and trout fishing way up north, beyond Vancouver. "I love that kind of thing," Hope said. "Would you like to go sometime?" Gray asked quickly. "It's not very comfortable, but I know you've been to Vietnam, and I know you sleep in tents." Hope did not reply.

Surrounded by sycophants, besieged by fans, and excoriated by foes, Hope responded by detaching even more. "I learned it was better not to engage in politics with him," said his son-in-law Nathaniel Lande. "I don't think he was truly and completely aware of all sides of the issue to have a diligent discussion." Sam McCullagh, his daughter Nora's husband, once mentioned at a family dinner how much he liked Robert Altman's film comedy *M*A*S*H,* and Hope jumped on him, arguing that the film didn't give a true picture of the dedicated work done in army hospitals. "That was the only time he ever pushed back with me," said McCullagh. "I was careful not to challenge him. I don't think he was challenged much, like a president of the United States isn't challenged. People deferred to Bob."

Which made a question-answer session with students at Southern Methodist University on January 29, 1971, all the more extraordinary. It was a friendly campus — the site of a theater named for him — and hardly a hotbed of antiwar activism. But amid the softball questions about his career and his comedy, Hope was drawn into a rare, and sometimes testy, debate over the war.

"If the people of Vietnam want to be Communists, why can't we allow them to be Communists?" asked one student. Hope replied that the United States was fighting to preserve Vietnam's freedom: "You cannot stand by and see a little child get crushed by a giant." Another student described his visit to the officers' training school at Fort Benning, Georgia. "I saw that giant you're talking about," he said. "I saw him in the senior officers who could laugh about wholesale slaughter of civilians. As far as I'm concerned, that giant, as much as I hate to say it, is the

675

United States Army." Hope responded with a rambling discussion of the My Lai massacre and the morality of war. "This is a cruel, lousy war," he said, "but war is war."

Hope was ill suited to this sort of debate. He had little understanding of the nuances, say, of whether the United States was trying to repel aggression in Vietnam or intervening in a civil war. He was mystified when his old friend Senator Stuart Symington grew disenchanted with the war and came out against it (though they remained friends). In 1970, Hope and Mel Shavelson were trying to develop a movie in which Hope would play a comedian who goes to Vietnam and is taken prisoner of war. After the invasion of Cambodia, Shavelson's secretary said she would no longer work on the film. Shavelson told Hope they should drop the project, and he reluctantly agreed.

"Money insulates you from a lot of things," said Shavelson, "not least of them public opinion. Bob never really understood the public thinking on Vietnam because he rarely discussed the war with anyone below a five-star general." Yet Hope wouldn't temper his hard-line views or stop speaking out about the war. "His attitude was we could finish it if we wanted to, make it end," said his son Tony. "He felt so strongly about it that he couldn't sit still and say nothing. We begged him to watch what he was saying. We warned him they'd blame the war on him. And they did."

The left demonized Hope; some began calling Vietnam "Hope's war." The right rallied around him. In a column for the *Arizona Republic,* Barry Goldwater wrote, "Anyone — and I don't care whether he is the president of the United States, the world's most popular entertainer or the least-known person — who dares to take a stand against the far left is immediately, viciously, libelously and scurrilously branded, and it is shameful the way Bob Hope has been treated." Dropping any pretense of neutrality, Hope worked openly for the reelection of President Nixon. In November 1971 he appeared at two "Salute to the President" fund-raising dinners on the same night — first in New York City, then hopping a plane to Chicago with campaign director Bob Dole, just ahead of President Nixon on Air Force One. When Hope received a humanitarian award from the National Conference of Christians and Jews, Jack Benny had the best line. Hope was born in England and "came to this country to entertain the troops at Valley Forge," Benny said. "He knew we were going to win that war."

The mail poured in, from both sides: letters from the wives of servicemen, praising him for his Vietnam trips ("I thank you, as I know every other wife, mother and girlfriend thanks

677

you, for bringing a little happiness to our men away from home," wrote Linda Faulkner of Kansas City, Kansas, whose marine husband saw Hope in Da Nang); attacks from the left for his disparaging jokes about hippies and antiwar protesters; criticism from the right for sharing a stage with "Communist sympathizers" such as Sammy Davis Jr. and the Smothers Brothers. Hope still tried to answer as many as he could with personal replies, even the negative ones, but by 1970 he had a form reply, with an edge of defensiveness: "The servicemen over there believe they are doing a necessary job, and they can't understand the draft-card burners and the anti-Vietnam demonstrations. They wonder if patriotism and love of one's fellow men have gone out of style."

Many of the letters asked him to help do something about the American prisoners of war being held by North Vietnam, in what many charged were inhumane conditions. One came from Mrs. James B. Stockdale, whose husband was the highest-ranking naval officer held as a POW and who was leading an effort to pressure North Vietnam to abide by the Geneva Conventions: "These men must be completely desperate, Mr. Hope, and they are the forgotten men in an unpopular war. Can you consider helping them by exposing Hanoi's treatment?" Hope decided to help by trying some freelance diplomacy.

His Christmas trip in 1971 again took Hope around the world, with Jim (*Gomer Pyle*) Nabors, country star Charley Pride, and singer Jan Daley among his entertainers. (Jill St. John also met up with the troupe for a show in Spain, and astronaut Alan Shepard made an appearance at Hope's last stop, at Guantánamo Bay.) When a show aboard the USS *Coral Sea* had to be scrubbed because of monsoon rains — the first time one of his Vietnam shows had to be canceled — Hope had some extra downtime in Bangkok, and he got in touch with the US ambassador to Thailand, Leonard Unger, who set up a meeting for Hope and the North Vietnamese envoy in Laos to discuss the POW issue.

The next day an Air Force plane flew Hope and his publicist, Bill Faith, to Vientiane, Laos. They were greeted there by US embassy officials, Admiral John McCain (whose son, the future US senator and presidential candidate, had been a POW since 1967), and the Reverend Edward Roffe, a Christian Alliance Church missionary in Laos, who served as interpreter. Hope, Faith, and Roffe were then driven from the airport to the home of the North Vietnamese envoy, Nguyen Van Tranh.

By all accounts, it was a cordial meeting. Tranh, a personable young man in his early thirties, told Hope he was a fan of the *Road* movies. Hope showed photos of his new grandson, Zachary, and said the war ought to be ended for the sake of the children on both sides. With no preset agenda for the meeting, Hope suggested enlisting American children to contribute their nickels and dimes to a fund to help rebuild homes and schools in the war-ravaged country. Tranh responded that the war could easily be ended if President Nixon would only agree to North Vietnam's seven-point plan at the Paris peace talks. Hope didn't even know what the seven points were, but he pressed his request to at least pay a visit to the POWs in North Vietnam and came away optimistic that he might have made some headway.

Hope's effort was private, done in secret and without official government sanction (though, with a US ambassador and an Air Force plane involved, it clearly had White House approval). But when he returned to Bangkok, the press had gotten wind of it, and Hope's meeting with the North Vietnamese became worldwide news. The White House, while not endorsing Hope's mission, said it "deeply appreciated" any gesture on behalf of the POWs. Hope's effort, however, came to naught. Before leaving Vietnam, he got word that his application for a visa to North Vietnam had been denied. "I'd known all along that my chances were slim," Hope wrote later, "but it was depressing just the same. I couldn't help feeling that all the talk in the press might have had something to do with Hanoi's negative reaction."

Hope made only glancing reference to the POW mission in his January special. As US forces were being withdrawn from Vietnam — only about one hundred thousand were still there, down from a peak of half a million — Hope found his audiences more relaxed and ready to laugh. "Actually, you guys are lucky," he said. "You *know* you're going to get home. But what hope is there for our men at the Paris peace talks?" In his closing remarks, Hope said the empty seats, in camps where he had once entertained tens of thousands, were a heartening sign: "Because every empty seat meant a guy who'd returned home, a GI who'd gone back to the world." And then a final sign-off, for what he expected would be his last trip to Vietnam:

All any of us wanted to do was make the burden lighter for those who are making the sacrifices. Maybe we don't all demonstrate or join parades, but we're all antiwar. Especially these guys right up close to it, the guys doing the miserable business and signing the receipts for it. And when people ask me is this our last trip, I can only hope that this is our last war.

Hope's Vietnam special of January 1972 was not the ratings blockbuster it had been the two previous years — only second in the ratings for the week, behind the new hit comedy *All in the Family.* Hope blamed it on his time slot — later than usual, at 9:30 p.m., eastern time. "I know one thing — I'd never put a show this important and with this work behind it on at that late hour," he wrote Jimmy Saphier. "I was very apprehensive about it before it was shown and certainly they'll never get me again in that spot." But the ratings slide was another sign that Americans were growing tired of Hope's war.

Nixon and Hope, two men under siege because of the war, grew closer as the debate over Vietnam grew ever more rancorous. Hope had dinner at the White House and at Nixon's retreat in San Clemente several times. They played golf together — Nixon once landed in a helicopter in Hope's backyard in Toluca Lake so he could play a round at Lakeside — and would see each other at Walter Annenberg's annual New Year's Eve party in Rancho Mirage. They corresponded frequently, Nixon congratulating Hope for various awards, sending condolences on the death of his brother Ivor, praising him for his Vietnam specials. The president showed up to support Hope at the grand opening of the Eisenhower Medical Center, for which Dolores had led the fund-raising campaign. When presidential assistant Dwight Chapin called two months before the opening to warn Hope that Nixon's schedule might prevent him from attending, Hope bristled. "It was, to say the least, an awkward phone call," Chapin related in a memo to his boss, H. R. Haldeman. "He indicated that of course if the President had to cancel, he would understand and they would do the best they could. However, he stressed that Mamie is expecting the President to come and everything is being geared around a Presidential appearance. . . . The result is — Hope has been warned, yet he still very much wants the President to try to work it out so he can be there." Nixon wound up making the event — along with Governor Reagan, Frank Sinatra, and most of the area's philanthropic and social mavens. Afterward, Nixon and Hope played golf together at the Eldorado Country Club, where Ike had been a regular.

Nixon had good reason to accommodate Hope. With the 1972 election approaching, the president was more intent than ever on using Hope to help make his case to the nation on Vietnam. On April 20, 1972, after Nixon had stepped up the bombing of North Vietnam in response to a major enemy offensive, Hope paid another visit to the White House. Nixon gave him a putter inscribed with the presidential seal and then brought him into the Oval Office for a chat.

"Sit down, let me tell you about the situation," Nixon began, in a conversation recorded on the White House tapes. Explaining the reasoning behind his response to the North Vietnamese offensive, Nixon said the enemy had calculated that "if they threw everything in, that I would not react," but were not prepared for the major escalation in bombing he ordered — from three hundred to nine hundred sorties a day. "If, after such a massive invasion, we just did tit for tat, it's no message. So what we are saying is, look here, if you're gonna play this kind of a game, we are going to hit you and more is to come."

Hope jumped in eagerly: "This is five years too late, this bombing! How can you not? It's like letting a guy who has a gun, let the fellow keep bringing ammunition, to fire at your house. It's stupid." He told Nixon of a conversation he had had with the late president Eisenhower four years earlier, in the backyard of Ike's Palm Desert home. "I said, 'If you were president today, what would you do?' And he said, 'I would invade North Vietnam and not be against using nuclear weapons.' "

"The point is, there is no choice," Nixon continued. "The United States cannot lose in Vietnam. We can't lose fifty thousand Americans and lose this war. This is where our Democratic critics are just dead wrong."

"And what about the future? What about Southcast Asia? The world?"

"What about the Mideast?" Nixon said.

"Your Jewish friends — you see a lot of those people. Let me tell you, if a Russian-supported invasion of South Vietnam by [North Vietnam] succeeds against the United States, what the hell do you think the Russians are going to do in the Mideast? They will arm those missiles over there, and man them with Russians in the UAR, and Israel is finished."

"Oh, God," said Hope.

Nixon bragged about his prowess as a poker player: "I can hardly remember a time when I was called that I didn't have the cards. We've got the cards now. And if they call us, and if these bastards continue to go down there and they do not come to the conference table and really negotiate, about everything including prisoners, we're going to continue to bomb the hell out of 'em, until we get an end. People say you lose the election if you do it, and impeachment. I don't give a damn. The main thing is, it's more important to save the country than to win an election."

The conversation wandered to Hope's relations with the press and Nixon's golf game. But the president hammered home his point one more time as he ushered Hope out the door: "And about Vietnam, just remember — we're gonna do what's right for this damn country, the hell with the election. You're the war hero."

Hope was a good messenger. He spoke out for Nixon's policies in his stage shows, at awards dinners, and in TV talk-show appearances. On October 26, 1972, a few days before the election, Nixon wrote Hope to thank him for the supportive comments he had made in accepting the Union League's Gold Medal Award in Philadelphia, and in an appearance on the *Merv Griffin Show:* "Your friendship and support are always welcome, but especially so during these last few days before November 7, and I just wanted you to know I am proud to have Bob Hope in my corner!"

The US withdrawal from Vietnam was continuing, even as the Paris peace talks dragged on without an agreement. Few entertainers were going there anymore. By mid-1972 the USO had only three clubs left open in South Vietnam, down from twelve at the war's height. But Hope had to see it through to the bitter end. In December 1972 he made one more trip to Vietnam, announcing in advance that it would be his last.

He lined up one big-name guest star: Redd Foxx, the former nightclub comic now starring in the hit NBC sitcom *Sanford and Son.* Known for his raunchy club material, Foxx ignored Hope's pleas to keep his material clean and did a stand-up act so rough it couldn't be used on the air. Lola Falana was back for a second year, along with singer Fran

Jeffries, Los Angeles Rams quarterback Roman Gabriel, and a selection of runners-up from the Miss America, Miss World, and Miss Universe pageants, dubbed the American Beauties.

Dolores also came along for the last Vietnam tour — meeting the troupe in Bangkok, so that Bob could "coax" her onstage from the audience for a song. The troupe nicknamed her Hambone, and Hope didn't do her any favors onstage either. While she sang "But Beautiful," he stood in the background behind her, idly swinging a golf club, in full view of the camera. Dolores's number is included in a transcript of his NBC special reprinted in Hope's Vietnam memoir *The Last Christmas Show.* But her song was cut from the final broadcast — as Dolores's numbers nearly always were when she joined Bob on his overseas tours. There was only one star in this family.

The tour began at Camp Shemya in the Aleutian Islands and included stops in Japan, South Korea, and the island of Diego Garcia in the Indian Ocean, with just one show in Vietnam, at Tan Son Nhut Air Base. "We figured it would be all over when we got here this time," Hope told the crowd. "But no luck. Not only did they fail to reach agreement in Paris, but now they're fighting over the hotel bill." In fact, a breakdown in talks had prompted Nixon to launch another major round of bombing just after Hope left on his tour. At Utapau, a B-52 air base in Thailand where Hope had often entertained, many of the flyers were missing because they were on missions over North Vietnam. At least fifteen aircraft from the base were lost.

Hope had an uncharacteristic diplomatic lapse on his last trip to Thailand, when he offended the locals by making jokes about the country's food, crowded living conditions, and no-holds-barred politics (which he compared to Thai kickboxing). After newspaper editorials claimed that he had insulted the country, the American embassy had to do some fast damage control, trotting out Hope for a Christmas Eve press conference in which he said he meant no offense.

But overall, Hope got a warm reception. "Back in the States, a negative press was writing that Hope was booed by the troops because he had spoken out in favor of our military presence. In fact, he was cheered wildly wherever he went," recalled Ray Siller, a writer who accompanied Hope on the tour. Siller was impressed with Hope's focus and stamina, even in the last days of his last Vietnam tour. On the way back home, Hope ordered a last-minute stop on Wake Island, and Siller had to gin up a monologue for him on the plane. With no time to put the jokes on cue cards, he simply read them to Hope from his notepad as they were circling the runway at midnight. Hope listened to them once, then asked for a second read-through. A few minutes later he went onstage and delivered all the jokes flawlessly, from memory.

It was an emotional farewell for Hope. At the end of the special that aired on January 17, 1973, he paid one last tribute to the soldiers he had entertained in Vietnam for nine straight Christmases: "Everywhere we witnessed the kindness and humanity of our GIs. They went out of their way to help the civilian population with their time, their money, and their goodwill. I can tell you that they're more concerned with building and healing than destroying." He read a long list of thank-yous — to his entertainers, his sponsors, the technical crew, President Nixon. "And especially to the millions of guys we played to in every latitude and every longitude around the world. Thank you for Christmases I'll never forget. Good night." And then it was over.

On January 14, 1973, three days before Hope's last Vietnam special aired, an agreement to end the war was finally reached at the Paris peace talks, and a cease-fire went into effect on January 27. Hope and Nixon talked frequently during this period. On January 9, a few days before the peace agreement, Hope called the White House to wish Nixon a happy sixtieth birthday, and the president told him that negotiations were "coming along." On February 15, Hope called again to share Nixon's jubilation over the homecoming of the first POWs released by North Vietnam. "You must be beaming all over!" cried Hope.

"It's so good for the country," Nixon said. "The country could not lose this war."

Hope exulted, "And it emanates from you! Your strength and how right you were!"

Even Dolores got on the phone to add her congratulations over the freed POWs. "I think they're gonna bring America back with them!" she said.

Three weeks later Hope was back at the White House, getting a briefing from Nixon on plans for an all-star dinner in May to celebrate the POWs' homecoming. "You must feel like eight zillion dollars, winding this thing up," said Hope. "What you did is something else."

"We now realize that all the heat was really worth it," said Nixon.

But a lot of work remained to be done — not just to patch up a badly divided nation, but to repair Bob Hope's career.

■ ■ ■ ■

VI
Ensuring the Legacy

TRYING TO RECOVER, AND
REFUSING TO QUIT

■ ■ ■ ■

CHAPTER 13
RESTORATION

"WHEN THE HOUSELIGHTS DIM
AND THE CAMERAS ARE TURNED OFF,
I'M JUST LIKE THE REST OF YOU."

Bob Hope's movie career ended with a sad flourish. *Cancel My Reservation,* his last starring vehicle, was the first Hope movie ever to open at New York's Radio City Music Hall. The venerable movie palace, the last in America to offer live stage shows along with its film presentations, was having trouble finding G-rated movies suitable for its family audience, and Hope's sorry effort was apparently one of the few to fill the bill. It opened in October 1972, accompanied by a stage show called, fittingly, "In One Era and Out the Other."

It had been three years since Hope's last movie, *How to Commit Marriage,* with Jackie Gleason. He had flirted with a couple of other projects since then: another film with Gleason, *The Bride Wore Blinkers,* about two con men who smuggle a racehorse into Ireland (Bing Crosby was penciled in to play an Irish priest); and a comedy by writer-director David Swift (*The Parent Trap*), with Hope as a small-town politician whose swing-

693

ing past comes back to haunt him. When neither got off the ground, Hope turned to a Western novel by Louis L'Amour that he had optioned, intending to produce it as a straight Western with other stars. Instead, he asked screenwriters Arthur Marx and Bob Fisher, who had worked on *I'll Take Sweden* and *Eight on the Lam,* to retool it as a comedy vehicle for himself.

Marx and Fisher protested that the story, about the murder of a Native American girl and the theft of tribal land by greedy real estate developers, wasn't suitable for a Hope comedy. But they came up with a treatment anyway, casting Hope as the stressed-out host of a TV talk show in New York City, who travels to Arizona for a rest and stumbles onto the tribal intrigue. Hope, eager for another film role, bought it. The film was produced jointly by Hope Enterprises and NBC and shot on location in Arizona in August and September of 1971, with a supporting cast that included Eva Marie Saint as Hope's wife, Keenan Wynn as a local sheriff, and Ralph Bellamy as the villainous real estate developer.

It was not a happy set. To direct the film, Hope turned not to one of his reliable old-timers — most of them by now retired or dead — but to a relative newcomer, TV director Paul Bogart (later the director of nearly a hundred episodes of *All in the Family*). The two were at odds from the start. Bogart was upset that Hope, in his usual manner, sent the script out to his writers for punching up and inserted gag lines wherever he could. Bogart fumed when Hope would arrive late to the set (in the broiling Arizona summer, he was the only one with an air-conditioned trailer) and would then ask Bogart to restage the scene he had just set up. They even argued about young costar Anne Archer. Hope thought she wasn't sexy enough. "She's a beautiful woman; what do you want her to do?" asked Bogart. Hope replied, "Can't she vamp a little, like Zsa Zsa?"

By the end of the filming, Bogart was a nervous wreck. "We argued about everything," he said. "The tensions were terrible. But he was in charge, and he wasn't going to let anybody tell him what to do. I kept calling my agent and saying, 'Get me off this thing.' He said, 'You can't.' I was condemned." Bogart was reduced to sending Hope letters, begging him to fix some of the more egregious things in the editing. The last straw came in New York City, where the film's final scene was shot on location in Rockefeller Plaza. Hope was late to the set as usual. While waiting, Bogart set up the shot, but when Hope arrived, he wanted it changed. Bogart exploded. "You are fucking impossible!" he screamed at Hope, as hundreds of bystanders watched from behind rope lines. After the

695

scene was shot and the film wrapped, Bogart checked himself into the hospital, suffering from pneumonia.

Cancel My Reservation was no better than it deserved to be. The mix of comedy and murder-mystery might have worked twenty or thirty years before, when Hope could do that sort of thing in his sleep. Now he actually does look asleep — tossing off gag lines mechanically, walking through a series of lame comedy set pieces (a breakneck ride on the back of a motorcycle, reprised from *I'll Take Sweden;* a climb to the top of a mountain to consult an old Indian guru, played by Chief Dan George). The film's run at Radio City was interrupted by a musician's strike, which shut down the theater for two days. Even without the labor problems, it was a box-office dud. On one Wednesday night, *Variety* reported, just six hundred of the theater's sixty-two hundred seats were filled.

After that, Hope and NBC dissolved their moviemaking partnership. Hope continued for years to look for other film properties. But except for a couple of cameo roles (as an ice cream vendor in 1979's *The Muppet Movie* and a golfer in *Spies Like Us* in 1985), *Cancel My Reservation* was his last big-screen feature. He desperately wanted to produce and star in a film biography of Walter Winchell, the famed gossip columnist whom he had known back in the Broadway days, but he couldn't get an acceptable script, and he was already too old for the part. Hope even tried to buy the screen rights to Neil Simon's hit Broadway comedy *The Sunshine Boys,* hoping to costar in it with Crosby. But Simon refused, unwilling to let his play about two bickering ex-vaudeville partners be turned into a vehicle for the *Road* picture team. "To my way of thinking, you and Bing would simply overpower the material," he wrote Hope, explaining his decision. The main characters were modeled on the vaudeville team of Smith and Dale, Simon said, and "not only are their appearance, mannerisms and gestures ethnically Jewish, but more important, their attitudes are as well. And if the audience would believe that Bob and Bing could portray two old Jews, then John Wayne should have been in *Boys in the Band.*"

The second inauguration of Richard Nixon, coming just as a peace agreement was being reached to end the Vietnam War, was a festive occasion in Washington, with a record five inaugural balls. Hope, Nixon's best friend in Hollywood, naturally had a big part in the celebration, joining Frank Sinatra as cohost of an "American Music Concert" at the Kennedy Center on the night before the inauguration, with the first family in attendance. But it was not one of Hope's finest hours.

For one thing, his cohost didn't show up. Sinatra, slated to emcee the first half of the show before handing off to Hope, canceled at the last minute, reportedly peeved because the Secret Service wouldn't allow comedian Pat Henry, one of his Vegas pals, to be added to the bill. Art Linkletter was a late fill-in, and he was impressed when Hope volunteered to take out some jokes from his monologue that overlapped with Linkletter's. But Hope was less cooperative about adhering to the strict schedule the Secret Service had set for the entertainment, timed to coincide with the comings and goings of the president and other dignitaries.

First, Hope was late getting onstage, causing an awkward delay as Nixon and the rest of the audience stood applauding for him, and the orchestra had to repeat the opening bars of "Thanks for the Memory" three times before he appeared. During his monologue Hope had trouble seeing the cue cards and kept calling for the lights to be turned up. Then, when he ignored warnings to wrap up his performance, his microphone was abruptly shut off and a curtain lowered behind him, as singer Vikki Carr came out for her number. When Hope finally retreated backstage, he threw a fit, reducing a young stage manager to tears. After Carr finished, Hope returned to the stage to do the rest of his truncated monologue, then abruptly left the theater. "The monologue was emasculated," recalled a member of Hope's entourage who was there. "He comes offstage pissed. The kid with the headphone starts crying. People are saying, 'Bob, calm down.' He says, 'Dolores, we're going over to see Van Cliburn.' And he walked out."

It was a bad omen for the start of President Nixon's second term. Before the end of the year, Hope's good friend Spiro Agnew was forced to resign as vice president, following charges that he had accepted bribes while governor of Maryland and as vice president. Then came the unfolding revelations about the Watergate break-in. Hope at first made light of the scandal that would ultimately drive Nixon from the presidency. "I want to thank the Watergate committee for making room for me," he said during the televised Watergate hearings. "Just shows, there's nothing one bunch of comedians won't do for another." But as the scandal widened, Hope grew increasingly uncomfortable with the subject. At a Weight Watchers rally at Madison Square Garden, he was booed for making some Watergate cracks that were deemed too pro-Nixon. "I wish they'd flush the whole thing and forget it," he said before a group of veterans in Columbia, South Carolina. Soon Hope had flushed Watergate from his monologues entirely, saying he thought the subject was overdone and the scandal blown out of proportion. "I think dragging this thing on for years and years is giving dirty politics a bad name," he told a *Playboy* interviewer in August 1973. "Every administration has been plagued by some kind of scandal or other. The whole thing has had a Mack Sennett feel to it. Actually, I don't know whether they ought to get them into court or central casting."

In the charged atmosphere of the times, Hope's jokes were sounding increasingly tepid and hackneyed — merely waving at topical issues, before deflecting them with formula gag lines. "The US is so short of oil, we may have to start draining Dean Martin's hair," he quipped during the 1973 oil crisis. "You've heard of Wounded Knee?" he said, referring to the Native American protest site in South Dakota. "How about the Battle of April 15 — Wounded Wallet!" His delivery too was growing more rigid and imperial: the joke, the stare, the laugh, the next setup. No more "savers" when he stumbled on a line, or when a joke fell flat — or much acknowledgment of the audience at all. He was Mount Rushmore with cuff links.

His TV specials as a whole were stodgier than ever. Guest stars such as Ann-Margret or John Denver would perform their musical numbers, exchange scripted patter with Hope, and read the cue cards in sketches. But Hope showed little spontaneity or connection with his guests. Jonathan Winters, one of the few younger comics Hope booked on his shows (with the exception of Phyllis Diller, stand-up comics were not allowed to do monologues on Hope's shows, so as not to compete with the star), was put off by Hope's inflexible working style. When Winters would stray from the script and improvise during a sketch, Hope would freeze him with a warning: "Stay on the cards, kid." "If the other guy got a laugh, it made him uneasy," said Winters. "Anybody who stepped into his arena bothered him. He was taken with himself and his own importance. He was not a fun guy to be with."

He wasn't a lot more fun at home. To celebrate his seventieth birthday, on May 29, 1973, Dolores organized a big family get-together, inviting cousins and their children from Cleveland and around the country to spend the July 4th week at their Toluca Lake home. It was a lively bonding experience for the clan; the kids were scattered in sleeping bags throughout the house, the backyard pool area was turned into a playground, and Dolores organized a series of day trips to Disneyland, Knott's Berry Farm, and other local attractions. Bob was there only in spurts. "He was usually at dinner, but very busy," recalled Avis Truska, the daughter of Hope's late brother Sid. "He'd sneak away and we'd say, 'Where's Uncle Bob?' When he was at dinner, he was often very quiet. I remember Dolores once said, 'Bob, why don't you say anything?' And he said, 'What do you want me to say?' "

Among the excursions Dolores arranged for the family was a trip to Palm Springs, for a tour of the extravagant new house she and Bob were building. Since buying their first home there in the 1940s, the Hopes had become honored first citizens of the ritzy desert community: Dolores a prime mover behind the Eisenhower Medical Center in nearby Rancho Mirage, and Bob host of the annual golf tournament that was the area's biggest national showcase. They threw many parties at their house on El Alameda street, including an annual Thursday-night dinner during the week of the Hope Classic — a convivial, serve-yourself affair, with Dolores helping cook the pasta, tables set up on the back lawn, and friends and family members mingling with the tournament golfers and Hollywood celebrities.

But Dolores wanted a bigger showplace, and to design it she hired renowned architect John Lautner. A disciple of Frank Lloyd Wright's, Lautner had designed a widely admired house in Palm Springs for interior decorator Arthur Elrod — a space-age structure with a conical roof and circular living room, which had been used as a set in the James Bond movie *Diamonds Are Forever.*

Dolores got Lautner to design a similar modernist house for the Hopes, with a twenty-nine-thousand-square-foot, dome-shaped roof, perched dramatically on a hillside overlooking the main highway below.

But on July 23, 1973, with construction well under way (and just three weeks after the Hope clan had come down for a tour), a spark from a welder's torch accidentally set fire to the plywood covering the roof. Every fire truck and volunteer firefighter in Palm Springs was called to the scene, as passersby watched the blaze from the highway below. By the time the fire was brought under control, an hour and a half later, the house was all but destroyed.

Hope's first instinct, naturally, was to make jokes about it: "We had a little problem with the Palm Springs fire department. We forgot to call for a reservation." His second was to file lawsuits. Construction was put on hold for years, leaving the charred shell of the house in full view from the valley below, an eyesore that prompted much grumbling from the locals. Building was finally resumed in 1978, after the Hopes had recovered $430,000 in damages — from the contractor, from the ironworks company that did the welding, and from Hope's own lawyers, who had neglected to buy fire insurance.

As he entered his seventies, Hope still looked

like a man at least ten years younger. He began using a new makeup man, Don Marando, who was doing Robert Goulet's hair at NBC when a Hope assistant asked if he would take a crack at Bob's thinning thatch. Marando took one look at Hope's "Eddie Cantor haircut — waitress black, twenty hairs on his head" — and said he couldn't do anything until Hope let it grow out. Three weeks later he was summoned to Hope's house at 10:00 p.m. "Can you do something now?" asked Hope. Marando set to work, applying some ash-brown color, using an ebony pencil in spots, leaving the longish sideburns gray, and giving it a blow-dry to fluff up the few strands that remained atop his head. (Marando also had a toupee made for Hope, but he never wore it.) Hope, the old vaudevillian, liked to do his own makeup, but Marando took over that as well: "Watching him throw on that pancake, I said, 'You remind me of a monkey throwing on shit.' " Marando was on call from then on, doing Hope's hair and makeup for nearly all his TV specials, traveling with him around the world, and becoming another fixture in Hope's large and loyal entourage.

Hope's age was also belied by his workaholic pace. Along with six or seven NBC specials a year and guest appearances on many more shows, Hope averaged at least three personal appearances a week: a nonstop schedule of trade conventions, college concerts, state fairs, Boy Scout jamborees, Rotary Club luncheons, cerebral palsy benefits, hotel-room engagements, and summer-theater gigs. His going rate by the early seventies was $30,000 a night, but he did many charity events for free and was always ready to hop on a plane to pick up another award or honorary college degree (one from Pepperdine in April 1973 was his twenty-second, according to the running count kept by his staff). With Vietnam finally behind him, Hope spent Christmas at home in 1973, for the first time in nearly twenty years. But he hardly took the holiday off, making a tour of veterans' hospitals in California and traveling to Washington to visit the National Naval Medical Center and Walter Reed Hospital. He even toyed with doing a Las Vegas show. Though Hope made frequent visits to Vegas (he was a fan of Shecky Greene's lounge shows), he had long resisted a Vegas hotel engagement, telling friends he would do one only if he got paid more than any other performer in Vegas history. Though hotels such as Caesars Palace and the MGM Grand pursued him, no one ever met his price.

He continued to pursue movie projects and tried to expand his TV footprint by setting up a development arm of Hope Enterprises — run for a time by Linda's husband, Nathaniel Lande, and later, after their divorce, by Linda — to develop other TV series for NBC. It had little success. One Hope-produced pilot called *The Bluffer's Guide*, based on a series of British how-to books, aired on NBC in May 1974, but it got bad reviews and didn't get picked up. A proposed sitcom about cabdrivers (years before *Taxi*), called *O'Shaughnessy and Leibowitz,* went through several incarnations, but it too was a no-go. Only one Hope-produced series ever made the NBC schedule: *Joe & Valerie,* a relationship sitcom that ran for eight episodes in the spring and fall of 1978 before being canceled.

Another thing that didn't slow down as Hope entered his seventies was his sex life. On the road or at home, Hope never seemed to lack for female companions. His girlfriends were mostly chorus girls, singers, beauty queens, and other showbiz wannabes, whose careers he often helped out and who sometimes appeared as an opening act in his stage shows. Several of these relationships lasted for years. Others were one-night stands, with the arrangements often handled by his trusted assistant and nominal tour manager, Mark Anthony — who was also in charge of supplying Hope's women with cash when they needed it.

Except for an occasional whistle-blower such as Jan King — a former Hope secretary who gossiped about his women in a 1991

706

story for the *Globe* tabloid — all of this was kept discreetly out of the public eye. Friends and coworkers indulged Hope's behavior, looked the other way, and frequently covered for him. Rosemary Clooney, a good friend of the Hopes, was in a Beverly Hills hair salon when she overheard a customer bragging about having spent the previous night with Hope. Clooney challenged the woman's story, claiming that she, Clooney, had been with Hope that night — then called Bob and warned him to be more careful. Lande, Hope's son-in-law, was on a flight from Los Angeles to New York City when his seatmate began talking about the weekend she had just spent with her "boyfriend," Bob Hope. The two shared a taxi from the airport to Manhattan, and before parting, Lande told the woman, "The next time you talk to Bob, tell him his friend Nathaniel Lande said hello."

Hope did little to hide his indiscretions when he was around people he trusted. Ben Starr, a writer who worked on film scripts and TV specials for Hope, was at a TV rehearsal with Hope when an attractive chorus girl walked by. Hope casually swiped his index finger across her belly as she passed. "It was his way of saying to me, 'She's mine,' " said Starr. A producer who was editing one of Hope's TV shows in the 1970s said Hope would routinely arrive each night with a different blonde on his arm. "We called them the Trixies," she said. Nor did Hope have any qualms about sharing the sexual opportunities. On one trip to London with Hope, makeup man Don Marando lamented that he needed some female companionship. Hope told him to go to the hotel bar at 8:00 p.m., and a woman in a red dress would be waiting for him. Marando made the assignation, and after dinner the two retired to his hotel room. Waiting for him there was a bottle of champagne and a note: "Good luck. Bob."

Even as the Watergate scandal began to overtake the Nixon presidency, Hope stood by his friend in the White House, defending him in public and bucking him up with encouraging notes in private. In March 1974, after Nixon appeared before a friendly business group in Chicago to defend his actions on Watergate, Hope dashed off a telegram to the president: "I now know why you were captain of the debating team at Whittier. I thought your Chicago appearance was magnificent. The best yet." In May, Hope sent Nixon's secretary Rose Mary Woods a clipping from the *St. Louis Globe-Democrat* in which Hope defended the president. ("I've heard fouler language every time I tip my caddy," Hope said of the expletive-laden White House tapes.) He told Woods to show the article to Nixon: "I would like the President to know how I really talk about him behind his back. . . . And I want you to know the audience applauded like mad when I said these things."

Hope didn't have much to say when Nixon finally resigned in August. "It was so sad for that poor bastard," he told the *Washington Post* a few months later. The two talked on the phone in December, Hope related, and Nixon seemed "very depressed. . . . I said, 'When are you going to come out to the Springs and play some golf?' He said, 'It'll have to be quite awhile.' "They met at a party in Palm Springs in March 1975, and Hope tried to cheer up Nixon with jokes: "I told him *The Towering Inferno* was the burning of the White House tapes. He didn't think that that was too funny."

Hope stayed friendly with the disgraced ex-president and in later years continued to stand by him. "I just think that Nixon got himself into a tough spot," Hope said, when asked about Watergate in 1977. "They hired those Mack Sennett burglars who went over there. When they got caught, Nixon tried to protect the staff — what you and I would do up to a point — and then he got to where he didn't know which way to go. If he knew the Supreme Court was going to let him down, he would have burned those tapes just like that."

With Nixon's resignation, Hope lost a

friend in the White House, but he gained an even better one. Hope had known Gerald Ford only slightly before he became president, but the two soon bonded over golf. Ford was a good golfer — capable of driving 250 yards, though he had a penchant for errant shots that gave Hope a chance to recycle the bad-golfer jokes he had once used for Spiro Agnew: "It's not hard to find Gerry Ford on the golf course. Just follow the wounded." The Fords vacationed in Palm Springs during their White House years, dining with the Hopes often, and retired to the area afterward, sealing the friendship. "Of all the Presidents," said Hope, "he is the one I can call a pal."

Hope was trying to keep a lower political profile in these years, hoping to put the partisan rancor of Vietnam behind him. But echoes of the Vietnam turmoil were hard to escape entirely. In April 1975 he found himself back at the center of a political storm, quite unexpectedly, at the Academy Awards.

Hope had not hosted an Oscar show since 1971, when his cracks about sexually explicit Hollywood films ("I go back to the kind of movie when a girl says, 'I love you,' and it's a declaration, not a demonstration") made him seem a little more old-fashioned than the Academy was perhaps comfortable with. But he was asked back as one of four hosts for the 1975 ceremony, along with Frank Sinatra, Shirley MacLaine, and Sammy Davis Jr. Hope's jokes about the year's big films were mostly innocuous. ("I think *The Godfather Part II* has an excellent chance of winning. Neither Mr. Price nor Mr. Waterhouse has been heard from in days.") The trouble came a few minutes after his opening monologue, when the award for best documentary feature went to *Hearts and Minds,* Peter Davis's sharply critical account of the US involvement in Vietnam.

The timing was piquant. Two years after the US withdrawal, South Vietnamese forces were rapidly collapsing in the face of a final Communist offensive. Three weeks later, on April 30, 1975, Saigon would fall, forcing the last US embassy personnel to make an ignominious escape by helicopter. "It is ironic that we're here at a time just before Vietnam is about to be liberated," producer Bert Schneider said in accepting the award for *Hearts and Minds.* Then he read a telegram from the Vietcong delegation to the Paris peace talks: "Please transmit to all our friends in America our recognition of all that they have done on behalf of peace. . . . These actions serve the legitimate interests of the American people and the Vietnamese people."

The statement caused a stir in the hall — and a bigger one backstage. Hope was furious that Schneider had used the Oscar podium to deliver what Hope considered a propaganda message from America's enemies. He told Howard Koch, the show's producer, that the Academy should issue its own statement disavowing Schneider's remarks. "Don't you dare!" cried Shirley MacLaine, a prominent opponent of the war. But Hope scrawled out a statement on his own, gave it to Frank Sinatra, who was about to start his portion of the evening, and insisted that he read it on the air. "If you don't read it, I will," said Hope.

Sinatra, a former Kennedy pal turned Nixon supporter, obliged. Appearing onstage a few minutes later, he told the audience, "I've been asked by the Academy to make the following statement regarding a statement made by a winner. The Academy is saying, 'We are not responsible for any political references made on the program and we are sorry they had to take place this evening.' "

Backstage, Shirley MacLaine tore into Sinatra: "You said you were speaking on behalf of the Academy. Well, I'm a member of the Academy and you didn't ask me!" (Her brother, Warren Beatty, later chided Sinatra from the podium: "You old Republican, you.") The controversy percolated for days. Hope denounced Schneider's statement as a "cheap, cheap shot" and said he wrote his response after getting telegrams backstage saying that "millions of viewers and the parents of fifty-five thousand American boys did not appreciate the Academy being used as a platform for propaganda from Hanoi." Yet even some of those critical of Schneider's remarks objected that Hope and Sinatra had taken it upon themselves to deliver a statement on behalf of all three thousand members of the Academy. Finally the Academy issued a statement endorsing the Hope-Sinatra reply, pointing out that Koch, as the show's producer, was "the Academy's authorized representative," and quoting bylaws stating that the "Academy is expressly prohibited from concerning itself with economic, political or labor issues."

The fracas was a vestigial reminder of the country's still-raw Vietnam wounds. But it soon died down, and so, eventually, did the passions. "Bob Hope's so mad at me he's going to bomb Encino," Shirley MacLaine joked after the ceremony. But she bore no lasting ill will toward Hope, who had helped her raise money for charities and whom she genuinely admired. "So he was screwed up about the war," she said years later. "Who wasn't?" Still, for the folks who put together the annual Oscar telecast, Hope was proving to be something of a liability. He would not be asked back as host for another three years.

By the mid-1970s, some of Hope's oldest friends, colleagues, and support people were starting to pass from the scene. In December

1974, Jack Benny, Hope's friend and onetime radio rival, died of pancreatic cancer. "He was stingy to the end," said Hope, in a eulogy written for him by Mort Lachman. "He only gave us eighty years, and it wasn't enough." Jimmy Saphier, the agent who had negotiated all of Hope's radio and TV deals since 1937, suffered a stroke in his office and died in April 1974, of what was later diagnosed as a brain tumor. (Louis Shurr, Hope's first movie agent, had died of cancer in 1968.) Marjorie Hughes, Hope's loyal assistant for thirty-one years and the linchpin of his superefficient office operation, retired in 1973. (Hope Enterprises left her with no pension, and she had to pester her former boss for months about it. Hope wound up writing personal checks to support her in retirement.) Bob's elder brother Jim, who oversaw the ranch Bob owned near Malibu dubbed Hopetown, died in August 1975 — leaving Fred, back in Cleveland, the only one of Hope's six brothers still alive.

And just before the start of the fall 1975 TV season, Hope had to say good-bye to many of the people who had worked with him for decades. He blamed it on his sponsor.

Hope had been shopping for a new corporate partner since 1973, when Chrysler ended its sponsorship of his TV shows (while continuing to sponsor his golf tournament). For two seasons Hope signed up sponsors on a show-by-show basis, among them Gillette, Timex, and Ford. Then, in early 1975, he negotiated a lucrative new deal with Texaco. The oil company agreed to pay $3.15 million for seven hours of specials in each of the next three seasons, plus another $250,000 annually to Hope for commercials and other duties as corporate spokesman. In return, however, Texaco wanted Hope to make a thorough housecleaning of his creative staff. His shows had clearly fallen into a rut, and the demographics of his audience were skewing older and older. Texaco thought the shows needed fresh blood.

The plan was to cut back on the number of specials and to make them more "special," hiring different producers for each. That meant saying good-bye to the man who had been producing all of them, Hope's longtime writer and confidant, Mort Lachman. Hope also fired his entire writing staff — veterans who had been with him for years such as Charlie Lee, Gig Henry, Les White, and Norm Sullivan. "It had to be done," Hope told UPI's Vernon Scott, "because I thought that after twenty-five years it was time to get a fresh format, some new ideas, a new style." In addition, with Texaco promising more PR support, Hope laid off his two longest-serving publicists, Frank Liberman and Allan Kalmus.

"Bob caved in," said Elliott Kozak, Saphier's former assistant, who had taken over his dealmaking duties. "It was too strong a deal. He didn't stand up to it." Kozak convinced Hope to rehire at least one writing team, Lee and Henry, to provide some continuity and veteran support for the newcomers being brought in. Both Liberman and Kalmus, too, were back working for Hope within a year. But the split with Lachman was unavoidable, and painful. Hope, always averse to confrontation, gave Kozak the job of breaking the bad news. Lachman was surprised and hurt, but he took it stoically. When Hope took him to play golf and tried to explain the decision, Lachman cut him off. "He was very sad, very close to a tear," Lachman recalled. "I said, 'I'm not interested in this whole conversation. Let's play.' We just played golf. And we left, and I told him we can still play golf anytime you call me. But it was a sad day." (They remained friends and golfing buddies, and Lachman had a successful post-Hope career as executive producer of such sitcoms as *All in the Family, Kate & Allie,* and *Gimme a Break!*)

Hope's first show under the Texaco banner, a belated season opener on October 24, 1975, was indeed more special, though hardly new: a two-hour compilation of highlights from his TV career, to mark his twenty-fifth anniversary on NBC. The three Hope specials that followed included a Christmas show, with guests Redd Foxx and Angie Dickinson; a concert special from Montreal, to raise money for the US and Canadian Olympic teams, with Bing Crosby among the guests; and a ninety-minute scripted show, in which Hope hosts a party at his home, where the guests (some fifty comedians, from Milton Berle to Freddie Prinze) are getting murdered one by one. The material was only marginally improved, but the shows at least had a fresher look, ratings were strong, and Texaco got its money's worth: Hope did nearly all the commercials as well, touting the company's oil-drilling operations in the Gulf of Mexico, pitching Havoline motor oil, and singing the praises of the "owners of America's oil companies" — stockholders like you and me.

The bicentennial celebration of 1976 gave Hope a chance to wave the flag once again, as host of a ninety-minute NBC special on July 4, *Bob Hope's Bicentennial Star-Spangled Spectacular.* It was one of his better shows of the era, with Hope and Sammy Davis Jr. playing anchormen of a revolutionary-era newscast, a spoof of the comedy soap opera *Mary Hartman, Mary Hartman,* and a funny Hope takeoff of Johnny Carson as host of an 1876 version of the *Tonight Show,* making jokes about Custer and griping about the tough studio audience. ("Better warm up the buckboard, Ed, they're getting hostile.") Hope

717

closed with a sentimental, Norman Rock-wellian tribute to the real "heroes" of America: "the guy in the bleachers with his kid, rooting for his team between bites on a hot dog . . . the man who fights the traffic every morning to get to work . . . These most uncommon common people are the heart of America, its hope and its future." It was Hope's plea to move beyond the divisive years of Vietnam and Watergate, and a heart-felt justification of his own life's work:

I like to hold up a mirror to our lives and see the fun in everything we do. Over the years I've gotten more than my share of laughs — about you and me and America and the way we live. But when the house-lights dim and the cameras are turned off, I'm just like the rest of you. Kid America? You bet your life. Love America? All the way.

For all the heat he had taken, Hope still saw himself as a unifying figure, an enter-tainer above partisanship — and, it seemed, above criticism. He hated bad reviews, and frequently got his writers and other staff members to write letters responding to them, often in the guise of ordinary readers or view-ers, the voice of the people. During the bicentennial summer, he entertained at a state dinner in Washington for Queen Eliza-beth and Prince Philip, hosted by President

Ford and the first lady. A few days after the event, which was televised on public TV, the *Los Angeles Times* ran two letters to the editor criticizing his performance. "I was shocked, disappointed and dismayed by the whole miserable mess, which has most certainly damaged the cultural image and prestige of our country," wrote one viewer. "Bob Hope should fire his writers, or, better still, retire gracefully."

A week later the *Times* printed three letters in response. One reader, identifying himself as one of Hope's writers (it was signed Charles Liebleck, evidently Charlie Lee), said that Hope "has entertained and brought the gift of laughter to more people in more places than any other single performer of our time" and pointed out that writing comedy is "much harder than writing bitchy letters to a newspaper." A second letter came from Geoffrey Clarkson — the pianist in Les Brown's band — who reported that he was at the state dinner and that "the Queen and Prince Philip enjoyed the entertainment immensely." A third letter asserted that Hope's "humanitarianism and talent are unquestionable, and to have such a great man as Bob Hope belittled is abominable." It was signed by Mark Antonio of Burbank, California — almost surely Hope's crony and longtime assistant Mark Anthony.

Hope was especially eager, in the post-

Vietnam years, to repair his image on college campuses, to show that he could still communicate with the young people who had turned against him because of his support for the war. His April 1975 special, *Bob Hope on Campus,* consisted mostly of a live performance at UCLA's Pauley Pavilion, where the audience was friendly and most of the gags were about the school's basketball team (John Wayne played Coach John Wooden in one sketch). But the show also included clips of Hope talking informally with small groups of students on other college campuses, such as Vassar and Columbia — awkward encounters, with Hope posing prepared questions such as "Is pot passé?" and "Who would you sooner be, Jonas Salk or Catfish Hunter?" (One student's reply: "Jonas Salk. Because he made it possible for more people to *be* Catfish Hunters." Right answer.)

Jimmy Carter's election as president in 1976 marked a new and unfamiliar challenge for Hope. A friend to every president since Truman, Hope was now faced with a president he had never met — one who didn't even play golf. The former peanut farmer from Georgia, who came from nowhere to win the Democratic presidential nomination in 1976, provided Hope with plenty of gag material. He joked about Carter's Southern roots ("When he prays, he calls God by his first name–Y'all"), his toothy smile ("He went to the dentist today to get his teeth cleaned; should be out by August"), and his colorful brother, Billy, the first presidential sibling with his own beer. But Hope, for the first time in many years, was left off the invitation list for the president's inauguration.

Not that Hope needed the extra activity. He was doing fewer specials now (four per season, down from six or seven), but working even harder to promote them. Before each one, he would do a round of phone interviews with TV columnists; make guest appearances on other variety shows; sit for interviews with talk show hosts such as Mike Douglas and Phil Donahue; and make his now-ritual drop-in appearance on Johnny Carson's *Tonight Show.* Hope continued to develop movie projects, commissioning a script for the Walter Winchell biopic from writer Sidney Boehm, which he found too "negative," and then a second one from Art Arthur, which came in at an unwieldy three hundred pages. Plans were announced for a Bob Hope Museum, to house Hope's voluminous collection of memorabilia — which he first wanted to build on fifty acres of his Malibu property, then on a plot of land in Burbank that he owned adjacent to NBC headquarters. Like so many other Hope projects, it never got off the ground. "The problem with Dad is that he would have these ideas," said Linda Hope.

"And he would call you from Peoria, Illinois, and say, 'I think we've got to get on this thing and start developing this or doing that.' And then he would be gone for a week or two weeks, and he's home for a few days, and in the meantime he had to do his real TV work, and he really had no time to develop the kinds of things that he may have dreamed of. He didn't have time."

By 1976 Linda was working for her father full-time. Her marriage to Lande (with whom she had a son, Andrew) had ended in divorce the year before — a split that took him by surprise. "I was in England writing a show," said Lande. "I came home to an empty house. She left me a note. It was all calculated and all devastating." (Linda later had a long-term gay relationship with TV producer-director Nancy Malone.) She always had an ambivalent relationship with her father; getting his attention was sometimes so frustrating, she told a friend, that she would purposely bounce checks, just so he would call her into his office to scold her. But after the divorce, she needed work, and her father put her in charge of program development for Hope Enterprises. She was paid little (only $600 a week at first), but she did a good job, overseeing the development of *Joe & Valerie,* the one series Hope's company managed to get on the air.

Her brother Tony might have seemed the

more logical Hope child to enter the family business. He worked for a while in business affairs at Twentieth Century–Fox and served as an associate producer on the TV series *Judd, for the Defense* and the 1971 Australian film *Walkabout*. His father depended on Tony for business advice, and some friends thought they recognized some of Bob's comic genes. Hal Kanter liked to tell the story of an encounter with Hope on the Paramount lot in the early 1950s. Kanter was wearing a bright red tie with red socks, and when Bob passed by, he commented, "My God, Kanter, that's the longest red tie I've ever seen." Years later, Kanter was at the Twentieth Century–Fox studios, again wearing bright red socks with a red sweater. This time Tony Hope saw him and wisecracked, "That's the longest red sweater I ever saw." Tony insisted he had never heard his father's line.

But Tony's career in show business came to an abrupt and not very happy end. In 1973 he teamed up with Barney Rosenzweig, a TV producer who had worked with Tony at Fox, to produce an independent film called *Who Fears the Devil?* It was a strange movie, based on a series of fanciful folktales by Manly Wade Wellman about an Appalachian balladeer who is transported back in time. After Rosenzweig kept lowering the budget to try to get backers, Tony Hope agreed to finance the film with $400,000 of his own money.

The production was beset with problems. Arlo Guthrie was originally cast in the lead, but he didn't work out and had to be replaced by an unknown. The dailies were not good, and the screenwriter pleaded for the director to be replaced. After it was finished, the film couldn't find a distributor, and Rosenzweig began peddling it himself, booking it in college towns across the Southeast — a grassroots technique that had been used successfully by the 1971 independent hit *Billy Jack*. But the movie died quickly, and Tony Hope lost his entire investment.

He took it hard. "He felt he failed, and he became bitter," said Rosenzweig. "We were having breakfast a year or two later. He said, 'Barney, we can't do this anymore. Because when I see you, I think of the movie, and when I think of the movie, I want to throw up.' " For the son of Bob Hope, the failure must have been especially difficult. "It had to be tough for Tony," said Rosenzweig. "Bob Hope was a tough taskmaster. I'm sure his father was brutal to him about it."

The whole episode left Tony — then living in Malibu with Judy and their two young children — broke and in debt, with no bailout coming from Dad. "Bob and Dolores thought everyone could make it on their own," said Judy Hope. She went back to work as a lawyer, making the long commute to downtown Los Angeles, while teaching part-time at Pepperdine University in Malibu. Then, in April 1975, a malfunctioning furnace in their home caught fire, and the house burned to the ground. Suddenly homeless as well as broke, Tony and Judy picked up and moved the family to Washington, DC.

Judy, who had connections in the Ford administration, went to work at the White House and became a partner in the law firm of Paul, Hastings, Janofsky and Walker. (She later worked on President Reagan's Commission on Organized Crime and in 1988 was nominated for a seat on the US Court of Appeals for the District of Columbia. The nomination was blocked by Senate Democrats.) Tony, meanwhile, bounced around in various jobs with such companies as Mutual of Omaha and Touche Ross. In 1986 he moved back to California to run for Congress, but lost in the Republican primary to an opponent who branded him a carpetbagger. Later he became the first head of the Indian Gaming Commission under President George H. W. Bush. But there was a sense of potential never quite realized. "Bob called Tony a lot," said Judy Hope. "When he wanted to buy a piece of property, Tony would go and look at it. When he had a radio station in Puerto Rico that had some problems, Tony worked them out. His dad trusted and relied on him. In a way, he shortchanged his own career for his dad."

■ ■ ■ ■

Hope's writing staff was going through a transition in the late 1970s. Old-timers Gig Henry and Charlie Lee were still around, but newcomers were filtering in. Gene Perret was writing gags for Phyllis Diller in 1969 when he sent three hundred unsolicited jokes to Hope for one of his Oscar appearances. Hope used ten of them on the air and told Perret, "It looks like you've been writing for me all your life." Perret continued writing jokes for Hope over the next few years, while on staff at *The Carol Burnett Show,* before joining him full-time in the late seventies. Bob Mills, a lawyer turned gagman, was writing for Dean Martin's celebrity TV roasts in 1977 when Hope hired him for a special. "I've got six more weeks on my Dean Martin contract," Mills said. Hope replied, "You work on Dean Martin during the day, don't you? Well, you can work on my stuff in the evenings." Mills stayed with Hope for fifteen years. Sitcom veterans Seaman Jacobs and Fred Fox also joined the staff, and later Martha Bolton, Hope's first full-time female writer. Other younger writers came and went, some hired for individual shows, others for a season or two.

All had to adapt to Hope's idiosyncratic working style. Even veteran writers never got

726

more than a one-year contract, which kept them on their toes and enabled Hope to dump writers who weren't measuring up. (For years some of the writers were even represented by Hope's own agent Jimmy Saphier — a conflict of interest if there ever was one.) The writers got used to the 24/7 schedule, the late-night phone calls, the oddly solitary working life. Unlike on other comedy shows, where writers would sit around a table and bat out scripts together, Hope's writers mostly worked alone, coming up with jokes on their own, then dropping them "over the wall" at Hope's Toluca Lake home office, where they might get chased by one of Bob's German shepherds.

The pace was intense. "He liked people who worked fast," said Perret. Hope might call for some jokes on a specific topic, then phone back a half hour later — no hello or greeting of any kind, just a command: "Thrill me." Hope once told his writers that he was appearing at a psychiatrists' convention, so they gave him a load of psychiatrist jokes. When Hope arrived at the event, he found out the audience was actually a group of chiropractors. The writers had thirty minutes to come up with a new set of jokes. Mills was once hosting a backyard barbecue when he got a call from Hope and heard music in the background: he was in the wings of some distant theater, minutes away from going onstage. On the way in from the airport, Hope told Mills, the traffic was terrible because all the streets were torn up, and he needed a line about it to open the show. "How much time do you have?" asked Mills. "About twenty seconds," said Hope. Mills came up with a couple of quickies ("between the hotel and here, the cabbie and I exchanged teeth three times"), then went back to his dinner guests. "I just made my entire salary for the year," he told them.

The old-timers sometimes tried to get away with recycling jokes from Hope's bottomless vault of funnies, but he had a photographic memory and usually rejected them. One time he asked his writers for some football jokes, and Mills sighed that he should just take some old ones out of the files. "Why do we have to write new ones?" Mills asked. Hope snapped, "I pay you with new money, don't I?" Yet Hope appreciated their hard work and didn't get down on them if they came up short. Perret once turned in a load of jokes and Hope asked if they were brilliant. "They're really not," Perret said. Hope told him not to worry: "The other guys will be hot."

The writers were responsible for virtually everything Hope said or that appeared under his name. They wrote his TV shows, monologues for his personal appearances, magazine articles that carried Hope's by-line, jokes that were fed to columnists such as *Variety*'s Army Archerd, acceptance speeches, commencement addresses, and eulogies. When Hope was a guest on other TV variety shows, he would get the script in advance and have his writers add new lines that he could throw into the sketches during rehearsals. (His practice of rewriting the lines annoyed some producers, who crossed Hope off their guest lists as a result.) Mills once got a request from Hope for some jokes about Pentagon generals. Not seeing any military events on his calendar, Mills asked what the occasion was. Hope said he was going to play golf with three generals and just needed some funny lines for conversation on the course.

Hope still moved at a pace that would have exhausted much younger men. He was on the road almost constantly — nearly 250 appearances in 1977 alone, from the National Dairy Congress in Waterloo, Iowa, to Queen Elizabeth's Silver Jubilee celebration in London. His TV specials, as a result, were getting increasingly short shrift.

The monologues were still a priority. For each one, Hope would cull through hundreds of his writers' jokes, picking the best thirty minutes' worth of material, then delivering it before a studio audience (usually Johnny Carson's *Tonight Show* audience, who would be asked to stick around for Hope after Carson's show was finished) before winnowing it down to seven or eight minutes that would make the final broadcast. As for the rest of his TV hours, Hope was paying only minimal attention. He didn't even try to learn his lines anymore; most of the rehearsal time was spent worrying about where the cue cards were going to be placed. He didn't like rehearsals that ran long. "Milton Berle liked to retake jokes — he'd say, 'I can do that one better,' " said Sid Smith, who began directing Hope specials in the late seventies. "Hope liked to do it once, and that's it. He didn't want to lose the spontaneity of the joke." He wasn't happy with guests like Lucille Ball, who rehearsed obsessively and would often stop to make suggestions on how the scenes could be improved. Grumbled Hope during one rehearsal, "She thinks I just got into this business."

He was not a temperamental star, at least by most inflated-Hollywood-ego standards. He projected an almost preternatural calm, humming an unidentifiable tune to himself constantly. But technical flubs or unforeseen delays could make him testy, and his fits of temper could be formidable. Dennis Klein, then a young comedy writer (and later the cocreator of *The Larry Sanders Show*), was in the greenroom for a *Tonight Show* taping in the late 1960s on a night Hope was a guest. Hope was used to royal treatment at the *Tonight Show:* always the first guest, always

730

leaving immediately after his segment was over, so that he wouldn't have to move down the couch and listen to other guests. This time, however, Hope was taken by surprise when Carson announced the show's first guest — not Bob Hope, but a monkey from the San Diego Zoo.

"What the fuck!" cried Hope, bolting from his chair and launching a profanity-laden tirade that left everyone in the room cowering. A *Tonight Show* assistant tried to calm him down, speculating that the animal was too skittish to wait any longer, or it was past feeding time. But Hope was "roaming the greenroom like an enraged animal, spewing invective," Klein recalled. Only when the monkey's segment was finished and Carson had announced Hope did he calm down — sauntering out onstage smiling, to the strains of "Thanks for the Memory," as if nothing had happened.

By mid-1977 one of Hope's pet movie projects finally seemed to be coming together: a reunion with Crosby in a new *Road* picture. London impresario Lew Grade was producing the film, which was based on a Mel Shavelson script called *Road to the Fountain of Youth*. Grade had even called the much-abused Dorothy Lamour to see if she could be coaxed back for one final reunion. The project got delayed when Crosby hurt his back after falling off a stage during a TV taping in March and needed a couple of months to recuperate. (Hope, a guest on the show, was among those who rushed to Crosby's side after the accident.) When Hope asked Crosby to appear at a charity golf tournament in June, he still wasn't well enough, writing Hope wanly, "It's unlikely that I'll be able to swing a stick by June — if ever." By the fall, Crosby had recovered enough to appear for two weeks at London's Palladium Theatre, after which he went to Spain for a few days of rest and golf. He was walking back to the clubhouse after a round on October 14, 1977, when he collapsed and died of a heart attack. The film was abandoned, and the *Road* team broken up for good.

Hope and Crosby were never close friends. They rarely socialized together and saw even less of each other in the later years, after Crosby moved to Hillsborough, outside of San Francisco, with his second wife, Kathryn, and their new family. But no one else in Hope's professional life meant more to him. He heard the news of Crosby's death while in New York City getting ready to do a benefit in New Jersey. (In a sad coincidence, his mother-in-law, Theresa De Fina, died on the same day.) He canceled his appearance, as well as one scheduled for the following night in Arizona, and flew back to Los Angeles. When Linda met him at the airport, she found her father as emotional as she had ever seen him: "He had tears in his eyes. You could see he was really hurting about it. At the same time, he said he felt bad he had left those people in the lurch. It was the first time I ever remember him canceling anything."

Hope issued a statement the next day: "The whole world loved Bing Crosby, with a devotion that not only crossed international borders, but erased them." Bing had insisted that his funeral be closed to all but family and the closest of friends. Bob and Dolores were among the small group of forty who attended the early-morning service at St. Paul the Apostle Church in Westwood. (Rosemary Clooney and Phil Harris were also there, but not Dorothy Lamour — a final snub from Bing.) Hope was in the middle of preparing his next NBC special, *The Road to Hollywood,* tied in with a new book about his movie career cowritten with Bob Thomas. Hope turned the special into a tribute to Crosby, retitled *On the Road with Bing.*

An anniversary, and the passage of three years, apparently dimmed the bad memories of Hope's last appearance at the Academy Awards, with his controversial role in the Bert Schneider affair. For the fiftieth-birthday Oscar ceremony on April 3, 1978, the Academy decided to bring back Hope as solo host one more time: a nostalgic tribute to the man who had done more than anyone else to make the annual awards telecast a national pastime.

At nearly seventy-five, Hope sounded a little disingenuous as he poked fun in his monologue at the parade of past Oscar winners trotted out for the anniversary: "It looks like the road company of the Hollywood Wax Museum." In truth, he had an off night. Hope was unhappy that he had to use a teleprompter instead of cue cards, and he appeared unusually transfixed by the camera. He sounded hoarse, and his delivery was stiffer and less supple than usual. For once, the Oscars' favorite host was showing his age. Still, he got off some good lines ("I haven't seen so much expensive jewelry go by since I watched Sammy Davis Jr.'s house sliding down Coldwater Canyon"), and he at least managed to stay out of the big political flap of the night — another inflammatory acceptance speech, this one by Vanessa Redgrave, who called members of the militant Jewish Defense League "Zionist hoodlums" and an "insult to Jewish people all over the world."

Marty Pasetta, who directed the show (one of the fourteen Oscarcasts he would handle), was impressed with how well Hope, despite his age, could roll with the punches — squeezing or stretching to fit the time as needed, adding jokes on the fly to respond to what took place during the show. "So many guys can't do that," said Pasetta. Johnny Carson, for example, who hosted the show for the next four years, was much less apt to improvise during the show. "Bob was a pleasure to work with," said Pasetta. "Johnny could be difficult at times. He wasn't as glib as Bob. He had more writers, and he needed the lines to be precise." Hope may have been looking like an anachronism by 1978, but his style stood the test of time — the gold standard, not just for Carson, but for every Oscar host who followed.

As Hope's seventy-fifth birthday approached on May 29, 1978, NBC suggested an all-star special to celebrate the occasion. Hope, who never liked to acknowledge his age, said no. "I can't go on television and tell the whole world I'm seventy-five years old," he told Elliott Kozak. But when James Lipton, a sometime actor, writer, and Broadway composer, who had produced Jimmy Carter's inaugural gala (and would later become better known as host of TV's *Inside the Actors Studio*), proposed a black-tie seventy-fifth birthday tribute at the Kennedy Center, with the proceeds going toward a new USO headquarters that would bear Hope's name, Hope couldn't resist. The show became the centerpiece for a weekend of birthday festivities and official tributes in Washington, another step in Hope's reemergence from the cloud of Vietnam.

"It's taken over a year," wrote Tom Shales in the *Washington Post,* "but the Carter administration finally established diplomatic relations with Bob Hope." To kick off the birthday weekend, President Carter hosted a reception for Hope at the White House, with five hundred Washington and Hollywood VIPs in attendance. "I have now been in office for 489 days," said Carter, on meeting Hope for the first time. "And when I've spent three more weeks, I will have slept as many nights here as Bob Hope." That evening, the Hopes hosted a private dinner at a restaurant in Alexandria, Virginia, owned by Dolores's nephew (and former Agnew aide) Peter Malatesta, with a guest list that included such Hollywood pals as Lucille Ball, Fred Mac-Murray, Phyllis Diller, Danny Thomas, and Elizabeth Taylor (now the wife of John Warner, soon to be elected senator from Virginia). "I'm pretty sure I'm seventy-five. But I've lied to so many girls," Hope said after the toasts, perhaps a little more lubricated than usual. "Of course, they always find out about one a.m. Dolores — that's a joke."

The next morning, Bob, Dolores, and most of the family were in the gallery of the House of Representatives, where Congressman Paul Findley of Illinois introduced a resolution saluting Hope on his birthday. (Hope woke up late and almost missed the 10:00 a.m. session. "Can't we change it to eleven?" he asked.) For forty minutes, the august chamber was filled with sentimental tributes and congressional mirth, highlighted by a chorus of "Happy Birthday" and some new verses for "Thanks for the Memory," sung by Minority Whip Robert Michel:

Thanks for the memory
Of places you have gone, to cheer our
   soldiers on
The president sent Kissinger, but you sent
   Jill St. John . . .

The three-hour special, broadcast live from Kennedy Center the following Monday night, was a fairly stodgy affair, done in what *Variety* described as "that peculiarly square and predictable style that seems to typify 'official' dress-up entertainment projects from the capital." George C. Scott led the parade of celebrities, ranging from George Burns to KC and the Sunshine Band, who offered reminiscences, songs, jokes, and clips of Hope's career highlights, as the guest of honor watched from a box next to former president Ford. The birthday special drew a mighty 27.1 Nielsen rating, the most watched program of the week and the best showing for a Hope special in years.

It validated the effort by Texaco and NBC to make Hope's specials bigger events. More of his shows were now done on location or pegged to an anniversary or other special occasion, many expanded to ninety minutes or even two hours. In February of 1978 he went on a five-city concert tour of Australia (with guests Florence Henderson, Barbara Eden, and Charo — and a young David Letterman among the writers) and turned it into a ninety-minute special that aired in April. In October he was the cohost, with Danny Kaye, of a two-hour special marking the seventy-fifth anniversary of baseball's World Series. Hope's own birthdays, meanwhile, became annual TV events, with Lipton returning to produce the celebration from a different locale each year — in May 1979 from the deck of the USS *Iwo Jima* in New York Harbor, with the Village People singing "In the Navy" to a shipload of rather bemused sailors.

Hope wasn't slowing down. He still took a hands-on role in nearly every aspect of his TV specials: monitoring the budgets, approving the network publicity, and calling in for ratings on the morning after the telecast. He demanded the same dedication from the people who worked for him. When he was unhappy with his ratings or thought he wasn't getting enough press, he would needle his publicists: "Are you still working for me?" or "Who's handling Sinatra?" Staffers got used to late-night phone calls from Hope, sometimes just to relate a joke he had heard on

738

the *Tonight Show*. "When he pays you a salary, he expects you to work around the clock," said Elliott Kozak, his agent, whom he put in charge of Hope Enterprises.

Kozak was a smart and loyal representative for Hope, and as close to him as anyone, but he had to put up with a lot. Once Hope summoned him to the house for a 9:00 p.m. meeting. Kozak already had dinner plans with his wife for their wedding anniversary and said he couldn't make it. "Oh, you don't have time for me anymore?" Hope snapped. They once got in a fight over a deal that Kozak negotiated for Hope to appear at the London Palladium. Hope wanted $50,000 for the show, but Lew Grade, its producer, said he could afford only $25,000. Hope relented, and the contract was drawn up. But months later, on the eve of his trip to London, Hope saw the contract and asked what happened to his $50,000. Kozak tried to correct him: "No, Bob, we asked for fifty, but they could only come up with twenty-five." Hope wouldn't budge: "You tell him he's gotta come up with the fifty thousand or forget about it."

Kozak, steamed that Hope was reneging on a deal that Kozak thought had been signed off on, had to go back and plead for another $25,000 from Grade — who came up with the money, on a promise that Hope would play another engagement at the Palladium

739

the following year. But Hope would not admit his mistake, insisting that Kozak had simply "got me the original fifty thousand." Kozak was angry and threatened to quit: "You don't trust me, and I break my back for you. I'm shocked and hurt after all these years." Finally Hope came the closest he could to an apology: "Let's just say it was a misunderstanding."

Kozak was soon out of a job anyway. In 1979, Hope replaced him as the head of Hope Enterprises with his daughter Linda, who had been in charge of program development. She protested that she wasn't ready for the job, but Hope insisted; he wanted someone he could trust in the position. The family ties, however, made their working relationship even more fraught than it had been between Hope and Kozak. They clashed openly on Linda's first big working trip with her father: his landmark 1979 visit to the People's Republic of China.

China was the last great frontier for Hope. Not long after President Nixon's breakthrough visit to the Communist country in 1972, Hope began lobbying to take an entertainment troupe there. (During a White House meeting with Hope in March 1973, Nixon put in a call to Secretary of State Henry Kissinger about the trip. Kissinger said the Chinese first wanted to see a tape of Hope's 1958 special from the Soviet Union.)

But not until President Carter established diplomatic relations with China in December 1978, and cultural exchanges between the two countries began in earnest, did Hope finally get approval for the trip.

He hired Lipton, his big-event specialist, to produce the show. Lipton and director Bob Wynn made an advance trip to China in April 1979 to scout locations and sign up Chinese performers. Back home, Hope lined up country singer Crystal Gayle, the singing duo Peaches and Herb (Hope thought their hit song "Reunited" was a good theme for the trip), and ballet star Mikhail Baryshnikov to join him on the tour. When Baryshnikov said he couldn't go because he had to appear with the New York City Ballet in Saratoga, New York, Hope called choreographer George Balanchine, with whom he had worked on Broadway in *Ziegfeld Follies of 1936,* and got him to rearrange the dancer's schedule so he could make the trip.

Dolores was along too (carrying cookies, crackers, and packets of Cup-a-Soup in her luggage, in case the food wasn't edible) when the troupe of forty-five arrived in Beijing on June 16, 1979. Few people in China knew Hope. When he and his entourage got off the plane, there was a flurry of excitement — for a delegation of Japanese diplomats who were on the same flight. Hope and his troupe spent four weeks in the country, shooting at such landmarks as the Great Wall, the Forbidden City, and Tiananmen Square. Hope played Ping-Pong with Chinese youngsters, joined an early-morning tai-chi class, walked the streets with Big Bird from *Sesame Street,* and discussed his movie *Monsieur Beaucaire* with a class of Chinese film students. Baryshnikov performed a scene from *Giselle* with a Chinese ballet student, and Dolores sang "Do-Re-Mi" from *The Sound of Music* to a group of schoolchildren. (Hope was mellowing: for once he didn't cut Dolores's segment from the final broadcast.) Chinese acrobats, comedians, puppets, and a trained panda performed. Hope did a monologue before a mixed audience of Americans and Chinese at the downtown Capital Theatre. To translate his jokes, he first tried subtitles projected on a giant screen, but found that the Chinese speakers in the audience were laughing before he got to the punch lines. Instead, Chinese actor Ying Ruocheng was recruited to translate each joke after Hope finished — thus giving him the pleasure of two laughs, in the right order.

Dealing with the Chinese authorities was a chore. They insisted on approving the entire script, which meant late nights going over the day's work, explaining jokes, and often fighting to keep them in. (For example, Hope made a wisecrack about a Chinese alcoholic drink: "I had one Mao-Tai, and my head felt like the Gang of Four." The censors made him take it out.) The Chinese crews that the authorities forced Hope to use weren't accustomed to the Americans' fast pace, and they seemed to purposely slow things down. "The Chinese were very, very difficult," said associate producer Marcia Lewis. "They wanted a successful show, but they didn't want to look cooperative." Some of the performers were balky too. The owner of the trained panda complained that he wasn't getting paid enough and said he would allow the show to use only half of the panda's act. After wrangling with him, Linda Hope agreed to take just the last half — but had the cameras record all of it, knowing that the animal would have to do its whole act from beginning to end anyway.

The crew had to resort to cloak-and-dagger tactics to get around some of the bureaucratic problems. After the Chinese found out that Hope had taped a sequence at the Democracy Wall, where Chinese citizens were allowed to post complaints about the government, they demanded the videotape of the segment. Director Bob Wynn wouldn't give it up. Then, after secretly sending it back to the United States in the luggage of a Los Angeles TV crew that was covering the trip, he gave the Chinese a blank tape instead — knowing they did not have the equipment needed to play it.

Relations between Linda, who shared a producer title with Lipton, and her father grew more tense as the trip went on. Bob was annoyed at the many delays and the rising costs, and Linda bore the brunt. Their arguments — often out on the hotel balcony, because Hope thought the rooms were bugged — became so heated that director Wynn had to step in and act as mediator. The final straw came at the airport in Shanghai, as the troupe was getting ready to leave for home. The Chinese demanded another videotape, of a Coke commercial that Hope had done at the Great Wall, as well as the equipment to play it on, which had already been loaded on the plane. As Linda argued with the officials and the plane sat on the ground, Bob stewed. "Dad was really aggravated with it," said Linda. "And he was aggravated with me — 'Just give them the tape!' "

The three-hour special that resulted, *Bob Hope on the Road to China,* was more of a diplomatic triumph than an entertainment one. Hope opens the show in front of the Great Wall, singing, "We're off on the road to China," to the tune of "The Road to Morocco," with new lyrics penned by Lipton. Hope has a few pointed monologue jokes that somehow eluded the censors: "Housing must be a problem here. By the time I got to my hotel there was a family of four living in my luggage." But for the most part, the diplomatic niceties and travel-brochure booster-ism make the show a little numbing. ("The Chinese are easy to like," says Hope. "They're ready to smile, they're courteous and helpful, and they make every effort to understand us.") What's more, the telecast, which aired on Sunday, September 16, 1979, was a disappointment in the ratings, ranking just twenty-sixth for the week.

Yet the China trip seemed to whet Hope's appetite for more diplomatic ventures abroad. He wanted to go to Moscow for the 1980 Olympics, but that was scuttled by the US boycott of the games following the Soviet invasion of Afghanistan. Instead, during the diplomatic chill that ensued, Hope went to Moscow to do a show for US embassy personnel. When Iranian revolutionaries stormed the US embassy in Tehran and held fifty-two Americans hostage for more than a year, Hope proposed a trip to Tehran to do a Christmas show for the hostages. An aide to President Carter worked with Tony Hope to try to arrange that or some other role for Hope in ending the hostage crisis, but nothing came of it. Hope had more success as an ambassador for golf: in September 1980 he went to London to host the first edition of the Bob Hope British Classic, a British counterpart to his popular Palm Springs pro-am tournament.

With the passions of the Vietnam era fading, there seemed to be more of an effort to recapture and pay homage to the Bob Hope of old. In April 1979 the Film Society of Lincoln Center staged a gala tribute to Hope, hosted by Dick Cavett — a big fan since junior high school, when he saw Hope give a concert in Cavett's hometown of Lincoln, Nebraska — and with Diane Keaton, Shelley Winters, Kurt Vonnegut, and Andy Warhol among the twenty-seven hundred fans in the audience. The centerpiece of the evening was a sixty-three-minute retrospective of Hope's film work, narrated by Woody Allen, who called Hope his favorite comedian and showed how strongly his own screen character had been influenced by Hope in such films as *Monsieur Beaucaire, My Favorite Brunette,* and the *Road* pictures. "When my mother took me to see *Road to Morocco,*" said Allen, "I knew exactly what I wanted to do with my life."

A tough *Rolling Stone* profile in 1980 rehashed some of the old Vietnam resentments, but other journalists seemed willing to let bygones be bygones. "Oh, go on, highbrows, take your great comedians and your intellectual clowns — but look at what America thought was really funny: Bob Hope," wrote Peter Kaplan in a fond 1978 profile in *New Times* magazine. "Age cannot wither, nor custom stale, the charm of Bob Hope," wrote Tom Dowling, in the *Washing-*

ton Star, during Hope's seventy-fifth birthday festivities. "[He] is, in short, a totem of every virtue held dear by the Elks, Moose, Kiwanii, Rotarians, Eagles, Odd Fellows and USO-ers. He's likable, quick on his feet, dependably salty when with the boys, safely correct when ladies are in the room, and a font of uplifting public-spiritedness when impressionable kiddies have their ears perked up. Like all men you can count on, he's as comfy as an old shoe."

By this time, he was an old shoe with a closet full of Guccis. In 1968, *Fortune* magazine put him on its list of the sixty-six wealthiest people in America, with a net worth estimated at between $150 million and $200 million — the richest entertainer in Hollywood. Hope routinely claimed such estimates were exaggerated, and since most of his holdings were in real estate, it was always hard to know precisely. But in 1979, after years of avoiding ostentatious displays of his wealth, he and Dolores oversaw the completion of their hilltop mansion in Palm Springs, which to many was the epitome of extravagance.

Construction on the house, on hold since the 1973 fire, finally resumed in 1978. Given the do-over, Dolores set about making changes in Lautner's severe modernist design, to cut costs and make it more user-friendly. She enclosed some open space (the original design necessitated going outside to get from the kitchen to the living area), made some changes in the exterior, and reduced the size of the upstairs. Lautner objected to many of the changes, and Dolores fired him — finishing up the house with another architect, and the help of her friend and decorator Laura Mako. "Mrs. Hope was kind of a frustrated architect," said Dolores's longtime assistant Nancy Gordon. "She had a very keen eye, and she was forever moving walls around here and there. I'm sure Lautner was frustrated. But she got what she wanted."

The house was still quite a statement, with its swooping, mushroom-shaped roof that reminded many of the TWA terminal at Kennedy Airport. It had a sixty-foot-wide central skylight, lavish separate bedroom suites for Bob and Dolores, two swimming pools (one indoors and one out), a small chapel for Dolores, a one-hole golf course for Bob, a massive outdoor fireplace, and an expansive slate patio, where party guests had a breathtaking view of the valley below. Many friends and family missed the old house on El Alameda (which the Hopes kept for guests), with its homier atmosphere and serve-yourself Italian dinners. Bob was one of them. "I love that little house," he told Andy Williams, a Palm Springs friend. "But Dolores wanted to have that big airplane hangar."

But he got used to it. The Hopes moved

into their new Palm Springs home in late 1979, threw a spectacular party there every year during golf-tournament week, and spent most of the winters there for the rest of their lives — a pleasure palace at last befitting Hollywood's royal couple.

Chapter 14
Legend
"NOW THAT'S THE WAY I SAY GOOD NIGHT."

For Bob Hope, who loved entertaining, craved live audiences, and could not conceive of a life in which he was not constantly in the public eye, retirement was never a serious option. His compulsive performing and need for applause became something of a punch line of its own. "Bob Hope would go to the opening of a phone booth in a gas station in Anaheim, provided they have a camera and three people there," Marlon Brando once sniffed. The joke was that Hope would hardly have disagreed. "Hell, if I did," he'd say when asked about retiring, "I'd have to have an applause machine to wake me up in the morning."

By the start of the 1980s, however, age was finally starting to wear him down — his hearing getting worse, his paunch bigger, the spring in his step decidedly less springy. Yet except for his ongoing eye problems, and a minor "cardiac disturbance" in October 1978 — paramedics were rushed to his hotel room when he felt dizzy following a performance in Columbus, Ohio — he was a remarkably healthy man. He almost never got colds. Though he was a night owl, rarely going to bed before one in the morning, he never had problems sleeping. His mornings would typically start late, between 10:00 and 11:00 a.m., with a breakfast of stewed fruit, decaffeinated coffee, and a B-complex multivitamin, which included 500 mg of vitamin C. He was a meat-and-potatoes man, with a special fondness for lamb chops and a weakness for desserts, especially lemon meringue pie. Even in his old age, he kept his dancer's body well toned with golf and daily massages; made a practice of hanging from a pair of rings each day to relax his back; and walked at least a mile or two before bed, no matter where he was in the world.

He was a man of action, seemingly never bothered by stress or self-doubt. "Damn it, make a decision," he once told a family member who was hesitating over a business deal. "If it's a wrong one, we'll make another." His recipe for a long life, he told a *Saturday Evening Post* interviewer in 1981, was to stay busy and get things done. "Procrastination is the number one cause of tension," he said. "It causes more heart attacks and strokes than anything else. You always worry about the things you put off. . . . I'm a great believer in getting things taken care of fast."

In 1983, the year he turned eighty, Hope made 174 personal appearances — including 86 stage shows, 42 charity benefits, 14 golf tournaments, 15 TV commercials, and 11 guest appearances on other TV shows, in addition to the 6 specials he did for NBC. He remained a hands-on manager of his own career. "The thing that impressed me about him," said Rick Ludwin, the NBC program executive in charge of Hope's specials in the 1980s, "here was a man who had already been a superstar in every form of entertainment there ever was, and yet he always made the phone calls himself. For every show, he would personally approve the print ad. The promo people would go over to his house, show him the mock-up of the ad and the rough cuts of the [on-air] promos, and he would make suggestions. And then the morning after a show aired he would call himself to get the overnight ratings. At that age, with that level of success, he was still out there hustling."

With his daughter Linda now running Hope Enterprises and serving as executive producer of his specials, the push to make them big events continued. There was a steady stream of tributes, anniversaries, retrospectives, and birthday celebrations. In January 1981 Hope hosted a two-hour special to mark his thirtieth anniversary on NBC-TV, a black-tie affair with such old friends as

George Burns, Martha Raye, and Milton Berle in the audience, giving him an obligatory standing ovation and joining him for bits onstage. That October he went to Grand Rapids, Michigan, to host the dedication of the Gerald Ford Presidential Library, another black-tie affair, with President Reagan, Lady Bird Johnson, Henry Kissinger, and a gaggle of world leaders on hand. ("That's why I'm up here," said Hope. "I wasn't big enough to be in the audience.") He did a show marking the sixtieth anniversary of the National Football League and another commemorating the twenty-fifth anniversary of NASA. During the 1980 presidential campaign, he starred in a scripted show in which he's drafted to run for president — with Johnny Carson putting his name in nomination, Tony Randall playing his campaign manager, and a host of other stars making cameo appearances.

His ratings were up and down, but at their best — especially the birthday specials and his Christmas shows, with Hope's annual introduction of the college football all-American team and the traditional "Silver Bells" duet with one of his guest stars — they were rare bright spots for NBC, which had sunk to a dismal last place in the network ratings. "We had so many problems at NBC when I got there, but he wasn't one of them," said Fred Silverman, the former CBS and

753

ABC programming whiz who became president of NBC in 1978 (and left three years later with the network still in third place). "You knew you would get a great rating with Bob's shows. We'd put them in sweet spots on the schedule." Hope was also great for the network's corporate image — always ready to appear at an affiliates' convention, press junket, or testimonial dinner, doing his bit for the network he stayed loyal to for more than fifty years.

Ronald Reagan's election as president in 1980 was a welcome restoration for Hope. After four years of Jimmy Carter, whom Hope never warmed to (a president who didn't play golf!), the White House was safely back in Republican hands. What's more, Reagan was an old friend from their early days in Hollywood, and a frequent target of Hope jokes since his days as California governor. Hope entertained at the 1981 Inaugural Ball (though Johnny Carson landed the emcee gig) and had little trouble refreshing fifteen years of Reagan material for the new resident of the White House. Hope joked about the president's Hollywood background ("Reagan has been rehearsing for the inaugural all week — he wanted to do it in one take"), his advancing age ("He's the only candidate who calls me Sonny"), and his wife Nancy's ritzy taste in White House decor. Yet Hope was a court jester careful not to offend. After making some cracks at a 1981 USO dinner about the first lady's plans to buy expensive new china, Hope wrote Reagan a note to make sure no feathers were ruffled: "I know that Nancy was shook up a little bit by some of those dish jokes, and I realize that I laid it on a little too strong. You can rest assured that I will not do another dish joke as long as I live." Reagan's good-natured reply: "Please don't concern yourself about the humorous barbs you directed toward the new White House china — after all, if you can dish it out, we can take it!"

Though they had known each other for years, Hope and Reagan were not especially close, and Hope didn't enjoy the kind of inner-circle access that he had during the Nixon administration. His chief role appears to have been as a supplicant for official presidential messages — to the minor annoyance of the White House staff. In 1981, White House assistant Dodie Livingston got a request from the Bob Hope British Classic for a message from President Reagan for its souvenir program. She declined, explaining that the president didn't do messages for ordinary benefits — "even if it is named for Bob Hope." Miffed, a Hope representative threatened to take up the matter with his friend Ed Meese and warned that "if a message wasn't provided, Bob Hope would never do anything else for the President." Livingston appealed to Deputy Chief of Staff Mike Deaver: "We've already done a couple of messages for events honoring Hope," she wrote in a memo. "Do you want us to stick to policy on this?" The handwritten reply, apparently from Deaver: "I'm afraid the President would like to do this."

Requests for presidential messages from groups honoring Hope kept coming: from the Golf Course Superintendents Association, the National Association for Sport and Physical Education, a Boys Club dinner honoring Hope as Los Angeles Citizen of the Year. Most were granted, grudgingly, with notes such as "Randy, don't overdo — we have done tons for him" and "Keep it *short.*" Hope did little actual campaigning for Reagan, but he seemed to consider himself an unofficial part of the team. "The thing I remember about Bob Hope is that he'd show up," said campaign strategist Stu Spencer. "We were in Cincinnati once for a campaign event, and the event guy says, 'Bob Hope's here.' So we're thinking, 'What the hell are we gonna do with him?' We put him on [the program] and he entertained and did fine. But the next morning, around six or seven a.m., I get a call from Hope: 'Let's go for a walk.' I'm beat up, probably hungover, and I go walking the streets of Cincinnati with Bob Hope. It was weird."

Reagan was there for Hope too. For his

eighthieth birthday celebration, Hope turned down a fervent bid from his hometown of Cleveland to host the event and opted instead for another big fete at the Kennedy Center in Washington, again produced by Jim Lipton. Reagan not only joined Hope in the guest-of-honor box, as such stars as George C. Scott, Lucille Ball, and Phyllis Diller paid tribute, but also taped an opening segment with Hope in the Lincoln bedroom, in which they reminisced about their early days in show business. It was the first Hope special ever to originate from inside the White House.

In December 1983, Hope made his first overseas Christmas tour since the Vietnam War. The new global trouble spot was Lebanon, where a terrorist bombing in October had killed 241 US marines stationed at the Beirut Airport, sent there as part of an international peacekeeping force following Israel's 1982 invasion of the country. The marines were still in shock from the tragedy, and their confused mission ended just a couple of months later, when Reagan brought the troops home. But for Hope it was a chance to get up close and personal with his favorite audiences once again, and to try to erase some of the bad memories of Vietnam.

He brought along a new generation of glamour girls, including teenage model Brooke Shields and TV stars Ann Jillian and Cathy Lee Crosby. Ten years removed from the unpleasantness of Vietnam, the entertainers relished the chance to join one of Hope's storied overseas missions. "I always felt your career wasn't complete unless you had at least one USO show with Bob Hope under your belt," said Jillian, who was a lively song-and-dance partner for Hope and led the traditional chorus of "Silent Night." Crosby, who had worked with Hope on her "Get High on Yourself" series of public-service TV specials, said yes to his last-minute invitation, even though she was in the hospital recovering from knee surgery and had to start rehearsals on crutches.

With Beirut considered too dangerous, Hope and his troupe were restricted to entertaining on the decks of US warships off the Mediterranean coast. (Hope was helicoptered alone into Beirut on Christmas Day for a tour of the battered Marine compound, and he taped a message for the troops.) The performers were impressed with Hope's stamina and dedication at age eighty — leading the group in climbing a rope ladder from a small ferryboat to one of the warships where they entertained, or keeping his cool when a red alert roused everyone out of bed in the middle of the night aboard the USS *Guam.* "He was bigger than life," said Crosby. "For me he was an inspiration."

The two-hour special devoted to the tour, which aired on January 15, 1984, didn't have the documentary-like urgency of his Vietnam shows. Hope and his troupe performed on well-lit stages instead of on jungle hillsides, and the show seemed more stage-managed throughout. Some of the service gags dated back at least a couple of wars, and Hope's ogling of the gals was as retrograde as ever ("Is that scenery or not, huh?"). But he seemed energized by the military audiences, and the special drew a solid 18.7 Nielsen rating — no blockbuster, but better than average for Hope's shows of the period.

Not all of Hope's international ventures turned out so well. Earlier in 1983 the Bob Hope British Classic, the pro-am golf tournament launched in 1980 in an effort to replicate Hope's Palm Springs event, ran into money troubles and had to shut down after just four years, £500,000 in debt. Hope got embroiled in the mess when it was revealed that he had been paid £124,000 in fees and another £75,000 in expenses, even as the tournament was hemorrhaging money. Hope claimed all the money paid to him went toward legitimate expenses: "When you're bringing stars over and taking care of them and their fares, it's a hell of a lot of expense there." Despite the financial mismanagement, the tournament raised £150,000 for charity — which mostly went to an organization for disabled children and for the restoration of the Eltham Little Theatre in Hope's hometown, which was rechristened the Bob Hope Theatre in a grand ceremony that Hope attended in September 1982.

Hope was having some financial headaches closer to home as well. He was growing disenchanted with his daughter Linda's management of his TV operations. He thought she was spending too much money. Linda blamed the problems on her father's overpacked schedule, which left him with little time to focus on his TV shows. "He was very demanding, in a way," she said. "He expected things to be ready and on time and on budget. But sometimes you had to pay more when you didn't get decisions until the last minute — sets getting built quickly because he hadn't had a chance to decide what the sketches were going to be. It would cost him money, and he wasn't happy about that. And I'd say, 'Dad, if you'd give more time to your television show, we could get this done and we wouldn't have a lot of this overage.' "

Their clashes got so bad that in 1983 Hope replaced Linda with Elliott Kozak, whom he had originally pushed aside to create a job for his daughter. For Kozak, who had moved to ICM after leaving Hope, the return brought a measure of vindication. Despite getting ousted by her own father, Linda stayed involved, forming her own production company with her partner Nancy Malone and continuing to develop projects for him (including a TV movie based on his life and career, which never got off the ground) before returning to the fold full-time a few years later.

The awards and honors continued to pile up, so many that Hope barely had time to acknowledge them. When the National Parkinson's Foundation, whose annual dinner he hosted for more than two decades, named a road near its Miami headquarters for Hope, he asked if the dedication ceremony could be held in the morning, so he could attend it on the way to the airport. While Miami mayor Maurice Ferré was making the formal presentation, Hope's limo waited nearby with the motor running. Sometimes the honors didn't live up to his exalted expectations. The USO, the beneficiary of Hope's seventy-fifth birthday celebration at Kennedy Center, had promised to name its new headquarters building after Hope. But he was disappointed to find out that the building had been downsized, to four leased floors of an existing DC building — and that President Reagan would be out of the country and unable to attend the dedication. In 1985, Hope received one of the prestigious Kennedy Center Honors — but only after several other Hollywood stars, among them Cary Grant, Gene Kelly, and Danny Kaye, had preceded him. And when Hope was inducted into the Television Academy Hall of Fame, in November 1986, he was just one of a group of seven that also included Johnny Carson, Ernie Kovacs, Jim Henson, and Eric Sevareid. Hope's staff worked diligently behind the scenes to make sure he got the final spot on the program, and a presenter of enough stature. (Lucille Ball did the honors, which satisfied him.)

The one place where Hope did not like to stand out was on the financial pages. He was dismayed in 1982 when *Forbes* magazine put him on its list of the four hundred richest Americans, estimating his net worth at $280 million. Hope, as usual, complained that the figure was too high and even challenged *Forbes* to prove it. "If my estate is worth over fifty million dollars, I'll kiss your ass," he told reporter Richard Behar. The magazine took up the challenge and assigned Behar to track down all of Hope's real estate holdings and put a value on them. After talking with real estate brokers, appraisers, Hope lawyers, and Hope himself (who displayed an intimate knowledge of his property holdings, down to their exact acreage), Behar concluded that, after some recent sales, Hope owned about eighty-six hundred acres, much of it inaccessible mountain and canyon land worth less than some earlier estimates. In the end, *Forbes* revised its estimate of Hope's net worth downward, to around $115 million.

"When we're proved wrong, we're glad to get it straight," said the magazine. "Thanks for the memories, Bob."

Yet he was certainly rich, and he traveled in rich circles. He was friends and golfing buddies with businessmen such as Bill Fugazy, the limousine-company magnate; ice-cream-store owner Tom Carvel; and Alex Spanos, the real estate developer and owner of the San Diego Chargers. Hope and Spanos even developed a little soft-shoe dance routine together that they would sometimes perform at benefits. Being friends with Bob Hope could be a heady, weirdly public experience. Dick Cavett, who got to know Hope while writing for Johnny Carson and later as host of his own talk show, was watching *Late Night with David Letterman* one night when Hope came on as a guest and casually mentioned that he was taking Dick Cavett to the Army-Navy football game. It was the first Cavett had heard of it. (He wound up flying to the game with Hope aboard the Nabisco corporate jet and eating bean soup with him in the stands during a boring game.)

Yet Hope was a showbiz aristocrat who considered himself a man of the people. He and Dolores sent out five thousand Christmas cards a year, to practically everyone they knew or had met in their travels. He would often drive himself to the take-out window of the local In-N-Out Burger or Bob's Big Boy.

Once while traveling in the South, Hope wanted to watch a Marvin Hagler boxing match, but couldn't get the satellite broadcast on his hotel TV set. His writers drove around the neighborhood, stopped in at the first house with a satellite dish, and asked the family living there if Hope could come watch at their house — which he did.

When the young stand-up comics who worked at the Comedy Store in Los Angeles went on strike in 1979, seeking to get paid for the first time, Hope sent a telegram backing their cause. "He supported the working-man," said Tom Dreesen, a leader of the strike, who appeared at benefits with Hope and played in his golf tournament. "I never heard him bad-mouth another comedian. And I can't say that for most of the comedians I've known." Hope once asked writer Gene Perret what he thought of a young comic Hope was thinking of booking as a guest. Perret wasn't that fond of him and replied judiciously, "Sometimes he's good, and sometimes he's not that thrilling." Hope's response: "Gene, that's all of us."

Hope became friends with younger entertainers such as Brooke Shields, the statuesque teenage model who became one of his favorite guests, and with whom he developed a close father-daughter relationship. "I'd come over to his house and he'd make me grilled-cheese sandwiches," said Shields. "When he wanted his ice cream, I'd bring him his ice cream. We were very close. I was kind of like a pet. Because of my age, he kind of let me in, in a sort of daughter-granddaughter way. I think he was even closer to me than he was to his own kids."

Another younger performer who became friendly with Hope in his later years was Dave Thomas, the *SCTV* comic who did a dead-on impression of him in sketches (most memorably, a parody of *Play It Again, Sam,* in which Hope, not Bogart, is the object of Woody Allen's infatuation). Thomas was sixteen when he first saw Hope in person, performing at the Canadian National Exposition in Toronto; Thomas accosted the star in his limousine after the show and tried to shake hands with him, only to have Hope roll up the window on him. When he met Hope years later — introduced by his friend Jeff Barron, another *SCTV* veteran, who was writing for Hope — Thomas showed him a videotape of some of his *SCTV* parodies. After watching them, Hope asked if he could get a copy. "Take the tape," Thomas said, adding jokingly that Hope could take the TV and the VCR too. "No," said Hope after a moment's thought, "I'll just take the tape." He was so used to getting freebies that he took Thomas seriously.

Thomas's impersonation of Hope was affectionate. But to many younger comics,

Hope in his old age was ripe for parody — an out-of-touch, cue-card-reading relic of a vanished show-business era. Casey Keller and Richard Albrecht were stymied when they were hired to write for Hope in the mid-1980s. They broke their writer's block only when they imagined they were writing bad jokes for Dave Thomas's parody-Hope. "She's the hottest thing to shoot out of Canada since hockey pucks," they had Hope say, for instance, to introduce a new Canadian singer. Hope loved the jokes. Said Keller, "Dave Thomas had a better handle on Hope than we did. We were writing for a Hope impersonator."

Hope's material, to be sure, was sounding awfully stale by this time. Producer Jim Lipton complained that Hope's writers were feeding his complacency by giving him variations on the same lines over and over. "I knew why they were doing it," said Lipton. "Because Bob would choose them — he was familiar with them, and he liked them. But I said, 'You're doing him a disservice. It's easier on you, but in the end it's unfair to Bob.' " The writers faced their own challenges in keeping Hope current. Once they gave him a joke that included the word *Formica.* Hope didn't know what it was. "It's fake wood," Bob Mills told him. "You'll never own any of it."

Hope, moreover, could betray a tin ear

when it came to contemporary sensibilities. On July 4, 1983, he entertained at a charity benefit aboard the *Trump Princess* in New York Harbor and ad-libbed a line he had just heard in the men's room: "Have you heard? The Statue of Liberty has AIDS. Nobody knows if she got it from the mouth of the Hudson or the Staten Island Ferry." The wisecrack, reported the next day in the *New York Post,* prompted a flurry of angry letters from gay activists and others who found it insensitive, and Hope was forced to apologize.

Nowhere was Hope's status as showbiz royalty more vividly on display than Johnny Carson's *Tonight Show.* Hope's frequent guest appearances on the show clung to a familiar, almost comical ritual. He would walk out to the strains of "Thanks for the Memory" — sometimes unannounced, sup-posedly a "surprise" guest. After some banter with Johnny, sprinkled with obviously pre-pared gag lines, he would introduce a reel of taped highlights from his upcoming NBC special. Then he would scoot away, always with somewhere urgent to go. One of those who grew tired of the routine was Johnny Carson.

Hope and Carson were NBC's two biggest stars, and they had much in common. They shared the same studio, designed for Hope back in the 1950s and taken over by Carson in 1972 when he moved the show to California, but always available to Hope for his specials. Their comedy styles were mirror images of each other: Carson did a more urbane and somewhat hipper version of Hope's monologues — joking commentary on the news, topical but scrupulously nonpartisan. They were strikingly similar personality types as well: cool, remote, and emotionally detached, ingratiating on the surface, but known intimately by only a few.

Yet there were crucial differences too. Carson was a drinker, a brooder, notoriously standoffish in social settings. Hope drank little, socialized easily, and loved being the center of attention. Beneath Carson's smooth exterior, one could sense the angst. Hope's superficial bonhomie hid no inner demons. Despite his debt to Hope as a performer, Carson never warmed to the older comedian, either personally or professionally. The *Tonight Show* host would often mimic and pay homage to the classic comedians he adored — Jack Benny, Groucho Marx, George Burns. He almost never referenced Hope. "Johnny admired Hope's place in show business," said *Tonight Show* producer Peter Lassally, "but he was not a great admirer of his work."

The coolness between them was in part a reflection of their rivalry. Carson was the only star at NBC who could challenge Hope for clout at the network. Yet Hope was still king, and Carson had to defer. Carson resented the way Hope could virtually book himself on the *Tonight Show* whenever he had something to promote, which seemed to be all the time. "We'd get a request," said Lassally, "and Johnny would go, 'Again?' And I'd say, 'Do you want to tell him no?' And he'd say, 'No. You can't turn down Bob Hope.'" Hope would bring in highlight reels from his specials that went on interminably. "We'd say, give us two minutes," said Jeff Sotzing, Carson's nephew and a *Tonight Show* producer. "He'd bring in five minutes, cut together with a rusty knife. That was frustrating." Once, after a Carson monologue that went over particularly well, Hope asked during a commercial break if he could use some of the laughter on his upcoming special. Flabbergasted, Carson said okay; later, on Hope's special, Johnny claimed he could hear Ed McMahon laughing at Bob's jokes.

Worst of all, from Carson's point of view, Hope was not a good guest. He came armed with scripted jokes and would rarely engage in any genuine conversation — especially in the later years, when his bad hearing complicated the give-and-take. "There was nothing spontaneous about Hope," said Andrew Nicholls, Carson's former co–head writer. "He was a guy who relied on his writers for every topic. Johnny was very quick on his feet. Very well read. He was a guy who learned Swahili, learned Russian, learned astronomy. He appreciated people who he felt engaged with the real world. There was nothing to talk to Bob about."

In the mid-1980s, with Hope's ratings starting to sag, NBC scaled him back to just four specials a year: a fall season opener, a Christmas show, the annual birthday special in May, and one more show slotted into February or March. Each summer Hope would meet with NBC programming executives — headed by new entertainment chief Brandon Tartikoff — to bat around theme-show ideas for the coming season: Bob tries to buy NBC, for example, or starts his own Ted Turner–style news network, or (around the time of the Iran-contra hearings) gets investigated by Congress. One year Tartikoff even suggested that Hope try to book the pope as a guest for his Christmas special. (Hope could deliver presidents, but Pope John Paul II gave him a pass.) In January 1986, Hope starred in his one and only TV movie, *A Masterpiece of Murder,* playing a washed-up cop who teams with a retired cat burglar (Don Ameche) to solve crimes.

"I'm still with NBC for three simple reasons," Hope said at the start of the 1985–86 season, his thirty-sixth with the TV network: "the creative atmosphere, the fine working conditions, and the pictures I took at the 1950 Christmas party." He could still deliver big ratings on occasion. His birthday special in May 1986 — from the Pensacola Naval Air Station, with Elizabeth Taylor and Don Johnson among the guests — drew a 39 percent share of the viewing audience, the highest of any Hope special in five years. But his routine shows were no longer doing well, and with NBC back on top of the network ratings race (led by its hit sitcoms *The Cosby Show* and *Family Ties*), programmers had to be careful where they scheduled them. "There might have been a time when you could broadcast a Bob Hope special any day of the week, any time of the night, and pull in an audience regardless of the competition," an NBC executive said in 1987. "Now we're looking at protective time frames."

The shows themselves were growing increasingly leaden: tired gags, corny sketches, with Hope looking more disengaged and cue-card-dependent than ever. *Variety,* reviewing his 1989 special from the Bahamas, chided Hope for "permitting his team of writers to throw together such a generally dismal collection of excuses for gags and uniformly horrible skits which could have been bettered by a reasonably talented high school sophomore."

Yet the shows were big moneymakers for Hope. When he went to overseas locales such as the Bahamas and Tahiti, the local tourist board would typically pick up the travel and

771

hotel costs (even though the network budget already allotted for them) and also pay Hope an extra fee for "promotional" work. That would cover most of the show's production costs, leaving virtually the entire license fee paid by NBC (around $1 million per hour) as clear profit for Hope. "The whole show would cost him essentially nothing," said Kozak. "We made out like bandits really."

Hope's fee for personal appearances was up to $75,000, and he was raking in even more money from commercials. In addition to his work for Texaco, Hope became a TV pitchman for California Federal Savings, and in the mid-1980s he signed a five-year deal to appear in ads for the Silver Pages, a new telephone directory from Southwestern Bell aimed at senior citizens. Kozak negotiated a sweet deal: Hope got $1 million a year for just a couple of days' work, and when Southwestern Bell ended the campaign prematurely, after three years, the company had to pay him $500,000 just to get out of the contract. (Kozak, who often felt underappreciated, was miffed at Hope's blasé reaction to the windfall. "He just takes the check," said Kozak. "No 'thank you.' I was so pissed that he didn't acknowledge what a hell of a deal that was.")

The legacy burnishing, meanwhile, continued at a steady clip. NBC renamed a street near its Burbank headquarters Bob Hope

Drive. A retirement community for Air Force veterans in the Florida panhandle was christened Bob Hope Village. In January 1988, Hope was guest of honor for the opening of the Bob Hope Cultural Center, a sixty-six-acre arts complex in Palm Springs — with President Reagan among the bigwigs in the audience, Van Cliburn playing the national anthem, and another slew of Hollywood stars on hand to pay their respects. He made *The Guinness Book of Records* as the recipient of more honors and awards than any other entertainer in the world. (Hope's publicists were always thinking. In the mid-1970s, the town of Hope, Arkansas — later to become famous as Bill Clinton's birthplace — invited Hope to its hundredth birthday celebration. Frank Liberman replied that Hope might come if the town would change its name to Bob Hope, Arkansas.)

Hope was back overseas at Christmas in 1987, traveling to the Persian Gulf (with Barbara Eden, Connie Stevens, and his granddaughter Miranda along for the ride) to entertain US troops aboard warships sent there in response to a threat by the Ayatollah Khomeini to cut off oil shipments. "I think this is appropriate," said Hope, aboard the USS *Midway,* "the oldest aircraft carrier meets the oldest operational comedian." Assuming it would be his last Christmas tour, Hope followed up with a book, *Don't Shoot,*

773

It's Only Me (written with Mel Shavelson), recapping his forty-plus years of entertaining the troops. Yet there would be one more, unexpected tour of duty: another Christmas trip to the Persian Gulf in 1990, where a US buildup of forces was under way in response to Saddam Hussein's invasion of Kuwait.

Hope by this time was eighty-seven and getting frail. His daughter Linda came along to provide support and produce the special, and Dolores joined them as well. Because of security precautions in the walk-up to the US invasion of Iraq, Hope and his entertainers (among them Ann Jillian, Marie Osmond, and the Pointer Sisters) were whisked from show to show by helicopter, often without being told their destination. Press coverage of the trip was severely restricted. (When reporters complained, Hope commiserated, "I live for the press. That's not my idea, believe me.") In deference to Islamic customs, moreover, the single women in the troupe were not allowed to perform in Saudi Arabia at all, but confined to shipboard shows and a stop in Bahrain.

Yet Hope weathered the trip well. "He was stronger than most of us," said Gene Perret, the writer Hope brought along. "He worked hard, did the monologues. He would do dance numbers with the women — which is not easy on a ship." Hope made the usual wisecracks about US servicemen on a mission far from home ("Where else can you see signs that say YANKEE GO HOME signed by Yankees?") and took a few jingoistic digs at Saddam Hussein (the Iraqi dictator should get a star on the Hollywood Walk of Fame, Hope said, "so we can all spit on it"). With the tight restrictions on what Hope could show of his travels, the ninety-minute special played more like a typical Hope variety show, with full-length numbers from most of the guest stars. Even Dolores, after being edited out of so many of Hope's earlier tours, was showcased in two numbers, including a duet with Bob on "White Christmas."

Hope's usual patriotic closing had a prosaic, almost boilerplate quality: "Let's pray that somehow or some way, we can destroy the menace that's causing the trouble over there and it won't be long before our servicemen and -women are back home where they belong." But the response from the troops was enthusiastic, the ratings decent — and, for once, the war over quickly. The US invaded Iraq, launching the first Gulf War, just days after Hope's show aired on January 12, 1991, and by April, Hope was able to host a homecoming special, featuring marines from the 29 Palms training center near Palm Springs, whom he had met in Saudi Arabia. Former president Ford and Jimmy Stewart were on hand for the show, and General Norman Schwarzkopf and Secretary of State

Colin Powell sent messages of thanks. Hope hailed the successful military campaign as "a whole new concept in politics" because President Bush "did everything he said he was going to do." Hope's last war, at least, ended in victory.

By the late eighties, Hope's physical decline was becoming noticeable even to casual viewers. Though he was still in overall good health, both his eyesight and hearing were deteriorating badly. He had another flare-up of his eye hemorrhaging in 1982, but this time in his right eye — previously his good one — and it seriously affected his vision. The cue cards had to be blown up extralarge so that he could read them, and they continued to grow as the years went on, the words scrawled by Barney McNulty in such gargantuan letters that a single joke would sometimes take up three or four cards.

Hope's hearing was getting worse as well. His ear specialist, Dr. Howard House, prescribed a hearing aid, but Hope was too vain to wear one. "I can still hear the laughs," he would tell friends. He had trouble hearing normal conversation, and it became hard for him to pick up the musical cues when recording songs for his specials. He was wandering off the beat so often that musical director Bob Alberti had to kneel beside Hope's cue cards during the tapings, giving him a visual downbeat for each line. And still Hope would sometimes lose the beat.

Producer Jim Lipton noticed the deterioration in the last birthday special he produced for Hope, from Paris in 1989. The monologue went so badly that Hope had to stay behind in the theater to rerecord some of the jokes. Lipton had written new lyrics for "Thanks for the Memory" in French, spelling them out phonetically on the cue cards, but Hope couldn't handle them. It was painful for both of them. "Great job," said Lipton, after Hope finished his monologue. "Aw, come on," Hope said. "I used to be twice as fast."

"Starting in the late eighties, it was affecting the work," said NBC's Rick Ludwin. "It would take him longer to do the monologue. He'd stumble over things. He'd get a little frustrated with himself. There was such goodwill on the part of the audience that they forgave him — they still loved that they were being entertained by Bob Hope. But the post-production on the show became more difficult, to sort of Scotch-tape together the monologue and have it appear as much as possible to flow logically."

The man once known as Rapid Robert was running down. His physical limitations were hard for him to accept, and he grew testy about them. Taping a sketch with Brooke Shields for one show, Hope kept missing his cue, and Shields tried to help by sneaking the line to him under her breath. Hope blew up at her. "He got really mad at me," she recalled. " 'What are you doing that for, you little idiot?' I just burst into tears because he had never yelled at me before. And then I realized he was mad at himself because he didn't hear the cue. I thought I was helping him. And it seemed that I was disrespecting him."

On the *Tonight Show,* his hearing problems were making his guest appearances even more of a trial than they already were. He often had trouble picking up Carson's questions, and Johnny had to stick precisely to the notes his staff gave him; if he asked a question out of order, Hope might answer a different question. Still, Hope kept coming on the show, his frailties on full display for the national TV audience. "If I ever end up like that, guys," Carson said to his writers, "I want you to shoot me."

Carson retired gracefully in 1992. But Hope soldiered on, battling not just his failing faculties but also network inattention. Writer Gene Perret had painful memories of one of Hope's last monologues. The fading star was shunted to a new studio, and when he arrived to do his monologue, a tiny crowd of only around fifty people was waiting in the audience. (NBC claimed the buses hadn't shown up.) Hope struggled to get any reaction from the sparse crowd, as Perret watched uncomfortably from the wings. Finally Hope stopped midway through, in distress, and called Perret over, asking him for some last-minute jokes about an award Johnny Carson had just been given by the outgoing president, Bush.

Perret quickly came up with a few lines ("Those lame ducks stick together"), and Hope got at least a few laughs before wrapping up the monologue. But afterward, when Perret asked Hope if he wanted to go over the videotape, as they usually did to start the editing process, Hope demurred, saying, "We'll do it later." For Perret, it was a poignant sign of defeat. "He knew it was a bad monologue. It was sad."

Along with the procession of awards and tributes that filled Hope's waning years were a couple of unwelcome distractions. One was a nasty dispute over something Hope had hoarded, and mostly guarded from public view, for years: his land.

By the 1980s the bulk of Hope's real estate holdings lay in the mountainous areas north and west of Los Angeles, a 240-square-mile area designated in 1978 as the Santa Monica Mountains Recreation Area. A state agency called the Santa Monica Mountains Conservancy was seeking to buy up as much of this land as possible, to preserve its pristine views, hiking areas, and endangered wildlife. But

Hope, who had watched the land appreciate wildly in value since he'd bought it in the 1950s and 1960s, was starting to sell it to developers — at prices far higher than what the conservancy could afford.

Several parcels had already been sold off. Hope got $13 million for one tract near Malibu Creek State Park, from a developer who built condominiums on it, and $10 million for another 195 acres in Calabasas, where a housing development was planned. But what set off a firestorm was a deal to sell the Jordan Ranch — a twenty-three-hundred-acre parcel in the Simi Hills north of the Ventura Freeway, which Hope had bought in the 1950s for a reported $300,000. In 1987 a Maryland-based developer called Potomac Investments acquired an option to buy the land from Hope for $25 million, pending approval of its plans to build a PGA-owned golf course on it, along with a development of more than eleven hundred homes.

Years of complicated negotiations followed, involving the developer, zoning officials, environmentalists, and Hope's lawyers. The plans for developing Jordan Ranch had a major stumbling block. The area lacked an access road to a major highway, and the only place to build one was through Cheeseboro Canyon — on land already owned by the National Park Service. So a land-swap compromise was proposed. The Park Service agreed to give up a fifty-nine-acre sliver of Cheeseboro Canyon to allow the developers to build an access road. In return, Potomac would donate the undeveloped half of Jordan Ranch — a picturesque area known as China Flat, long prized by environmentalists — to the state so it could be preserved as parkland.

The proposed deal split the environmental community. The Santa Monica Mountains Conservancy and the Sierra Club backed the plan, reasoning that giving up a small slice of national-park land in return for preserving China Flat was worth it. But other environmentalists hotly opposed the deal, arguing that the government had no right to give up any national-park land to pave the way for a housing development in the area.

The dispute boiled over in early 1990, covered extensively in the local press and on TV news. Hope was cast as the environmental villain, a greedy landowner who cared more about golf courses than protecting California's natural beauty. "No one has a larger ownership of land in the Santa Monicas, and yet has not given up one inch," said Margot Feuer, of the Save the Mountain Park Coalition. "What is it that drives this man?" An editorial cartoon in the *Los Angeles Times* showed a map of the Santa Monica Mountains Recreation Area, with the topographical details replaced by an eighteen-hole golf course. The caption: "Faith, Hope and Damn Little Charity." One Saturday morning protesters showed up in front of Hope's Toluca Lake home: HONK IF YOU THINK BOB HOPE HAS ENOUGH MONEY read one sign. The controversy raged in the letters columns of the *Los Angeles Times.* "Hope doesn't owe anyone anything," wrote one reader. "But if he doesn't see the desperate need to maintain a buffer of open space around Los Angeles and more importantly, respond with a gift of land to the Santa Monica Mountains National Recreational Area, I for one am going to be sorry I ever went to any of his films, or watched any of his numskull TV specials. Thanks for the memories! Thanks for nothing!"

Hope was dismayed to find himself in the role of an environmental meanie. He had a perfect right to profit from the land investments he had made decades ago, he argued. "I didn't hold it for twenty-five years and pay taxes on it just to give it away," he told a reporter. His lawyers reminded people of all the work Hope had done for charity and claimed that he had already given away fifteen hundred acres of his land in various places, including the eighty acres in Rancho Mirage that he had donated for the Eisenhower Medical Center.

But the environmental protests succeeded in scuttling the land-swap deal, and Hope soon backed down. After another round of negotiations, a new deal was worked out, with Hope and the developer making major concessions. Potomac agreed to move its housing development and golf course out of Jordan Ranch altogether, combining it instead with another development being planned for Ahmanson Ranch, in Las Virgines Canyon. At the same time, Hope agreed to sell all of Jordan Ranch, along with the rest of his property in the area — including the 4,369-acre Runkle Ranch farther north and 339 acres overlooking the ocean in Malibu's Corral Canyon — to the government for parkland. Hope would get $29.5 million, substantially below the land's market value, and the state would get a huge swath of mountain and canyon land protected from developers for good.

More zoning battles, objections from environmentalists, and lawsuits followed. But Hope was instantly transformed from environmental villain into public-spirited land donor. "In preserving these open spaces, Bob Hope is making a special gift to all Californians," said California governor Pete Wilson, when the deal was signed in November 1991. For Hope, the financial sacrifice must have been painful, but it was worth the restoration of his public image. "The knocks he's taken from environmentalists for not wanting to give up the properties for so long finally got to him," a Hope associate told the *Los Angeles Times.* "Here you have this national hero who has given generously of himself his entire life, and I think he figured the criticism just wasn't worth it."

Hope's image took some blows on another, more personal front around the same time, as some serious breaches appeared in the cone of silence that had long shrouded his extramarital sex life. First, in 1991, one of his former secretaries, Jan King, regaled readers of the *Globe* tabloid with an account of Hope's womanizing, which she helped cover up for years. Two years later, Arthur Marx, drawing on King's account as well as his own interviews, published a gossipy tell-all biography, *The Secret Life of Bob Hope.*

Marx's bio, brought out by the small New Jersey publisher Barricade Books, was an uneasy mix of gossip and reporting, sloppily written and wildly unbalanced — with pages and pages devoted to minor Hope dalliances as if they were Soviet spy cases. Hope refused to comment on the book, and his publicist Ward Grant dismissed it as "just a lot of old stuff, nothing new." One libel suit was brought against it, by Hope's former son-in-law, Nathaniel Lande, who disputed some allegations about his relationship with the family and won a $10,000 judgment in a jury trial. Yet Marx's account of Hope's womanizing was never seriously challenged, and most of those in Hope's inner circle who would talk candidly agreed that it rang true.

Even in his eighties, Hope still had a roving eye. His last girlfriend, according to both Marx and Hope publicist Frank Liberman, was Sandy Vinger, a former writer on his California Federal Savings commercials, who was his frequent companion in the 1980s. In 1994, when Hope was ninety-one, she filed a breach-of-contract suit, claiming that Hope had hired her in 1974 as an "assistant and companion," on the promise that he would support her for life. The suit was dismissed in 1996 after an undisclosed out-of-court settlement. The amazing thing is how little of all this made its way into the mainstream press. Even in the age of tabloid television and a far-more-aggressive gossip industry, Hope's all-American image, for most of his fans, remained unsullied.

Hope's all-American family, meanwhile, was going through its own trials. His youngest daughter, Nora, had divorced her first husband, Sam McCullagh, after ten years of marriage (and one daughter, Alicia) and married Bruce Somers, the ex-husband of actress Suzanne Somers, a college friend of Nora's. Her second marriage exacerbated Nora's already-strained relationship with her mother. Dolores, the strict Catholic, disapproved of the divorce, and she didn't get along with Nora's new husband and three stepchildren.

According to a friend of Nora's, the discord came to a head when Dolores told Nora that Bruce and the stepchildren were not welcome at an upcoming holiday get-together. Nora never spoke to her mother again. She eventually cut off contact with her father and the rest of the family as well — even her brother Kelly, with whom she had been close.

The abrupt renunciation of her adoptive family was inexplicable to many in the Hope circle. Nora had been a favorite of Bob's — high-spirited, fun, eager to please her dad. But she chafed under her mother's stern discipline and was never comfortable living in the aura of her father's celebrity. "I remember always Nora not being at all happy with the public persona and what was required," said Linda Hope. "Her dream was to marry a shoe salesman and live in a little house with a white picket fence and have nothing to do with all the Bob Hope hoopla." Nora's friend pinned much of the blame for the rift on Somers, her second husband, who convinced her that the relationship with her family was toxic and that she needed to break from them.

For Dolores the estrangement was obviously painful. For Bob, maybe less so. Whatever angst it caused him was kept, as always, well hidden. "I don't think it really deeply affected him," said Linda. "It affected my mother more. But maybe he just didn't talk about it." Nora later divorced Somers, sought out her birth parents, and continued to reject any attempts by friends and family to reestablish contact. She didn't attend Bob Hope's funeral, or Dolores's eight years later.

Hope's ninetieth birthday, on May 29, 1993, presented a challenge for NBC. A big celebration was clearly called for, but Hope's eyesight and hearing were so bad that he could no longer carry a show on his own. Instead, the network prepared an elaborate three-hour special for which Hope would largely be a bystander. He and Dolores were seated at a table on a wing of the stage, as a parade of celebrities (including taped messages from President Clinton and all five living ex-presidents) paid tribute to him. To help him follow what was going on, and for the few segments in which he briefly participated, producer Don Mischer put a small IFB microphone in his ear, so that Linda, sitting in the control room, could brief him on who was there and what was happening.

Even Hope's limited role caused some anxiety. Johnny Carson agreed to do a monologue on the show (the first and only one he would do after leaving the *Tonight Show*) on the assurance that Hope would not do one as well; despite his frustrations with Hope, Johnny didn't want the master to be embarrassed. George Burns, seven years older than Hope, was apprehensive about the small bit of comedy business that had been written for the two of them. "I don't know if I can do this because his timing is really off," he told Mischer. In the end, Burns, seated next to Hope, did all the talking. When Hope got up onstage for a little patter with Dorothy Lamour, he stepped on one of her lines.

Still, the ninetieth birthday special — which aired Friday night, May 14, and beat the competition in the ratings — was a well-produced and entertaining show. Dance production numbers were interspersed with clips from Hope's movies, TV shows, stage career, and overseas tours, introduced by guest stars ranging from Roseanne Arnold to Walter Cronkite. Dolores sang "Paper Moon," the first number Hope had seen her perform in a New York nightclub back in 1933. Through some video trickery, Lucie Arnaz replaced Shirley Ross in the "Thanks for the Memory" scene from *The Big Broadcast of 1938*. Servicemen from each of the four wars in which Hope had entertained came onstage to convey their thanks. Longtime colleagues such as Barney McNulty, Hal Kanter, NBC's Rick Ludwin, and even Hope's handyman did brief walk-ons to wish him happy birthday. Hope took it all in amiably, smiling and nodding with approval, occasionally getting misty eyed, and gathering himself for a few words of thanks at the end. At three hours, the show seemed to never end, but it was a tasteful and often touching farewell.

Except that it wasn't a farewell. Hope refused to quit, continuing to do specials that tested the creativity of Linda and NBC to find formats that would demand little of him. More shows were essentially compilations of old clips, or "young comedians" specials, in which Hope would simply be trotted out to introduce a lineup of new standup comics. His Christmas show in 1993 was a visit to the Hope home (actually an NBC studio set) for a family get-together, featuring Hope's children and grandchildren and drop-ins by such stars as Loni Anderson, Barbara Eden, and Joey Lawrence, with Bob largely an onlooker. For friends and fans alike, the spectacle was getting painful. "Bob Hope could have done what Johnny Carson did — kind of step aside," said David Letterman in a *Rolling Stone* interview. "I watched a lot of his early films over the holidays on AMC, and, Jesus, talk about a guy who was sharp and on the money and appealing and fresh and charismatic. Then I saw Bob Hope's [Christmas show] and it was tough to watch. If it had been a funeral, you would have preferred the coffin be closed. I mean, can he be gratified by that?"

The family gently tried to coax him into retirement. "I said, 'Dad, you don't want to keep on with this,' " Linda recalled. " 'This is not you. You don't want people to remember you at less than your best.' And he'd say, 'Yeah, but I've got a deal with NBC.' He was just so habituated to doing this kind of thing that I think it was very difficult for him to let go of it." Handling him, never easy for his producer-daughter, became even tougher. During the taping of a young-comedians special in 1994, Dave Thomas witnessed a tense encounter when Linda tried to set up a shot for her father to say a quick good-night. "I'm not doing that!" he snapped at her. Linda backed off and went on to other matters. A few minutes later, Hope took the microphone, the cameras scrambled into place, and he wrapped up the show with a few jokes. "Now that's the way I say good night," he told Thomas, as he sat back down. "Not like goddamn Walter Cronkite."

He continued to make his annual appearances at the Bob Hope Desert Classic, hitting a drive on the first tee to launch the tournament, before retiring for the rest of the event. He had one last hurrah in February 1995, when three living presidents — Clinton, Ford, and Bush — played a round with Hope and the tournament's defending champion, Scott Hoch. Though he could barely play anymore, Hope puttered around the course with them, hitting most of his drives from the middle of the fairway and skipping a couple of holes. His friend Andrew Coffey, who was at the wheel of his golf cart, had to drive halfway onto the greens, so Bob wouldn't have to walk too far to putt. Hope was ready to quit after nine holes, but President Clinton was enjoying it so much he said he wanted to play eighteen. "Dammit," Hope grumbled, as he returned to the course. Hope retired after a few more holes, and President Bush won the presidential match with a round of 92, beating Clinton by a stroke.

Clinton, a lifelong fan of Hope's, had first met the comedian in the late seventies, when Clinton was Arkansas governor and they had dinner together on the town square in Fayetteville after a Hope appearance at the University of Arkansas. A few months after the Palm Springs match, they had another chance to bond on the golf course when Hope was traveling to Washington and called Clinton at the White House to ask if he had time for nine holes. "I practically fell out of my chair," Clinton recalled. "But it happened to be a day when I had some free time. So I cleared the schedule and took him out to the Army Navy club [in Arlington, Virginia] because it was close." Though the ninety-two-year-old Hope could barely see, he could still hit the ball. On a narrow 173-yard par three, with woods on the left and a steep hill on the right, Clinton was astonished to see Hope drive the ball dead straight onto the green.

"He could see the ball below his feet, but

he had no distance vision," Clinton said. "We got up to the green, and the young fellow who was with him was helping him aim his putts. And I said, 'Bob, you have a twenty-foot putt, slightly uphill, and it's gonna break about six, maybe eight inches max, to the left.' He said, 'I got it.' The guy lined him up, he hit the ball to two inches, and tapped in for a par. For a guy his age, it was just amazing."

Back at NBC, Hope's specials — now mostly shunted to low-viewership Saturday nights — were getting the worst ratings of his career. After his ninetieth birthday special NBC was rumored to be ready to retire him, but the network was careful not to force the issue. "Brandon Tartikoff regarded Bob Hope as an institution and part of the DNA of NBC," said Ludwin. "There was never a thought of canceling him." But clearly he couldn't continue much longer. In 1995, as he was planning a trip to Europe for a special to celebrate the fiftieth anniversary of VE Day, Dolores finally threw up her hands. "We're doing this one," she said. "But this has got to be the last." That December, for the first time since 1950, there was no Bob Hope Christmas special. An NBC spokesman explained that a mutual decision had been made to "devote our energies toward specials in 1996."

An exit plan was quietly worked out. "There

came a point where all the parties involved decided that it was really tough to go forward," said Ludwin. "We discussed with Linda and the press reps how we wanted to handle it. Because when you're dealing with someone who has been in business at NBC for six decades, you have to handle it diplomatically." Ludwin remembered how Lucille Ball, when her ratings at CBS were falling, announced that she was leaving the network. "I thought to myself, 'What a classy way to handle this. What network could fire Lucille Ball? She had to fire the network.' So I thought to myself, 'That's the way this has to be handled. No one can fire Bob Hope. He has to fire us.' "

One last special was scheduled: a retrospective of Hope's presidential humor, tied in with his soon-to-be-published book, *Dear Prez, I Wanna Tell Ya!* On October 23, 1996, one month before the telecast, Hope took out a full-page ad in *Variety,* the *Hollywood Reporter,* and the *Los Angeles Times* — paid for by NBC — announcing that it would be his last NBC special. "Guess what? I've decided to become a FREE AGENT," the announcement read. "My thanks to NBC, for making it possible to be part of your lives all these years. It's been a great ride. Now, caddy, hand me my 7-iron."

His publicist Ward Grant stressed that

Hope was not retiring, but would be touring to promote his new book, updating his autobiography, and overseeing the release of his specials on home video. Hope was resistant to the bitter end. "It was sort of a mutual thing," said Linda Hope of the retirement scenario, "although Dad was less mutual about it. If NBC had said, 'We'll do another year,' Dad would have done it."

Hope's final NBC special, *Laughing with the Presidents,* aired on November 23, 1996. Tony Danza was the host, introducing film clips of Hope's encounters with presidents and engaging in a bit of carefully edited conversation with him. The good-bye was painless, if anticlimactic. "This TV entry? An amusing look at Hope's tilting with Presidents," said *Variety* in its review. "His comedy and his career? Both terrif."

The last few years were not pretty. Hope's eyesight and hearing were going, and signs of dementia were starting to appear. In his few public appearances, at various benefit dinners and ceremonial events, Hope could seem confused or disoriented. His short-term memory was spotty, and he had trouble recognizing people — though it was difficult to tell if the problem was his eyesight or his mind.

Remarkably, he could still pull himself together in front of a microphone. In January

1997 he appeared briefly onstage at a benefit performance given by Dolores and Rosemary Clooney in Palm Springs. After Bob's retirement, Dolores had decided to restart her long-dormant singing career, and she recorded an album of standards, *Now and Then.* She and Clooney then prepared a nightclub act together, which they debuted at Palm Desert's McCallum Theatre, to a sold-out crowd. At the end of the show they called Bob onstage.

"Backstage he was not in good shape," recalled Michael Feinstein, the cabaret singer, who became close to both Bob and Dolores in the later years. "We were worried. But, wouldn't you know it, once he was introduced, he went right to center stage, took the microphone, and he was right there." He joined Clooney in a duet of "It's De-Lovely," his old number from *Red, Hot and Blue.* The gimmick was that Bob merely repeated each *it's,* with Clooney picking up the rest of the lyrics. Before they started, she took out her score and gave him one the size of a postage stamp. "Can you spare it?" Hope quipped.

At other times, however, he could seem like a very old man. He was in the audience when Rosemary and Dolores opened their show together at New York City's Rainbow and Stars. Dolores appeared first, singing "Paper Moon" and "I Thought About You" and teaming with Clooney for Sondheim's "Old

795

Friend," before turning the show over to Clooney, the headliner. The *New York Times* gave Dolores a nice review: "Her timbre was clear and strong, her intonation pitch-perfect," wrote critic Stephen Holden. But Hope couldn't help upstaging his wife, even in his dotage. Bill Tush, an entertainment reporter who was covering the event for CNN's *Showbiz Today,* recalled the uncomfortable scene when Hope, apparently unable to hear, began talking loudly during Dolores's numbers. She gamely ignored him, before finishing her set and returning to the table.

"Mrs. Hope joined Bob at his table and Rosemary sang," Tush recalled. "Then I could hear him — 'What are you doing? Stop that!' I looked, and she was rubbing his head, lovingly. 'Stop kissing me. Stop that!' It really got embarrassing for everybody, and finally they got up to leave. I couldn't help but look. When he stood up, his pants were undone. He pulled them up to button them. Meanwhile Rosemary kept the show going. Mrs. Hope and a handler helped Bob out. He was stooped over and still yelling things out, like 'Leave me alone! I'm okay!' Out the door they went, and that was the last time I saw Bob Hope. What a way to remember."

At home he settled into a comfortable routine. He still slept late, waking between 10:00 and 11:00 a.m. His caretaker, J. Dennis Paulin, would read to him from the morning

Los Angeles Times, and large-print editions were made of business documents that he needed to see. He would watch *Jeopardy!* on TV (with headphones, so he could hear) and still took his late-night walks, though they were usually indoors now — up and down the aisles of the local Vons supermarket in Toluca Lake, or, when he was in Palm Springs, through the terminal building of the Palm Springs Airport. Sometimes, in Toluca Lake, Paulin would let him take the wheel of his golf cart and drive the five blocks to Lakeside for a couple of holes of golf. Paulin had a key to the back gate and could cut onto the course and look for a vacant hole where Bob could play, then take him back to the clubhouse for a fake Brandy Alexander. In 1996, after a lifetime of dilatory churchgoing, Hope acceded to his devout wife's wishes and was baptized into the Catholic Church.

Reports of his failing health, along with photos showing his stooped frame and red-rimmed eyes, would occasionally surface in the tabloids, with dire headlines about his "tragic last days." On June 4, 1998, AP actually reported his death by mistake, when an advance obituary for him was inadvertently posted on the Internet. When the House Republican leader, Representative Dick Armey, heard the news, he passed it on to Representative Bob Stump, the Republican chairman of the Veterans' Affairs Committee, who delivered a eulogy on the floor of the House. "We're all going to miss him," said Stump, praising Hope as "the best friend anyone in uniform ever had." When reporters began phoning, Linda calmly informed them that her father was having breakfast.

He made a few trips to Washington for events honoring him — including a visit to the White House, where President Clinton signed a congressional resolution making Hope the first Honorary Veteran of the US Armed Forces — but Dolores did most of the talking. After returning from a trip in June 2000, for the opening of the Bob Hope Gallery of Entertainment at the Library of Congress, Hope had a major health scare. Some renovations at the Toluca Lake house were not finished, and the Palm Springs house was closed for the season, so when he returned, Hope moved temporarily into the old house on El Alameda street. There he began having stomach pains and was rushed by ambulance to the Eisenhower Medical Center, suffering from gastrointestinal bleeding. Family spokesmen minimized the event, but he was seriously ill. "He was in very critical condition," said Paulin. "It was a pretty harrowing event." Hope recovered, but after that needed full-time nursing care.

He lingered for three more years — bedridden most of the time, but brought out by Dolores in a wheelchair for family get-togethers. In July 2001, Pentagon officials came to the house in Toluca Lake to present him with the Order of Horatio Gates Gold Medal, for his work raising the morale of US soldiers around the world. In April 2003, as his hundredth birthday approached, NBC marked the occasion with one more tribute special, *100 Years of Hope Humor.* He got more than two thousand birthday cards — from President George W. Bush and Queen Elizabeth, among others — and at least thirty-five states proclaimed his birthday "Bob Hope Day." "His eyes light up with each thing I tell him," Linda told *Variety,* "and they bring a big smile to his face." On the day he turned one hundred, the milestone his grandfather never quite reached, he had his favorite dinner of roast lamb with mint jelly.

He lived just two months longer. On Sunday night, July 27, 2003, with family members and a few household staff gathered at his bedside in Toluca Lake and Dolores holding his hand, Bob Hope died peacefully, officially of pneumonia. The family waited until early morning to notify the police, who had a security plan in place and set up roadblocks around the house to keep away gawkers and the press. Some TV news crews beat the roadblocks and camped outside anyway.

The funeral was low-key, with a hundred

family members, household staff, and caregivers gathered at 6:00 a.m. Wednesday morning in the chapel at St. Charles Borromeo Church. Hope's two sons, Tony and Kelly, and his grandson Zach, spoke briefly at the thirty-minute service. Hope could have been buried with pomp at Arlington National Cemetery, or in the Hollywood showplace for dead celebrities, Forest Lawn. But Dolores opted for quieter dignity, and his flag-draped coffin was transported in a police motorcade to the San Fernando Mission Cemetery, in Mission Hills, California, where he was laid to rest.

A month later, on August 27, the family held a larger, invitation-only funeral mass at St. Charles Borromeo. The eulogists included Senator Dianne Feinstein and General Richard Myers, chairman of the Joint Chiefs of Staff. Mickey Rooney, Kathryn Crosby, Tom Selleck, Raquel Welch, Brooke Shields, Nancy Reagan, and former president Gerald Ford and wife, Betty, were among those in the audience. "He was leading us to something deeper than laughter — joy," said Cardinal Roger Mahony, archbishop of Los Angeles, who conducted the service. Later in the afternoon, a more raucous memorial was held at the Academy of Television Arts & Sciences, where friends and colleagues — including Sid Caesar, Jack Carter, Lee Iacocca, and Larry King — paid tribute with stories and jokes. "I couldn't be here in spirit, so I came in person," said Red Buttons.

His oldest son, Tony, died unexpectedly of a heart aneurysm just a year later, at age sixty-three. Dolores lived long enough to celebrate her own hundredth birthday and then some (she died in September 2011, at age 102). Linda, the daughter who tended to her father so loyally in his final years, took charge of the legacy, orchestrating the tributes that dribbled on for years and tending to his estate, estimated at around $300 million at the time of his death.

His death triggered the usual round of media tributes that routinely follow the passing of any major showbiz celebrity: the front-page obituaries, the encomiums from colleagues and friends, the endless loop of film clips on the entertainment shows and cable news channels. There was more, befitting a national hero. The flags were lowered to half-staff. "Today America has lost a great citizen," said President George W. Bush in a statement. Former president Clinton praised Hope's "matchless legacy of laughs to people all over the world." Nancy Reagan said, "Losing him is like losing a member of the family."

Yet the response to Hope's passing seemed restrained, almost dutiful. The master of comic timing had, quite simply, lingered too long, the memories of his great years tarnished by his long and very public decline. The *New York Times'* obituary for Hope had been sitting on the shelf so long that its author, former film critic Vincent Canby, had himself been dead for three years. *Time* magazine gave the comedian of the century a polite but meager one-page send-off. (The death of George Harrison, the third-best Beatle, rated a cover story.) NBC, having just aired its hundredth-birthday tribute to Hope in April — and rerun it on his birthday in May — opted not to gear up another one. Instead, on the evening after his death, the network ran a two-minute "salute" to Hope at the beginning of prime time — then returned to regularly scheduled programming.

In the years that followed, even the people most indebted to Hope seemed to take him for granted. Younger stand-up comics, when asked about the comedians who influenced them, would cite rebel role models such as Lenny Bruce, and occasionally an old-timer such as Groucho Marx or Jack Benny. Almost no one mentioned Bob Hope — an odd omission, considering that he essentially invented their art form. His movie work never enjoyed a revival-house rediscovery or received the kind of film-buff attention accorded more fashionable comics — W. C. Fields or the Marx Brothers — or the silent-film clowns. Unlike Lucille Ball, Jackie Gleason, and other comedy stars of TV's golden age — who starred in sitcoms that lived on endlessly in cable reruns and thus gained new generations of fans — Hope appeared mainly in variety shows that have been out of circulation for years, leaving most younger audiences with little memory of him, except in his declining later years.

Yet the show-business world he left behind would not have been the same without him. Every late-night talk-show host who does an opening monologue is tilling the ground that Bob Hope first plowed. Every year's burst of Oscar frenzy — the obsessive handicapping of nominees, tracking of odds, dissection of the studios' Oscar campaigns — can be traced back, at least in part, to Hope's role in making the Academy Awards show an annual must-see event. The entire image-making industry that rules Hollywood — the publicists, agents, managers, and studio executives who create the stars, shape their careers, and protect their private lives — is an elaboration of the publicity and brand-building machinery that Hope pioneered.

His passion for public service had a lasting impact as well. During the Iraq War, comedians as distant from his sensibility as David Letterman and Stephen Colbert carried on his tradition of traveling to the war zone and entertaining the troops. When George Clooney, at the 2010 Emmy Awards, accepted a Bob Hope Humanitarian Award for his work for human rights and disaster relief around the world, he took a moment to credit the award's namesake — Bob, and Dolores too — for their charitable work and for embodying, as Clooney put it, "the best version of the term *celebrity.*"

Even his long, long good-bye was somehow inevitable and fitting. Hope needed to keep performing because he couldn't stop believing that the audience needed him. It was understandable for an entertainer who never forgot the days when a visit from Bob Hope meant everything to a lonely soldier on a distant battlefield, or an anxious family gathered around the radio in times of national crisis.

In 1943, on his first tour of England during World War II, Hope and his entertainment troupe were traveling from camp to camp through the moors of Devonshire. But they couldn't go everywhere, and one unit of six hundred men found out that Hope was going to miss them. Disappointed, they heard that he was doing a show ten miles away, and the entire camp, officers as well as enlisted men, marched the ten miles across the wild moors to see him. But when they arrived, they found that the show was indoors and packed to capacity, with no room for them. All they could do was turn around and start the ten-mile trek back.

After the show Hope was told of their disappointment. He commandeered a couple of jeeps, piled his troupe into them, and caught up with the soldiers, still trudging back to their camp. With a few boards laid out across the jeeps for a stage, Hope did a forty-minute show for the men in the driving rain. "I love the English weather," he cracked, wearing a tin hat borrowed from one of the GIs. "It's so dependable." By the end of the show, Frances Langford's hair was streaming wet across her face, and Tony Romano's guitar was so drenched he had to spend half the night drying it. The applause was like nothing they had ever heard.

"Never make 'em think you don't care," Hope once told a reporter, explaining why he always signed autographs. "Your time's not your own. You owe 'em." They owed him too. He may have taken a little too long to leave the stage, but at his peak — a peak that lasted longer than almost anyone else's — he was the best version of celebrity. He was there in spirit. And he was there in person.

ACKNOWLEDGMENTS

This book would not have been possible without the generous help and cooperation of Linda Hope, Bob Hope's daughter. She sat for several hours of interviews; allowed me access to her father's papers, both at the Library of Congress and at the Hope home in Toluca Lake; and in general made sure all doors were open to me during the researching of the book. I am enormously grateful and honored that she placed her confidence in me to tell the story of her father's extraordinary life and career. For someone as dedicated as she is to her father's legacy, it must have been difficult at times to relinquish control and trust a journalist to tell that story fairly and honestly. I sincerely hope the finished product justifies her trust.

I am grateful also to the many other members of the Hope family who shared their recollections and insights with me, especially Bob's surviving son, Kelly Hope, and grandchildren Miranda and Zachary Hope. I also

807

want to thank Jim Hardy, Jan Morrill, and all the staff members of Hope Enterprises for their help during my reporting and research.

I am appreciative and touched that so many former colleagues and friends of Bob Hope's were generous enough to spend time with a strange reporter, ransacking their memories to help me piece together my story. Many of them were, understandably, quite old, and it saddens me that so many have passed away since our interviews. I feel privileged to have been able to record some of the last reminiscences of a vanishing show-business generation.

Much of my time was spent in libraries, and I want to thank all the people who facilitated my work. Mike Mashon, head of the Library of Congress's National Audio-Visual Conservation Center, in Culpeper, Virginia, was a gracious host for my many days of research there. Sam Brylawski and Alan Gevinson, curators of the two Hope exhibits assembled for the Library of Congress, were invaluable in guiding me through the mountain of material. Rebecca Jones was an always-congenial minder while I was in Culpeper, and Karen Fishman kept me focused while I was at the main library in Washington, DC.

At the Paley Center for Media in New York City, where I spent many long hours watching and listening to Hope TV and radio programs, I'm grateful to Richard Holbrooke for making the process so pleasant and efficient, and to Carrie Oman, for always opening the doors. For research help, I would also like to thank Bill Hooper, custodian of the magazine archives at Time Inc.; Angela Thornton and Susan Weill, in the *Time* magazine research library; Karen Pedersen, at the Writers Guild of America library; Ann Sindelar at the Western Reserve Historical Society library; Jim Ciesla, who tracked down some key Cuyahoga County court records for me; and the entire staff of the Motion Picture Academy's Margaret Herrick Library, for making sure I always wrote in pencil.

I'm a writer who likes doing my own research, but I could not have done as thorough a job without the help of three people: Caroline Stevens, who supplemented my work at the Library of Congress, both in Culpeper and Washington; Konni Corriere, who prowled some of the back shelves at the Margaret Herrick Library; and Nona Yates, who was an expert guide through the California court and real estate records.

Alan Blackmore, a retired schoolmaster in Weston-super-Mare, England, has done more work on the Hope genealogy than anyone else, and he was an invaluable resource in sorting through the family's history in England. He also provided me with a copy of Jim Hope's unpublished memoir, "Mother

Had Hopes," with its fascinating chronicle of the family's early years in England and later in Cleveland.

I am indebted to Meg and Kay Liberman, who gave me a copy of their father Frank Liberman's unpublished memoir, with its thoughtful and candid reminiscences of Hope and his world. Elizabeth Frank was kind enough to transcribe for me some key passages from the journal of her father, Melvin Frank. I spent an entertaining afternoon in Los Angeles with Miles Krueger, Broadway archivist extraordinaire, who showed me the only surviving footage of Hope's appearances on Broadway. Richard Behar, my former *Time* magazine colleague, excavated his notes and tape-recorded interviews for the article he wrote on Hope's finances for *Forbes* magazine. Michael Feinstein supplied me with rare early recordings of "Thanks for the Memory" by Al Jolson and the songwriters Robin and Rainger. And my brother Paul Zoglin helped me navigate the genealogical archives and locate many key census and immigration documents.

Jim Shepherd, of the Bob Hope Theatre in Eltham, England, and local historian John Kennett were welcoming hosts and tour guides on my visit to the town where Hope was born. In Cleveland, Mike Gavin was most helpful in showing me the neighborhoods where Bob grew up, providing me with

810

family photos, and in many other ways.

Jeff Abraham, one of the great students of old-time comedy, was an irreplaceable resource throughout, leading me to countless new finds, recordings, and sources. Stephen Silverman, of *People* magazine, provided me with insights into the Hope family and introductions to several relatives who became valuable sources. Dick Burgheim, the great Time Inc. editor, my former boss at *TV-Cable Week* and author of a 1967 *Time* cover story on Hope, was an inspiration and sounding board for me throughout. And Bill Faith, author of the most definitive Hope biography to date, was most generous in giving his time and help to a fellow biographer.

In addition to the people quoted in the book, many others were important in connecting me with sources, providing background, and helping me develop my ideas. Among them I would especially like to thank Mary Altman, Robert Bader, Gary Giddins, Gloria Greer, Joanne Kaufman, Dennis Klein, Kristiina Laakso, Robert Morton, Richard Niles, Robert Osbourne, Marvin Paige, Hermine Rhodes, Jeff Ross, Richard Schickel, Marion Solomon, Maureen Solomon, and Bill Zehme.

At Simon & Schuster, I am forever indebted to David Rosenthal, who commissioned this book and shared my conviction that a major biography of Hope was overdue, and to his successor, Jonathan Karp, who showed such enthusiasm for a project he inherited. I was incredibly lucky to have an editor, Priscilla Painton, who is also a great friend and a longtime colleague from *Time*. She was an astute and constructive critic of the book, a godsend during some of the tough times I endured during its writing, and an absolute pleasure to work with from beginning to end. Her assistants, Sydney Tanigawa and Sophia Jimenez, along with the entire production staff at Simon & Schuster, made the process as easy as I could imagine.

My agent, Kris Dahl, was, as always, a great rock of support and dedicated friend every step of the way. I will always be grateful for her advice and unshakable faith in me, both on this book and over the years.

Finally, I must thank the most important person in my life, my wife, Charla Krupp, who died of breast cancer during the writing of this book. We were married for nineteen years, and she was my greatest editor, adviser, cheerleader, and life inspiration. She read early drafts of the first few chapters of this book, and her tough criticism inspired me to keep striving to meet her high standards, even in her absence. I cannot express the sorrow I feel that she is not here with me to share what she helped produce. I only hope that it carries some of her spirit, as I do every moment of every day.

NOTES

Introduction

"World's Last Bob Hope Fan": Onion, July 31, 2002, http://www.theonion.com/articles/worlds-last-bob-hope-fan-dies-of-old-age,3061/.

"To be paralyzingly": Christopher Hitchens, "Hopeless," Slate.com, August 1, 2003, http://www.slate.com/articles/news_and_politics/fighting_words/2003/08/hopeless.html.

"I grew up loving him": Woody Allen, interview with author.

"Do you think anybody here knows": Larry Gelbart, interview with author.

"the unabashed show-off": Leo Rosten, "Bob Hope: Gags and Riches," *Look,* February 24, 1953.

"Bob had no intellectual curiosity": Katherine Green, interview with author.

"Everybody came to attention": Sam McCullagh, interview with author.

"He was funnier than the monologues": Gelbart, interview with author.

a starstruck stewardess fawned: Arthur Freeman, letter to the editor, *Times of London,* July 31, 2003.

The bishop who was to introduce Hope: Recounted by Nathaniel Lande, interview with author.

"Once you worked for Hope": Hal Kanter, interview with author.

"What time can you get here?": Frank Liberman, unpublished memoir.

"Now you're talkin' ": Ibid.

"Bob, this gal comes from New York": J. Anthony Lukas, "This Is Bob (Politician-Patriot-Publicist) Hope," *New York Times Magazine,* October 4, 1970.

"the world's only happy comedian": Lupton A. Wilkinson, "Hope Springs Eternal," *Los Angeles Times,* December 7, 1941.

"Deep down inside": "Fish Don't Applaud," *Time,* October 25, 1963.

every morning Bob Hope would get up: Elliott Kozak, interview with author.

"Playing the European theater": Bob Hope, *I Never Left Home* (Simon & Schuster, 1944), 15.

"It is painfully obvious to us": Richard Schickel, *Intimate Strangers: The Culture of Celebrity* (Doubleday, 1985), 217.

"I believe this operation can take place": Letter

from Howard Luck, October 1969, Hope archives, Library of Congress.

"This is just to thank you for the lemon pie": Letter from Hope, July 10, 1974, Hope archives.

"She is in the hospital": Letter from Donna Moore, October 8, 1967, Hope archives.

"Dear Kelly: Remember me?": Letter from Hope, October 24, 1967, Hope archives.

Chapter 1: Opening

"Lord Hope, 17th baronet": Birmingham News Age-Herald, December 15, 1935, Hope archives.

"lured the aristocratic scion": Brooklyn Daily Eagle, undated, Hope archives.

the family moved from Borth: The account of Avis's early years comes largely from Jim Hope's unpublished memoir, "Mother Had Hopes," which is based primarily on the recollections of his mother. Some of it is corroborated in a report on Hope's genealogy done for the Hope family by Research International in 1979 (Hope archives).

The records of the parish school: Alan Blackmore, interview with author. A grade school would presumably be more scrupulous in obtaining the correct birth date of its students.

suggests that Avis was most likely taken: Ibid.

By the time she appears: 1891 census records,

815

administrative county of Glamorgan, Wales. Avis may also be listed in the 1881 census for Borth as well, but the entry is confusing. A nine-year-old girl whose name appears to be "Ivis Towis," born in Middlesex, London, is recorded as a "boarder," living with a woman named Jane Lewis and her son John. Intriguingly, a man named Abraham Lloyd Lewis and his family are living on the same street.

"Why, she's just a baby": J. Hope, "Mother Had Hopes," 19.

"I have not seen a handsomer man": Ibid., 50.

"You know you're the only girl": Ibid., 88.

"When he would be in the house": Ibid., 134.

"I was defending my dogs": Bob Hope, *Have Tux, Will Travel* (Simon & Schuster, 1954), 11.

"Whose lovely little girl are you?": J. Hope, "Mother Had Hopes," 188.

"The very air in America": Ibid., 192–94.

"We started planning and figuring": Ibid., 195.

"Gone to Canada": Alan Blackmore, interview with author.

"Everybody on the ship was in sympathy": J. Hope, "Mother Had Hopes," 200.

Leslie is the fifth of six: Ship manifest, USS *Philadelphia,* March 21, 1908.

"I'll swear she looked": J. Hope, "Mother Had Hopes," 203.

Cleveland was not a bad place: William Ganson Rose, *Cleveland: The Making of a City*

(World Publishing, 1990), 600–607, 679–88.

The bustling area . . . was becoming known: Charles Asa Post, *Doan's Corners and the City Four Miles West* (Caxton, 1930).

"Euclid and Cedar had Brush arc lights": Map of Doan's Corners, circa 1900, Western Reserve Historical Society library, Cleveland, OH.

"not only an artist with the stone-cutting tools": Hope, *Have Tux,* 14.

"I remember Dad saying": Ibid., 19.

"For when he was sober": J. Hope, "Mother Had Hopes," 329.

"I have seen Harry in a great group": Ibid., 266.

"She had the kind of skin": Ibid., 209.

"unless we put our bare bottoms": Ibid., 233.

"Ach! How many Hopes": Ibid., 313.

"Looking back on my Cleveland boyhood": Hope, *Have Tux,* 18.

"You sat in front of me": Letter from Jessie Morris-Harman, September 9, 1971, Hope archives.

"He was a big show-off": Timothy White, "The Road Not Taken," *Rolling Stone,* March 20, 1980.

"If you want to be a success": Hope tells the Rockefeller anecdote in *Have Tux,* 27, among other places.

"As his leisure increased": Grace Goulder, *John D. Rockefeller: The Cleveland Years*

817

(Western Reserve Historical Society, 1973), 233.

"We would hang around the corner": Letter from Norman J. Freeman, January 18, 1973, Hope archives.

"Don't worry about Leslie": William Robert Faith, *Bob Hope: A Life in Comedy* (Da Capo Press, 2003), 11.

"you and 'Whitey' fattened me up": Letter from Isabele M. Goss, April 7, 1964, Hope archives.

"My father had a Buick": Letter from William Hoagland, February 3, 1967, Hope archives.

he was sent to reform school: Boys Industrial School, Inmate Case Record #20546, vol. 26, Ohio Historical Society.

"adjudged a delinquent": May 17, 1918, Juvenile Court records, Cuyahoga County, OH.

"I guess it's no secret": Typewritten jokes for Boys Club appearance, May 4, 1967, Hope archives.

readmitted to the school: Boys Industry School, Inmates Case Records. In the faded records, the last digit of the date of Hope's final release is unclear; it is either 1920 or 1921.

Jack was trying to rescue a fellow soldier: J. Hope, "Mother Had Hopes," 337.

"Leslie was a good worker": Ibid., 343.

"It is not true my nose": Hope, *Have Tux,* 10.

818

"Bob helped out weekends": Maurice Condon, "They Remember Bob," *TV Guide,* April 16, 1966.

"He was a good young fighter": Ibid.

"I probably outweighed Hope": "Two Recall Assists for Bob Hope," *Cleveland Press,* April 20, 1960.

"In the first round I played cozy": Hope, *Have Tux,* 8.

Les and Whitey were walking: Various accounts of the attack are given in *Have Tux, Will Travel* (9), "Mother Had Hopes" (317–20), and the *Cleveland Press* (undated, Hope archives).

"He's not half as good as you": Hope, *Have Tux,* 6.

"Lester Hope will teach you to dance": Business card, Hope archives.

"Lester Hope . . . started a new contest": "Council Takes No Action to Halt Dancing Contests," *Cleveland Plain Dealer,* April 17, 1923.

"Mildred was tall, blonde": Hope, *Have Tux,* 38.

"She worshipped Leslie": J. Hope, "Mother Had Hopes," 360–61.

"He would follow me home": Faith, *Life in Comedy,* 13.

Mildred claimed that Les . . . kept all the money: Ibid., 14.

" 'This is a little dance' ": Hope, *Have Tux,* 39.

"When we came out to do": Faith, *Life in Comedy,* 14.

"We wore brown derbies": Hope, *Have Tux,* 40.

"The whole offering is built": Cleveland Plain Dealer, August 28, 1923.

Chapter 2: Vaudeville

In 1900 the United States had an estimated two thousand: The statistics and other details of vaudeville's early years are drawn largely from Trav S.D., *No Applause, Just Throw Money: The Book That Made Vaudeville Famous* (Faber and Faber, 2005).

"Tab shows were a special part": Hope, *Have Tux,* 41.

"Frankly we had all thought Lefty Durbin": Faith, *Life in Comedy,* 16.

"By the end of the week the towels": Ibid., 17.

At a hotel in Bedford: Hope describes the affair and the hotel incident in *Have Tux,* 44.

she broke off the relationship: "Hope's Morgantown Saga Reviewed," *Morgantown Post,* April 28, 1966, Hope archives.

Hope's partner died: The description of Durbin's death is drawn from Hope's own brief account in *Have Tux,* 45; Faith, *Life in Comedy,* 18–19; and Jim Hope's recollections in "Mother Had Hopes," 359–60. Lawrence Quirk, in *Bob Hope: The Road Well-Traveled* (Applause Books, 2000), 26–

27, gives the most uncharitable view of Hope's actions.

"George was pink-cheeked": Hope, *Have Tux,* 45.

dubbed "Dancers Supreme": Advertisements for *Jolly Follies,* Hope archives.

"After that we told Maley": Hope, *Have Tux,* 46.

The team added bits of comedy: Hope, *Have Tux,* 49.

"The most versatile couple"; "they stopped the show"; "For the premier honors": Undated newspaper clips, Hope archives.

"I taught myself to play": Hope, *Have Tux,* 49.

"Because it'll go to his head": Personal reminiscence of the reviewer of Hope's book *The Road to Hollywood, Daily Variety,* July 26, 1977.

One of their models was . . . Duffy and Sweeney: Hope describes their act with much affection in *Have Tux,* 52–53.

"Our act opened with a soft-shoe": Ibid., 55.

State Theater; Oriole Terrace; Stanley Theater: Contracts for Hope and Byrne's Detroit and Pittsburgh appearances, Hope archives.

"the thinnest man in vaudeville": Hope, *Have Tux,* 57; publicity shots of Hope and Byrne, Hope archives.

"If you're only half as good": Hope, *Have Tux,* 56.

"the greatest draw attraction"; "The finish is a

wow": Review reprinted in an advertisement for the show in *Variety,* March 18, 1925.

"They have some fast dances": Unidentified newspaper review, Hope archives.

"At first it was a funny sensation": Hope, *Have Tux,* 56.

By 1925, only a hundred all-live: Trav, *No Applause,* 250.

More than 260 shows . . . opened on Broadway: Larry Stempel, *Showtime: A History of the Broadway Musical Theater* (W. W. Norton, 2010), 207.

Getting cast in the show: Hope and Byrne's abbreviated stint in *Sidewalks of New York* is recounted in Hope, *Have Tux,* 60–61; and Faith, *Life in Comedy,* 24.

"You ought to go West": Hope, *Have Tux,* 65.

Hope called an agent in Cleveland: Hope describes his pivotal engagement in New Castle in *Have Tux,* 65–66, among other places.

a suave comedian named Frank Fay: Trav, *No Applause,* 183, 233. Glimpses of Fay's work as a vaudeville emcee can be seen in the 1937 film *Nothing Sacred* and other movie roles from the 1930s.

"I think I'll try it alone": Hope, *Have Tux,* 66.

"Without him I'm nothing": Quirk, *Road Well-Traveled,* 38.

After the split, Byrne spent a few years: Byrne obituary, *Variety,* December 28, 1966.

"My mother told me": Avis Hope Eckelberry, interview with author.

"If I don't get any work by Saturday": J. Hope, "Mother Had Hopes," 386.

"I went out, bought a big red bow tie": Hope, *Have Tux,* 67.

"Audiences knew that white performers": Robert W. Snyder, *Voice of the City: Vaudeville and Popular Culture in New York,* 2nd ed. (Ivan R. Dee, 2000), 120.

"Don't ever put that cork on": Hope, *Have Tux,* 67.

"I couldn't get in anybody's door": Ibid., 68.

"I used to dance on that corner": Miranda Hope, interview with author.

"Late of Sidewalks of New York": Advertisement in *Chicago Tribune,* June 25, 1928.

"I thought Bob had more": Hope, *Have Tux,* 75.

billed him on the marquee as "Ben Hope": John Lahr, "The C.E.O. of Comedy," *New Yorker,* December 21, 1998. Hope repeated the anecdote many times, with varying responses from the theater manager.

"I had to tell you that you didn't make it": Letters from Harry A. Turrell, January 12, 1970, and October 24, 1975, Hope archives. Hope gives his own account of the Stratford engagement in *Have Tux,* 69–72.

signing a contract with the Stratford: Marcus Loew Western Booking Agency contract, Hope archives.

"I learned a lot about getting laughs": Hope, *Have Tux,* 71.

"He was a bright package": Lahr, "C.E.O. of Comedy."

"a new twentieth-century aesthetic of shazz and pizzazz": Trav, *No Applause,* 161.

He also had a new partner: Hope describes their act, though little about Troxell, in *Have Tux,* 72.

"When I walked out before my first Fort Worth audience": Hope, *Have Tux,* 74.

As Hope recalled the events: Ibid., 77.

"I offered Lee Stewart $35": Letter from Dolph Leffler, May 13, 1959, Hope archives.

"How's the audience here?": Hope, *Have Tux,* 77.

"No, lady, this is not John Gilbert": Ibid., 78.

"Hope, assisted by an unbilled girl": Variety, November 6, 1929.

The salary: a hefty $475 a week: Contract with Keith–Albee Vaudeville Exchange, Hope archives.

$100 a week, according to Hope: Hope, *Have Tux,* 80.

Hope crisscrossed the country: Map of Hope's 1929–30 vaudeville tour, "Bob Hope and American Variety," Library of Congress exhibit, available online at http://www.loc.gov/exhibits/bobhope/index.html.

"socked in heavy on the laugh register": Billboard, November 23, 1929.

"This act flows": Variety, June 11, 1930.

"Do us a favor, take it out": Hope, *Have Tux,* 82.

"Girl with Bob Hope": Mollie Gay, "Clothes and Clothes," *Variety,* November 27, 1929.

he accompanied the offer with a marriage proposal: Rosequist gives her account of the incident in Faith, *Life in Comedy,* 41.

"She was quick and intelligent": Hope, *Have Tux,* 72.

"He was a great joke mechanic": Ibid., 85–86.

A typical Boasberg telegraphed pitch: "Bob Hope and American Variety," Library of Congress exhibit.

"Bob Hope closing 28 minutes": Variety, February 11, 1931.

Some of the old neighborhood gang: Variety, February 25, 1931.

"From the moment she took her seat": J. Hope, "Mother Had Hopes," 394–95.

went there on a rescue mission: Mike Gavin, interview with author.

"What's going on behind the curtain?": Hope describes their bits in *Have Tux,* 92–93.

"A part of my new idea": Ibid., 92.

"I had to pound his eardrums": Ibid., 98.

"He almost kissed me": Faith, *Life in Comedy,* 49.

Hope later disowned it: Hope, *Have Tux,* 95.

"I was numb": Ibid.

"They say that Bob Hope": Quoted by Hope, ibid., 96.

Bob played a hotel desk clerk: Script for desk-clerk routine, "Bob Hope and American Variety," Library of Congress exhibit.

"The sting of some of his gags": Variety, November 6, 1929.

"Act needs a lot of watching": Bureau of Sunday Censorship report, "Bob Hope and American Variety," Library of Congress exhibit.

"I'd never seen anything so awful": Hope, *Have Tux*, 87.

"Ups-a Daisy . . . Smiles": The Internet Broadway Database, and contemporary reviews, clearly record Hope's participation in both shows, making it especially odd that neither Hope nor any of his biographers have ever mentioned them.

Chapter 3: Broadway

New York City . . . was suffering: Edward Robb Ellis, *The Epic of New York City: A Narrative History* (Carroll & Graf, 1966), 531–34.

"For most Americans, 'café society' ": Neil Gabler, *Winchell: Gossip, Power and the Culture of Celebrity* (Knopf, 1994), 185.

until it began affecting his singing voice and he gave them up: Charles Thompson, *Bob Hope: Portrait of a Superstar* (Fontana/Collins, 1982), 234.

"Actually it was rather frightening": Faith, *Life in Comedy,* 52.

Hope again had to vamp for time: Hope's role in the show is described by Hope in *Have Tux,* 99–101; Faith, *Life in Comedy,* 52–54; and in a script excerpt in "Bob Hope and American Variety," Library of Congress exhibit.

"An agreeable but far from brilliant": Howard Barnes, *New York Herald Tribune,* September 7, 1932.

Commercial radio . . . was quickly reaching critical mass: Gerald Nachman, *Raised on Radio* (Pantheon, 1998), 16–25.

the Major appropriated most of the good jokes: Hope, *Have Tux,* 104–5.

"Here's a picture of a girl": Fleischmann Hour script, Hope archives.

"It all seemed so strange": Faith, *Life in Comedy,* 54.

"Goofy, self-assured, ingratiating": Variety, March 21, 1933.

"Son, I haven't eaten": The routine is quoted in the papers of Mort Lachman, Writers Guild of America archives.

Hope . . . chastised himself: Hope, *Have Tux,* 106.

"The gags weren't very funny": Faith, *Life in Comedy,* 56.

"One answer to what's wrong": Variety, November 21, 1933.

Hope and Richie Craig . . . devised a revenge scheme: Faith, *Life in Comedy,* 60–61.

Hope would always defend Berle: Elliott Kozak, interview with author.

Hope made the largest single contribution: Variety, January 23, 1934.

Max Gordon was casting a new Broadway musical: Gerald Boardman, *Jerome Kern: His Life and Music* (Oxford University Press, 1980), 334–41.

"Do whatever you can": Faith, *Life in Comedy,* 59.

"An impossible, impossible man": Quirk, *Road Well-Traveled,* 69.

"Extremely unimportant": Quoted in Ethan Mordden, *Sing for Your Supper: The Broadway Musical in the 1930s* (Palgrave Macmillan, 2005), 53.

"The humors of Roberta": Brooks Atkinson, *New York Times,* November 20, 1933.

longer than any other book musical: Mordden, *Sing for Your Supper,* 55.

"I've always said that Bob Hope": Thompson, *Portrait of a Superstar,* 32.

"I had Marilyn Miller's old dressing room": Hope, *Have Tux,* 111.

"I hadn't caught his name": Faith, *Life in Comedy,* 62.

"Nana was the heart and soul": Reminiscence by Mildred, Hope archives.

a columnist called her the female Crosby: Gary Giddins, *Bing Crosby: A Pocketful of Dreams* (Little, Brown, 2001), 561.

"I hadn't seen that particular girl": Hope, *Have Tux,* 112.

Their marriage license . . . identifies the couple: Erie County Marriage License Bureau, Erie, Pennsylvania.

When the marriage license was unearthed: Arthur Marx, *The Secret Life of Bob Hope: An Unauthorized Biography* (Barricade Books, 1993), 71–72.

according to an Erie official: Associated Press, July 31, 2003.

"I was in a thick pink fog": Hope, *Have Tux,* 112.

"Because I couldn't wait": Hope interview with Alan King, "Inside the Comedy Mind of Bob Hope," 1992.

"announced their engagement yesterday": New *York Herald Tribune,* August 4, 1934.

"guilty of extreme cruelty": Divorce petition, September 4, 1934, Cuyahoga County Court of Common Pleas.

The judge found in Hope's favor: November 19, 1934, Cuyahoga County Court of Common Pleas.

"It was in the early 1930s": Letter from Henry B. Johnson, June 21, 1968, Hope archives.

"It was great hearing from you": Letter from Hope, August 20, 1968, Hope archives.

Milton Berle, told Arthur Marx: Marx, *Secret Life of Bob Hope,* 81.

doing Dumb Dora routines with a new partner:

Reviewing a vaudeville show in Brooklyn on July 24, 1935, *Variety* notes, "Joe May and Louise Troxell do their familiar flip comic and dumb gal routine, next to closing."

"When Deb went away": Letter from Louise Troxell, 1976, Hope archives.

"Dolores Hope — Godparent": Death certificate for Deborah Halper, County of San Diego, CA, October 20, 1998.

Kirsten Flagstad, who sang: J. Hope, "Mother Had Hopes," 412.

"It was murder": Hope, *Have Tux,* 283.

"What he expected was perfection": Faith, *Life in Comedy,* 67.

"Come right over"; "They gave her a little more production": Hope, *Have Tux,* 114.

"A likely picture bet": Variety, October 9, 1935.

"On song values she's in the same category": Variety, December 4, 1934.

turned down an offer . . . to costar: Described by Al Melnick, Shurr's West Coast partner, in Marx, *Secret Life of Bob Hope,* 84.

"When they catch Dillinger": Bob Hope and Bob Thomas, *The Road to Hollywood: My Forty-Year Love Affair with the Movies* (Bookthrift, 1979), 16.

"Sam's ability to squeeze a buck": Ibid., 17.

"I'm the star": Hope, *Have Tux,* 116.

"If he'd had a good score": Ibid.

"merriest laugh, song and girl show": Quoted

in Faith, *Life in Comedy,* 68.

"Mr. Hope, as usual, was amiably impudent": Percy Hammond, *New York Herald Tribune,* November 9, 1934.

"the guy responsible for my success": Faith, *Life in Comedy,* 69.

"Hope is intermittently very funny": Variety, January 15, 1934.

"thick, spoonbread Southern accent": Hope, *Have Tux,* 118.

"Bob Hope is a likeable fellow": New York Radio Guide, March 30, 1935.

she became a flamboyant: An obituary in the *New York Times,* August 20, 1995, recounts her colorful life. Many letters to Hope from Wilder are found in the Hope archives.

"It's all right for the established comedians": Unidentified newspaper article, Hope archives.

"He just doesn't look like a comedian": Radio Stars, September 1936, Hope archives.

"Before 1940, don't be surprised": Dick Templeton, *Cincinnati Radio Dial,* March 19, 1936, Hope archives.

Hope said he gave Arden the line: Hope, *Have Tux,* 119–20.

"A jovial and handsome": Brooks Atkinson, *New York Times,* January 31, 1936.

"It was a kick": Hope, *Have Tux,* 122.

During a performance in Philadelphia: Ibid., 121.

The show . . . had another rough voyage to

Broadway: The problems of *Red, Hot and Blue* are recounted in Mordden, *Sing for Your Supper,* 246–48; and Faith, *Life in Comedy,* 77–80.

"Trow me da book": Hope, *Have Tux,* 123.

"I've been with Bob a long time": Ethel Merman, as told to Pete Martin, *Who Could Ask for Anything More* (Doubleday, 1955), 129.

"He lay down by the footlights": Ibid., 135.

"I probably kidded around": Faith, *Life in Comedy,* 80.

"he told me that he and Ethel": Liberman, unpublished memoir.

"coyly engaging": Time, November 9, 1936.

"generally cheering": Brooks Atkinson, *New York Times,* October 30, 1936.

"urbane, sleek, and nimble": Quoted in Faith, *Life in Comedy,* 80.

silent footage shot by a young theater enthusiast: Ray Knight collection, courtesy of Miles Krueger, Los Angeles.

"roly-poly Bob Hope": Time, November 9, 1936.

"I was an entirely different fellow": Brooks Riley, interview with Hope, *Film Comment,* May–June, 1979.

of the 125 major benefits: Faith, *Life in Comedy,* 81.

"Hollywood was for peasants": Hope and Thomas, *Road to Hollywood,* 18.

Jack Benny, who turned it down: Mary Livingstone, *Jack Benny* (Doubleday, 1978), 94. Livingstone also says that Benny "didn't think he could handle" the romantic ballad he was required to sing — "Thanks for the Memory."

"Please advise Bob this is the great opportunity"; "Advise Bob Hope part Paramount has for him": Telegrams from Louis Shurr, July 14 and 15, 1937, Hope archives.

"We've always hated the idea": Quoted in Faith, *Life in Comedy,* 88.

Chapter 4: Hollywood

"The most obstinate, ornery": David Chierichetti, *Mitchell Leisen: Hollywood Director* (Photoventures Press, 1995), 112.

"my most embarrassing moment": Ibid., 110.

"It's not easy to say, 'I love you' "; "No, it's not funny": Roy Hemming, *The Melody Lingers On: The Great Songwriters and Their Movie Musicals* (Newmarket Press, 1999), 199, 200.

"I rehearsed Bob and Shirley": Chierichetti, *Mitchell Leisen,* 111.

"everything comes through the eyes": Hope, *Have Tux,* 133.

"We didn't know we wrote": Chierichetti, *Mitchell Leisen,* 111.

"When I saw the rushes": Hope and Thomas, *Road to Hollywood,* 21.

"I don't think it's so much": Hope, *Have Tux,* 132.

"Bob, your whole personality": Faith, *Life in Comedy,* 93.

"log-size chip on my shoulder": Hope, *Have Tux,* 131.

"It's amazing that you can be a star in New York": Robert Coleman, *New York Daily Mirror,* September 8, 1937.

greeted by a Paramount publicist: Faith, *Life in Comedy,* 91.

Paramount Pictures was a good place to land: Ethan Mordden, *The Hollywood Studios: House Style in the Golden Age of the Movies* (Fireside, 1989).

being eyed for a Damon Runyon story: *Hollywood Reporter,* July 29, 1937.

"Bob Hope, fine Broadway comic": Ed Sullivan, *New York Daily News,* January 6, 1938.

"Hope, like Crosby, is just having": Paramount press release, 1938, Academy of Motion Picture Arts and Sciences (AMPAS) archives.

"I found him a shrewd boy": Hope, *Have Tux,* 232.

"I had watched Hope at the Capitol": Faith, *Life in Comedy,* 84.

"The monologue is now showing signs": Samuel Kaufman, *New York Sun,* July 17, 1938.

"A comedian won't be able to take the stage": Coleman, *New York Daily Mirror,* September

8, 1937.

"He had never been able to understand": Edgar Thompson, unidentified newspaper column, Hope archives.

"He took an old form": Coleman, *New York Daily Mirror,* September 8, 1937.

the two would spend two or three late nights: Hope, *Have Tux,* 209.

"Hope appears too adaptable": *Variety,* January 26, 1938.

The head of Lucky Strike: Faith, *Life in Comedy,* 97.

"big hit tune of 1938": Jolson radio performance, December 30, 1937, Michael Feinstein archives.

"All loose ends and tatters": Frank Nugent, *New York Times,* March 10, 1938.

"You'll rave over Bob Hope": Ed Sullivan, *New York Daily News,* undated column, Hope archives.

"Bob is our American Noël Coward": Hedda Hopper, undated column, Hope archives.

spent ten weeks on radio's Your Hit Parade: Hemming, *Melody Lingers On,* 200.

"Our favorite gulp": Damon Runyon syndicated column, March 13, 1938.

Hope on the differences . . . Hope's guide to comedy slang: Paramount publicity material, AMPAS archives.

"Move over, boys": quoted by Wilkie Mahoney in letter to Hope, August 28, 1958, Hope

835

archives.

went to producer Lewis Gensler: Faith, *Life in Comedy,* 95.

"a pleasant comedian completely bested": Howard Barnes, New York Herald Tribune, April 28, 1938.

an offer from Universal: Hope and Thomas, *Road to Hollywood,* 28.

"Paramount signed me": Script for Paramount appearance, Hope archives.

"Everyone goes to bed": Ibid.

only enough money for one pair of dress pants: Anecdote related by Liberman, unpublished memoir.

hopped in his 1937 Pontiac: Faith, *Life in Comedy,* 98.

had considered Milton Berle and Fred Allen: Charles Luckman, *Twice in a Lifetime* (W. W. Norton, 1988), 141.

"to prevent your being a smart aleck": Faith, *Life in Comedy,* 100.

starting salary of $1,500 a week: Hope later recalled it as $2,500, but this is the figure cited by Luckman, *Twice in a Lifetime,* 141.

"No comic had ever tried . . . All these comedy minds": Hope, with Melville Shavelson, *Don't Shoot, It's Only Me* (Putnam, 1990), 29, 33.

coming close to hiring Ozzie Nelson: Variety, August 9, 1938.

introducing him as a famous Italian tenor: Bob

Colonna, *"Greetings, Gate!": The Story of Professor Jerry Colonna* (BearManor Media, 2007), 42–43.

found out the rights would cost him $250: Faith, *Life in Comedy,* 104.

"That small speck": Variety, October 5, 1938.

"My idea was to do": Hope, *Have Tux,* 214.

"When you wrote for Hope": Peter Kaplan, "On the Road with Bob Hope," *New Times,* August 7, 1978.

"he seemed a little concerned": Melville Shavelson, *How to Succeed in Hollywood Without Really Trying* (BearManor Media, 2007), 36.

"He had no sense of time": Sherwood Schwartz, interview with author.

"What took you so long?": Ibid.

make paper airplanes out of the writers' paychecks: A widely repeated anecdote, in Marx, *Secret Life of Bob Hope,* 122; and elsewhere.

"I'll leave it in the mailbox": Shavelson, *How to Succeed,* 37.

"We'd go to a hotel": Schwartz, interview with author.

"What we didn't realize . . . it was Bob's excuse": Lahr, "C.E.O. of Comedy."

"It never occurred to us": Shavelson, *How to Succeed,* 37.

"Two things: Sam Goldwyn and Bob Hope": Maureen Solomon, Shavelson's former as-

sistant, interview with author.

"There was no separation": Schwartz, interview with author.

"Hope is the ordinary actor type": Melvin Frank, private journal.

"My father really loved Hope": Elizabeth Frank, interview with author.

"He still had a tendency to go overboard": Marx, *Secret Life of Bob Hope,* 125.

Hope exploded: Schwartz, interview with author.

A 1939 poll of radio critics: Nachman, *Raised on Radio,* 143.

"In previous pictures": Frank S. Nugent, *New York Times,* December 8, 1938.

"Looks like Bette Davis's garage": Mason Wiley and Damien Bona, *Inside Oscar* (Ballantine Books, 1986), 89.

"Bob Hope didn't get an Oscar": George E. Phair, "Hollywood Hides Heart Under Hokum," *Daily Variety,* February 24, 1939.

"I want you to know": Hope and Thomas, *Road to Hollywood,* 32.

in Chicago, Hope's show earned $44,500: Variety, July 12, 1939.

"A little pin money": Letter from Kenneth Smith, Hope archives.

"start brushing four times a day": Faith, *Life in Comedy,* 108.

got the Ohio clan together: Ibid., 108.

"As always, Hope isn't inclined": Variety, July

26, 1939.

"I'm used to this sort of thing": Thomas M. Pryor, "Bob Hope and a Series of Interruptions," *New York Times*, August 6, 1939.

"Crisp instructions were sent": "Studios Call Stars Back from War-Menaced Europe," *Los Angeles Times*, August 26, 1939.

Among the 2,331 passengers: "Queen Mary Brings 2,331 Here Safely," *New York Times*, September 5, 1939.

"Many of the British people": Hope, *Have Tux*, 167.

Hope did an impromptu show: Ibid., 167–68.

"We were getting along fine": Ibid., 287.

"We took his own characteristics": Lahr, "C.E.O. of Comedy."

"the extreme wisdom of comedians": *Variety*, October 4, 1939.

boosted him into tenth place: *Variety*, January 3, 1940.

Chapter 5: Actor

The names of the winners . . . had prematurely been revealed: Wiley and Bona, *Inside Oscar*, 98.

"ten best actors of the year": Hope's lines reported in *Daily Variety*, March 1, 1940; and Wiley and Bona, *Inside Oscar*.

"Bob Hope . . . was his lifesaving self": Hedda Hopper, *Los Angeles Times*, March 4, 1940.

Their chemistry so impressed: Hope and

Thomas, *Road to Hollywood,* 33.

The idea took more than a year: The rather convoluted genesis of *Road to Singapore* is drawn from Paramount records at the AMPAS library; Faith, *Life in Comedy,* 116; and Giddins, *Bing Crosby,* 564–65.

"For a couple of days . . . tore freewheeling into a scene": Bing Crosby, as told to Pete Martin, *Call Me Lucky* (Da Capo Press, 1953), 157.

"I kept waiting for a cue": Dorothy Lamour, as told to Dick McInnes, *My Side of the Road* (Prentice-Hall, 1980), 88.

"If you recognize any of yours": An oft-repeated anecdote, in Faith, *Life in Comedy,* 116; and elsewhere.

"I had a great staff": Hope interview, *Film Comment,* May–June 1979.

"The Road *pictures had the excitement":* Hope and Thomas, *Road to Hollywood,* 35.

"How fast was I going, Officer?": Giddins, *Bing Crosby,* 580.

"That scene was like a piece of music": Hope and Thomas, *Road to Hollywood,* 36.

By April, Paramount was already planning: Variety, April 10, 1940.

"Bing loved to hunt and fish": Giddins, *Bing Crosby,* 561.

"Bing was a cold tomato": Sherwood Schwartz, interview with author.

"What the hell are you doing that for": Liber-

man, unpublished memoir.

"Bob wanted everything that Bing had": Hal Kanter, interview with author.

"It was the only time I saw Bob": Ibid.

On his first stop in Joliet . . . there were lines around the block: Hope with Shavelson, *Don't Shoot,* 61–62.

With a guarantee of $12,500: Variety, May 15, 1940.

"Bob Hope is blazing Hot": Variety, May 22, 1940.

"It was my first experience": Hope with Shavelson, *Don't Shoot,* 61–62.

"He had his job, and she had her job": Tom Malatesta, interview with author.

"She longed for romance from this man": Lahr, "C.E.O. of Comedy."

When he saw that the boy had a ski nose: Hope, *Have Tux,* 289.

"I haven't made a comedy"; "That's all fine": Ibid., 156–59.

"Its lightness and levity throughout": Variety, June 12, 1940.

especially well with "the under-21 mob": Variety, June 26, 1940.

put the squeeze on Pepsodent: Variety, June 19, 1940.

"Everyone would write down": Thompson, *Portrait of a Superstar,* 50.

"Who do you think you are — Harpo?": Hope with Shavelson, *Don't Shoot,* 64.

841

"I want to thank both political candidates": Ibid., 65.

"The Democrats really put on": Ibid., 67–68.

"We are getting many protests": NBC memo, November 19, 1940, "Bob Hope and American Variety," Library of Congress exhibit.

President Roosevelt . . . launched a massive war mobilization effort: Background on the home front in the years leading up to and during World War II is drawn largely from Doris Kearns Goodwin, *No Ordinary Time: Franklin and Eleanor Roosevelt: The Home Front in World War II* (Simon & Schuster, 1994).

"did Selznick bring them back?": Accounts of the ceremony in Wiley and Bona, *Inside Oscar,* and *Daily Variety,* February 28, 1941.

he entertained at a reported 562 benefits: "Hope for Humanity," *Time,* September 20, 1943.

Lamour . . . tried to keep up: Lamour, *My Side of the Road,* 98–99.

seventy-two of them had to be removed: Paramount publicity material, AMPAS archives.

"some of the most uninhibited": "The Groaner," *Time,* April 7, 1941.

plans for a third in the series: "Road to Moscow New Crosby–Bob Hope Trek," *Los Angeles Times,* March 24, 1941.

"I thought David was going to knife me": Hope,

Have Tux, 148.

"Why should we drag the whole show": Hope with Shavelson, *Don't Shoot,* 73.

"I got goose pimples myself": Ibid., 74–75.

"It was our job to talk to the men": Schwartz, interview with author.

Even the term GI: Hope with Shavelson, *Don't Shoot,* 76.

Pepsodent printed 4 million copies: Daily Variety, September 29, 1941.

"I was such a beautiful baby . . . I remember my first appearance . . . Fan mail is like bread and butter": Bob Hope, *They Got Me Covered* (Bob Hope, 1941), 10, 32, 66.

"You can say it's about a quarter of a million": Time, July 7, 1941.

"It's not very often that I get mad": Bing Crosby, letter to the editor, *Time,* August 4, 1941.

Paramount's No. 1 star and ranked fourth: Variety, December 31, 1941.

"Other top-line funnymen": Wilkinson, "Hope Springs Eternal."

"We were all too shocked": Hope with Shavelson, *Don't Shoot,* 80.

Chapter 6: War

Hollywood was a changed place after Pearl Harbor: Otto Friedrich, *City of Nets: A Portrait of Hollywood in the 1940s* (Harper & Row, 1986), 101–3.

"to ensure completion of films": Variety, December 17, 1941.

"Sacrifices will have to be made": Daily Variety, December 8, 1941.

car chases were banned . . . as was the filming of battle scenes: Louella Parsons, syndicated column, January 17, 1942.

Hedy Lamarr and Lana Turner sold bonds: Friedrich, *City of Nets,* 105–9.

Jack Benny . . . found the raucous crowds too disruptive: "Radio, Vaudeville & Camps," *Time,* April 13, 1942.

"I find these audiences . . . like a tonic": "Bob Hope Typical Soldier Entertainer," *Los Angeles Times,* June 15, 1942.

"We are all soldiers now": Daily Variety, January 20, 1942.

In Houston, the crowds packed the fairways: Unidentified Houston newspaper article, February 13, 1942, Hope archives.

"If anything it was Bob Hope's Victory Caravan": Daily Variety, May 1, 1942.

Hope came home physically exhausted: Daily Variety, June 23, 1942.

The war didn't deter a record crowd: Wiley and Bona, *Inside Oscar,* 118–20.

Carroll . . . telephoned to thank Hope: Hope and Thomas, *Road to Hollywood,* 44.

some British military officers, who complained: Variety, April 15, 1942.

"Not only the funniest Bob Hope picture": Rich-

ard Griffith, "*My Favorite Blonde* Shows Bob Hope at Comedy Peak," *Los Angeles Times,* April 13, 1942.

It broke records . . . and outdrew Hope's previous hits": Variety, May 6, 1942.

one of Hope's former movie stand-ins . . . suggested: Faith, *Life in Comedy,* 140.

The trip was almost scrubbed: Hope gives detailed accounts of the Alaska trip in *I Never Left Home,* 194–202; and *Don't Shoot,* 90–93.

"It was a pretty scary night": Bob Gates, interview with author.

"I wouldn't trade this trip . . . Hollywood won't see so much of Hope": Variety, October 14, 1942.

"He was rejected every time": Dorothy Kilgallen, undated newspaper column, Hope archives.

"The greatest good you can do": Ed Sullivan, undated article in *Photoplay,* 1943.

No. 1 program in radio's Hooper ratings: Variety, October 21, 1942.

The camel improvised the spit: Hope and Thomas, *Road to Hollywood,* 47–48.

"There were never less than three telephones": Faith, *Life in Comedy,* 146.

Hope got a call from a Paramount wardrobe boy: Ibid., 146–47.

The evening began with privates Alan Ladd and Tyrone Power: Wiley and Bona, *Inside Oscar,*

128–29.

Hope even squeezed in some last-minute reshoots: Daily Variety, June 15, 1943.

"Take care of yourself"; "You know I will": Faith, *Life in Comedy,* 147.

"I couldn't let this exciting world": "How Mrs. Bob Hope Is Pitching on the Home Front," *Screenland,* August 1943.

"there is no soap in the King's bathroom": Hope, *I Never Left Home,* 33.

"I was sorry I wasn't able to tell him": Ibid., 39–40.

"He finished out of the money": Time correspondent files, August 1943, *Time* archives.

"We soon discovered you had to be pretty lousy": Hope, *I Never Left Home,* 46.

In one ward Langford began to sing: Time correspondent files, August 1943.

The prime minister did a double take: Hope, *I Never Left Home,* 87.

"The most wonderful thing about England": Faith, *Life in Comedy,* 149.

"When the time for recognition of service": John Steinbeck, *New York Herald Tribune,* July 26, 1943.

an officer lent him: Hope, *I Never Left Home,* 99–100.

"Frances and I were standing": Ibid., 130.

"I was bouncing like a rubber ball": Sidney Carroll, "Where There's Life," *Esquire,*

January 1944.

"He is what the psychologists call": Ibid.

"It not only gives you a feeling of security": Hope, *I Never Left Home*, 157.

"A very wonderful guy": *Time* correspondent files, August 1943.

"I want you to tell the people": Stanley Hirshson, *General Patton: A Soldier's Life* (Harper, 2003), 399–400.

"Bob came on the grandstand": Letter quoted in Hope, *I Never Left Home*, 205–7.

"After you've listened to a raid . . . the most frightening experience": Ibid., 162.

"I was in two different cities with them": Ernie Pyle, *New York World-Telegram*, September 16, 1943.

"Don't you know there's a war on?": Hope, *I Never Left Home*, 170.

"He flattered us"; *"We're too strong for 'em"*: Ibid., 178–79.

"When we were lost over Alaska": Ibid., 182.

"From the ranks of show business have sprung heroes": "Hope for Humanity," *Time*, September 20, 1943.

The two worked together through the fall: Faith, *Life in Comedy*, 156–57.

"I saw your sons and your husbands": Hope, *I Never Left Home*, vii.

"A zany, staccato but often touching account": Tom O'Reilly, *New York Times Book Review*, June 18, 1944.

"I think I was suffering": Hope with Shavelson, *Don't Shoot,* 125.

drew an astonishing 40.9: NBC advertisement, *Daily Variety,* March 6, 1945.

"Have plane coming north tonight": Hope, *Have Tux,* 248.

"In those days they were enormous": Faith, *Life in Comedy,* 158–59.

"Some days I became almost as nonchalant": Hope and Thomas, *Road to Hollywood,* 57.

"The next day it was all patched up": Lamour, *My Side of the Road,* 140.

"We had Barney along": Bob Hope, "Now They Call Me Trader Corn," syndicated newspaper column, November 12, 1944.

"Probably the biggest boost to our morale": Eugene B. Sledge, *With the Old Breed: At Peleliu and Okinawa* (Presidio Press, 1990), 34–35.

"When did you get here?": Hope with Shavelson, *Don't Shoot,* 144.

"You had to be careful": Patty Thomas, interview with author.

"Bob would tell people": Ibid.

"Hey, Dad, I think we're in trouble": Ibid.

Barney Dean, who was petrified . . . some American cigarettes . . . local dance hall in gratitude: Hope with Shavelson, *Don't Shoot,* 144–45.

"He's so used to seeing Bob going away": "Bob Hope and Troupe Return from Pacific," *Los*

Angeles Times, September 3, 1944.

"I don't see how we can let you do that": Faith, *Life in Comedy,* 162.

"Just now I've been to Toronto": "Bob Hope 'Suspends' Studio — That's His Version, Anyway," *Hollywood Citizen-News,* November 9, 1944.

"I'm not underrating the importance": "Hope Suspends Studio, Studio Suspends Hope!," *Los Angeles Times,* November 12, 1944.

"Some of the servicemen are boys": "An Open Letter to a Radio Star," *Catholic Pilot,* November 17, 1944.

"I think if we came out with some publicity": NBC memo, "Bob Hope and American Variety," Library of Congress exhibit.

"I think it is only fair to me": Unidentified wire story, Hope archives.

"most consistently violates": "Unchristian Hope?," *Time,* December 11, 1944.

"Risqué stories — phooey": Undated letter to Hope, Hope archives.

"as unfair a charge": Ivan Spear, *Boxoffice,* December 30, 1944.

had to take off five days for an eye operation: Daily Variety, May 9, 1944. Neither Hope nor any of his biographers mention the episode.

"showed that you have been under a terrific strain": Letter from Dr. Hugh Strathearn, January 12, 1945, Hope archives.

Hope's contract gave him 50 percent: Letter of

agreement to Hope from King Features Syndicate, April 21, 1944, Hope archives.

Hope returned to host the Academy Awards: Quotes and anecdotes from the ceremony from *Daily Variety,* March 16, 1945; and Wiley and Bona, *Inside Oscar,* 146–47.

Hope signed a new seven-year contract: Daily Variety, May 7, 1945.

"When a star of Hope's stature": Quoted in Faith, *Life in Comedy,* 169.

he spotted Maurice Chevalier in the audience: Hope tells the Chevalier anecdote and offers a defense of Chevalier's wartime activities in *Don't Shoot,* 155–56.

"Everything was different": Hope, "It's Great to Be Home," unidentified magazine article, December 9, 1945, Hope archives.

"Those boys in the stadium rose twenty-five feet": Hope, It Says Here column, August 15, 1945.

Hope's official itinerary had him continuing: Bob Hope Itinerary, 1941–1951, Hope archives. It lists stops for Hope in Germany, France, and Austria through at least August 31. Yet *Daily Variety* reported on August 22, "Bob Hope arrived in New York yesterday after completing his USO tour of Europe and expects to leave for the coast immediately." According to *Daily Variety,* he arrived back in Los Angeles on August 30, the day his official itinerary has him appearing at Stadt Stadium in Munich.

"It was a pleasure to hear from you": Letter to Hope, December 8, 1944, Hope archives.

Chapter 7: Peace

"Why isn't Hope doing": Faith, *Life in Comedy,* 172.

still dominated by the same prewar stars: George Rosen, "This Is Where They Came In," *Variety,* December 19, 1945.

Hope said it would never get past: Hope and Thomas, *Road to Hollywood,* 59.

the largest contract for radio talent: Daily Variety reported the figures, January 17, 1945. Luckman, in *Twice in a Lifetime* (177), says the amount "to the best of our knowledge" was the largest ever to that point.

projected to reach $1.25 million: "Hope Springs Financial," *Newsweek,* May 6, 1946.

Hope would typically arrive in town: Time correspondent files, July 1946.

"I can't even remember what city": St. Louis *Globe-Democrat,* June 25, 1946.

grossing $500,000 in ticket sales: Variety, July 10, 1946.

He split his show-business endeavors: "Hope, Inc.," *Time,* November 18, 1946.

"Wherever he goes, the whole board of directors": Douglas Welch, *Seattle Post-Intelligencer,* quoted in Faith, *Life in Comedy,* 179.

851

"We made him remove the wig": Time correspondent files, November 1946.

he would always take a drive and walk the property: Payson Wolfe, Hope attorney, tape-recorded interview with Richard Behar, 1983.

"If they would give me one spot"; "Mr. Hearst is very pleased": Letters between Hope and Ward Greene, 1946, Hope archives.

"I used to climb over the fence": "Hope Sets New High in Gate Crashing," *Los Angeles Times,* June 23, 1946.

"We didn't really do the Hollywood": Linda Hope, interview with author.

"She wasn't easy": Ibid.

"Dolores had a voice": Rory Burke, interview with author.

"She was a mother of the period": Robert Colonna, interview with author.

"My mother would say . . . sit up straight": Linda Hope, interview with author.

"Mother was a pistol": Tom Malatesta, interview with author.

"I've worn out four agents": Jim Hope letter, May 15, 1946, Hope archives.

Marie . . . claimed she had been underpaid: Daily Variety, June 15, 1942.

Bob turned down the paper's request . . . "It was a silly thing": Faith, *Life in Comedy,* 180–81.

Producer Paul Jones didn't like . . . the studio

brought in Frank Tashlin: Hope and Thomas, *Road to Hollywood,* 60–61.

"He was a wonderful comic actor": Woody Allen, interview with author.

he never worked for a major director: Tashlin probably came the closest, and Raoul Walsh (years before his great films) directed *College Swing.* But no Howard Hawks or Leo McCarey or Billy Wilder. Even Jack Benny did a film for Lubitsch.

"Monsieur Beaucaire, *as now enacted*": Bosley Crowther, *New York Times,* September 5, 1946.

"That rumbling yesterday": John L. Scott, *Los Angeles Times,* August 23, 1946.

"He used to say that he carried two watches": Lamour, *My Side of the Road,* 152.

$72,000 under *budget:* Paramount production records, AMPAS library.

"The best picture Monsieur Robin": Louella Parsons, undated newspaper column, Hope archives.

returning to Broadway: Daily Variety, March 11, 1947.

making a trip to Europe and North Africa: Daily Variety, January 6, 1947.

stayed at the palatial estate: Faith, *Life in Comedy,* 187.

Hope got so sunburned: Daily Variety, July 24, 1947, *Time* correspondent files, July 1947.

Jimmie Fidler . . . gave Hope an early warning:

Letter from Fidler, November 29, 1946, Hope archives.

Hope was branded the most tasteless come-dian: "The RAP," *Time,* November 17, 1947.

an innuendo-laden free-for-all: Arthur Marx quotes extensively from it in *Secret Life of Bob Hope,* 224–27.

The network bleeped out Hope's line: Daily Va-riety, April 23, 1947.

Hope told Sinatra . . . The line got bleeped: Va-riety, May 14, 1947.

"You could enjoy it": Jack Gould, *New York Times,* September 29, 1946.

" 'sad saga of sameness' ": Variety, September 24, 1947.

"I can tell the seasons": "Irium-Plated Alger," *Time,* April 10, 1944.

The travel issue came to a head: Daily Variety, November 6, 1947.

had to miss the first week's broadcast: Daily Variety, November 11, 1947.

Fred Williams . . . keeled over drunk: Hope, *Have Tux,* 217.

Queen Elizabeth reportedly "laughed so hard": Daily Variety, November 28, 1947.

"Look at him": Hope recounts the dialogue in *Have Tux,* 224.

"The most important thing for us in America": Faith, *Life in Comedy,* 192.

"The only sad thing about coming to Clare-

854

more": Ibid., 188.

Paramount had initially vowed: Hedda Hopper, *Los Angeles Times,* October 5, 1946.

"Bing and I hardly left the set": Hope and Thomas, *Road to Hollywood,* 63.

"They could have considered a four-way split": Lamour, *My Side of the Road,* 160.

"Crosby's attitude toward Dorothy Lamour": Liberman, unpublished memoir.

"My friendship with Bob": Marx, *Secret Life of Bob Hope,* 232.

"I never liked Bing": Marcia Lewis Smith, interview with author.

the two at least temporarily patched up: Faith, *Life in Comedy,* 189.

"Bob is very much worried": Letter from Hugh Davis, December 11, 1947, AMPAS archives.

Colonna . . . was ready to leave: Robert Colonna, *Greetings, Gate!,* 166; and interview with author.

"He is definitely out to remove": Hollywood Citizen News, undated article, Hope archives.

"Unpack": Hope, *Have Tux,* 251.

"He was trying something quite novel": Gelbart, interview with author.

"there were product payoffs": Si Rose, interview with author.

"He was demanding": Gelbart, interview with author.

"Bob's staff would circle around him": A. E.

Hotchner, *Doris Day: Her Own Story* (Morrow, 1976), 109.

"we'd always see a gal with him"; "Some of the guys are participating": Rose, interview with author.

"they did one take": Jane Russell, interview with author.

"Bob, you get back here": Ibid.

"A triumphant travesty": Howard Barnes, *New York Herald Tribune,* December 16, 1948.

had been planning to take Dolores: Faith, *Life in Comedy,* 196.

Dolores, who went to Christmas mass: Dorothy Reilly, wife of Air Force colonel Alvin Reilly, interview with author.

"It was an adventure": Rose, interview with author.

"the greatest filibuster of all times": Los Angeles Times, December 26, 1948.

Hope asked his driver to find the radio station: Faith, *Life in Comedy,* 197–98.

"Here is a perfect example": United Airlines advertisement, *Daily Variety,* April 18, 1949.

"We often flew through storms": Hotchner, *Doris Day,* 106.

the two began a relationship: Payton's affair with Hope is described in John O'Dowd, *Kiss Tomorrow Goodbye: The Barbara Payton Story* (BearManor Media, 2006), 65–68; and by Payton herself in "Have Tux, Will Travel . . . and That's What Bob Hope

Did with That Blonde," *Confidential,* July
1956.
"You can't make money like that": John Crosby,
New York Herald Tribune, March 1, 1949.
"The Hope success should inspire": Hollywood
Reporter, January 20, 1949.
a deal to lease seventeen hundred acres: Time
correspondent files, August 1949; and
Faith, *Life in Comedy,* 201.
NBC also stepped up: Faith, *Life in Comedy,*
200.
another fight with Luckman . . . over the taping:
Daily Variety, June 6 and August 12, 1949.
"If your economy-minded production heads":
Faith, *Life in Comedy,* 202.
"lifts comedian Bob Hope": Time, June 27,
1949.
the three combined to boost Hope: Phil Koury,
"New Box-Office King," *New York Times,*
January 8, 1950.
Hope was hesitant: Hope, *Have Tux,* 200.
"We'll move your pin": Ibid., 201.
"Get me some soup": Ibid., 203.
"The Bob Hope Christmas stint": Daily Variety,
December 29, 1949.
"His professional jaunts have astonished":
Koury, *New York Times,* January 8, 1950.

Chapter 8: Television

"I remember how my head jerked": Faith, *Life*
in Comedy, 207.

"Never trust a politician": Ibid., 209.

"I started in this sort of racket": Otis J. Guernsey Jr., "Bob Hope Takes Times Square by Storm," *New York Herald Tribune,* March 5, 1950.

Hope set house records: Daily Variety, March 2, 1950.

"Where was Hope": Advertisement in *Variety,* March 15, 1950.

"It was very intuitive and correct": Tony Bennett, interview with author.

In May 1948 . . . only 325,000 TV sets in American homes: "The Infant Grows Up," *Time,* May 24, 1948.

By the end of 1949, that number had grown: Radio Electronics Television Manufacturers Association figures, http://www.earlytelevision.org.

The radio audience was dropping: Jeff Greenfield, *Television: The First 50 Years* (Harry N. Abrams, 1977), 44.

"The only radio comic": Walt Taliaferro, *Los Angeles Daily News,* May 30, 1949.

"I want to take a little bet": Letter from John Royal, June 29, 1949, "Bob Hope and American Variety," Library of Congress exhibit.

"Berle can have that medium": Letter from Hope, ibid.

Hugh Davis . . . came to visit Hope: Hope, *Have Tux,* 237.

more than had ever before been spent on a single hour: Time correspondent files, April 1950.

"I'm being underpaid": Time correspondent files, April 1950.

"It was very difficult": Mort Lachman, video interview, Academy of Television Arts & Sciences (ATAS) archives.

"His hand was soaking wet": Carl Reiner, interview with author.

"seemed subdued and uncertain": "The $1,500-a-Minute Program," *Life,* April 24, 1950.

"petrified with fear": John Lester, *New York Journal-American,* quoted in Faith, *Life in Comedy,* 213.

"I couldn't believe how nervous": Faith, *Life in Comedy,* 214.

"It was really caveman TV": Gelbart, interview with author.

"I used to work very fast": Hope, *Have Tux,* 238.

a deal that guaranteed Hope $3 million: Variety, May 17 and September 27, 1950, January 10, 1951.

Hope struck a new deal with Paramount: Variety, September 6, 1950.

MacArthur had requested . . . But Hope prevailed: Daily Variety, October 11, 1950.

"He held us spellbound"; "Most of them are so young": Hope, It Says Here column, Octo-

ber 23, 1950.

"How long have you been here?": Hope with Shavelson, *Don't Shoot,* 181.

"The only thing we're going in for": "Bob Hope and Marilyn Maxwell in Wonsan Before Leathernecks," *Los Angeles Times,* October 27, 1950.

"I always had the feeling": Hope with Shavelson, *Don't Shoot,* 183.

sued . . . for making jokes: New York Herald Tribune, June 29, 1950.

"Writers got $2,000 a week": John Crosby, "Radio's Seven Deadly Sins," *Life,* November 6, 1950.

Hope sought $2 million: Daily Variety, November 17, 1950.

eventually dropped the suit: Variety, May 26, 1951.

"He was the worst egomaniac": Quirk, *Road Well-Traveled,* 222.

"I have learned that there is absolutely no truth": Quoted in Faith, *Life in Comedy,* 223.

"Our mission in life": Liberman, unpublished memoir.

"The boss knew a number of people": Faith, *Life in Comedy,* 223–24.

"I think he's a great man": Joan Barthel, "Bob Hope: The Road Gets Rougher," *Life,* January 29, 1971.

"If he's had romances": Betty Beale, "And Here's a Lady Who Loves Him," *Washing-*

ton Star, May 24, 1978.

"It never bothered me": Lahr, "C.E.O. of Comedy."

"I'm sure that my mother knew": Linda Hope, interview with author.

"She had grace under fire": Rory Burke, interview with author.

SLEEP IN A WIGWAM TONIGHT: Liberman, unpublished memoir.

called Maxwell the second most serious: Ibid.

ranked him as Britain's No. 1 box-office star: Guardian, December 28, 1951.

"had lapses into feebleness": Quoted in *Time* correspondent files, April 1951.

"If little that Hope gave us": Guardian, April 25, 1951.

Hope impulsively promised: Faith, *Life in Comedy,* 224–25.

"Bob was really great to us kids": Thompson, *Portrait of a Superstar,* 94.

"Hope never looked like a serious contender": Variety, January 30 and 31, 1952.

"How hard can you hit": Ibid.

got his rescue man, Frank Tashlin: Hope and Thomas, *Road to Hollywood, 76–77.*

"95 minutes of uninhibited mirth": Variety, July 16, 1952.

Prompted the Catholic Legion of Decency: Variety, August 6, 1952.

Hope . . . said he was going to lay off television: Daily Variety, December 7, 1951.

"I didn't think it fair": Lamour, *My Side of the Road,* 190.

"I haven't seen this much of Bob": Kathryn Crosby, *My Life with Bing* (Collage, 1983), 197.

"Realizing how important it was": Lamour, *My Side of the Road,* 198.

Starr had to threaten to sue: Ben Starr, interview with author.

"He still holds Hollywood like King Kong": Carrie Rickey, interview with author.

"I think it's Americanism" . . . *Many in the audience booed:* Undated wire-service story, *Time* archives.

the FCC at the last minute withheld: Variety, November 25, 1953.

Hope wanted the cards as big as possible: Barney McNulty, video interview, ATAS archives.

"It's not only a challenge, but it gives Bob": Variety, October 13, 1952.

"Hope at his old-time radio best": Variety, November 12, 1952.

"Seldom has the immediacy": Jack Gould, *New York Times,* March 23, 1953.

"socko almost all the way": Variety, March 25, 1953.

"Why didn't you play this well yesterday?": Bob Hope, as told to Dwayne Netland, *Confessions of a Hooker: My Lifelong Love Affair with Golf* (Doubleday, 1987), 75.

didn't attend a single meeting: Daily Variety, June 11, 1953.

the first monthly installment . . . sold 5.2 million copies: Army Archerd, Daily Variety, February 16, 1954.

"That breezy Bob Hope": Hope, Have Tux, v–vi.

"He told me he starts with his feet": Arlene Dahl, interview with author.

"Bob was doing about twelve other things": Thompson, Portrait of a Superstar, 107.

"misses as often as it clicks": Daily Variety, March 1, 1954.

"Aside from a few scattered laughs": Hollywood Reporter, March 1, 1954.

"only asking for good stories": Hedda Hopper, Los Angeles Times, October 6, 1954.

"Let them sue me": Faith, Life in Comedy, 253.

"In television in America": Time correspondent files, November 1954.

"As an evening's entertainment": Daily Variety, December 8, 1954.

"Entertainment will continue to be": Daily Variety, November 24, 1954.

saying he wanted to take a break: Daily Variety, February 1, 1955.

"It didn't really affect me for three days": Faith, Life in Comedy, 255.

"The gang at Lakeside will tell you": Jack Hellman, Daily Variety, February 14, 1955.

Hope agreed to a new five-year contract: Daily

Variety, June 9, 1955.

Mel Shavelson and Jack Rose . . . came to see him: Shavelson describes the scene in *How to Succeed in Hollywood,* 60.

Cagney took no salary: Ibid., 61.

"I think the way things are going": Louella Parsons, *Los Angeles Examiner,* Pictorial Living, June 26, 1955.

"A commanding abandonment of the buffoon": Daily *Variety,* May 26, 1955.

"Hope can now hold up his head": New York Daily News, quoted in Faith, *Life in Comedy,* 253.

"The family changed in the 1950s": Malatesta, interview with author.

"She looked at the report cards": Kelly Hope, interview with author.

"This trashy magazine": Linda Hope, interview with author.

Chapter 9: Ambassador

Bob Hope applied for a visa: Daily Variety, November 15, 1955.

"greatest I've ever seen": Daily Variety, May 7, 1956.

"I've seen many a curtain go up": Daily Variety, November 15, 1955.

didn't even return his phone calls: Hedda Hopper, *Los Angeles Times,* December 24, 1954.

drew a protest from the cameramen's union:

Daily Variety, January 7, 1955.

"In an era when even the best": "Bob Hope and the 7 Year Itch," *Variety,* March 6, 1957.

drew protests from both Canadian and British fans: "Canadians Irked by Bob Hope's Royalty Jokes," *Los Angeles Times,* November 17, 1955.

When Hope looked at the books: Memo from Jimmy Saphier, March 14, 1957, Hope archives.

"I'm a hit but going broke": "Bob Hope Going for Broke on TV," *Daily Variety,* December 27, 1956.

Under the new deal, NBC would pay: Daily Variety, February 6, 1957.

"The land purchase was done directly": Tom Sarnoff, interview with author.

"Bob was known to hang on to his real estate": Art Linkletter, interview with author.

"He was very patient"; "Thank God I had grown up": Eva Marie Saint, interview with author.

"Leave it to Bob Hope": Variety, June 20, 1956.

"too much the type of entertainment": "Has Video Staled Screen Quipping?," *Variety,* August 1, 1956.

Hope merely suggested a few "hokey thoughts": Hope and Thomas, *Road to Hollywood,* 85–86.

"I had been sold a false bill of goods"; "the biggest egomaniac": A. Scott Berg, *Kate Remembered* (Berkley, 2004), 232.

"After only two days I realized": Michael Freed-
land, *Katharine Hepburn* (W. H. Allen,
1984), 141.

Hepburn was "a gem": Hope and Thomas,
Road to Hollywood, 86.

*"This is to notify you"; "I am most understand-
ing":* "Ex-Partners," *Time,* October 15,
1956.

"The notion of these two characters": Bosley
Crowther, *New York Times,* February 2,
1957.

Filming was scheduled to begin: Hope gives a
long account of the *Paris Holiday* troubles
in *I Owe Russia $1200* (Doubleday, 1963),
81–107.

"Each time I pack my bags": Hopper, *Los
Angeles Times,* December 25, 1957.

He had renewed his application: Hope, *I Owe
Russia,* 11–17; and Faith, *Life in Comedy,*
257–58.

"What does your Mr. Hope want to do": Hope, *I
Owe Russia,* 13.

"This was to prevent us": Ibid., 216.

"I still don't know who went through": Ibid., 235.

"Can you believe it?"; "Congratulations": Lachman, interview with author.

"What we are trying to do is to state": Hope, *I
Owe Russia,* 252.

"I wish there'd been a lot more Russia": Cecil
Smith, *Los Angeles Times,* April 8, 1958.

"Who would have thought": Gould, *New York*

Times, April 7, 1958.

Sitting next to Mrs. Khrushchev: Hope describes the encounter in *Don't Shoot,* 231–34.

"Guys ask me all the time": Weekend 7, no. 42 (1957), Hope archives.

Timex . . . dropped him after just one month: Daily Variety, October 21, 1957.

"It's getting out there in person"; "I sit in my office": Pete Martin, "I Call on Bob Hope," *Saturday Evening Post,* April 26, 1958.

Hope told Millar (without irony): Faith, *Life in Comedy,* 272.

"The walls of the room . . . started closing in": Hope, *I Owe Russia,* 166.

"Stop lying to me": Ibid., 186.

"Bob Hope to Fly East": Beverly Hills Citizen, March 2, 1959.

Several people offered to donate: Get-well letters, Hope archives.

"If I had taken a day off": Louella Parsons, "Faith, Hope and Charities," *Los Angeles Examiner,* Pictorial Living, March 29, 1959.

Hope "seemed depressed": Vernon Scott, UPI, March 2, 1959.

"He's quieter now"; "Nobody moved as fast": Vernon Scott, "Bob Hope — on the Road to Retirement?," *Los Angeles Examiner,* May 10, 1959.

"I felt . . . people were always looking past me":

Timothy White, *Rolling Stone,* March 20, 1980.

Hope chewed out Bill Faith: Faith, *Life in Comedy,* 274.

"Bob Hope is the champ": George Rosen, "Familiarity Breeds TV Fame," *Variety,* February 10, 1960.

"Don't you think this is a rather strange way": Letter from Jimmy Saphier, August 5, 1959, Hope archives.

"It's a little straight": Hope and Thomas, *Road to Hollywood,* 88.

"I don't want it to be the Road": Ibid.

"Was I Lucy?": Ibid., 89.

Hope wanted instead . . . Frank ended up using his own: Thompson, *Portrait of a Superstar,* 129–30.

"I entertained his father!": Hope, *I Owe Russia,* 187.

a deal that Hope publicly complained about: Dan E. Moldea, *Dark Victory: Ronald Reagan, MCA and the Mob* (Viking, 1986), 142–43.

"Lenny, you're for educational TV": San Diego *Union,* April 6, 1978.

Chapter 10: King

"It was scary": Janis Paige, interview with author.

"Everybody hated Zsa Zsa": Andy Williams, interview with author.

"He said, 'Jan, she's throwing hysterics' ": Paige, interview with author.

"Bob Hope is such a good American": "Sinatra Suspects Had Earlier Plot," *New York Times,* February 28, 1964.

"If there is anybody who has": *Daily Variety,* March 6, 1962.

in Seattle, drawing crowds so big: *Daily Variety,* July 13, 1962.

who would take Hope . . . to Jack Ruby's nightclub: Tony Zoppi, interview with author.

Hope did the show, unaware that Nichols: Many letters and clippings in the Hope archives chronicle this misconceived event, including a wrap-up by Tony Zoppi in the *Dallas Morning News,* July 2, 1962.

"Let's face it, Bob": Letter from Warren Leslie, July 5, 1962, Hope archives.

"I can't wait till I get home": *Time* correspondent files, June 8, 1962.

"He was just a doll": Jack Shea, video interview, ATAS archives.

"This is one of the only bills"; *"The president was a very gay"*; *"I feel very humble"*: *New York Times,* September 12, 1963; and *Time* correspondent files, September 12, 1963.

"Hope is the closest anybody": George Rosen, "Of Hope (Bob) and Fulfillment," *Variety,* April 26, 1961.

"This is all the talent we have, fellas": *Time* correspondent files, September 1963.

"When things go wrong": Ibid.

Hope would call and bark: Mort Lachman, interview with author.

Bob would sometimes squeeze Mort's arm: Time correspondent files, September 1963.

Lachman was miffed and quit . . . went back to Hope: Lachman's break and reconciliation chronicled in *Daily Variety* stories, March 25, April 13 and 15, 1964.

around $350,000 per hour, plus another $50,000: Rosen, *Variety,* April 26, 1961.

too steep for Buick: Variety, March 22, 1961.

"He's shallow in the sense": Time correspondent files, September 1963.

"When he's not quipping": Ibid.

no whistling . . . or hats: Liberman, unpublished memoir.

"If it were Danny Thomas": Time correspondent files, September 1963.

"Bob who?": Art Schneider, video interview, ATAS archives.

"From now on, don't argue": Hal Kanter, interview with author.

"Are you telling these interviewers": Liberman, unpublished memoir.

"There's always some guy": Time correspondent files, September 1963.

"I never put in another expense account": Sid Smith, interview with author.

When Alberti arrived . . . Hope asked why: Bob Alberti, *Up the Ladder and Over the Top* (Bob Alberti, 2003), 136.

Even a family member . . . was startled to get a bill: Nathaniel Lande, interview with author.

"We were paying it off": Dorothy Reilly, interview with author.

"Why did he care?": Bob Mills, interview with author.

"Thanks a lot, kid": Janis Paige, interview with author.

"Well, if they settle for anything less": Time correspondent files, September 1963.

"Emotionally he's still the vaudevillian": Ibid.

"Dad was always of the mind": Linda Hope, interview with author.

"Even within the family": Justine Carr, interview with author.

"He was an impersonal guy": Malatesta, interview with author.

"We sat down for dinner": John Guare, interview with author.

"You could imagine Theresa": Ibid.

"It was not a house full of undercurrents": Ibid.

"They obviously had a lot of money . . . The Hopes were very supportive . . . He was very kind to me": Tony Coelho, interview with author.

"Your hospital needs a new wing?": Dwight Whitney, "Bob Hope," *TV Guide,* January 16, 1965.

"It was something that obviously called out": Linda Hope, interview with author.

"Bob admitted to me that the great love": Liberman, unpublished memoir.

Frankland died of a drug overdose: "Britain's First Miss World Killed by Drug Overdose," *London Telegraph,* December 18, 2000.

"Bob Hope lives in his own world": Dana M. Reemes, *Directed by Jack Arnold* (McFarland, 2012), 152.

Hope proposed a gala premiere: Memos from Arthur Jacobs, January 1959, AMPAS archives.

"I explained to Bob that the magazines": Ibid.

"The film industry needs a positive approach": *Variety,* May 9, 1962.

"It'll be Southern California's answer": Peter Bart, "Bob Hope to Build Own Disneyland," *New York Times,* July 31, 1965.

The Bob Hope Desert Classic had its origins: The tournament's history is recounted by Larry Bohannan in *50 Years of Hope* (Pediment Publishing).

The mammoth field included: Bill Shirley, "Pros to Tee Off at Desert Today," *Los Angeles Times,* January 22, 1965.

"He never came to a board meeting": Ernie Dunlevie, interview with author.

"without doubt one of the best": Eddie Gannon, interview with author.

"He could hit the ball farther": Lachman, interview with author.

"He would do a benefit": Linda Hope, interview with author.

"He was a fair golfer": Arnold Palmer, interview with author.

"Palmer got the blue-collar guys": Dunlevie, interview with author.

once on a course that filled the inside: Hope, *Confessions of a Hooker,* 8.

Chapter 11: Patriot

the Air Force limited Hope's troupe: Variety, December 20, 1961.

"Hope did a valid service": Dorothy Reilly, interview with author.

a marine who claimed he had "hitchhiked": Faith, *Life in Comedy,* 284.

"Christmas without Bob Hope": Variety, December 11, 1963.

"one of the roughest we've ever had": "Dick, Please Be Good, So I Can Bow," *TV Guide,* April 11, 1964.

"Bob Hope is so established": Jack Gould, *New York Times,* January 18, 1964.

"greater than that normally used": UPI dispatch, *New York Times,* December 25, 1964.

for every five thousand men: Faith, *Life in Comedy,* 298.

they found a chaotic scene: The Brinks bombing was widely reported at the time. More complete accounts of it are in Bob Hope, *Five Women I Love: Bob Hope's Vietnam Story* (Avon, 1966), 111–21; and Faith, *Life in Comedy,* 299–300.

"We had no electricity": Mort Lachman papers,

Writers Guild of America archives.

"tiny room, with one Coke bottle": Janis Paige, interview with author.

"We supposedly had thirty thousand men"; "I started complaining"; "He was definitely not a hawk": Jill St. John, interview with author.

"Shortly after the explosion": AP, March 17, 1967.

The cue-card stand had collapsed: McNulty gives his version of the widely repeated story in a video interview, ATAS archives.

an "altogether asinine": Howard Thompson, *New York Times,* August 12, 1965.

"Hello, Yankee dogs!": Bob Thomas, AP, July 21, 1965.

It was a rough trip from the start: The 1965 Vietnam tour is recounted at length in Hope, *Five Women;* as well as in Faith, *Life in Comedy,* 306–8; and Lachman's papers, Writers Guild archives.

"In case of an attack": Jack Jones, interview with author.

"Tension became almost unbearable": Hope, *Five Women,* 169.

"It was one of the most emotional": Jones, interview with author.

"He was a happy, positive force": Ibid.

Bing Crosby sent him a letter: AP, *Los Angeles Times,* December 31, 1965.

Jack Shea . . . reluctantly told Hope: Jack Shea, video interview, ATAS archives.

"On January first I would take a thirty-day leave": Art Schneider, video interview, ATAS archives.

"Because of his continued and patriotic": Congressional Record, January 27, 1966.

"frequent visitor to Vietnam"; "Camp Runamuck"; "It's on the paper": Variety, April 6, 1966.

He taped a half-hour TV program: Variety, February 16, 1966.

"Can you imagine returning": Bob Hope, "An Open Letter About Our GI's," Family Weekly, June 12, 1966.

"One group is fighting": Faith, Life in Comedy, 311.

"People seem to forget": Peter Bart, "Cold War Alters a Hollywood Law," New York Times, August 5, 1965.

"They call you a comedian": Jack Warner, letter to Hope, December 26, 1963, Hope archives.

More than 62 percent said yes: Faith, Life in Comedy, 312–13.

"a couple of the Washington boys": Ibid., 312.

only 60 percent of the seats . . . at the Yale Bowl: Variety, July 27, 1966.

some stars turned him down: Tom Buckley, "Hope Says Some Performers Refused Vietnam Trip," New York Times, December 22, 1966.

The new Miss World . . . nearly backed out:

AP, "India's Miss World Reconsiders Plan for Trip to South Vietnam," *New York Times,* November 28, 1966.

He played the straight man": Phyllis Diller, interview with author.

Hope just missed . . . Lynda Bird Johnson: Bob Hope, as told to Pete Martin, *The Last Christmas Show* (Doubleday, 1974), 209.

give him small parts . . . and sent regular "royalty" checks: Robert Colonna, *Greetings, Gate!,* 217; and interview with author.

"She was charming and lovely": Lachman papers, Writers Guild archives.

"The last thing those guys needed": Sally and Ivor Davis, "Always Another Show to Play," *Chicago Tribune,* April 2, 1978.

In Bangkok, Hope and his troupe: Accounts of the 1966 tour in Hope, *Last Christmas Show,* 209–27; and Lachman's papers, Writers Guild archives.

"We saw the show site": Lachman papers, Writers Guild archives.

"This is what has to win it": Hope, *Last Christmas Show,* 223.

"Bob and Westy would sit up talking": Lukas, "This Is Bob (Politician-Patriot-Publicist) Hope," *New York Times Magazine,* October 4, 1970.

"Everybody I talked to there": Hal Humphrey, *Los Angeles Times,* January 18, 1967.

"I'd rather be a hawk": UPI, *New York Times,*

December 31, 1966.

"When you get guys like Eisenhower": Bob Hope interview, *Playboy,* December 1973.

"He was very supportive": Coelho, interview with author.

"If Kennedy had lived": John Johns, interview with Hope, *California* magazine, March 1977.

"It was difficult for him": Linda Hope, interview with author.

Her father gave the blessing: Account of the wedding from Judith Richards Hope, interview with author.

"When you come onstage": Raquel Welch, interview with author.

"He never got ruffled"; *"I was over there to entertain"*: Ibid.

"the land of rising commitment": Hope, *Last Christmas Show,* 243.

"embarrassing"; *"ungracious"*: Gould, "Will Emmy Do Better Than Oscar and Tony?," *New York Times,* April 28, 1968.

"It was difficult to be funny": "Forty Is a Dangerous Age," *Time,* April 19, 1968.

"I went with Bob because": Faith, *Life in Comedy,* 318.

"What a boon he is": *Variety,* January 17, 1969.

"I wanted to get married under a tree": Nathaniel Lande, interview with author.

"Texas wouldn't rent us the Astrodome"; *"Linda, Linda"*: Army Archerd, *Daily Variety,* Janu-

877

ary 13, 1969.
"You'll make a Republican": Lande, interview with author.

Chapter 12: Partisan

"See what one dinner": Lukas, "This Is Bob," *New York Times Magazine.*
"The humorous 'one-liners' ": Letter from Agnew, December 31, 1968, Hope archives.
"We hated writing for a repressive": Lukas, "This Is Bob."
"He took natural advantage": Dwight Chapin, interview with author.
"Where There's Death": A letter to Hope from a University of Michigan student apologizing for the leaflets, Hope archives.
"Hell, I'm for peace": Faith, *Life in Comedy,* 332.
"It's those small minorities": Ibid., 329.
"rigged clips": Daily Variety, November 13, 1969.
"I have no doubt that Hope": Daily Variety, November 14, 1969.
One of the Golddiggers . . . unfurled: Connie Stevens, interview with author — though Faith, describing what was apparently the same incident in *Life in Comedy* (333), attributed the disruption to one of the Golddiggers trying to get Nixon's autograph.
Hope . . . was so late getting there: Faith, *Life in Comedy,* 334.

President Nixon . . . threatened to fire: H. R. Haldeman, *The Haldeman Diaries: Inside the Nixon White House* (Putnam, 1994), 111.

described it as only a "smattering": Faith's account of the incident is in *Life in Comedy*, 335.

"After about fifteen minutes": Timothy White, *Rolling Stone,* March 20, 1980.

"I happened to be walking": Connie Stevens, interview with author.

"They were severely wounded": Ibid.

"A few kids, about five": Barthel, "Bob Hope: The Road Gets Rougher," *Life.*

"the coldest, most unresponsive"; "It had been a wipeout day": Hope, *Last Christmas Show,* 290.

"Our response . . . came out of fear and loneliness": White, *Rolling Stone,* March 20, 1980.

showed a loss of $274,000: J. L. Kubin, secretary for Hope Enterprises, relates these figures in a memo to NBC's Tom Sarnoff, Hope archives.

For the 1969–70 season, his average rating soared: Variety, April 29, 1970.

"one of those curiously lackadaisical": William Tusher, *Hollywood Reporter,* March 20, 1970.

"everyone has hurriedly gotten together": John Mahoney, *Hollywood Reporter,* April 13, 1970.

"They are so prejudiced": Letter from Jimmy Saphier, April 15, 1970, Hope archives.

"This kind of bitchy, ill-tempered": Letter from Charles Lee, Hope archives.

"This is one day we're not trying": Carol H. Falk, "Comic Bob Hope Calls His Rally Nonpartisan, but Some Are Dubious," *Wall Street Journal,* July 3, 1970.

"designed to show a phony national consensus": "Rennie Davis Scores Honor America Day," *New York Times,* June 25, 1970.

Demonstrators . . . started early: John Herbers, "Thousands Voice Faith in America at Capital Rally," *New York* Times, July 5, 1970.

Hope was driven: Faith, *Life in Comedy,* 345.

When it was over, demonstrators broke through: Faith, *Life in Comedy,* 346.

JOHN WAYNE IS A RACIST: Wiley and Bona, *Inside Oscar,* 437.

Shirley MacLaine yelled: "Mocking the Mockery," *Time,* April 20, 1970.

old-timers such as Bob Hope were "unacceptable": Variety, September 2, 1970.

"I have seen Bob Hope": Colonel Edward M. Kirby, *Variety,* September 9, 1970.

"He just doesn't understand": Lukas, "This Is Bob."

He talked to his attorney: Faith, *Life in Comedy,* 350.

"I just hated to get involved": Leroy F. Aarons, "Bob Hope: A Gadfly to Hawk," *Washing-*

ton *Post,* August 18, 1970.

"It's not American students": Timeri Murari, "The Great White Hope," *Guardian,* November 21, 1970.

Hope . . . learned of the show in advance: Faith has a long account of Hope's *This Is Your Life* segment in *Life in Comedy,* 351–68.

he was interrupted by a handful of women's liberation activists: Accounts of the incident by Nicholas de Jongh, "Beauty O'ershadowed by the Women's Lib," *Guardian,* November 21, 1970; and Faith, *Life in Comedy,* 366–67.

"the worst theatrical experience": Christopher Walker, "Miss World Was Not Amused," *Observer,* November 22, 1970.

"You'll notice about the women": Faith, *Life in Comedy,* 367.

"I didn't talk to the military brass": Bob Thomas, AP, January 14, 1971.

"Hope is not only an entertainer": Jack Gould, *New York Times,* January 31, 1971.

"I thought your closing remarks": Letter from Richard Nixon, January 20, 1971, Hope archives.

"The growing unpopularity of the war": Variety, January 20, 1971.

"out of touch with today's soldier": Variety, February 17, 1971.

not *invited to . . . the Ohio State Fair: Variety,* July 7, 1971.

"uncritical endorsement of the . . . Indochina war": Grace Lichtenstein, "Church Council Bars Award to Bob Hope," *New York Times,* March 18, 1971.

"I couldn't say anything against": AP, March 19, 1971.

called the Vietnam War "a beautiful thing": Barthel, "The Road Gets Rougher."

claimed he had been misquoted: Kenneth J. Fanucchi, "Bob Hope Denies He Called War in Vietnam 'Beautiful,' " *Los Angeles Times,* March 17, 1971.

Her tape recorder had actually run out: Joan Barthel, interview with author.

"Do you have a lunch date tomorrow?": Barthel, "The Road Gets Rougher."

"I learned it was better not to engage": Lande, interview with author.

"That was the only time": McCullagh, interview with author.

"If the people of Vietnam want": Transcript of appearance at Southern Methodist University, January 29, 1971, Hope archives.

Shavelson told Hope they should drop: Davis, *Chicago Tribune,* April 2, 1978.

"Money insulates you": Ibid.

"His attitude was we could finish it": Ibid.

"Anyone . . . who dares to take a stand": Faith, *Life in Comedy,* 371.

"He knew we were going to win": *Daily Variety,* September 29, 1971.

"I thank you . . . for bringing a little happiness":

Letter from Linda Faulkner, January 1, 1970, Hope archives.

"The servicemen over there believe": Hope form reply, Hope archives.

"These men must be completely desperate": Letter from Mrs. James Stockdale, February 17, 1969, Hope archives.

The next day an Air Force plane: Accounts of the POW meeting in Hope, *Last Christmas Show,* 326–29; and Faith, *Life in Comedy,* 374–77.

"I'd known all along": Hope, *Last Christmas Show,* 331–32.

"I know one thing": Hope letter to Jimmy Saphier, March 3, 1972.

"It was . . . an awkward phone call": Memo from Dwight Chapin to H. R. Haldeman, September 30, 1971, Richard Nixon Presidential Library.

"Sit down": White House tapes, conversation 714–22, April 20, 1972, Nixon Library.

"You're the war hero": Ibid.

"Your friendship and support": Letter from Nixon to Hope, October 26, 1972, Nixon Library.

By mid-1972 the USO had only three: Variety, April 26, 1972.

At least fifteen aircraft . . . were lost: Hope, *Last Christmas Show,* 344.

an uncharacteristic diplomatic lapse: Jack Foise, "Hope Forced to Explain His Jokes to Ruffled Thais," *Los Angeles Times,* December 25, 1972.

"Back in the States, a negative press": Ray Siller, e-mail to author.

Siller had to gin up a monologue: Ray Siller, interview with author.

Hope called . . . to wish Nixon a happy sixtieth birthday: White House tapes, conversation 35-108, January 9, 1973.

"You must be beaming all over!" White House tapes, conversation 43-109, February 15, 1973.

"What you did is something else": White House tapes, conversation 872-19, March 8, 1973.

Chapter 13: Restoration

another film with Gleason: Daily Variety, June 17, 1969.

a comedy by writer-director David Swift: Variety, January 20, 1971.

Marx and Fisher protested: Marx, *Secret Life of Bob Hope,* 416–18.

The two were at odds; "We argued about everything": Paul Bogart, interview with author.

"You are fucking impossible!": Ibid.

just six hundred . . . seats were filled: Variety, October 18, 1972.

"you and Bing would simply overpower": Letter from Neil Simon, January 24, 1973, Hope archives.

Art Linkletter . . . was impressed: Linkletter,

interview with author.

First, Hope was late: The account of Hope's troubles at the inauguration comes from Maxine Cheshire, "Backstage, Offstage, Onstage," *Washington Post,* January 22, 1973; and a member of Hope's entourage.

At a Weight Watchers rally . . . he was booed: Variety, July 18, 1973.

"I wish they'd flush the whole thing": Variety, June 20, 1973.

"I think dragging this thing": Interview in *Playboy,* December 1973.

"If the other guy got a laugh": Jonathan Winters, interview with author.

"He was usually at dinner": Avis Truska, interview with author.

Every fire truck and volunteer firefighter: "Showplace Home of Bob Hope Destroyed in Palm Springs Fire," *Los Angeles Times,* July 25, 1973.

Construction was put on hold . . . recovered $430,000 in damages: Peter Aleshire, "But I Wanna Tell Ya About This House," *New West,* September 11, 1978.

"Eddie Cantor haircut": Don Marando, interview with author.

"Watching him throw on that pancake": Ibid.

only if he got paid more than any other performer: Elliott Kozak, interview with author.

Rosemary Clooney . . . challenged the woman's story: Anecdote related by Michael Fein-

885

stein, interview with author.

The next time you talk to Bob": Lande, interview with author.

"It was his way of saying": Ben Starr, interview with author.

Waiting for him there: Marando, interview with author.

"I now know why you were captain": Typewritten draft for telegram, March 15, 1974, Hope archives.

"I would like the President to know": Hope letter to Rose Mary Woods, May 31, 1974, Hope archives.

"It was so sad for that poor bastard": Tom Donnelly, "Bob Hope: I've Enjoyed All of It," *Washington Post,* February 14, 1975.

"I told him The Towering Inferno": "Hope, Wayne Talk Politics," *UCLA Daily Bruin,* April 14, 1975.

"I just think that Nixon got himself": Johns, *California,* March 1977.

"Of all the Presidents": Bob Hope, *Dear Prez, I Wanna Tell Ya!* (Hope Enterprises, 1996), 99.

The statement caused a stir; "Don't you dare!": Accounts of the Schneider brouhaha in Wiley and Bona, *Inside Oscar,* 504–7; and *Daily Variety,* April 10, 1975.

a "cheap, cheap shot"; "the Academy's authorized representative": Ibid.

"So he was screwed up": Shirley MacLaine, interview with author.

"He was stingy to the end": The eulogy is contained in Lachman's papers in the Writers Guild archives, strongly implying that he wrote it.

she had to pester her former boss: Letters from Hughes to Hope, November 1974, Hope archives.

Texaco . . . agreed to pay $3.15 million: Faith, *Life in Comedy,* 392.

"It had to be done": Ibid., 393.

"Bob caved in": Kozak, interview with author.

"He was very sad": Lachman, video interview, ATAS archives.

"I was shocked, disappointed and dismayed": Letter from Felix De Cola, *Los Angeles Times,* July 15, 1976.

"much harder than writing": Letters to the editor, *Los Angeles Times,* July 24, 1976.

"the Queen and Prince Philip enjoyed"; "to have such a great man as Bob Hope": Ibid.

"The problem with Dad": Linda Hope, interview with author.

"I was in England writing a show": Lande, interview with author.

She was paid . . . only $600: White, *Rolling Stone,* March 20, 1980.

"My God, Kanter": Hal Kanter, interview with author.

The production was beset with problems: Barney Rosenzweig, interview with author.

"He felt he failed": Ibid.

"Bob and Dolores thought everyone": Judith Richards Hope, interview with author.

"Bob called Tony a lot": Ibid.

"It looks like you've been writing for me": Gene Perret, interview with author.

"I've got six more weeks": Bob Mills, interview with author.

"He liked people who worked fast": Perret, interview with author.

the audience was actually a group of chiropractors: Gene Perret and Martha Bolton, *Talk About Hope* (Jester Press, 1998), 26.

"How much time do you have?": Mills, interview with author.

"I pay you with new money": Perret and Bolton, *Talk About Hope,* 15.

"The other guys will be hot": Perret, interview with author.

Hope said he was going to play golf: Robert L. Mills, *The Laugh Makers: A Behind-the-Scenes Tribute to Bob Hope's Incredible Gag Writers* (Robert L. Mills, 2009), 16.

"Milton Berle liked to retake jokes": Sid Smith, interview with author.

"She thinks I just got into this business": Howard Albrecht, interview with author.

"What the fuck!" cried Hope: Dennis Klein, interview with author.

"It's unlikely that I'll be able": Bing Crosby, letter to Hope, May 3, 1977, Hope archives.

"He had tears in his eyes": Linda Hope,

interview with author.

"The whole world loved Bing Crosby": Daily Variety, October 17, 1977.

but not Dorothy Lamour: Lamour, *My Side of the Road,* 222.

Hope was unhappy that he had to use a teleprompter: Kaplan, *New Times,* August 7, 1978.

"So many guys can't do that": Marty Pasetta, interview with author.

"I can't . . . tell the whole world I'm seventy-five": Kozak, interview with author.

"It's taken over a year": Tom Shales, "Bob Hope Breakthrough," *Washington Post,* May 24, 1978.

"I'm pretty sure I'm seventy-five": Faith, *Life in Comedy,* 403.

"Can't we change it to eleven?": Ibid.

"that peculiarly square and predictable style": Variety, May 31, 1978.

"Are you still working for me?": Liberman, unpublished memoir.

"When he pays you a salary": Kozak, interview with author.

"Oh, you don't have time for me anymore?": Ibid.

"he's gotta come up with the fifty thousand": Ibid.

"You don't trust me": Ibid.

Nixon put in a call: White House tapes, March 8, 1973, Nixon Library.

Hope called choreographer George Balanchine: James Lipton, *Inside Inside* (New American Library, 2008), 216–17.

When he and his entourage got off the plane: Accounts of the China trip in Lipton, *Inside Inside;* Mills, *Laugh Makers;* and interviews with Linda Hope and Marcia Lewis Smith.

"The Chinese were very, very difficult": Marcia Lewis Smith, interview with author.

Linda Hope . . . had the cameras record all of it: Linda Hope, interview with author.

"Dad was really aggravated": Ibid.

An aide to President Carter worked with Tony Hope: Judith Richards Hope, interview with author.

"When my mother took me to see": Film tribute to Hope, Film Society of Lincoln Center archives.

"Oh, go on, highbrows": Kaplan, *New Times,* August 7, 1978.

"Age cannot wither": Tom Dowling, *Washington Star,* May 26, 1978.

Fortune *magazine put him on its list:* Arthur M. Louis, "America's Centimillionaires," *Fortune,* May 1968.

"Mrs. Hope was kind of a frustrated architect": Nancy Gordon Zaslove, interview with author.

"I love that little house": Andy Williams, interview with author.

Chapter 14: Legend

"Bob Hope would go to the opening": Quoted in Joan Collins, *Second Act* (St. Martin's Press, 1996), 112.

"Hell, if I did": Al Martinez, "Comedy in Motion," *TV Guide,* October 25, 1980.

stewed fruit, decaffeinated coffee, and a B-complex multivitamin: Jolie Edmonson, "Where There's Hope, There's Life," *Saturday Evening Post,* October 1981.

"Procrastination is the number one cause": Ibid.

Hope made 174 personal appearances: Faith, *Life in Comedy,* 415.

"The thing that impressed me": Rick Ludwin, interview with author.

"We had so many problems": Fred Silverman, interview with author.

"I know that Nancy": Letter from Bob Hope, October 22, 1981, Ronald Reagan Presidential Library.

"Please don't concern yourself": Reagan reply, October 27, 1981, Reagan Library.

"Do you want us to stick to policy on this?": Memo from Dodie Livingston to Mike Deaver, April 10, 1981, Reagan Library.

"Randy, don't overdo"; "Keep it short": Various memos, Reagan Library.

"The thing I remember . . . is that he'd show up": Stu Spencer, interview with author.

"I always felt your career": Ann Jillian, inter-

view with author.

"He was bigger than life": Cathy Lee Crosby, interview with author.

Hope got embroiled: Guardian, December 20 and 21, 1983.

"When you're bringing stars over": Ibid.

"He was very demanding": Linda Hope, interview with author.

he asked if the dedication ceremony . . . was disappointed to find out that the building: Faith, *Life in Comedy,* 416–17.

Hope's staff worked diligently: Ibid., 418.

Forbes *magazine put him on its list:* "The Forbes Four Hundred," *Forbes,* September 13, 1982.

"I'll kiss your ass": Richard Behar, "How Rich Is Bob Hope?," *Forbes,* October 1, 1984.

"When we're proved wrong": "On Trusting Bob Hope," editors' note, *Forbes,* October 1, 1984.

It was the first Cavett had heard of it: Dick Cavett, interview with author.

His writers drove around the neighborhood: Mills, interview with author.

"He supported the workingman": Tom Dreesen, interview with author.

"Gene, that's all of us": Perret, interview with author.

"I'd come over to his house": Brooke Shields, interview with author.

"Take the tape": Dave Thomas, interview with author.

"Dave Thomas had a better handle": Casey Keller, interview with author.

"I knew why they were doing it": James Lipton, interview with author.

"It's fake wood": Mills, interview with author.

"The Statue of Liberty has AIDS": Quirk, *Road Well-Traveled,* 305.

"Johnny admired Hope's place": Peter Lassally, interview with author.

"We'd get a request": Ibid.

"We'd say, give us two minutes": Jeff Sotzing, interview with author.

Hope asked during a commercial break: Anecdote related by Bob Dolan Smith, e-mail to author.

"There was nothing spontaneous": Andrew Nicholls, interview with author.

Tartikoff even suggested that Hope try: Memo from Rick Ludwin, July 26, 1983, Hope archives.

"There might have been a time": Margy Rochlin, "Funny Man," *Los Angeles Times Magazine,* February 1, 1987.

"permitting his team of writers": Variety, April 19, 1989.

"The whole show would cost him": Kozak, interview with author.

"He just takes the check": Ibid.

In the mid-1970s, the town of Hope: Memo from Frank Liberman, Hope archives.

"I live for the press": Philip Shenon, "A

Curtain Falls on Bob Hope's Show," *New York Times,* December 26, 1990.

"He was stronger than most": Perret, interview with author.

Alberti had to kneel: Alberti, *Up the Ladder,* 135.

"Great job"; "Aw, come on": Lipton, interview with author.

"Starting in the late eighties, it was affecting": Ludwin, interview with author.

"He got really mad": Shields, interview with author.

"If I ever end up like that": Andrew Nicholls and Darrel Vickers, interview with author.

The fading star was shunted; "We'll do it later": Perret, interview with author.

But what set off a firestorm: The dispute is chronicled in numerous *Los Angeles Times* articles in 1990 and 1991, as well as Tom Johnson, "Bob Hope's Last Road Show," *Los Angeles* magazine, November 1990.

"No one has a larger ownership": Alan Citron, "Park Advocates Pressure Bob Hope for Land Gift," *Los Angeles Times,* March 7, 1990.

HONK IF YOU THINK BOB HOPE: Johnson, "Hope's Last Road Show."

"Hope doesn't owe anyone": Stephen Padgett, letter to the editor, *Los Angeles Times,* March 16, 1990.

"I didn't hold it for twenty-five years": Johnson, "Hope's Last Road Show."

"Bob Hope is making a special gift": "Hope Signs Deal to Turn His Acreage into Parkland," *Los Angeles Times,* November 8, 1991.

"The knocks he's taken": Ron Russell, "Of Faith, Hope and a Little Charity Parks," *Los Angeles Times,* November 14, 1991.

"just a lot of old stuff": *Santa Monica Daily Breeze,* October 24, 1993.

"Her dream was to marry a shoe salesman": Linda Hope, interview with author.

"I don't think it really deeply affected him": Ibid.

Johnny Carson agreed . . . on the assurance: Don Mischer, interview with author.

"I don't know if I can do this": Ibid.

"Bob Hope could have done": Bill Zehme, "Heeeeeerrrre's Dave," *Rolling Stone,* February 18, 1993.

"I said, 'Dad, you don't want to keep on' ": Linda Hope, interview with author.

"I'm not doing that!": Anecdote related by Dave Thomas, interview with author.

Hope puttered around; "Dammit," Hope grumbled: Andrew Coffey, interview with author.

"I practically fell out of my chair": Bill Clinton, interview with author.

"He could see the ball below his feet": Ibid.

"Brandon Tartikoff regarded Bob Hope": Ludwin, interview with author.

"We're doing this one": Related by Michael Thompson, the Hopes' estate manager at

the time, interview with author.

"devote our energies toward specials": Los Angeles Times, November 30, 1995.

"There came a point where all the parties": Ludwin, interview with author.

"I've decided to become a FREE AGENT": Ad in Variety et al., October 23, 1996.

"It was sort of a mutual thing": Linda Hope, interview with author.

"This TV entry?": Daily Variety, November 20, 1996.

"Backstage he was not in good shape": Feinstein, interview with author.

"Her timbre was clear": Stephen Holden, New York Times, May 23, 1997.

"Mrs. Hope joined Bob": Bill Tush, e-mail to author.

Paulin would let him take the wheel: J. Paulin, interview with author.

AP actually reported his death by mistake: Bob Pool, "Yes, America, There Is *Still* Hope," Los Angeles Times, June 6, 1998.

"He was in very critical condition": Paulin, interview with author.

"His eyes light up": Army Archerd, Daily Variety, May 28, 2003.

"I couldn't be here in spirit": Patricia Ward Biederman, "Friends Recall Hope with Tears, Laughter," Los Angeles Times, August 28, 2003.

The New York Times' *obituary:* Vincent

Canby, "Bob Hope, Comedic Master and Entertainer of Troops, Dies at 100," *New York Times,* July 28, 2003.

Time *magazine gave the comedian:* Richard Schickel, "Bob Hope: The Machine-Age Comic," *Time,* August 11, 2003.

one unit of six hundred men . . . marched the ten miles: Time correspondent files, August 1943.

"Never make 'em think": Kaplan, *New Times,* August 7, 1978.

BOB HOPE'S MAJOR WORK

MOVIES

Going Spanish (short, 1934). Educational Films. Director: Al Christie.

Soup for Nuts (short, 1934). Universal. Director: Milton Schwartzwald.

Paree, Paree (short, 1934). Warner Bros. Director: Roy Mack.

Calling All Tars (short, 1935). Warner Bros. Director: Lloyd French.

Watch the Birdie (short, 1935). Warner Bros. Director: Lloyd French.

Double Exposure (short, 1935). Warner Bros. Director: Lloyd French.

The Old Grey Mayor (short, 1935). Warner Bros. Director: Lloyd French.

Shop Talk (short, 1936). Warner Bros. Director: Lloyd French.

The Big Broadcast of 1938 (1938). Paramount. Director: Mitchell Leisen.

College Swing (1938). Paramount. Director: Raoul Walsh.

Give Me a Sailor (1938). Paramount. Director: Elliott Nugent.

Thanks for the Memory (1938). Paramount. Director: George Archainbaud.

Never Say Die (1939). Paramount. Director: Elliott Nugent.

Some Like It Hot (1939). Paramount. Director: George Archainbaud.

The Cat and the Canary (1939). Paramount. Director: Elliott Nugent.

Road to Singapore (1940). Paramount. Director: Victor Schertzinger.

The Ghost Breakers (1940). Paramount. Director: George Marshall.

Road to Zanzibar (1941). Paramount. Director: Victor Schertzinger.

Caught in the Draft (1941). Paramount. Director: David Butler.

Nothing But the Truth (1941). Paramount. Director: Elliott Nugent.

Louisiana Purchase (1941). Paramount. Director: Irving Cummings.

My Favorite Blonde (1942). Paramount. Director: Sidney Lanfield.

Road to Morocco (1942). Paramount. Director: David Butler.

Star Spangled Rhythm (1942). Paramount. Director: George Marshall.

They Got Me Covered (1943). Samuel Goldwyn. Director: David Butler.

Let's Face It (1943). Paramount. Director: Sidney Lanfield.

The Princess and the Pirate (1944). Samuel

Goldwyn. Director: David Butler.

Road to Utopia (1946). Paramount. Director: Hal Walker.

Monsieur Beaucaire (1946). Paramount. Director: George Marshall.

My Favorite Brunette (1947). Paramount. Director: Elliott Nugent.

Variety Girl (1947). Paramount. Director: George Marshall.

Where There's Life (1947). Paramount. Director: Sidney Lanfield.

Road to Rio (1947). Paramount. Director: Norman Z. McLeod.

The Paleface (1948). Paramount. Director: Norman Z. McLeod.

Sorrowful Jones (1949). Paramount. Director: Sidney Lanfield.

The Great Lover (1949). Paramount. Director: Alexander Hall.

Fancy Pants (1950). Paramount. Director: George Marshall.

The Lemon Drop Kid (1951). Paramount. Director: Sidney Lanfield.

My Favorite Spy (1951). Paramount. Director: Norman Z. McLeod.

The Greatest Show on Earth (1951, cameo). Paramount. Director: Cecil B. DeMille.

Son of Paleface (1952). Paramount. Director: Frank Tashlin.

Road to Bali (1952). Paramount. Director: Hal Walker.

Off Limits (1953). Paramount. Director:

George Marshall.

Scared Stiff (1953, cameo). Paramount. Director: George Marshall.

Here Come the Girls (1953). Paramount. Director: Claude Binyon.

Casanova's Big Night (1954). Paramount. Director: Norman Z. McLeod.

The Seven Little Foys (1955). Paramount. Director: Melville Shavelson.

That Certain Feeling (1956). Paramount. Director: Norman Panama, Melvin Frank.

The Iron Petticoat (1956). Paramount. Director: Ralph Thomas.

Beau James (1957). Paramount. Director: Melville Shavelson.

Paris Holiday (1958). United Artists. Director: Gerd Oswald.

Alias Jesse James (1959). United Artists. Director: Norman Z. McLeod.

The Facts of Life (1960). United Artists. Director: Melvin Frank.

Bachelor in Paradise (1961). MGM. Director: Jack Arnold.

The Road to Hong Kong (1962). United Artists. Director: Norman Panama.

Critic's Choice (1963). Warner Bros. Director: Don Weis.

Call Me Bwana (1963). United Artists. Director: Gordon Douglas.

A Global Affair (1964). MGM. Director: Jack Arnold.

I'll Take Sweden (1965). United Artists.

Director: Fred de Cordova.
Boy, Did I Get a Wrong Number! (1966). United Artists. Director: George Marshall.
Eight on the Lam (1967). United Artists. Director: George Marshall.
The Private Navy of Sgt. O'Farrell (1968). United Artists. Director: Frank Tashlin.
How to Commit Marriage (1969). Cinerama. Director: Norman Panama.
Cancel My Reservation (1972). Warner Bros. Director: Paul Bogart.
The Muppet Movie (1979, cameo). ITC Entertainment. Director: James Frawley.
Spies Like Us (1985, cameo). Warner Bros. Director: John Landis.

BROADWAY SHOWS

Sidewalks of New York (October 3, 1927–January 7, 1928). Book, music, and lyrics by Eddie Dowling and James Hanley.
Ups-a Daisy (October 8–December 1, 1928). Music by Lewis A. Gensler, book and lyrics by Clifford Grey and Robert A. Simon.
Smiles (November 18, 1930–January 10, 1931). Music by Vincent Youmans, lyrics by Clifford Grey and Harold Adamson, book by William Anthony McGuire.
Ballyhoo of 1932 (September 6–November 26, 1932). Music by Lewis A. Gensler, lyrics by E. Y. Harburg, book by Norman H. Anthony.
Roberta (November 18, 1933–July 21, 1934).

Music by Jerome Kern, book and lyrics by
Otto Harbach.

Say When (November 8, 1934–January 12,
1935). Music by Ray Henderson, lyrics by
Ted Koehler, book by Jack McGowan.

Ziegfeld Follies of 1936 (January 30–May 9,
1936). Music by Vernon Duke, lyrics by Ira
Gershwin, book by David Freeman.

Red, Hot and Blue (October 29, 1936–April
10, 1937). Music and lyrics by Cole Porter,
book by Howard Lindsay and Russel
Crouse.

RADIO PROGRAMS

The Intimate Revue, sponsored by Bromo-
Seltzer, NBC (January 4–April 5, 1935).

Atlantic Family Show, sponsored by Atlantic
Oil, CBS (December 14, 1935–September
3, 1936).

The Rippling Rhythm Revue, sponsored by
Woodbury soap, NBC (May 9–September
26, 1937).

Your Hollywood Parade, sponsored by Lucky
Strike, NBC (December 29, 1937–March
23, 1938).

The Pepsodent Show, Starring Bob Hope,
NBC (September 27, 1938–June 8, 1948).

The Swan Show, Starring Bob Hope, NBC
(September 14, 1948–June 13, 1950).

The Bob Hope Show, sponsored by Chesterfield, NBC (October 3, 1950–June 24,
1952).

The Bob Hope Show (mornings), sponsored by General Foods, NBC (November 10, 1952–July 9, 1954).

The Bob Hope Show, sponsored by General Foods, NBC (January 7, 1953–July 1, 1953).

The Bob Hope Show, sponsored by the American Dairy Association, NBC (September 25, 1953–April 21, 1955).

TELEVISION MILESTONES

The Star-Spangled Revue, sponsored by Frigidaire (April 9, 1950). First Hope network TV special, broadcast live by NBC on Easter Sunday.

The Colgate Comedy Hour (October 1952– June 1953). One of several rotating hosts on his first regular series.

Academy Awards (March 19, 1953). Host of the first televised Oscar ceremony.

Hope in Greenland (January 9, 1955). First televised holiday tour for the troops.

The Bob Hope Show, sponsored by Chevrolet (1955–57), Plymouth (1958), and Buick (1958–61). A monthly fixture on NBC, and Detroit's favorite TV star.

Bob Hope in Moscow (April 5, 1958). First network TV show from behind the Iron Curtain.

Bob Hope Presents the Chrysler Theatre (September 1963–May 1967). Host of weekly dramatic anthology series, the start of a long association with Chrysler.

Bob Hope Desert Classic (February 1965). NBC covers the first edition of Hope's Palm Springs golf tournament.

Hope in Vietnam (January 15, 1970). Special on his 1969 Christmas tour draws the largest audience for any entertainment show in TV history to date.

A Quarter Century of Bob Hope on Television (October 24, 1975). First Hope special sponsored by Texaco.

Academy Awards (April 3, 1978). Last of Hope's nineteen appearances as Oscar host.

Happy Birthday, Bob (May 29, 1978). First of his annual birthday specials, live from the Kennedy Center in Washington.

Bob Hope on the Road to China (September 16, 1979). First American TV special from the People's Republic of China.

A Masterpiece of Murder (January 27, 1986). Hope's first and only television movie.

Bob Hope: Laughing with the Presidents (November 23, 1996). Last TV special.

ABOUT THE AUTHOR

Richard Zoglin is a contributing editor and theater critic for *Time* magazine. His book *Comedy at the Edge: How Stand-Up in the 1970s Changed America* is considered the definitive history of that seminal era in stand-up comedy. Zoglin is a native of Kansas City, Missouri, and currently lives in New York City.

The employees of Thorndike Press hope you have enjoyed this Large Print book. All our Thorndike, Wheeler, and Kennebec Large Print titles are designed for easy reading, and all our books are made to last. Other Thorndike Press Large Print books are available at your library, through selected bookstores, or directly from us.

For information about titles, please call:
  (800) 223-1244

or visit our Web site at:
  http://gale.cengage.com/thorndike

To share your comments, please write:
  Publisher
  Thorndike Press
  10 Water St., Suite 310
  Waterville, ME 04901